FREEDOM SONG

A Personal Story of the 1960s Civil Rights Movement

MARY KING

William Morrow and Company, Inc. New York

Library of Congress Cataloging-in-Publication Data

King, Mary.
    Freedom song.
    Includes index.
    1. King, Mary.   2. Afro-Americans—Civil rights.
3. Civil rights workers—United States—Biography.
I. Title.
E185.98.K56A3   1987   323.1'196073'073   87-5484
ISBN 0-688-05772-1

Printed in the United States of America

First Edition

1 2 3 4 5 6 7 8 9 10

BOOK DESIGN BY MANUELA PAUL

FREEDOM SONG

This book is dedicated to the civil rights workers
who gave their lives in the struggle
and in some way touched my life;
most of them have never told their stories.

Herbert Lee, black, shot to death at a cotton gin in Amite County, Mississippi, on September 25, 1961.

William L. Moore, white, shot to death at Attalla, Alabama, while protesting segregation, on April 23, 1963.

Medgar Evers, black, killed by a sniper's bullet in Jackson, Mississippi, on June 11, 1963.

Louis Allen, black, shot to death in Amite County, Mississippi, on January 31, 1964.

James Chaney, black, beaten and shot to death in Neshoba County, Mississippi, on June 21, 1964.

Andrew Goodman, white, beaten and shot to death in Neshoba County, Mississippi, on June 21, 1964.

Michael Schwerner, white, beaten and shot to death in Neshoba County, Mississippi, on June 21, 1964.

Jimmy Lee Jackson, black, shot by a state policeman in Marion, Alabama, as he helped his mother, who had been clubbed by police, on February 18, 1965, and died eight days later.

James Reeb, white, died of injuries resulting from a beating by four whites after eating at a black café, in Selma, Alabama, on March 11, 1965.

Viola Liuzzo, white, shot to death while driving back to Montgomery after transporting participants in the Selma, Alabama, march on March 25, 1965.

Sammy Younge, black, shot to death while attempting to use a segregated rest room in Tuskegee, Alabama, on January 3, 1966.

Martin Luther King, Jr., black, assassinated in Memphis, Tennessee, on April 4, 1968.

PREFACE

Mary King is like her ancestors. She walks a very straight line for a long time. She was always like that: solid, linear, historical, careful, analytical, objective, thorough. And stouthearted. This is, I think, a good book. It is personal, of course. Everyone's memories, everyone's slice of it, are personal, different. But she has spoken well and carefully to a good many of the major questions of the period. This book will be widely read in years to come, disputed and quoted as an authority. Primarily, however, its value will be in keeping alive a period and a movement which are rapidly becoming forgotten or misunderstood.

The movement today is commonly known as the civil rights movement, but it was considerably more than that. To me, it was everything: home and family, food and work, love and a reason to live. When I was no longer welcome there, and then when it was no longer there at all, it was hard to go on. Many of us in this situation, especially the southern whites, only barely made it through. I count myself lucky to be a survivor.

The movement was a special time and place of rapid events and extreme integrity. One thing led to another and it was all underground, illegal, dangerous, and on the road. There was a lot of bumming of cigarettes from each other and long cross-country drives in the night to meetings. It was outrageous, really. Exciting, liberating, spicy, when we were young and in the South. The movement—sometimes I have longed for it so profoundly. The only nostalgia that compares is for my grandmother's backyard when

I was a child—the pomegranates and ripe figs, roses and sweet peas, ferns and irises and crepe myrtles and oleanders, pecans and walnuts and swings and wet grass on little bare feet in the summertime. The movement was rich like that. And in like manner there is no going back.

There was a comfort in that time that was born of the absolute certainty that what I was doing was the right thing to be doing. Mary and I were the golden girls and nothing could touch us. Looking back we marvel at our courage, but at the time there was no courage, no fear. We were protected by our righteousness. The whole country was trapped in a lie. We were told about equality but we discovered it didn't exist. We were the only truth tellers, as far as we could see. It seldom occurred to us to be afraid. We were sheathed in the fact of our position. It was partly our naïveté that allowed us to leap into this position of freedom, the freedom of absolute right action. This is where it was truly safe.

I think we were the only Americans who will ever experience integration. We were the beloved community, harassed and happy, and poor. And in those little, hot black rural churches, we went into the music, into the sound, and everyone was welcome inside this perfect place. We simply dropped race.

We loved the untouchables. We believed the last should be first, and not only should be first, but in fact *were* first in our value system. They were first because they were redeemed already, purified by their suffering, and they could therefore take the lead in the redemption of us all. We wanted to turn everything not only upside down, but inside out. This is not mild stuff. It is not much in vogue now. We believed, even before the Beatles, that love, not power, was the answer. All the debates about nonviolence and direct action and voter registration, in my view, were really about whether love or power was the answer. And we did love each other so much. We were living in a community so true to itself that all we wanted was to organize everyone into it, make the whole world beloved with us, make the whole world our beloved.

The movement in its early days was a grandeur that feared no rebuke and assumed no false attitudes. It was a holy time.

I think for Mary this book demonstrates a coming full circle, coming to terms with those times, herself.

When we were debating how to continue to work and create together at Waveland, Mississippi, after the summer of 1964 (which was a momentous time and a period when we couldn't seem to get at deciding what to do anymore), I remember talking about circles. Instead of lines, boxes, and hierarchy in the diagrams of how to organize SNCC, I was drawing circles indicating people working together with the circles overlapping other circles as we all generated programs and things to do together. That was how the movement should have been. Our side lost at the time. But we were right in the end. Hierarchy didn't take.

But things do not always fall apart. Sometimes what looks like falling apart is only part of a coming full back around. I think we have to hope for that, for a time when the truths women and old organizers know will be honored and the secret compassion we have secured in our hearts will find value in the population, among the people. Or that the people will find we have shared this all along.

In the midst of the dissolution of the movement, it became more and more difficult to ask what was to be done, to keep working. This was the problem that led to Mary's and my writing about women. It was so painful to see all the floundering about, trying to figure out what to do, to be burning out oneself, and to see the community dissipating. It seemed like we should keep talking about what was really happening, what really mattered, and thus hold together.

It says a great deal about SNCC that we could raise these concerns, hitherto so private, so publicly. Yet, this is what we had learned in SNCC: to raise basic questions with astounding implications and to share ourselves without restraint.

For a brief time, art, religion, and politics were one. Those of us with SNCC in the South in those days were political, it is true, but more radically, we were midwives to a great upheaval, uprising, outpouring of the human spirit. This was the spirit of the thousands and thousands of poor southern blacks who were in fact the movement. The form, the style, the very life of the movement, was theirs. They were there when we got there and there when we left. Many of them could not read or write and they could barely speak the English language. They will never see this book. They, and not we, were the heroes, the heroines. I was privileged to have been their servant for a while. To them, for all I learned from them and for all the beauty I witnessed, I extend my most sincere and humble thanks.

—Casey Hayden
(Sandra Cason)
Atlanta, Georgia
April 8, 1986

FOREWORD

Mary King, Ella Baker, and Casey Hayden were all quite different, but in 1960, as I began to meet these remarkable women, they all set off one defensive reaction: They were too much like my mother.

Strong women were the backbone of the movement, but to young black men seeking their own freedom, dignity, and leadership perspective, they were quite a challenge.

Mary King and Ella Baker were preachers' daughters, and Martin King and Wyatt Walker were preachers' sons. Each was struggling to reconcile one's own mission with the domineering parental ego. It was inevitable that these personal dynamics would produce separate organizations for the freedom struggle.

Even so, I could not escape. I ended up working directly with Septima Clark and Dorothy Cotton, two of the strongest women to emerge in the movement. Men and women struggling for freedom, but gradually becoming aware that freedom might mean different things for men and women, is an untold story of the civil rights movement.

So little is known, and even less is understood, about the complexity of forces that changed the American southland in the 1960s. *Freedom Song* (or Freedom Sisters as Chapter 12 might be called) makes an informed and involved comment that will shed new light on the movement for historians and hopefully will inspire a new generation, black and white, to continue the struggle.

"The struggle," a euphemism that expressed a kaleidoscope

of motives, drives, and yearnings, coalesced into a marvelous movement of change without violence and encompassed a moment in time that not only changed laws in relation to black people, but opened a Pandora's box of freedom-loving expectations for others, especially women.

Mary King was one of those young white women who gave themselves to the struggle for the rights of poor blacks only to discover that the same forces and many others in our society conspired to build even stronger barriers against women's fulfillment.

Erik Erikson, in his psychohistorical studies of Martin Luther and Gandhi, explores those inner drives and relationships that contribute to the style and substance of leadership and the shaping of history. We were no less driven by our own needs to resolve parental conflict and sibling rivalry. Race and sexual differences were always the explosive content that shaped our responses to the societal conflict and legal barriers.

The interorganizational tensions and rivalries that were often given enormous ideological and political significance by the press also emerged as a part of the interpersonal dynamic of male-female, black-white, adolescent-young adult characters of the individuals involved. The leadership versus participatory models of decision-making that evolved in SCLC and SNCC are also bound in the personal struggles of the respective individuals.

Mary King humanizes these conflicts and demythologizes them to the extent that the heroes of the period emerge rather as remarkable individuals who allow their own lives to respond to the social demands of their environment. The strength of character that gave a heroic response to the violence and hatred of racism was indeed forged by the simple commitment "to be present" with people in need.

America needs to know about the Amzie Moores, Ella Bakers, Casey Haydens, Bob Zellners, Annelle Ponders, and many other "Saints of Rank and File," to use the phrase of Peter Marshall, as well as the Martin Luther Kings, Julian Bonds, or Andrew Youngs who have emerged as the visible images of the period.

But even Julian and Martin emerge not as saints or superheroes, but as searching, dedicated individuals with many of the frailties of the rest of humanity.

Freedom Song is a remembrance and a prophecy. It warms us to the glory of times recently past, but it does so in such a way as to assure us that humanity once again is capable of raising such giants of the times from the ranks of ordinary people.

We see them struggling in the Philippines and in South Africa. Hopefully, even in these United States, we can give *Freedom Song* a global chorus as we stand with those in need across our planet.

—THE HONORABLE ANDREW J. YOUNG
Mayor of Atlanta, Georgia
November 14, 1986

ACKNOWLEDGMENTS

Over the years, many individuals suggested that I write this book, but Marcia Donnan Wood was the first person who sat me down and specifically encouraged me to commit myself to the project. I did not make a firm decision, however, until one night during an intimate dinner in San Francisco in 1980 when Laurel Sheaf bore down on me, importuning me that this book was no longer an option that I could take or leave. Didn't I understand, she admonished me, that it was an *obligation*—I had no right to withhold my experiences and must let others share them.

Clayborne Carson of the history department of Stanford University encouraged me in this endeavor for several years. Howard Zinn of Boston University similarly heartened me. I have relied in some instances on the research of these two historians to fill in certain gaps left by my own papers. To both of them I extend my appreciation for their stimulation and confidence.

Professor Michael Thelwell of the W.E.B. Du Bois Department of Afro-American Studies at the University of Massachusetts gave me his time, his energy, and his heart in reviewing the manuscript.

I am grateful to historian Bernice Johnson Reagon of the Smithsonian Institution for her comments and for reviewing the choices and lyrics of the freedom songs I selected in the context of the manuscript.

I would also like to thank the lawyers, scholars, and readers who read part or all of the manuscript and identified areas that needed elaboration. They include: Barbara Blum, Julian Bond, Wiley A. Branton, Charlie Cobb, Marian Wright Edelman, Christine Moss Helms, my brother John Norman King, Joyce Ladner, Dorothy Holland Mann, Donella H. Meadows, Charles Morgan, Jr., Jean Wheeler Smith, and Susan Williams.

My close friend and colleague Margery Tabankin has deepened the bonds between us and earned my profound gratitude by reading the manuscript at different stages and making many astute observations. Special thanks go to two friends, Odeh F. Aburdene and Dan E. Moldea, who emboldened me in this project and are always unbridled in their comments on my work.

My personal collection of documents has been donated to the Social Action Collection of the Wisconsin State Historical Society at Milwaukee. The society's Social Action Archivist Sarah Cooper spent three days working alongside me, sorting and copying my files from the years 1962 through 1966. Her assistance in organizing the letters, personal notes, news releases, reports, staff-meeting minutes, affidavits, lists, and files that I had gathered enabled me to penetrate and use my own papers to provide many of the primary sources employed in writing this book. Barbara Kaiser of the historical society aided me as well.

Suzanne Thorin and Bruce Martin of the research staff of the Library of Congress have my appreciation for granting me a scholar's study desk and for facilitating my ability to use the book and microfilm facilities of the national library. David Beasley, research librarian of the New York Public Library, provided help and documents for which I am grateful.

Of the many persons who gave me specific help—the details of which each of them knows—there are some I would especially like to thank. They include: Sana H. Sabbagh; Victor Gold; Laurence R. Birns of the Council on Hemispheric Affairs; J. Herman Blake, president of Tougaloo College; Jeffrey Clark; the South Africa-born human-rights activists Dawn Zain of Kuala Lumpur and Jessica Strang of London; Annette Jones White; and William and Gerald Dunfey. Caroline Wellons stayed in my home and diligently worked through the night for over one month to assist me. Amy Carter gave me a useful reaction.

Whenever I was intimidated by the scope of the civil rights movement with its impact on hundreds and thousands of individuals and communities, I remembered the advice of Stoney Cooks that I was responsible only for what I experienced.

Gerard F. McCauley, my literary agent, has my deep appreciation for representing me. I also thank him for introducing me to my editor at William Morrow and Company—Lisa Drew. Her belief in me provided the opportunity to tell my story, and she has earned my admiration, respect, and affection as a superb editor and friend.

Many talented individuals at William Morrow took a keen interest in the preparation of this book and their contributions often went beyond the call of duty. David R. Means gave thorough, ready, and solid assistance no matter how often I requested help. Maria Epes showed sincere personal involvement and genuine concern for bringing the interior design, maps, and photography sections to a high standard. Deborah Weiss gave excellent and reliable assistance in copyediting. Daniel Garrett and Cheryl Asherman offered their judgment, skills, and advice.

To my father, Luther Waddington King, go unique thanks for the consistency of both his scholarly and emotional support. He tirelessly proofread the manuscript at each phase of its development, making me feel that nothing in the world was more important, and encouraged me over and over again.

My husband, Peter Geoffrey Bourne, who offered valuable insights and buoyed me up when I was discouraged, also helped me with the grieving process that accompanied the writing of this book.

Finally, I must express grudging acknowledgment to a horse. A golden Welsh cob named Sunshine Star—in a mare's anxiety over her foal—threw me from a canter in a pasture in western Wales, fracturing my hip and ankle. The accident and ensuing surgery forcibly slowed me down, painfully allowing me months of introspection. As I recovered in the solitude of an isolated seventeenth-century farmhouse near Tregaron, I was able to complete this book with the moral support of Dai Williams from Brynteg at Cwrtycadno and Glenys Lloyd of Llanio Isaf, and with the typing assistance of Linda Howells of Llanfair and St. David's University in Lampeter, Dyfed, Wales.

—M.E.K.

CONTENTS

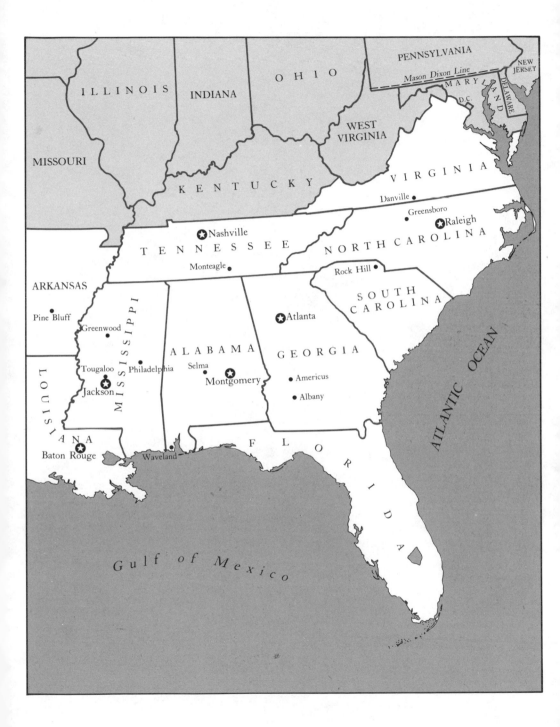

INTRODUCTION

I have chosen *Freedom Song* as the book's title because of the prominent place held by songs about freedom in the American civil rights movement. The repertoire of "freedom songs" had an unparalleled ability to evoke the moral power of the movement's goals, to arouse the spirit, comfort the afflicted, instill courage and commitment, and to unite disparate strangers into a "band of brothers and sisters" and a "circle of trust." The freedom songs were a contemporary expression of the old spirituals—one group of songs from a significant black choral tradition universally recognized as one of the most profoundly moving and expressive bodies of music in the world. The spirituals were created out of a blend of the African and American experiences and matured in the fierce fires of southern slavery.

During the human-rights struggle in the 1960s, the freedom songs uplifted us, bound us together, exalted us, and pointed the way, and, in a real sense, freed us from the shackles of psychological bondage. They captured and kept alive the yearnings, dreams, and fervency of a people under stress. Indeed, the civil rights movement was fueled by the singing of black people. Traditional spirituals and gospel hymns were used exactly as they had come down through the years, or were adapted or completely rewritten. Freedom songs were also composed anew. A strong black tradition of composing in performance and in the midst of need led to new words being added or a line being changed to address a specific issue. Song leading became an organizing tool, helping to mobilize the dedicated or to motivate the reticent. Never has there been a social or political struggle as rich in protest songs as the southern civil rights movement, because of the magnificence of black congregational singing, nourished as it was by a legacy of struggle, resistance, endurance, and faith. It was a movement that could be said to have had its own culture. Freedom songs both gave and reflected back the political fire and spiritual longings of countless individuals in untold mass meetings, addressing real frustrations whether of making a personal commitment or of fear and dread.

This is a personal account. Mine is not a definitive history of the civil rights movement, something that I believe no participant in the struggle writing out of memory and experience could produce. Furthermore, I am a white woman writing about my experiences working in a mostly black, largely male-led organization. While this is one person's story, inasmuch as I have attempted to present my experiences in an accurate and clear historical framework, it is also a partial history. If not a history of the movement, and much less so of black people, it is in part a history of the most enigmatic, elusive, and perhaps consequential of the key activist groups in that struggle, the Student Nonviolent Coordinating Committee (SNCC).

I have done a great amount of research, yet, as the book is autobiographical, I have not forgotten internal research into my own thinking, growth, and development, focusing on my perceptions of issues, events, and people as the movement changed and evolved. Although it is often hard to remember how one thought before absorbing subsequent knowledge, I have tried to convey the level of awareness (or lack of it) that I had at the time.

Hoping to give a sense of what it was like inside the conflict, I have included as many primary sources as possible from the movement itself and writings by people who were at that time in its midst. Most of these sources are from my own papers. Given the pressures we were under, our itinerancy, and the scope of the unrest, no individual participant's resources could be exhaustive. Mine aren't either, but for over two years I was at the center of my organization's Communications section and much of the material on paper produced by my group in that period was either written by me or went through my hands.

This account is told from my point of view but sometimes

the ground on which I stand shifts. I have tried to combine an account of what I experienced, a personal discussion of my inner state, a statement of what was happening around me, a record of my perspective and analysis, and also some distant historical views. Therefore, I speak in different voices. My words are sometimes those of the storyteller, occasionally painfully personal; here and again they are reportorial with personal involvement; and sometimes they are historical. I have tried to strike a balance between personal memoir and historiography. In four of the early chapters, I have interwoven my family background so that the reader will understand who I am, my values, why I did what I did, and why I draw certain conclusions.

A direct correlation exists between oppression and secrecy. We were aware that no democratic movement could succeed if contained within itself; if we could not expose the evil of oppression and our struggle against it, we could not effect change. My job in the movement was Communications, translating experience into words. First I documented, and then I transmitted these words, moving them through the news media so they could influence attitudes, thinking, and action. I did not accuse—I described. My role was systematically to gather and dispatch information on behavior that would reveal the mind-set of those who supported the brutal status quo. Disclosure about the actions of the perpetrators of injustice requires them to look at their deeds in the light of a larger morality. Without the flow of revealing data, they are not forced to reexamine their offenses. The biographers of Mohandas Gandhi claim he knew and played this card well, urging workers at the start of campaigns first to document, and then to communicate. The government of South Africa showed how dangerous is simple information, and how critical in the fight for justice is the flow of words about repression and the people fighting it, when it banned the world's news media.

Years after the events that inspired this book, I find myself once again translating experience into words—it has become habitual for me.

I have tried to remain true to the situation as it was when I was involved. This has posed some difficulties with word usage. Except in direct quotations where *Negro* was used, I have employed the term *black* because it is the word now claimed by those to whom it refers. On the other hand, in the 1960s we used the term *chairman* for the elected leader of our group and I have not changed it to *chairperson*, in light of later practice, because it was the title at that time.

Nomenclature aside, on a deeper level, I have attempted to represent forces and people as we saw them during the conflict. Examples include our perceptions of the Reverend Dr. Martin Luther King, Jr., and of the Kennedy and Johnson administrations. I have sought to allow the honesty and integrity of those views to stand untrammeled by later experience. Many writers have offered interpretations and extrapolations on the period, and others have written legends, but I have felt that my obligation is to tell my story with authenticity, trying to be true to my point of view in that time.

I have worked equally hard to portray accurately my own political and intellectual development. It is amazing to me now to think how little I had to offer the movement when I joined it at the age of twenty-two other than passionate belief; yet it was my very naïveté that sustained me, undaunted and not comprehending the obstacles from within or without. Only rarely have I mentioned my later life, wanting this account to have its own completeness. Toward the end of the last chapter, however, where I make certain evaluations and sum up the impact of my experiences, I must necessarily speak from the perspective that I gained subsequently.

Some readers will wonder if there weren't more expletives and profanities, more scatological language, more caterwauling, in such an explosive and rousing movement. There was plenty of street language, racy badinage, bellowing, and just plain "cussin' " and shouting within our ranks. But when I took notes at the time, I normally left such expressions out as extraneous. In remembering what people said, I have usually forgotten obscenities, probably because they added nothing to meaning, unless a fresh or unique formulation impressed me.

Racism has been the great moral issue of the twentieth century, and remains the central paradox and contradiction of American democracy. All that any of us could do was to decide to participate and then to do so with actions both big and small, to have intense loving relationships with ourselves and others in the struggle (including sibling rivalry with other organizations), and to create a forward thrust that often brought results but at various times could do no more than destine that progress would follow.

Although we underwent external and internal schisms, defeats, and deterioration, there was, finally, no failure in what we wrought. We lived life at its fullest while being engaged with the deep perplexities and political questions of our time.

The civil rights group with which I was associated for almost four years of my life—the period about which I write—was labeled radical. For most people this term connoted militancy. More properly, what made SNCC radical was that it sat astride some of the major philosophical and political gulfs of this era. These included relationships between blacks and whites, the choice of nonviolence as opposed to violence, the question of reform versus revolution, decentralized local authority as contrasted with centralization, relationships between women and men, democracy or authoritarianism, and the question of leadership from the people or leadership from above.

Containing these conflicts and polarities within its small, highly visionary, young, diverse, and rebellious staff, it was inevitable that our organization could not last. Its relevance is that, even as we approach the final years of the twentieth century, these transcendent global questions are still not resolved. Its enduring significance is that, within the American context, we raised these quandaries, projecting them into contemporary political debate, in some ways contributing to the terms of the discussion that continues to this day.

During his 1980 presidential campaign Ronald Reagan, then governor of California, sought out the obscure town of Philadelphia, Mississippi, in rural Neshoba County, to launch his bid for the highest office in the land. Why, I wondered, would he choose an insignificant town where, sixteen years earlier, three of my fellow civil rights workers had been murdered?

It would have been impossible to go to Neshoba County for political purposes in 1980 and not be aware of what had happened there. Indeed, as columnist Anthony Lewis observed on September 22, 1980, in *The New York Times*, "The likelihood, moreover, is that the staff members who arranged Reagan's trip did know." Using the code words of the white South that stood for opposition to equal rights on racial matters, Governor Reagan stated, "I believe in states' rights," and he declared that, as president, he would do everything he could to "restore to states and local governments the powers that properly belong to them." Thus, it was obvious that his intention was not to remind America of the struggle to achieve basic rights for blacks in America or to show that his sympathies were with the three idealistic young men who had lost their lives in 1964. Was this merely an insensitive political ploy? Was this his idea of how to ask for the support of the whites of Mississippi and elsewhere in the deep South? Was it conceivable that he would want to send a message that his administration would stand with those who would make a rearguard action against the rights of blacks?

For those who were aware of what had happened in Neshoba County, and as columnist William Raspberry of *The Washington Post* and others wrote at the time, the act suggested that his sympathies were with those who committed the murders. Therefore I had to ask myself: Had the nation forgotten? When I considered this question, it burned to the touch. How could America forget? The possibility seared like acid in an open wound.

Later it seemed to me a dreadful paradox that what appeared to be an appeal to racism should go relatively unnoticed while President Reagan's visit to the cemetery at Bitburg in 1985 should produce a firestorm of criticism because some of those buried there included SS officers. Was it just that President Reagan wanted the support of the German people for himself and for his friend, their chancellor, as he had wanted the votes of white Mississippians? In both instances, was he saying, albeit in a clumsy way, Let bygones be bygones?

When Senator Jesse Helms of North Carolina was fighting against making the birthday of the Reverend Dr. Martin Luther King, Jr., a national holiday, President Reagan was asked at a news conference whether he thought Dr. King had communist sympathies. "We'll know in about thirty-five years, won't we. . . . There is no way that these records can be opened. Because an agreement was reached between the family and the government, with regard to those records." Did he really think that any southern black, much less Dr. King, needed communist inspiration in the conflict over constitutional rights?

On another occasion, manifesting a point of view that had some popularity in his administration, President Reagan said he favored the "unamended Constitution." That would mean the U.S.

Constitution minus the Bill of Rights. Given the admiration around the world for our Bill of Rights, why advocate the Constitution stripped of its finest raiments?

Perhaps my account, *Freedom Song,* can make a contribution to assuring that the United States does not forget, and, indeed, that it properly celebrates the movement that remains, worldwide, a high-water mark for human rights. For, like a bright moon revealed by clouds that have suddenly parted, lighting up the night, it is a painful but ultimately glorious struggle of which the American people can, in the final analysis, be proud.

It must not be forgotten.

—MARY ELIZABETH KING
Washington, D.C.
September 9, 1986

FREEDOM SONG

CHAPTER 1

MOVEMENT

I know, I know we'll meet again,
I know we'll meet again,
And then you and I will never say good-bye
　　when we meet again.

Well, you come from Atlanta, Georgia, oh yes,
And I'm from Memphis, Tennessee,
We both met in the Mississippi jail
　　because we want to be free.

Well, when I left Mississippi, oh yes,
I traveled to Tennessee.
There I worked with the SNCC
　　fighting for our dignity.

We've been together in this jailhouse, oh yes,
And now we too must go.
But we will be alone after you've gone,
My friend, I'm gonna miss you so.

　　—Nashville freedom song from the sit-ins by
　　James Bevel and Bernard Lafayette, 1960

Toward the end of four years of college, I made a trip
that changed my life. During the Easter break of 1962,
I was one of ten students from Ohio Wesleyan University who
with a professor traveled to Nashville, Atlanta, and Tuskegee,
Alabama. My participation in this "study tour" was the outgrowth
of a stirring that started in childhood. It was the beginning of a
series of exhilarating events and experiences that would try and
test me.

　　Over two years before, on February 1, 1960, four students at
North Carolina's all-black Agricultural and Technical State University in Greensboro, having debated and planned, had decided
to go downtown and ask for a Coca-Cola at a Woolworth's all-
white lunch counter. They were unaware that their action would
trigger the sit-in movement and lead to the formation of a new

civil rights organization. Ezell Blair, Jr., Franklin McCain, Joseph McNeil, and David Richmond met in their first semester; they studied together, ate together, and discussed issues, including segregation, together. Their action wasn't yet called a sit-in; it had no name. It was four freshmen, bolstering one another's nerve, whose tactic was simply to stay when asked to leave. The effect on me, watching the four freshmen on the evening news in my dormitory during my sophomore year in college, was electrifying. News stories, television footage, and radio coverage must have struck thousands of other students similarly.

I wanted to take part in this new phenomenon, but the opportunity for contact with the ground swell did not come for two years until the study-tour group pulled out of the central Ohio college town in station wagons. We covered 1,860 miles. We stayed at black colleges such as Fisk University, Clark College, and Tuskegee Institute, and we visited white schools such as Vanderbilt University, Agnes Scott College, Georgia Tech, Emory University, and Berea College. I met students, faculty, civil rights leaders, mayors, chiefs of police, business leaders, clergy, community leaders, human-relations groups, and newspaper editors.

By the end of the trip, I knew that the civil rights convulsions in the South marked a new epoch and that the United States would never again be the same. The sit-ins had launched the new decade. One era was drawing to a close and another was beginning. I was also convinced, with the tenacious certainty of youth, that it was there that I belonged—with the civil rights movement.

In Nashville our group of ten white and black students and faculty adviser Miriam Willey, from the college's philosophy and religion department, met and talked with two young black activists named John Lewis and Bernard Lafayette, both of them graduate students preparing for the ministry. They were poised, modest, self-confident, and clear-minded. John seemed a little shy. Both of them, I learned, had been "Freedom Riders" the previous year and had traveled by bus from Washington, D.C., to Jackson, Mississippi, in a racially integrated group. They had suffered violent beatings. By the time I met them, they had each been arrested many times for nonviolently protesting segregated public facilities. John and Bernard explained that they were affiliated with a group whose name was a mouthful—the Student Nonviolent Coordinating Committee (SNCC), pronounced "snick." It was head-quartered in Atlanta and they recommended that we stop by the office.

When we reached Atlanta we visited the organization and I saw how the small headquarters staff of sixteen was coordinating communications among hundreds of campuses and communities where student groups were confronting segregation. I walked gingerly up the stairs into the grimy office wondering what the nerve center of the black sit-in movement would look like. Papers were strewn across every desk with unstudied abandon. Telephones were ringing, wastebaskets bulged with trash, and file-cabinet drawers gaped open. A mimeograph machine monotonously whooshed paper through its rollers in the background, and a radio somewhere thumped a heavy beat. The floors looked as if they had not been scrubbed since installation, and the windows were opaque with dust. I did not see anyone who was white there among the young black people rushing around that day.

James Forman, the group's executive secretary, welcomed us, casually rounding up folding chairs and pulling them into a circle. He was in his mid-thirties, had high cheekbones, and a slightly protruding paunch; he was easygoing and warm but struck me also as audacious. Older than anyone else there, Jim explained that SNCC had forty-one full-time staff members. In eight Mississippi towns, it was operating voter-registration programs; it also had similar activities in Dallas County, Alabama, and in Terrell, Lee, Baker, and Dougherty counties in southwest Georgia, and had one project in South Carolina. Programs of "direct action" such as sit-ins and other forms of confrontation, Jim said, operated in Little Rock and Pine Bluff, Arkansas; in Nashville; in Baltimore; and in Gadsden, Talladega, and Huntsville, Alabama. That day I also met a strikingly self-possessed young man, Julian Bond, a smooth writer with a wry sense of humor who served as SNCC's press secretary.

In downtown Atlanta, we met a white woman named Connie Curry who was a member of the student group's executive committee. Eugene Patterson, the editor of *The Atlanta Constitution*, saw us as did other moderate leaders of the white community. We met with representatives of a dozen separate civil rights and human-relations groups including those sponsored by the Quakers and the Mennonite Central Committee. Across the city, we visited the headquarters of the Southern Christian Leadership Conference (SCLC), which was headed by a young minister named Martin Luther King, Jr., and met with SCLC staff as well as other black leaders and professors in the city.

In Alabama, we visited Tuskegee Institute, a major black institution of higher learning, and I met researchers and local leaders. They explained how their small black town of Tuskegee, then possessing the highest ratio of black to white citizens in the United States, had been gerrymandered to prevent black political participation.

We had planned to travel on to Birmingham but were advised in Atlanta that we should not go there since the police knew of our integrated group's coming and had formally declared that they would not provide protection. For the first time, this brought me face to face with a common method used by law officers to maintain the system of segregation—by simply removing themselves they could let mobs and thugs attack with impunity, ensuring brutal reprisal against those who dared to deviate from the system of segregation.

On that Eastertime study tour in 1962, I also met a woman who fascinated me. Named Casey Hayden, she was an unself-consciously beautiful slender blonde with translucent skin and a low-voiced and throaty laugh. Her symmetrical features were arranged with appealing fragility. From Victoria, an east Texas town near Louisiana, she was lanky and had a wide-stepping walk like someone who had grown up with horses all her life, although she hadn't.

I met Casey for the first time at a lunch seminar in a restaurant on Hunter Street in Atlanta; she looked the epitome of southern propriety, dressed in a blanket-plaid black and yellow woolen skirt and a yellow sweater, her blond hair cascading over the epaulets of her trench coat. I learned that her grandfather had been the sheriff of Victoria. What she had to say, however, was as unorthodox as her looks were traditional. She made an immediate and profound impression on me as she described to our group how she had spent the previous year traveling to southern campuses.

Casey's traveling had been paid for by a grant from the Field Foundation awarded to the National Student Young Women's Christian Association (YWCA) for a special human-relations project. In 1962, "human relations" was the euphemism used for race relations, and Casey had traveled to southern white campuses in the name of examining academic freedom. The topic of academic freedom provided cover for her, she explained, since she would not have been allowed to visit white campuses to talk about race. What she found, she told us quietly but forcefully in her east Texas accent, was "appalling." In university after university, academic freedom had been sacrificed on the altar of racial segregation. She spoke bluntly, but with a quality of clear-sightedness and an ability to see to the heart of the matter that was to become very familiar to me over the next few years. Casey described social-science professors afraid to discuss race and the effects of segregation, and white students and professors feeling abysmally alone when they questioned the validity of racial segregation. She told of how the fear of being labeled communist, a tangible threat, kept scores of professors from speaking out on southern campuses on the issue of race.

There was something about Casey's sincerity that magnetized me and drew me to her. As the meeting, which had several other speakers, broke up, I made a point of approaching Casey to ask her advice on how I could organize a student group at Ohio Wesleyan to support the sit-ins. "The first thing to do is to pull a group together," she said, starting to laugh. "Then give yourselves a name," she continued, chuckling brightly at the simplicity of what she was saying. "Have a meeting, form committees, and issue a release or statement of your goals."

That study tour was a turning point in my life. Of all the individuals and groups that I met on the trip, the young people associated with the Student Nonviolent Coordinating Committee had the most significant effect on me. They touched me. SNCC gripped my imagination. I had vaguely known that it was born as a result of the sit-ins. Yet, only as a result of my meeting John Lewis, Bernard Lafayette, Jim Forman, and Julian Bond, was I able to see how youthful, bold, and idealistic was this group. It was different in its dynamism and outlook from the other more staid civil rights groups I had encountered. In these SNCC workers I sensed high energy, self-assurance, impatience, and determination. I identified with them. I saw myself in them. Although it was small, SNCC seemed potent.

As a result of feeling that I actually knew John, Bernard,

Julian, and Jim as individuals, as persons, as people who were intense like me, committed and concerned, my life was changed. I decided then, right there on that trip, that I wanted to work for SNCC.

When I returned to Ohio Wesleyan University, I wrote a newsletter distributed on campus. It read in part:

> It occurs to me that the most profound commitment and courage to be found in America today is present in the section of the country traditionally regarded as the most stagnant. In the area of action in human relations, the south is leading our country. We must respond with the same courage. . . .

As I finished my senior year and awaited graduation, I could scarcely contain myself. I was intent on returning to Atlanta. First I did exactly as Casey had suggested. I organized a group of sixty students, recruiting them to work on a variety of projects, such as working to change the university's policy of rooming black freshmen in single rooms or only with each other, and its policy of limited enrollment for blacks. Never in the Methodist university's history had there been more than thirteen black students at any given time in a student body of two thousand. With Casey's advice strongly in mind, and by dint of sheer intention, I taught myself how to run large meetings, use parliamentary procedure, set up a committee structure, issue press releases, and call a press conference. I also designed and made the logo for our mimeographed materials.

I was amazed at the interest our Student Committee on Race Relations (SCORR), a fast-moving and kinetic group, attracted on campus, and I was surprised by our successes. Before city and state sponsorship of public education, the Methodists had operated many private schools and seminaries; education had a prominent place in the spread of Methodism across the country in the nineteenth century. Ohio Wesleyan University was founded in 1842 and a large number of missionaries were dispatched from there. After the start of the Peace Corps in 1961, for years this school was the college with the highest per capita proportion of its graduates enlisting in the national volunteer service corps.

Yet, according to my standards and despite this evidence of

public-mindedness, I found the student body as a whole preoccupied with their own ambitions. There were some notable exceptions; I sought out most of them and they became my friends.
Among them were two black students, one the son of a Methodist
bishop, Edward G. Carroll, Jr., and the other the daughter of a
professor at the University of Louisville, Ursula Parrish. My pal
Trish Van Devere would surprise me three years later when I
looked up on a stage in Mississippi and found her, by then an
accomplished actress, in a production of John O'Neal's Free
Southern Theater. But like many campuses, then, the student
body seemed mostly uninterested in current issues, and exces-
sively concerned with its social life. Sororities and fraternities added
to the constraints. At the end of my junior year, I "deactivated"
from my sorority because it would not admit a Nicaraguan student
named Angie who had dark skin. The administration was even
more conformist than the student body and I was always crossing
swords with the dean of women because I chafed under the university rules for women.

The professors, however, were dramatically different from the
stodgy administration. Most of the faculty members that I knew
were academically outstanding, inquiring, and wide-awake. Although I majored in English literature, most of my friends among
the faculty were in the social sciences including Butler A. Jones,
a black professor who was chairman of the sociology department.
I held student jobs in the Institute for Practical Politics and the
Citizenship Clearing House with Professors Fred Burke and Arthur Petersen. I developed lasting relationships with some professors, unrelated to my budding activism on matters of race, and for
many years afterward corresponded with the chairman of the English department, Benjamin T. Spencer. In my senior year, I was
president of the English Writers Club, a group that brought authors and poets to campus.

It surprised me that the Student Committee on Race Relations took flight at all. The student newspaper, *The Transcript*,
reported our doings on its front page on May 2, 1962, and quoted
me as saying, "We are not interested in flagrant demonstrations
but we want to work with deliberation and effectiveness. We hope
to achieve support for national student movements, a change in
the university housing situation for minority students, and a change
in the climate of opinion and attitude on our campus by giving

Negro and foreign students greater social mobility." This last point referred to exclusion from sororities and fraternities.

In June 1962, having been graduated, I turned over the leadership of the committee to someone else and was sitting on the main street of Delaware, Ohio, in the bus station across from the administration building of the college, waiting for the bus that would take me home. I was planning to go to graduate school at either Emory University in Atlanta or Tulane University in New Orleans, only so that I could establish a base from which I hoped to work my way into the civil rights movement and to SNCC.

I was neither worldly nor wise. In his literary criticism seminars, Dr. Spencer pushed me hard on what he called "self-knowledge" as the starting point for critical and analytical thought. One day, wavering between exasperation and endearment, he said, "You're always asking cosmic questions, Mary!" My political exposure was woefully meager and my only experience was in that sheltered campus environment, even though I had held two of the best student jobs available and the only ones with any semblance of political significance. I came from a minister's family and a home of high purpose, moral values, and life lived in the raw with the suffering of parishioners, but it was short on political sophistication. I had indignation and determination, and the beginning of a sense of direction.

I thought of myself as a "pilgrim soul" from a favorite poem, "When You Are Old," by William Butler Yeats, who wrote to his heroine, Maud Gonne, "One man loved the pilgrim soul in you." I was, in fact, setting off on a lifelong search for meaning. I thought I could find it in the civil rights movement, yet I knew that I couldn't walk up to SNCC's door, knock, and expect to be welcomed. The organization was tiny, there were only two whites working for it, Bob Zellner and Dorothy Miller, and I knew instinctively that SNCC people had to trust me before I would be accepted and that trust takes time and can't be rushed. As I was musing over my hopes, wondering how I could win SNCC's confidence through my plan, someone from my dormitory tracked me down and located me in the seedy bus station where I sat surrounded by luggage and brown cartons containing my books.

A telephone call from Atlanta came through the coin box from a Miss Rosetta Gardner, the director of the College Division of the Young Women's Christian Association (YWCA) in the south-

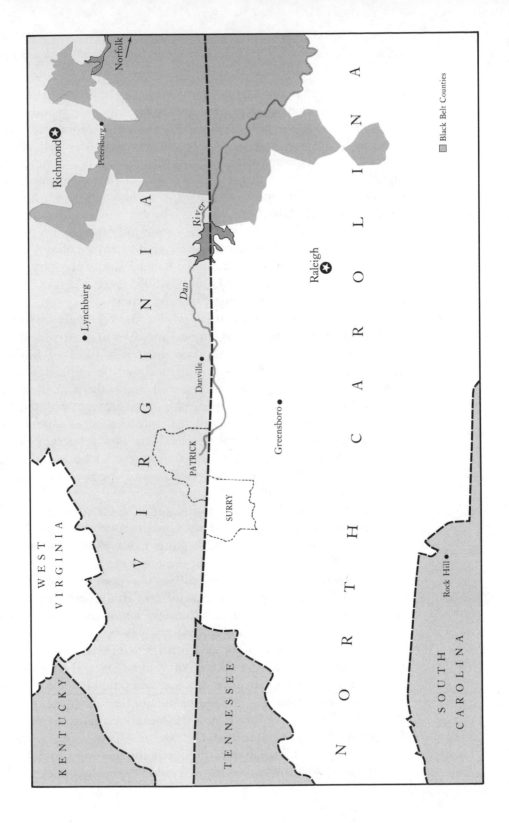

ern region. The polite and polished voice of the seasoned executive explained that she had met me on my Easter trip and asked if I would be willing to fly to North Carolina to a conference where I would be interviewed by two of her advisers, Miss Ella Baker and Professor Howard Zinn. I said yes. Could I fly there that night? The National Student YWCA, Miss Gardner explained, was considering inviting me to replace Casey Hayden on its human-relations project as she was leaving with her husband for Ann Arbor, Michigan. The next step was for me to be interviewed.

I was stunned. Replace Casey! I could hardly believe it. My heart leaped and, without hesitating, I said I would ship my books home on the bus as planned but I would catch the next plane from Columbus to the Raleigh-Durham airport.

I was about to meet a woman who would be vitally important to the civil rights movement and to me. When I arrived at the conference center and was taken to meet Ella Baker, I found a middle-aged woman with a downturning smile, beautiful dark skin, and a high forehead. She was dressed modestly in a blue-patterned dress but it was not until she stood up that I noted her dignified carriage. She impressed me immediately as a person of wisdom and intellectual honesty. Perhaps as a reflection of my own limited experience, she appeared to me to be a sage. Her voice was deeply resonant, her diction and speech self-assured. She radiated confidence.

Ella Jo Baker had been a debater in high school and was valedictorian of her class at Shaw University in Raleigh, North Carolina. Born in 1903, the granddaughter of slaves, she had wanted to be a medical missionary but her dreams were thwarted by family obligations. She went instead to New York where she lived in Harlem and became an organizer for the Roosevelt administration's Works Progress Administration (WPA) on consumer education, later organizing consumer cooperatives in Philadelphia and Chicago. She had been involved with the southern Young Women's Christian Association (YWCA) off and on since the 1920s and 1930s. As a young woman, she worked as a field secretary for the National Association for the Advancement of Colored People (NAACP). During the 1930s and 1940s, she organized many of the NAACP chapters south of the Mason-Dixon Line as far as Texas, often traveling alone, clandestinely seeking more members for what was then considered a subversive organization. She later became director of branches for the NAACP and participated in the founding of the Congress of Racial Equality (CORE) in 1942. Believing that the NAACP had become too bureaucratic, she resigned in 1946. When the Southern Christian Leadership Conference (SCLC) was organized in 1957, Miss Baker arranged a series of mass meetings for the new entity; and, in 1958, she established its office in Atlanta and became its first full-time executive secretary, subsequently acting as an adviser to its president, the Reverend Dr. Martin Luther King, Jr.

She left the leadership conference in 1960 by mutual agreement. "I had not planned to stay," she told the filmmaker and journalist Joanne Grant in the documentary film *Fundi: The Story of Ella Baker*. She described her encounters with SCLC:

> I was difficult. I wasn't an easy pushover. Because I could talk back a lot—not only could, but did. And so that was frustrating to those who never had certain kinds of experience. And it's a strange thing with men who were supposed to be "men about town"; if they had never known a woman who knew how to say No, and No in no uncertain terms, they didn't know what to do sometimes. Especially if you could talk loud and had a voice like mine. You could hear me a mile away sometimes, if necessary.

I was soon to realize that everyone called Ella Baker, whether she was present or not, "Miss Baker." It was an expression of respect for this mature woman of stature. In the South, the prevailing practice of the time was for whites to address black people by their first names only, with no title. It was a method of diminishing their status—or insulting them—and with only rare exception that pattern was followed even in addressing black physicians and lawyers. Even though many in the movement knew her well, the acute sensitivity in the black community to this universal offense was reflected in the way she was always addressed. I don't remember anyone familiarly calling her "Ella."

I was later to learn more of her story as I began to interact with her. Unnoticed by many Americans, the first sit-in on February 1, 1960, caught Miss Baker's instant attention and she began to plan. As surely as it struck her, the first such protest must have been even more galvanizing to the black college students of the South for whom there had been few outlets for action. In the years immediately leading up to this period, landmark events were changing the social terrain for black Americans, but they provided little opportunity for individual involvement. The Supreme Court's five landmark school desegregation decisions, popularly known by the first to be handed down as *Brown* v. *Board of Education of Topeka*, had occurred in 1954; the Mississippi killing of a four-teen-year-old black boy named Emmett Till, for allegedly whis-tling at a white woman, happened in 1955; the Montgomery bus boycott began in 1955; and the desegregation of the Little Rock schools took place in 1957. But it was not until the first sit-in that a way of individual engagement that had meaning as part of a regionwide phenomenon was created.

The sit-ins had started two and a half years before my meet-ing with Miss Baker. During the two weeks following the news about the first sit-in at Greensboro, North Carolina, the idea had spread to Nashville; to Orangeburg, South Carolina; to Texas; and elsewhere, activating students in fifteen cities in five southern states. Within two months, thirty-five thousand students were putting themselves on the line. By the end of 1960, seventy thou-sand students, most of them black but, increasingly, some of them white, had sat-in and thirty-six hundred student demonstrators had been arrested and jailed. By the end of 1961, hundreds of lunch counters in the mid-South and the border states had been deseg-regated, although little had changed in the Deep South states of Alabama, Georgia, Louisiana, Mississippi, and South Carolina.

I was to find out that two and a half months after Greens-boro, on Easter weekend of 1960, April 15–17, funded by eight hundred dollars from the Southern Christian Leadership Confer-ence, Ella Baker had called together a meeting at her alma mater in Raleigh. It was attended by what Miss Baker recalled as two hundred student delegates from fifty-eight southern communities in twelve states as well as white student supporters from nineteen northern campuses and thirteen observer organizations. Called the Southwide Student Leadership Conference on Nonviolent Resis-tance to Segregation, the meeting at Shaw University began on Good Friday and ended on Easter Sunday. Miss Baker had wanted the new student movement to have a chance to take stock of itself; the acts of conscience of the students were taking place in isolation yet there was a connection. She was also concerned that

SCLC was not as involved in the sit-ins as she thought it should be. To a degree, she felt the student movement lacked its own direction. She also thought the students had a right to make their own mistakes.

Believing that you must "work with people where they are," Miss Baker screened out the northerners in attendance in Raleigh and had them meet by themselves. "They were more experienced than the southerners," she said, "and their ability to articulate themselves would have been intimidating to the southerners."

I would subsequently hear often about the speech made by Miss Baker that called for the entire social structure to be changed. She urged that the student movement should be concerned with "more than a hamburger and a Coke"—about more than the right merely to eat at a lunch counter. Perhaps this was the first indication that the new group that would grow out of this conference would eventually go far beyond mere desegregation. A thirty-one-year-old black divinity student named James M. Lawson, Jr., recently expelled from then mostly white Vanderbilt University in Nashville for advocating nonviolent resistance, made a ringing and militant speech on nonviolence. Some in attendance thought that Jim was challenging the Reverend Dr. Martin Luther King, Jr., one of the representatives of SCLC who was present and who also spoke, for the leadership of the fledgling student movement. This reflected the relative modesty of Dr. King's role in 1960. He was neither the dominant force nor the figurehead of the civil rights movement, although he was clearly the symbolic personality produced by the Montgomery bus boycott. He attended the Raleigh meeting as one of three SCLC representatives, and, particularly to those delegates who were from Dr. King's hometown of Atlanta, he was but one more talented minister.

Again and again I was to hear how representatives also attended from the NAACP (or, as it was widely called, "the N double A") and CORE. Each of these organizations' representatives was jockeying at that 1960 meeting in the hope that the student movement would become affiliated with his organization. SCLC's delegates—the Reverend Dr. Martin Luther King, Jr., the Reverend Ralph Abernathy, and the Reverend Wyatt Tee Walker, who was himself replacing Miss Baker—sought to bring the student movement under SCLC's wings. Although she thought the leadership conference should be more involved in the sit-ins, Miss

Baker did not think it should take over the student movement. It was her refusal, at a private meeting in the residence of the president of Shaw University, to go along with SCLC's plan to attach the student sit-in movement, that was responsible for its remaining autonomous and not becoming part of the leadership conference. Miss Baker's stance wedged open the space for the new entity to emerge, and the student delegates turned away from affiliating with the more priestly and patriarchal SCLC. Having failed to incorporate the students, the three ministers left Raleigh before the conference ended.

It was only later that I would realize that this regal woman I was meeting for the first time was the one who allowed the Student Nonviolent Coordinating Committee—a scrappy, unkempt, fearless, and ragtag group that at times held the rest of the movement and the nation by the scruff of the neck during the 1960s—to come into being.

Perhaps this action of Miss Baker's was the origin of a pervasively negative attitude toward her that I encountered in subsequent years among staff members from SCLC. The Ella Baker that I knew would never have acted on the basis of personal whim or opinion; she had too much intellectual honesty. In refusing to go along with SCLC's design, I believe, she was reflecting the opposition among the students toward being subsumed. It has been rare in the years since to hear proper acknowledgment of the contributions Ella Baker made to the American human-rights struggle.

Two years before I came on the scene, the net result of the conference in Raleigh was a decision by the students to have no formal relationship with SCLC but, rather, to maintain friendship with all civil rights groups and to remain independent. That conference created the Temporary Student Nonviolent Coordinating Committee and decided it would be based in Atlanta. When the temporary committee met in May 1960 at Atlanta University, however, it elected someone from Nashville as its chairman—Marion Barry, a tall, handsome Mississippi-born farmer's son and nattily dressed graduate student in chemistry at Fisk University who was, years later, elected mayor of Washington, D.C. This represented a compromise struck between the two most significant student sit-in groups at the time, the Nashville Christian Student Movement led by Marion Barry, John Lewis, and Diane Nash, and the Atlanta Committee on Appeal for Human Rights, which included Julian Bond, Lonnie King, Marian Wright, and Bernard Lafayette. "Nashville had the troops and the Atlanta Committee had the money," was the way that one SNCC worker subsequently described the compromise.

In October 1960, another meeting of several hundred student delegates (many of whom had participated in the Easter conference) was held at Atlanta University. Omitting the word "Temporary," they established the Student Nonviolent Coordinating Committee, composed of representatives of southern campuses, on a permanent basis. SNCC had one delegate from each of sixteen southern and border states and the District of Columbia plus observers from CORE, SCLC, the National Student Association, the NAACP, the YWCA, the American Friends Service Committee, and the Southern Conference Educational Fund. The first voting delegates, several of whom would become my friends, were: Bernard Lee and Jesse Walker from Alabama; Lorenzo J. Brown from Florida; Marian Wright, Julian Bond, and Lonnie King from Georgia; Edward B. King, Jr., from Kentucky; Clarence Mitchell III from Maryland; David Forbes from North Carolina; Charles F. "Chuck" McDew from South Carolina; Marion Barry from Tennessee; Virginius Thornton from Virginia; and Henry James Thomas from the District of Columbia. Each state had one vote.

The coordinating committee had few powers because the local student groups were to remain autonomous, but it elected an executive committee. That body in turn elected as its chairman the brawny athlete with darkly brooding eyes from South Carolina State College at Orangeburg, Chuck McDew, who used to interject the phrase, "Tell the story!" whenever he was moved. He remained in that position until June 1963. One of the very few black activists of the sit-ins who had grown up in the North, in Massillon, Ohio, Chuck chafed under the rigid segregation of South Carolina and was arrested three times during his first three months there. When told by visiting white Protestant ministers at the campus during Religious Emphasis Week that he could not join their churches, he promptly converted to Judaism when a rabbi among the visitors said that he would be welcome at his synagogue.

Workshops at the October 1960 conference were led by Diane Nash, a beautiful and determined student leader from Fisk; Ben Brown from Clark College in Atlanta; and Chuck McDew; as

well as Sandra Cason (who was, after her marriage to Tom Hayden, known as Casey Hayden) of the University of Texas. Also
participating was Timothy Jenkins, the vice-president of the National Student Association. Jim Lawson spoke at the second conference as well, this time decrying that so many students had
allowed themselves to be bonded out of jail by their elders who
should have, Jim insisted, instead been working to end segregation. Jim's challenge launched SNCC's distinctive "Jail—No Bail"
policy, which, reinforced by several episodes, was for years afterward a key difference between SNCC and SCLC.

The first published description of the new organization stated:
"Its purpose is to coordinate activities, analyze the status of the
movement and map plans for the future. It is self-directing, but
welcomes the participation and assistance of supporting observer
groups." The new "self-directing" entity was already showing the
characteristics that would attract me to it and mark it for the next
several years. Ella Baker's thinking had taken hold—SNCC was
to have "a suggestive rather than directive" role, and was to reflect "group-centered leadership."

Immediately after I met with Ella Baker in North Carolina in
June 1962, she introduced me to Professor Howard Zinn, who,
although white, taught history at Spelman College, a black wom-
en's college in Atlanta. He was a tall, lean, and readily accessible
teacher who was both relaxed and thoughtful at the conference
sessions. I remember his discussion of "natural law," as a higher
law that transcends the conventions, case law, statutes, and
changing institutions of customary law. This was the basis of the
civil disobedience used in nonviolent resistance, he explained. I
later found out that Ella Baker and Howard Zinn were the two
senior advisers to SNCC.

During the interviews, Miss Baker, Professor Zinn, and Miss
Gardner of the Student Y each questioned me intensively about
whether I would be willing to take the risk of traveling from city
to city with a young black woman who had also recently been
graduated from college. They wanted to pair two recent graduates
as an integrated team for the human-relations project. Our formal
purpose, they explained, would be to assess the extent of academic freedom in southern colleges, continuing the work that Casey
had done; the other purposes for the project would become clear

shortly. Miss Baker, Miss Gardner, and Professor Zinn each warned me that my partner and I would be endangering ourselves, that they could not guarantee our safety, and that we might be attacked or beaten for traveling together. This project, although modestly described in the formal wording of the proposal to appease the officers of the philanthropic foundation funding it, was intended to break down some of the barriers erected by the system of segregation in southern universities.

The project was not to be one of direct action, they stipulated, yet, in those days, two young professional women, one white and one black, traveling together by bus, train, and airplane in the South for any purpose, represented a head-on conflict with legalized segregation. The machinery that kept this system in place operated through the overt, legal channels of segregated education, health care, and transportation; denial of voting rights; and infringement of the constitutional rights of free speech and assembly. But it was also maintained through extralegal, covert means—unlawful detention, police tyranny, terror, firebombing of homes, and killing. Those sworn to uphold the law looked the other way, or, worse, cooperated with the terrorists and vigilantes who carried out their vengeance.

In *Deep South*—the classic 1941 study based on two years of fieldwork said to have been carried out in Natchez, Mississippi—the social anthropologists Allison Davis, Burleigh B. Gardner, and Mary R. Gardner described the social strictures of a southern city:

> It is considered entirely correct for the white person to resort directly to physical attack upon the Negro. . . . The white must always be ready to maintain his superordinate position, even by physical violence. . . . The Negro victim then becomes both a scapegoat and an object lesson for his group. He suffers for all the minor caste violations which have aroused the whites, and he becomes a warning against future violations. . . . Thus he lives under the shadow of an ever present threat. He is a Negro, and woe unto him if he forgets; if necessary, the whites can and will enforce their authority with punishment and death.

In the ten southern states in which I would be traveling, 261 counties then had fewer than 15 percent of voting-age blacks registered to vote as a result of this systematic, carefully administered intimidation. Local governments were, in many places, known to be controlled by members of the Ku Klux Klan. Whites did not shake hands with blacks, much less dine with them or sit together in public conveyances. The sight of a black person (who was not in a servile role) with a white might result in immediate violence or later reprisal such as loss of a job for either or both.

Having mentally accepted the consequences of traveling with a black woman, for reasons I cannot explain and perhaps irrationally, I had little fear of physical danger. I knew that I was putting myself into jeopardy. But it seemed to me then, as it seems to me now, that since we all must die, the question is not how you die but how you live. Far more important to me than fear was my belief that I might give my life more meaning and fulfillment if I could participate in this great human-rights encounter.

I was willing to take on the possibility of being killed—as many known and unknown civil rights activists in fact were. It was a decision that I made in serious contemplation. I knew that neither of my supervisors, Miss Baker and Miss Gardner, would send our team into hostile circumstances with abandon, yet I also knew that the violent punishment of those who defied the system of segregation was random and unpredictable. Although segregation was anti-American and stood in opposition to the guarantees of the U.S. Constitution and the provisions of the Bill of Rights, segregationists had the cover of local law and were often in collusion with law officers. No one could say with certainty that I would finish the project alive.

I was honored to be replacing Casey and felt privileged to be working with Miss Baker. I had neither sought the assignment nor asked for it; it had just happened. Yet it was everything I might have hoped for. I was committed, with blind single-mindedness, to working for the civil rights movement, but until this opening occurred, I had had no idea how I would make my way into it. Now I had found the first inroad. My big problem still lay ahead—how to become trusted enough to be invited onto the staff of the Student Nonviolent Coordinating Committee.

My commitment to working for the civil rights movement had been developing since childhood. When I was ten years old, I learned that I was related to Henry Clay, the noted nineteenth-century statesman, through my father's Virginia family, and I de-

cided to write about him when I was required to pick a topic for
a composition in my fifth-grade class in Manhattan. This led me
to the first research I had ever done, and I spent time in the
library reading books about my kinsman. Although he came to
national fame as a Kentuckian, his family had always been from
eastern Virginia, as far back as the officer from whom he (and
therefore I) was descended who fought in Nathaniel Bacon's Rebellion in 1676 against the British colonial governor of Virginia. I
discovered in those musky-smelling antiquated books with their
peculiar engravings that Henry Clay's father, the Reverend John
Clay, a Baptist minister in Hanover County, Virginia, had been a
slaveholder, and that Henry Clay had later owned slaves. Dashing
home to confront my father with this information, I learned to my
consternation that it was true. My father explained that Clay had
been opposed to slavery, had worked for gradual emancipation,
and had freed some of his own slaves. He wanted, however, to
preserve the Union at all costs, and his successful promotion of
the Missouri Compromise of 1820 hindered the spread of slavery
and deferred the outbreak of the Civil War. (Later I learned that
this compromise slowed the start of war until 1861, by which time
the northern and north-central states had become so much stronger
than the South in industry and population that northern victory
preserving the Union was assured.)

This research, if you can call it that, started my thinking and
reading at an early age about race and justice. Even earlier, as
soon as I had learned to read, almost everything else lost its attraction for me. I had little interest in dolls, in part because I had
three younger brothers who were the real thing, crying and squab-
bling, but I read books one after another, which I borrowed, three
or four each Saturday, from the public library around the corner.
After I finished my cleaning chores at home on Saturday morn-
ings, I spent the afternoons with the librarians.

My favorite book was *All About Us*, by Eva Knox Evans, published in 1947. It was a Christmas present given to my brothers
and me when I was seven years old by the deaconess of the church
my father served as pastor. I now understand that it was a child's
introduction to the principles of anthropology, as the author wrote:

> All of us had the same first grandfathers and grandmothers.
> We were descended from them as well as the children in

Borneo and West Africa and Russia and Japan. . . . There
are snooty people who think they are better than other people because their ancestors were white. . . .

    We all know that two chemicals—carotene and mela-
nin—decide the color of skin. . . . It covers our flesh and
bones and that is all it is good for. It has nothing to do with
our insides or our brains.

I read and reread this book dozens of times in childhood, and
knew and loved every illustration explaining Indians, blood types,
immigration, manners, slavery, hair, and shapes of heads. Its closing sentence was, "Every living person is kin to us, and we are
related to everybody in the whole world." At seven years of age,
that became my creed. Years later, it is still an underpinning belief.

    Anyone looking at me from a distance would have thought it
was a crazy decision for a twenty-two-year-old white woman, newly
graduated from college, to go to work for the most militant of the
civil rights organizations and one that was composed mostly of
black males. But it was not a hard decision for me at all. The
decision part was easy; finding my way into the movement and
becoming accepted would be the difficult part. There was little
rebellion in my decision. I was in fact being a dutiful daughter.

    Both my parents were taking graduate degrees throughout
most of my childhood and the crumbs dropped from their studies
in anthropology—predicated on the equivalency in value of all
cultures—into the dinner table discussion. We often read selected
topics from an enclycopedia to each other at mealtime. My sense
of geography is still shaped by the miniature research projects on
"new places" in the world that each of my brothers and I presented to the family, a game of discovery that celebrated the differences among peoples and cultures. Before we feel asleep at
night, my father told us a "magic story" that lasted for years, far
longer than a thousand and one nights—his own variation of *The
Flying Carpet*—in which my brothers and I would travel to Siam,
Persia, Kashmir, the Ivory Coast, or Peru, and land, the carpet's
powers making us invisible, to watch and learn from the customs
of the people as he described them.

    It was my father's optimism and idealism that had shaped
and preconditioned me so that in the eventful Easter week of
1962, two years after the start of the sit-ins, when I met John

Lewis, Bernard Lafayette, Jim Forman, and Julian Bond, I would draw the conclusion that I should go to work for SNCC.

In a sense, I was shaped for that decision from the time I could talk. As I was growing up, my father would not let me forget that, as a youth in Virginia, he never heard mention of the Gettysburg Address until he accidentally stumbled on the oration in the library at Washington and Lee University. This was not because he was a poor student. On the contrary, he was shortly to be graduated with the two highest honors possible from a college considered one of the best in the South, when he came upon Lincoln's speech. It seems almost unfathomable now but Lincoln's historic address preceding the Emancipation Proclamation had never been discussed in his Virginia public-school education nor in any of his liberal arts courses at Washington and Lee, and, even more surprising, it had never been mentioned in any of the textbooks used in his education. To my father, a scholar, this omission was proof that racism and segregation affected southern whites as it did blacks, denying both groups full humanity. If, he reasoned, in the interest of justifying segregation, the basics of American history had been denied and distorted in one of the South's best universities, then all southerners were the losers. "I would rather be robbed than rob, and I would rather have been enslaved than to have enslaved," he would tell me, believing it more destructive to the human spirit to be the oppressor than the oppressed.

I was not left to absorb these principles passively. My father, the Reverend Dr. Luther Waddington King, was an expatriate southerner who had come to Manhattan to attend seminary for the ministry and remained in New York so he would be able to serve racially and ethnically integrated parishes. A Methodist minister's work is inextricably tied to belief, and the children of ministers are exposed to continual dialogue about the meaning of human existence.

My father preferred for me to sit up close to the front of the church sanctuary, on the right, but near the pulpit, so that he would be able to watch my face reacting to his sermons as he preached. He said my face reflected what I was thinking. My father's sermon would be carefully constructed throughout the preceding week, building to a climactic Saturday night when my three brothers and I were supposed to be more quiet than usual so as not to disturb his final preparations. Sometimes he would review the next day's sermon with my mother in his study.

My father earned his Ph.D. degree from New York's Columbia University and studied at Union Theological Seminary at a time when Paul Tillich and Reinhold Niebuhr were on the faculty. The names of these theologians were household words in our home and their thinking influenced me through my father. Tillich was forced to leave Germany in 1933 because of his antagonism toward the Nazis. He taught the history of theology at Union, and many regard him as a major thinker of the twentieth century on a world scale. Reinhold Niebuhr was an ethicist who, interested in the practical application of Christianity, said, "Our capacity for justice makes democracy possible; our inclination to injustice makes democracy necessary." He refused, Robert McAfee Brown later wrote, "to separate the world of faith and the world of politics." I used to see my father reading the Bible in Hebrew and Greek to understand its exact textual meaning and checking phrases that were in dispute among theologians with his knowledge of Latin, French, and German. He had also studied comparative religion, and his sermons were richly textured with lessons from other cultures and systems of belief from all over the world. From the time I was four years old until I left home for college at eighteen, I sat with my mother in the selected church pew listening to my father's sermon every Sunday morning. My three younger brothers, William, John, and Edward, said I was the apple of my father's eye.

I took my father's sermons very seriously—they were so carefully prepared and inspiring. Equally, my father seemed to care about what I thought of each sermon. This was a significant experience for a young girl, to have her opinion sought on her father's sermons. Yet, even as he was seeking my opinion, his sermons were influencing me. He engaged my mind. He made me think. He also made me feel that what I thought was important. Personal piety was gravely insufficient in my father's view and didn't count with him unless it was translated into daily life and action. The gospel was to him the radically transforming news that each individual is precious in God's sight, and therefore personal salvation was all but meaningless to my father if it was devoid of concern for fundamental justice for others.

His view of social justice included women. My father intro-

duced me to the mystery of one of the puzzling verses of the Old
Testament, Jeremiah 31:22—"For the Lord has created a new
thing on the earth: a woman protects a man." It would be decades, he said, before scholars would unravel the full meaning of
this little-noted verse.

My father also did for me what fathers may more ably do
than anyone else for their daughters: He made me believe deeply
that I was as good as any man. This is one area in which fathers
can excel—a father can make a young girl believe more profoundly in her own worth than her mother can, because the mother
inherently shares her own second-class status as a woman in the
larger society.

So it was hardly a surprise that after returning to Ohio Wesleyan University following the Easter 1962 trip, I could barely
concentrate on my studies long enough to complete and collect
my obligatory degree. I was determined to join the civil rights
struggle. Even in this I was a purist though, and only SNCC would
be pure enough for me.

The air was hazy over the sprawled city of Atlanta as Rosetta
Gardner, Roberta Yancy, and I drove in from Tennessee in June
1962. We were heading for 41 Exchange Place, Southeast, my
base for the next year working on the human-relations project with
the two of them and Ella Baker. The freeways leading into Atlanta spiraled themselves into arching and turning patterns creating an easy path for traffic in and out of the city. My first
impressions are hard to reconcile with the city I know now.

Downtown, the metropolis was a combination of old and new,
an uneasy balance between the South of firecracker stands, barbecue shanties, and Confederate regalia, and the urban culture of
modern buildings, commercial banking, commodity trading, and
construction. An enormous Coca-Cola sign marked a central fork
off Peachtree Street. The name "Peachtree" was used in thirty-
seven different streets, a taxi driver told me—Peachtree Place,
Peachtree Circle, Peachtree Court, Drive, Crescent, and I suppose somewhere there was a Peachtree Alley.

On a major artery downtown, a "Johnny Reb" restaurant blatantly hawked the cooking and atmosphere of the unreconstructed
South. Rich's department store loomed as a chic but constrained
emporium that sold middle-range looks but not the latest fash-

ions, wanted by a city ambivalent about whether it lived in the past or the present. It would be important not to be too flashy in Atlanta.

In the open-air farmers' markets of the city, stalls sold cut sugarcane stalks, sorghum, blackstrap molasses, okra, and dried black-eyed peas. Crawfish and chitterlings were heaped there, too, along with hot sausage to be sold by weight from hanging scales. Chicken gizzards and plucked wings lay before the customer on neatly arranged trays.

On the avenues, white women wore teased mountainous beehive hairdos and prim sleeveless dresses, some walking in mincing steps on high heels. White men tended to be drably dressed in light-colored serge suits, thick-soled shoes, and nylon shirts, their hair in crew cuts or slicked down with pomade. The feet and ankles of black women on the avenues in Atlanta told a different story. They revealed a childhood low in calcium and a lifetime of standing in someone else's kitchen in poorly fitting shoes. I noticed legions of black women waiting in line for the buses that took them to the fashionable white homes on the other side of Atlanta where they worked, their feet splayed and ankles gnarled. Their shoes were fallen flat in the arches and sprawled at the toes. At night they would return to their own homes to carry out again the same housework they had done all day.

White Atlantans liked to remind you that the city had been burned by General Sherman one hundred years before and had to be built anew. As it was reestablished, it was segmented into rigid racial divisions. A certain tightness in white Atlanta was reflected in the repressed languor of the women and taut-lipped faces of the passers-by, as if struggling for control over something undefined. Taxis were abundant, although they were best hailed by phone; fares were cheap and drivers polite, as long as a black person did not get into a cab with a white driver. There was, as in all southern cities of the time, no subtlety in the signs segregating the city: COLORED or WHITE ONLY for lavatories, waiting rooms, doctors' offices, railway stations, water fountains, restaurants, and movie theaters. It was a precisely quartered, drawn, and diced city checkered into separate white and black worlds.

Nonetheless, Atlanta was viewed in the early 1960s by some southerners as a "beacon." This was the word I heard as I started traveling across the ten states in the southern region for the human-relations project. I was to hear it from blacks as well as moderate elements of the white community including professors, journalists, and the clergy who were struggling with what they delicately termed the race question. One of the reasons Atlanta was viewed as a "beacon" was that in its black section, unlike those of most American cities of that time, some businesses were owned and operated by blacks, with the margin of profit going to a growing black middle class. Dozens of black entrepreneurs had opened banks, restaurants, shops, dry-cleaning establishments, and pharmacies that catered to the needs of the black community. Although relatively few in number, the success of these small businesses was an emblem.

When I first moved to Atlanta in 1962, Ella Baker and Rosetta Gardner wanted me to live in the white community. They had some notion that I might influence someone or penetrate somebody's thinking. That was wholly unrealistic. I had a spacious garden apartment near Agnes Scott College, but I was bored and unhappy. None of my black friends could visit me, and I spent all my spare time away from there. I convinced Miss Baker and Miss Gardner that I would be more productive if I could live where my friends from SNCC were living and so I moved into the black community in Atlanta after two months in Decatur.

I might as well have been moving into a country in Africa, Asia, Latin America, or the Middle East. At first, I was apprehensive; I didn't know if I would be welcomed or spurned. It didn't seem, however, to cause much commotion. Yet, there was one aspect that vexed me. It took me a long time to become accustomed to a penetrating stare as black people residing on the west side of the city where I lived looked at me as I walked down the street. It was not a hostile gaze; it was intense and curious. Ella Baker explained to me that people were staring at me to see whether I was actually white, or whether I was one of the members of the black community who was in some small percentage Negroid, therefore legally considered to be black, yet someone who could "pass" for Caucasian and move in and out of the white community at will. In my own mind, I called this piercing inspection "the look." It was almost a prurient leer. Are you passing? asked "the look." This scan reflected that perverse logic of societies that give disproportionate weight to the "taint" of what is considered racially inferior blood, indirectly attributing greater power to those bloodlines than is realized. I was embarrassed by "the look" because it revealed to me how much some blacks had internalized self-deprecating attitudes. Once I understood "the look," I saw that it was not only legal segregation that needed to be overturned but certain attitudes of blacks, deeply affected by pernicious racism, as well as the domineering attitudes of whites.

There was another reaction to me on Hunter Street that bothered me more than "the look." This was when a man averted his eyes and looked hard at the ground rather than make eye contact. In 1962, when I arrived in Atlanta, some of the black men passing by me as I went to a pharmacy or shop, would step off the sidewalk into the street out of my path. Under the mores of the Deep South, they were required to "give way" and not establish eye contact with a white woman. These conditioned behaviors had not been as evident in Richmond, Fredericksburg, or other mid-South cities with which I was familiar. In the "Old South," slaves were taught not to look their master or mistress in the eye because that would imply social equality; this sanction was a convenience for slave owners because they could be partially dressed in the house but slaves would be expected not to look at them. Also, decades of killing, castrating, or terrorizing black men, often on flimsy or fabricated charges of molesting or raping white women, had produced this protective reaction. The downward glances of some black men on Atlanta's streets were probably a hangover of servant manners as well as a guard against being considered "sassy" or "uppity." Even in the commercial districts of Atlanta, black street cleaners and elevator operators did not look white people in the eye and behaved deferentially toward them. "Not only must the Negro observe these rules of deferential speech and conduct," *Deep South* had observed, "but he must observe them wholeheartedly and with no apparent reservations . . . willingly and cheerfully."

I was told that the city had twenty-two black millionaries. When I asked some of my new friends in SNCC about them, the answer usually came with a wry laugh, "Oh yes, they live in the 'golden ghetto,' " referring to a state of mind as well as a section of the black community. I was surprised to find such a large elite with exclusive social registers, debutante balls, and strong social mores forming a subculture within a subculture—a bizarre parody of white culture. Since so many of this group's privileges, attitudes, and preferences were derived from mimicking the dominant white culture, it was important to the ultimate success of the movement that some of its sons and daughters forsake polite society to join the front lines of the movement. I could already see from the friendships I was developing with SNCC staff that the group of activists trickling into SNCC from Howard University in Washington, D.C., was important for this reason. Not only was their education more comprehensive but they represented conservative bastions within the black community that had achieved a good standard of living despite the racial constraints of white culture and were ambivalent about confrontations that might jeopardize their hard-won gains.

The telephone call from Atlanta in June 1962, diverted from the dormitory at Ohio Wesleyan to the coin box at the bus station where I was waiting, was in retrospect even more significant for me than the fact that it provided the conduit for me subsequently to work for SNCC. The YWCA human-relations project, as it turned out, also exposed me at a critical juncture to an international organization run entirely by women.

Thus it was that both Casey Hayden and I came into the civil rights movement through a completely female-led organization, one whose purpose was leadership development for women and girls. We saw the whole YWCA at work, from the policy-setting national governing board to the southern-region campus division or, as it was called, the "Student Y." The National Student YWCA, one segment of the large domestic organization, was more enlightened and progressive than its male counterpart, and it was entirely led by women.

Rosetta Gardner, the director of the southern region of the Student Y, was an outstanding and upright black woman executive. This was my first off-campus job and I didn't know much about office procedures, much less how I would carry out this assignment. Yet I never hesitated or doubted that I could do it, so clear and strong was my belief in my purpose. It never occurred to me that I could fail. It was from Rosetta that I learned advance preparation. She used to tell me, "Mary, be sure you have several speeches ready in your hip pocket for different occasions." Off I went to make speeches, never thinking about how extraordinary this was. Happily, I did not know enough to realize how little I had to offer other than enthusiasm and energy.

The human-relations project allowed me to be shaped and influenced by the fine mind of Ella Baker, whom I now see as one of the dominant personalities in twentieth-century American political struggles, and one of the major voices for blacks in this century. On a daily basis, I was exposed to the personal modesty and the reasoning power of Miss Baker.

The black intern working on the human-relations project turned out to be Roberta Yancy, nicknamed Bobbi, a smart young woman from Pittsburgh with an air of nonchalance and a caustic sense of humor who chortled cynically. She wore her medium-brown hair pulled back behind her head and had just been graduated from Barnard College in New York City. Periodically, Miss Baker would stop whatever Bobbi or I was doing and probe with a series of questions. With Socratic persistence, in her resonant and commanding voice, she would query, "Now let me ask this again, what is our purpose here? What are we trying to accomplish?" Again and again, she would force us to articulate our assumptions. Sometimes I felt intimidated by her scrutiny.

Miss Baker had a beautiful high-contoured forehead, a gracefully defined mouth, and she carried her small frame with natural unstudied elegance. Her posture was always erect, conveying self-confidence. She might have seemed imperious if you did not know how down-to-earth she was. What might be considered self-evident was never self-evident to Ella Baker; it had to be explained and make sense in the telling. Bobbi and I were never allowed to go for long without phrasing our intentions and reexamining our strategies.

At a very important period of my life, Miss Baker tempered my natural tenacity and determination with flexibility and made me suspicious of dogmatism. "The problem in the South," she once mused, "is not radical thought. The problem is not even conservative thought. The problem in the South is not enough thought." She taught me one of the most important lessons I have learned in life: There are many legitimate and effective avenues for social change and there is no single right way. She helped me see that the profound changes we were seeking in the social order could not be won without multiple strategies. She encouraged me to avoid being doctrinaire. "Ask questions, Mary," she would say.

I learned later that it was Ella Baker who resolved a major conflict that occurred within SNCC in 1960. The battle was over whether the organization should pursue as its primary strategy the type of direct-action demonstrations represented by the sit-ins or whether it should embark on longer-term voter registration in pursuit of political power. After three acrimonious days of debate at a meeting at Highlander Folk School in Monteagle, Tennessee, Miss Baker unraveled the problem when she pointed out that SNCC could do both. One might wonder why she let the arguments run on for so long, but Miss Baker preferred not to interfere by offering advice. She later said that her intervention over this division was as "instructive" as she had ever been. Her flexible solution may now appear to be the obvious resolution but, at the time, this question before the green and youthful organization resulted in paralysis.

Miss Baker also played her Socratic role as SNCC's senior adviser. Sometime later I was to see the carefully honed nature of her guidance in the way she would handle one intense staff meeting toward the end of 1963, as we debated the feasibility of a gigantic Mississippi Summer Project for 1964. Miss Baker stopped the meeting short where it was taking place in the basement of Frazier's Lounge on Hunter Street in Atlanta. Acting as if she needed the information only for her own purposes, she closed her eyes, slowly tilted her head back in thought, and, uttering each word decisively with her flawless diction and cultured voice, said, "I never remain associated with any organization for long without asking the question, What is our purpose?" Her eyes still closed, she asked, "Let me pose this question once again, What is it, exactly, that we are trying to accomplish?" Sensing that this was a watershed decision for us—as indeed it would be for the whole civil rights movement—Miss Baker's searching forced another round of discussion on the reasons for enlisting one thousand white student volunteers. All of the reasons were elucidated by various participants again, and, in this process, consensus was reached. I watched as Miss Baker, without being instructive or judgmental, and without even offering her opinion, but using only her nondirective approach, thus gave the final push in support of the plan for the summer project.

As I settled into my new work in Atlanta, I realized that the human-relations project office was one of many such programs located on Exchange Place, Southeast, in Atlanta. Georgia Bureau of Investigation (GBI) agents were frequently parked in front of the building, photographing from their cars those of us going in and out. They considered the building a nest of vipers. Head-quartered in that several-story edifice in Atlanta's commercial area were Quaker organizations such as the American Friends Service Committee, run by Jean Fairfax; the Society of Friends; Connie Curry and the National Student Association; Leon Marion and the World University Service; and our Campus YWCA regional office. I remember being photographed by the GBI. Knowing that they were in collusion with local vigilante groups as well as with the Federal Bureau of Investigation (FBI), who we also knew had us under surveillance, I was certain that my photograph, and that of others working in the building, was being flashed on the screen of nocturnal Ku Klux Klan meetings to identify us for their tar-geting. (The Klan had been organized in the spring of 1866 when a group of former Confederate soldiers formed the first chapter in Pulaski, Tennessee, under the leadership of Colonel Nathan Bed-ford Forrest. By 1867, it had spread throughout the South and was viewed as "the white man's hope," a view that many still shared in 1962.)

Bobbi and I used to visit Connie Curry's tiny cubicle at 41 Exchange Place. We had lunch brought in to us because Bobbi and I could not eat together in downtown Atlanta. We usually spent the time doubled over in laughter because of Connie's ex-plosive and indefatigable sense of humor. As a member of the executive committee of SNCC, she had many friends in the or-ganization and we watched as she was frequently called on to solve problems that cropped up.

Connie, a plucky white North Carolinian, drove a terra-cotta-and-cream-colored Karmann Ghia sportscar that I considered out-rageously racy for someone who was under surveillance. I was amazed by her defiance in cavorting about in the car with its small brass plate mounted on the dashboard engraved with the words, THIS CAR WAS MADE FOR CONNIE CURRY. I once rode with Connie to a racially integrated meeting at Penn Center at Frogmore, a beautiful moss-draped campus in the Sea Islands of South Caro-lina established in 1862 by women missionaries as a school for freed slaves, which was used in the 1960s for retreats by different groups in the movement. The jokers who tap our phones will know where we're going and why, I thought, and all the way from Atlanta I was sure we would be stopped because her car was so identifiable.

Bobbi and I had to write reports for the human-relations project. After a meeting between Benedict College, a black school, and the University of South Carolina, then all-white, Bobbi and I described the situation in reporting to the Field Foundation:

> The meeting dealt with formation of the Student Committee to Observe Order and Peace (SCOOP) at the University of South Carolina. Attention was given to the role that Negro students could play in aiding SCOOP's cause and an attempt was made to gain clear insight into the problems faced by a Negro campus financed by the state. Part of the meeting's significance lay in the fact that we were able to bring together a new group of students. . . . The direct confrontation which ensued at this meeting is one of the high points of our experience thus far.

One invitation we received to visit a campus together was from Queens College, a white women's school in Charlotte, North Carolina. James Meredith's desegregation of the University of Mississippi (Ole Miss) on October 1 of that same year, had sent a jolt through the campus of Queens College. Although he had been accompanied by two hundred fifty federal marshals, this was not sufficient to prevent rioting and two deaths. Bobbi and I wanted to know exactly what sort of environment we were walking into, and prior to our visit we had a survey distributed to the student body through the local Student Y to assess student reactions to the events of Ole Miss. After the visit, in our next report to the Field Foundation, on December 21, 1962, we wrote:

> We received an invitation to visit the campus together as an interracial team with the entire campus ready and prepared for our coming. . . . At the end of our address in the compulsory chapel, during which students who we thought were doing homework were actually taking notes, there was applause which was later indicated to be a very unusual occurrence. There can be little doubt that the visit to Queens College was the most gratifying visit we have made so far. . . .
>
> We were invited to speak to three sociology classes and one informal discussion where questions were honest and probing. While the campus climate cannot be described as sophisticated . . . the astuteness of the questions asked in-

dicates . . . a keener awareness than can probably be found
in most southern colleges. . . . A Committee to Study Integration has been formed. . . . The question of alienation
from family and probability of intermarriage arose frequently. . . . One of the students who accompanied us to
the airport remarked at the end of the visit, "You probably
don't realize this, but your coming on campus together
means more than six speeches made separately. It is too bad
you have to work separately most of the time."

Bobbi's and my overall assignment in the human-relations
project was, however, more difficult than even the perceptive Ella
Baker had anticipated. Although we frequently traveled together
to the same city—provocative enough in most situations—we were
not able to visit white campuses together as had been hoped, except for Queens College, because white colleges would not invite
both of us. We had planned to start an underground group composed of students from Millsaps College, a private white school
in Jackson, Mississippi, and others from Jackson State University,
a school for blacks in the same city. But the staff of the Millsaps
Campus Y, who served as my entry to the Methodist college, were
afraid of losing their jobs, finding themselves ostracized, or being
forced to leave Jackson. I was apprehensive, too. Within thirty
minutes after leaving Bobbi with students at Jackson State, I noticed a police car trailing me. It followed me until I left the city.

The atmosphere at most colleges, black and white, was oppressive. At Southern University, a state school in Baton Rouge,
Louisiana, the largest single black school in the country with an
enrollment of five thousand, over two hundred students had been
expelled for participating in sit-ins. The faculty adviser to the Y
there, an unctuous woman, told Bobbi about one of the student
leaders, Java Thompson: "She went to one of those big Y meetings last year and came back filled with ideas about the sit-in
movement." At white schools, the environment was stultifying.
One young woman gushed to me after I spoke at Ole Miss,
breathlessly exclaiming, "Oh, you're from Atlanta. I've always
wanted to go to Atlanta. You know, it's the city of *Gone with the
Wind*." Then she added ruefully, "I guess it's changed some since
the war though," meaning the Civil War.

I had experiences similar to those Casey had described. When one university professor with whom I was meeting realized that I wanted his opinion on race relations, he stood up and closed the door to his office before he would speak. In a sociology class I observed at another college, I watched as a student raised her hand and questioned the professor about whether the cost of "separate but equal" educational systems wasn't an enormous financial burden for a state that was already behind on expenditures for education. "I can't answer that question," the professor replied.

Despite all the obstacles in our path, Bobbi and I organized one workshop for students from nine black and white colleges in Atlanta in November 1962 and another seminar the following March in Gatlinburg, Tennessee on voter registration, tutorial programs, and fair housing. Still another workshop, featuring the progressive southern white author Wilma Dykeman Stokely, was held at Maryville College in Maryville, Tennessee. Bobbi and I brought into the program John Lewis of SNCC, who was black, and Bob Zellner, his white fellow worker, to give participating students some exposure to the verve and spirit of SNCC. We developed a similar interracial program for the University of North Carolina at Chapel Hill. One of the most successful efforts was a workshop at Memphis State University on "The Search for Southern Identity" that Ella Baker and I organized for December 1, 1962. I remember how thrilled I was to introduce Miss Baker at a white state university just a few miles from the border of Mississippi.

Ella Baker was convinced that conferences and meetings could be life-changing and she cherished a deceptively simple idea that linking people who were interested in social change, but existed in isolation, could speed its progression. One workshop that Bobbi Yancy and I organized at Duke University in the spring of 1963 was, like the others, for the purpose of bringing together southern black and white students who, although concerned individuals, were not themselves taking stands of courage in their communities. Bobbi and I chose the students to be invited, having met them while making speeches at various campuses in the preceding months. This would have been the first time for both the black and the white participants that they had been able to meet a university-level student of another race. As a result of speaking with each other about race relations, the participating students, we hoped, would be more likely to overcome their fear and exert some influence when they returned to their campuses.

I had by then seen it happen repeatedly; if you brought the right resource people together with selected participants, you could create an experience that let them see the problem and their own potential for effectiveness in an entirely new way. Later I realized that even SNCC's frequent and combustible staff meetings fitted in with this view of Miss Baker's that bringing people together was vital. Such gatherings were also personally important, she believed, because they could determine life decisions; my Easter trip to Nashville, Atlanta, and Tuskegee fitted that pattern. I began to incorporate this approach into my own organizing strategies.

Bobbi and I also distributed a six-page newsletter, called "Notes from the South," to campus groups across the country. The title of our mimeographed missive now has the ring of a report from a foreign country; indeed there was a sense of alienation from the rest of the country felt by many enlightened blacks and whites throughout the region then. In this publication, we reported on litigation, student direct action, token integration occurring at selected colleges, and what SNCC was doing.

Part of our approach, as Ella Baker and Rosetta Gardner had designed the project, was for Bobbi or me to make speeches in student chapels, since they usually required mandatory attendance by an entire campus. The Student Y was frequently the only place on a campus where social-change issues were discussed. Bobbi and I would telephone the faculty adviser and try to elicit an invitation to speak through the Campus Y or the dean's office. I would typically speak on the topic of academic freedom because it was acceptable whereas the theme of racial justice was not. Even so, I would make enough references to segregation that the speech acted as a stimulant to those who were interested in this subject. My remarks were like a dragnet because they provoked a response from those who were receptive and the mention of race invariably produced responses afterward from faculty, administration, and students who would step forward. A group always huddled at the front of the auditorium or chapel waiting to talk with me after my remarks, and it was from among those who responded that I would draw a group together, first making sure that they knew each other and were aware that they had company on the same campus.

Sometimes I used our project funds to invite one or two of

the most promising individuals from a campus to a Southwide or national conference so they could see they were not alone. The isolation felt by thoughtful southern whites who questioned racial segregation was paralyzing, and one of the most important results of our project was to break their sense of painful loneliness by putting them in touch with others for mutual support.

During my year of traveling to campuses in ten southern states, Bobbi Yancy and I were able to organize underground groups of black and white students at the black Benedict College and the white University of South Carolina, both in Columbia. We were also able to develop a secret group in Tuscaloosa at Stillman College for blacks, and at the University of Alabama, which was white.

It wasn't often that I could suggest that a group from a white campus start meeting with black students and faculty from a nearby college because it was too dangerous. Meetings would have to take place covertly, at night, usually with the white students and faculty going onto the black campus—the reverse would have resulted in physical violence and arrests. Arrests meant expulsion from school. It was crucial, Ella Baker and Rosetta Gardner believed, that the human-relations project help southern whites to know educated black counterparts in the same town and develop genuine relationships with them as human beings. This had been made virtually impossible in the South by the labyrinth of laws and customs designed to prevent such parity. The resulting estrangement had prevented even gradual remission of attitudes and weakened and made impotent the moderate leadership of both the white and black communities. This had left segregation fixed as the law of the land, with its actual enforcement allotted to the hands of sanctioned desperadoes.

Public speaking was never easy for me. But I have a credo that you should always make yourself do what you are afraid to do. As I reasoned, I would never be a great orator like Henry Clay. Therefore, I decided to speak from the heart, believing that my ideas and sincerity were all I had to offer, not my delivery. Every speech paid off. Someone hungry for reinforcement always came up to talk with me. I also discovered that if a question-and-answer period could be arranged, I would have much better interaction with the audience, which was of course the whole point. Speaking extemporaneously and answering questions was easier and made me feel more comfortable than when I was proceeding through a formal address. If only there was a Q and A, I'd be home free!

Years later I read several articles in popular magazines that reported polling and public-opinion research surveys showing that many people fear making public speeches more than anything else, including death or injury. By that time I was making more than fifty speeches a year all over this country and overseas as a senior government official. Even as speechmaking became easier the more I did it, I never lost my dread immediately before standing up and talking for twenty or thirty minutes, and my basic approach never changed from the one I had worked out for the human-relations project.

First, I would convince myself that precisely *because* I was afraid I therefore *had* to speak my convictions. You should make yourself do what you are afraid to do, I would tell myself. Second, I would take five very deep breaths, counting slowly, to relax the muscles of my diaphragm. Third, I would say to myself, Just speak from the heart. In 1976, I was asked to give one of the addresses at the Democratic National Convention in New York City's Madison Square Garden to over ten thousand milling people and the national television audience. As I waited on the podium, my legs quivering and feeling as if there were no breath in my lungs or oxygen in the air, I employed the same three-step approach I had used for those lonely speeches on southern campuses.

During my year of working with Ella Baker and Bobbi Yancy in the human-relations project of the YWCA, I spent weekends volunteering at the SNCC office on Raymond Street in Atlanta, stuffing envelopes, putting out mailings, and doing whatever had to be done. Bobbi and I were invited to all the SNCC parties on weekends and we even hosted one ourselves, for which Bobbi baked an enormous candied ham. At that party, I met individuals beyond the SNCC circle like Randolph Blackwell, then director of field operations for the Voter Education Project, and Vernon Jordan, who was at the time with the NAACP. I began to make friends among the SNCC staff. Although I didn't recognize it then, my association with Ella Baker was giving me the priceless imprimatur I needed to win the trust and confidence of, first, Jim Forman and then Julian Bond.

Nonetheless, I was worried about how I could accomplish my goal of working for SNCC. The staff was small and tight, and there were only a handful of whites. My Field Foundation grant was scheduled to end in June 1963. Determined to stay in Atlanta and find my way into the movement, I was still unsure of how to get myself onto the SNCC staff. After weeks of racking my brains over this problem, I finally made up my mind to meet with Jim Forman and discuss it with him. I needn't have worried. He was immediately receptive and offered me a position on the staff. Jim suggested that I talk with Julian Bond; he thought I might be the ideal person to replace Dorothy Miller, who was leaving for another assignment; Dottie had been working with Julian, managing the flow of information to the news media in SNCC's Communications operation since 1961. Julian was agreeable, and so I was added to the SNCC payroll at the subsistence stipend of twenty dollars a week before deductions, a drop of two thirds from my modest pay on the human-relations project. Exultant, I joined the SNCC staff in Atlanta when my foundation grant expired in June 1963, and went to work assisting SNCC's press secretary Julian Bond.

In pausing for a few pages to consider the Student Nonviolent Coordinating Committee, we should remember that when it emerged from the sit-ins at the start of the 1960s, little other civil rights activity was visible. Awakening black youth across the region, the sit-ins took the existing civil rights organizations completely by surprise. No one was more astonished than the relative newcomer to the civil rights scene, the Southern Christian Leadership Conference, which, along with its eloquent leader, the Reverend Dr. Martin Luther King, Jr., had emerged from the Montgomery bus boycott of 1955, the first mass action by American blacks. After the success of the boycott, SCLC and Dr. King began to develop a leadership network through the black churches in the region, but nothing remotely resembling the Montgomery confrontation was on its drawing boards for the future when the sit-ins burst into force. The National Association for the Advancement of Colored People had thousands of members and hundreds of court cases under way in the South but no specific action targets. The Congress of Racial Equality, formed in 1942 (the group that had first used the tactic of the sit-in in the 1940s), had some direct action planned but CORE was largely a northern organization. SNCC came on the scene with its own bravado and reinvigorated the quiescent southern civil rights drama. It became the most creative, daring, and ingenious of the civil rights organizations of the 1960s.

The students who survived the sit-ins went on to a baptism by fire in the Freedom Rides. The rides, initiated by CORE, were modeled after a 1947 nonviolent direct-action journey of reconciliation. Following bloody confrontations with mobs as the buses carrying integrated groups of Freedom Riders pulled into bus stations in Anniston and Birmingham, Alabama, and after pressure from the Kennedy administration for a "cooling-off period," CORE abandoned this tactic as too dangerous. SNCC workers Diane Nash in Nashville and Ruby Doris Smith in Atlanta mobilized to continue the rides and CORE was displaced as the guiding force. Spurning all advice that the rides were too perilous, SNCC continued the protest (while retaining the nominal support of CORE and SCLC).

The prison where most of the Freedom Riders ended up for forty-nine days—Mississippi's dreaded Parchman penitentiary—was reminiscent of a medieval dungeon. Over three hundred activists stayed in prison in Mississippi that summer rather than pay bail, and on September 22, 1961, the Interstate Commerce Commission (ICC), having been swayed by the Justice Department, issued a regulation banning separate facilities for whites and blacks in bus and train stations. More resolute as a result of their traumatic experiences, these students converted SNCC from a loose and vague coordinating mechanism into a dedicated cadre of shock troops for "the movement." The sit-ins had amazed everyone and opened a new chapter in post-Civil War black struggle. The Freedom Rides brutally seasoned many of the same students into inveterate resisters, and they came out of the summer of 1961 determined to mount a war of nerves against the savage status quo.

Assuming responsibility for the Freedom Rides gave SNCC a sense of identity, a feeling for its own leverage against the inertia of other groups, and a grasp of its ability to produce action from the ambivalent Kennedy administration. It also sharpened SNCC's image of itself as militant and "self-directing."

Both the sit-ins and the Freedom Rides represented tactics of "direct action." A combination of figures including Attorney General Robert Francis Kennedy, Harry Belafonte, and Timothy

Jenkins now suggested that SNCC should emphasize voter registration instead. Tim taciturnly refused to call himself a law student and always said pointedly that he was "studying for the *law*."
A lean and brilliant black man with great presence, Tim was the
officer of the National Student Association who represented NSA
at SNCC meetings; he formally proposed that the organization
adopt voter registration as its primary strategy. The more religiously inclined SNCC staff, including Marion Barry and the
Nashville group, held firmly to the radical moral vision of the sit-
ins and thought voter registration was a ploy suggested by the
Kennedy administration because it would bring SNCC into less
conflict with white southern communities. SNCC's dilemma over
whether it should pursue direct action or voter registration was, as
I have mentioned, resolved by Ella Baker at a staff meeting at
Highlander Folk School. The decision that the student movement should do both was made on August 11, 1961, after three
days of turbulence; SNCC would work on voter registration in
Mississippi and southwest Georgia and carry out direct action
everywhere else. Diane Nash was put in charge of direct action
and Charles Jones, from Charlotte, North Carolina, was to run
voter registration.

Charles Sherrod, a divinity student from Petersburg, Virginia, was hired as SNCC's first "field secretary." This was the
title used for staff who were based in local communities across the
South. Having been a Freedom Rider, Sherrod (as he preferred
to be called) studied theology at Union Theological Seminary in
New York City before joining SNCC. Despite the hazards that it
posed in an area regarded as the second or third most dangerous
part of the country for blacks, Sherrod insisted that the Southwest
Georgia Project should always have a racially integrated staff. One's
means had at all times to reflect one's ends, he argued.

Robert Moses, a doctoral candidate at Harvard University from
New York City, was already in Mississippi developing voter-registration programs with a key local leader named Amzie Moore.
In September 1961, James Forman came from Chicago to join the
staff as executive secretary and, having earned the confidence of
both direct-action adherents and voter-registration proponents, he
was able to infuse the organization with new administrative and
fund-raising prowess. SNCC began making the transition from a
slack coordinating committee for dispersed student groups to a

fully staffed operation, based in Atlanta, with field secretaries located throughout the region organizing projects in either direct
action or voter registration.

The SNCC staff by June 1963 saw themselves no longer as
students but as staff organizers, and declared so at a Southwide
meeting in Atlanta; they were influenced in part by Ella Baker's
concept that indigenous leadership was inherent in every individual and community and could be released by skillful behind-the-
scenes organizing. In southwest Georgia, both voter registration
and direct action were to be combined. But in Mississippi, direct
action was less possible because of extreme danger from head-on
confrontations, and other tactics were developed that reflected
SNCC's increasing turn toward organizing for political power.

In 1960, in Cleveland, Mississippi, Amzie Moore had emphasized to Bob Moses, SNCC's Mississippi director, the need for
voter registration, rather than direct action, in Mississippi and urged
that it be accomplished by a large contingency of student volunteers. Voter registration was also more desirable to Bob, who
strongly shared Ella Baker's view of leadership. In the autumn of
1963, a mock election, or "Freedom Ballot," in Mississippi demonstrated the desire of disenfranchised Mississippi blacks to vote.
The mock election also laid the foundation for black citizens in
the state later to enter congressional races for the first time since
Reconstruction, although as protest candidates. Subsequently, alternative Freedom Schools for education in civics, as well as community centers and libraries, were developed by SNCC in
Mississippi.

In 1964, principally with SNCC's assistance, the Mississippi
Freedom Democratic party was formed, and, based on meticulous
documentation for submission to the Credentials Committee of
the regular Democratic party, a formal "Challenge" was mounted
against the regular all-white Democratic party delegation to the
national convention in Atlantic City, New Jersey. A racially integrated delegation, selected through proper and open elections,
asked to be seated instead of the all-white regular delegation that
forbade black participation. Yet the Challenge was rejected. This
strategy, of trying to make the party reform itself, failed; disenchanted, SNCC would from that point on emphasize a strategy of
separate political organizing.

Simultaneously, SNCC's research staff, headed by a former-economics professor, Jack Minnis, drew attention to the concept developed by political scientist Floyd Hunter that there existed in every political entity an unseen but underlying "power structure," a term popularized by SNCC and used throughout the decade.

The Atlantic City effort at realignment of the Democratic party fell short, but SNCC experienced great success in accomplishing its other goals in its Mississippi Summer Project of 1964, in which nearly one thousand nationally recruited volunteers, most of them white, joined the effort to fulfill Amzie Moore's dream. Three of them were killed, but, as the eyes of the world focused on Mississippi, the spine of violence against blacks in that state was finally broken.

This victory was, however, followed by a period of tumultuous upheaval as the organization thrashed out its identity, internal structure, and future direction. A series of strained and contentious meetings during 1964 and 1965 sought to clarify such issues. SNCC operations now reflected a strategy that, while neither trim nor tailored, was aimed at achieving political power for blacks. It was during this period of intense debate on the structure of the organization that Casey Hayden and I—increasingly concerned about self-determination for women in the context of a community committed to equality and social justice—summarized our thinking in a memorandum that we sent to forty women organizers across the country. Many of them would subsequently report that it was a major catalyst sparking their own early organizing around women's issues.

By late 1965, SNCC organizing was almost wholly directed at parallel political organizations, with plans for a separate new political party, the Black Panthers, in Lowndes County, Alabama. In electoral politics, there was a new sally: Julian Bond's ultimately successful campaign for the Georgia State Assembly. Although something of the old concept of direct action resurfaced in the gigantic march from Selma to Montgomery, Alabama, that year, the event grew out of two years of sustained organizing through SNCC's voter-registration program there. SNCC staff began to talk about "taking over the courthouse," its jargon for achieving political power. And another phrase popularized by SNCC would soon catch attention—"Black Power."

* * *

I had succeeded in my goal of becoming a member of SNCC's staff, when, not long after, a second happy development occurred—Casey Hayden asked me if I would like to share an apartment with her. Casey had gone north with her husband, Tom Hayden, and returned a year later without him. She was the first white person in Georgia to have a black attorney, Howard Moore, represent her in a divorce case. She went to work with Jim Forman, handling fund-raising and contacts with external groups. She was called northern coordinator; she also corresponded with campus groups and handled liaison with the National Council of Churches, the National Student Association, and other organizations that supported SNCC. I cannot explain why I was so drawn to Casey. Perhaps she was the sister I had never had.

I had strong feelings about almost everyone in SNCC. Closeness among us developed fast. Everything was telescoped and there was no time for the normal evolution of relationships; bonds formed quickly and deeply. We were emotionally encapsulated within the community that we had constructed and into which we were cordoned; and we felt both isolated from and vulnerable to the outside world. What sustained us from day to day was an intense feeling of interdependency—the sense that we had only one another to rely on—and a spirit of comradeship. We could not trust anyone else. We had to trust each other and we did. It was a rare and precious time that none of us would ever recapture.

When I looked into Casey's blue eyes, I thought of Ralph Waldo Emerson's observation that eyes are the window to a person's soul. "What a world! What a world!" she would say when anything went wrong, and then she would laugh long and resonantly with her clear blue eyes dancing. She had come into the civil rights movement by way of the Christian Faith and Life Community at the University of Texas, an ecumenical campus group that had produced many activists. As a young student, Sandra Cason had met and married Tom Hayden, a founder of the Students for a Democratic Society and author of the Port Huron Statement—the guiding issuance for SDS and much of what was later called the New Left—who afterward married Jane Fonda and was elected state assemblyman in California.

Two years earlier, during the period when over thirty-six hundred southern students had been jailed for sitting-in and thousands more were risking incarceration, Casey once enthralled a

national student audience. In her speech, she described an encounter between Henry David Thoreau and Ralph Waldo Emerson, two of the New England Transcendentalists. Thoreau had
been jailed in Massachusetts for advocating civil disobedience, when
he was visited by Emerson, his friend and colleague. Describing
Emerson peering through the bars at his associate in the dismal
cell, Casey echoed Emerson's admonishment, "What are you doing
in there, Henry?" To the hushed audience of six hundred attending the National Student Association congress, Casey's voice re-
verberated with Thoreau's taciturn response, "What are *you* doing
out there, Ralph? What are *you* doing out there?"

After she and I decided to share an apartment, we went
downtown to the rental office for a housing project that was located in the southwestern section of Atlanta, off Gordon Road. It
was the best housing we could afford on our stipends. As it was,
the twenty-dollar weekly subsistence I received as a member of
the headquarters staff was higher than what most SNCC staff received because the cost of living was higher in Atlanta. A SNCC
field secretary was paid $10 a week—$9.64 after deductions. Staff
in the Atlanta office couldn't live off the land like a field secretary
working in what we called "the rurals." Of course, if you were in
jail, you didn't get anything.

At the rental office, Casey and I encountered a blond clerk
with lacquered bouffant hair, penciled eyebrows, and a sharply
pointed brassiere who became hostile when she looked at us and
suddenly realized, by the southwest Atlanta address we had requested, that we two white women wanted to rent in a black
housing project. She must have thought we were whores although
the taboos on sexual relations between white women and black
men normally prevented even white prostitutes from accepting
black business. The anthropologist authors of *Deep South* had eth-
nographically noted that incest was "viewed with less horror than
infraction of the caste sex taboos" of race. When Casey and I had
the temerity to ask for three gallons of pale apricot paint so we
could cover the sickening green color of the apartment, the clerk
became agitated. The same scornful treatment was afforded us by
the employees of the telephone and utilities companies as we went
to open accounts with them.

Our neighbors in the housing project off Gordon Road were
diffident and left us alone. No one ever asked us what we were

doing there, reflecting the split consciousness in the black community about civil rights. The view from the ground-floor apartment looked out on a cemetery across the road. There was no paving among the buildings of the housing project, only the tamped-down red clay of Georgia that spattered sorrel-colored mud when it rained. Often, it seemed when we were most exhausted, we received strange phone calls from men who obviously thought we were prostitutes. Living in that project was one way I came to understand the almost pathological preoccupation of a few black men then with long-forbidden sexual contact with white women. "White pussy," they hissed and spat into our phone, "white pussy." They whispered obscenities and talked in anatomical terms that perplexed me as I didn't know many of the words.

Casey and I worked long hours at the Raymond Street headquarters of SNCC in southwest Atlanta, and when we arrived home at the small apartment we would share the cooking and cleanup. During these evenings we read and discussed the works of the French author Simone de Beauvoir and the South African author Doris Lessing. Our copy of Beauvoir's *The Second Sex* was underlined, creased, marked up, and finally coverless from our study of it. It had caused an uproar when it appeared in 1949 by condemning marriage as a form of slavery. Beauvoir wrote, "One is not born, but rather becomes, a woman. No biological, psychological or economic fate determines the figure that the human female presents in society; it is civilization as a whole that produces this creature."

Whether it was Beauvoir's *The Mandarins* and *She Came to Stay*, or Lessing's *A Man and Two Women*, Casey and I had an insatiable appetite for these two authors and especially for Beauvoir's global perspective. Beauvoir expressed the fundamental existentialist belief that the human race is responsible for its own destiny, and she wrote that it may make of its history "a hopeless inferno, a junkyard of events, an enduring value."

The novels among these books all had something in common: The significance of the female characters was not due to their relationship with a lover, husband, brother, or father—although the story often involved these relationships. The women were thus not in the role of what Beauvoir called "the other"; their existence was not defined by a man. They defined themselves. We cautiously lent our dog-eared copy of Lessing's *The*

Golden Notebook, with its broken yellow buckram spine, in succession to Jim Forman, Bob Moses, Mendy Samstein, Andrew Young, Mike Thelwell, and other men who we thought might be able to appreciate it.

I had first been introduced to Simone de Beauvoir by Miriam Willey, professor of philosophy and religion at Ohio Wesleyan University while I was a student there. As the faculty member who led the trip where I met the four SNCC workers, Miriam had also introduced me to dry sherry at her home in Delaware, Ohio, and used to talk candidly about the discrimination and condescension she faced as a woman professor. She thought the college suffered from too much "moral authoritarianism." In retrospect, I think it was academic authoritarianism and male authoritarianism that rankled Miriam.

Long before feminist theologians began to probe centuries of ecclesiastical practices that sought to justify the church's patriarchal hierarchy and, indeed, its suppression of women, Miriam was doing her own biblical analysis and found it empowering to women. She talked with me almost as if I were her peer, and her confidence in me and her opening up to me began to alter my view of the world. As a result of those evening discussions over slender glasses of pale sherry, I had become conscious of double standards all about me, one standard for men and another for women. Miriam never made me feel sorry for her or for myself. She opened my eyes so that I would not be swept along like flotsam, unaware, drifting in a sea of male bias. She helped me learn that I couldn't battle on all issues and would have to pick my fights. It was Miriam who made me realize that moral indignation without political shrewdness is worthless. This was a lesson that the civil rights movement only deepened and reinforced, and it was crucial to my becoming the person that I am.

While lending Lessing's *The Golden Notebook* to our male friends, we started lending Beauvoir's *The Second Sex* to other women we could convince to read it. As important to Casey's awakening as Miriam had been to mine was Dorothy Dawson from Austin, Texas. While rooming together at the University of Texas, Casey and Dorothy had begun discussing the second-class status of women. During this period, Dorothy was working with Connie Curry in the NSA project and she, too, was involved in our conversations about women.

Betty Friedan's *The Feminine Mystique,* which sent shock waves across American suburbs that same year, seemed irrelevant and marginal to us. Although I later realized its significance with some sectors of American women, it was amazing to us that black women in the United States were not cited once. Our own civil rights movement was not mentioned, even though it was then roiling the structures of the South. Friedan's suburban emphasis seemed out of touch with the social and economic issues that concerned us and utterly unrelated to the questions of political and personal self-determination that were beginning to preoccupy us.

Casey and I confided in each other. She was just enough older than I to be my peer but at the same time my mentor. We shared our hopes, our fears, our anxieties, and our dreams. Although it is not always easy for me to talk openly because I am protective of my feelings, Casey's radiance and magnanimity gave me assurance and helped me grow. It was my experience of her loyalty to me and the courage of her example that led me to conclude that loyalty and courage are two of the most important attributes of character. I was to learn, however, that my courage is more apt to show from how I act—in my decisions, what I undertake, how I follow through, and in the way I commit my time—than it is from what I say publicly.

CHAPTER 2

DANVILLE

In Danville on June the tenth
In the year of sixty-three,
From Bible Way Church to the courthouse
Some people marched to be free.

As they fell down on their knees
Led by Reverend McGhee,
He looked up and cried, "Lord, please,
We want to be free."

They heard the voice of Chief McCann
As it cut across the prayer,
I'll never forget those violent words,
"Nigger, get out of here!"

And as they heard those brutal words
They didn't turn around.
The water from the fire hose
Knocked them to the ground.

And as they fell down on the ground
They were hit with billy sticks.
I'll never forget that terrible sound
As the people's heads did split.

Don't you stumble, brother, don't you falter,
O mother, don't you weep.
We're climbing up to our freedom
Although the road is steep.

On June thirteenth we marched again
They used the tear gas bombs.
The grand jury indicted us
On five thousand dollars bond.

In Danville town's corrupted courts
We got no justice done.
We were found guilty before the trial
And the judge he wore a gun.

—MATTHEW JONES,
The Freedom Singers, 1963

My great-great-great-grandfather Wright Johnson pulled on his sturdiest boots. The soles had been repaired again and again, and, in preparation for this trip, they had again been resoled. He was wearing heavy homespun wool pants, a homespun wool jacket with wide lapels, a white shirt with billowing sleeves, and a sash tied loosely at the neck. His deerskin jacket was made from a buck he had shot himself, as were his gloves. He pulled low on his forehead a raccoon hat that would shield him from the rain. As he sat on the edge of his handmade wooden bed, he placed the last few items including his Bible in his satchel of wild boar skin.

It was the winter of 1836. He stepped out of his log house built from hewn timbers in Surry County, North Carolina, near the state line just below Patrick County, Virginia. He was leaving behind his wife Nancy Wilkes who came from Wilkes County, North Carolina. Her light blond "flaxen hair" caught the light as she stood in the window to wave good-bye. He closed the hatched door, thinking to himself, It smells like snow—in that peculiar vernacular of farmers and those who live close to the land and can sense when it's going to snow. Ahead of him lay a 275-mile walk to be ordained a deacon in the Methodist Church.

Wright Johnson had been preaching for many years as a licensed lay preacher, or "local preacher," to use the church term. His grandfather had been an officer of the Virginia militia who fell in Braddock's defeat in the French and Indian War in 1755. But now Wright Johnson wanted to be an officer in the army of the spirit—he was determined to become a full-fledged minister in the first of the two categories of ordination provided by the Methodist *Discipline* and would soon be able to administer the ordinances of baptism, marriage, and burial of the dead.

The records of the "class meeting" that he supervised some years later at the Mount Hermon Methodist Church in Surry County foreshadow my own interest in human rights and show an openness of spirit that was ahead of his time. Among those noted in the meticulously kept attendance records for 1849, with a cursive "P" for present and "A" for absent, are two black women members of his class, listed as "colored members." It was commonplace before the Emancipation Proclamation for slaves to attend church with their masters, sitting in a separate balcony, which can still be seen in some church buildings. But the class meeting was an altogether different phenomenon. At the heart of membership in the early Methodist Church was the idea of close personal fellowship obtainable only in a small group. Ministers—sometimes called circuit riders—traveling the frontier on horseback with twenty, thirty, or more preaching places could not know each member individually. Class meetings were an important supplement with class leaders chosen to act as lay pastors. With usually no more than twelve members, class meetings gathered weekly for Bible study, individual witness, prayer, discipline, spiritual guidance, and problem solving. These were close personal sessions—not formal worship in the sanctuary—in which everyone knew everyone else intimately, and class or social distinctions were set aside as each member participated freely. The doctrine of free grace for all brought about an insistence on the worth of each person under God. Despite the emphasis on democracy and participation, during the years before the Civil War black or slave members would have been restricted to sitting in balconies during regular worship. The fact that these two black women, "colored members," were regular members of my great-great-great-grandfather's intimate class meeting is surprising, at a time when the United States had admitted little more than half its eventual quota of states to the Union.

The circuit riders and their assistants—the class leaders and lay preachers—were involved in the total fabric of eighteenth- and nineteenth-century American society. They agitated for improved social conditions, they were booksellers, and through their camp meetings they helped lay the groundwork for democratic self-government. They also acted as physicians of sorts in emergencies.

Starting out on that overcast day in 1836, Wright Johnson walked from Surry County approximately seventy-five miles to Danville in Pittsylvania County, Virginia, breaking his journey by staying overnight with kinfolk along the way. When he reached Danville, he spent an extra day resting in the home of a friend. Carrying his boarskin satchel, he set out the next morning to walk the additional two hundred miles to Norfolk. He walked and walked, staying one night with a cousin and another night with strangers who took him into their home, sensing his faith, his determination, and understanding his mission. Weeks later, both his boot soles and his body thinner, he reached the meeting of the Virginia Annual Conference of the Methodist Episcopal Church at Norfolk. After due examination and the recommendation of his peers, he was ordained by Bishop Elijah Hedding as a deacon of the church on February 17, 1836. The Reverend Wright Johnson then left Norfolk and walked the 275 miles back again across southside Virginia, stopping in Danville, to return home to his ministry.

Exactly 127 years later, I arrived in Danville, a tobacco and textile city of forty-five thousand, on June 22, 1963, in a shimmying red truck. I was traveling with Sam Shirah, a white native of Alabama, and another child of a Methodist minister, who had once been a student of George Wallace, later the avowedly segregationist governor of Alabama. Wallace had been his Sunday school teacher in the town of Clayton. Sam joined the SNCC staff in May 1963 and led a Freedom Walk of ten persons into Alabama, a protest that had continued the "walk" of Baltimore postman William L. Moore, a member of CORE, who was murdered on an Alabama highway at Attalla carrying signs protesting racial discrimination. As a result, Sam had spent thirty-two days on death row in the Kilby corrections facility, where the Scottsboro Boys were incarcerated—the nine black youths who were charged with the rape of two white women on a freight train in 1931 and, despite medical testimony to the contrary, were sentenced to death until the decision was reversed by the Supreme Court in 1932. We left the Atlanta SNCC headquarters, driving to New York City with an old friend of mine, Alan Hogenauer, in order to pick up the red truck that had been donated to the movement. Jim Forman thought the truck ought to be assigned to the Danville project and told me, as he dispatched us, that SNCC workers Ivanhoe Donaldson, Bob Zellner, Dorothy Miller, and Avon Rollins were expecting us at the local office in Danville.

At midnight on June 19, Sam and I climbed into the donated red truck, leaving Manhattan through the Holland Tunnel for an overnight drive to my parents' home in Virginia. On June 21, possessing the high energy of youth that draws little distinction between night and day, we roared out of Spotsylvania County at 9:30 P.M. and arrived at the movement headquarters in Danville early the next morning. As we entered the city—briefly the last capital of the Confederacy—I peered at it sprawling on the banks of the Dan River. The main industry in Danville, the Dan River

Mills, was considered by the local chamber of commerce to be the largest "single-unit textile mill in the world," and it was the Dan River Mills that ran the town.

I was looking for four churches of which my grandfather, the Reverend William Luther King, had been the pastor in the 1920s—Stokesland, Olivet, Fairview, and Design congregations of the "Danville Circuit" of the Methodist Episcopal Church, South. In the back of my mind was my great-great-great-grandfather's journey on foot through Danville and the handmade deerskin gloves from the buck he had shot.

I still have Wright Johnson's oatmeal-colored deerskin gloves with their crude but sturdy dark-brown stitches. I had often fingered those gloves as a child. When I began to ponder myself in place and time, the deerskin gloves gave me hints and clues to the question that started in childhood and persisted into my late twenties: Who am I? They told me that I came from people who lived in wilderness and helped to open up the country. Because of what I knew about Wright Johnson's steps, the gloves revealed tenacity and resourcefulness. They also said that my family lacked earthly riches but could survive on the land. From what I knew about the man who shot the buck and made the gloves, they told of a family with dignity and integrity that derived from a deep religious faith.

We passed Stratford College. This junior college was a continuation of the former Randolph-Macon Institute, a private and of course racially segregated and exclusive "ladies' seminary" affiliated with the Methodist Church. By special permission, my father, then a boy of thirteen, was allowed to attend along with his sister without having to pay tuition. This must have been a blessing because my grandfather's salary was then not much more than one hundred dollars a month. My father had been one of only two boys to have had that special status on the all-girls campus, the other being the son of Mr. Charles Evans, the principal of Randolph-Macon Institute.

I remembered that I had been to Danville only twice before, once as a small child and later, at thirteen, on the way to a reunion of my father's family in Patrick County, Virginia. Because of my experiences the previous year traveling with the human-relations project, I figured that I had only a few hours in Danville to observe and get my bearings before I would be targeted by the police. I knew that once I visited the movement's headquarters, from then on I would be marked and under scrutiny. I searched the city, imagining my father's boyhood days, my grandparents' lives, and, before that, Wright Johnson's sojourn there.

Sam and I arrived at the High Street Baptist Church where Dorothy Miller would brief us on what had happened so far. We arrived at 8:00 A.M. on Saturday morning. Less than an hour later, I heard the Danville police, upstairs, kicking in the main door to the sanctuary of the church to arrest three SNCC workers who had been indicted by the grand jury.

I had come to Danville to run SNCC's local Communications operation. I would manage everything related to the information we gave the news media representatives who were based in Danville and act as the telephone link between our Danville office and SNCC headquarters in Atlanta, from where Julian Bond would back me up if I was having trouble breaking a story. Dorothy Miller had been responsible for this function but was leaving for Massachusetts to enlarge the Boston Friends of SNCC group, one of our northern support organizations.

The following Monday morning, June 24, I attended a hearing before federal judge Thomas Jefferson Michie of the U.S. District Court for the Western District of Virginia. In the federal courthouse in Danville, motions were filed by several attorneys to remove the cases of two local men, jailed by Judge Archibald M. Aiken, from the state courts to the federal system. I watched a beautiful young black woman with presence named Ruth Harvey Charity, a local attorney who was the first woman lawyer in the city, making the motions. She and a team of noteworthy outside attorneys—Len Holt, William Kunstler, Arthur Kinoy, Professor Chet Antieu, Shellie F. Bowers (later a District of Columbia Superior Court judge), and Phil Hirschkopf, then a law student— were, along with five other local lawyers, to make a series of legal pirouettes that summer in Danville. The noted black attorney Leo Branton, brother of lawyer Wiley A. Branton, also came to Danville for a period from Los Angeles. Bill Kunstler treated me like a daughter and Ruth Harvey was warm and responsive to me, but it was Len Holt who would help me when the time came to escape across the river.

I had been in Danville for exactly two days. As I walked down the corridor to the courtroom of the federal courthouse, one of two tobacco-chewing Danville police lounging there called out loudly, "Mary King!" I was stunned. Even though I had tried to prepare myself mentally for being placed under close watch by the police in Danville, here was the evidence. I shuddered involuntarily. Forty-eight hours after my arrival, the police recognized me and knew my name.

Frustration had been brewing in the black community for some time. Inspired by the sit-ins that had started in 1960 not far away in Greensboro, North Carolina, the black leadership of Danville took action. For several months, there continued an intense legal skirmish concerning the main public library—the site of the final full cabinet meeting of the Confederacy—because blacks in Danville were not allowed to use this library. They were forced to use a pathetic branch typical of those to which blacks were relegated all over the region. Faced with a court order to desegregate, won by the NAACP, library officials closed the building from September through November 1960. It was then reopened on an integrated basis; however, all the chairs had been removed. For months afterward, admission to this previously free public library cost $2.50 for a one-year card.

One third of Danville's population was black. In addition to their being disenfranchised, everything in the city was segregated. Streets in the black community were unpaved and badly lighted. Garbage was collected there less frequently than in the white community. Blacks were restricted to balconies in theaters. Restaurants, hotels, and motels bore WHITE ONLY signs. Restrooms at public facilities and gas stations were segregated. Physicians and dentists had two separate waiting rooms, one for whites and one for "colored." The train and bus stations had separate waiting rooms on either side of the station, similarly labeled. All the schools were segregated except for one state-financed vocational school for high school graduates that had admitted two black students the year before. By 1963, one of these had dropped out leaving one sole black student in the entire area studying in an integrated institution.

Toward the end of May 1963, soon after television coverage flashed around the world showing police dogs and fire hoses being used by Police Chief Eugene "Bull" Connor against peaceful demonstrators in Birmingham, two black Protestant ministers in

Danville led a demonstration at the municipal building. They were requesting equality in municipal employment, an end to school racial segregation, and desegregation of restaurants, hotels, and motels. Dorothy Miller began to tell Sam Shirah and me her story as we sat together in the basement office of the High Street Church. Dottie was small and stocky with shoulder-length brunette hair. She had a forthright manner. A practical young white woman from New York City, Dottie had a contagious laugh that broke easily and she liked to laugh at herself. She had already learned from working with Julian—as I would soon learn—to understate her descriptions. Yet, even though unadorned, her tale was gory.

The Reverend Lawrence Campbell and the Reverend Alexander I. Dunlap had decided to lead a march daily from May 31 to June 5, 1963, with each march emphasizing employment of black citizens. Dottie helped to make some of the demonstrators' signs; they had asked for jobs as firefighters, meter readers, police officers, secretaries, and clerks in municipal offices.

Shortly after the first march, the Commonwealth's Attorney drew up an injunction against the key figures, and copied it, filling in the names of others who had marched. In short order, nearly two hundred people had been arrested for violating the injunction.

On June 5, according to Dottie's account, their patience wearing thin, the Reverend Mr. Campbell, the Reverend Mr. Dunlap, and several students asked to see Mayor Julian R. Stinson, who could not be found. The group said politely that they would wait and sat down on the floor. The police assaulted them, knocking the Reverend Mr. Dunlap down a flight of stairs and choking a young woman, who, forgetting her lessons in nonviolence, hit one of the policemen with her purse. Dottie burst into uncontrolled laughter at this part of the story, identifying with the young woman's exasperation and impatience shown by such a futile move. The young woman and the two clergymen were arrested, Dottie explained, the two ministers having been indicted by the grand jury for "inciting to riot" and "inciting or encouraging a minor to commit a misdemeanor," and bail was set at $5,500 for each. This was a high bail at that time.

The day after those arrests, June 6, was the day that the Reverend Mr. Campbell telephoned Jim Forman in Atlanta and fervently begged for help, saying that Danville was becoming another Birmingham. Jim sent the first field secretary to Danville on June 8; and another fourteen SNCC workers, including Dottie and me, were to follow throughout that summer.

A local newspaper, *The Roanoke Times*, editorialized on June 7:

> Danville is now going through its ordeal of racial tension
> brought on by those not content to rely upon the procedures
> of law to gain what they assert to be Negro rights. The
> demonstrators have taken the issue out of the courts and
> into the streets. . . . The Negroes of Danville will have to
> realize that the only sound basis for obtaining the recogni-
> tion they seek is by appeal to the courts. . . . When any
> body of citizens takes it upon themselves to determine
> which laws they will obey and which they will defy we ap-
> proach social anarchy.

Again the decision was made to march on the municipal building, and on Monday afternoon, June 10, thirty-seven individuals were arrested.

"Suddenly," Dottie said, her hands gesticulating, "police officers snaked large coils of fire hoses into position on the steps of the city hall. As the demonstrators continued walking, the fire hoses were turned on them full blast and police started openly beating them with clubs."

That night, sixty-five black citizens—plus one lone white SNCC worker, Dorothy Miller—walked five abreast from the Bible Way Church to the city jail. Led by the Reverend Hildreth G. McGhee, they sang hymns and circled the jail once, passing several impassive policemen. As they began a second walk around, Chief of Police E. G. McCain arrested twenty-four-year-old SNCC field secretary Bob Zellner, who had been photographing the demonstration (and whom Dottie would marry later that August). The chief ordered the Reverend Mr. McGhee to stop the singing. The minister instead passionately raised his voice in a loud prayer for the police "who know not what they do," and implored divine forgiveness for them. The next thing Dottie knew, he was being led away by the police and fire hoses were turned on full force toward those who remained. Police, including hurriedly deputized city employees, clubbed those who dodged under cars to escape the pressure of the fire hoses.

As Dottie described it in a pamphlet called *Danville, Virginia* written by Dottie and published by SNCC in August 1963:

Chief McCain bellowed, "Let 'em have it" and firemen turned hoses on the people, many of them women and teenagers. Nightstick-wielding police and deputized garbage collectors smashed into the group, clubbing Negroes who were bunched for safety against parked cars. Some were washed under the cars; others were clubbed after the water knocked them down. Bodies lay on the street, drenched and bloody. Police and garbage collectors chased those demonstrators who were able to walk for two blocks.

Forty-eight of the sixty-five demonstrators were wounded and treated at Winslow Hospital—in its segregated and understaffed section for blacks. The force of the water was so strong that it tore the dress off Gloria Campbell, the wife of the Reverend Mr. Campbell. Two were severely injured, and many were hospitalized. A total of fifty individuals were arrested that day.

The following day, the bombastic words of Mayor Stinson appeared in *The Washington Post:* "We will hose down the demonstrators and fill every available stockade." The mayor denied there was any problem in the city and blamed instead "a couple-hundred hoodlums" for the demonstrations. Yet even Danville's two local newspapers, *The Register* and *The Bee,* admitted that "demonstrators were dispersed with the use of hoses and nightsticks."

On June 11, the next day, Dottie was among two hundred individuals marching to city hall who still called for equality in public hiring but were now also protesting against police brutality. Many of those pacing back and forth in front of city hall were bandaged; one teenager walked with the aid of a crutch. Again, the mayor refused to see them.

Dottie continued her saga. On June 12, Jim Forman arrived from Atlanta and was arrested at the entrance of a Howard Johnson's restaurant on a charge of trespassing. He was released on bail, and the next day, June 13, he and Dr. Milton Reid, Virginia representative of the SCLC, joined the Reverend Lendell W. Chase, pastor of the High Street Baptist Church, in a leadership huddle. The Reverend Mr. Chase, president of the Danville Christian Progressive Association, the local organization behind the movement in Danville, led a procession of two hundred and fifty citizens to see the mayor. They waited in front of the barred doors of city hall as several hundred sandwiches prepared at the High Street Church and soft drinks were brought to the demonstrators. At eleven o'clock that night, Dottie continued, as some had stretched out to sleep the fire trucks again appeared. Police arrived on the street wearing helmets. Fire hoses were once again unwound. Police burst from inside city hall onto the steps, clubs in hand.

Dottie recounted how the two ministers and Jim Forman quickly consulted with each other as the marchers gripped the railing on the stairs and covered their faces.

"Some took flight," Dottie noted. "But more than eighty were prepared to face three high-pressure fire hoses about fifteen feet from their faces—close enough to break bones, puncture skin, fracture skulls, and blow eyes out. Jim was at his best," Dottie exclaimed. "Suddenly, he broke ranks, rushed over, and excitedly challenged the police chief." This diversion was designed to give the remaining demonstrators a break so they would have time to get out of the way of the power hoses—which they did. "If Jim hadn't made that move, many people would have been seriously injured, some perhaps might have died."

First Amendment rights were also dampened in Danville. William Chapman, a serious young reporter who observed much of that traumatic summer in Danville, and who later that July would talk quietly with me while I walked a picket line, filed his story on the events of June 13 with *The Washington Post*. He dryly noted, "Eight reporters who had been told to wait for Mayor Stinson's latest comments in the City Council chamber were told by a police officer that they could not leave the room while the demonstrators were being cleared off the steps." The reporters, held in a form of house arrest in the council chamber, were allowed to leave but not until after the steps of city hall had been cleared of Danville's nonviolently protesting black citizens.

That night's mass meeting in a Baptist church in the black community saw police with submachine guns set up roadblocks near the church. Nearby a riot tank with four mounted machine guns was poised, silhouetted against the darkened Danville sky.

The city was under siege. Looking as if a police convention were in town, uniformed officers lingered in small groups on the

streets or watched in police cars gyrating around the textile-man-
ufacturing city. State troopers patrolled in arrogant, slothful abun-
dance. Middle-aged white municipal employees, hastily deputized
and pressed into service, loitered about the town. Fire trucks
clanged and careened around the corners of the city. There were
even signs of a military mobilization taking place: Armed personnel were sighted about the town, and helicopters on the outskirts
spasmodically broke into clatter. I felt the city might blow apart.
This was the first time I had been surrounded by police, state
troopers, and deputized militia, and heard choppers in the distance. I had never felt besieged before. I noticed a tightening
nausea in my stomach. So this is what it is to be in dread, I thought;
this is the sickening feeling of fear.

The police in Danville were ingenious and inventive in their
harassing tactics. They did something that I have never seen anywhere else. They "followed" us in front. A favorite device of
police everywhere in the region was to follow civil rights workers
closely from behind to intimidate them. Usually, in most towns
and hamlets, police cars would hug the rear of our cars, watching
carefully for any petty violation upon which they would flash their
lights and sirens, swooping down upon us to make an arrest. But
in Danville, the police followed us in front. They would move
one of their cars, crawling, out into the street before one of our
cars and slow down until there was less than six feet of clearance.
Because the law required the driver to signal a left or right turn
fifty feet before turning, the police could always tell which way
our car was turning from their rearview mirrors, and, of course,
failure to use the blinking signal, or a hand signal, guaranteed that
we would immediately be arrested. Any other petty violation also
resulted in arrest—for example, not stopping long enough or pulling too far out into the street at a stop sign. For a SNCC worker
to drive a car in Danville meant that you had to be ready to be
arrested, because it was inevitable that sooner or later the police
car "following" in front would see a violation. This form of harassment was exasperating. It thwarted me, it made me nervous,
yet there was no way I could elude it.

There was, however, one section of the black community in
Danville where police cars never followed the movement's vehi-
cles, either in front or from the rear. There was a street that led
across a deep ravine, an unpaved road beside the Dan River. Once

on the other side, the only way out was back along this single
road that crossed the ravine. As soon as it was evident to the
police that we were starting toward that particular street, their cars
would drive off. In this section of the black community, everyone
knew the SNCC workers, white and black, by sight, and they
recognized the donated cars we were driving. They welcomed us.
We were nestled under their blanket of protection. Since the police would not venture there, I asked why. The other SNCC
workers said it was because the police knew that they might be
picked off by sniper shots in that part of town. This was new to
me. Nonviolence was the philosophical framework of the movement, but across that darkened ravine, in the dead of night, no
one could account for everyone's actions. There was not necessarily any contradiction or conflict felt by a black southerner who
professed nonviolence but also believed in self-defense. Later, in
Mississippi, this juxtaposition would become even more evident.
One of the first things I did on arrival in Danville was to learn
how to find my way through the city back to this single road across
the ravine that led to safety. I would never have armed myself,
but I wasn't averse to someone else's protection. I knew every
route to that escape.

Civil rights workers from outside Danville were farmed out
to various families who welcomed us into their homes. One family
after another made room for members of the SNCC staff in Danville, who numbered less than fifteen at any given time. These
families, sometimes showing courage by taking us into their homes,
gave us each a place to sleep, and they fed us physically and
spiritually from whatever their own spare resources might be. The
family I stayed with had pictures of President Kennedy in the
living room and embroidered antimacassars on the backs of
the sofa and chairs. The folks were warm, caring, and inquiring.

The local leadership wanted backup, support, and acknowledgment of the seriousness of its struggle. But we on the SNCC
staff were certainly not necessary to fuel the fires raging in the
hearts of Danville's black citizens, and we weren't the ones taking
the major risks. Across the South, editorials of both moderate and
extremist newspapers inveighed against SNCC and SCLC workers as "outside agitators," denying both the indigenous nature and
validity of the struggle. It was often, as in Danville, local people
who fired the tinders of a movement, and no organizer sent from

Atlanta could make headway without strong desire from a community for change, or without the willingness of the residents to put themselves in jeopardy. SNCC workers didn't live in Danville. The local people were in more danger than we were. This was a mass movement and it was larger than all of us.

The singing of black people was an integral part of the movement that cannot be forgotten by anyone who participated. It is with me always, half-conscious, dreamlike, full of feeling, murmuring in my psyche, reverberating in my mind. Because of the grandeur of congregational singing in black culture, there has never been a protest movement as rich in song as was the civil rights movement. The outpouring of freedom songs went to the core of the struggle and expressed, as nothing else was able, the hope, belief, desire, passion, dreams, and anguish of the conflict.

Some of the songs sung in the movement were familiar to me from the Virginia camp meetings of my childhood—lined meter hymns like "Amazing Grace." But most of the freedom songs were linked to the history of black singing during slavery through the spirituals. "These songs remained in the black community after the days of slavery were over, to be adapted and changed again and again in time of crisis," historian Bernice Johnson Reagon, a former SNCC worker, wrote in her dissertation. Having been expelled from Albany State College for her participation in the Albany, Georgia, Movement, Bernice had gone on to Spelman College and was awarded a doctorate from Howard University. A perceptive black woman whose spoken voice is as mellow and evocative as her singing voice, Bernice was a song leader in her hometown of Albany, Georgia. One of the early participants in the student sit-ins, she was also a member of The Freedom Singers, a special musical group developed by SNCC that reflected the central importance of music by using the freedom songs as an organizing tool.

Sensing the mood of the people or the demands of the situation, whoever was acting as song leader in a mass meeting seemed to know which choice to make. It might be "Marching to the Freedom Land" if the mood was one of ebullience, or "Woke Up This Morning with My Mind on Freedom." If the community was feeling combative, it might be "Ain't Going to Let Nobody Turn Me Around," or "We Shall Not Be Moved."

The more intense the problems, the more the singing reflected the trauma, obstacles, and emotions of the moment. In trying hours and when the community was filled with dread, the song leader might take the mass meeting into "Wade in the Water." This was a spiritual with a haunting minor key about the troubled waters that you inevitably have to go through if you want change:

See those children dressed in red.
God's gonna trouble the water.
Looks like the children Moses led.
God's going to trouble the water.

Wade in the water, wade in the water, children,
Wade in the water.
God's gonna trouble the water.

Tell me who's coming all dressed in white.
God's gonna trouble the water.
Well it looks like children fighting for their rights.
God's gonna trouble the water.

Wade in the water, wade in the water, children,
Wade in the water.
God's gonna trouble the water.

Jordan River is chilly and cold.
God's gonna trouble the water.
It chills my body but not my soul.
God's gonna trouble the water.

Wade in the water, wade in the water, children,
Wade in the water.
God's gonna trouble the water.

Another spiritual we sang was like a dirge. I remember it with shudders: "It may be the last time we see each other." Its selection reflected the fact that the community thought it had reached a time of terrible suffering and didn't know what was going to happen. I don't recall ever hearing this sung at any mass meeting except when people were reckoning with great risk. It was about facing fear, and people cried—I cried—because they truly didn't know if they would see each other again.

It may be the last time we can sing together,
    May be the last time, I don't know,
It may be the last time we pray together,
    May be the last time, I don't know.

It may be the last time we walk together,
    May be the last time, I don't know,
It may be the last time we dance together,
    May be the last time, I don't know.

It may be the last time we meet together,
    May be the last time, I don't know.
It may be the last time we march together,
    May be the last time, I don't know.

People seated themselves everywhere during mass meetings—hanging off the balcony, thronging down the side aisles,
sitting in the open windows, squatting on the stairs up to a chancel, and sometimes leaning into church windows from overhanging tree boughs. A few electric fans usually stirred the heat, and
throughout the congregation women would gracefully ply hand-
held fans made of palm or paper for small breezes of relief. In the
summer, I would feel the perspiration trickling down my back,
my blouse sticking to the wooden pew. Normally, people came
an hour or two before the meetings began in order to find good
seats and take part in the early singing, which required little to
stimulate it. There were never any rehearsals. Tremulously at first
and then gathering potency, the heat and the emotions of the
meeting would come together as if in union. People swayed to
the rhythm, punctuating the songs or the speeches when they
were moved with "Amen," "I know," "Oh yes," "Say it."

In black choral singing, new verses could come from anyone
who was singing, the rest of the singers simply following once
they caught the new line. Little interest was ever given to a freedom song's authorship. Bernice has noted, "Each execution or
performance of the song made a new song, which changed with
each singing. Singers felt free to mix verses, make up new ones,
add new inflections without much attention to the individual who
had originally brought it to its status as a freedom song."

One of the strongest characteristics of black choral singing is
that it requires the participation of all. Every voice was lifted in a
mass meeting whether resonant or quivering—it made no differ-

ence. There are no auditions in black congregational singing. I had sung alto in my church choir, and my mother and I harmonized when we sang at home, but in the black community my voice seemed thin and usually lacked the timbre of the voices around me. Nonetheless, swept up and carried away, I would sing with all my strength, and with my mind, my emotions, my body, my whole being brought together, shivering with the joy of total expressiveness and lost in the momentary unity of belief, feeling, and music.

Voices occasionally flowed together in unison, but more often than not they expanded into the harmony of several parts, all blending in rich vocal texture. Occasionally they broke into rhythmic shouts. Syncopated hand clapping drove some songs; others moved with tragic elegiac dignity. Sometimes the song leader would lead the crowd in a freedom chant. Hundreds of people murmured, "Freeeeedom! Freeeeedom! We want freeeeedom!" It became a roar.

Every mass meeting ended with "We Shall Overcome," the signature anthem of the civil rights movement, which has since gone on to become a theme song of other international struggles. Originally sung as "I'll Be All Right" or "I'll Overcome," according to Bernice Reagon this was a root song in the standard repertoire of many black Baptist and Methodist churches in the United States. She says that "oral testimony indicates wide usage of this version by the turn of the twentieth century." And she notes that the black Food, Tobacco, and Agricultural Workers Union of Charleston, South Carolina, adapted this old hymn for their strike against the American Tobacco Company that lasted from October 1945 through April 1946. Some believe, according to Bernice, that it came to Charleston from the union's sister black local in Winston-Salem, North Carolina, at the R. J. Reynolds Tobacco Company. The Charleston strikers won and both the factory and union were integrated.

Later, some of the union members took it to Highlander Folk School in Tennessee, from which organizers carried it across the South to other labor-union meetings. By that time, it had lost the singular expression and had become "We Will Overcome." "In the black tradition," Bernice maintains, "there are no 'we' songs. The use of 'we' is considered noncommittal because groups are made up of individuals who must commit personally themselves and 'I' is not viewed as individualistic or in opposition to the collective. Whenever you hear a black song that uses 'we,' it means that someone white changed 'I' to 'we.' "

The folklorist and singer Pete Seeger told Bernice that he had changed it to "We Shall Overcome." Guy Carawan started to use it in 1953. As musical director for Highlander, it was Guy who introduced it to the student sit-in movement at the April 1960 Raleigh conference. That episode sealed its use as the theme song of the civil rights movement. When Guy led the student sit-in leaders in this exalting hymn at the pivotal conference, everyone stood spontaneously, crossed their arms to hold hands in the process, and swayed from side to side, starting the ritual that has accompanied the hymn's use ever since.

The Albany, Georgia, protest that began in December 1961, added another dimension. Student government leaders at all-black Albany State College had been suspended for sympathy demonstrations following their action in response to a telephone call from Julian Bond in Atlanta asking their support of the sit-ins. According to Bernice, who was one of the students jailed during the Albany protest:

> This campaign coming out of the heart of the Black Belt of
> southwest Georgia brought to bear all of the richness and
> creativity of the southern black culture on the freedom
> songs. They were all brought more fully into the fold of the
> black choral musical tradition regardless of their history.
> "We Shall Overcome" became impregnated with additional
> slurs and improvised musical punctuations. "My Lords," "I
> know that" and intricate "ohs" appeared at the beginning of
> lines and at musical hesitations and rests between phrases.

This stately anthem is moving, majestic, and always overpowering to me. The leaders at any civil rights meeting would close by crossing their arms, holding hands with the person next to them, and then, swaying side to side to the slow refrain, everyone would follow. With hundreds of people singing and moving slowly in unison, the hymn gradually built to a crescendo, as individuals called out particular stanzas, or sang one they had just made up, and the chorus followed. It was never sung lightly or oversung as it is sometimes now. This was not a popular ditty but a serious, sonorous, and resonant reaffirmation. We were singing an oath of mutual support. "When you get through singing it," SNCC worker Reginald "Reggie" Robinson once told a reporter, "you could walk over a bed of hot coals, and you wouldn't feel it."

The power of the feelings and memories I associate with this sublime anthem are so strong that, more than twenty years later, within the first few bars, a tear rolls down my cheek and probably will for the rest of my life. In those days, tears often glistened on the faces of the grown men and women around me and those who were leading from the chancel.

We shall overcome,
We shall overcome,
We shall overcome, some day.
Oh-h, deep in my heart,
I do believe,
We shall overcome, some day.

We are not afraid, we are not afraid,
We are not afraid today.
Oh-h, deep in my heart, I do believe,
We shall overcome some day.

We are not alone, we are not alone,
We are not alone today.
Oh-h, deep in my heart, I do believe,
We shall overcome some day.

We'll walk hand in hand, we'll walk hand in hand,
We'll walk hand in hand today.
Oh-h, deep in my heart, I do believe,
We shall overcome some day.

The truth will make us free, the truth will make us free,
The truth will make us free some day.
Oh-h, deep in my heart, I do believe,
We shall overcome some day.

Black and white together, black and white together,
Black and white together today.
Oh-h, deep in my heart, I do believe,
We shall overcome some day.

We shall all be free, we shall all be free,
We shall all be free some day.
Oh-h deep in my heart, I do believe,
We shall overcome some day.

By the time I arrived in Danville, on June 22, 1963, there were mass meetings at churches in the black community almost every night. These began in response to the arrests of June and continued throughout July and into August. The mass meetings and the singing of freedom songs were a form of inchoate planning for the community. This was group decision-making with no gavel, no parliamentary procedure, and no agenda. It was a time when the community gathered emotionally around a goal and agreed to take the risks involved and accept the consequences. The soul-stirring singing, a crucial part of the black community's mobilization in Danville as everywhere, bonded participants together emotionally, giving individuals strength, and forming a collective shield. Most of the mass meetings I participated in during that summer were led by the local clergy. But some were led by SNCC workers Ivanhoe Donaldson and Bob Zellner.

When you encountered Ivanhoe, you were running into an intense young twenty-two-year-old man with an internal generator whose button was never switched to "off." Despite his radiation of energy, Ivanhoe looked unimpressed with himself. Always thinking about something, he had a jaunty walk in which he would throw his shoulders forward expressively. With strong eyes, light skin, and a receding hairline, the jut of his prominent jaw gave his face power and fitted his stubbornness well. I thought Ivanhoe was brilliant in his ability to analyze any situation, and indeed he came as close to being a theoretician as anyone in SNCC. Although he could often be crotchety, fussing and fidgeting about this or that, when he dissected a problem Ivanhoe used clinical logic. He had a method of arguing in staff meetings by which he put all apparent self-interest aside. When he spoke, it was with detachment, uncluttered by his personal opinion. Always avoiding press conferences or other public appearances, he preferred to be the strategist behind the scenes.

Ivanhoe had grown up in Harlem and joined SNCC after "dropping out" of Michigan State University—a badge of honor to us because it signified that he had put his future on the line

for his beliefs. At Michigan State, Ivanhoe had roomed with Er-
nest Green, one of the Little Rock Nine who desegregated the
schools in the Arkansas capital in 1957 and later became assistant
secretary of labor in the Carter administration.

At our modest office in the basement of the High Street Baptist Church, more than once I watched Ivanhoe balled up on a
sagging couch, rocking his head in his hands from the pain of a
migraine headache. He was in and out of the Danville jail often
that season. A volunteer from New York City—whose name I cannot remember but who suffered a detached retina as a result of
being beaten in the Danville jail—told me Ivanhoe lay curled up
on the prison floors of the cell they shared, suffering from the
headaches. Whenever Ivanhoe had one of these episodes, it reduced him to a state of cantankerous withdrawal. His normally
energetic stance, that of an analyst with a good sense of operations, crumpled under the pain.

Ivanhoe was also irascible at times. He scared me at first because I sometimes found him yelling and shouting at me, while I
was unable to figure out what I had done wrong, what had stimulated his reaction, or even what it was we disagreed about. I
don't like concentrated aggression directed at me and he made
me extremely uncomfortable when I couldn't understand why he
was angry at me. Yet despite these occasional one-sided spats, I
felt affection for Ivanhoe. He had a compassionate side, and I
liked him.

His driving style was exasperating, like that of a New York
City taxi driver—he kept one foot on the brake with the other
pulsating on the accelerator. With this approach, it was fortunate
that he had an automatic transmission and didn't have to use a
clutch! With shoulders hunched over the wheel, peering intently
through the windshield, Ivanhoe would careen around street corners, lurching the car from sudden bursts of speed into abrupt
stops. Since I felt fear much of the time I was in Danville, when
Ivanhoe was driving I often became nauseated.

Bob Zellner was an engaging twenty-four-year-old white Alabaman and son of a Methodist minister. He had a muscular frame,
dimpled cheeks, a boyish grin out of one side of his mouth, and
the cowlicks of a farm boy in his brown hair. Bob talked with an
Alabama twang. In Danville, Bob was a fixture at the nightly mass
meetings. The black community, allowing for a range of skill,

generously accepted him as a song leader. Regionwide, he was almost alone as a white staff member in being allowed to play this role.

Bob had sensitivity and unstudied native charm. His emotions were accessible to himself and to everyone else through his open face. Everyone liked the fact that a "white boy" could show such "soul." His humor was self-deprecating and few whites showed as little self-consciousness. When he was asked to lead the singing, Bob would walk humbly to the front of the church, look down at his chunky shoes, and then roll his head back, twisting it slightly to one side while he closed his eyes. As he started to sing out of one corner of his mouth, with his head back, his arm would begin to move with the rhythm. As his feelings began to take over, his arm rhythmically pulsing, the people allowed him to lead them. One of Bob's favorite songs, "Been Down into the South," developed out of a traumatic set of experiences that had occurred the year before.

In 1962, after standing trial in McComb, he and Chuck McDew had gone by bus to Baton Rouge to visit SNCC worker Dion Diamond, who was being held under a record $14,000 bail. They were told by the jail officials, "You can't visit Dion; coloreds' day is Thursday." Bob and Chuck, dressed in suits and ties, left the jail and returned carrying paperback books and newspapers for Dion as well as copies of *The Nation* and other items. As they approached the jail, they were arrested and charged with vagrancy. The next morning, they discovered that their bail had been set at the unheard of amount of $24,000 and their charges changed to "criminal anarchy." Separated from Chuck, Bob was kept awake all night and threatened with castration by the white men in his cellblock. Finally moved into solitary confinement, to his relief, Bob discovered that his cell was next to Chuck's. "I couldn't see Chuck's face but I could catch the reflection of his hand waving at me in the fire extinguisher; I was so moved to know that he was beside me." High school students were brought through the Baton Rouge jail on tours to see the two "criminals and communists." At Chuck's cell they were told, "Here's our Negro communist"; at Bob's cell the students were shown "our white communist." Some of the students asked Chuck, "Say something in communist!" He responded in Yiddish, *"Kish mir in tuchas!"* meaning "Kiss my ass," and the students left, pleased.

"Chuck and I started singing every freedom song we could remember through the walls to each other," Bob recalled years later. "The first one we sang was 'Woke Up This Morning with My Mind Stayed on Freedom' because it was so rousing and hopeful, and got us moving around":

Woke up this morning with my mind (my mind it was)
   stayed on freedom,
(Oh, well I) woke up this morning with my mind
   stayed on freedom,
(Oh, well I) woke up this morning with my mind
   (my mind it was) stayed on freedom,
Hallelu, hallelu, hallelu, hallelu, hallelujah!

Well I walk, walk, walk, walk, walk,
   with my mind on freedom,
Walk, walk, walk, walk (I walk) walk, walk.

Ain't no harm to keep your mind stayed on freedom,
(Oh, well it) ain't no harm to keep your mind
   stayed on freedom,
(Oh, well it) ain't no harm to keep your mind
   (my mind it was) stayed on freedom,
Hallelu, hallelu, hallelu, hallelu, hallelujah!

Walkin' and talkin' with my mind stayed on freedom. . . .

Singin' and prayin' with my mind stayed on freedom. . . .

When they ran out of freedom songs, they started making them up. Bob remembered a hymn, "Been Down into the Sea," from the Methodist camp meetings of his childhood at Blue Lake, Alabama. "I made up a new version that Chuck and I later taught to everyone":

I haven't been to heaven but I think I'm right,
   Been down into the South,
There's folks up there both black and white,
   Been down into the South.

[*Chorus follows each verse:*]
Hallelujah, freedom, hallelujah, freedom,
Hallelujah, freedom,
Been down into the South.

I wanna go to heaven, but I wanna go right,
   Been down into the South,
I don't want to go without my civil rights,
   Been down into the South.

I been knockin' on doors and spreadin' the news,
   Been down into the South,
And wearin' big holes in the bottom of my shoes,
   Been down into the South.

Yes, I've got big holes in the bottom of my shoes,
   Been down into the South,
But this is one battle that we can't lose,
   Been down into the South.

If you don't think I've been through hell,
   Been down into the South,
Just follow me down to the Baton Rouge jail,
   Been down into the South.

By the summer of 1963, Bob had twenty-five charges against him stemming from his movement activities in McComb, Mississippi; Baton Rouge, Louisiana; Albany, Georgia; Montgomery and Talladega, Alabama; and more would be added to his ledger in Danville.

Avon Rollins was a SNCC field secretary from Knoxville, Tennessee. He had clear medium-brown skin, hair that curled, and a medium build. Sometimes Avon affected a tougher-than-thou attitude exaggerated by a slight tilt of his head which beckoned as if saying, Come and get me. He and I, however, got along very well. He was kind to me and we were pals.

One day, when neither Ivanhoe Donaldson nor Bob Zellner was in Danville, Avon was calling the shots. A mass meeting had been arranged for that night by several of the local ministers. Many people were still in jail and several of those wounded by the fire hoses still wore casts and bandages. Within the black community there was further tension because the local leadership wanted the Reverend Dr. Martin Luther King, Jr., to come to Danville to speak and lead a demonstration, and all that they had gotten for their efforts was the state representative of SCLC who traveled out from Petersburg south of Richmond. The pleas to the leadership conference, many felt, had thus far gone unanswered. (Eventually, Dr. King did come to Danville to speak.) While Danville as a site didn't have the same long-term advantages that other localities had, nor was the movement there initiated by one of the early student sit-in groups, nevertheless SNCC had made a commitment that promised personnel, resources, and backup from the operation in Atlanta.

Avon decided that it was time for a local press release to be issued—probably because, with the others out of town, he could write his own quotation. He approached me where I was writing in the movement office. A creaking old fan on my desk shimmied every time it revolved to one side, giving me the feeling that it might topple of its own fanning.

"Let's put out a news release," Avon said.

"We don't have anything to say right at this minute," I responded.

I had been taught how to write a proper news release by Carl Braden of the Southern Conference Educational Fund (SCEF) when he had come to visit Bob Zellner and Sam Shirah. Sitting with me in Danville after I first arrived, Carl drilled me and drilled me in the format of a news release until I could write one fast, without deliberation, almost by instinct putting the most important facts first.

"We've got somethin' to say," Avon countered. "I want to be quoted saying that there will be blood in the streets if our demands aren't met."

"That seems a bit strong," I replied. "Do we really want to up the ante like that now, Avon? 'Blood in the streets'?"

The fan nearly tumbled. I stared at it. Implicit in Avon's quotation was the threat of violence originating from the black community. While there was always this implied threat, dating back to slave rebellions during slavery days, there was widespread and deep-seated reluctance in the movement in the early days— for moral, philosophical, strategic, and tactical reasons—to make the threat explicit. Practically speaking, we also didn't know how fierce the retaliation against us might be in Virginia. There was some ambivalence among our ranks in attitudes toward nonviolence. For many SNCC workers, particularly the group that came from Nashville, nonviolence was an all-encompassing way of life. Others found nonviolence to be more an expedient position than a philosophical commitment. No one professed violence.

An element of threat crept into the movement's rhetoric every once in a while. At the demonstration on June 11, the students marching could not resist singing, "We're going to set the world on fire—some day." The movement was, after all, made up of human beings whose emotional makeup was composed of a broad palette that included all feelings. Although I worked to overcome it, I myself and, I suppose, everyone else at times felt bitterness, outrage, and hostility. It was sometimes hard to control such emotions and harness the accompanying energy needed to achieve a strategic goal. Even I had felt a certain smugness at learning that some local blacks in various communities were bearing arms—it provided useful contrast. It also served notice that the patience of blacks was not unlimited.

"You're underestimating what could happen in response if we appear too provocative," I said. "Virginia might be as bad as Mississippi. We already know Danville's as bad as Birmingham."

I did not feel good about this taunting quotation of Avon's. I was learning to fight in this war by the use of words, but it appeared to me that this exercise would be an empty charade. It seemed to me that the local people had suffered so much already that we should be careful not to engender more resistance if it had no point. On the other hand, Danville was my first field assignment and I didn't yet have the confidence to challenge someone I regarded as an old hand. Furthermore, policy-making in SNCC seemed obscure to me and I was not sure yet how to raise such a disagreement.

"Let's go ahead with it," Avon argued. "It's time we got serious. We've gotta get tough. This nonviolence stuff is going to our heads. I'm fed up and tired of playing around with these . . . on the police force and in city hall." And he let out with a string of expletives.

I relented. I wrote the release announcing that there would be renewed efforts to bring the municipal authorities to face the grievances of the black community and quoted Avon on the possibility of blood running in the streets. One of the volunteers helped to mimeograph the release and distributed it to the reporters assigned to cover Danville. I had come to know many good reporters that summer, but three in particular stand out in my mind: Susanna McBee and William Chapman of *The Washington Post* and Richard Valeriani of NBC television news.

The next thing I knew, Jim Forman, who had returned to the Atlanta headquarters, was on the phone from Raymond Street, bellowing into the receiver at the top of his voice, "What the hell's going on, Mary?"

"Hi, is that you, Jim?" I asked, dodging.

"What's this blood-in-the-streets business? Where'd that come from?" he yelled.

"Avon thought we should put out a stronger release. He says we're losing momentum in Danville. Ivanhoe and Bob weren't here. I argued against it, but Avon was adamant," I responded.

"Damn! 'Blood in the streets.' Don't you realize, baby? Those bastards are gonna come down on you with tanks!" he blasted.

Then, lightly at first but getting louder, from the receiver I could hear Jim's voice start to cackle in his characteristic laugh. Jim could always laugh at himself no matter how serious the situation, and even when he was angry he was always warm and open toward me. I explained what had happened and his anger dissipated. He told me that a reporter had called him in Atlanta to ask if this release marked a change in SNCC's nonviolent policy. Jim had felt caught without warning. He, of course, hadn't known of the release. My apprehensions subsided. As he relaxed a little, talking on the phone, he even started to enjoy our dilemma and see humor in the situation. He was acutely aware that in the relationship of the local movements to the Atlanta headquarters there arose constant friction between local needs and perspectives, which we were philosophically pledged to support and develop, and the requirements facing the headquarters staff to coordinate, raise money, and speak representationally on a national basis. SNCC operated with so much local autonomy that he knew better than anyone that I didn't have to clear the release with Atlanta. He told me that he understood, furthermore, how I had gotten squeezed by Avon, and closed the telephone call affectionately, making me feel good at the end. He was sensitive to people.

As it turned out, Avon was hoist with his own petard as the Danville-based reporters swirled around him demanding to know what he meant. He ended up cornered as he clarified and reclarified—the next thing to prevarication in my view—lamely saying that it was really just his fear of local white retaliation that he was talking about.

* * *

As thoughtful and realistic as my father was about the region's history—bearing in mind that some white southerners com-
prehended the venality and repression of the South better than
anyone else—I think that even he was astonished by the chronicle
that I recounted to him. From Spotsylvania County, Virginia, my
father wrote the governor of the state, strongly protesting the police brutality in Danville. The governor's assistant, Carter O.
Lowance, responded on July 10, 1963, that my father had "a distorted report on the demonstrations," and said that he was forwarding my father's letter to the mayor of that city. On July 18,
Mayor Julian R. Stinson answered my father in Spotsylvania
County:

> It is my considered feeling that you would never have made
> such accusations had [*sic*] any real knowledge of the se-
> quence of events occurring here since demonstrations began
> on May 31.
>   It is impossible at this time for me to give you the de-
> tails necessary to prove that in actuality the police have
> demonstrated remarkable restraint during a very difficult pe-
> riod. In the last few weeks, lawless mobs have undertaken
> to break up and destroy the orderly pattern of life in exis-
> tence here between the colored and the white population
> since reconstruction days. . . .
>   Suffice it to say, as Mayor I have no choice other than
> to maintain law and order in this city even though a small
> proportion of our Negro citizens would prefer otherwise.

My father was the sixth minister in five generations of his
Virginia and North Carolina family. I felt an irony in having been
sent to Danville. Later that autumn, I wrote my English professor
Benjamin Spencer at Ohio Wesleyan University, "I guess I felt a
very real imperative to work in Danville."

When I mentioned to local reporters from the city's newspapers, *The Danville Register* and *The Bee,* my grandfather's ministry
in Danville in the 1920s and my father's attendance at Stratford
College, they sneered in disbelief and contempt. Their response
revealed their lack of objectivity; it would have been easy for them
to check my assertions. They simply didn't want to believe that
a white with some connections to Danville would side with the
"nigras." It was inconceivable to them. Yet my father's paternal

family dates back to the seventeenth century in the five-county area around Danville on either side of the state line.

Those six ministers from the Danville area in five generations made me feel that I had a right to be there. Before my father, there was my grandfather, the Reverend William Luther King. His brother, Granville Booker King, and his half brother, Benjamin Cranford, were both ministers. My grandfather's first cousin, William Sherman Epperson, was an ordained Presbyterian minister and the son of John Epperson, who fought with the Union army during the Civil War and whose brother William Epperson was a Confederate soldier (such split loyalties were sometimes found in southern families). The sixth was Wright Johnson.

There, in the south-central part of Virginia, about five miles from the North Carolina border, I felt close to my paternal great-grandmother, Justina Norman. She was the forebear who made the strongest impression on me when I was growing up. I pictured her as having a back as straight as a ramrod, perfect and proud carriage, and probing blue eyes. I have today her beautiful silver engraved watch, with its cornflower-blue enameled numbers, which still keeps time, and her brass thimble which is the only one I use. I saw her in my mind as the sovereign of her family, stern, hardy, indomitable, but loving in her expressions and invincible in her faith. Born in 1850, she was eleven years old when the Civil War started. She once read the Bible through day by day and chapter by chapter, on her knees by a kerosene lamp. She had read the Bible in its entirety eighteen separate times, but "after that I lost count of how many times," she told my father. In the custom of her day, she kept a switch from a cherry tree by her side at the dining table, and any of her sons forgetting his manners would suddenly hear the swishing of the switch through the air and feel the sting of the thin cherry branch across the knuckles. Since my parents neither whipped nor hit me, I used to cringe when I thought of those cherry switches and their tender destinations and the more serious leather-belt whippings behind the woodshed for more grave infractions—like "talking back."

I am convinced that some of my tenacity comes from Justina Norman. Once I have made a decision and embarked on a goal, I proceed toward it much as she must have read the Bible on her knees, by sheer determination.

Justina Norman's father was Isaac Norman, a Methodist lay

preacher—a vital figure in the church societies of the rural areas of North Carolina and Virginia where ordained ministers were scarce. Her three sons became ministers, one of those my grandfather. So strong was her faith that when my father, as a young man, in 1935, accompanied her up the aisle at the Petersburg funeral of another son, Granville, she looked down into the open coffin and instead of being swept away with grief, she smiled broadly and said, "I'll see you soon, son. I'll see you soon." Four years later, she died.

In this, however, I am unlike my great-grandmother, for I am still grappling with my mortality. The civil rights movement helped because it sharpened my focus on the issue of how I live rather than the question of how I die. But I have not yet achieved her peace of mind and acceptance of death.

My grandfather William Luther King was born at The Hollow (now Ararat) in Patrick County, Virginia, the second county west of Pittsylvania County, of which Danville was the largest town. With no public schools in the immediate post-Civil War period, obtaining an education was difficult in the isolated communities of the foothills of the Blue Ridge Mountains in Virginia. He was taught at the Friends Mission by Quaker missionaries who, with slender resources, educated him well. After graduating from a missionary school in Nyack, New York, now known as Nyack College, he was ordained as a Methodist minister. When he was assigned to Amherst County, Virginia, he rode horseback to the churches under his authority; in my favorite photograph of Pa King, as my brothers and I called him, he is seated on his horse, Lady, a four-gaited partner who took him from church to church.

Time moves slowly in such rural communities. Fifty-eight years after my grandfather had been assigned to another parish, my father drove up a mountain road in Amherst County looking for the Macedonia Methodist Church my grandfather had served. He asked two men sitting on a porch for directions, explaining, "My father was Preacher King." Peering at my father intently, one of the men responded, "I know you, Luther," as if nearly six decades had not passed. "How are your sister and brother, Esther and Norman?"

Pa King married a generous-spirited Presbyterian of Quaker heritage from Salem, New Jersey, Mary Ann Waddington. In 1897, when she was fourteen years old, my grandmother started keeping a diary. As I read it, she reminds me of myself, ravenously consuming books throughout her adolescence. On Friday, January 8, 1897, she wrote, "I finished *The Last Days of Pompeii* tonight"; five days later she had read *Little Women*. On January 24, she "ate hickory nuts and read the Bible all this afternoon." She was also like me in that she was able to assume responsibility very young. On January 29, "Miss Linda absent from school today because of snow. Only eleven pupils so the teacher asked me to take her classes and I did." This happened again on February 5: "Well, Miss Linda taught Miss Casper's room and I taught her room. I made out pretty well except getting a headache." On Tuesday, May 25, 1897, my grandmother turned fifteen, and wrote, "64° at 5.45 A.M. Weather clear. Today is my birthday. Aunt Han gave me five cents Saturday for my birthday and that is all the presents I received." Two months later she noted, "I gave $1 for the relief of the famine in India today"; this was a gargantuan sum for a fifteen-year-old considering the five cents she received for her birthday. My grandmother also could be a workhorse, as can I; elsewhere that year she mentions helping to mow seven loads of wheat one day, as well as threshing wheat and oats. One day in September she wrote, "We killed twenty-four pairs of chickens . . . receiving thirteen cents a pound." On December 1, she told her diary she was reading *Uncle Tom's Cabin*.

By the time she was training to become a teacher in "normal school," from which she was graduated in 1903, she showed herself to be even more like me in her concern for issues. These diaries reflect the way she wrestled with two looming questions of her day: evolution and the existence of the devil. She wrote each night of her discussions with other students and her teachers. On Sunday, January 11, 1903, she wrote, "I want to settle the question of my belief." The next day's entry read, "Effie says if her father thought I believed in the theory of evolution he would not let her go with me." On Friday, March 13, she penned, "I went over to school at 3 o'clock to hear a talk on settlement work in the slums." She wrote on April 3, "We went to the auditorium for an address by Booker T. Washington. It was very fine." She was a young woman concerned about the issues of her day as I would be a half century later. April 11's entry read as follows: "This afternoon I . . . went around to Mr. Louderbough's, the Presbyterian minister at Salem. Had the long promised talk about

evolution. Personally he does not accept the theory, he does believe in verbal inspiration, a personal devil and demoniacal
possession."

On Saturday, May 9, she wrote, "My application for position
of principal of the Hancock's Bridge School has been accepted at
a salary of $38 a month." She often said that if she hadn't been a
teacher, she would have been a lawyer, something to which few
women then aspired. On May 19, she penned, "Started to read
McCash's 'Religious Aspect of Evolution.' " The account for
Monday, May 25, said, "Daisy Freeland was over this evening
trying to make me give up the study of evolution." At approximately the period in my life when I was deliberating Albert Camus and the French existentialists, and considering my own
religious doubts, she was weighing similar concerns. On Sunday,
July 5, her entry read, "I didn't receive any help from the Com-
munion. I don't know what I do believe or what I don't believe.
I *do* believe in a God, other than that I do not know." The account for Wednesday, September 9, was significant: "Miss Harris
introduced me to the new Methodist minister Mr. King this afternoon." He was my grandfather.

There was about my paternal grandparents a sense of peace
and an unhurried grace that even now, when I think about them,
casts a glow over whatever I am doing. My grandfather had a
smile that came from deep within and I never saw him angry. My
grandmother was warm and affectionate. They both had a quiet
composure. Anger was alien to them; they tried instead to understand, to comprehend. I have sought to teach myself to react as
they did, often without success. I have learned from them to attempt to understand hostile behavior. When I have been attacked
behind my back,. experienced the jealousy of others, or been undermined, I try hard not to react emotionally but to understand
why people do as they do. Whether I comprehend it or not, I
rarely waste time on vengeance.

As a child I went to "camp meetings" in the summer. My
grandfather was the president of the ongoing yearly evangelical
camp meeting in Spotsylvania County; I sat on the hard wooden
benches of the "tabernacle" with my family as he preached and
prayed, exhorting, and encouraging personal testimony. I don't
know which had more lasting effect, my having been forced at a
tender age to think about good and evil or my having learned

discipline early from sitting straight for hours on bare pews.

It was my grandfather who awakened in my father his sense of justice, thereby influencing me. I have long thought that—had they known—my grandfather and grandmother would have been proud, despite the weight of the mores of their day, that I added my shoulder to the civil rights movement. My grandfather possessed something for which there is no other word but wisdom. He used to observe to my father while he was still a child that the idea of the southern gentleman was often a myth. "Many a slave was more of a gentleman than his master," my grandfather observed during the early part of this century. When demogogues inveighed against "social equality" of the races and "race mixing" (along with "school mixing" and "job mixing," a favorite term of headline writers for southern newspapers until the 1960s), my grandfather quietly said to my father that he thought that was very strange because obviously, judging from the ranges of skin color abundant in the South, there had been a great deal of "social equality" in the past.

It was Justina Norman King Cranford's grandfather, the Reverend Wright Johnson, who had walked 275 miles to Norfolk to be ordained and walked all the way back. The handwritten records of the Virginia Methodist Conference in the library of Randolph-Macon College at Ashland contain the documentation of his ordination. Saying grace was not enough; Wright Johnson knelt at the table to give thanks before meals and also used to get out of bed in the middle of the night to pray some more. Born in 1778, he preached until he was ninety years old. Then, in 1868, as he was walking along a country road, he suddenly threw up his hands in the air, looked heavenward, shouted "Glory!" and dropped dead.

In the way that families transmit values and blend memories of the past with daydreams of the future, creating a sense of potentiality, I feel Wright Johnson's influence in me—his pursuit of a cosmic dimension in ordinary life, his discipline, his firmness once he had made a decision, and his persistence. Perhaps Wright Johnson also unwittingly reinforced in me a feeling that my parents imparted to me—that there was special purpose for my life—when I learned that he used to pray, "God bless my children and my children's children and their children on down through the generations." I was going to need that.

In preventing blacks from registering to vote, Virginia had

used almost every ruse imaginable. Well after the Civil War, to disenfranchise blacks it had passed a poll tax and other exclusionary legislation. The poll tax was an effective bar against blacks and others who could not afford such a tax. In 1932, for example, the year my father in Virginia helped elect Franklin Delano Roosevelt president, the poll tax was a dollar and a half annually. If you had neglected this tax since the last presidential election, you had to pay a total of six dollars to vote that year. This was at the worst part of the Great Depression when black domestic servants earned as little as fifty cents a day and black yardmen or gardeners were paid perhaps sixty cents daily. What laundress or field hand would have walked miles to a remote poll to put down six dollars to vote? In many southern states, whites did not have to comply with literacy tests because there was an exception: If your grandfather had voted, you could vote without following the new requirements. Obviously, these "grandfather clauses" served only whites, so only they could vote.

Virginia used the poll tax in this manner until sometime after 1965 when it was finally outlawed by the Voting Rights Act. Poor whites were obviously disenfranchised this way, too—a not unintended effect. I was told in 1963 that the commonwealth of Virginia had also concocted a technique called blank-page registration in which there was no form to fill out and the page was blank; no matter what the applicant wrote in response to the registrar's questions, if he or she were black, it would be wrong. Although in the early 1980s the state, under the leadership of Governor Charles Robb, finally overcame much of the residue from these practices, the net effect of decades of such exclusionary laws is that, even today, the right of suffrage in rural areas of Virginia is still considered by many to be an elite affair: Voter registration is frequently restricted to courthouses that are difficult for the rural poor and elderly to reach, and registration has sometimes been scheduled to take place solely during business hours, so that working people will be discouraged from meeting the requirements to vote.

The public-relations assistant to the mayor of Danville was—without any attempt to disguise the relationship between the municipality and the industry that ran it—also the public-relations director for Dan River Mills. At the time of our demonstrations, the mills employed at least twelve thousand individuals and the year before had sold over $173 million worth of fabric and yarn. Of the mills' twelve thousand employees approximately eleven hundred were black, most of them doing menial work, and the highest-ranking position held by a black was as a machinist who was paid $80 a week. As an adjunct to the demands for fair employment in the municipal services that were at the heart of the Danville protest, the local leaders of the black community decided to press for fair employment at the mills, easily the city's largest employer. A plan was put into action to have daily pickets immediately outside the main entrance to the mills. Most of the SNCC workers as well as some out-of-town volunteers took turns walking the picket line along with local people. Even though my job was communications in Danville, I took my turn at the demonstration.

As I walked with the pickets, I thought of my father who as a schoolboy of thirteen was awakened each morning by the cotton mills' powerful steam whistle that could be heard more than a mile away. Picketing was not exciting. It was not fun. It was not even interesting. It was boring, tiresome, dull, and tedious. It was drudgery to me. That was when I first realized that I could accomplish more on the phone than in the street. Direct action without good communications was of little consequence.

On July 9, 1963, we announced a boycott of the products of Dan River Mills and on July 17 there were sympathy demonstrations in New York City sponsored by the International Ladies Garment Workers Union (ILGWU) and the New York Friends of SNCC organization. This boycott marked a new achievement for SNCC, and the organization began to give more attention to economic discrimination. The Danville boycott, although small by later standards, was the antecedent to the long and successful boycott of the J. P. Stevens textile company which almost twenty years later was necessary to bring about fairer employment practices and proper health benefits for mill workers suffering from brown-lung disease contracted in inadequately ventilated textile-mill environments.

Bob Zellner had escaped Danville, fearing, he later told me, for his life. A couple of days later, Dottie Miller had to flee as well. Having learned that the grand jury was about to indict her,

Dottie sped from the city accompanied by SNCC photographer
Danny Lyon. They were driven out of town, hiding on the floor
of a car, at high speed by a local resident. At the airport, Danny
was so certain that Dottie's name would be recognized and they
would be apprehended and returned to the grand jury, that he
decided to make her airplane reservation under a pseudonym. In
his state of agitated nervousness, casting about for an obscure name
to hide her identity, the only name he could think of to reserve
her seat under was "Joanne Woodward." Dottie still signs her
letters to Danny with the name of this actress.

Late in July, Leonard W. Holt, a clever and assertive black
attorney from Norfolk who was associated with both CORE and
the National Lawyers Guild, rushed into the movement headquarters to see me. Grabbing my arm, Len pulled me up out of
my seat so that I was standing and staring him right in the eye.
He said, "Mary, you're about to be indicted for acts of violence
and war."

"You've got to be kidding, Len," I said.

"I'm dead serious," he answered.

"Come on," I said. "I've maintained a very low profile. I've
been handling Communications. I talk on the phone to the press.
I organize press conferences. I'm on the phone to Atlanta. I write
releases. I come straight to the office in the morning and stay here
most of the day. Lunch is carried in. I've been on the damn phone
almost since I got here."

He was listening to my protest with a playful smile about to
break from the corners of his mouth. Len didn't think I was taking his warning seriously enough. It was not that I didn't recognize that draconian measures were being used against us by the
city; rather, I fantasized that because of the low profile I had
adopted, I would somehow escape them.

"When I leave at night," I continued, perturbed, "I go straight
to the mass meetings and then home to the family I'm staying
with. I've taken part in as few demonstrations as possible because
I thought it was more important to keep Communications functioning. They've got nothing on me," I said, "n-o-t-h-i-n-g."

Speaking patiently, Len said, "Remember how the city council
passed an ordinance making all picketing, demonstrations, and
marching illegal without permits, and then they arrested me at
city hall for violating the injunction to make the point?"

"Yes."

"Remember how the grand jury handed down indictments against local leaders, SNCC workers, and SCLC staff?" Len asked. "Remember how the next day the police kicked in the door of the High Street Baptist Church to arrest three SNCC workers who had been indicted?"

"I was right downstairs," I answered.

"You know Judge Michie signed an injunction charging the entire movement with conspiracy to violate federal laws, prohibiting demonstrations? It had the effect of making it illegal to *breathe* in the city of Danville."

"Yes," I said, woefully.

"Well, the grand jury's reconvened and they're at it again. They're about to indict you."

I could feel sweat start to bead on my upper lip and forehead. My stomach was knotting. My knees felt weak.

If I stepped back and looked at myself from a distance, I saw someone sincere and committed, but also determined, reliable, tenacious, and dedicated. It came as a shock to my self-image suddenly to see myself through the eyes of our opponents: lawbreaker, "nigger lover," deviant, and radical. These were all terms that had been used by various antagonists. I had not yet learned to laugh at such epithets.

Years later, I had. In 1976, a hate sheet of the White Citizens Council in Shreveport, Louisiana, published a long article about me, which stated, "The most powerful woman in the Jimmy Carter apparatus is the same white woman who ran with a pack of Negro criminals during the 1960s." The article said SNCC "seethed with hatred for the Christian white people of the South and their traditions." It blamed Stokely Carmichael and me, a "grinning wide-eyed white woman" with a "fierce glare," for the "ruin, riot, rape and revolution in the Deep South." (I found out about this article because it was broadcast in full, for fifteen minutes, from a radio station in Mount Airy, North Carolina. The station's owner, Ralph D. Epperson, subsequently contacted me to apologize for the many errors it contained. During the discussion with him, I realized that he was a distant cousin.)

But at the moment in Danville, I was sensitive. For example, I was especially hurt by the response of one of my aunts, to whom I felt very close; she reacted to the events in Danville and the use of fire hoses by saying, "You must have deserved what happened." She also wrote, in commenting about the injured in Danville, "I think some of these people have a martyr complex and regard these battle scars as a status symbol." And she stung me when she said disparagingly, "You are outside agitators."

Through the Danville experiences, I was beginning to understand with my heart and my stomach rather than only with my mind exactly how different American justice was for blacks and those in the civil rights movement than for whites in general. Viscerally, I began to comprehend the enormity of the distortions created in the American justice system by racism.

Many in the movement relished the opportunity for outright confrontation with the law. Taking on the unfair system of justice and going to jail was a way of asserting oneself and of venting indignation; moving into action was a good way of preventing anger from becoming corrosive. For some, going to jail may even have been a way of fighting fear, a counterphobic defense. I felt that the functions I was performing were more useful than my going to jail.

The hideous possibility of being raped now flashed through my mind. It seemed to me that as a white woman I would probably not be as brutally treated as nonwhite men who might be jailed. I did not think I would be beaten or killed. Yet I had heard several firsthand accounts of brutal jail rapes. Worse, I had heard about rough vaginal searches performed as part of the intake process on some of the women in the Freedom Rides—a form of torture—after the buses reached Jackson and the women were put in stockades or jailed. This was a cruelly violent means of retaliation. Annie Pearl Avery had told me that acid had been poured on the genital tissues of some of the women arrested in Jackson. Could I handle that kind of assault if something like that happened to me? I wondered, worried. I was not sure. It frightened me to think of such a violation and wanton brutality.

Almost worse than anything physical, though, was my anxiety about whether I would be able to stand the strain. Would I be able to handle the isolation? Would I break down? Could I be true to my principles? How much could I take?

Within SNCC we had informal internal divisions of responsibility, usually undiscussed. Some of us went to jail, and some of us remained in other functions. Someone had to handle the news media and jostle with the FBI. If, for your own reasons, you

needed to change roles, it was understood. You could switch any-
time you wanted to. It was up to the individual. No one said you
had to go to jail—although everyone accepted it as possible at
some point. Competition and bragging were frequent in the
movement as to who had been jailed or beaten the most. It was
acknowledged to require courage. Yet, no one ever made me feel
that I had to prove myself by going to jail. And I never thought I
had to prove myself in this way.

Now, the information I was hearing from this movement lawyer, Len Holt, presented me with a dilemma. If I stayed in the
office directing Communications, I would be indicted and locked
up, and unable to continue my work. I didn't fool myself into
thinking that my going to jail would be a statement of any importance; it would hardly be noticed. There were, by the time of the
march on Washington later that summer, over six hundred people
charged with more than twelve hundred offenses in Danville. If,
however, I left Danville, I would no longer be effective there.
Not to be able to keep up the activities to which I was pledged
created great anxieties.

"I think you ought to get out of town," Len was saying to
me, pulling me back from my thoughts. "Right now. Don't wait.
Once you're called before the grand jury, you'll be indicted for
sure."

"What are they going to indict me for? Talking on the phone
to reporters? Writing news releases? Calling a press conference?
Going to mass meetings? Walking on the picket line at the mills?"
I asked.

"Mary, damn it. Shut up. What they're going to indict you
for is inciting to acts of violence and war," Len sputtered.

Len enunciated the words staccato, lawyerlike. I took greater
notice.

"Given their pattern, they don't need any more reason to
indict you than the fact that you're here with SNCC. That's plenty
in their eyes," Len said. "I'll help you get across the Dan River.
There's a convent run by some nuns who can take care of you
until it's safe to return."

"You come and defend me, Len," I protested, "and we'll
fight it out. Maybe Ruth Harvey, Bill Kunstler, and Arthur Kinoy
would be willing to help. I haven't done anything indictable. This
is preposterous," I insisted.

"Nope. Nothing doing, Mary; we've already got over two

hundred trials growing out of the injunction," Len responded. "You're not entitled to have an attorney present in the courtroom. It doesn't make any difference to these people what you say anyway. No matter what you say, they've got you."

The Corporation Court grand jury had found and dusted off an archaic Virginia statute that held that it was illegal "to incite the colored population to acts of violence and war against the white population." This was the statute passed after the Nat Turner slave uprising in Southampton County in southside Virginia in 1831 and was the basis on which John Brown was hanged following the Harper's Ferry raid. Each of the fourteen individuals charged under this statute so far that summer of 1963 had been placed on $5,000 bail. When the grand jury held its hearings leading to the June 21 indictments, no one subpeonaed was allowed to bring an attorney. Corporation Court judge Archibald M. Aiken presided over the state court with a pistol strapped to his waist. Len Holt, while acting as attorney, was himself served with an indictment in the middle of the courtroom and spent three days in jail.

After thinking it all over, I decided to leave. I raced back to the home where I was staying and threw my few things into a bag. As I hunched down low in a car, in the well of the passenger's seat, out of sight, one of the local people drove me through town and across the Dan River to a Roman Catholic convent in North Carolina.

The nuns welcomed me with keen interest. They gave me a clean simple room with a narrow bed covered with spotless sheets. The sisters, most of them North Carolinians and all of them white, were, interestingly, very sympathetic to the civil rights movement but were distant from it in their self-imposed monasticism. They were hungry for information, wanting it as reinforcement for their thinking and discussion. I fed them with stories, vignettes, graphic scenes, and detailed accounts. They in turn fed me. They served me an unforgettable meal of succulent corn, tomatoes, beans, and other vegetables they had grown themselves in their garden, along with fried chicken from hens they had raised. I can taste that fresh corn and tomatoes now. Never having enough time for proper meals in the vortex of the movement, and always yearning for a delicious spread, I gorged myself on the nuns' southern cooking. I fell asleep in mid-afternoon, more exhausted than I realized, relaxing now in the sweet haven the nuns offered me. I relished the fragrant air, the tranquillity of the herb garden outside my room, and the brilliantly cobalt-blue sky. It had been a long time since I had thought about the color of the sky.

Meantime, the grand jury was meeting. It handed down the indictment against me for "inciting to acts of violence and war." But, by the time they had taken this action, I was across the meandering Dan River on the other side of the state line, in North Carolina, safe in the shelter of the convent.

Despite constant and humiliating harassment from the Danville authorities, the legal initiatives of the movement lawyers were clever as they handled the cases growing out of the city council ordinance and injunction, and the indictments stemming from them. Perhaps the most brilliant maneuver was the employment of a federal statute used in Mississippi that had been passed by the Reconstruction Congress in 1866 that allowed a defendant who was charged with a crime in a state court to remove the case to a federal court by filing a petition in federal court and a notice in state court. The team of attorneys filed the motions in Danville's federal court to remove the cases of the defendants from the Corporation Court and place them in the federal court system. Federal judge Michie's injunction against the Danville movement was later found to be unconstitutional.

Ruth Harvey Charity subsequently wrote in "Danville Movement," an article she co-authored with Christine Davis and Arthur Kinoy, in the July/August 1982 edition of *Southern Exposure*:

> Less than one percent of the 236 cases that grew out of the movement were overturned. The sentences were immediate. Even though all of the cases were appealed, they eventually still came up on the calendar before Judge Aiken. His response in 1966, and as late as 1974 when the last appeal was denied, was the original sentence [forty-five days] with few or no suspensions.

In the last century, white abolitionists of the underground railroad helped blacks escape across a river from Kentucky to freedom in Ohio. In Danville, one hundred years later, an efficient and articulate black lawyer helped a twenty-three-year-old white woman escape from a warlike city across a river and the state line to freedom.

CHAPTER 3

DELTA

We've been 'buked and we've been scorned,
We've been talked about sure's you're born.
But we never will turn back,
No, we'll never turn back
Until we've all been freed
And we have equality.

We have walked through the shadows of death,
We've had to walk all by ourselves.
We have hung our head and cried
For those like Lee who died,
Died for you and died for me,
Died for the cause of equality.

"We'll Never Turn Back," song by
Bertha Gober of SNCC, 1963

After escaping from Danville, I returned to Atlanta and took up where I had left off working with Julian Bond in Communications. I could now produce a news release in minutes, had met members of the national news corps who were based in Atlanta, and started writing special reports including an account of what was happening in Americus, Georgia, where black children were in jail and three of our workers were being held under the death penalty. Jim Forman and Julian Bond both liked my Americus report and, in the autumn of 1963, they asked if I would go to Mississippi to prepare a brochure; I think it was to be SNCC's first printed leaflet. I was pleased. Based upon a 1961 agreement, white SNCC staff were not allowed to work in that state until October of 1963 as it was considered likely to increase the frequency of acts of violence. It was a sign of confidence in me that they had asked me to go to Mississippi.

I was eager to spend some time there. Even in the heart of SNCC, there was a mystique associated with the state. Casey Hayden was the first white SNCC worker that Bob Moses had asked to move there and she wrote me on October 29, 1963:

Well, well, here I am in Mississippi. . . . I went after I
talked with you, to the Delta—Greenwood, Itta Bena—surrounding fields full of cotton and heat and on highways
lined with cotton; along the highways there is a little white
line of cotton that has blown off cotton trucks. And the
fields—goddam those fields—are full of tired stalks and
white tired heads of cotton and dark tired heads of cotton
pickers. The weather in the Deep South has not been written about enough. Whether hot or cold, rainy or sunny, it
always feels as if there is no relief coming, no change ever
to come. . . .

As for the Revolution: It is proceeding in its broken
down fashion and we won't ever really win down here not
really, but a few people are changed and their lives are
richer because they see that it's worth fighting to change
things. That, said Frost, has made all the difference.

And, Mary, as Chatfield says, perk up. They are going
to serve wine later on.

I wanted to see Casey and also to visit a friend of ours named
Jane Stembridge who was preparing the training manual for volunteer teachers who would arrive the following summer. Jane was
the second white member of our staff to be based in Mississippi,
and although the presence of a white woman in the black community had often intensified the virulence of reprisal, Casey and
Jane were old hands and maintained such a low profile that their
presence was not considered endangering to others. Jane came to
Jackson to meet me and offered to drive up into the Delta with
me. She was a gifted writer and I wanted to consult with her
about the leaflet despite the fact that brochures didn't fit Jane's
style of writing.

"To make a flyer, it takes at least one gimmick," Jane said
cynically. She was even more of a purist than I. "There's no gimmick; these people are starving and they're cold."

"Jane, how can we expect the rest of the country to understand the need for this struggle if they don't know how bad things
are in Mississippi?" I asked her. "We can't expect national support if people don't know the need."

For Jane Stembridge, writing was a natural form of expression. I thought she had a unique way of looking at a situation. I
urged her to write, especially from Greenwood, which, as our state
headquarters, we thought of as the capital of the Delta.

In a November 15, 1963, letter from Greenwood, Jane bristled, angrily revolting against frustration:

> I want you to know that I am not making a carbon copy of
> this letter because when one makes carbon copies, one is
> either assuming that one has something to say, or is assum-
> ing that we are involved in a business that keeps records.
> We do not keep records like that.
>
> If you want the record, it's inside of me and I can write
> it out again and can write through this night or any other
> night five thousand pages of people and faces and long lines
> stretching from Yazoo City to Greenville and backed up to
> Itta Bena, wrapping around Winona and ending up at my
> front door—cold and hungry and tired and waiting.

While a student at New York City's Union Theological Seminary, Jane had been asked to become SNCC's first executive secretary in the period following the formative Easter weekend meeting in April 1960. Starting in early June of that year, she opened SNCC's first office in a cramped corner of the SCLC Atlanta headquarters. Jane was small and stocky. Her blond hair stuck out in uncontrollable wisps, looking as if it had been hacked off by blunt scissors. Perhaps, unable to see the back of her head, she had reached around and cut it off hank by hank. Jane's blue eyes had a penetrating and hypnotic quality. She had grown up in Georgia; her father was a Southern Baptist minister who had followed the "call" to churches all over the state.

Jane was torn by her own search for identity, as a woman, as a white southerner in conflict with the immorality of segregation, and as a poet-philosopher in a movement she feared was in danger of becoming mechanistic. I used to sense her conflicts and feel for her but there was not much that I or anyone could do to resolve them. For five years, she moved toward and away from SNCC, never far from its orbit but sometimes withdrawing for a period. "Paris must be preferable to Greenwood," Jane wrote me on November 19, "but when I was in Paris they burned a bus in Alabama and I came home—*home?*" She was dislocated from the southland of her birth, but, on the other hand, she disagreed with what she described as the "Christmas boycotts and theories of race" aspect of the movement. Hers was the radical moral vision of the early student movement of the sit-ins.

I think Jane took seriously the biblical injunction not to put one's faith in princes, that is, political leaders. It was she, I believe, who wrote the anonymous editorial for the volume one, number three, October 1960 edition of SNCC's newspaper *The Student Voice*, defining nonviolence as a mind-set in which "each person has personhood"—including the segregationist. "The movement is more than a social force," that editorial asserted; "it is people sitting, people standing, people waiting, people giving, people hoping. It can be a vision of the self into the self and an acceptance of the other."

During this period, I was becoming increasingly political in outlook and less moralistic. As a result of my experiences in Danville, I had seen that the real social anarchists were, not the civil rights workers castigated by the local newspapers, but actually the men sitting on the bench and running city hall. The ignominious refusal of the judges, political figures, and mill owners to respond to the grievances of the black community made me wonder how useful were peaceful appeals to conscience where racism was institutionalized. Danville made me want to dislodge the pistol-packing judges and mayors who blasted fire hoses, not supplicate them to change. I was, along with the rest of SNCC, beginning imperceptibly to shift my outlook to a more political orientation.

Jane, however, was experiencing conflicts about this direction of SNCC and had written me from Greenwood:

> I wanted to write something for you about food and clothes,
> but it is hard for me to be a writer of leaflets. I am such a
> bad politician. Lillian Smith, call her Miss Lil for warmth
> (she likes it too), told me that when I begin to be political,
> I begin certainly to lie because poetry is in opposition to
> ideology. She used to refuse to talk with me when I became
> political.

Lillian Smith had been one of the speakers at SNCC's October 1960 meeting, and she, another white writer from Georgia, was Jane's friend. She was the author of *Forbidden Fruit*, a controversial book that discussed the taboos against interracial sexual liaisons and the interracial sexual attraction that resulted and played such a strong part in the violence of the South. Lillian Smith's collection of books and library at her Rabun County, Georgia,

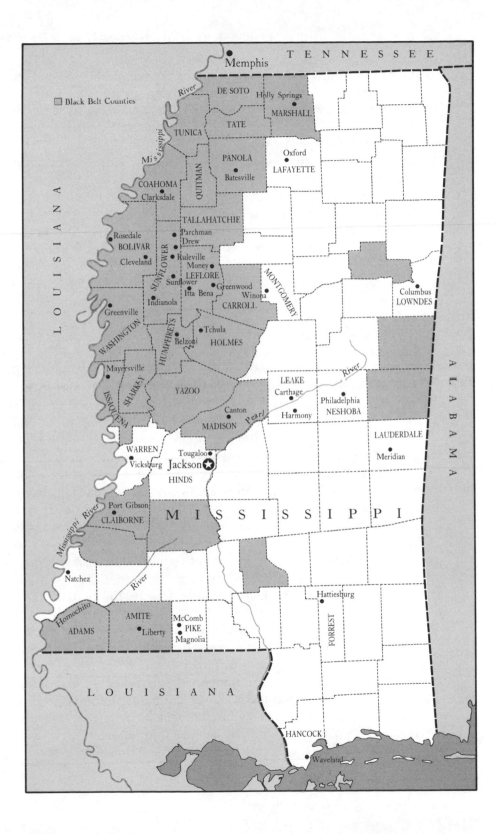

home were burned down as a result of her ventilating this subject.

"Perhaps we will be remembered for our freedom songs and hymns," Jane wrote me that autumn, "but we have to remember there is something greater than a folk song and that is a poem." She found poetry everywhere. She heard it in the cadences of the speech of community people. She found it sitting over coffee. Hers had no literary tradition, no school of thought, no indebtedness to style, and no knowledge of devices. Jane told me it was her way of keeping herself honest, along with a few people in the movement among whom she circulated her poetry. She brought out feelings of protectiveness in me. I sensed her vulnerability and her striving, and wanted to help. I used to encourage her to write poetry because I thought that no matter how wretched our circumstances, difficult our mission, or formidable our goals we still needed the clarity and insight of a poem.

Jane and I drove north out of Jackson on U.S. Route 49 and up into the Mississippi Delta, heading for the Greenville and Greenwood SNCC offices. Until that trip, I had been only to Biloxi and Gulfport, on the more tolerant Gulf Coast, and to Jackson and Tougaloo near the center of the state. Since this was my first trip to the Delta, we decided to take additional time. Once out of Jackson, we were driving on an unpopulated and undulating rolling stretch of highway flanked on both sides by masses of kudzu vines. A tenacious clinging vine that needed little water, kudzu was introduced as a measure to combat soil erosion. It grew quickly and overcame everything in its path. Taking over trees, ditches, hills, stumps, gulleys, mounds, and even telephone poles, it gave the feeling of an uncontrollable green shroud creeping across the land. It was as if the energy of nature were as much out of control as the outlaw forces at work in the state.

As we entered the Delta, I was struck by the bluffs of Yazoo City; part of the town was built on a low-lying flat area on the shore of the Yazoo River, while another section was perched on surrounding hills. When we reached the hamlet of Midnight, I sensed we were entering a different geographical mentality because of the increasing numbers of small, decrepit weatherboarded shacks dotting the edges of the fields. Periodic stretches of swampy thickets with cypress and palmetto trees gave me a feeling of what the terrain had looked like before the Delta was cleared and levees constructed against the Mississippi's flooding.

The Yazoo River emerged and then disappeared. Black people walked alongside the road, their feet their means of transportation. A line of seven black children walked single file and barefoot on a railroad track, balancing themselves with their arms out, in perfect formation with the tallest first and the shortest last.

We passed two Indian burial mounds before we reached Indianola. You couldn't help noticing the imprint of Indian names on the land in Mississippi. Every other town and river reflected the Indian nations that had once had sovereignty there.

The farther Jane and I went into the Delta, the more I retreated into my own thoughts. Jane was not uncomfortable with silence. She could be quiet with me for a long time.

Mississippi exemplified violent racism. Between 1890 and 1920, according to historian Howard Zinn, approximately four thousand Negroes had been put to death in the South without benefit of trial, and Mississippi accounted for a good proportion of these. Many of the deaths were from hanging, but some victims had been burned at the stake. Mississippi was at the center of America's twentieth-century paradox: legalized segregation and disenfranchisement in the land of freedom. It seemed as if I were standing on the edge of a volcano, peering down into a foul-smelling bottomless crater with a rising stench.

The cultural anthropologists who wrote *Deep South* described white attitudes about the subordinate position of blacks as

> based upon immutable factors, inevitable and everlasting. To them, the Negro is a lower form of life, biologically more primitive, mentally inferior, and emotionally undeveloped. He is insensitive to pain, incapable of learning, and animal-like in behavior.
>
> The belief in organic inferiority of the Negro reaches its strongest expression in the common assertion that Negroes are "unclean." In spite of their widespread use as nurses and servants, there remains a strong feeling that the color of the Negroes is abhorrent and that contact with them may be contaminating. . . .
>
> The whites frequently relate specific instances of Negro behavior as "proof" of their theories. . . . He is lazy and will not work except under the compulsion of force or immediate need; he is irresponsible and does not anticipate or plan for future needs; he is dependent upon the whites and

prefers this dependence to the struggle of existing in the
present society without their protection. . . . Owing to his
inherent inferiority, he can never become a mature individual, completely socialized according to white standards, and
must forever remain a child.

Were we being naïve? I asked myself. Perhaps it was merely
a romantic notion that a group of young people could quell this
monstrous hatred. The land oozed with blood spilled in slavery
times from thousands of black slaves toiling in fever-infested
swamps, clearing, draining, tilling, and later in backbreaking
chopping and picking of cotton. The earth had already been
browned by the blood of the Indians. Mississippi's history was a
narrative of blood and subjugation. Could we, a few dozen SNCC
staff, provide a structure and a framework onto which Mississippi's black population could walk, one that would be strong enough
to support them in rising up and insisting that they whose fore-
bears had built this land be accorded all the rights of citizenship?
    I asked Jane, Are we being naïve? I could always share my
doubts with her. She grinned at me, her blue eyes open wide,
and answered by quoting some lines from the poet Friedrich
Hölderlin that Casey had sent her:

> And tenderly I pledged my heart to
> the grave and suffering land and often
> in the consecrated night I promised
> to love her faithfully until death,
> unafraid, with her heavy burden of
> fatality, and never to despise
> a single one of her enigmas.
>
> Then did I join myself to her
> with mortal cord. . . .

There was, however, little that was enigmatic about Mississippi's "heavy burden of fatality." Rather, it was an economic and
political arrangement with deadly consequences. Jane and I arrived in Indianola, the county seat of Sunflower County, which
arose near Indian Bayou around 1830, and then we reached the
town of Sunflower where more cotton per acre was grown, on
the plantations that surrounded the town, than anywhere else in

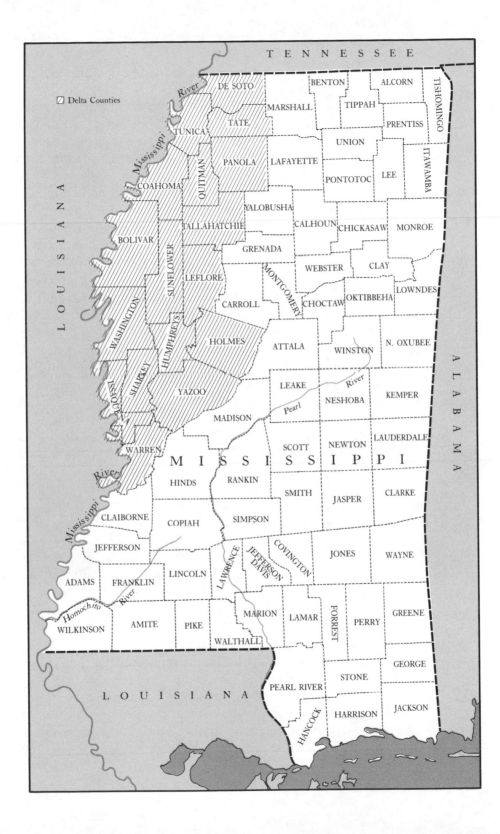

the state. Three quarters of the people living in Sunflower County were sharecroppers who paid a share of the crop in return for primitive subsistence housing. They were advanced seeds, insecticide, and fertilizer against their earnings from the upcoming harvest, but tenant farmers rarely worked their way out of debt or obtained any ownership or equity in the land arrangement. Slightly over 1 percent of the eligible black voters in Sunflower County were registered to vote; out of 13,524 potential nonwhite voters, only 164 were registered. The tenant farmers were part of a system of land-based slavery without chains; they lived in a county that was three quarters black and were denied the most basic right of democracy—the vote. Their disenfranchisement is one of the reasons that Senator James O. Eastland—who owned a fifty-eight-hundred-acre cotton plantation on the outskirts of Doddsville in Sunflower County—was able to serve in the U.S. Senate for thirty-six years and had such firm control of the powerful Judiciary Committee, as well as the Internal Security Subcommittee from which he regularly attacked what he saw as the threat of communism.

Some of the SNCC field secretaries tried to make inroads on the plantations around Indianola, Sunflower, and Ruleville, but it was treacherous work. They had to wait for dusk to walk into the plantations. In the last rays of light, they sought out the unpainted and uninsulated tenant cabins. They went from door to door, politely asking if they could step inside and talk about registering to vote. Some sharecroppers were afraid and wouldn't admit them to their cabins. Others said yes and invited them in. It was slow organizing. First you had to develop trust, then you had to stimulate confidence. There was a moral burden, too—no field secretary could ask sharecropping families to take the risks of registering to vote without acknowledging that as a result they might be driven off the plantation with nowhere to go, with no housing, no food, no job, and with only what amounted to our intangible support.

Of Mississippi's eighty-two counties, in only six were more than 15 percent of voting-age blacks registered to vote. Approximately 6 percent of the state's nonwhite adult population, or slightly over 25,000 of 421,866 adults, was registered to vote. In the Delta, however, where the proportion of the population that was black was higher, comprising most of the Second Congressional District, it was worse; thirteen out of the district's twenty-four counties had fewer than 1 percent of voting-age blacks registered to vote at the time of the 1960 census. Issaquena and Tate counties had not one black person registered to vote, and seven other Delta counties allowed less than a handful of blacks to do so.

In addition to the brute intimidation used to keep the voter rolls white, Mississippi law required that a twenty-one question form be filled out by any individual wishing to register to vote. This gave complete administrative control to the voter registrar— in Mississippi, the clerk of the court—because the potential registrant would be asked to interpret any of the 285 sections of the state constitution chosen by the clerk who had complete authority to determine if the interpretation was correct. Furthermore, in state elections, a poll tax was required (the Twenty-fourth Amendment to the Constitution affected only federal elections).

Jane had described the situation to me in one of her letters:

> Cotton's been picked. Most of it was picked by machine
> anyway, but those who had a little work last month don't
> have any now. And it's winter. It's one thing to go out and
> look for work in winter if you've got some warm clothes to
> put on while you walk the streets looking. The people here
> are cold and they're hungry. There's *nothing* to stop the
> wind when it starts coming across the long flat Delta.
>
> The people have gone down to the courthouses of this
> state and they have tried to register and vote. They have
> been time after time after time. When you go and try to
> vote down here, they publish your name in the newspaper,
> and you have lost your job. There's not much work anyway.
> If you lose your job, you won't likely find one until cotton's
> ready again. That's a long winter.

Frequently, the SNCC staff were forced off the Delta plantations with rifles stuck in their ribs by white foremen or guards. It came as a shock to me that many of the plantations were owned by northern insurance or timber firms and had been for thirty years or more. Some of the corporations were foreign-owned. I remember seeing in the town of Scott the placards of the thirty-eight-thousand-acre Delta and Pine Land Company Plantation and being told by a visiting journalist that it was owned by a Manchester, England, concern. Those guards routing our staff from plantations with dogs and Winchester rifles or double-barreled shotguns were not necessarily the hired hands of old planter families; in many instances they were corporate employees. This strengthened my belief that it was the violent history of its economic system rather than the behavior of individuals that had so oppressed Mississippi's black citizens.

Much of the Mississippi Delta had in fact been cleared and drained from an impenetrable morass of sloughs and swamps by black slaves. Some of the land had been cleared through a convenient arrangement created by the state legislature whereby convict-labor gangs could be cheaply leased from the state by private planters. The swampy flood plain called the Delta was the last part of the state to be settled because of the annual flooding from the spreading Mississippi River and the constant threat of malaria and yellow fever. Until the early nineteenth century, the plain stretching north for two hundred miles from the juncture of the Yazoo and Mississippi rivers to Memphis had belonged principally to the Chickasaw tribe, as well as to the Chakchiuma, the Ibitoupa, and the Taposa. In the lower Delta, on the Yazoo River, lived the Yazoo, Tiou, Griga, Koroa, and Tunica tribes.

The process of the white settlement of Mississippi told a ruthless story. From the time of the French explorer Pierre le Moyne, Sieur d'Iverville, who founded the first permanent white settlement in the lower Mississippi valley, and who first encountered the Biloxi tribe on the Gulf coast in 1699, it took less than one hundred fifty years for most of Mississippi's Indians to be either killed or driven off, leaving only their names on the land. The Yazoo were virtually annihilated after 1729 by the French. In 1730, a succession of French victories over the Natchez left some of the tribe to be sold as slaves while the others were scattered westward. The Tunica were largely subjugated by 1763 and later departed for Louisiana to be absorbed by French and black communities. After the eastern Atlantic colonies had won independence from British rule, the Choctaw, the largest Mississippi tribe, and the Chickasaw were pushed farther and farther west as a result of the spread of white, often slave-owning, settlements. An 1801 treaty gave the U.S. government right-of-way on the Natchez Trace—the wilderness trail of the Natchez tribe that ran north to where the Tombigbee River meets the Tennessee River near Muscle Shoals. The trail was widened by U.S. soldiers in order to accommodate wagons and soon brought traders, settlers, and outlaws. The Choctaw gave up their southern Mississippi lands and then were removed to Oklahoma after their chiefs, including Greenwood Leflore after whom Greenwood was named, signed the Treaty of Dancing Rabbit Creek in 1830.

The Spanish had first claimed the area in 1540, when Hernando De Soto entered the Mississippi region. Later the French contested for rule but yielded to the British, who then departed as the result of the War of Independence. French planters tried to raise tobacco and indigo with the labor of slaves and destitute peasants dispatched to improve their holdings in America. From 1800, however, until the time that I arrived in Mississippi, cotton was dominant. Agriculture meant cotton and cotton meant cheap labor. With the improvement of the spinning machine in the latter half of the eighteenth century, the refinement of the cotton gin to separate the seeds from the fibers, and the horticultural improvement of the stock, cotton was installed as economic ruler of the state—King Cotton they called it. Between 1794, the year Eli Whitney patented his gin, and 1804, the value of the American cotton crop was estimated to have leaped from $150,000 to $8 million a year. With that catapult, demand for cheap labor became the main force in the cultivation of cotton and slavery became entrenched.

The Civil War left slaves free on paper but unemployed and unorganized. It took very little time for former masters, the landowners, and former slaves to fall back into a similar economic arrangement in a form of semislavery, called the tenant-credit system, that lacked only the former system's shackles. High cotton prices following the war, the pressures on the market by merchant-creditors who stepped in to advance credit on future cotton, and the war-weariness of planters, all led to maintaining a one-crop system. When the swamps of the Delta were cleared for cotton, it required draining the land and then protecting it against flooding by the Mississippi River. Levees had to be built and drainage guaranteed. Most of this was accomplished by the arduous toil of black people. By the time of the Great Depression in the 1930s, forty-seven of every one hundred people in the state were tenants according to the Works Progress Administration, some of them white, a higher proportion than anywhere else in the United States. In ten of the most densely populated counties growing cotton, 94 percent of the farm population were tenants before World

War II. The figures were roughly the same when I first went to the Delta and much of the Delta was 75- or 80-percent black. The arrangement I was encountering had been implemented, with little change as the decades passed, a century before.

I noticed a certain quality to the light in this section of the state; there seemed to be more illumination in the atmosphere. Perhaps it was the flatness of the alluvial plain creating the sensation that it was brighter in the Delta than elsewhere. Bayous cut through the land like arteries. The cotton fields in late summer looked snowdrifted with white bolls but in winter they were sad-colored with the previous year's cotton stalks strewn recklessly across the furrowed ground. Against the sweep of gray- and gold-rippled sky, tenant-farmers' cabins leaned drunkenly on the encircling trees.

I think I have felt colder in Mississippi than anywhere else I have ever been, because our light clothing and the uninsulated housing were so inappropriate to the actual temperature and dampness. I went through one winter wearing a rubberized slicker from an army-surplus store as my overcoat. To stay warm, I usually wore it inside homes and offices as well as outside. This made me perspire under the unventilated rubber material, and then, when I went outside, I would be colder than before. Virtually all of the houses were heated by gas heaters or occasionally a more expensive electric heater. These heaters threw warmth out into a limited radius but the uninsulated houses couldn't retain the heat. Homes had hot pockets near the gas heater and the rest of the house was cold. A characteristic sound and a particular smell accompanied these heaters. Jane Stembridge described this:

> There is a fine gas heater here, you remember? We are snuggling. We are talking. We are being quiet. It is better than a conference. It is even better than a mass meeting. It is better than anything I have done in three weeks—coffee and Willy Smith and Dick Frey and the sound that a gas stove makes.

From November through February in Mississippi, the black community, poor whites, and movement staff all huddled. We moved from huddling around one gas heater to huddle around the next.

Winter was wet as well as cold, which meant that the chill

penetrated. One night in 1964, I drove in a freezing downpour with Tom Hayden who was visiting from his SDS organizing in Newark, New Jersey. We went along the Natchez Trace from Natchez to Jackson in a Volkswagen with broken windshield wipers. As the rain fell on the windshield, it froze. The only way the driver could see was to reach out with the free hand to wipe off the icy rain. We were both trembling with cold and drenched and had to take turns driving so each of us could, in turn, thaw out one arm. As soon as I got one limb warmed, the other was cold.

No one with whom we worked seemed to have enough food or clothes to last through the winter. Jane wrote me when I returned to Atlanta from our fall 1963 trip:

> About the Delta: you would like to see it with frost on the fields. Except it just reminds you of people beginning to be colder than before. The sky is very blue and smoke is coming out of chimneys, out of kitchens. We do need food and clothes so bad. . . . There won't be enough food, nor enough warmth for this winter as there wasn't for last, nor for the one before that. . . .

Inside uninsulated sharecropper cabins, several layers of newspaper were sometimes taped onto the walls when the family was too poor to buy tar paper or crude insulation. There was a neatness and a certain patterning in the placement of the paper used to install this barrier against the wind. A wall lining of newspaper and a gas heater were all that many black families in the Delta had for warmth against the winter. Usually their clothing was made not of wool but cotton because it was cheaper.

I was interested in the inventiveness of poor sharecroppers in making life more tolerable for themselves. One shack was roofed in five different shades of tar paper laid out like a plaid—red, green, blue, brown, and beige—and had powder-blue painted chairs on the crooked front porch. Elsewhere, patterns were swept into dirt floors to mimic the swirls and flourishes of carpets. Driving along highways, I saw dead trees decked with bright-blue milk-of-magnesia bottles. Dozens of cobalt-blue empty bottles stuck onto the tips of bare branches caught the sunlight and sparkled like Christmas-tree decorations. Elsewhere, hundreds of bottle caps from Fanta, Dr Pepper, Coca-Cola, and other soft drinks were pressed into the earth forming an imitation pavement for a mock patio in front of the porch. Sometimes old hubcaps from the wheels of automobiles were nailed into the sides of tenant cabins. They stared at you like a hundred cyclopic eyes looking out across the Delta.

Ingenuity found expression in other ways. I can never forget a small round-faced woman named Hannah with a broad smile and who smoked a pipe. She was a tenant farmer near Itta Bena—the tiny town in the Delta where Marion Barry grew up—whose name, meaning home in the woods, was chosen by the Choctaw chief Greenwood Leflore, the man who signed away the Choctaw land at Dancing Rabbit Creek. Hannah and I struck up an easy intimacy; she was so open with me. She innocently explained to me that after she and her husband had finished a day's work in the fields, with their twelve children hoeing or chopping cotton alongside them, she would urge him to make love. There was no other diversion such as reading or television. "When ah gits home, ah grabs him and says, Mack, let's *do* it," she told me, her eyes sparkling. For the evening meal, Hannah would make pies in their wood-burning stove. She made pies of sweet potatoes, Irish potatoes, black beans, white beans, pinto beans, navy beans, blackbirds, and on down a list of twenty-two different tarts she named from crops that the family grew or birds that the boys shot with slingshots.

Hannah's day was nothing but uninterrupted work. She was bowed down in servitude to the landowner, to her husband, and to her twelve children—and did far more work than any of them did. "Sometimes ah gits so tired ah cain't 'member theah names—then ah calls 'em Cupcake or Peaches." Pleasure was found somewhere along the way in lovemaking with her husband despite the lack of privacy in their dirt-floor cabin. I was subsequently to observe that although her life in the Mississippi Delta was similar to the lives of peasant women today in Africa, Asia, the Middle East, and Latin America, it differed in two significant ways. First, she was not by ancient custom required to feed her husband first, her children second, and herself last with whatever remained, as is still the case for perhaps one third of the planet's population of women. Second, she did not have to be sexually subservient; lovemaking could be at her instigation.

Like most tenant-farming families, Hannah's children spent more time in the fields than at school, a situation made easier by the state legislature's shortening the school year for black children to facilitate their agricultural work. (In many counties in the South, the school year was eight months for white children and six months for blacks; the rationalization given was that blacks paid less in taxes. County school supervisors often acted with impunity, closing black schools early to make the children available for fieldwork.) From shortly after dawn until long after sundown, Hannah was at work. Her husband was not slothful, either. He used the hours when he was not in the fields to repair implements, help in the garden, bring in the wood, and work on the 1940 Ford whose immobilized axles were stretched across cinder blocks in the backyard and whose destiny down any road seemed improbable to me. Yet the significant burden of food production and preparation for the fourteen members of the family was primarily Hannah's, with help from the children especially in cleaning up with pump-drawn water.

Rural electrification had still not reached Issaquena and Sharkey counties when I went to see Unita Blackwell in the summer of 1964. These two isolated rural counties near the southern point of the Delta appeared to me to be largely private hunting preserves. Of Sharkey County's 1,316 occupied houses at the time, 1,039 were lived in by tenant farmers who labored on the land in exchange for rent, ensnared in the credit system that rarely allowed them to work their way out of debt. Unita Blackwell was a statuesque and strong black woman, stable and unassuming but with a dynamic presence, who would, a little over a decade later, be elected mayor of Mayersville, the county seat of Issaquena County, a county in which not a single black person was registered to vote the night I stayed with her. It was so rural that Mrs. Blackwell not only had no telephone, she had no address. Driving south from Cleveland in the Delta, I passed a service station on the right named Tony's. I went one quarter of a mile beyond to a stop sign with the printed side facing away from the highway. After a sharp right, hers was the first house, a weatherboarded frame dwelling with a green Chevrolet truck in front of it. When I visited Mrs. Blackwell, her home and all the surrounding houses were still kerosene-lit. She wanted to give me her bed, but I resisted and finally talked her into letting me sleep on the floor. I did not want to impose on her, insistent as she was about giving me the best she had to offer.

I wrote down my observation about her then: "Mrs. B. is critical to the movement in Mississippi now and regarded so by all the staff." I remember something more than the value of the role she played as a local organizer, and her strength and solidity; I remember how many of the individuals I came to know like Unita Blackwell were in their own way intellectuals, reflecting upon and analyzing their circumstances, weighing their values, and giving thought to the meaning of what they did.

My favorite time of day is just before sundown in high summer when the long golden and peach-colored rays of the sun cast a halolike glow over everything they touch. It was in Rosedale, the largest town in the Delta, on the Mississippi River between Greenville and Memphis, at this special time of day that I learned about poverty and pride. Casey Hayden and I had gone there for a precinct workshop and were to stay overnight with one of the local women who participated in the workshop and who offered us lodging. She lived in a modest uninsulated frame house on the outskirts of Rosedale. Her house was bathed in those long rays of summer as we were introduced to her five small children and sat down to talk for a while. She was proud to have a freezer. Very few black families at that time in Mississippi could afford both a refrigerator and a freezer. If they were able to buy one of these, they generally purchased the freezer because it would hold more and each item could be thawed as it was needed. A refrigerator couldn't preserve food over a winter—for example, a bushel of carrots—but a freezer could. When our hostess proudly opened the freezer to show it to us, though, there was only one thing to see: Sitting alone on the frosted bottom of the chest was a saucepan half-filled with boiled dried beans. This was the only food in the house other than a jar of peanut butter and half a loaf of bread.

When it was time to go to bed, I realized that she and the five children normally all slept together in the double bed. That night, however, she was going to give Casey and me the bed, and she and the children would sleep in the living room on a bedspread laid out on the floor. We told her that we instead would take the living room. I felt awful about casting her and the children onto the floor. We insisted. She insisted. Finally, I saw by her firmness and the look in her eyes that she genuinely wanted to give us the best that she had. It was important to her sense of who she was that she was able to offer us the double bed, and I suddenly saw that if we refused it, we would hurt her feelings. I learned a lesson that night: Be careful about rejecting someone's hospitality or generosity out of concern for their welfare; evaluate the sincerity of the offer; it may be an error to impose your sense of what is right. The next morning, Casey and I were awake at dawn, and, without rousing the children sprawled out on the living-room floor, we thanked our hostess and drove back to the Jackson office.

Again and again, I encountered extraordinary generosity from abysmally poor people. I was impressed by how giving and compassionate was the black community of Mississippi. This made me worry, however, that I was in danger of reverse stereotyping. In the same way that prejudice is a simple defense mechanism transferring hatred and fear onto others by generalizing, wasn't it possible that I might generalize, too—not out of ignorance or fear, but out of another emotion, out of hope? Wasn't I looking for nobility where there was simply humanity? Yet, I continued to experience the selflessness of people who had even less than the woman with her freezer in Rosedale. I did not want to indulge in the obverse of racism and glorify the poor, for that too would be a form of dehumanization. But with my own eyes I saw how hard poor people worked and how generous toward me were those with no earthly goods, living as they did in the most stark poverty in the United States.

In part, those who live in rural and agrarian communities are accustomed to reciprocity; their survival may depend on assisting each other. At least, that was how I analyzed it then. Years later, the distinguished Washington civil-liberties lawyer Charles Morgan, Jr., one of a handful of southern white attorneys who risked their careers to defend us, showed me public-opinion research data from several surveys. Responses to researchers' questions revealed that black women formed the category of Americans who were most concerned about the welfare of others and most willing to act on that basis—in other words, the group that would be considered the most generous.

I did not pity the poor with whom we worked. One reason for this lies with a book that Casey and I were studying: *Let Us Now Praise Famous Men,* a record of southern cotton-tenant families in the 1930s, written by James Agee and with photographs by

Walker Evans. Agee called it "an independent inquiry into certain normal predicaments of human divinity." I could identify with one of Agee's conflicts, which concerned his use of the printed word, as an outsider, to convey the reality of the people about whom he was writing and his feeling that he was an intruder on the sanctity of the families he described. This limned my own struggle to be effective as I worried that I might be an interloper. Agee also made a contribution to a dialogue that Casey and I were having about the redemptive power of suffering, which we found all about us in the generosity of spirit of impoverished black Mississippians. Furthermore, although now dated, Agee wrote with a strong grasp of the unity of suffering of both black and white in the South and showed respect for the beauty and dignity of the poor that transcended their circumstances. He understood that people outside the mainstream of American prosperity could yet be richer in spiritual gratification. Once I grasped that, I never felt sorry for the people with whom we worked.

"Poverty negates the strength of being poor," Jane Stembridge wrote me. The "strength of being poor" was nowhere more evident than in the Mississippi Delta, and no one personified this quality of inner determination and resiliency, coupled with magnanimity of spirit, better than Mrs. Hamer, a woman who would play a special leadership role in the civil rights movement in Mississippi.

Fannie Lou Hamer was a timekeeper and sharecropper who had worked on the Marlow plantation in Ruleville for eighteen years. In the summer of 1962, she was fired by the landowner and forced to leave her "furnish." This was an arrangement in which tenant farmers worked the land in return for a house and credit against the products of their labors. The reason for his action was that she had gone to the Sunflower County courthouse and registered to vote. On September 10 of that year, night riders fired sixteen times into the home of a friend in Ruleville where Mrs. Hamer had been staying after she was evicted, the shots entering the wall one foot over where her head normally rested as she slept. She was, fortunately, not there that night.

When I met Mrs. Hamer in November 1963, she was in her mid-forties. Although she was not tall, she was large-boned and strongly built with baleful eyes and a grieving gaze; her hands were big working hands with enlarged joints. Everything about her suggested strength of character as well as physical stamina, and the more you knew her the more you felt her vitality, warmth, and spiritual strength. She was the last of twenty children, born in 1917 into a Montgomery County family of six girls and fourteen boys. She started picking cotton at the age of six and by the time she was thirteen, she was picking two hundred or three hundred pounds of cotton a week. One of her legs was withered from polio contracted as a child and she walked with a limp.

I have always felt that what happened to Mrs. Hamer on June 9, 1963, intensified her limp. She and five others were returning to Greenwood from a meeting in South Carolina when the bus stopped in Winona, Mississippi, and some of them went into the white waiting room. The police arrested the entire group, including Mrs. Hamer who had stepped off the bus to see what was going on. In the Winona jail, Annelle Ponder, a beautiful dark-skinned graduate of Clark College in Atlanta and voter-education worker for SCLC was separated from the rest of the group, and she was beaten to the point that she could barely speak. I remember hearing Mrs. Hamer talk about how she could hear Annelle crying and screaming, praying for God to forgive the men who were beating her. Mrs. Hamer was taken to another cell where there were three white men and two black prisoners. One prisoner was handed a blackjack and told to "make that bitch wish she was dead." He beat her all over her body with the blackjack while one of the other men held her feet down to prevent her from moving. The blackjack was then passed to the other prisoner to continue the beating. Mrs. Hamer was left unable to walk.

The following day, a group of SNCC staff drove to Winona. Among them was Lawrence Guyot, a robust and feisty young SNCC worker, smart, ebullient, tenacious, and someone that I never in four years saw intimidated. In trying to visit the movement prisoners, Guyot (as he preferred to be called) politely but sternly refused to say "sir" to a state trooper who then slapped him about and turned him over to a group of White Citizens Council members. They beat Guyot until he couldn't lift his arms or open his eyes. When Mrs. Hamer was released from the Winona jail two days later, it was only to learn from James Bevel of the first planned assassination of a political figure in the civil rights movement.

Just after midnight, June 11, Medgar Evers, then thirty-seven

years of age and for nine years the Mississippi field secretary for
the NAACP, was killed by a sniper's bullet fired from ambush in
front of his home in Jackson, Mississippi. The NAACP and SNCC
were at opposite ends of the pole on ideas about how to produce
social change, but this division no longer mattered in the wake of
Medgar's death. Street protests the next day resulted in 158 arrests (13 of which were of clergymen). Several hundred black
teenagers were stopped by a 100-man police force equipped with
riot guns and automatic rifles.

About six months later, on December 7, 1963, I was on the
phones in Atlanta when Annelle Ponder called from Greenwood
to report on the hearing that had taken place that week regarding
the arrests and beatings of the previous summer in Winona.

"All of those who were charged were freed on all seven counts,
Mary!" Annelle said, her velvet voice now sober and contained.
"All the evidence we presented seems to have accomplished
nothing. Euvester Simpson, Guyot, James West, Rosemary Freeman, the two Negro prisoners, Mrs. Hamer, the white waitress,
the white owner of the restaurant—all of them testified, but it
seems to have done nothing. Even the FBI showed pictures of
our people after they had been beaten and testified to that effect."

"This is terrible. It makes me feel so angry, Annelle," I said.

"What's worse," she replied, "there's no appeal, so all of
those charged with the beatings are free."

Two days later, Dick Frey, a white SNCC field secretary and
a mainstay in the Greenwood office, called me and said that
Roosevelt Knox, a twenty-three-year-old black man from Kilmi-
chael in Montgomery County, Mississippi, was the prisoner who
had beaten Mrs. Hamer the previous June. "He testified at a brutality trial in Oxford that he had indeed beaten the other prisoners
but that the police had given him the blackjack and made him do
it," Dick told me.

When I first met Mrs. Hamer, I asked if she knew of any
black women in the Delta being involuntarily sterilized. I had
recently read that in Fauquier County, Virginia, and in a number
of other locations in the South, some black women were forced to
undergo sterilization in order to receive hospitalization for their
last childbirth and to remain eligible for federal and state entitlement programs. Mrs. Hamer said this had happened to her as a
young woman and told how, without her understanding the con-

sequences, the local doctor in Ruleville had her sterilized after she had two children. I took down an affidavit from her on the episode, hoping I would someday be able to use it to bring this situation to light. I later learned that the town physician was the son of Congressman Jamie Whitten, who had represented that district since 1941.

Fannie Lou Hamer became a SNCC field secretary after she was forced to move off the Marlow plantation. She was constantly subjected to threats. For example, more than two years after her eviction, in March 1964, word was sent to her through a friend who still worked on the Marlow plantation: "Mrs. Hamer thinks she is a big woman now but she'll be killed." If this sort of harassment bothered her, Mrs. Hamer never let anyone know it; with her large-socketed, sad eyes, she was a source of strength and resourcefulness for others.

One example of this quality involved a woman named Betty Carter, who lived on the Coleman plantation in Leflore County and had nine children. The plantation owner told her that he had found out about Mrs. Carter's attempt to register to vote on March 4, 1964, and said he wasn't having "that mess" on his plantation and that she would have to give him $115 and move. Leflore County then had 3,545 houses, of which 3,066 were occupied by sharecroppers under the tenant-credit system. In the off-season, Mrs. Carter was supported by her thirteen-year-old son who worked for thirty cents an hour, ten hours a day, seven days a week, cleaning bricks and feeding cows. Despite her circumstances, she had been refused eligibility by the local administrators of the federal-state welfare program. In her need to find other housing, she turned for help to Mrs. Hamer, who diligently talked to people on her behalf until she was able to make another arrangement for the hardworking family.

Mrs. Hamer tempered her resolve with restraint. A group in Illinois sent to Ruleville a truckload of clothing that was being stored at the home of a Mrs. Earl Johnson. The mayor took it upon himself to announce over the radio that clothing was being given out at Mrs. Johnson's; he did this obviously for the purpose of creating a crowd and unrest. The original plans called for the clothes to be given out that day but not in that manner. By early afternoon, over fifty automobiles and a large crowd had gathered. Mrs. Hamer, with characteristic humility, telephoned the SNCC office and asked what she should do. They told her, also characteristically, to handle it as she saw best. She walked over to the Johnson home, caught the attention of the crowd that by then filled the street, and made a speech, declaring, "The mayor can't tell Negroes what to do. If you all would just go down to the courthouse to register to vote, we wouldn't have a mayor doing things like this to us." The crowd became quiet, an orderly process was worked out, and the clothes were distributed.

I found myself moved by Mrs. Hamer's character and courage. I felt that I was growing as a result of my contact with her. She personified grace and honor, and, much as James Agee had described a tenant farmer in *Let Us Now Praise Famous Men*, she possessed "extreme dignity, which was as effortless, unvalued, and undefended . . . as the assumption of superiority which suffuses [the] rich and social."

One individual emerged that autumn as having great significance for me and for the civil rights movement. His name was Robert Parris Moses. By October 1963, my work in Communications required that I regularly talk to him from Atlanta by telephone. He was to make a profound impression on me.

Bob Moses was unique. He had a purity of thinking and a power of mind that were exceptional. His logical way of reasoning was made even more effective by his other, special qualities: his deep sense of human dignity, his political shrewdness, and his prescience. When he spoke, I felt he had reached deep down inside himself and that whatever he was talking about, he had been thinking of for weeks. There was a nondefensiveness about Bob that expressed itself in the way he carried his stocky frame— his shoulders and torso were held open in an unprotected manner as if he had nothing to hide—and never in the four years that I knew him in the movement did I see him defensive. His eyes focused steadily on you, a few freckles scattered across his brown complexion.

When Bob joined the movement, he left behind his job teaching mathematics at the prestigious Horace Mann School in New York City and his advanced studies for the doctor of philosophy degree at Harvard University. Growing up in Harlem, he had watched both his mother and his father crushed by their meager jobs, but his own intelligence had seen him through the competitive examination to enter New York City's Stuyvesant High School. Through his intellectual prowess alone, he had been accepted at Hamilton College in upstate New York where he majored in philosophy, and he received a master's degree from Harvard University in 1957. He subsequently became a doctoral candidate at Harvard, a statistical rarity for a young black at that time. The sit-ins started just a few months after his mother died of cancer at the age of forty-three, shortly after she and Bob's father had had their first vacation. Moved by the news accounts of southern blacks challenging the laws of segregation, Bob came south, slipped into a demonstration at Newport News, Virginia, and returned to New York where he talked with Bayard Rustin—a Freedom Rider in CORE's first such protest of 1947, a Quaker, and a theoretician on nonviolent resistance—about the student movement.

Coming to Atlanta in the summer of 1960, two years before I did, he and Jane Stembridge worked together in a corner of the SCLC office, sending out SNCC mailings. When I arrived, there was an amusing story still being told about Bob's appearance. I suppose it was natural that a certain amount of the anticommunism rhetoric that greets attempts at reform in the United States affected the black community, too, in the early 1960s. The charge of communism was so promiscuously used that it began to take on the connotation of anything unusual. When Bob first started working for SNCC, Lonnie King, an exuberant and volatile activist and one of the first student leaders in Atlanta, went around saying, "Bob is so quiet and intense that he must be a communist."

Bob traveled to Mississippi on his own funds to select those to attend the key conference that the Temporary Student Nonviolent Coordinating Committee was planning for October 1960 in Atlanta. In Mississippi, he met Amzie Moore. Thoughtful and secure, hefty, and having survived as the local NAACP chief in the Delta town of Cleveland, Amzie was a man of physical and moral stature who had unassailable authority. When I later drew up a list of "key local people and key staff" for the national news corps, I put Amzie at the top of the page. Bob respected him and it was always to Amzie that Bob gave the credit for setting the framework for SNCC in Mississippi. Amzie urged Bob to stay away from direct action as too dangerous in Mississippi and, instead, together they planned a voter-registration program for the state. Southwest Georgia was the only other place where the move-

ment, through SNCC, was then using voter registration as its point
of focus.

Bob was brilliant, but, more important, he was original in his
thinking and inventive. He examined everything SNCC was doing
and was ready to admit error. Bob was also unafraid. He inspired
confidence. When individuals outside the movement—journalists
or church representatives—described Bob, they invariably called
him either a mystic or a saint. Local people in Mississippi used to
say that he was "Moses in the Bible."

Bob was reserved. He showed his immense personal power
and strength through a quiet, monotonal tranquillity. In the same
way that one listens more attentively to a whisper, people were
drawn to Bob—he was so unobtrusive that in his quiet self-possessed stillness, he fixed additional attention on himself. He seemed
entirely nourished from within.

If Bob walked into a room or joined a group that I was in, I
felt my chest muscles quicken and a sudden rush of exhilaration.
He inspired me and touched me. I trusted Bob implicitly and felt
deep affection for him. He was only thirty years old but I considered him prophetic.

Bob was once asked at a conference, "Exactly how do you
organize?"

"By bouncing a ball," he answered quietly.

"What?"

"You bounce a ball. You stand on a street and bounce a ball.
Soon all the children come around. You keep on bouncing the
ball. Before long, it runs under someone's porch and then you
meet the adults."

It was a simple answer, so simple that if you were not thinking about what he was saying, you would miss it. Yet it was quintessentially profound. That was Bob's way.

Bob had been deeply affected by the death of a black farmer
in Amite County, Mississippi, and he carried the awareness of the
murder of Herbert Lee with him wherever he went. It is worth
digressing to include the story here, because, as with everyone
else who knew Bob Moses, Lee's death had a serious impact on
me through Bob.

The events that led up to Lee's killing began on August 15,
1961, after Bob returned to Mississippi from the crucial staff
meeting where Ella Baker resolved the dilemma of whether SNCC

would emphasize direct action or voter registration. Bob accompanied a farmer and two middle-aged women to the courthouse in a town ironically called Liberty, the county seat of Amite County. All three of them were students in the SNCC voter-registration school that had opened in McComb in adjacent Pike County on August 7, 1961, and he was going with them to the Amite County courthouse to help them register to vote. Bob recounted the story in Howard Zinn's book *SNCC: The New Abolitionists:*

> They were literally paralyzed with fear. So after a while I spoke up and said they would like to come to try to register to vote. . . . I told him who I was and that we were conducting a school in McComb, and these people had attended the school, and they wanted an opportunity to register. . . . Finally finished the whole procedure about 4:30; all three of the people had had a chance to register— at least to fill out the form. This was a victory.

On the way back to McComb, Bob was arrested by a highway patrolman they had seen in the circuit clerk's office and was arrested in McComb on a charge of interfering with an officer.

The second of SNCC's original field secretaries to be hired after the 1961 Freedom Rides, Reggie Robinson, an energetic and genial black business student from Baltimore, had joined Bob and John Hardy, from the Nashville student movement, to open the first voter-registration school in Pike County. Later in that eventful month, another voter-registration school was set up on the farm of E. W. Steptoe in Amite County. Mr. Steptoe was the local president of the NAACP, a warm man with hollow cheeks and prominent ears. He had a wide ingenuous smile, and was a person of stamina and quiet courage. He was also generous. I remember how, one blistering summer day, he dug a huge hole in the ground, slaughtered one of his calves, and pit-barbecued it over sizzling red-hot embers to feed the entire Mississippi staff.

During that same August of 1961, Bob again accompanied to Liberty two individuals who had studied at the school on Mr. Steptoe's farm to try to register. According to Howard Zinn's account, "There he was attacked on the street, by Billy Jack Caston (cousin of the sheriff and son-in-law of a state representative named Eugene H. Hurst) who proceeded to hit Moses again and again with the butt end of a knife." Bob required eight stitches in his

scalp from the beating but made a point of returning immediately
to Liberty so the local people wouldn't think he was frightened.
After washing the blood out of his shirt at Mr. Steptoe's farm, he
attended a mass rally at which Jim Bevel spoke.

Marion Barry had come into McComb to hold workshops on
nonviolent direct action. Inspired by this, two slight but gently
rugged eighteen-year-old McComb high school students, Curtis
Hayes and Hollis Watkins, who were among the first group of
SNCC field secretaries locally recruited and trained by Bob, sat-
in at the Woolworth's lunch counter. This was, according to Howard Zinn, "the first such act of defiance in the area's history" and
they were arrested for breach of the peace and sentenced to thirty
days in jail. Now, McComb saw another "first"—Bob Moses filed
charges of assault and battery against Billy Jack Caston. He was,
not surprisingly with the hate-filled atmosphere of southwest Mississippi and his political connections, acquitted. Bob himself was
attacked so many times that year that he often had to hide among
the hanging suits and dresses on the racks in a black-owned dry-
cleaning establishment in McComb.

Reversing the usual pattern, this time voter-registration activities led to sit-ins. In McComb, a plucky fifteen-year-old local girl
named Brenda Travis was sentenced to one year in a state school
for delinquents after a sit-in. Voter-registration activities proceeded in Amite, Pike, and Walthall counties, on the state line
with Louisiana, with local people coming in ones and twos to study
for the weighted registration process. A field secretary from New
York City, Travis Britt, was beaten into semiconsciousness at the
courthouse in Liberty. John Hardy who, along with another SNCC
worker, MacArthur Cotton, was running the voter-registration school
in Walthall County, was pistol-whipped by the county's voter registrar and then arrested for disturbing the peace. The frightening
accumulation of these incidents was starting to scare even further
the local black residents who already lived in fear.

They had good cause. Bob told Howard Zinn what happened
next as recorded in *SNCC: The New Abolitionists:*

> The boom lowered on September 25; Herbert Lee, a Negro
> farmer, was killed in Amite County. I was down at Steptoe's
> with John Doar from the Justice Department and we asked
> Steptoe—was there any danger in that area—who was caus-

ing the trouble, and who were the people in danger? Steptoe told us that E. H. Hurst, who lived across from him, had been threatening people and that specifically people said that he, Steptoe, Herbert Lee and George Reese were in danger of losing their lives. . . . The following morning about twelve o'clock, Dr. Anderson came by the voter-registration office and said a man had been shot in Amite County. They had brought him over to McComb and he was lying on a table in a funeral home in McComb and he asked me if I might have known him. I went down to take a look at the body, and it was Herbert Lee. There was a bullet hole in the left side of his head, just above the ear. He had on his farm clothes.

Subsequently, according to Bob, he and some other staff drove out after dark for four or five nights going from one home to another trying to find witnesses who had seen Lee killed. They found three farmers who had seen the shooting and told the same story. The men had been waiting in line at the cotton gin in early morning when Herbert Lee pulled up in a truck loaded with cotton; E. H. Hurst drove up behind him in an empty truck.

Hurst got out of the truck and came up to Lee, who was sitting in the cab of his truck, and began arguing with him. Hurst gesticulated, pulled a gun from under his shirt. Lee said he wouldn't talk to Hurst unless he put the gun away, and Hurst put the gun under his coat. Then Lee slid out of the cab on the side away from Hurst. Hurst ran around in front of the cab, took his gun out, pointed it at Lee and fired.

An all-white coroner's jury ruled that the killing of unarmed Herbert Lee was justifiable self-defense and, one month later, the grand jury refused to indict Hurst.

Howard's book includes the rest of Bob's account:

Lee's body lay on the ground that morning for two hours, uncovered, until they finally got a funeral home in McComb to take it in. No one in Liberty would touch it. They had a coroner's jury that very same afternoon. Hurst was acquitted. He never spent a moment in jail. . . . I remember reading very bitterly in the papers the next morning, a little

item on the front page of the McComb *Enterprise Journal*
said that a Negro had been shot as he was trying to attack
E. H. Hurst. And that was it. Might have thought he'd
been a bum. There was no mention that Lee was a farmer,
that he had a family, nine kids, beautiful kids, and that he
had farmed all his life in Amite County.

Bob was later told by a black witness named Louis Allen that
he had lied at the coroner's inquest out of fear of reprisal, but that
he would be willing to tell the truth to a federal grand jury if he
were protected. When Bob asked the Justice Department to provide protection, however, he was told that there was no way it
could offer this and that it probably wouldn't make any difference
because Hurst would be found innocent. Allen told the grand jury
the same lies he had earlier given, and Hurst was exonerated. Bob
told us that Allen's jaw was later broken by the deputy sheriff
with a flashlight after the FBI disclosed to the lawmen that Allen
had lied. On January 31, 1964, Allen was shot and killed outside
his home by three blasts of a shotgun.

Although Bob had remarkable equanimity, I always knew that
he was profoundly touched by Lee's death. Bob told Lee's story
often and was convinced that his death resulted from his having
opened doors for the SNCC staff. Herbert Lee had helped them
make contact with local people and organize the voter-registration
meetings.

A week and a half after Lee's slaying, 115 high school students marched through McComb to protest the death of Lee and
the expulsion of their fellow student Brenda Travis. Bob Moses,
joined by Chuck McDew, Bob Zellner (the only white field secretary in SNCC at the time), and others went with them. Bob
Moses, Chuck, and Bob Zellner were all attacked. Nine of the
SNCC staff, including Bob Moses, were arrested and jailed. Separately, more than a hundred of the high school students walked
out when given an ultimatum by their principal that they were
not to demonstrate. An alternative school—called Nonviolent High
School—was set up in Pike County. It was attended by students
who refused to sign a statement proscribing their participation in
future demonstrations. Bob Moses taught algebra and geometry;
Dion Diamond taught physics and chemistry; and Chuck McDew
taught history.

In late October, Bob, Chuck, and Bob Zellner along with nine local residents were found guilty of the charges associated with the McComb march and, unable to raise fourteen thousand dollars to keep them free pending appeal, Bob and the others spent the next several months in jail. In November, Bob was able to sneak a message out of the jail which made its way from hand to hand and eventually into the Atlanta SNCC headquarters:

> We are smuggling this note from the drunk tank of the county jail in Magnolia, Mississippi. Twelve of us are here, sprawled out along the concrete bunker: Curtis Hayes, Hollis Watkins, Ike Lewis and Robert Talbert, four veterans of the bunker, are sitting up talking—mostly about girls— Chuck McDew ("Tell the story") is curled into the concrete and the wall; Harold Robinson, Stephen Ashley, James Wells, Lee Chester Vick, Leotus Eubanks, and Ivory Diggs lie cramped on the cold bunker; I'm sitting with smuggled pen and paper, thinking a little, writing a little; Myrtis Bennett and Janie Campbell are across the way wedded to a different icy cubicle.
>
> Later on, Hollis will lead out with a clear tenor into a freedom song, Talbert and Lewis will supply jokes, and McDew will discourse on the history of the black man and the Jew. McDew—a black by birth, a Jew by choice, and a revolutionary by necessity—has taken on the deep hates and deep loves which America and the world reserve for those who dare to stand in a strong sun and cast a sharp shadow. . . .
>
> This is Mississippi, the middle of the iceberg. Hollis is leading off with his tenor, "Michael, row the boat ashore, Alleluia; Christian brothers, don't be slow, Alleluia; Mississippi's next to go, Alleluia." This is a tremor from the middle of the iceberg—from a stone that the builders rejected.

Northern cities are inhabited by many black Mississippians who moved there seeking jobs and opportunity. Prior to the civil rights struggle, which provided an avenue for confrontation, the only course available to many blacks had been to leave the South. As early as 1964, Bob Moses sought to formulate a means of stemming the flow of southern blacks to Chicago, Detroit, New York, and Boston by revitalizing rural southern living.

Bob expressed his views as he swayed gently from a swing

that hung from a gnarled oak tree on a hot day in Mississippi in 1964. I remember thinking that, growing up in Harlem, he would not have been able to swing in the shade of a low-hanging tree kicking up the golden dust beneath his feet where the grass had worn bare. If the emigration to northern slums by people in search of jobs could be slowed, Bob maintained, and if agribusiness could be contained to allow small farmers to survive, life might be qualitatively better in the South. This would require decent wages, desegregation of education and its improvement, as well as equal access to federal grants and entitlement programs. Illiterate people do not know how to fill out forms. By and large, black people in Mississippi did not know about Social Security and could not sign up for it, to say nothing of the Agricultural Extension Service, Soil Conservation Service, or the Farmers Home Administration. This information had been closely held and they lacked the tools to ferret it out. In urban ghettos, Bob argued, families disintegrate from economic pressure; life is filled with the stress of overcrowding, crime, unemployment; no one has any roots, nor sense of community. In Mississippi, blacks belonged. They had built the state. Whatever had been developed in Mississippi was a tribute to them as much as, and even more than, anyone else.

Bob Moses stood out as one of very few individuals in the movement who tried to look at long-range goals beyond the daily circumference of the struggle. He was also the first person I heard to argue that once desegregation had been accomplished in the South, the eventual quality of relationships between the races would be finer and more durable than in the North. Once the traumas of adjustment were past, integration would be more successful in the South, Bob maintained, because whites knew blacks and blacks knew whites, unlike the theoretical relationships between the races and lip service to equality of people elsewhere in the country. The enormous disparity between rich and poor in the United States could also, he believed, be more humanely overcome in the South where black people had a real stake in what had been developed.

The high percentage of blacks in the Mississippi Delta counties led Bob to comment on the long-term prospects for democracy. At the time, Washington, D.C., did not have "home rule" and it was not yet being seriously advocated. "The test of democracy," Bob used to say, "is whether or not the District of Columbia—seventy percent black and the nation's capital—will be allowed to govern itself." If the Congress would not permit home rule, democracy would be shown to be corrupted by racism and there could be little hope for the Black Belt—the string of counties with 70 or 80 percent black populations that trailed like a sash across the mid-girth of the Deep South. Little did we suspect that one of our own staff, Marion Barry, would later be elected mayor of Washington, D.C., or that, in 1974, the Congress would vote home rule.

Despite his trenchant mind and his prescience, Bob Moses had, however, overlooked the severity of one major problem that would loom for the black citizens of the Delta—the effects of agricultural business technology. Within less than two decades, most of the sharecroppers would be displaced by harvesting combines and automated equipment; many would slowly lose their toehold in the land their grandparents and great-grandparents had cleared as slaves. Large numbers went on to Chicago; Detroit; Gary, Indiana; and other industrial cities. Of those who had already abandoned the fields and farms of the state, Bob worried about their survival and the quality of their uprooted life. We rued their departure. We feared that more displacement would occur unless the pattern was reversed, but we didn't realize how fast or how relentlessly it would become a reality. Despite all the doors opened by the movement, despite its compelling vision of human worth, and despite its creativity, we were not analytical enough, shrewd enough in our strategies, or tenacious enough to reverse these effects. And, we had extremely powerful economic opposition.

When Jane Stembridge's next letter arrived, she reminded me of Hölderlin: "The important words, the ever-present ones, the hold-up-the-banner words, the ones for winter time in Greenwood and within my heart, are, 'And tenderly I pledged my heart to the grave and suffering land. . . .' "

CHAPTER 4

JAIL

You know I'm tired of segregation and
    I want my equal rights
Segregation did me wrong, made me leave my
    happy home,
That's why I'm fighting for my rights,
    Fighting for my rights,
You know I'm fighting for my rights,
    Fighting for my rights.

My mother, yeah, she told me
    And she was very brave
Child, if you don't get your freedom
    I'd rather see you in your grave.

Well, my father, yes, he told me
    A long, long time ago
Child, if you don't fight for freedom
    You'll be a slave forever more.

Well, my cell it had two windows
    But the sun could never come through
And I felt so sad and lonely
    You know I didn't know what to do.

That's why I'm fighting for my rights,
    fighting for my rights
You know I'm fighting for my rights,
    fighting for my rights.

—Adapted by Charles Neblitt and Charles Wingfield
    from the Ray Charles song, "Lonely Avenue"

I was smoking two packs of Pall Malls a day, long
slender cigarettes with a lengthy draw, unfiltered for
the additional kick. My consumption had more than doubled. I
was drinking my coffee black—six or seven cups a day. Having
left Danville and returned to Atlanta, I shared the Communications office with Julian Bond. In the beginning, I was naïve; my

Black Belt Counties

TENNESSEE

NORTH CAROLINA

Rock Hill ●

SOUTH
CAROLINA

★ Atlanta

G E O R G I A

ALABAMA

STEWART

WEBSTER

● Americus

SUMTER

QUITMAN

TERRELL

LEE

CRISP

RANDOLPH

Sasser ● ● Leesburg

CLAY

CALHOUN

Albany ●

DOUGHERTY

WORTH

EARLY

BAKER

MILLER

MITCHELL

COLQUITT

SEMINOLE

DECATUR

GRADY

THOMAS

BROOKS

FLORIDA

Atlantic Ocean

commitment was based on my heart and the values derived from my family background. Yet I had grown rapidly from my experiences in Danville and had not only gained confidence but valuable skills. Before Danville, I had virtually no comprehension of the judicial system, but the city under siege gave me a crash course in how it could be used as an instrument of injustice. I had also seen firsthand how ruthlessly First Amendment rights could be abused in the defense of segregation. This lesson was intensified by my exposure to events later that autumn in southwest Georgia.

I spent several days in Sumter, Lee, Dougherty, and Calhoun counties, as well as "Terrible" Terrell County, writing a special report on the situation in the town of Americus. I drove south from Atlanta with Joyce Barrett, a vivacious brunette staff member from Philadelphia with pixielike hair. Once in Albany, the center of SNCC's Southwest Georgia Project, I met up with Penny Patch, a quiet white field secretary whose pallid complexion belied her steely tenacity, and Joni Rabinowitz, also white, another earnest staff member who was working there.

Joyce gave me a long account of Charles Sherrod's initiation of the project when he and Cordell Reagon, both of them black SNCC workers, arrived in October 1961 to open an office in Albany. They had come to conduct workshops in nonviolence, start voter registration, and assist the indigenous Albany Movement that antedated SNCC—a swelling tide of high school and college students who had become involved through the local NAACP youth chapter.

Two sets of jailings had occurred in December 1961 when Eliza "Goldie" Jackson, who served as secretary of the Albany Movement, sent a telegram to Dr. King. She wired, pleading with him to come into Albany because of a desperate need to bring national attention to the efforts of a small struggling local movement that had over seven hundred people in jail. He came to Albany and accomplished this to the satisfaction of the activists, and in January 1962 Andrew Young opened a citizen registration school in Dorchester. This particular local movement tackled a whole city's segregated structure by a complex interaction of organizing with litigation. I believe it was the first local protest to challenge an entire municipality, in contrast to the Montgomery bus boycott, for example, which was an assault on the segregated bus system.

One of the great freedom songs of the movement came from southwest Georgia. It was initially sung at the mass meeting in the Union Baptist Church of Albany following the first march of the Albany Movement in December 1961. Charles Jones had asked Bernice Johnson, then a student at Albany State College (later Bernice Johnson Reagon), to lead a song. Bernice raised a haunting and lyrical spiritual. As she started into the first line, she realized that the word *trouble* in the original was not right for the situation and changed it to *freedom*. One of my clearest and most lasting memories from the movement is of hearing Bernice's rich and warm solo voice—rising from wherever in a room she was standing—swelling slowly, filled with meaning and without accompaniment, singing this song:

> Over my head, I see freedom in the air,
> Over my head, I see freedom in the air,
> Over my head, O, Lord, I see freedom in the air,
> There must be a God somewhere.
>
> Over my head, I see victory in the air,
> Over my head, I see victory in the air,
> Over my head, O, Lord, I see victory in the air,
> There must be a God somewhere.

A recurring problem for SNCC organizers was that local residents often withheld their trust believing that they would be abandoned when trouble arose. It had taken a long time for Sherrod with his modest demeanor, skin the color of toast, and pleasant bespectacled face—SNCC's first field secretary—at twenty-two years of age to gain acceptance by Albany residents. They were convinced he would leave them at the first sign of difficulty. He decided it was important to show that he identified with them, intended to stay, and would share in whatever suffering lay in store. One of his first breakthroughs in achieving trust occurred following a night when Sherrod had talked at length with a man who kept repeating to him, "People treat me like a dog." Again and again, he asked Sherrod plaintively, "Do I look like a dog? Do I look like a dog?" Many had witnessed that discussion of several hours as Sherrod kept pushing his eyeglasses up on his nose, eyes focused intently on the man. Afterward, word sped through the community that the SNCC people really cared.

On September 9, 1963, I wrote my former professor Benjamin Spencer, a white Kentuckian who was married to an Alabaman:

> One of the most basic things we're fighting for is simply the
> right to dissent. For example three of our workers are now
> facing a possible death penalty in Americus, Georgia. They
> were part of a demonstration the night of August 8 and were
> beaten in the streets by police and arrested for "inciting to
> insurrection," a capital crime in Georgia under the old law
> used against slave insurrections and revolts. They have been
> in prison now since August 8 and the lawyer has been able
> to see them only once. Not only did the judge refuse to set
> bond at their commitment hearing, but in addition he
> placed a peace bond on them totaling $120,000. . . . We're
> working on a habeas corpus now. . . .

The three workers incarcerated were Donald Harris, a sophisticated black graduate of the Fieldston School and Rutgers University who had unstudied elegance and wore dark-rimmed eyeglasses; Ralph Allen, a white student on leave from Trinity College in Hartford, Connecticut; and John Perdew, also white, a thoughtful student from Harvard University, who was originally from Colorado. Ralph had been beaten on the street in Americus, the county seat of Sumter County, the preceding April, when he accompanied a woman to the courthouse to register to vote. According to my estimate, the three men might be locked up for two years. They were arrested on August 8, when police waded into 250 peaceful demonstrators in Americus, dispersing them by brandishing billy sticks and firing pistols into the air. They slugged their way through the crowd to Don, beating him in the street, and dragging him to the police car; then they trampled Ralph and John. The next night, most of the 175 who demonstrated were arrested by police armed with guns, clubs, and battery-operated electric cattle prods. Twenty of them, young girls aged nine to thirteen years, were sent to the Leesburg, Georgia, stockade in Lee County and held for as long as one month in a cell eight feet by ten feet by thirty feet with no beds, springs, or mattresses, and with only two broken and clogged commodes.

I took several depositions, including the following:

Robertina Freeman, being duly sworn, deposes and says: I am thirteen years old and was in the Leesburg stockade. . . . There were two toilets and they were stopped up when I got there. They wouldn't work. At first they had to use them because they had nothing else. . . . But soon they were overflowing and couldn't be used anymore. Then the girls started urinating in the drain near the shower. . . . The guards took away our remaining beds because we were singing and praying. So then we started sleeping on the floor with no mattresses, no beds, no blankets, no sheets, no nothing. The floor was wet with the waste material.

Bobby Lee Jones, being duly sworn, deposes and says: I am nineteen years old. . . . We were in the city jail of Americus one night when they brought in about fifteen girls who had been demonstrating. They had been burned by cow prods and were sore from being hit. They put all the girls in a room about eight feet by twelve feet where they were refused medical care.

We regarded southwest Georgia as the most dangerous place in the region, second only to Mississippi. This impression stayed with me for many years. In 1971, well after my 1963 Americus report, I was visiting Atlanta as an official of the U.S. Office of Economic Opportunity in Washington, when my future husband, Dr. Peter Bourne, introduced me to Georgia's new governor, Jimmy Carter. Before the meeting, Peter told me he believed the governor had potential for a national role. But when I learned he was from Sumter County, I groaned, "Oh, no, I *know* southwest Georgia," visualizing the young girls in jail in Sumter and Lee counties and remembering the capital charges against our workers and $120,000 in peace bonds.

Until that meeting with Governor Carter, the only white officials from southwest Georgia I had met were like those reflected in a story told by Charles Jones, a handsome, fair-skinned black field secretary, the son of a Presbyterian minister in Charlotte, North Carolina. He had searching blue eyes, high energy, and intensity. Charles captured attention when he walked into any room. A crucial player in SNCC's voter-registration activities, he spent much of his time in the Southwest Georgia Project. During my first visit there, he quoted the police chief of Albany, Laurie Pritchett, in adjacent and equally reactionary Dougherty County:

"It's just a case of mind over matter. I don't mind and you don't matter."

Dr. Spencer responded to my letter:

> I cannot believe that any kind of sadism can exceed that of the resourceless white southerner whose ego has no other support than the humiliation he can inflict on the Negroes. . . . Heroism has not gone out of American life, but, ironically, it seems to me, it has been most magnificently displayed by the young Negro children of the South during the past five years.

The experiences of southwest Georgia led Sherrod to write a freedom song:

> I became a young man, proud as I could be
> Used to hear them saying, "Hang him on a tree,"
> Tree limb couldn't hold me, segregation tried,
> Jumped the gun for freedom, getting closer every stride.
>
> *Chorus after every verse:*
> Nothing but a soldier, soldier
> Nothing but a soldier, soldier
> Nothing but a soldier, soldier
> Can make it in, can make it in.
>
> Folks say don't go marching without an alibi,
> But I say give me freedom before the day I die,
> We don't need the H-bomb, rockets do not serve,
> We have got nonviolence, packs more power for every
>   nerve.
>
> Hoses were a-spurting, police everywhere,
> Dragged me to the wagon, stripped my underwear,
> Dogs tore off my clothing, cow prods burnt my flesh,
> Cops beat me with blackjacks, they were stomping on my
>   chest.
>
> Blood ran down my forehead, blood ran down my back,
> Threw me in the jailhouse, face down on the rack,
> Told Judge Jim Crow slowly, I may not be brave,
> You can jail my body, but I'll never be your slave.

The story in Americus was so horrific that, fearing the disbelief of SNCC's readers, I wrote the report distantly, relying on excerpts from notarized affidavits, tape recordings by a volunteer named Alan Ribback, photographs by Danny Lyon, and quotations from a news conference held by witnesses in Atlanta on September 9. Julian Bond liked the seven-page report and the fact that I hadn't expressed my opinion but limited myself to the facts. This account, dated September 24, 1963, was the first item that had gone out from SNCC with my by-line and, although I didn't have much time to dwell on it, I felt extremely proud and happy.

My intellectual growth was rapid too, much of it concerned with the link between belief and action. Casey and I, having read *The Plague* by Albert Camus at night, were now reading and deliberating his books *The Fall* and *The Rebel*. He was preoccupied with achieving a balance between moral purity and political effectiveness, a question that absorbed me. Keeping these two imperatives in proportion would become a persistent tension in my process of personal development in the movement. How I resolved this pressure would determine how I would handle certain choices for the rest of my life.

We were also reading the Spanish scholar Miguel de Unamuno and his essays on preservation of personal integrity despite a world of problems and compromise. Calling himself a "sower of doubt and agitator of consciences," Unamuno believed that there was nothing more important than searching for one's own truth, no matter how trying. He made an observation with lasting meaning for me when he commented that a new friend had enriched him not by what he gave him, but by what he caused him to discover in himself. Casey was causing me to discover insights into myself—and I, in her. Everything in SNCC was causing discovery in me—in my understanding of the underlying forces at work that degraded black people, in working relationships, in political analysis, and in my world view.

From the minute I reached headquarters the first thing in the morning until I left late at night, the telephone was cradled between my ear and my left shoulder leaving my hands free to type and take notes. I had attended a fancy high school where entrance was by competitive examination, but it didn't teach the two subjects that might have done me the most good—typing and automobile mechanics—so I typed with two fingers, as I still do, but fast. For much of almost four years, the length of time I worked for the civil rights movement, I remember the telephone crooked in my neck. It became an extension of me, like an arm or a leg.

Atlanta was a different city then. Roosters crowed at dawn each morning in the backyards in the black community where I lived and hens cackled away the daylight hours in bliss. They might as well have been in a farmyard as in a major city of the southland for this section of Atlanta with its unpaved streets and little houses was still semirural.

Only one doorway from Hunter Street, the long rambling thoroughfare of merchants that wound through the segregated southwestern black section of the city, stood the ramshackle mint-green two-story building that was headquarters of the staff of SNCC. Located on the west side of Atlanta just beyond a long arching overpass from the downtown area, the only white people who ventured near there, other than one or two white staff members at the SNCC office, were men making utility repairs or deliveries to shops. This section of the city was ignored by the municipal white power structure that was largely unaware of its existence, and it seemed that no one in central official Atlanta except a few journalists, one or two city politicians, and perhaps the FBI knew what went on in the chaotic second floor above the tailor shop at 6 Raymond Street, Southwest, which we soon enlarged to include 8½ Raymond Street as well. Our yearly budget in 1963 was approximately $250,000, virtually all of it in contributions from individuals, churches, and private organizations.

A few blocks away was the Atlanta University complex, the largest black institution of higher learning in the world. The campus, composed of seven colleges, teemed with students from all over the country, many of them the first of their families to attend college. There, too, few who were studying or teaching at those seven colleges knew what happened in our mint-green building. Much of the black middle class was politely defending a gradual approach to social change and blaming themselves for their own underdevelopment. The students or faculty who did know about SNCC were often embarrassed or ashamed by the confrontations provoked from Raymond Street. A couple of hundred brazen Atlanta University students had joined the sit-ins and formed the Atlanta Committee on Appeal for Human Rights, but, by and large, the somnolent reaction of the black middle class reflected its isolation from the awakening of black college students.

I remember *Time* magazine describing our building as a "windowless cubicle." That was wrong. Julian and I shared the front right-hand office and its two windows above the tailor shop. Every time the wind shifted, smoke from the pit of Alex's Barbecue Heaven wafted through our second-story window. The barbecue was just around the corner from our slightly sloping street that ran at a right angle to Hunter Street. When the scent was particularly pungent, our small office building would temporarily empty as SNCC staff people trickled out to bring back barbecued spareribs or chicken to their desks and satisfy the yearning stimulated by the piquant smell. Alex's barbecue had a large blackened stone oven-pit, large enough for a person to stand in and over fifteen feet wide, where wood fires hissed as the juices of spareribs and chicken doused with Alex's own blend of sauce dripped from the grill.

Since Atlanta could be temperate even in winter, I opened the window a crack on Saturday, December 21, 1963, when I was working alone in our section. Julian was press secretary for SNCC, yet I now sometimes ran the Communications operation by myself, and whether or not I acted as spokesperson for the organization would be my own judgment call. There were often times, however, when only Julian could go on record because he had been speaking for the organization since its start in 1960.

The smoke from Alex's Barbecue Heaven seeped lazily into the Communications office. I had worked late the night before, putting out what the news media called "actualities" to radio stations across the country, including the West Coast, which was fortunately three hours behind us. This meant a "feed" to radio stations, individual telephone call by call, containing a taped direct quotation from one of our staff on the scene. The radio stations were pleased to have such individualized treatment; they received a semiexclusive account, and we were able to get our report played in the major media markets, breaking our stories nationally even if the Associated Press or Universal Press International wire services wouldn't carry them. This allowed us to penetrate radio news. All it took were some defenses against boredom and a simple hookup from a tape recorder into the phone.

I was still feeding tapes to radio stations by rote, tired, when Jim Forman strolled in to see me.

"Sweetheart," he said, using an affectionate term as he normally did. "Would you like to meet a member of the new Kenyan cabinet, the minister of home affairs, Oginga Odinga?"

Jim conveyed affection although he was tough and acerbic when he needed to be. While he talked with you alone, he focused solely on you and was gentle and absorbed. Normally found wearing ordinary workman's overalls, with his hands hanging loose in the pockets, portly and smoking a pipe, Jim was approachable. Yet, as our executive secretary, he could adopt the mien of a grizzly. He was thirty-five years old which made him more than ten years older than the rest of the organization. He had been born in Chicago but was sent back to Mississippi to his grandmother's care at eleven months, and grew up in Marshall County. More sophisticated and experienced than any of the rest of us, he had served in the U.S. Air Force. He received a degree in public administration from Roosevelt University in Chicago and then attended Boston University on a grant from the institution's African studies program, one of the few such units then found in American universities. Jim also spoke French. In the fall of 1960, he left his job teaching school in Chicago and went to Fayette County, Tennessee, to help set up a program to house sharecroppers evicted from their tenancies because they had tried to register to vote. An embittering experience in Monroe, North Carolina, the following year, in which he was beaten with the barrel of a gun and nearly killed, while police stood by watching, led him in the fall of 1961 to become SNCC's executive secretary.

Jim's brown face with high cheekbones was beaming with excitement. "How'd you like to meet Oginga Odinga?" Jim asked.

"Tell me about him."

"He just accepted his country's seat at the United Nations and has been touring the United States," Jim responded. "Atlanta's the last stop on his trip. He's also vice-president of the Kenya African National Union called KANU. He was a Mau Mau leader before independence and he's influential in the new Kenyan government."

"When are we to meet him?" I asked.

"Today. This is the first visit of an African liberation-movement leader to the South."

"I thought the State Department wasn't letting Africans travel in the South because the government can't assure their safety."

"You're right. Washington refused to let him travel by surface even though he wanted to see the countryside by train or bus, because he'd be vulnerable. They made him fly to Atlanta on a direct flight. That's all they're willing to take responsibility for—a straight flight from Washington to Atlanta, one airport to another. He can go on from Atlanta to New Orleans the same way, but they won't let him out on the ground."

"When's the meeting?" I asked.

"Couple of hours, baby. Odinga specifically asked to meet with us. I guess he identifies with SNCC more than other groups. Everyone in the office who can go should go."

"I'd like to meet him."

Jim always tried to make a connection between what we were doing and what was happening in Africa, with his knowledge of the continent and its history. "The Mau Mau had a ferocious reputation," he continued. "The world reaction to sixty-eight European deaths in Kenya was incredible. But no one raised an outcry internationally about the black Kenyans killed in that struggle or one million Algerians who died at the hands of the French or thousands of Africans who died in the Congo and southern Africa."

"Pure racism."

"So you'll go, baby?"

"Wouldn't miss it. Should we take some gifts?"

"What do you suggest?"

"A record of freedom songs and a book."

Jim moved out of the office to talk to other staff.

My interest was piqued by the thought of our meeting the Kenyan leader who came to Atlanta to meet with us. Almost the entire headquarters staff and several visiting field staff put on their coats and jackets and crammed into donated automobiles. We drove across the Hunter Street overpass into white Atlanta and traveled north, heading straight up Peachtree Street. It was four days before Christmas and Atlanta was bustling with the final stages of Christmas preparations. Store windows were decorated with evergreens, tinsel, red ribbons, Christmas lights, and trimmings. Pedestrians were rushing about, carrying shopping bags from Rich's and Davison's department stores stuffed with brightly wrapped packages. Children had the giddy air of expectation that goes with that time of year.

Finally we came to the Peachtree Manor Hotel, which was

located at what was then 696 Peachtree Street, Northwest. This was the lone integrated hotel in the city, a development that had occurred only the preceding year. I had been stunned to learn when I moved to Atlanta in 1962 that there was only one in the "beacon" of the South. Arriving there, we left our cars in the parking lot between the hotel and the Toddle House coffee shop and made our way through the entrance into the drab lobby of the modest hotel, gathering ourselves around the Christmas tree.

His Excellency Oginga Odinga appeared, and our group of perhaps two dozen staff surrounded him, filling the small lobby. He was wearing several layers of flowing white embroidered robes and a decorative white-and-gold hat shaped like a pillbox. In his hand was a ceremonial fly-swisher made of horsehair, also white, that he carried as a symbol of office as did his head of state Jomo Kenyatta. The white robes and regalia set against his dark skin made him strikingly handsome and our eyes were fixed on him. The minister had been sworn in as a member of Kenya's new postindependence cabinet only six months earlier, following years of struggle to free the East African country from British control.

We presented him with our gifts including the record and, as Jim explained freedom songs, he singled out four of the members of SNCC's singing group, The Freedom Singers, who happened to be in Atlanta that day resting from a concert tour. In an unplanned response, The Freedom Singers—that day Charles Neblitt of Carbondale, Illinois; Matthew Jones of Knoxville, Tennessee; Cordell Reagon of Nashville; and Phyllis Martin—broke spontaneously into song and led the group in several freedom songs, bringing a warm rush of feeling.

One was a traditional song modified for the Freedom Rides by members of CORE:

> Freedom, freedom, freedom's coming and it won't be long,
> Freedom, freedom, freedom's coming and it won't be long.
>
> Took a trip down Alabama way,
> Freedom's coming and it won't be long,
> Met much violence on Mother's Day,
> Freedom's coming and it won't be long.
>
> We took a trip on a Greyhound bus,
> Freedom's coming and it won't be long,

To fight segregation, this we must,
Freedom's coming and it won't be long.

On to Mississippi with speed we go,
Freedom's coming and it won't be long,
Blue-shirt policemen meet us at the door,
Freedom's coming and it won't be long.

Judge say local custom shall prevail,
Freedom's coming and it won't be long,
We say "No" and we land in jail,
Freedom's coming and it won't be long.

Hey, Mister Kennedy, take me out of misery,
Freedom's coming and it won't be long,
This evil segregation, look what it has done to me,
Freedom's coming and it won't be long.

Cordell Hull Reagon, a wiry and baby-faced stylish student leader from Nashville who had become involved with the movement at the age of sixteen, led off another song in solo. His head thrown back, eyes slightly closed, the sinews of his light brown neck pliant and strong, Cordell sang a parody of a song originally performed by Little Willie John that was popularized by the Nashville student movement and that Cordell had learned from James Bevel and Bernard Lafayette. He let his voice linger on the word "bone":

Well I went down to the dime store to get myself some
eats, they put me in the jail when I sat on them folks' seat.

You better le-e-e-e-e-eave segregation alone, because
they love segregation like a hound dog loves a bone, a
bone, a bone, a bone, a bone, a bone, a bone, a bone.

Well I went down to the dime store to get myself a Coke,
the waitress looked at me and she thought it was a joke.

You better le-e-e-e-e-eave segregation alone, because
they love segregation like a hound dog loves a bone, a
        bone, a bone.

Oginga Odinga smiled broadly, enjoying himself. He joined us on some of the verses of a traditional song adapted by the movement:

We are fighting for our freedom, we shall not be moved,
We are fighting for our freedom, we shall not be moved,
Just like a tree, planted by the water,
We shall not be moved.

Black and white together, we shall not be moved,
Black and white together, we shall not be moved,
Just like a tree planted by the water,
We shall not be moved.

We'll stand and fight together, we shall not be moved,
We'll stand and fight together, we shall not be moved,
Just like a tree planted by the water,
We shall not be moved.

Then the Kenyan leader recited poetry and demonstrated how the fly-swisher was used ceremonially. He led us with his fly-swisher in chanting "Uhuru," meaning "Freedom" in Swahili.

This meeting was, in fact, the first concrete contact between the American civil rights movement and the newly emerging African states and liberation movements. Notwithstanding our pleasure in meeting the leader from Kenya, it was the struggle in Algeria that seemed the most important of the several anticolonial conflicts then occurring on the African continent. Jim Forman's allusions to the protracted and bitter war in Algeria lodged in me. The struggle of the Algerians against the French made me optimistic that we could ultimately win in the United States where the structure of our legal canon and the judiciary held out hope for eventual justice.

I was excited by the December meeting with Oginga Odinga partly because of a book that was then making the rounds in the movement. Earlier in 1963, Frantz Fanon's *The Wretched of the Earth*, a mournful and persuasive exposition on colonialism, had appeared in English. Copies were extremely hard to come by. I could not buy my own personal copy until one year later, but I borrowed one. It followed my study of *The Rebel* by Albert Camus, also about Algeria.

Slowly, people were reading and quoting Dr. Fanon, a black psychiatrist born in Martinique who went to Algeria to practice psychiatry. He died tragically in 1961 from leukemia at the age of thirty-six in Washington, D.C.'s DuPont Plaza Hotel after having been brought to Walter Reed Hospital. Fanon's book, a dense exploration of the effects of imperialism on the colonized, had an immediate impact on our thinking.

The Wretched of the Earth changed me and modified SNCC. There was one inescapable conclusion from exposure to Fanon: The most important innovations were not necessarily external but had to take place internally—in the self-concept of black people. Reading Fanon, I saw that barriers lay within as well as without and began to believe that our energies would also have to be directed at attitudes, especially the self-contempt and assumptions of inferiority produced by centuries of oppression.

I began in my own mind to feel that the framework through which I was looking at the civil rights movement was limited, and started questioning whether we needed more penetrating tools for conversion of the forces against us than desegregating public conveyances and interstate travel. After the Freedom Rides in 1961, although Charles Sherrod emphasized voter registration in southwest Georgia and Bob Moses was doing the same in Mississippi, the rest of SNCC and its affiliates continued with direct action in the tradition of the sit-ins—picket lines, kneel-ins, wade-ins, demonstrations, boycotts—mainly with targets of restaurants, hotels, and public transportation. In addition to its philosophical roots, part of the reason for this approach lay in the modicum of regulation provided by the Interstate Commerce Commission (ICC), the oldest U.S. federal regulatory agency, established in 1887. The ICC oversight of interstate travel gave us one of our few handles for injecting meager federal leverage into our struggle.

Now, direct action was beginning to seem insufficient to me because it could not change the fundamentals of who had power and who controlled whom. With my reading of Fanon, perhaps my romanticism about the movement started to change. I certainly began to think in longer-range terms. Considering the instruments available to the movement, I became more interested in the potential of voter registration and its ultimate impact on policy in the United States. This line of thinking led me straight to a concern for breaking down the seniority system in the U.S. Congress—the arrangement that allowed control of three fourths of the key committees in the House and Senate to be maintained year after year by officials elected from southern districts and states heavily populated by blacks. I remember the day Tom Hayden detailed for me the demographics of how many of those who controlled the Congress were unchallenged at the polls because of racial disenfranchisement.

Because of the seniority system, the major civil rights bills enacted by the Congress in the 1960s became law only by strategies to bypass the Senate Judiciary Committee, which Senator James Eastland of Sunflower County, Mississippi, controlled rigidly until his retirement in 1978. Senator Eastland served for six years as president pro tempore of the Senate—a post that kept him fourth in line in the succession to the presidency should something happen to the president, vice-president, and speaker of the House—under Presidents Richard M. Nixon, Gerald R. Ford, and Jimmy Carter. Beginning twelve years after this period, as a senior official in the Carter administration, I was required to appear regularly before sixteen committees and subcommittees of the U.S. Congress. This was an irregularly high number for any government department but our subcabinet agency had both domestic and overseas programs. I embarrassed myself two or three times during that four-year period when, chagrined and exhausted by the impediments and intricacies of the more democratic new system resulting from the weakening of the seniority system in the 1970s, I found myself longing for its old less democratic efficiency so I could get the appropriations for my programs and go home.

The Wretched of the Earth was a milestone for me in the personal transition I was still making from thinking moralistically to thinking politically. In my mind's eye, I was shifting the way I saw myself from that of an activist on the side of right to that of a political strategist. It was the first step in the process that led to the way I see myself now, as someone working to accomplish goals that are connected to policy and power. While it would take years of experience to solidify, after reading Fanon I was never the same again. I saw the depths of the impact of the French on the Algerian psyche and realized that an appeal based on rightness is not enough. I started to view myself as a serious political being functioning in a democratic system that must be forced to change or to live up to its promise.

Reading this book also brought my sophistication in political analysis to a new level of understanding. Another of the changes set off by Fanon was that I was becoming more international in my outlook. I was receptive to internationalism because my parents had raised me to be what they called "a citizen of the world," but now Fanon brought the African movements right into my own sphere.

He linked us in the American civil rights movement at once and intimately with the anticolonialism sweeping the African continent, which we had glimpsed on television and in news reports, because he provided insight into the thinking of Algerians engaged in the war. I remember race as being less significant an issue in Fanon than the impact of cultural dominance on the minds of the colonized. I observed that women shared some of the characteristics of the colonized, and men, those of the colonizers.

Although it took another full three years to play out, I was not the only one shifting as a result of Fanon's book. The questions he raised spurred people in the movement to wrestle with new issues that would send SNCC in two directions. One was the beginning of a concern with identity; the rhetoric that accompanied this probing opened the door for the black nationalism that emerged in 1965. A second direction was toward another form of nationalism that was land-based and had to do with local leadership, local and community control, and neighborhood "turf."

One aspect of Fanon's thinking would four years later become influential with a generation of black nationalists for whom his book became almost a bible. Concerned with the *psychological* freeing of people who had been subjected to the "superiority" of the colonizers, Fanon believed, as a result of the Algerian strife, that when both sides faced each other with guns, all pretensions to supremacy would be stripped away, an inherently positive experience for the colonized. Furthermore, he thought that mobilization for war not only carried with it potential defeat of those who held themselves to be superior, it also provided a structure and framework for the new society that would follow the unrest.

While Fanon gave us a general philosophical framework for SNCC's solidarity with African liberation movements, the meeting with Minister Oginga Odinga before Christmas 1963 was itself a catalyst. Our session with the former Mau Mau figure was a tinder that ignited SNCC to its wider circumference.

Suddenly, as our meeting with the Kenyan was drawing to a close, two members of our gathering decided to get a cup of coffee at the Toddle House restaurant next door. The waitresses refused to serve them. Our group was made up entirely of blacks except for two whites, Nancy Stearns and me, and Ed Nakawatase, an American of Japanese descent from Camden, New Jersey. Someone who saw what was happening came into the hotel lobby where we were finishing our meeting and told us that a spontaneous sit-in was in progress. It didn't take us long to decide to join them. The situation was clear. This diplomat, minister of the Kenyan government, vice-president of a victorious national party, leader in a national liberation movement, and now ambassador to the United Nations would not have been able to get a cup of coffee. We made an immediate group decision. Without hesitancy, we left Oginga Odinga at the hotel, walked across the parking lot, entered the restaurant, sat down on the stools at the long lunch counter, and asked for cups of coffee.

The waitresses with their bleached blond hair and pink aprons started moving about frantically, nervously cleaning and recleaning bottles of ketchup, wiping the Tabasco sauce bottles over and over, filling toothpick holders, and checking the levels of the salt and pepper shakers, all the while studiously avoiding looking us in the eye. Unlike most sit-ins, this one had little commotion. There were no thugs hanging around or local rednecks (named for their sunburned necks exposed while driving tractors) harassing us. We were polite. The sit-in was restrained. For a while there was some question as to whether we would actually be arrested. I harbored the fantasy that the city of Atlanta might not stoop to something so old-fashioned as arrests for a sit-in because I wanted to get back to the office and continue the telephone feeds to the radio stations. From the whispered discussions among the waitresses, however, it became apparent that the police had been called and were on their way.

Two paddy wagons pulled up and several police officers entered the restaurant and began arresting us. Without consultation with each other, but because of previous training and preparation, each of us went limp as we were arrested, making no resistance but refusing to cooperate by walking to the paddy wagon. This meant that the police had to carry us one by one from the coffee shop into the waiting wagons. Twenty-one of us were hauled off to the Atlanta city jail, nicknamed Big Rock, downtown near the gold-domed capitol building of the state of Georgia. It was ugly and forbidding. We also refused to cooperate there and had to be carried into the processing sections as well. Two of our group were vindictively dragged feet first by the police and injured.

I was roughly handled but not hurt. My main worry at that moment was whether they would let me keep my toothbrush and Chapstick with me. We used to laugh that one never went anywhere in the movement without a toothbrush in case one found oneself locked up. To this day I still carry a toothbrush with me. I didn't wear much lipstick but used Chap Stick to prevent cracking of the skin on my lips. Would they take that from me? That was the big issue I was worrying about. We were each of us in turn dumped on the floor of the processing "tank" where we sat, serious and reserved. No one was outwardly upset.

Sprawled around on the floor of the Atlanta city jail tank were people who will always be heroes to me. The years have softened the hard edges of internal disagreements and petty disputes, and as recollections of the tensions of the moment have evaporated, what has remained is a distillation of the essence of each person in my memory; the unimportant has been forgotten but the true character remains.

Jimmy Bolton was a youth of nineteen from Atlanta, meticulous, highly energetic with a bounce to his walk, tenacious in follow-up, and willing to carry out in good humor whatever task had to be done. He seemed strangely out of place having nothing for his active hands to do now, but his agreeable demeanor hadn't changed. Judy Richardson was a sprightly and beautiful young woman from Tarrytown, New York, also nineteen, whose happy, buoyant, and joking nature was contagious. She had an impish quality and sat with a seeming determination to find something that was fun in all this. Charlie Cobb sat guilelessly, a hint of a smile breaking at the corners of his mouth, taking in every detail. There was a quality of innocence about Charlie, a nimble and self-contained twenty-year-old. William Porter was rotund. Sometimes he could be grumpy and belligerent but now he sat quietly with a baleful look. Annie Pearl Avery from Birmingham was scrappy, hotheaded, and knew no fear. I had seen Annie Pearl jump up, battering the chests of police, elbows flying, nostrils flaring, and eyes flashing, when her twenty-year-old emotions overtook her judgment. Now she was fidgeting restlessly. Worth Long, contemplative and thoughtful, was a gifted twenty-seven-year-old occasional poet from Little Rock, Arkansas. He sat peering through his glasses at the gray concrete floor, philosophically mulling over the situation. Ivanhoe Donaldson, then twenty-two years of age, was thinking; he seemed to relish the irony of our having been arrested after meeting with an African leader.

We talked quietly among ourselves, agreeing that we would stay in jail and accept no bail. This was vintage SNCC. Others in the movement could be bailed out, but our policy was still "Jail— No Bail."

When the processing began, without warning Nancy Stearns and I were taken off separately. I felt a tightening in my stomach and shoulders when I saw that the authorities planned to segregate us and put us in the section of the institution for white women. My heart sank. This was awful. I wanted to be with Judy Richardson, Annie Pearl Avery, and Phyllis Martin. Grimly, I had already concluded that the worst thing that could happen was for Nancy and me to be thrown in with the white prisoners.

As they took away my purse, I managed to shift the two objects I was worried about into the pockets of my dress. They fingerprinted us and filled out papers. We gave our names, and ages, and then Nancy gave her address in Berkeley, California. My address in Atlanta caused sneers as the officers recognized that I lived in a black section of the city. I was twenty-three years old and Nancy was twenty-four. When filling out the papers, they asked us with boredom what race we were. Nancy and I turned and looked at each other intently for one second. Without any verbal communication, we both blurted out "Negro!" in the parlance of the day, desperately hoping they would keep us out of the white section and put us in with the other women so we could be together. They did not.

"Here's some damned white girls who say they're colored," one of the officers processing us called out jeeringly to his superior in another room. "Whatcha want us to do with 'em?" They looked at us with hostility and scorn and charged us with violation of the state's antitrespassing law. This was a statute that had been passed in March 1960, one month after two hundred Atlanta students, with soldierlike coordination had moved into ten downtown restaurants resulting in seventy-six arrests. Nancy and I were placed under $100 bail. Unbeknownst to Nancy and me then, most of the other nineteen SNCC workers arrested gave their names as Freedom Now in a gesture of defiance.

Nancy and I were crudely searched by two brittle female prison wardens, called matrons, but they let me keep my toothbrush and Chap Stick. We were shoved through one barred door after another, up some stairs, down darkened corridors with bare low-watt bulbs, through windowless antechambers, and finally into the hands of some other leathery matrons who controlled the white women's section of the jail. I had completely lost my sense of direction and didn't know where in the building we had been taken. A heavy barred door slammed behind us loudly, sending reverberations through the wing. Under normal circumstances I have low blood pressure, but now I was beginning to feel even more subdued and physiologically depressed, as if all my organs and systems were slowing down.

Nancy and I were not close friends and I did not know her well. What would I do spending time with no diversions, with someone I didn't know? What fun it would have been to be locked up with Judy Richardson and Annie Pearl Avery! They both liked to amuse themselves and others with antics, cutting up, making jokes, and in general finding something to laugh about. Right now, I thought, Judy, Annie Pearl, and Phyllis are probably expressing their anger at the humiliations of the processing by laughing, playful bellicosity, and mocking the men who dealt with them and the matrons who searched them.

The matrons led Nancy and me to two metal cots next to each other with lumpy mattresses stretched over what looked like chicken wire. I slowly took stock of my surroundings. Nancy and I lay down on the cots, which had no sheets or pillows. Overhead, ceiling lamps burned with low wattage. They were covered with the wiring used on basketball courts to protect against their being smashed. The windows were crossed with massive bars. We must be on the top floor, I thought, because I could see no surrounding buildings. The walls were a dirty shade of mustard and the floors looked stained. I glanced at the other women there, lying down or sitting sullenly on metal cots that stretched out along two sides of the large cellblock; there were perhaps twenty women and several empty cots. Most of them seemed to have a toughness about them but I was not sure whether it was resignation, fatigue, or meanness. I figured they were prostitutes and petty thieves.

Suddenly, without warning, one of the women picked a fight with another. Both of them were approximately fifty years of age.

I watched the aggressor push her burning cigarette into the lower arm of the other woman and grind it out, twisting the butt back and forth to gouge and burn the flesh. The other woman shot up off the bed, screaming in pain and fury and hit back. The matrons rushed in to break up the fight. I shuddered.

"Nancy," I whispered urgently, "these women will never understand why we're here. It's hopeless, pointless; it would be foolish even to try to explain."

"I agree," Nancy responded. "But they'll probably ask us how we got locked up. What'll we say?" Nancy was a law student at the University of California at Berkeley. She had angular features, wavy hair that fell below her shoulders, and was slender.

"I don't know," I said in a low voice. "But if we tell them the truth, the chances are very good that they'll treat us like that," I said, nodding toward the woman who had been burned and was now being accompanied by the matrons to the front of the block. "We'll be in trouble. That's probably why they put us in here separately. Those sanctimonious cops downstairs did this on purpose, hoping we'd get beaten up." It was common knowledge that white men in the movement were often tossed into white cellblocks specifically for the purpose of provoking violence. It saved the police the time and trouble of beating them up themselves. Police all over the South knew that a white man in jail for civil rights activities would be beaten and sometimes nearly killed by other whites in antipathy. Bill Hansen, SNCC's white Arkansas state director who was arrested more than two dozen times during his SNCC years, had his jaw broken in such a jailhouse beating. Bob Zellner had several times been subjected to cell-block beatings deliberately stimulated by the police, who encouraged the other white prisoners to attack him. Very few white women in the movement had been arrested at that time, however, and there wasn't the same inevitability about our treatment. I didn't know how much we had to fear and I wasn't eager to test the reactions of this surly bunch of hardened women with grainy complexions.

"What will the matrons say about our being here?" Nancy asked. "If they tell, we'll have no recourse."

I whispered, "It will probably be a while before the women here start to probe. Let's lie low and keep our eyes and ears open. In the meantime, if we're asked, let's just say what our charge

was—trespassing—without explaining the circumstances. Some of
the women in here might have been picked up on the same charge
themselves. We may not have to explain after all. We don't have
to volunteer that it was a sit-in."

Nancy nodded. I was beginning to feel good about her. She
seemed solid. I was relieved that I hadn't been thrown in there
alone and I began to see how cooperative and intelligent Nancy
was. In the days and nights that followed, I grew to know her as
a serious and committed person. She later went on to become a
civil-liberties lawyer in New York. Our ruse worked. When asked,
we drily responded that we had been charged with trespassing.
Apparently the matrons kept the nature of our arrest to themselves.

All night the ceiling lamps burned. The low wattage was too
dim to read by in the daytime and too bright to sleep with at
night. I was having trouble sleeping anyway. I was anxious and
afraid even before seeing the cigarette burned into the woman's
arm. Several fights broke out over stolen cigarettes, imagined in-
sults, supposed provocations, accidental brushes, and some purely
antagonistic behavior. The next morning I was feeling terrible. I
hadn't slept and I was hungry. I was worried about undressing to
shower in the bathroom because I thought someone would steal
my clothes, so I didn't shower. I was still sizing up the situation
and absorbing details that would make it possible for me to cope.

We were suddenly ushered from the cellblock into an ante-
room with gray metal tables and benches. All the prisoners were
lined up and each given a pan three inches deep and roughly five
by five inches square, along with a spoon. Into these stainless
steel pans was poured a thick, ugly stew with some undercooked
kernels of corn floating on the top. I tried to eat it. I have always
thought myself fortunate that I do not have a finicky stomach. I
can travel anywhere in the world and be at home with whatever
is served in any village, no matter what it is or how poorly prepared. I pride myself on this adaptability. In those days, at SNCC
staff meetings, as you looked around the room, you would see
bottles of Maalox and other antacid compounds being lifted for a
swallow of relief for a tense stomach. Many of my fellow SNCC
workers had stomach problems or ulcers. But somehow I went
right through the movement years unscathed by these disorders
and I never once had indigestion or even lost my appetite. Often

it was impossible to eat nutritionally balanced meals, but the important thing was that despite what I might be feeling—apprehension, anxiety, fear, tension, dread, sorrow—it did not affect my stomach.

I tried to spoon up some of the glutinous stew. It was foul. I looked at Nancy across the table; our eyes locked. I looked sharply at the stew and then at the ceiling. She nodded and obviously felt the same. I thought about how much better fed were my grandfather's hogs at the hamlet of Burgess Store in Northumberland County, Virginia. We used to feed them "slop" made of the scraps from our meals; it would have been better than this. I tried to drink the coffee too, but it reminded me of tar and I could only manage a couple of acidic swallows. At least there was some bread, like dried-out Wonder bread. As bread, it was sorry, but it was something.

I began to look at the other women more carefully as some of my anxiety started to subside. By now I was thinking that we might be able to hold our own, not attracting much attention, not making any points or trying to assert ourselves in any way, sticking to ourselves but not appearing disdainful, friendly enough but not trying to make any friends, and not doing anything that might antagonize. The matrons didn't seem to have it in for us. I began to relax slightly, although, in general, I felt miserable.

As arraignments started, I began to learn more about the situations affecting the individual women prisoners. Several were there for passing bad checks. This was something entirely new to me; it had never occurred to me that people were arrested for bouncing checks. Clearly, this was an offense that was related to one's social class. Some of the women with such charges were in difficult circumstances involving the necessity to obtain food or other essentials for their children after having been abandoned. One young woman with a pasty complexion resulting from malnutrition had lifeless hair, a tattered blue dress, and sunken eyes. She cradled her knees and rocked back and forth on her cot moaning about her babies left behind. She told a woeful story of abandonment, job losses, ill children, and misery, and of pleading with the policemen when they came to arrest her on the bad-check charge, crying, "Who will take care of my sick babies?"

Many of the prisoners were alcoholics and were caught in a cycle in which they were arrested and rearrested. Some of them obviously had come to accept being in the city jail as their due—this was better shelter than they otherwise might have had. One woman bragged about how many times she had been locked up as a drunk. "This place is more like home than home is to me," she said.

Another, who looked like an aging ballerina, wore a pale pink dress and had shoulder-length black hair tied back with a ribbon that hinted at former elegance. She had the carriage and grace of a dancer. She paced up and down the cellblock, railing at Chief Judge Robert E. Jones for taking her off Antabuse and thus causing her downfall. This referred to an innovative program that was the one bright spot in the otherwise dismal Atlanta city-court system. Alcoholics were offered the chance of taking Antabuse—a chemical that induces vomiting if alcohol is subsequently drunk—and supportive counseling, as an alternative to serving a prison term for public drunkenness. (Ten years later, I found out that this unusual program had been originated by my husband-to-be, Peter Bourne, whom I did not yet know.)

Some of the other alcoholics had been picked up on charges of vagrancy because they had less than five dollars on their person or for creating a public disturbance. There were also, as I had thought, several prostitutes, most of whom talked about their pimps scurrilously and with raw disparagement. Others were there for petty crimes such as shoplifting. No one in that cellblock had a serious offense. Of all the women prisoners, the prostitutes were the ones who seemed to have the most self-confidence.

It began to dawn on me that although many white male prisoners would have committed violent crimes, women incarcerated in jails and prisons at that time were more likely to have been the victims than the perpetrators of violence. As I began to look at these women as human beings rather than antagonists, they no longer seemed threatening to me but, instead, pathetic.

Nancy and I were taken to our arraignment hearing and allowed momentarily to join the others in our group. I was happy to be reunited. To my surprise, I found that the day after our arrests, several others had continued our sit-in at the Toddle House and had been arrested, including John Lewis, a young man who was the apotheosis of nonviolence and played a substantial role in the early SNCC years.

*   *   *

This was the twenty-seventh arrest for John Henry Lewis. He was the divinity student who had impressed me deeply when I met him at Fisk University in Nashville, in the spring of 1962, during the study tour when I decided to work for the movement. Although his courage was legendary, he was a quiet, even tender, person whose innocence sometimes made him vulnerable to manipulation. Stocky, dark, and gentle, he would later describe himself in political campaigns as a "tugboat," an apt phrase that suggested his sturdiness. He was born in Dunn's Chapel, a rural community near Troy, Alabama, and was one of ten children. His mother was a laundress and his father was a tenant farmer who also drove a school bus. Managing somehow to save three hundred dollars, his parents were able to buy a 110-acre farm when John was a small child. On that farm, the family grew cotton, corn, and okra, and raised chickens. For as long as he could remember, John had wanted to be a minister. When he was four years old, he preached to a chicken on the farm and "baptized" it. Having watched christening by immersion with his Baptist family, John set about to follow the preacher's example and baptize the chicken the same way. But he held the hen under the water so long that it drowned.

A graduate of the American Baptist Seminary in Nashville, John was an organizer of the Nashville student movement and a participant in the original workshops there that had studied the philosophy of nonviolence two years before the sit-ins started. As a youth of fifteen and sixteen, he had been deeply touched by the personal example of Martin Luther King in the Montgomery bus boycott, which had occurred fifty miles north of his home. John later helped write the "rules" of conduct for the sit-ins, incorporating much of the nonviolent Montgomery approach. As one of the original Freedom Riders in May 1961, he was instrumental in continuing the rides, after CORE wanted to discontinue them, contending that the protest had become too dangerous. He was the first of the riders to be mobbed and beaten in Rock Hill, South Carolina, as he approached the rest room when the Greyhound bus arrived. After the buses were halted in Birmingham and SNCC took over the rides, John was brutally beaten by a crowd in Montgomery, Alabama.

I had seen John kneel and look his adversary in the eye, it seemed without blinking, as billy sticks crashed down on his forehead breaking the skin and sometimes blinding him with his own blood. Again and again he would be thrust forward by a group to lead a demonstration because of his inner determination and tranquillity under adversity. I don't think it was possible to frighten John, so intense was his commitment. This was one of the qualities that led to his being elected chairman of SNCC in June 1963. His purity made him appear more militant politically than he actually was, and thus he was a good compromise candidate. John was not naïve but he made no claim to political shrewdness. What he had was character and courage, which he gave with raw, uncalculating largess. He had already been arrested twenty-four times when he was elected chairman. Not staking out a position as a strategist or theoretician, the sincerity of John's commitment and the ardor of his example made him acceptable to everyone to chair SNCC, including those who were more impatient, less religiously oriented, and more sophisticated.

It is worth pausing to look back on the most difficult passage of John's leadership, which had come four months earlier, during the march on Washington in August 1963. The Reverend Dr. Martin Luther King, Jr.'s, birthday is now a national holiday and, although his "I Have a Dream" speech is the lasting motif of the march on Washington worldwide, it was not mentioned until page 13 of the main story on the event by Robert E. Baker in *The Washington Post* on August 29, 1963, and then only to note that Dr. King was one of the speakers. Susanna McBee's account, on page 14, reported that "the loudest and most consistent applause came for Dr. King whom [A. Philip] Randolph introduced as the 'moral leader of the nation.' " As a result of Dr. King's speech, he rose on the scene and became regarded as the major personality of the civil rights movement, and many then came to view him as Randolph had described him—the moral leader of the nation. In both Baker's and McBee's stories the next day, however, actual quotations from John's speech and descriptions of the alteration of it at the last moment received noticeably more paragraphs of coverage than did Dr. King's. For SNCC, the march produced a canker that never healed and inflicted pain on the organization for years to come. This was because of changes that John made under pressure from other figures participating in the event.

Those who view the Kennedy administration as an activist force say that the young President needed the march to give impetus to the civil rights bill that the administration had recently introduced. Others thought that the civil rights movement required the march in order to demonstrate against the administration's slowness and inaction. Something dramatic was indeed needed for an uncomplying Congress that was, by definition, not representative of the important black minority in America and was dominated by openly racist representatives and senators from the Black Belt whose long tenure gave them command of three quarters of the House and Senate committees. Whether President Kennedy was being helped or being put on the spot depends entirely on your vantage point. For us, it was the latter. Although there was some internal disagreement, we in SNCC were mainly of one accord on the value of the march—we didn't think it had much.

We saw one quarter of a million people of all races, creeds, and walks of life arriving by buses, trains, and cars (few could afford to fly) in Washington to walk together. *The Washington Post* reported 1,514 buses, 21 special and 18 regular trains, and "some came by bicycle, motorcycle and scooter." Yet, at the time, it sickened much of SNCC to see labor-union and liberal resources that had spurned our requests, often refusing to help us, being poured into what we regarded as a symbolic gesture. The United Auto Workers and other labor unions achieved visibility at the march, but many of them had rejected Jim Forman's requests for funds. The AFL-CIO did not support the march and never assisted SNCC. While money flowed for the one-time spectacle, we were desperate for cars, vans, buses, mimeograph machines, typewriters, and paper (oh, precious paper!). We were working where no other organizations had projects. It was not long before this period that SNCC field secretaries Sam Block and Willie Peacock were still riding mules for transportation in Mississippi.

The youngest speaker at the march was our chairman, John Lewis, twenty-five, and his speech was censored. Attacked by Roman Catholic Cardinal Patrick O'Boyle, who, reflecting the position of the Kennedy White House, said John's remarks were too hostile and bitter against the federal government, the cardinal threatened to withdraw himself from giving the invocation and the support of the Catholic hierarchy if John delivered his text as prepared. Curiously, John had been the only one of the many speakers who had actually followed the ground rules worked out in advance and had circulated his speech—none of the other speakers distributed theirs.

John's speech authentically reflected SNCC's thinking, and our viewpoint was from the Black Belt where the system of segregation was imposed in Manichean manner. These were the counties that SNCC had adopted as its organizing challenge. To us, the federal government's policy of noninterference meant that it actually supported the system we were trying to assault. Ours was a perspective on constitutional authority that had been shaped by lawyers close to SNCC who had been exposed to the thinking of Howard University Law School in Washington, D.C. This school after World War II had become the nation's leading proponent of an aggressive challenge to the legal system to extend constitutional guarantees.

As the forces on all sides built prior to the climactic march, the turbulence created by Cardinal O'Boyle's offensive became a maelstrom. Yielding to excruciating pressures from the Kennedy administration, by now construing the march as a push for its legislation, Jim Forman, Courtland Cox, Joyce Ladner, and John Lewis held a meeting behind the Lincoln Memorial and capitulated. They decided to go along with Bayard Rustin who was the march coordinator, A. Philip Randolph who was director of the march and head of the Brotherhood of Sleeping Car Porters, Dr. King and Ralph Abernathy of SCLC, and Eugene Carson Blake of the National Council of Churches in editing John's speech. They later explained that John would not have been allowed to speak if his remarks had not been altered. They removed this key sentence: "I want to know: Which side is the federal government on?" and deleted John's use of the word "masses" and his call for a social revolution.

Also changed was John's withholding of enthusiastic support for the pending legislation, and gone were his words, "In good conscience, we cannot support the administration's civil rights bill, for it is too little and too late," which reflected our belief that the Kennedy language was inadequate. The legislation treated a person without a sixth-grade education as illiterate; we believed that only age and residence should be the qualifying factors for the right to vote. The phrase, "We support it with great reservations," was substituted instead. Also removed was his observation that "not one thing in the bill will protect our people from police brutality" and his allegation that President Kennedy had "consistently" appointed racist federal judges.

John did, however, talk about a pathetic action of the Department of Justice when it prosecuted nine civil rights workers in late 1963, after the picketing of a white grocery store, entailing the use of over thirty FBI agents against us. He referred to this shameful episode:

> In Albany, Georgia, nine of our leaders have been indicted not by Dixiecrats but by the federal government for peaceful protest. But what did the federal government do when Albany's deputy sheriff beat attorney C. B. King and left him half dead? What did the federal government do when local police officials kicked and assaulted the pregnant wife of Slater King and she lost her baby?

John had written, "We have been told to stay patient, but for many of us, patience is a dirty word." Later, John said that Bayard Rustin had told him that the Roman Catholic hierarchy didn't like that phrase because they believed in patience.

One week prior to the march, John had seen a televised news story from what was then Northern Rhodesia and is now Zambia in which a demonstrator was carrying a sign saying ONE MAN, ONE VOTE. John wrote, " 'One man, one vote' is the African cry, it should be ours." That, at least, was not removed from the edited speech and SNCC's widespread use of this slogan was thus initiated. Despite its unconscious use of the male gender to ears now sensitized to sexist language, at the time it was considered a strident rallying cry.

This episode of the censored speech remained an open wound within SNCC because the actions of a few in changing the speech flew in the face of the organization's democratic tradition. The question was painfully asked an untold number of times over the next few years: Who gave John and Jim and the others permission to make those changes?

Many in the organization, including me, would have preferred that SNCC simply not participate. I viewed the demonstration as a siphoning off of energy and resources. Because of the rump rewriting, the event also turned out to undermine trust within our ranks.

John Lewis's commitment to nonviolence was not mindless; I could often see him working in a form of meditation to achieve his strength and the peace of mind he required for nonviolence. I was glad that he had joined us in the Atlanta city jail. More than anyone else in the entire civil rights movement, he personified the spirit of nonviolence.

Back at headquarters in Atlanta, a national campaign was being constructed around our arrests. On Christmas Eve, Dick Gregory's wife Lillian and Prathia Hall were arrested. With them was Roberta "Bobbi" Yancy who had also gone to work for SNCC at the end of the human-relations project. A novel twist was added that would alter some of the tactics of working for social change when, before leaving to sit-in at the Toddle House next to the Peachtree Manor Hotel, John Lewis, Lillian Gregory, Bobbi Yancy, and Prathia Hall had bought shares in Dobbs House, the Tennessee company that owned Toddle House. They were therefore arrested in a restaurant they partly owned. At "Big Rock," they were each placed in solitary confinement. Dick Gregory flew into the city to witness his pregnant wife's arraignment.

Meanwhile, Julian Bond put out a special edition of our weekly newspaper, *The Student Voice*, to our growing mailing list all over the country: CHRISTMAS IN JAIL blared the front-page headline. Jim Forman sent telegrams to then Undersecretary of State for African Affairs G. Mennen Williams asking him to "remove Atlanta from the itinerary of future African visitors to the United States" and declaring that "Atlanta is the most segregated city in the South for its size." Jim also publicly issued "profound apologies" to Oginga Odinga "for any embarrassment you might have encountered here in Atlanta as a result of the arrests" and sent wires to President Lyndon Johnson urging a public accommodations law. Minister Odinga denounced racial matters in the United States as "very pitiful." Demonstrations were now being staged at Atlanta mayor Ivan Allen's office and at his home. At the city airport, demonstrators carried signs declaring WELCOME TO ATLANTA—A SEGREGATED CITY. In front of city hall, SNCC workers stood with large signs bearing this message: DEMOCRACY ON THE LINE. WHY ARE 21 STUDENTS IN JAIL?

"Christmas in jail" was becoming a battle cry across the country, although I had no knowledge of this until later. Emer-

gency circulars were printed at Raymond Street and sent in bulk
to Friends of SNCC groups in the major media centers. Sympathy
demonstrations started in Hartford, Connecticut; Philadelphia; and
New York City. "Atlanta is on the move. We can use all people
who are willing to demonstrate and go to jail, without bail," one
brochure sent to thousands read. Good tactician that he was, Jim
Forman had seized on the watchword "Christmas in jail" and was
blending a new level of programmatic astuteness with his sense
of timing. SNCC literature now called for demonstrations at 255
Toddle Houses in thirty states and Washington, D.C., and at their
parent company, Dobbs House, which had eighty-seven restaurants in twenty-eight cities.

The campaign would continue to build, with demonstrations
two weeks later resulting in twelve of the Dobbs House restaurants being closed. The emphasis then shifted to an "open city"
drive to make Atlanta an integrated city. A coalition of national
and local black organizations, called the Atlanta Summit Leadership Conference, had earlier attempted some negotiations on desegregation, but the combined force of the "Christmas in jail"
declaration and the Dobbs House offensive had shifted expectations into another gear. Dissatisfaction at the slow pace of change
was spreading in Atlanta's black community. By mid-January, Mayor
Allen told the city's board of aldermen that he would seek a local
public accommodations ordinance if "voluntary desegregation" did
not take place soon. The Reverend Wyatt Tee Walker, administrative assistant to Dr. King; Leon Cory, Georgia State NAACP
field secretary; the Reverend John Morris, an Episcopalian church
leader; Harry Boyle; and several others had now joined the group
in jail, but bail had by then been raised to $1,000. The campaign
widened to target the Heart of Atlanta Motel, Krystal's restaurant,
and the Holiday Inn. Signs read, ATLANTA'S IMAGE IS A FRAUD.
John Lewis eventually was able to negotiate an agreement with
Dobbs House suspending demonstrations. This new type of corporate targeting was a direct forerunner of later campaigns such as
the boycott of Nestle, the Swiss maker of infant formula mar-
keted under false pretenses throughout the developing world, and
subsequent organizing against toxic waste in the 1980s.

Nothing of this national "Christmas in jail" campaign was
known to Nancy and me, still being held in the segregated wom-
en's section of the Atlanta city jail. Within its tawdry and sullen

walls, I used a dime to place the phone call that the authorities were obligated to let me make—I had been saving it—and called the SNCC office. As soon as someone answered, Jim Forman rushed onto the line. His voice was solicitous. He sounded concerned.

"I'll bail you out of jail if you like, baby," Jim said. "Your Uncle Billy died and if you want to go to the funeral I'll have you out in hours."

I choked. I had seen my uncle at Thanksgiving and he was sick, it was true, but I didn't think that he was that ill. "He died, Jim? You say he died?" His voice becoming even more caring, Jim explained that my parents had telephoned him.

I made a fast decision. I decided that I had already accomplished whatever was to be achieved by my arrest and accepted his offer.

"He was my only uncle, Jim, and I think I ought to be with my father now," I told him.

My father's brother, Norman Granville King, whom my three brothers and I called Uncle Billy, was only forty-seven years old. He had served as a sergeant in the Army fighting the Japanese at Leyte and on Okinawa in World War II. Having smoked cigarettes heavily since he was drafted, he had died of lung cancer. I adored him, his sense of humor, and his irreverence for convention. His one defense against the inevitable problems of life was to find something to laugh about and he had tales, stories, and jokes in response to every situation. He seemed never to take anything seriously. No matter how deep his troubles or trying the circumstances, he would grin out of the side of his mouth, light up a cigarette, and find a way to joke about it. Now, I couldn't believe he was dead.

I went back to my cot, told Nancy, and wept. A short time later, I was bailed out and led from the city jail. In order that Nancy should not be left alone in "Big Rock," she too was soon out on bail. I must admit that I was very happy to be out of prison after what must have been four or five days, yet I was also despondent at the reason. My uncle's death was hard for me to accept. He was so young. I have since known many people who reminded me of him with their flair for soothing trauma with humor, but no one I have ever known has had such a nonmalicious ability to find laughter in the midst of tragedy.

After going by the office to see Jim and Julian Bond briefly, I went back to the apartment and packed the best dress I had—a simple black wool jersey dress I had made myself with my Aunt Sookie's help over Thanksgiving—and one pair of black Dior pumps I had found on sale in New York City. I have never felt that there was any moral virtue in dressing "down" and have always been amused by those who dressed shabbily as a way of demonstrating their beliefs. Dressing drearily shows nothing about a person's stands or beliefs.

I wanted to be taken seriously, not as someone working out a phase of postadolescent rebellion, and when I dealt with the public I wanted people to respond to my ideas, my convictions, what I stood for, and not to react to the way I was dressed. Perhaps I diverged from many SNCC staff in this attitude, as most of the men wore work shirts and overalls, and certainly my concept was different from that of the white volunteers who joined us later in denim blue jeans. My own exposure to rural Virginians, black and white, had taught me that all people, including farmers, field hands, and factory workers, aspire to dress well. It is a misunderstanding of the ethos of the poor to think that they want organizers and people in leadership to dress for their sake. Poor black women did not wear pants in those days, and so, in order not to separate myself from them, I usually wore skirts and blouses. Had I worn overalls or pants as a supposed statement of "identification" with the poor, I believed it would have distanced me rather than brought me closer. Even though I had no money and only three or four items of clothing, I tried to dress as well as I could.

It boiled down to whether I wanted to make myself feel good or to be effective. I learned in those days to ask myself this question: Am I indulging myself and trying to make myself feel good or am I trying to accomplish something? I still stop and pose this query to myself and make decisions based on my answer. If I had worn the blue jeans that I liked in high school and cannot do without at home today, it would have been self-indulgent and would not have contributed to my effectiveness.

I must have learned this basic view from my father, who, even on his pathetically low Methodist-minister's salary, bought his suits only from the best tailors he could afford, wore well-made shirts, and always had his best pair of shoes polished and well-heeled. He in turn had learned this from his father, who even during the Depression carried out his ministerial duties dressed as well as he could be, his clothing carefully repaired and re-re-paired, sometimes cutting up old starched collars to be inserted inside his shoes when the soles had worn through. "You have to show respect for the people you are serving," my father would say when I, as a child, watched him care for his clothes. He had only one pair of gold cuff links, which my mother had given him soon after they married, but he has worn those same cuff links ever since. Strangely, years later, these principles still seem sound to me. So, although there wasn't much in my suitcase as I flew to Richmond, what I did have would have passed muster under any conditions.

Arriving at the home of Uncle Billy and his wife, Amy, my aunt, I took a nap upstairs. After I woke up, I started down the stairs. I saw my father's sister, Aunt Sookie, Aunt Amy, and other members of my father's family gathered together and sensed tension in the atmosphere.

I was anxious about this homecoming. I had made the decision to be bailed out, and yet, emotionally, I was still with those in jail. My parents fully supported me; in fact, my father said he had never been more proud of me. But many of my father's family were "unreconstructed" southerners and were not uncomfortable with the status quo. They liked things the way they were. One of my aunts had already written to me about the movement, jabbingly and with disapproval: "What is this freedom they're always talking about?" My emotions were raw from having been in jail—it had been stressful and ugly, made worse by the authorities isolating Nancy and me from the others. Now the last thing I wanted was to be chided by unsympathetic family members. My aunt and cousins were also descendants of the same Wright Johnson who included "colored members" in his class meetings in the middle of the nineteenth century. But somehow, some of my father's family were not sympathetic to the struggle for social and racial justice, while for my father it was a chord that ran through his entire adult life.

As I slowly started down the stairs of the house that was set back one fifth of a mile from the highway deep in the Virginia woods, and within minutes of the sites of the major Civil War battles of Chancellorsville, the Wilderness, and Spotsylvania

Courthouse, I was reserved and restrained. Normally I would have
been outgoing. Now I was quiet and took each step slowly, reluctantly. I felt apprehensive. Around me I could see my uncle's
collection of musketry, minié balls, ramrods, shells, gun caps, and
other remains of the Civil War that surface after heavy rains on
our land (bought by my grandparents for five dollars an acre during the Great Depression). There were daguerreotypes, cannon-
balls, canteens, Union and Confederate belt buckles, and other
relics about the house. I was uncertain about what this unpredictable interlude would yield.

Suddenly, my mother walked into the room and sensed the
strain and tautness. Then, clapping her hands together lightly as
if to attract attention by applause, she punctuated the silence by
brightly exclaiming, "So—there's my little jailbird!" Walking over
emphatically, with a spirited gait, to where I stood at the bottom
of the stairs, she threw her arms around me in an exaggerated
hug. Everyone was watching. There was a moment of silence and
of hesitation and then, to my surprise, I heard laughter. The tension was shattered. Relief flooded the house. Each person em-
braced me in turn. Everyone was talking. In one spontaneous,
unplanned, and instinctive response, my mother had broken
through the constriction and stiffness of the moment, mentioning
the unmentionable and annulling the condemnation.

A few days later I wrote to Ellen Ratkovich Hill, one of my
closest friends at college, about my uncle:

> He was the Civil War buff of our family. He took with him
> more knowledge about this county and our family than all
> the rest of us had put together. Because he died just one
> month after being diagnosed, no one was able to take down
> the things he knew. He left a large outbuilding filled with
> Civil War relics and family possessions, the history of which
> only he knew.
>
> My father, as he had done for his father, conducted the
> committal service at the cemetery. The train of cars that fol-
> lowed us to the cemetery was more than fifty cars long. He
> was buried in our family lot in the Spotsylvania Confederate
> Cemetery, between regiments from South Carolina and
> Louisiana—boys half as old who had been killed in the sev-
> eral battles of the area.

Ella Baker, Birmingham, Alabama, 1964 © *Danny Lyon/Magnum*

Bob Moses, Mississippi, 1964 © *1964 Steve Shapiro—Black Star*

Dorie Ladner *(left)* and Casey Hayden (Sandra Cason), 1963
© *Danny Lyon/Magnum*

SNCC staff singing freedom songs, Raymond Street headquarters, Atlanta, Georgia, 1963

Left to right: Courtland Cox, MacArthur Cotton, Jim Forman, Marion Barry, Lester McKinney, Mike Thelwell, Lawrence Guyot, Judy Richardson, Jean Wheeler Smith © *Danny Lyon/Magnum*

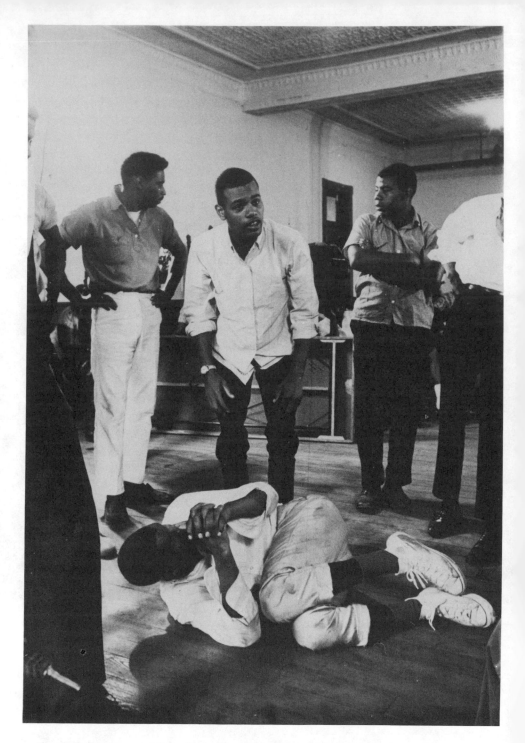

Cordell Reagon training Danville, Virginia, residents how to minimize injury if attacked with firehoses, or by police, onlookers, or police dogs in nonviolent demonstrations, July 1963 © *Danny Lyon/Magnum*

Mock voting in the protest Freedom Ballot, Mississippi, November 1963 © *Matt Herron—Black Star*

Bob Zellner leading freedom songs at a Danville, Virginia, mass meeting, July 1963, with Ivanhoe Donaldson *(left)* and Matthew Jones *(right)* *Marjorie Collins*

Bernice Johnson Reagon: "Over my head, I see freedom in the air. . . . O Lord . . . there must be a God somewhere." © 1965 Bob Fletcher: a SNCC Photo

Registering to vote © Matt Herron—Black Star

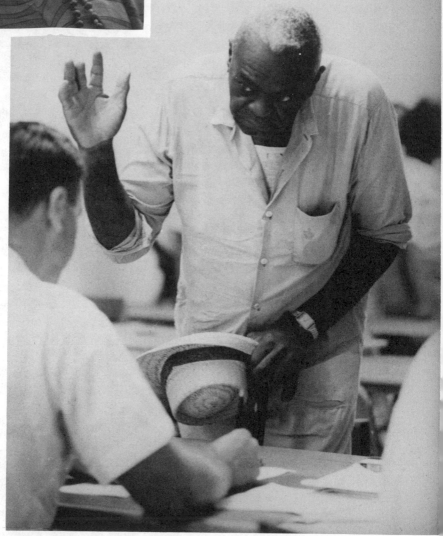

Voter registration, Mississippi, 1964 © *1964 Charles Moore—Black Star*

Jim Forman, Montgomery, Alabama, 1965 © *Charles Moore—Black Star*

CHAPTER 5

BIRTHRIGHT

I'm on my way to the Freedom Land,
I'm on my way to Freedom Land,
I'm on my way to Freedom Land,
I'm on my way, Great God, I'm on my way.

If you don't go, don't hinder me,
If you don't go, don't hinder me,
If you don't go, don't hinder me,
I'm on my way, Great God, I'm on my way.

I'll ask my mother, would you come with me,
I'll ask my mother, would you come with me,
I'll ask my mother, would you come with me,
I'm on my way, Great God, I'm on my way.

If she can't go, I'm gonna go anyhow,
If she can't go, I'm gonna go anyhow,
If she can't go, I'm gonna go anyhow,
I'm on my way, Great God, I'm on my way.

—Adaptation of spiritual

Perhaps my mother's sympathy was historic recall from her own family, from events that had happened before her birth and were ultimately the cause of her coming to the United States where she would meet my father who was then in seminary when she was in nursing school. My own interests seem to have been foreshadowed and suggest that my feminism is linked to four girls in turn-of-the-century South America. Despite scientific evidence to the contrary, I wonder whether there might be a genetic memory that carries values, experiences, and insights much as physical characteristics are carried on the shafts of chromosomes.

My great-grandparents, my mother's maternal grandparents, were Don Gabriel Burgos Grimaldo and Doña Elisa Burgos de Urueña. They were from Tolima, a picturesque region southwest of Bogotá in Colombia, South America. My great-grandfather was a general in Colombia's army and mayor of the town of El Carmen de Apicalá. Don Gabriel excelled at mathematics and was also an accountant with fine handwriting. He was born into the family of ten children, five girls and five boys, of José Pio Burgos and Josefita Grimaldo de Burgos. Their wealth and upper-class background meant that they virtually owned their part of Tolima and in effect owned—in a form of serfdom—those who lived there. "The town belonged to José Pio Burgos," one of my great-aunts once mentioned to me. Doña Elisa, my great-grandmother, had seven sisters and five brothers. Her parents, Cristobal Urueña and Marta Barreto Echeveria de Urueña, were from the region of Tolima.

It was a family that might have produced another phantasmagorical novel by Gabriel García Márquez—Nobel laureate and distant cousin through Doña Elisa's sister Elena's marriage to Rodolfo Arteaga. The combined twenty-one sisters and brothers of Don Gabriel and Doña Elisa included army generals, poets, opera singers, lawyers, cattle raisers, and physicians. Doña Elisa's cousin Fabio Lozano was minister to Peru. The family was enterprising and cultured. El Carmen de Apicalá was a lush locale where verdant fields sheltered partridges and flowers nestled in its folds. The family's estate, or *finca*, was called La Calera (The Quarry), named for a limestone quarry on the land. The main house was huge with large rooms elegantly furnished; it sprawled with inner courts which had pools of running water and fountains where daily baths were taken. A brook meandered through the estate with hidden pools for bathing. Horses were stabled and fruit trees abounded. Servants, possessing various categories of skills, grew the produce, tended livestock, slaughtered animals, watched over the horses and carriages, prepared the food, cared for the house and its contents, hand-embroidered the linens, and designed, sewed, and laundered the family's clothing.

Don Gabriel's brother, Pio, wrote a book of poetry that was published in 1921, called *Flores del Crepusculo* (*Flowers of the Twilight*), a copy of which, well-worn, I have. In his poetry Pio writes of ideal love, honor, illusion, truth, the spring, death, gardens, memories, youth, the women in his life, Tolima, and other vaunted poetic conventions of his day.

My mother's mother, María Luisa Burgos, was the first of four daughters to be born into the cradled comfort of La Calera. There followed Carmen, Lucila, and Ester. The four girls had a glorious childhood with picnics and barbecues arranged by the servants in different parts of the estate and outings on horseback. They wore loose-fitting *chinges* similar to sack dresses to bathe in the brook. They were born into privilege and enjoyed enchanted girlhoods. Dances, parties, and music filled their days. Beneath the patina and veneer of opulence, however, lay the absolutism, rigidity, and narrow-mindedness engendered by Roman Catholicism as practiced then in Colombia long before the liberalization brought about by the Vatican II Council.

(To maintain perspective, it is worth noting that it was front-page news in *The New York Times,* on September 9, 1964, when Pope Paul VI deigned to permit some nuns—the "flowers of the church"—and leaders of Roman Catholic women's organizations to attend the Ecumenical Council as "auditors" in some sessions "on matters of interest to them.")

Don Gabriel and Doña Elisa, especially since they had no sons, wanted their four daughters educated. This was not customary around the turn of the century; in fact it was astonishing. Some would have said it was aberrant. A series of tutors were engaged. One was the Italian artist Ubaldini. Another was Salvador Enrique Iregui, professor of Romance languages at the University of Antioquia, who had been educated at Geneva, Switzerland, and spoke and wrote in six languages, including German and English. The four girls were given piano lessons and were taught French, history, composition, and mathematics as well as painting.

Their education could not continue at home beyond a certain point and my great-grandparents wanted to have their daughters formally educated. At last they found that some Presbyterian missionaries from the United States, whom they had first met in the 1890s, would continue their education. This was in stark contrast to the Jesuits and other Roman Catholic teaching orders and institutions, which refused to help. All four girls were admitted to the Colegio Americano, a secondary school run by the Presbyterian missionaries in Bogotá. Carmen went on to the National School of Dentistry and became the first woman in Colombia to receive a diploma as doctor of dental surgery. Ester also attended the dental college but did not finish the program. My great-grandparents were both deeply grateful for the Presbyterian missionaries' willingness to complete the formidable task of education they had undertaken for themselves.

One evening at dinner Don Gabriel remarked, "The kindness and bounty of the Presbyterian missionaries to us has been extraordinary. All of the missionaries, but especially the Reverend Thomas Candor and his wife, have cared for María Luisa, Carmen, Lucila, and Ester as if they were their own daughters."

"I agree," responded Doña Elisa. "I am proud to have been associated with such wonderful people, and the training they have given our girls is excellent."

Don Gabriel became pensive for a moment and suddenly said, "That's it! We shall become Presbyterians. We will convert!" imperiously making his announcement with the full authority that his time and culture deeded to him. "We received no help from the Church and the priests in fact discouraged us," he declared.

Doña Elisa, a skillful manager of the estate, thought for a moment and concurred. "I believe you're right, Su Merced," she said, using the archaic expression that still survives in some circles in Colombia meaning Your Mercy or Your Honor. This formal manner of address was the way that members of the family routinely showed respect for one another. "What better way to express our appreciation and loyalty to these remarkable people," she said. "Let us then become Presbyterians."

At the time of this writing, my eighty-seven-year-old great-aunt Ester, the youngest of the four sisters, tells me she remembers, as if it were yesterday, that day early in this century when her father made the decision that the family would become Protestant. It was a decision that would become a burden for the family because Protestants were the targets of severe persecution. From the time they converted, life for Gabriel, Elisa, María, Luisa, Carmen, Lucila, and Ester became, as my great-aunt says with emphasis, "miserable." They were attacked within family circles for becoming Protestant, and, beyond the family, they were ostracized. They encountered attitudes of intolerance, parochialism, bigotry, and hostility. They felt caged by contempt wherever they went.

"We were no longer invited to parties, dinners, dances, or fiestas," Aunt Ester says. "At family gatherings such as baptisms and weddings, other members of the family would come up to each of us and castigate us. My cousins used to tell me that my soul was going straight to hell."

In 1952, as a child, I read a front-page story in *The New York*

Times that Protestants were being stoned in Colombia by Roman
Catholics. Later, I learned that a process of meticulous documentation of violence in Colombia was carried out by the parents of a
friend, Fred Goff, who came to assist SNCC in Mississippi as a
volunteer in 1963. I met Fred's father, the Reverend James Goff,
in Nicaragua, in 1984, as he was leading a demonstration of Americans, many of them Protestant missionaries or Quakers, who were
opposed to U.S. policy in Nicaragua, in front of the U.S. Em-
bassy in Managua. As Presbyterian missionaries themselves, the
Goffs had taught at the Colegio Americano and knew of the Candors' work. The article on stonings of Protestant Colombians in
The New York Times that had made such an impression on me as a
girl was probably a result of the careful assemblage of data by
Fred's parents.

The violence against Protestants was related to Colombia's
history. One brutal decade of conflict between the Liberal and
Conservative parties is called the period of La Violencia because
of the killings, assassinations, and destruction of villages and towns
that accompanied the years 1948 through 1958. This time of un-
declared civil war saw crucifixions, scalpings, disembowelments,
and bayoneting of infants, and resulted in nearly three hundred
thousand people being killed. The country had been torn by violent rivalry between the Liberals and the Conservatives since the
mid-nineteenth century; in fact, Colombia's twentieth century
opened with a three-year civil conflict called the War of a Thousand Days in which over one hundred thousand died. (An agreement adopted by leaders of both parties on July 20, 1957, has now
led to a sharing of power that is still in effect in some ways.) Close
to the surface of this otherwise fascinating, variegated, and richly
textured country and culture are depths of indecent intolerance—
legacies of the rule of both the Spanish colonizers and ultrareac-
tionary elements of the Roman Catholic Church.

My great-aunt Carmen was graduated from dental school in
1916 as the bitterness of family members intensified and external
ostracism of the Burgos family was becoming more vicious. In the
tradition of the Grand Tour in which the sons of the aristocracy
were sent to Europe to be exposed to the customs and manners
of the Continent, Don Gabriel decreed that he would take his
family to the United States as a graduation gift for Carmen. In
retrospect, he must have had more than presents or the exposure

of travel in mind. The family embarked by steamer from Barranquilla and arrived in New York City to begin their visit. As events unfolded, they decided to stay. They left behind La Calera, Carmen's dentistry practice, the missionaries who had quite literally changed their lives, and a standard of living impossible to match without a cohort of servants. Don Gabriel also abandoned a half interest in an emerald mine as the sole partner with his cousin. Then, as now, roughly 70 percent of the land in Colombia was owned by 10 percent of the people.

My mother, Alba, was six years old when she walked off the gangplank of the steamer berthed in the Hudson River harbor of New York City, dressed in a pleated navy-blue skirt and white middy blouse with button-up shoes. She and her mother—my grandmother, María Luisa—had come along for Carmen's graduation-gift trip (Lucila and Ester had gone to New York earlier). Her father, Salvador Enrique Iregui, stayed behind. It was he who had taught Spanish to the Candors and other Presbyterian missionaries at the Colegio Americano, and it was as the French tutor of the four girls that my grandmother had met and fallen in love with him. He married María Luisa. I think the family felt he was not of sufficient social standing for the match, although my mother says the archives in Bilbao, in the Basque region of Spain, show that he was paternally descended from some of the French and Spanish nobility living on both sides of the Pyrenees. At any rate, for reasons I have never been able to pry out of those who would have known, my grandmother must have wanted the excuse of the graduation-gift trip to leave him, and he remained in Colombia. The separation was painfully accepted by my mother.

In one of his few letters that got through Colombian censorship, my grandfather, Salvador Enrique Iregui, wrote to my mother in English from Colombia in 1945 about "religious liberty," which, he said, "there is not at present":

> The Roman Catholic Church is every day more powerful
> and fearful. The Spanish Government of Francisco Franco
> exercises a great influence here on conservative newspapers
> and they send money for *falangismo* propaganda (Spanish
> Nazis or fascism). The newspapers insult Protestants, social-
> ists, and the Government in the most open and dreadful
> manner. The missionaries are attacked if they go out of the

town and are bitterly persecuted; the native Protestants that
dare to go to the country are nearly killed, stoned and
beaten.

Also in 1945, Professor Iregui published an article that he
dedicated as follows: *"A mi hija que una ola tormentosa se llevo al
otro lado del mar."* "To my daughter whom a great tidal wave has
carried to the other side of the sea." In sending my mother that
article, he wrote:

> I am old and weak, feeble, and the snow of life is crowning
> my head. My life is peaceable and honorable but difficult
> and I have to work hard and to be badly paid, but I am as
> free as I can be. . . . Some day you will receive news that I
> have left for the country from which no one returns; but be-
> fore that, please receive my love and my kindest regards for
> you and your children for whom I wish all and best bless-
> ings from God.
>   Your always loving father . . .

María Luisa, my grandmother, along with the rest of the family, started an entirely new and shockingly different life in New
York City. She went from a culture and society in which she addressed her parents as "Your Honor" to the brute crush of life in
Manhattan. She became a staff missionary with the New York
City Mission Society, an interdenominational agency that still works
on the front lines of urban problems in New York. She remained
in this staff position until she could no longer work because of
crippling arthritis.

My grandmother was a devoted city missionary but, although
no one ever said so to me, I know that the adjustment to life in
North America was excruciating. The four sisters had birdlike grace,
cultured gentility, and their hard-won educations, yet they could
do little for themselves when they arrived in New York. They did
not know how to cook, bake, sew, clean, mend or launder their
clothes, shop, or handle any of the myriad tasks needed for daily
life. Gradually they learned the hard way how to fend for themselves. My grandmother, as the oldest of the four sisters, had the
greatest problems. Ironically, in seeking to minister to the needs
of others as a staff member of the mission society on the Lower
East Side, she had to relinquish personally meeting her own chil-

dren's basic needs. My grandmother was granted a scholarship to pursue studies in religious education at New York University, but the terms of the scholarship required that she live with the other students on Gramercy Park in downtown Manhattan. In her absence she left her second child, two years old and named Gabriel after his grandfather, at her parents' home in the care of a family member. On the advice of a friend of the family, she arranged for her daughter, eight years of age, to be admitted to a Methodist institution in Westchester County, New York, with the assurance that the school offered an excellent opportunity for the young girl. The traumatic unfolding of results from these well-intentioned plans for her children is reminiscent of a Greek tragedy. While she was away, her little son fell to his death out of a window. The three-year stay of her daughter—my mother—at the school traumatized her and left scars that affected her sense of security and therefore touched me.

Great-aunt Ester says Don Gabriel came to the United States with a chest full of gold coins, approximately five million pesos, or about four million U.S. dollars then. But if this is true, he managed the money with patriarchal impunity and no sense of accountability to the rest of the family, and with no real strategy for survival in the new country. They lived well for several years, but after that there was apparently nothing left of the fortune. My mother distantly remembers talk of a robbery and never saw one cent of it. All I have inherited is Aunt Carmen's diamond ring and Pio Burgos's book of poetry.

My mother courageously worked and strove to develop her own solid career in public health and the teaching of nursing. She studied anatomy at the College of Physicians and Surgeons of Colombia University and gained two degrees, while teaching full time, rearing four children, and being a minister's wife—a job in itself. She accomplished all these things entirely on her own—with my father's genuine moral and active support—but with no help from her own dislocated family. She also studied to become an artist and painter with a resulting prodigious artistic output, despite all her other responsibilities.

As a child I was puzzled by the mysteries of my mother's story. I was also irritated by the silences that would intrude when I asked questions. There was no narrative. I had to piece it together bit by bit, teasing out fragments one at a time. My grandmother and the graceful great-aunts were of little help.

"What difference does it make, my dear?" Aunt Ester, still beautiful at eighty-seven years of age, inquires.

"It would enrich my life to know, Aunt Ester," I reply and then perhaps learn one more facet.

For a family to put female education and religious tolerance ahead of wealth was contradictory to the materialism of the world I saw around me and conflicted with the predominant values of post-World War II America in which I was growing up. I was fascinated that my mother's family would leave the pampered gentility, brooks, and horses of La Calera, life in El Carmen de Apicalá and their other home in Bogotá, in exchange for the awesome adjustments required for life in the hurly-burly of New York. There must be more to this, I thought. Maybe this tale of high principles and strong values was fanciful. Maybe there was more, hidden from view.

Knowing that families employ selective memory, screen out the negatives, and romanticize the past, I went to Colombia in 1971 to meet my cousins who had known Don Gabriel and Doña Elisa. In giving me their version of what happened, they not only confirmed the account I had laboriously stitched together, adding details, but also, individually, they each repeatedly used the word *oportunidad*—"opportunity." They were saying that Don Gabriel and Doña Elisa traded their land and position for opportunity for their daughters. To my great-grandparents, however, this was not opportunity in the material sense but opportunity as a value—an evanescent and elusive goal—as well as life free from the bigotry and rejectionism of Catholicism as it was practiced in Colombia in the early years of the twentieth century.

While millions of Huguenots, Quakers, Jews, and the persecuted of other faiths had migrated to America from western Europe, eastern Europe, and the Soviet Union in search of religious liberty, my mother's family are the only people I have ever known who emigrated to the United States from South America in pursuit of religious freedom.

As far as I have been able to discover, even in those secret corners of the family where unspoken yearnings, pain, and remorse were involuntarily disclosed, none of them has ever regretted the difficult exchange they made. Despite my grandmother's suffering and inability to adjust fully to the new life, the radiance of her faith showed me, even as an uncomprehending child, the spirit that caused this family to make its tidal wave of a move. The night she died, the nursing staff in the hospital heard my grandmother singing hymns. The price the family paid for the education of its women and religious freedom was high, and I was to be the real beneficiary of it.

For reasons I came to understand only as an adult, communication with my mother was not always easy. The problems of her childhood were never fully resolved, as her uprooted family faced the difficulties of coping with the stresses of a life vastly different from the one they had left behind. Her grandfather became a surrogate father and for a while brought real happiness into her life—until tragedy struck again. He became paralyzed on one side of his body and was unable to speak. Previously her grandmother had suffered the amputation of a leg and was confined to a wheel chair. Much of the care of both invalids now fell upon my mother in her after-school hours, while the adults were away at their jobs.

The members of my mother's family were not pretentious in the slightest. Quite the opposite, they worked hard to put the past behind them. The swallowed pain and silences, however, that were a part of their moving forward with their lives, came to be a confusing burden for me as a child growing up and seeking to discover my own identity. The silences snuffed out the understanding that was needed when, as a child and later as a young woman, certain questions and references—even a fleeting expression across my face in response to something spoken—troubled my mother. Not understanding her life story, the *ola tormentosa* and its consequences, nor seeing the written correspondence with her father until I was fully grown, I couldn't comprehend her suffering. When she became tense as I asked her questions about her childhood, I recoiled. I felt anger rather than sympathy. In those moments I pledged to be more like my father—even-tempered, able to think before reacting, taking stress in stride. My mother's very suffering and the pain she struggled to overcome created distance rather than closeness between us.

In the deepest parts of me, I made a decision. It was a pact with myself. I was determined to mobilize myself on demand to get the job done, handle the public requirements of whatever I was committed to, and teach myself to be disciplined. I didn't want to have my mother's emotional vulnerability and was afraid I would, if I didn't work to overcome it. I trained myself to be able to act under psychological pressure and the stress of enormous responsibility. I taught myself to continue functioning no matter what I was suffering and to put my commitments first. The civil rights movement gave me the ideal testing ground with all its exhaustion, strain, and tension. The demands were inordinate and there was very little in the way of extended release. Just because I was white, I could not slip away from the black community into the white community and achieve another state of mind like shedding a jacket—not that I ever wanted to. I carried with me everywhere, even in solitude, a sense of myself as working for the movement. The struggle gave me the chance to learn to push past my emotional limits—if I did my job just a little bit better or worked a little longer, I might save someone's life or avert a tragedy.

Jim Forman would authorize rest and recreation for us, referring to it as "R and R" following the military usage, but we were to ask only if we were in bad shape. I never asked. I never even considered it. There was something in me bearing down. These were special circumstances. A convergence of forces had been building for decades. This was an extraordinary moment. It was an opportunity that had to be seized. I wouldn't give in to tiredness. Learn, I would say to myself. Learn. Learn how to handle the exhaustion. Learn how to pull more energy from within, from deep within. This moment will not come again, I told myself.

Although I trained myself relentlessly not to break down, not to give in to fear, to handle stress, and to fulfill my obligations, looking back over my life now I realize that I failed, to a certain extent, in carrying this off. Those who know me best say I choke up easily, am frequently moved, and flare up when crossed by someone close to me—similar to my mother—despite my public equanimity and drive. On the other hand, this quality is balanced in both of us by a quick subsidence. Had I completely succeeded in suppressing the emotional vulnerability of my mother in myself, I might also have denied the inheritance of some characteristics of hers that are responsible for whatever successes I may have had in my life.

For many years I thought it was only my father's idealism and passion for justice that had made it probable that I would undertake a series of almost impossible causes. But now I remember my mother's rising voice when she would hear me say, I can't. "What's that?" she would interrupt. "There's no such word in the English language as *can't*. The word does not exist, Mary. You can." Perhaps it was an echo of her grandparents concept of *oportunidad*.

The more time passes, the more I realize how much she has given me and in how many positive ways I am like her. Not only did my mother give birth to me and at one point hold my entire being in her two hardworking hands; she nurtured me through childhood and gave me perhaps the most important thing of all—unquestioning acceptance. She has never been judgmental and has always been proud of me even when I made grave errors.

When my mother broke the tension at my uncle's funeral in Virginia by calling me a jailbird, talking openly about my being locked up in the Atlanta city jail, she ignored and demolished the barely controlled disapproval of the rest of my father's family by using her special understanding of what is important and what is not. With her plucky and spontaneous way of screwing up her courage to do what she believes must be done, she did what no one else could do. Not for one minute would she allow anyone else's attitudes to impinge on her daughter's ability to act out her beliefs.

It is she who shaped the practical side of my nature. She gave a pragmatic edge to my idealism that helped me aim for achievable goals. This was crucial to my internal struggle to learn how to balance purity of belief with effectiveness. Her whole life has been a demonstration of how to perform many tasks at once— a tendency I acquired from her. It is also from her that I learned to drive myself mercilessly to meet a deadline or complete an agreement no matter how exhausted. Without this quality, without this pragmatism and realism, I could not have survived the civil rights movement intact.

CHAPTER 6

COMMUNICATIONS

Governor Wallace, you never can jail us all,
Governor Wallace, segregation's bound to fall.

I read in the paper
Just the other day
That freedom fighters
Are on their way
They're coming by bus
And airplane too
They'll even walk
If you ask them to.

Well this is the message
I want you to hear
You know I want my freedom
And I want it this year
So you can tell Jim Clark
And all those state guys too
I'm gonna have my freedom
And there's nothing they can do.

You can push me around
You can throw me away
But I still want my freedom
And I want it every day
You can tell Jim Clark
And Al Lingo
It's time for them
To end Jim Crow.

Governor Wallace, you never can jail us all,
Governor Wallace, segregation's bound to fall.

—By James Orange, used in Selma, Alabama,
in 1964 and 1965, adapted from the rhythm-
and-blues song "Kidnapper"

 Public awareness was crucial to our strategy. Without
national exposure and mobilized public opinion, there

was no point to the struggle. The sacrifice would be lost in oblivion. The news media were therefore essential, for how else would the American people, including many white southerners, know about the machinery of injustice that tyrannized blacks in the South? How else would we produce the nationwide awakening that would, through massive disapproval and application of pressure on the federal government, extract the fangs of the system that kept black people in a state of slavery without the chains?

The civil rights movement could not succeed without significant coverage by the national news corps, but to accomplish this aspect of our strategy would not be easy. The primary reason for this difficulty was that the activities and grievances of the black community were not considered newsworthy. We would have to overcome this fundamental obstacle that stood in the way of mobilizing public opinion. To do this, SNCC created a function called Communications that was based in its Atlanta headquarters. It was to play a little-understood but key role in the conflict. How it did this is an important part of the larger saga of the civil rights movement.

"BE SPECIFIC. ASK QUESTIONS. SUMMARIZE OFTEN." The words leaped out from a mimeographed circular about gathering news information that I sent from the Communications office in the Atlanta headquarters in 1964 to all of SNCC's field offices across the southern states and to each of the local offices in Mississippi. These were instructions that I asked to be followed when Julian Bond, I, or someone else called from the Communications office:

> Distinguishing phrases must be used. There is a difference
> between being shot at, being shot, and shot down; between
> being hit with fists and beaten with blackjacks; between
> being taken into custody and being arrested; between city,
> county, and state police.

I asked for information: What? Where? When? Who? How? I explained that "this means names, ages, dates, locations, background, and organizational affiliation." I suggested underlining important data, pointed out that "all interpretative statements (not specific facts) should be attributed to someone," and advised that headlining would be useful.

It's difficult to grasp now that anything as pedestrian as registering potential voters or as prosaic as gathering in a church could have been a life-threatening act in the United States of America only twenty-five years ago, when, particularly in rural areas, law enforcement agents collaborated with vigilantes and terrorist groups. Whatever small protection we had came through news reports that brought our actions to the attention of the nation and broke the cover of secrecy. So little has been written about the civil rights movement from the inside that it is fair to say that, with the exception of those involved at the time, no one knows how important the effective use of the news media was to our safety, and even our lives.

Whenever a field secretary was jailed or a church mass-meeting bombed, whenever night riders struck or firebombings occurred, whenever a local leader's home was shot into, or any other serious act perpetrated, Julian Bond and I went into high gear. The presence of a reporter at a jail or a telephone inquiry from a newspaper was often the only step that let a local sheriff know he was being watched. Our job, in mobilizing the press, was to make local law officers feel that they were under scrutiny, thereby providing a measure of safety for civil rights workers.

My memorandum to the field offices was followed by an "urgent memo" from Jim Forman to all field staff. In it, he said that it was mandatory to follow the procedures I had earlier outlined. Jim went one step further and urged SNCC workers to pose as journalists—something that Julian and I were routinely doing: "If the incident is an arrest, start calling the *jail* posing as a reporter for an Atlanta or Washington or New York newspaper. This is extremely important. Police may modify violence. Try to get information."

First from Atlanta, in 1963 and the first half of 1964, and then from Jackson, in the rest of 1964 and 1965, I spent my days and nights telephoning our field offices or receiving incoming phone calls, and then telephoning the news media to place the stories obtained from our field secretaries. It was normal for me to work seven days a week and from twelve to sixteen hours a day. The information that I collected from the field offices was compiled into a daily "WATS Line Report." As I or someone else finished the compendium, I slipped a carbon copy into a personal file in the left-hand drawer of my desk along with other papers that I was collecting for my own records. I had no plan for using these documents; I merely thought they were worth keeping.

In 1963, SNCC introduced a technological change that increased the effectiveness of the Communications office by installing three Wide Area Telephone Service—WATS—lines, special trunk lines that allowed us to call all over the country for a set monthly rate of what I think was approximately three hundred dollars for each line. This advance made a tremendous difference to us because it meant we could telephone long-distance without considering the individual cost of each call. No WATS lines installed by the American Telephone and Telegraph Company ever got more use than SNCC's.

To reduce the cost even further, Julian and I set up a list of dummy surnames, using the names of trees, so that we could refuse to accept incoming collect phone calls with reversed charges, only to re-dial the call on the WATS line seconds later. A collect call from John Chestnut might mean that Atlanta should telephone Ruleville, Mississippi; a collect call from John Maple might mean that we should get back to the Greenville office; reversed charges from John Pine might mean that Julian or I should call McComb. We used this technique as long as we could until the local operators figured it out.

What did we do with the information we collected? This WATS line system was a vital connection among individual field secretaries, local offices across the region, state offices, and the headquarters. We used this lifeline for a host of purposes—to coordinate action, gather information or news stories as they occurred, break those items into the news media, send messages, issue telegrams, call press conferences, lessen reprisals, and sometimes to save lives.

On Monday, October 7, 1963, Jim Forman telephoned me in Atlanta from Selma, Alabama, the seat of Dallas County. Selma was an Old South city with a population of twenty-nine thousand on the Alabama River, approximately fifty miles west of Montgomery. Howard Zinn described it in *SNCC: The New Abolitionists:*

> Selma was a slave market before the Civil War. In one
> three-story house, still standing, four or five hundred Ne-
> groes were kept at one time to be exhibited and sold. The

TENNESSEE

Monteagle

MISSISSIPPI

ALABAMA

GEORGIA

Gadsden

Anniston

Birmingham

Talladega

Tuscaloosa

PERRY

Selma

DALLAS

Montgomery

Tuskegee

LOWNDES

WILCOX

River

Alabama

Mobile

FLORIDA

Gulf of Mexico

☐ Black Belt Counties

town became a military depot for the Confederacy. At the
turn of the century, it was a lynching town. By the 1950s,
the lynching had stopped, but the threat of it remained.
Selma became the birthplace of the Citizens Council in Alabama, wrapped tight in the rules of race.

It was also the birthplace of Eugene "Bull" Connor, Alabama's director of public safety, who earlier that year had unleashed
police dogs and fire hoses on SCLC demonstrators in Birmingham.

Jim told me that there were three hundred or four hundred
people on line at the Dallas County courthouse trying to register
to vote. The county was 57-percent black. The 1960 census found
that of 15,115 voting-age blacks in this Black Belt county, only
242—or 1.6 percent—had been allowed to register to vote, while
59.7 percent of Dallas County's 14,400 eligible whites were registered to vote. Three youths had just been arrested: William Gray,
twenty-one years of age; Fred Moss, nineteen; and James Mur-
ray, twenty-three. They were charged with unlawful assembly for
walking across the street from the courthouse with signs reading,
REGISTER TO VOTE. Jim also told me that, at approximately the
same time, field secretary Prathia Hall had been arrested at the
home of a local leader, Amelia P. Boynton. The charge against
her was unclear.

Prathia was a persuasive young black woman from Philadelphia, Pennsylvania, and the daughter of a minister. She was a
powerful and moving speaker. Prathia possessed a perpetually serious expression that made her seem mature beyond her years.
She had a heart-shaped face; high, rounded, applelike cheekbones; and a strong and proud carriage. In December 1963, I heard
her deliver a speech at a black church in Atlanta that epitomized
another SNCC quality—the attempt to tell the truth even if it
wasn't polite:

> Negroes must also bear the blame for the desecration of hu-
> manity that is segregation. For we have been silent much
> too long. We've been preoccupied with telling our city
> power structure not what it needs to know, but what it
> wants to hear. We are here today because we can no longer
> bear the shame of our guilt, because delay means compro-
> mising our dignity . . . we are here today to serve notice on

the city of Atlanta and the state of Georgia. We are tired of segregation and we want equality now.

Prathia received her bachelor's degree from Temple University in Philadelphia, where she majored in religion and political science, and went on to graduate studies there at the Conwell School of Theology. In August 1962 she decided to take leave of her theological studies and join the SNCC staff, and later became a member of SNCC's executive committee. Helping Charles Sherrod to pilot SNCC's twenty-two-county Southwest Georgia Project, Prathia was one of three voter-registration workers wounded by night riders' shots in Dawson, Georgia, in the summer of 1962. By the time she was arrested in Selma, in the autumn of 1963, she had been locked up many times.

When Jim Forman left the line of almost four hundred people stretching around the Alabama courthouse in Selma and walked over to the water fountain for a drink, Sheriff James Clark of Dallas County pushed him in the side with a billy stick. Jim reported to me that there was general harassment. For example, when he went with some local people to help them register to vote at the courthouse, Deputy Sheriff J. E. Holston said they could not go in and directed them to the front door. At the front door, however, a law officer named V. B. Bates told them they couldn't enter. Back at the side door, a member of the sheriff's posse dramatically barred the entrance, his flagrant gesture flashing a tattoo on his arm. Jim reported that Maryland state representative Verda F. Welcome, a black woman elected from Baltimore's fourth district, was expected in town to give moral support.

Then Jim reached the action part of his telephone call and directed a battery of requests to me: "Mary, can you get UPI and ABC into Selma? Please telegraph again to Bobby Kennedy requesting federal marshals and ask them for a temporary restraining order. Tell Julian to do something about the federal-marshals business. Tomorrow I'm going to call for federal referees."

Jim read me his own telegram sent to Attorney General Robert F. Kennedy:

"WHY CAN'T THE JUSTICE DEPARTMENT TAKE STEPS TO HAVE SHERIFF JAMES CLARK OF DALLAS COUNTY, ALABAMA, PLACED UNDER AN IMMEDIATE TEMPORARY RE-

STRAINING ORDER? THE SHERIFF AND HIS DEPUTIES ARE
CONSISTENTLY ARRESTING AND INTIMIDATING PEOPLE
WHO ARE IN THE PROCESS OF REGISTERING TO VOTE IN
SELMA TODAY. I CAN'T UNDERSTAND WHY THE FEDERAL
GOVERNMENT CAN'T PROTECT THEM AND PERSONS AT-
TEMPTING TO HELP CITIZENS TO REGISTER AND VOTE."

An hour and a half later, at 3:30 P.M., Worth Long telephoned me from Selma. Worth, a twenty-seven-year-old black poet
from Arkansas, had bookish eyeglasses that intensified the
thoughtful impression given by his solid, stable demeanor. Speaking carefully and clearly, Worth said, "The people at the courthouse have been standing in line all day without food." James
Baldwin, the author; Mrs. Boynton; Professor Howard Zinn;
Carver "Chico" or "Chuck" Neblitt of The Freedom Singers; and
Jim Forman left the line and walked over to Sheriff Clark. They
asked him if they could step out of line to talk with some of the
others who had been there all day. The sheriff intimated that if
they did, they would be arrested. So Avery Williams of SNCC
staff, a cheerful twenty-year-old student from Alabama State University and originally from Gadsden, Alabama, and Chuck Neblitt
who was also twenty and from Southern Illinois University at Carbondale, went with clipboards and voter-registration forms to the
line, carrying concealed sandwiches beneath the clipboards.

Worth saw Chuck fall when fifteen state troopers surrounded
the two men. They were both badly beaten and stamped on, especially Chuck, and were then arrested. Worth told me, "Eleven
of the state troopers' cars are now double-parked in front of the
courthouse, but two men from the Justice Department have arrived and are observing—a Mr. Wisterstrom and a Mr. Hender-
son." In his measured voice, Worth asked me if I would fire off a
telegram demanding the immediate arrest of Sheriff Clark.

In the WATS Line Report, I suggested that three steps be
taken by each of our Friends of SNCC offices and, since these
reports also functioned as internal staff communication, asked that
any staff member talking with the Friends offices pass on these
ideas:

1. Throw up picket lines at any federal building with signs
saying "One Man—One Vote"; "Arrest Sheriff Jim Clark

Who Places Himself Above Constitutional Law"; and "Why Won't the Federal Government Protect People Trying to Vote in Selma, Alabama?"

2. Call for telegrams from all over the country to go to the Justice Department asking for arrests and a restraining order.

3. Make sure that the wire services' stories are carried by the local newspapers and keep the pressure up on regional bureaus of the wire services.

I quickly sent telegrams to President Kennedy; his brother the attorney general; and to Berl I. Bernhard, a presidential assistant:

URGENTLY REQUEST FEDERAL MARSHALS IN SELMA, ALA-BAMA, FOR FREEDOM MONDAY, OCTOBER 7. WE EXPECT LARGE CROWDS OF NEGROES AT THE COURTHOUSE TO REGISTER TO VOTE.

IT IS REPORTED THAT DALLAS COUNTY SHERIFF JIM CLARK PLANS TO MAKE ARRESTS. THE RIGHT TO VOTE MUST BE PROTECTED BY THE FEDERAL GOVERNMENT.

I phoned the Friends of SNCC offices in twelve northern cities with news details. I emphasized the importance of putting pressure on the UPI and the local ABC-network affiliates. My records don't say exactly whom I reached that day, but I often spoke with Roberta Galler in Chicago and remember Lucia S. Hatch in Princeton. I then went back to telephoning other SNCC field offices. Dinky Romilly, who had just joined the staff and replaced Casey Hayden as northern coordinator on October 10, 1963, when Casey left for Mississippi, was not yet on the job. Casey or Dinky often handled the news calls to the Friends of SNCC.

I also telephoned the FBI in Atlanta, the Justice Department in Washington, the southern bureaus of the AP and the UPI in Atlanta, and each reporter on my key list of news-media contacts.

This roster was what I considered my "hot list," the sheet that hung in front of me at the office and next to my apartment telephone containing daytime and nighttime telephone numbers for both live- and print-media journalists. I inherited Dorothy

Miller's list, and as editors changed assignments the roll was changed. For example, when Georgie Anne Geyer, who covered the Albany, Georgia, movement for *The Chicago Daily News*, was reassigned, her name was lifted. Even today, I can see in my mind's eye my version of the typed list: Karl Fleming and Joe Cumming of *Newsweek*, Claude Sitton of *The New York Times*, Larry Still of *Jet* magazine, Fred Powledge and Walter Rugaber of *The Atlanta Journal*, Dudley Morris of *Time*, Nick Von Hoffman of *The Chicago Daily News*, I. F. Stone and his biweekly, and others. At the bottom of the list were additional scribbled-in names of those who moved in and out on assignment—Richard Valeriani and Jack Perkins of NBC, Paul Good of ABC. The list lengthened during the summer of 1964 and, at different points, included others. Some whom I warmly recall include James Millstone of *The St. Louis Post-Dispatch*, Peter Jennings of ABC, John Herbers of *The New York Times*, Andrew Kopkind of *The New Republic*, Sue Cronk, and the author John Hersey, a man whose person and writings impressed me greatly.

Not every situation was as ironic nor as headline-grabbing as Selma's, where, on October 7, 1963, a group of Justice Department lawyers and FBI agents coolly observed as local police dragged SNCC workers down the steps of the federal building, jabbing them with electric cattle prods as they sought to bring food to potential voter registrants waiting in line. The lawyers and agents were responding to months of agitation by SNCC for a federal presence during voter activity but at this time they only watched.

News story after news story—about arrests, beatings, firebombings, night riders, church burnings, and the economic reprisals that represented more subtle efforts to squash local movements—made the national news through the network of connections that Julian Bond and I managed. This trellis of press contacts was a necessity. To the national press, these were local stories; to the news corps in the region they were not stories at all because of whom they were about—members of the black community. In rare accounts of a criminal court case, black people were referred to disparagingly in the press as "the Smith woman" or "the Williams man." Few of the big-city southern daily newspapers, with the usual exception of *The Atlanta Constitution*, carried mention of the stories we were trying to break. The AP and

UPI wire services, even though disseminating their accounts from bureaus in all of the state capitals staffed by regular employees, often depended on local reporters, or "stringers," to file stories with the regional bureau. Thus, whatever the wire service carried was often written by a reporter from a local newspaper such as *The Jackson Clarion-Ledger* or *The Selma Times-Journal;* because of the ingrained bias of reporters writing for these local newspapers, these could scarcely be construed as straight news stories.

Most of the time neither the AP nor UPI would make any mention of the latest violence. Here is where Julian's and my network of connections came into play. We would call our Friends of SNCC offices in northern cities and ask them to telephone the regional AP or UPI wire-service bureaus to inquire if the particular news item was being carried. SNCC's northern coordinator—in succession, Casey Hayden, Dinky Romilly, and later Betty Garman—sometimes helped with these calls. When the Friends of SNCC inquired of AP or UPI, their questions would usually prompt the news bureaus in those cities to teletype a query to the Atlanta regional bureau of both wire services. Having received such requests for information from their regional offices in the Northeast, the Middle Atlantic, the West Coast, or the Middle West, the Atlanta AP and UPI wire-service bureaus would be obligated to carry a dispatch over their national wires. To do that, they would have to ask a state bureau or request that an affiliated newspaper send a stringer to the site to file an account. Getting a reporter, any reporter, to the scene could save lives, and did.

Public exposure was critical for the success of our strategy but in no area was the role of the news media more necessary than when civil rights workers were jailed. Sheriffs, their deputies, and the so-called courthouse crowd (which Bob Moses once described as "the old farmers and the young ones and the thugs, an all-man male chorus") who lingered about the county seats watching for action might beat our staff or provoke their beating with impunity—unless they believed that they were under some form of surveillance.

A little over one week after that Selma attempt to register voters, on Tuesday, October 15, 1963, John Lewis telephoned me from a pay phone in Selma, Alabama. At 6:15 A.M., the first persons had arrived at the courthouse to stand in line to register.

At 7:30 A.M., Sergeant Bates of the city police force arrived and called forward those white people who were queued up on the side of the building. After giving them numbered cards with low numbers, he handed out high numbers to blacks. There was one improvement, however; they could now leave the line to eat or use a bathroom, reserving their place according to their number. John said that the next day they would have to cash in the old numbers and obtain new numbers. Only sixty cards had been passed out. At 3:00 P.M., those queued up who did not have a number were told to leave. There were by then 325 people standing on line outside the courthouse and 250 others inside. The police shifted the line around through an alley and into the county building so that from the street there did not appear to be a long line. Now, however, all but 60 were forced to leave as part of the county's general harassment; one waited from 7:30 A.M. and was then asked to leave. *The Selma Times-Journal* reported that 31 people were registered to vote on that day, the first 12 of whom were white.

John Lewis also reported to me that John Doar, deputy director of the Civil Rights Division of the Department of Justice, had arrived in Selma from the Justice Department in Washington, D.C., for a hearing in federal court. He filed a motion for a preliminary injunction against county officials and the state solicitor to enjoin them from interfering with potential voters and voter-registration workers. But, John said, Judge Daniel H. Thomas refused to admit any testimony on recent brutality and, in fact, limited testimony to incidents of the previous August and then refused to give a ruling. The hearing had resulted from a writ of mandamus filed in the Fifth Circuit Court of Appeals, and now the judge had taken it under advisement, meaning that three weeks would probably pass until a ruling would be issued. John mentioned that John Doar suggested that each person who had been refused registration should write a letter to the judge with specific information on the rejection based on the Civil Rights Act of 1960, keeping one copy and forwarding the other to the Justice Department. This letter-writing approach had already been used with some benefits in Perry County, Alabama, and in Louisiana.

The rest of that evening's compilation from the calls on the WATS line was a mixture. In Greenwood, Mississippi, there was a citizenship class. In Holly Springs, the president of Rust College had become our new contact. People in Batesville were afraid of reprisal if they invited Aaron "Doc" Henry to speak. From Columbus, Mississippi, the report came in: "Dr. E. J. Stringer can't arrange a speaking opportunity for Doc Henry and doubts that we will get a place because of fear; the ministers might allow it but the lay trustees of local black churches would not, especially the Baptists." In Cambridge, Massachusetts, Dorothy Miller found space that could be rented cheaply from the American Civil Liberties Union so we could open a Friends of SNCC office there. Someone left a message that Larry Still of *Jet* magazine would be traveling with Karl Fleming of *Newsweek* and they would be in Jackson to cover Aaron Henry. Mike Miller, an astute and capable white organizer from California, was planning to assemble a team of reporters to accompany Doc Henry. John Lewis telephoned later to say that the Reverend Dr. Martin Luther King, Jr., had given a speech at the First Baptist Church in Selma in which, John reported with elation, "he called SNCC a sister organization and said it was doing a fine job." The last entry of the evening was a cryptic note to Jim Forman to call Selma tomorrow about enlarging our operation there.

The following day was much the same. The typewriter on which I composed the reports was faulty. Its capital letters jumped up a half space giving a crazy confusion to the accounts—all of our typewriters were donated, so characters were frequently missing and something was usually dysfunctional. There was one account that a Reverend Mr. Powell, a black minister located near Selma, had successfully organized twenty tenant farmers. They were all in debt, however, to a white man named McHuggart, who owned the property they farmed; they had borrowed from him in order to obtain seed, fertilizer, and insecticide. In a twentieth-century manifestation of semislavery, on some Alabama plantations U.S. currency was not used; tenant farmers were paid in tin tokens disbursed by the foremen, which they traded in at the plantation store. Under this system, they were to pay Mr. McHuggart back from their first produce sold; the problem was that they could almost never work their way out of debt. Here was another catch: Mr. McHuggart would put any of them and their families off the land if they registered to vote. One family had already been displaced. Nonetheless, with the Reverend Mr. Powell's support, these farm families were now ready to stake everything in an attempt to register, but they wanted some help.

In Gadsden, Alabama, the voter-registration office was now open for two weeks at the beginning of each month. At the mass meeting in Greenwood, Mississippi, three hundred people turned out. This was as great a showing, the report noted, as when Dr. King and the Reverend Fred Shuttlesworth of SCLC had spoken in Jackson to a packed mass meeting of three hundred individuals crammed into the church where Medgar Evers, slain by a sniper's bullet in Jackson on June 11, had been a member. Also in Jackson, a man was shot in the leg outside a restaurant, but Mike Miller said he would handle the press from there.

There was a sense of immediacy in the reports: "We need money. We are almost in the 'starving bracket' now. In Selma, five young black women have been trying to register every day this week. Each time the numbers are passed out, they seem to run out exactly at the moment they reach these young women."

When Communications wasn't functioning as a life-saving apparatus, our operation was gathering affidavits, publishing special reports, monitoring daily events in the lives of far-flung field secretaries, and servicing the information needs of the national news corps. Communications had, since SNCC's formation, also published our newspaper called *The Student Voice*. In 1964, we took an important step and started printing this weekly tabloid on our own photo-offset presses. They were run by a leggy, energetic white staff member named Mark Suckle who sprouted a thatch of flaming red hair. The information for all of these activities, however, was funneled through the WATS-line telephoning process.

One of our field secretaries, MacArthur Cotton, had gone to McComb, Mississippi, and telephoned me for the WATS Line Report. MacArthur was born in Kosciusko in the northeastern part of the state. A student at Tougaloo Southern Christian College before he joined the SNCC staff, MacArthur had olive skin, curly hair, and heavy-lidded eyes. I respected MacArthur with his husky and brave yet sweet gentleness. He was a heroic figure. I can never forget his telling me how, while imprisoned in Mississippi's Parchman penitentiary for participating in the Freedom Rides, he was hung by his thumbs in punishment for leading the other Freedom Riders in singing freedom songs.

The Wats Line Reports showed the routine activities of our movement as well as its heroism. On Saturday, October 19, 1963, MacArthur arrived in McComb, in the southwest section of Mississippi, an area suspected of harboring more vigilante and terrorist groups than the rest of the state. A railroad and manufacturing center, McComb was the largest town on the Illinois Central Railroad line between New Orleans and Jackson. When MacArthur telephoned, it was always with a mixture of the pressing and the humdrum. He had arrived in McComb and found a place to stay, but the landlady wanted eight dollars in advance for rent. Since he had only seven dollars, he gave her that amount but she wanted the other dollar and, he asked, would we please send him some cash right away. He hadn't eaten for a day and would like the money to be wired to him. The situation in McComb was very tense and several incidents had occurred there recently. A sixty-five-year-old white man had raped a young black girl but the authorities refused to do anything about it. An elderly black citizen was beaten by a white man but the matter was ignored.

Back in Selma, two youths who were affiliated with SNCC, Wilson Brown and Alvery Wilson, were stopped by police who searched their car. When the officers found SNCC literature and a draft report on the situation in Selma that Wilson was writing, they said, "You damn niggers ought to keep your asses at home and out of trouble. If I had a pair of scissors, I'd cut your penises off one by one," and then booked them for reckless driving and vagrancy. That was probably a polite rendition of the police officers' comments. Foul and obscene language was the norm for police but when it was telephoned in to me, I usually edited out the gratuitously vulgar language for the written report.

Worth Long telephoned me in Atlanta from Selma as two mass meetings were starting on the evening of Wednesday, October 23, 1963. There were five hundred people at the mass meeting in the First Baptist Church and six hundred at the convocation in Brown AME (African Methodist Episcopal) Chapel. John Lewis was speaking and stressing voter registration. Fifty state troopers headed by state public safety director Al Lingo had arrived that morning, apparently at the request of Sheriff Jim Clark, and were standing in readiness at the national guard armory. There had been no demonstrations but, nonetheless, seventeen youths were arrested for truancy and two twenty-one-year-olds were booked for contributing to the delinquency of minors. The young people were stopped by police and asked, "Do you want to go to school or to jail?" They chose jail. *The Selma Times-Journal* reported that the sheriff had ordered the arrest of Benny Tucker, a twenty-one-year-old SNCC worker, who sought sanctuary at the First Baptist Church with Worth.

"Selma is an armed fortress," Worth told me. "Everywhere you go, you see Alabama state patrolmen, the sheriff, his three-hundred-man posse, or the city police. Hundreds of cars are packed with police. We've just seen two cars drive by, one without a license, loaded with rifles, as the mass meeting started. With nineteen arrested, the student strategy committee says, 'We can't turn back!' They say instead, 'We'll intensify efforts regardless of Al Lingo, Sheriff Clark, or even Governor Wallace himself. How can we stop now?' "

I closed that Wednesday's report with a warning: "It is expected that there will be trouble." Then I went into frenzied action telephoning my key list of news-media contacts, the wire-service regional bureaus, the Friends of SNCC offices, and the FBI. Wednesday was a good day of the week for breaking stories and I wanted to take advantage of it.

Although they were mostly humorless and devoid of commentary, there were occasional lapses in the WATS Line Reports. So it was one autumn day when we had received no response from Selma: The evening report read, "Selma—no answer (Where art thou, Selma? You are like the spring, out of season.)"

The FBI, supposed to be upholding the Constitution, was a major factor in the thwarting of constitutional rights for blacks in the South. Julian Bond and I made it a practice to report any incident or atrocity to the FBI, a formality we knew in advance would be futile, because of the frequent collusion between the FBI and local law officers. In its 1960 report, the U.S. Civil Rights Commission politely noted that the FBI was closely allied to local police forces because of mutual need in the solving of ordinary crimes. Yet, SNCC workers knew, there was a simpler explanation—the FBI agents in the South tended to be segregationists. Whenever I telephoned the FBI, they seemed more interested in recording my name, address, date and place of birth (presumably for the dossier of one Mary Elizabeth King) than they were in obtaining the facts that I was calling to report. I would try to put the facts across, offering details of each incident, but these points were brushed over as the agent zeroed in on me. Even though

Julian and I thought that it would do no good, SNCC had embarked on the wobbly path of hope that the FBI could eventually be forced to do its proper job, and we believed that we should lay the groundwork by providing the agency with a steady flow of information. We informed the bureau methodically of every incident. It was boring and sometimes humiliating, but we were still a reformist movement seeking to change existing institutions. I thought it was required of us to act on the theory that the FBI, the federal agency charged with upholding U.S. law, would actually do so.

Sometimes I fantasized about the extent of the influence Julian and I could exert across the country with our WATS lines. There we were hunched over two telephones on an obscure street in southwest Atlanta. Yet we were mobilizing support groups in all the key cities around the country, contriving to make it impossible for the wire services to walk away from a story, rousing the national press corps into action, trying to prod the FBI into doing right. All of this we did with but two telephones crooked in our necks.

In retrospect, I realized that this gave me a sense of what might be called personal power—that is, the ability to effectuate—that few people my age had the opportunity to experience, for I came to expect to read the results of my telephone call in *The New York Times* the next day. It took me almost ten years to realize it, but a strange thing was happening. I was developing from this work a need that was subsequently to influence many life decisions. Before I was barely into my twenties, the skills I had acquired allowed me to have an effect on certain national issues that many people far older than I and in more powerful positions did not have. I began to hope that, whatever I was doing with my life, I would not only be breaking ground, but would be making broad positive impact.

Bob Moses telephoned me on that same Wednesday, October 23, 1963, to report that six people had been arrested in Indianola, Mississippi, the county seat of Sunflower County, and home county of Senator James Eastland. Promotional literature for the town maintained that its primary businesses were cotton ginning and compressing as well as the "administration of justice." On this day, apparently, "justice" meant arresting six individuals aged sixteen to forty-two for distributing leaflets without a permit. The six local blacks were participating in the special mock election, the Freedom Vote for Governor, that Bob and the Mississippi SNCC staff had organized to draw attention to the desire of the state's black citizens to exercise their right to vote. In Clarksdale, Bob said, five had been arrested under the same charge, including one student from Yale University, Dick Van Waggoner.

Bob described the preparations for the mock election in Mississippi simply and precisely. The Freedom Vote (or Freedom Ballot) was a mock gubernatorial election devised by Bob and the Mississippi staff during the autumn of 1963 to coincide with the regular election as both a form of protest and a means of preparation. Since southern blacks were customarily said by white politicians to be "content with the way things are," a mock election would offer the disenfranchised a chance to demonstrate to the country their desire to exercise democracy's most basic right. It would also strengthen the case for federal marshals or greater federal involvement which the Kennedy administration, despite having the power, had been loath to mandate. Perhaps, most important, it would teach people who had been excluded from the protections of the Constitution how to participate in voting. With Amzie Moore's advice in mind, the SNCC program in Mississippi had been built around voter registration since Bob first visited the state in 1960. His deliberate efforts and those of the small cadre of locally recruited field secretaries, however, were showing few numerical results. This was because of the cumbersome 21-question registration form and requirement to interpret any one of the 285 sections of the state's constitution. In addition, the beatings, arrests, firebombings, shootings, night riders, and economic reprisals had their effect. The Freedom Ballot was deceptively simple. It was adopted as a tactic to increase pressure on the state, but the mock election would also lay the groundwork for all of our political programs to come.

Bob slowly described the activities of the students from Yale and Stanford over the telephone. The enlistment of student volunteers had also been part of Amzie's early counsel. These particular students participating in the 1963 Freedom Vote had been recruited at Yale and Stanford by Allard Lowenstein, a forceful and sometimes churlish activist who was subsequently elected to Congress from Manhattan. Bob reported that he, Stephen M. Bingham—nephew of Congressman Jonathan Bingham and a student at Yale University—and another Yale student had been arrested at midnight the night before for "running a stop sign," on a corner where there was no such sign. Bail of eight dollars each had been posted so they could continue working on the mock election. Al Lowenstein had been arrested in Jackson the previous night on a charge of violating the city-curfew law along with Yale student John Speh. They were bailed out at sixteen dollars each the next morning by Doc Henry, the gubernatorial candidate in the Freedom Vote. The experiences of the mock election involving these students led Bob to devise the Mississippi Summer Project, as conceived by Amzie Moore, to involve a thousand students and take place the following summer.

While Bob was planning a press conference in Jackson on the arrests and allied efforts by officials to impede the mock election, I started to work arousing interest by the news media—"flacking the press." I divided our key-contact list with Julian Bond and we telephoned each of the journalists on the list. I telephoned my two favorite journalists, Claude Sitton, *The New York Times* bureau chief in Atlanta, and Karl Fleming of *Newsweek*. They had earned this special status in my mind because these southerners had again and again proved themselves fair-minded and willing to battle for placement of stories that seemed neither urgent nor newsworthy to their New York editors.

I used to visualize New York City as the communications center of the planet. As I pictured it, Julian and I were like David up against Goliath, only we were contesting skyscrapers filled with editors sporting green eyeshades and plastic cuffs to protect their shirt sleeves from smudging. These editors, in my mind's eye, were busily lining out with red pencil anything that might arouse sympathy in the copy sent by their correspondents in the South, or they were dropping stories of the civil rights struggle unceremoniously into their trash bins. One reporter showed me the story on Mississippi he was filing with his editors at *Time*. It was well-researched and rousing copy with breadth and depth. When I saw later what the editors ran, it had an unrecognizable pall.

It would be inaccurate to say that Julian and I had total faith in the news media. Many instances of indifference or even malice linger in my memory. Even now, I remember the day in 1963 that I picked up Roland Evans and Robert Novak, the syndicated Washington columnists, and read how they attempted to discredit the movement by describing SNCC as the "nonstudent violent coordinating committee."

Concerning those journalists and columnists who were seriously interested in covering the movement, Julian and I had drawn an invisible line in the sand barring emotional investment in the stories they were filing. I suppose they felt the same way about us. We came to respect individuals like Claude Sitton and Karl Fleming and, later, Paul Good of ABC-TV, who broke with his network because he believed its editorial position was not positive enough on the struggle.

I also thought highly of a reporter named Fred Powledge of *The Atlanta Journal* and another, Jack Nelson of *The Atlanta Constitution*, both men of integrity and ability. Fred's reportage was accurate enough that he was wooed away to *The New York Times*. Jack was born in Talladega, Alabama, and had won a Pulitzer Prize for his story on Georgia's central state mental hospital. He later became Washington bureau chief for *The Los Angeles Times*. Fred and Jack were among a small group of southern white reporters from rural backgrounds who showed discernment and courage in standing up against the prevailing bias. As time has sifted and sorted my experiences, the four white southern reporters among the national news corps who stand out in my memory as having shown unusual perception and understanding—Claude Sitton, Karl Fleming, Jack Nelson, and Fred Powledge—still have my admiration.

Julian never showed anger but I am positive he felt what I did, continual consternation over the lukewarm, equivocating stories most reporters wrote. It may not have been fair for us to feel this way. Nicholas Von Hoffman probably thought he offered strong coverage through *The Chicago Daily News*, but most of the time when I was dealing with Nick, I was furious that he would not go further or make more definitive statements. I remember Jim Forman's exasperation with him for the same reason.

Yet it was through these experiences of handling the national press, despite my being so young, that I learned not to let my anger stand in the way of pursuing my goal or getting the job done. I would say to myself, Don't waste time getting aggravated, Mary, just use the press—get the story out; don't indulge your feelings. Looking back, I can understand Nick's efforts to remain "objective." I probably judged him harshly precisely because I sensed that he was sympathetic.

*   *   *

We were dependent on the news media. It grated on me, but it was true without question. We needed the media to cover the social upheaval and register the suffering from the many forms of retaliation employed against those trying to change a racist system. In addition, we relied on the media to create the impression that state, county, and municipal law officers were being observed. We also required coverage for the monumental public-education campaign that the civil rights movement had undertaken—it was the only way we could do what Ella Baker stressed: Make the rest of the country shoulder responsibility for the continued degradation of black lives in the Deep South.

In order to make the system of segregation a national problem, rather than a regional one, we had to have public information flowing on a massive basis. Using the tools of telephones and typewriters, the civil rights movement represented one of the first deliberately organized citizen efforts to use the power of electronic and print media systematically to change national opinion. One person more than anyone else was responsible for originating and developing the creativity of this approach—an enigmatic and handsome young man named Julian Bond.

Fror the beginning, dependency on the news media was recognized by SNCC. The first issue of its newspaper, *The Student Voice*, published in June 1960, contained the report of the committee on communications at SNCC's founding conference in Raleigh, North Carolina, and described the communications functions SNCC should carry out:

> The Committee on Communications recommended:
> A. The publishing of a newsletter to be distributed within the movement and to supporting groups. It should contain, among other articles, news reports sent in from areas all across the South.
> B. A system of flash reports to alert the nation of emergencies and serious developments.
> C. The release of press statements on the movement.
> D. The issuing of public and interpretive statements.
> E. The development of public relations pamphlets.

There is more to placing news stories, however, than issuing releases. Julian and I had to be believable. This required that we meticulously check the facts we passed on to journalists and that we verify all the information contained in each news release. I picked up Julian's style of editing as the excited, occasionally agitated, and sometimes tremulous telephone reports came in from the field. In every contact with any field secretary, we tried to emphasize the importance of being specific and differentiating terms by the questions that we asked. The accounts we ended up writing were unemotional and often dry.

It was sink-or-swim learning for me. There was no time for deliberation. I had to catch on and do it with speed. Strangely, I felt there was equity in this because Julian treated me as his peer. Never once can I remember Julian exaggerating anything. In fact, we tried as much as possible to minimize. We held back our opinions. Sometimes our news releases contained provocative quotations from John Lewis or Jim Forman, and, if asked, Julian or I would express our opinion for a direct quotation. But when trying to stimulate the news media, we were cautious, deliberate, and thorough. Credibility was everything. It would take only an instant for one error or overstatement to destroy that. Eventually we reached the point where Julian or I could get any story placed that we deemed important. Of course, this process of gaining credibility was accompanied by the greater sophistication of the SNCC staff, coverage in the live media of major confrontations and increased broadcast of Dr. King's orations, and the diligence of the Friends of SNCC groups. Once this credibility was acquired, it was precious.

Whether Julian's personality influenced this particular approach or his personality was influenced by his handling of the news media, it is hard to say. Both are probably true. Julian Bond was ideally suited for the role of Communications director. Slender, debonair, and six feet one and a half inches tall, Julian had a polish that belied his youth, and he could think fast on his feet. Imperturbable and urbane, he had a wry sense of humor. His adroit wit came easily and he never appeared to be troubled. He had a clipped manner, rarely expressed emotion, and used his refined voice and speech tonally to make humorous side comments. He also had one other curiously attractive and intriguing characteristic—Julian had an air of diffidence accompanied by a sidelong glance. This is still one of his most appealing features.

The first issue of *The Student Voice*, in June 1960, contained a poem by Julian:

> I too, hear America singing
> But from where I stand
> I can only hear Little Richard
> And Fats Domino.
> But sometimes,
> I hear Ray Charles
> Drowning in his own tears
> or Bird
> Relaxing at Camarillo
> or Horace Silver doodling,
> Then I don't mind standing a little longer.

Julian was born with all the faculties needed to become a major figure on the American scene. His father was the distinguished black educator Horace Mann Bond, and his mother came from the elite of Nashville's black community. Julian honed his journalistic skills as a reporter with *The Atlanta Inquirer,* a weekly that was an outgrowth of the Atlanta student movement. He left Morehouse College before graduating, to go to work for the movement. Like many others active in the sit-ins who had so much to lose, this scion of the black upper class put commitment ahead of personal gain and dropped out, thereby paradoxically earning greater respect.

Years after working with Julian, I stumbled across some lines he had written at the time, when he was twenty-three years old, in a small anthology of black verse that Casey Hayden gave me:

> Look at that girl shake that thing.
> We can't all be Martin Luther King.

In another verse he called Ray Charles "the Bishop of Atlanta."

Julian was the youngest person and first black ever to have his name placed in nomination for the vice-presidency at the Democratic National Convention in Chicago in 1968 when he was twenty-eight years old. His suave demurral that he was too young, as indeed he was according to the U.S. Constitution, caught the eyes of the national audience.

After SNCC embarked on a course that was more political than its early days of direct-action programs, Julian was elected in 1965 to the Georgia State Assembly. With Ivanhoe Donaldson initially serving as his campaign manager, followed by Charlie Cobb, and with five hundred dollars borrowed from SNCC for qualifying fees plus another hundred dollars to open an office, the campaign was launched. This election was a benchmark in the organization's turn toward seeking political power. Julian was prevented from taking his seat, however, until 1967 by state legislators who objected to his opposition to the war in Vietnam. His resulting lawsuit was rejected by a three-judge panel in federal court, but in the meantime he was twice reelected to the seat he could not fill. He finally took office in 1967 as a result of a landmark Supreme Court decision, and he served in the Georgia State Assembly for twenty years.

I admired Julian and his reserve. I have rarely liked anyone so much. He was talented and articulate. He also managed always to stand above the fray of daily conflict. I liked that quality about him. I decided that I, too, should work on achieving more distance from needless conflict.

His political stance was like his sidelong glance—he almost never took a hard stand or positioned himself on one side or another of any raging SNCC issue; if pushed to speak on a pending policy question, he would most likely respond with an observation. It was as if he wouldn't allow himself to be sullied by dissension. Julian had so much to be conceited about and yet he was wholly unpretentious. He was also maddeningly self-contained, so much so that one longed to feel close to him.

Sometimes I dreamed about Julian with ill-concealed distress over my inability to know him deeply. A key broke off in my hand in one of my dreams, and in another I was searching for him but unable to find him. In one dream I was looking for a word in an unabridged dictionary while he sat writing at his desk opposite mine, but as I struggled, endlessly turning page after page of the massive tome, frustrated, I could not find the word. I spent most of my waking hours with Julian and had so much respect for him, and yet there remained large areas about him that I could not penetrate.

Meanwhile, despite harassment and intimidation, the protest Freedom Vote for Governor, scheduled for November 5, 1963, was under way in Mississippi. The campaign had all the right elements and necessary drama to enable us to call to the attention of the press the increasingly frequent arrests and the strong desire of Mississippi blacks to vote. We decided to go for broke. The results of the mock election would reveal the falsity of the argument that black people were happy with their lot.

In Mississippi, the tension built as the telephone reports continued to pour in. Four individuals were arrested in Hattiesburg for distributing literature on the mock election. Matteo Suarez, a dynamic and colorful CORE worker, was "escorted" out of Meridian by the police and told not to return. Local people in Yazoo City were afraid to participate because, in 1955, a number of them had signed a petition on desegregation of facilities and, as a result, all of them had lost their jobs. Six individuals were arrested in Greenwood including Ivanhoe Donaldson. Amzie Moore was sending us six tapes of research he had done in the area. Dr. King and Aaron Henry were both speaking in Yazoo City. Some printed materials had arrived at their destination and the word came in: "The posters look great; everyone is elated. We plan to send them to the Mississippi-based news correspondents and have them posted on every tree in the Delta!"

Doc Henry, the Clarksdale pharmacist and longtime NAACP activist as well as the alternative candidate for governor in the mock election, spoke on education in one of his speeches. "Mississippi has the poorest educational system in the country," the forty-one-year-old president of the state chapter of the NAACP declared:

> The state is trying to support two educational systems when both of them added together don't add up to one good one. In 1962, the city of Greenwood spent one hundred sixteen dollars per white child per year and only forty-six dollars and forty-two cents per Negro child. In 1962, Leflore County, in which Greenwood is located, spent one hundred seventy-five dollars and thirty-eight cents per white child and only nine dollars and fifty-three cents per Negro child per year. . . . We have got to fix it so the white man has no choice but to make it equal expenditure for both. The only way is to put black and white in the same classroom.

Southwide, the picture was bleak for school desegregation. The number of black children attending public schools with white children in seventeen southern and border states increased by 9,298 in the school year ending in 1963. Most of that increase, however, occurred in only one state, Maryland, where the number rose by 7,026.

Intimidation was beginning to take its toll in Hattiesburg. In this industrial and factory city set in the middle of a small-farming district with peach orchards and stands of longleaf pine, local blacks were starting to back away in fear from the mock election. On Monday, October 28, 1963, Lawrence Guyot's usually spirited manner was subdued because of "general police intimidation."

That afternoon, Guyot said, police went into the Whirly Bird Café in Hattiesburg with a warrant. They entered the kitchen, turned over the garbage on the floor, and handled the food in the refrigerators. They stood up on the counters and walked about, scuffing them with their boots. When the police left, they took a bottle of whiskey and arrested Mrs. Norwood, the owner, charging her with possession of alcohol. Her bail was set at $1,000. They singled her out because hers was the café where the students from Yale had gone for lunch. Police also arrested a student from Yale Divinity School named Jon Else; Gerald Bray of Detroit; and a local youth named Doug Smith. Guyot was worried. This troubled me because the twenty-three-year-old native of Pass Christian, a small town on the Gulf Coast, was normally optimistic. I empathized, seeing his determination and drive affected by worry that the mock-election tactic might fail because of reprisal. People were beginning to return the ballot boxes for the mock election (these had been distributed throughout the black community), he said, dejected over police harassment. Guyot always rebounded, however, with even greater determination.

I went to work flacking the Hattiesburg story and received another account the next day when Danny Lyon, a brilliant photographer who came to work for SNCC in 1962, called me in Atlanta. Part of my job, on an increasing basis, entailed obtaining photographs that we could use in *The Student Voice* and in reports. We were now printing our own news releases with a simple photo-offset press. Danny was an incorrigibly energetic artist who not only served as our principal photographer but also shared an apartment in Atlanta with John Lewis. The Black Star photographer Matt Herron also photographed for us and later Joffre Clark, Robert Fletcher, Cliff Vaughs, and other young photographers joined the crew.

Danny was driving to our office in Hattiesburg to photograph a mass meeting being held that night in support of the Freedom Vote. I asked him to go there because I sensed there might be something uglier beneath the surface than we had thought, in the eastern part of the state, and I would the following summer be proved grimly correct. Danny reported, his trembling voice aroused by the danger, that four fire trucks now blocked our office and police had cordoned off the Masonic Temple where the meeting was to be held that night. Three firemen and Sergeant Creel of the city police had just walked into the office there and one of them said, "Why don't we condemn the place right now?" Although the situation was very tense, with police patrolling with dogs in their cars, Danny told me, astonishingly, that the mass meeting would continue as planned, and, he announced with satisfaction, shouting the words, "People have begun to vote!" He also mentioned that John Rosenberg and Robert Owen of the Justice Department had arrived in Hattiesburg—but only to observe.

By this time we had received reports of more than one hundred individuals harassed by Mississippi police in all sections of the state who attempted to prevent local people from casting their protest ballots in the boxes that were generally placed, as if in a regular election, in churches and schools in the black community. On November 2, 3, and 4, "vote-mobiles" traveled to rural areas to receive ballots. Arrangements were also made for "underground ballots" to be sent and received through the mail where people could not cast their mock votes in the open.

A temporary injunction against all civil rights groups was issued in Jackson. Jane Stembridge was arrested in Greenwood and held under $1,000 bail. George Greene was arrested in Natchez and held under $5,000 bail. Because they were conspicuous, the ten Stanford students and twenty from Yale were getting a full dose of Mississippi justice at every turn.

Bob Moses asked me to send a telegram to the Justice Department. I wrote, IF VOTER REGISTRATION IS TO BE MEANINGFUL, THERE MUST BE OPPORTUNITY FOR POLITICAL ACTION. WE URGE YOU TO INTERVENE ON BEHALF OF DEMOCRACY. Eleven arrests had occurred in Clarksdale alone in connection with the mock-election campaign.

Arrests picked up in Greenwood and Oxford. A Stanford student, Hugh Smith, was shot at in Tate as he accompanied local people to participate in the Freedom Vote. John Lewis was escorted out of Rosedale by police. In Cleveland, Mississippi, SNCC workers were not allowed by the police to get out of their cars.

In Port Gibson, SNCC worker George Greene and Yale student Bruce Payne were accompanying Ella Baker who was traveling to Jackson from Natchez when two carloads of white men followed them for forty-seven miles and, when they stopped for gas, beat Bruce while the others restrained George. Bruce said later, when they finally made it to Jackson, that the only thing that saved them, as they slipped in and out of traffic and ran red lights, was George's "excellent driving." The following day the same men forced Bruce and George from the Natchez Freedom Vote-Mobile and beat them both after forcing them off the road against a bridge. When they were finally able to get their vehicle onto the road again, the assailants shot at them three times.

As we tried to turn the attention of the national news media toward the mock election, it was clear to Julian and me that the students from the North and the West Coast gave us leverage that was otherwise missing in the city room of a newspaper or in a regional bureau of a wire service. As a result of striving to get press coverage of the Freedom Ballot, I realized with a sinking feeling of finality how permeated by racism the country was; it was much easier for the Friends of SNCC groups outside the South to badger their local wire-service outlet in the hometown of a person who was white. This recognition that northern whites could command greater press attention was another one of the factors that led Bob Moses to design the massive Mississippi Summer Project. We would, however, be using the implicit racism of the press, and its failure to see atrocities against black people as newsworthy, to fight racism.

On Tuesday, November 5, 1963, the results of the Mississippi mock election began to be tallied. By nine o'clock that night, Mendy Samstein telephoned me that 71,942 individuals from two hundred communities throughout the state had cast ballots. These were extraordinary results, given the extent of the state's efforts to intimidate people.

Interestingly, the effects of the mock-election turnout stimulated other southern communities toward increased legal voting behavior. In Pine Bluff alone, across the Mississippi River in the

Arkansas Delta, 7,300 people turned out for a bona fide election in which a forty-four-year-old black dentist ran for city council. The usual turnout, reported to me by the Arkansas SNCC staff, would have been between 500 and 1,000. Dr. W. L. Molette received only 2,881 votes out of 7,334 ballots cast, but this in itself represented profound change in the willingness of the black community to take risks. Our white Arkansas director, Bill Hansen, was less sanguine about the results and grumbled, "All we did was bring the white folk out." Bill was a terse Cincinnatian, unimpressed with himself and everyone else, who, at the time I had first met him in 1962, had already been arrested nineteen times.

In Selma, Alabama, Worth Long told me, even though only sixty numbers were given out each day for those hoping to register for the actual election, the sums were slowly mounting up, starting with October 15 when five blacks had been processed and registered to vote in Dallas County. Each day between eight and twenty-two were registered. On November 5, as the results of the mock election were being counted in Jackson, twenty blacks applied to register in Selma and nine were accepted. Two days later, Worth reported, forty-two black employees of Dunn's Rest Home, all women, lost their jobs because they had attempted to register to vote.

On Thursday, November 7, an exultant Dona Richards, a graduate of the University of Chicago, telephoned. She gave me the final count of the mock election. Despite all of the official efforts to halt the protest election and with not a whisper, much less a presence, from the Justice Department, eighty-two thousand black persons in Mississippi had cast mock ballots for Aaron "Doc" Henry for governor and the Reverend Edwin King, the white chaplain of Tougaloo College, for lieutenant governor.

Yet, despite the consistent lack of initiative from the Kennedy administration, back in Selma Judge Daniel H. Thomas made a statement to the Dallas County grand jury comparing the Kennedy brothers to the Mafia and the Cosa Nostra. One week later, President Kennedy was shot and killed.

In the Atlanta SNCC headquarters, we were glued to a borrowed television set. I had been spending a good portion of my time trying to rouse the Justice Department, providing a trail of information to the FBI, reporting every major incident to John

Doar, in addition, of course, to stimulating news coverage of the activities exploding across the South. A constant theme of Julian's and mine was that the federal government was doing little to safeguard constitutional rights. President Kennedy often came under attack from me, and even more so from others, for failing to put real force behind his words. Now he was gone. (See Chapter 7 for more detailed discussion of the Kennedy civil rights record.)

Even before he was pronounced dead, I left the group around the television set and went back to my desk. Having been bitterly critical of President Kennedy's nonaction, I was now gravely concerned that we might be in for worse. Our lively and rambunctious office had quieted. I telephoned Dorothy Dawson, the former roommate of Casey's, and Robb Burlage, both of whom were among a small group of individuals active with Students for a Democratic Society who were close to SNCC; the group also included Todd Gitlin and Tom Hayden. Robb had been a political science student at Harvard and was then with the State Planning Commission of Tennessee. What does this portend for civil rights? I asked them. Will Lyndon Johnson's presidency set us back? Robb and Dorothy responded that little would change in the way of policy now. They cited opposition to the Texas anti-lynch law in Johnson's Senate race. I decided that what Robb and Dorothy had said was worth circulating and drafted an internal staff memorandum passing on their observation that Johnson was a brilliant opportunist and that if SNCC thought it couldn't trust Kennedy, it should be prepared to trust Johnson only half as much.

Three days later, I wrote Jim Forman a policy memorandum suggesting that an upcoming conference we were planning in Washington, D.C., be shifted to allow staff time for "sounding out Johnson's allies, and trying to get the lie of the land politically now." I was beginning to feel more self-confident about analyzing the forces affecting the civil rights movement and my ability to play a role in the policy-making of the organization. I suggested, "There is no one in Congress that we can trust at this point. A probable congressional shake-up will keep traditional liberal support in abeyance"; and I said someone needed to start looking up LBJ's record on civil rights. I also raised a concern—growing out of my increasing understanding of the counterpoint between the states and the federal government—suggesting that we should assume from now on that the state governments in the South would try to play off Johnson's weaker position on civil rights. I closed the November 25, 1963, memorandum with a quotation from a telephone conversation with Bob Moses:

> "The conference may be the one place in the whole country where people can get together and talk . . . without having to pay homage which is trivial . . . banalities. It just doesn't seem that anywhere in the country we have a counterbalance to the idea that if a president dies, he was a hero therefore we must now eulogize him. So if there are any real issues at the bottom of this, we must cover them up and avoid real confrontation because it divides. See, SNCC doesn't have to go through that."

In the next five days following President Kennedy's assassination, the bodies of five black men turned up floating in the tributaries of the Homochitto River in the Natchez area of Mississippi. When Bob Moses first told me about his, I was stunned. I was afraid that this signaled the new ruthlessness, on the part of the state's terrorist elements following the presidential assassination, that I had been worried about, and that we faced an upsurge in social depravity and brutalization in the southwest section of Mississippi. I decided to do everything in my power to get these five black deaths reported in the news as, I hoped, a deterrent to further lawlessness. I didn't even discuss it with Julian. By now, I felt confident enough to make that decision on my own.

The intention of terrorism is always, by senseless atrocities against innocent victims, to shock and cow the rest of the populace. How would I be able break this story? This was precisely the sort of thing that never appeared in the press. "In Natchez," Bob reported, "the black community is withdrawn, fearful, and silent. Don't even bother to try to find someone for attribution for a quotation," he told me. What reputable journalist could I locate who would report these deaths? For the next several days, I talked with reporters about these five likely murders, in the course of keeping them informed about other incidents. No one would use it. No one was even curious. There was no evidence. It was only an allegation. The feeling came over me, slowly dawning, that some of the reporters responded as they did because they were afraid for their own safety if they went to Natchez to verify the account.

This is when Claude Sitton became a hero to me. Only Claude, alone among the members of the national news corps, was willing to find a way to work into the copy he was sending to *The New York Times* my allegation of the facts concerning the five deaths in Natchez.

Claude would return to *The Times* as national news director in October 1984, but, while he was still southern correspondent, in 1963, he had traveled to southwest Georgia to cover a mass meeting at a church in the town of Sasser. With Claude that night was Bill Shipp of *The Atlanta Constitution* and Pat Watters of *The Atlanta Journal*. While they were in the church, three white sheriffs and a dozen deputies entered, including one big uniformed deputy who strode up and down the aisles of the church slapping an eight-cell "Louisville slugger" flashlight against his palm. One of the sheriffs, Zeke Matthews of Terrell County, stepped forward and questioned the reporters about their presence. As those assembled, including Charles Sherrod, local people, and the reporters, left the church, the sheriffs and deputies made threatening remarks such as "I'm gonna have a piece of your ass, boy!" and the like.

During the mass meeting, the air was let out of a tire of Claude's rented station wagon and sand was poured into the gas tank. After that night, Claude's coverage lost the distant, flat quality of most news reportage of the time and leaped to life. He had come to understand in a personal way the nature of the opposition to full black participation in the political and social life of the country, and his accounts were subsequently crackling with episode after episode that gave his readers a genuine sense of the high stakes involved.

Bill Shipp had written one tendentious editorial after another alleging that there existed communist influence in the civil rights movement. Throughout those years of the early 1960s, he "Red-baited" us, at times giving the farcical impression that those of us involved in the struggle were automatons directed by remote control from Moscow. Julian and I assumed that most of his "disinformation" came from the House Un-American Activities Committee (HUAC). On that particular night in Sasser, however, when Shipp accompanied Claude Sitton, he was sitting in the church when the sheriffs interrupted the meeting. He was also there when Claude discovered the tire and the sand in the gas tank. That time, Bill Shipp wrote a fair editorial.

No reporter ever gave us everything we wanted. I suppose this was built into the situation. Too cautious and restrained, in our view, all of them demanded verification beyond what was reasonable, given the fearful circumstances of the time. Looking back, I have to admit that my hopes were unrealistic—and insatiable— because no journalist could have reported the movement with the tenacity and fervor I thought it deserved. Yet, when Claude Sitton was the only journalist to allude to the five deaths in Natchez, he won a fast friend in me. Seventeen years later when the fifteenth anniversary of VISTA (Volunteers in Service to America) took me to Raleigh, North Carolina, as a government official, I made certain to visit Claude, then editor in chief of *The News and Observer*.

Our job in Communications became more difficult as SNCC's strategies diversified from the assimilationist direct action of the sit-ins and Freedom Rides to our subsequent pursuit of more political objectives. Some of these difficulties were highlighted by a telephone discussion I had with SNCC field secretary Frank Smith.

A wiry, thoughtful, Morehouse College graduate, Frank was smart and self-assured. Originally from near La Grange, Georgia, he married another SNCC field secretary, Jean Wheeler, and later became an elected member of the Washington, D.C., City Council. Frank telephoned me in late November 1963 and discussed two matters neither of which would have been considered worthy of news coverage, but I thought they were important. First, progress was being made in the opening of lending libraries for black communities in Mississippi. The initial one set up in Greenwood, inside the Freedom House, was finished and some of Greenwood's donated books, mostly from the Friends of SNCC groups, were being moved to Columbus, near the Mississippi-Alabama line. These libraries, albeit modest, were significant because the segregated state public-school system was pathetic. Most of the teachers were products of an abysmal system where the state legislatures spent little on education, with this inadequate amount unequally applied to maintaining two systems. The doctrine of segregation was still justified as offering "separate but equal" facilities, an absurd characterization that was an outright falsehood. There were no "separate" libraries for black people other than an occasional paltry mobile van in the larger cities, where second-hand books were passed down from white libraries when they were too worn for their use. The SNCC staff's efforts to open libraries across the state gave a point of focus for northern donations, provided an expression of the desire for education by Mississippi's black citizens, and served as a statement that SNCC sought fundamental long-term change.

Jane Stembridge wrote me from the Greenwood office in late 1963: "This afternoon, about thirty kids came in to get some library books and it was a very loud and happy time. I was glad to be here when they came and to hear what they had to say. That is the most important event. . . ." It was an "event" if you looked at it against the backdrop of tedious long-term political organizing, like a sprint in contrast to the race of a long-distance runner. It was not, however, a news story.

The other issue Frank discussed with me in the fall of 1963 was the new interest of adults in taking action on civil rights following the Freedom Vote. "Before the mock election, the students were working the adults into their program," he said. "Now, the opposite is happening." As our coordinator in the First Congressional District, Frank reported that there would be a new series of meetings with various adult groups during the week. *The Student Voice* was now going to more older people in the district. "We're trying to create a solid base among adults and it's looking good," Frank noted. This was significant, but it also wasn't going to be of interest to the news media. Neither would Hunter Morey's report that two local individuals in Greenville had agreed to be named publicly in a school desegregation suit if Jack Greenberg and the NAACP Defense Fund, Inc.—the "Inc. Fund"—would agree to handle it in addition to their suits pending in Jackson, Biloxi, and Clarksdale. It was striking to me that two black citizens would be willing to step forward in Greenville, because they would probably lose their jobs the next morning or face some other immediate reprisal, but, again, it was not a news story. Frank wasn't looking for kudos; he liked the role of behind-the-scenes organizer as SNCC had fashioned it, and was one of the advocates of SNCC's abandoning direct action and adopting a strategy of achieving political power. He knew I couldn't peddle these two stories to the news media, but he wanted the rest of the headquarters staff to know what was happening through the WATS Line Report.

Part of the difference in perspective about what was important and what was not lay in the difficulty the news media always face when confronted with a process rather than an incident. What Frank Smith was describing was procedural; it was part of a larger developmental process, not a specific happening that could be tied to a time and place.

In contrast, from Danville, Virginia, on November 22, 1963, Avon Rollins reported that a white volunteer and three Roman Catholic priests had been arrested after the volunteer had been hit on the side of his head by police. That specific occurrence was something with which I could arouse the interest of the news media, including the Catholic Church's own large and extensive press outlets. I would also be able to make some inroads with the press the next day when seven students from Southern Illinois University and twenty students from Lane College were arrested in Jackson, Tennessee—although even this story lacked real appeal to the news media because the majority of the students were black.

To what extent did the appetites of the news media influence what we served up to them? From the vantage point of over twenty years, and not only viewed through memory but also through the unchanging texts of the WATS Line Reports I carefully tucked into my drawer, I must conclude that SNCC had its own strong sense of integrity in withstanding an almost irresistible pull to shape events, confrontations, demonstrations, and encounters to suit the media. It is surprising to me, considering the tempestuous nature of those years in the movement, how true we were to our own standards. Once something significant had happened, Julian and I, along with Mark Suckle, the photographers, Julian's always-cooperative brother James, Jerry DeMuth, and others supporting the Communications operation would attempt to make the best use of the opportunity. Of course, our state directors and the SNCC staff as a whole learned very quickly, and perhaps intuitively, what was of interest to the news media and what was not. Although this awareness may have shaped some aspects of our programs and was consciously a basis for planning the Mississippi Summer Project of 1964, it did not dominate SNCC's decision-making process.

Any significant social change in the United States requires mastery of communications and effective use of the news media, unless you are relying solely on achieving change through litigation. Even then, on a long-term basis, courts are inevitably affected by prevailing social attitudes. After all, segregation had been legal for much of our country's history and was given second life by the Supreme Court's *Plessy* v. *Ferguson* decision in 1896, which upheld the constitutionality of "separate but equal" seating on trains. Appointees to the federal bench taking office today will be sitting well into the twenty-first century and these appointments could reflect a repudiation of the values of the civil rights movement unless there is vigilance. Forces will periodically revive to create a mind-set in the country that if you support social reform you must be a communist.

The skillful use of the news media for public education is the modern equivalent of the "pen," and the pen is still mightier than the sword. The courts can change and ultimately will reflect the popular will. The First Amendment, guaranteeing the right to free speech, will always be the most important constitutional principle, upon which all the others are grounded. One of the lasting lessons of the civil rights movement is that attitudes of Americans can change and individuals can mobilize on a national basis if they have accurate information about injustice. The news media and the technologies of mass communications are malleable—they can be used for purposes of progress or for purposes of regression and, increasingly, they can be used on an international basis. The civil rights movement showed that the free press and the technology of communications are among the most ineluctable strengths of the Western democracies.

CHAPTER 7

GENESIS

Paul and Silas, bound in jail,
Had no money to go their bail,
Keep your eyes on the prize, hold on, hold on,
Keep your eyes on the prize, hold on, hold on.

The only chain that a person can stand
Is the chain of hand in hand,
Keep your eyes on the prize, hold on, hold on,
Keep your eyes on the prize, hold on, hold on.

We're gonna board that big Greyhound,
Carryin' love from town to town,
Keep your eyes on the prize, hold on, hold on,
Keep your eyes on the prize, hold on, hold on.

We're gonna ride for civil rights,
We're gonna ride both black and white,
Keep your eyes on the prize, hold on, hold on,
Keep your eyes on the prize, hold on, hold on.

We've met jail and violence too,
But God's love has seen us through,
Keep your eyes on the prize, hold on, hold on,
Keep your eyes on the prize, hold on, hold on.

—Adaptation of traditional song, 1960

 As sit-ins opened the decade of the 1960s in the United States, much of the rest of the world was preoccupied with the tide of anticolonialism, probably the single most significant global phenomenon since World War II. On February 1, 1960, when four freshmen sat down at Woolworth's in Greensboro, North Carolina, the nation of India had been independent of the British for thirteen years, Algeria was still embroiled with France in what has been called her "savage war of peace," Ghana had freed itself of British rule, and the youthful Fidel Castro had just ousted the dictator Batista to establish his revolution in Cuba.

For those who cared to see what was happening, powerful

anticolonial movements and forces pressing for national liberation were, throughout major portions of the Southern Hemisphere, irrevocably changing the map of the world. With these movements came halting infant steps toward mass education, universal suffrage, adult literacy, and public-health campaigns. The sun finally set on the British Raj in India on August 15, 1947. In 1949, a revolution in mainland China closed the doors of that country to the West. The decade of the 1950s brought reports of wars of independence, and the newly developing medium of television showed the installation of an African head of state in Ghana and rejection of the French in Guinea; debates in the United Nations brought the struggle in Algeria and other wars of liberation into the living rooms of American families.

For the first time, black Americans read news stories datelined Accra, Nairobi, Lagos, and Katanga. They watched Gamal Abdel Nasser defy the British in his speeches, and then they observed as he nationalized the Suez Canal. Before their eyes, blacks in America saw vast postcolonial changes being initiated. Individuals like Mohandas Gandhi, Nehru, Nasser, Sukarno, Mao Zedong, and Ho Chi Minh provided new leadership in the non-Western countries of the world and gave voice to millions from whom little had previously been heard in Western capitals. Anticolonial movements were permanently changing the global patterns of leadership, and, although most Americans have still not reckoned fully with the implications of this sea change, the world was altering once and for all.

It was inevitable that black people in the United States—exposed to the effects of anticolonial movements in Africa, Asia, and Latin America—would someday turn around, take a look at the United States, and begin to demand their constitutional rights. A movement that was anticolonial in nature would develop in the United States because blacks, generally speaking, were to white America, particularly in the rural South, what black Africans were to the European colonialists—a source of cheap, subjugated labor tantamount in many respects to slave labor, long after the abolition of slavery. American blacks naturally identified with anticolonial movements because of this basic similarity, but there were also striking differences. Blacks born in America didn't need a new state; they did not have to fight for a constitution but merely to make its protections work for them.

This assertion was considered subversive only because of *who* was advocating those rights.

The civil rights movement in the United States, as a tangible phenomenon—a chain of events involving the awakening of hundreds upon hundreds of southern black communities—was sparked and catalyzed by the anticolonial movements of the post-World War II period. But the civil rights movement did not come into being fully grown. Its roots sprang from the bitter seeds of the region's history of slavery, the Civil War, the period of Reconstruction, and the marked racial oppression of the 1890s.

Of course, like most white Americans, I knew little or nothing of this background of oppression and resistance. American society was in fact *antihistorical* in conspiring that we should not know, and, as events were to unfold, we were to pay a price for that ignorance. While I was aware that an irrational and disgraceful racial injustice was woven into the fabric of our society and had distorted and reduced the lives and possibilities of our black citizens, I had no real knowledge of the history and evolution of this reality other than having read my grandfather's hand-marked and underlined biography of George Washington Carver. (It is a tribute to his own intellectual power and curiosity that my southern-born and -bred grandfather had owned and studied such a book.)

Like many of my generation, my first graphic confrontation with this social evil came from an incident in Mississippi in September 1955 that, concerning as it did someone who was also a teenager, had a powerful and traumatic effect. A fourteen-year-old black youth named Emmett Till had come from Chicago to visit his relatives near the little town of Money, Mississippi, in the Delta. Three white men grabbed him from a private home and dumped him in the Tallahatchie River, a crude heavy weight tied to his neck with barbed wire. His crime? A rumor that he whistled at a white woman. Although black men had been killed for similar rumors over the years, this slaying occurred following the Supreme Court's landmark school desegregation decision and the Montgomery bus boycott, and this time the story was carried by the national news media.

Following this event, I spoke to my social studies class at New York City's special High School of Music and Art, using *Life*

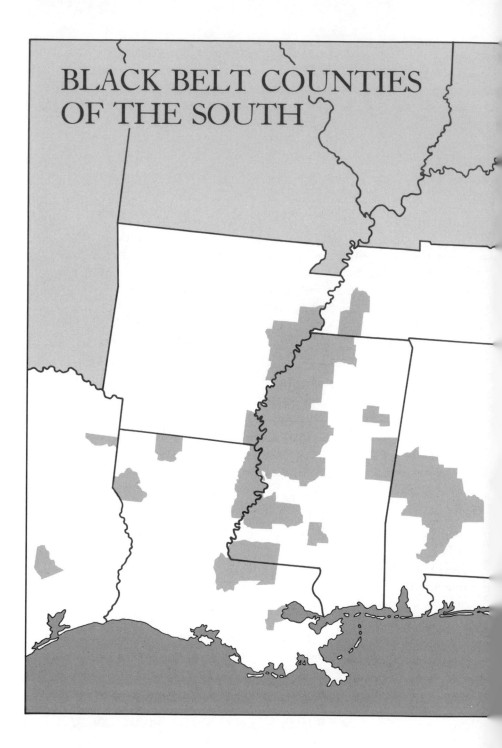

BLACK BELT COUNTIES
OF THE SOUTH

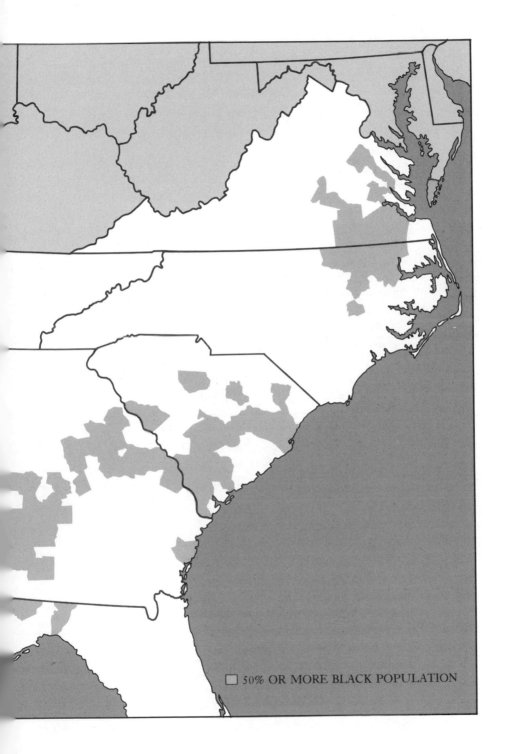

☐ 50% OR MORE BLACK POPULATION

magazine's article about the murder as my source. My voice broke as I told the class, most of whom were, like me, fifteen years of age, that he was only one year younger. This was my first speech about an issue of justice and it may have represented a predecision leading to my working for the movement, because critical choices are often made early in life. (Years later, as a presidential appointee responsible for the Peace Corps, I learned while visiting volunteers in Africa and Latin America that a great number of them made the decision to sign up when they were ten or twelve years old.)

Apart from the sickening assault on my consciousness of Emmett Till's death, and later my growing realization that something wonderful and powerful was happening in the South with the sit-ins, I had no understanding of the genesis of the modern civil rights movement. I am reasonably sure that not too many of the young men and women with whom I was later to be associated in the movement did either. This helps to explain in part why we were so naïvely optimistic that courage, determination, and sincerity could change, forever, the phenomenon of racism. We were not aware of how deep were its roots and how pervasive and tenacious a grip it had and still has on the psychic life of the nation.

In retrospect, I can now see that many of the shoals and rocks against which our organization would later founder had a deep historical basis. For "Those who do not remember the past," George Santayana said in *The Life of Reason,* "are condemned to repeat it." I believe, therefore, that it is important to sketch in here some of the history we did not then know. What follows is not an attempt to summarize in a few pages the complex, bitter, and infinitely moving struggle of black Americans. It is simply a brief discussion of some of the ideas, forces, and conflicts that created our organization in the form that we knew it—and that later would change it profoundly—because the unique struggle that took shape in the American South between 1955 and 1965, reaching its fullest expression in the direct-action nonviolent movement that flourished between 1960 and 1965, had deep origins.

It began, literally, when two battered English cargo ships arrived in Jamestown, Virginia, in 1619, bearing twenty African captives in their holds, the rest of their slave cargo having died. These captives from West Africa were the vanguard of millions more representing the only immigrant population of America that did not wish to come here. Yet their presence has affected the history, culture, and present reality of this nation to a greater extent than has any other minority. Also, their own perception of their relationship to this society, as an inevitable consequence of the way they came here and the treatment to which they have been subjected, is the most ambivalent. One of the problematic questions that would arise in 1965 related directly to this ambivalence. How should black people in the United States understand their relationship to this society? Were they in fact Americans, that is, citizens, like everyone else? Or were they a captive people, oppressed and excluded, whose ultimate liberation could only be found outside the mainstream of white society? (It is sad and ironic that even as I write, twenty-five years later, compelling arguments can still be fashioned for either position after examining the domestic policies of the United States.)

Until 1864, the Afro-American experience was that of slavery, with people legally defined as property—chattel—to be sold, deeded, bequeathed, and disposed of like sheep or cattle. The history of the resistance of black Americans to this condition must be the subject of other books, but it is useful to note here that the earliest civil rights activity took the form of flight, purchase of one's freedom, lawsuits and petitions for rights (unsuccessful), strikes, work stoppages, and, as a final desperate strategy, armed insurrection. What is clear is that our black countrymen and women never accepted the definition of their place, value, and existence imposed on them by slavery. This is evident in the record of the two hundred thousand blacks who flocked to the call of Frederick Douglass in 1862 to "strike a death blow to slavery." Many historians now maintain, furthermore, that it was the black Union soldier who turned the tide of the Civil War.

Blacks' sense of themselves as Africans in America, and as human beings with worth and dignity, was preserved in a religion-based culture of profound spiritual power and moral authority that is expressed in the most evocative and hauntingly inspiring tradition of music that the modern world has seen. The exposure of young white Americans to the power and resonance of this rich culture and its freedom songs was one of the great and enduring rewards from involvement in the civil rights movement.

Abolition and its disappointments and broken promises, the psychic and economic disruption of the South, and a national ca-

pitulation to a white supremacist view of reality, created the preconditions of the civil rights movement and the racial landscape
of the 1950s and 1960s. It was the young Republican party of
President Abraham Lincoln that held power during the Civil War
and its aftermath. The question that they and white America confronted in 1864 is the one we faced in 1960 and that we still face:
What is the proper, just, and honorable place for blacks in American society? Obviously, since we still confront it, it has never
been satisfactorily answered.

Many white Americans felt in 1864 that a population of some
five million black people could not be assimilated into the United
States. These Americans proposed many solutions, for example,
colonization to Africa or to Central America. Others felt that blacks
should by right enjoy all the freedoms and opportunities of American citizens and that, to this end, the South should be reconstructed in order to make that possible. This policy was adopted
by the Republican administration and a noble attempt to implement it—one that might well have succeeded—was made. The
problems were formidable. The white South, with its protocols of
racism and white supremacy, was defeated and resentful. The black
population was in chaos and displaced by the war, and was mostly
illiterate as a result of the policy and laws of the antebellum slave-
owning society. Yet, for some thirty years, as long as the policy of
the national administration was to affirm and ensure the democratic civil rights of freedmen and freedwomen, vast, indeed almost unbelievable, progress was made.

As was to happen one hundred years later, white Americans
of conscience came South and joined hands with blacks to create
schools, colleges, clinics, communities, and a free society. Blacks
voted, ran for office, and developed political skills and an enlightened leadership that gave the lie to racist assertions of inherent black inferiority. Many of the black colleges and universities
mentioned in this book have their origins in this period—Fisk,
Howard, Tougaloo, Stillman, Benedict, Spelman, Morehouse. They
were the products of black and white cooperation similar in some
ways to the 1960s civil rights movement.

It is perhaps the greatest single tragedy of American history,
the most shameful failure of national imagination, decency, and
spiritual will, that this effort at democratic and egalitarian reconstruction of the southland was betrayed and abandoned. Had it

not been, the South would have transcended its history and outgrown its biases; it would have flourished, developed, and overcome its black, *and* white, impoverishment; and the black
community would have taken its rightful place in American society and been spared an added century of suffering, oppression,
and bloodshed; and contemporary America would be a vastly
healthier and more humane society, and probably more prosper-
ous as well.

But this was not to be. The freedmen and freedwomen naturally voted Republican, the party of Lincoln, as did their white
allies, by no means all of whom were of northern origin. A political coalition under federal military protection held power in the
South and engineered the Reconstruction. The minority Democratic party was all white and maintained a not-so-secret alliance
with white secret societies and terrorist groups like the newly created Ku Klux Klan, which was organized around a racist platform
that asserted, "The South is a white man's country and by God
we'll rule it," "The South shall rise again," and other such slogans. The U.S. Congress during the 1890s permitted the white
south to reduce blacks to a state of peonage, to disregard their
civil rights, and to disenfranchise them by statute, intimidation,
and force.

In the 1890s after federal troops had been withdrawn, through
the use of threat, fraud, and violence, the southern Democratic
party of the "Dixiecrats" came to power. By the systematic disenfranchisement of black voters, the Dixiecrats wielded unchallenged
political might in the region for over seventy years, from 1890 to
the late 1960s. Even more significantly—entrenched in its chairing of powerful congressional committees—the party of Senator
Theodore Bilbo, Senator James O. Eastland, and Governor Ross
Barnett, in shameful alliance with powerful Democratic party machines of the big northern cities, dominated the Congress right up
to the time of Lyndon Baines Johnson's presidency. Thus began
for blacks in the 1890s what the Reverend Dr. Martin Luther
King, Jr., called "the long, dark night of oppression." Not only
did the Dixiecrats roll back Reconstruction, but, by adopting a
host of statutes and outlawing everything interracial, they, like
the government of South Africa, institutionalized racial injustice
and the symbolic inferiority of "the Negro" in the total and discriminatory separation of the races. In this way was southern seg-

regation established, made possible with the systematic deprivation of the fundamental entitlement of citizenship in a democracy—the right to meaningful political participation.

By 1910, nearly ten million black Americans, or over 90 percent of the black population, lived in the segregated South. All power was in white hands, protocols of racism covered all aspects of behavior, and every institution of society was neatly if unequally divided into "white" and "colored." Economic life for blacks was dominated by the peonage and sharecropper system little different from its predecessor slavery, and education was stifled. No organized, purposeful way of bringing about change was possible since, in the black community, one lived under the terror of random and arbitrary violence, of having one's physical security subject to the whim of those who hated one, and knowing that due process—the protection of the law, police, and the courts—did not extend to blacks.

What was more problematic for blacks, and to the enduring disgrace of the nation, was that this took place with the tacit support and complicity of the U.S. Congress, successive White Houses, and, in addition, the Supreme Court. Indeed, as waves of black emigrants escaped north to "the promised land," they discovered that southern racism and views of appropriate race relations had found significant support in northern public opinion. Though not enshrined in statute, discrimination was cruel and real. The half-million blacks who streamed to cities of the North between 1910 and the 1920s, partly as a consequence of World War I, found poor housing, residential and educational segregation, job discrimination at the hands of white employers and the trade unions, plus hostility or worse, brutality, from police. Certainly the situation provided almost unimpeachable evidence supporting the views of those who asserted that on the issue of race white America was beyond redemption.

As late as 1946, New York congressman Adam Clayton Powell was leading demonstrations and boycotts to get the white-owned businesses on 125th Street in the heart of Harlem to hire blacks. The significant difference was that blacks enjoyed the right to vote and to run for public office. Yet even this basic freedom was ironically limited by the relatively small numbers of blacks in the North compared to the South. Nonetheless, many of these immigrants entered the mainstream of the American industrial economy, their children were educated into the middle and professional classes, and they became the nucleus of the emerging black middle class, so called.

The colossal betrayal of the hopes of freedom during the decades around the turn of the century had many effects on the attitudes of black Americans. The wholesale national rejection of black rights and entitlement, and the systematic attempt to crush the spirit and aspirations of a people, fueled ambivalence long present in the black psyche. A division of perception in the black community over identity, aspiration, and ultimate solution was as old as slavery. Some Africans had refused to learn English, adopt Christianity, or refer to themselves with other than African names. Others assimilated into an Afro-American culture. During the fight for abolition in the 1840s and 1850s, the great Frederick Douglass fought for freedom and full civil rights and responsibilities for blacks as Americans. His friend, Dr. Martin Delaney, a physician and novelist, however, argued for separation and led an expedition to explore the delta of the West African country of Niger in search of an Afro-American homeland. These two giants of black history, while holding irreconcilable views on the subject, respected each other. Douglass, in speaking of Delaney, reportedly said, "Every morning I thank God I am a man. Dr. Delaney thanks God he is a black man." Even before this period, in 1832, David Walker issued a call to the black race for revolutionary struggle and a black nation, made necessary, he averred, by the unrelenting oppression of blacks.

This division courses throughout the history of black people in the United States. Leaders like Booker T. Washington and his nemesis, W.E.B. Du Bois, despite their differences over means, believed that blacks must work out their destiny in America, struggling in the Western Hemisphere for full citizenship and acceptance. That current in black thought produced many prominent leaders. Dr. Du Bois in 1905 created an integrated organization that evolved into the NAACP by 1910 and that pressured the courts against discriminatory legislation and practice. In 1911, the National Urban League was formed in New York City to address the economic and social needs of black immigrants arriving from the South. These organizations, one concerned with legal and political rights, the other absorbed by economic and educational realities, became the strong pillars of the struggle to "integrate" millions of black people into American society.

Dr. Delaney also had his adherents. In the 1920s, during a

period of race riots and Ku Klux Klan militance, the Back to Africa movement burst on the scene. The Jamaican Marcus M. Garvey derided any attempt at coexistence. White racism was so pervasive and worldwide, Garvey argued, that the only hope for blacks was a return to the continent of their origin. "Africa for the Africans," was his call. He appealed to racial and national pride for a strong and independent black homeland. This bold cry struck a responsive chord with great numbers of American blacks and the Garvey movement grew phenomenally with two million, he claimed in 1919, enlisted for the Universal Negro Improvement Association. Later, Garvey contended that as high as six million people were involved in as many as nine hundred branches.

Virtually every trend and fluctuation in the modern civil rights movement had its roots in the struggle of generations of black leadership, slowly gathering consciousness and confidence for over a century. In 1942, a call for a march on Washington presaged the time twenty-one years later when one quarter of a million people would march on the nation's capital.

Even the Supreme Court's momentous five landmark decisions in 1954, customarily referred to as *Brown* v. *the Board of Education of Topeka,* ordering the desegregation of public schools, had their roots in the past. Washington, D.C.'s, Howard University Law School, a leading school of constitutional law, had since the 1930s focused on aggressive interpretation of the Constitution. Major black figures like Justice Thurgood Marshall and Charles Hamilton Houston, former dean of the law school, had for over twenty years carefully initiated cases in the courts, culminating in the suits—utilizing research by sociologist Kenneth Clark—that yielded the Supreme Court's rulings.

Until 1928, members of the black community who were able to vote had largely voted Republican because it was the party of Lincoln. It was Franklin D. Roosevelt's election in 1932 that shifted most of their votes into the Democratic column. President Harry S. Truman, the first American president since Lincoln to have a policy on civil rights, in 1948 signed an executive order desegregating the armed forces that had a significant effect on black service personnel and their families. Something else occurred. Blacks serving in the military in World War II and the Korean War, especially those who went overseas, and particularly those who served in Europe, experienced being treated like any other American soldiers by people of other nationalities.

Yet the impulse to separate nationhood has persisted throughout modern black history. It is a drift given logic and strength by white intransigence and institutionalized racism. During the height of the 1960s civil rights unrest, it was most cogently represented by the Nation of Islam and the charismatic minister El Haji Malcolm X.

The movement of which I was a part would thus, sooner or later, with a historic inevitability of which I was utterly unaware, become enmeshed in this conflicting and divergent tendency.

Many undocumented cases of personal resistance to the laws of segregation took place during the 1940s and 1950s. At some time a collective point of saturation would be reached. This did not occur, however, until the response that greeted an event that took place on Thursday, December 1, 1955, in Montgomery, Alabama. On that day, a tailor's assistant named Rosa Parks decided she was too tired to stand all the way home as she had been ordered to do by the bus driver to free a seat for a white male passenger. The black users of the Alabama capital's public-transportation system, about 70 percent of its riders, were forced to pay at the front of the bus and then step back out into the street and reboard through the rear door. Even if the first four rows reserved for whites only were empty and the unreserved section for blacks filled, blacks had to stand. Mrs. Parks's refusal to act in accord with the laws was iconoclastic; however, it was not, as many people think, totally spontaneous. She had previously attended Highlander Folk School, the training institute for union organizers in Monteagle, Tennessee, that had for years provided opportunities for interracial dialogue in a rigidly segregated South. There she met director Myles Horton and Septima P. Clark.

Mrs. Parks had also worked with E. D. Nixon, a regional official of the Brotherhood of Sleeping Car Porters and a leader of the state and Montgomery NAACP, as the secretary of the local organization, and knew that he had been looking for a test case. Several individual violations of the laws of segregation had occurred in Montgomery prior to Rosa Parks's action, but she was the first to be booked for an offense against the segregation statutes. Her step sparked the first overt community mobilization of American blacks and involved fifty thousand people; however, had there not been an E. D. Nixon, she might simply have served time in jail and her action might have gone unrecorded.

Mr. Nixon, who was described by Roy Wilkins as "straight as a ramrod and brave as a squad of Marines," is an important figure. He is significant not merely for his specific contributions to the Montgomery bus boycott and therefore the modern civil rights movement, but because of the manner in which his entire adult life was representative of a black tradition of resistance that is not widely enough recognized.

In the United States, we quite justly make much of our freedoms. We celebrate the Constitution that defined and codified these freedoms, and pay heed to the American tradition of honorable dissent that extended, deepened, and secured these freedoms in social practice. When this tradition—one sometimes honored more in the breach than in observance—is mentioned, the roll call is usually white and includes names like Henry David Thoreau, William Lloyd Garrison, Susan B. Anthony, Eugene Debs, Norman Thomas, and A. J. Muste. For racial balance, the list is leavened with the occasional Frederick Douglass, Harriet Tubman, or Martin Luther King, Jr.

There is another tradition, uncelebrated and obscure, one of black southern grass-roots protest and resistance that is no less important and that runs from Nat Turner and the nameless slave preachers and exhorters up through the Amzie Moores, Fannie Lou Hamers, and E. D. Nixons that you have met in these pages. These are southern black people—usually of humble origin and little formal education—born into the politically and socially most oppressive and psychologically debilitating circumstances, reinforced by the constant threat and infliction of lawless violence, to which this country has ever subjected any group of its citizens. Yet these "simple" people demonstrated the moral courage, wisdom, and resourcefulness to organize and inspire resistance. They also had the faith, the grandness of spirit, and the warm humanity to avoid the bigotry and hatred against which they struggled and by which they were oppressed. Their courage, valor, and forbearance, and the legacy they have left us, place them solidly among the genuine aristocracy of the American dream.

Mr. Nixon was an exemplar of this tradition. Born at the turn of the century into the terror and isolation of post-Reconstruction Alabama, he had no more than twelve months of formal education, so he set about educating himself. As a young man, he heard a speech by the dynamic black labor leader A. Philip Randolph,

which, in his words, "changed my life." He had never, he recalled, heard a black man speak so eloquently, so analytically, so
persuasively, and so fearlessly of the causes of his condition and
how they might be changed. The young Edgar Daniel Nixon,
who was a muscular six foot three inches, dark-skinned, with intense eyes and the gruff gravelly voice and grammar of a Delta
blues singer, determined to devote his life to fighting segregation.
"I decided then and there that I'd give a lick to old Jim Crow
every chance I got," Mr. Nixon remembered.

As a sleeping-car porter during the 1930s and 1940s, he was
part of the small group of black men who had the opportunity to
travel outside the isolated, race-obsessed caste system of Dixie.
Sleeping-car porters were able to see that segregation was neither
universal nor inevitable. Mr. Nixon recalled that the porters
would systematically collect bundles of newspapers and magazines, black as well as white publications and anything that could
enlighten their solitary southern kinfolk, and would tie them up
with string and throw them out to the remote black crossroads,
settlements, and towns through which the trains would pass.

Back home in Montgomery, such was his reputation for militance that he was elected to many terms as an officer of the
NAACP. It was during one of his periods as president that Rosa
Parks was arrested. Mr. Nixon had found his chance. After bailing
her out of jail, he remembered, he went home, took out a map of
Montgomery, a set square, and a compass, and sat down at his
dining table.

"I calculated," he said, "that there was no place in Montgomery that a person couldn't walk to work from if they really wanted
to." Next, Mr. Nixon made a list of the twenty or so leading
black ministers in town and began systematically to telephone them.
The one at the top of the list did not answer so he called the
others. Having worked his way down through the names, he went
back to the first number, that of the eloquent, well-educated new
minister who had recently come to the pulpit of the Dexter Avenue Baptist Church. When he explained his idea, the minister
was quite interested and would indeed attend the meeting. "Mighty
glad to hear that, Reveren' King," said Mr. Nixon, " 'cause I
done already told the others that the meeting be at your church."

During one of several meetings, Mr. Nixon, not being a
preacher, was sitting in the balcony listening to the deliberations

of the clergymen. As they discussed his idea, many expressed grave doubts and a caution that seemed to him to approach timidity. He thought he saw his opportunity slipping away and felt it necessary to intervene with some fervor.

"I figured," he recollected, "that I had to do something. Besides, I was a little hot. Guess I spoke kind of rough to them. Told them they was not acting like men but like scared little boys as if they was scared of the white folks." One minister responded with equal heat. The Reverend Martin Luther King, Jr., forcefully spoke up that he certainly was no one's boy nor was he scared. "Mighty glad to hear that, Reveren', 'cause now I'm nominating *you* to be president of the Montgomery Improvement Association." The rest is of course history.

Mr. Nixon, incidentally, was also politically smart enough to "forget" to telephone in a report of these meetings to the NAACP national office in New York City until the boycott was a *fait accompli*. He explained that he just wasn't sure if their emphasis on litigation and the courts could embrace the direct community action he envisioned and figured it would be easier to explain afterward than to get permission before.

Mr. Nixon was one of the progenitors of the Montgomery bus boycott and one of the architects of a distinguished American career of protest, that of Martin Luther King, Jr. By his life of perseverence, he was one of the important heroes in the American struggle to realize its dream of freedom and democracy.

With the cooperation of the city's eight black taxi companies who formed themselves into a jitney service offering rides at the bus fare of ten cents, and with their strength of numbers, the black community was able to sustain the boycott economically. The case went to court and eventually reached the Supreme Court, which ruled against the city and in favor of the boycott. Out of that major struggle, the young minister who had accepted an invitation to serve the Dexter Avenue Baptist Church in Montgomery, with the understanding that he would also be working to finish writing his doctoral dissertation, became its symbolic personage, and the Southern Christian Leadership Conference (SCLC) was born.

The Montgomery bus boycott had another effect. It signaled earlier black leaders of all political viewpoints—and whites who had been active in various progressive movements in what was

once a political Left in the United States—that there was again a
vehicle for their hopes for a more just society. The brilliant Bayard Rustin, for example, a black socialist, who was a conscientious objector in World War II and spent twenty-eight months in
jail during the war, had in the 1920s been a disciple of A. Philip
Randolph. Bayard came to Montgomery to consult on the organizational techniques of nonviolence and decided as a result to resign from his responsibilities at the War Registers League to work
for Dr. King. Another such figure was Stanley Levinson, a former
supporter of the Communist party. He, too, came to help the new
leadership conference, urging it not to make the same mistakes
that he and others had made, and eventually he became one of
Dr. King's closest confidants.

It was an era when change was sweeping the nonwhite world.
A few months before Rosa Parks refused to give up her seat,
twenty-nine nations of the Third World, representing 1.3 billion
people, gathered in Bandung, Indonesia, in April 1955. This conference condemned colonialism in all forms and amounted to a
rejection of the formal alliances of the Western nations. It created
for the first time a unified force in the developing world—in effect, a global association of nonwhite people—and launched the
nonaligned movement. It also lifted the Algerian struggle from a
conflict of the Maghreb to an international cause. Whether Rosa
Parks and E. D. Nixon personally took heart from the Bandung
conference I do not know, but it would be hard to argue that
there was absolutely no connection. The year after the bus boycott began, in 1957, Ghana secured its independence, and, in 1958,
Guinea's head of state Sekou Toure urged his West African country to vote against continued French control and it did.

The parameters of nonviolence for the civil rights movement
of the 1960s were established by the Montgomery bus boycott in
1955 and 1956. To the extent that there is a moment in time in
which these boundaries for action were drawn, it would coincide
with the instant when the young Montgomery pastor would become recognized as a national leader.

There are, even in the most intricately organized movements—which the American human-rights struggle never was—
events that cannot be planned and episodes that could not have
been anticipated or stage-managed. These occasions emerge sud-

denly from the stream of history like a shining rock from the foaming surface of a rushing river. They result from the confluence of personalities, events, and powerful opposing currents at a specific place and time. In the seconds and circumstances of coming together, the lives of people, the course of movements, and the destinies of nations are changed.

Such a moment came when the Montgomery bus boycott was less than two months old, and I shall tell the story as it has been passed through the oral tradition among my friends in SNCC. Against all predictions and despite the political, legal, and economic maneuvers of the white establishment, the black community in Montgomery had pulled together and stood firm. Their young leader had advanced his philosophical and spiritual position of nonviolence, the redemptive power of love, forgiveness, and persistence. The struggle had been peaceful despite provocation and occasional violent retaliation against the boycott, yet the city remained unyielding. Everything was at an impasse and a stalemate. Perhaps the boycott would now falter and its spirit dissipate.

The national news media had begun to pay a certain amount of bemused attention to the Alabama capital—maybe something more significant than anticipated was happening there. Perhaps it bore watching. Reporters and television crews were present that Sunday night late in January 1956 when a mass meeting was called for one of the Montgomery black churches. The rally had hardly begun when word reached the gathering that the home of the Reverend Dr. Martin Luther King, Jr., had been bombed. Members of his family were thought to be inside the wreckage.

When the young minister reached his house, followed by people streaming from the church and the television crews, he was reunited with his shocked but unharmed family. He found that a crowd of black folk had already gathered there. Some of them were armed with broken bottles carried in their hands, but most of them brandished firearms and were exceedingly angry. To some observers it seemed that the long-expected, long-dreaded race war was at hand. As many had predicted, the nonviolent movement had led to this final provocation. The mood of the group was bitter and resentful, and for revenge in kind and without mercy. That was the moment.

What followed took place in the full glare of television klieg lights. The next day, the nation and the international news circuits were made witness to an event of moral greatness—a spontaneous, heartfelt, and natural act of grace and magnanimity of spirit. A little-known Baptist clergyman—a black man and grandson of slaves—stood in the iron Alabama darkness, on the porch of his bombed-out home, looked into the vengeful eyes of his much-provoked kindred, and spoke to them of forgiveness, of restraint, of the redemptive power of righteousness, and of love: "My brothers and sisters, we must not allow ourselves to do as they do, to hate as they hate."

Such was the power of his sincerity and his evident faith in the path he had chosen that the people put aside their anger and went home and laid down their weapons. The country saw and marveled. It was, if not Martin Luther King's greatest speech, his finest hour, and the memory was imprinted in the minds of many Americans.

Over the next four years, prompted by the success of the Montgomery bus boycott, and affected by the sweeping anticolonialism reverberating throughout the Southern Hemisphere, students in black southern colleges and universities—usually in complete isolation from each other, and in small groups of twos and threes and fours—began to consider what steps they should take.

On February 1, 1960, the four freshmen attending North Carolina Agricultural and Technical State University in Greensboro, after a "bull session" discussion among themselves, reached their decision. Joseph McNeil and Ezell Blair, who were roommates, and their friends Franklin McCain and David Richmond, decided that they would sit down at a segregated lunch counter. They would ask to be served and would just sit and sit and sit.

Disparate groups of students had been invisibly and without coordination preparing for individualized action. There had been isolated protests. But now, following the action of the North Carolina A & T students, in spontaneous combustion, thousands of students moved into action based on a pure and simple belief that the laws of segregation were morally wrong. The United States had a young President in John Fitzgerald Kennedy, and the first generation of blacks born since the start of World War II was starting to flex its muscles.

The sit-ins stunned the established black organizations, including the newest addition, the Southern Christian Leadership Conference, which had emerged from the Montgomery unrest. The NAACP, with its large membership, had litigation pending on the dockets of courts throughout the region, but no specific action was planned. CORE had come into being in 1942 and had some action targets but it was essentially a northern organization. SCLC was concentrating on developing networks through the black churches of the South, but nothing similar to the Montgomery bus boycott had even been considered.

When the four freshmen made their move, very little was visibly occurring. In the months prior to February 1960 and the Greensboro initiative, Atlanta's two daily newspapers, *The Constitution* and *The Journal,* were reporting only occasional news stories pertaining to desegregation efforts. In the preceding month of October, for example, six headlines related to desegregation. After the sit-ins began, the change was dramatic; the two newspapers reported one volley of action after another. By February 17, front-page headlines in the final editions of *The Constitution* and *The Journal* read:

NEGROES PLAN SCHOOL PUSH THIS MONTH

LUNCH COUNTER SITDOWN ERUPTS IN RACIAL MELEE
[PORTSMOUTH, VIRGINIA]

RUSSELL LOSES BID TO DELAY DEBATE ON RIGHTS 61:28

CHANGE LAWS OR CLOSE SCHOOLS, SIBLEY WARNS

OLD SOUTH STANDS ALONE

RIGHTS FORCES SHIFT ATTACK

The Greensboro sit-ins burst like the proverbial cannonball across the bow of the decade of the 1960s. When SNCC was formed as a loose confederation of local student movements in October of that first year of the decade, six months after the April conference that Ella Baker convened at Shaw University, only one of the four A & T students, Ezell Blair, attended the meeting and he did not seek a leadership position. By the end of that year, seventy thousand students had joined sit-ins protesting segregated facilities in one hundred cities throughout the South. Starting out as a small and amorphous mechanism in contact with this dispersed student

activism across the region, SNCC quickly became the most militant of the civil rights organizations.

Who were the seventy thousand students? Mostly black, although joined by some whites like the handful of women who
sat-in from Randolph-Macon Woman's College in Lynchburg,
Virginia, they were young people who dared to put their futures
on the line. The children of veterans of World War II, they were
upwardly mobile, many of them striving to escape the rural poverty and limited options of the Black Belt, and they were frequently
the first of their families to attend college; their long-suffering
parents had often sacrificed everything to give them a university
education. Sitting-in and becoming politically active meant they
might be arrested, to say nothing of being subjected to brutality.
An arrest record, given the conservatism of southern black colleges, would jeopardize or destroy their ability to finish college. I
remember John Lewis telling me that his parents thought the worst
thing that could possibly happen to him was if he were to go to
jail; yet, to John and thousands of other students, jail rapidly became a way of life after February 1960, whether it was for a weekend, a week, or for months.

While the anticolonial movements on the rest of the planet
set the basic framework for the American civil rights movement,
the period of McCarthyism in the United States in the 1950s had
sharpened the focus of Americans, who, as a result, realized that
there could be serious threats to constitutional guarantees. Mc-
Carthyism was an issue about which I was greatly concerned. My
father had often discussed with my brothers and me at the dinner
table the vulgar excesses of Senator Joseph McCarthy when he
attacked some of the Protestant clergy, especially Bishop G.
Bromley Oxnam of the Methodist Church. McCarthy was echoed
in the House of Representatives, when a member vilified Oxnam
saying, "The bishop serves God on Sunday and the communist
front the balance of the week." An exchange often talked about
in my family was as follows: Stanley High, a maverick Protestant,
wrote an article for *Reader's Digest*, in February 1950, called
"Methodism's Pink Fringe" in which he smeared progressive elements of the Methodist Church. Bishop Oxnam contacted the
magazine and asked to be allowed to publish a statement that
reflected the denomination's correct position. *Reader's Digest* flatly
refused. My mother still writes back to *Reader's Digest* whenever

she receives a subscription solicitation, declaring that she will never subscribe because it carried an unfair attack on the Methodist Church. Discussions of McCarthyism and the dangers it posed to ministers, their families, and, in an ultimate sense, to everyone, were frequent within our family. We obtained a television set for the first time to be able to watch the hearings of McCarthy's committee.

My first public act of conscience was to lead a demonstration protesting renewed action of the House Un-American Activities Committee (HUAC), at Ohio Wesleyan University, on the main street of the drowsy town of Delaware, Ohio, in 1960. McCarthy had been thoroughly discredited by thirty-six days of Congressional hearings against Army officers and civilian officials in 1954 and died in 1957 but HUAC was again stirring, seeking to expose communists. (It was not finally abolished until January 1975, its ignominious name by then changed to the House Internal Security Committee.) It must have come as a great shock to the lumbering dean of women that anyone attending this fine school with its tradition of decorum would want to condemn HUAC, much less support the southern student sit-ins. University administrators at that time did not expect to see student activism and, unlike the situation with students in Europe then and in the United State today, student activism was still an aberration. Yet, evidence of a possible recurrence of McCarthyism was, I thought, a grim threat to our democratic ideals, and the danger that the Republican senator personified was still alive to me. Benefiting himself from the protections of the First Amendment guaranteeing freedom of speech, he trampled these safeguards for others like swine squashing through the mud of a pigsty, and I thought it could happen again. I screwed up my courage, gathered some other students together, and led a picket line in front of the Student Union building protesting a recent initiative of HUAC.

The rampage of McCarthyism from 1950 to 1954 was useful in at least two ways. It alerted millions of Americans to the jeopardy in which constitutional rights could be placed, and their concern set the stage for active national support of the southern civil rights movement. It also showed what could happen when enough individuals with power, such as business executives, members of Congress, and the nation's military leaders, became embarrassed by the antics of Senator McCarthy and HUAC—they halted the excesses. This awareness arose not long after the 1954 Supreme

Court decision desegregating public education; many Americans thus concluded that visibility for human-rights and civil-liberties issues was possible once more. Eventually, by the time of the passage of the Civil Rights Act of 1964 and the Voting Rights Act of 1965, we would see something similar happen as sufficient numbers of individuals with power began to decide that black people had spilled enough of their own blood.

Perhaps my passionate contempt for HUAC was not typical of most SNCC workers, since McCarthyism did not appear to be closely related to the day-to-day struggles for existence in the black community, although I do recall that Stokely Carmichael had taken part in anti-HUAC demonstrations in high school. A few of our staff had actually grown up with parents who had been communist, had been accused of being communist, or were hounded during the McCarthy era because of their friendships and associations—such as Constancia "Dinky" Romilly, daughter of Jessica Mitford; Dorothy Miller of New York City; and Deborah Amos, a black SNCC worker from Philadelphia. They knew firsthand about the traumas associated with that period. Although for most SNCC staff, 80 percent of whom were black, it might have been remote, the ghost of McCarthyism strengthened the determination of many people across the country to support the civil rights cause—with money, action, and with litigation—because this was a movement to restore and preserve essential constitutional guarantees.

In fact, the civil rights movement was a thoroughly American stirring to reaffirm democracy and make its ideals a reality for a segment of the population that had been excluded. The nineteenth-century French political writer and observer of the American scene, Alexis de Tocqueville, looked at the United States as an outsider. One of his insights was that individualism was a potential threat to the nation's strength. He identified three entities preventing the American character from drifting into narcissistic individualism: the family, religious traditions, and voluntary associations, especially those at the local level that addressed political concerns. Writing in *Democracy in America,* Tocqueville observed, "The Americans combat the effects of individualism by free institutions. . . . Americans of all ages, all conditions, and all dispositions, constantly form associations."

The sit-ins were squarely within the voluntary tradition that

Tocqueville identified. They were a distinctively American response to a dilemma: If you've got a problem, get a group together, and take action. The sit-in movement and its most important outgrowth, SNCC, represented a thoroughly American problem-solving and organizing phenomenon.

Although not convinced that the country's legal system and independent judiciary could be made to work in the interest of justice, we nonetheless hoped and believed that we could force it to start dispensing justice for blacks. Some outstanding southern judges sitting on the federal bench in the South had made a number of admirable decisions, for example, Frank M. Johnson, Jr., in Alabama; J. Waties Waring in South Carolina; and J. Skelly Wright in Louisiana.

In retrospect, however, I criticize myself for being naïve and provincial in failing to recognize at the time exactly how important the American system of law and the independent judiciary would be to many of the movement's successes. These were two of the strongest positive forces that would come into play for us. But I was young and impatient. Five years for a piece of litigation to move through the courts seemed inexorably slow. Life appeared to stretch on forever. Also, like most SNCC workers, I lacked perspective. Recognition of the staunch underlying importance of American rule by law had to wait years until I had traveled in much of the world where legal institutions afford little or no certainty of justice and where there are weak or captive judicial systems.

The movement and the many outstanding lawyers who were part of it such as C. B. King, Frank Hollowell, and Howard Moore brought the egregious discrimination against blacks to the attention of the nation and produced a galaxy of cases to be litigated through the courts. Although many areas remain in which there is still unconstitutional discrimination, the soundness of the fundamental structure of law has hastened the demise of explicit segregation. Subtler mutations of racism still await resolution, and litigation may not be so surgically effective against less discernible forms of discrimination.

The civil rights conflict was a startling and unassailable demand to make the rhetoric of the Constitution real for those with dark skin. One of the significant reasons the American civil rights unrest remained a struggle for reform and never became a revolution was that the nation's powerful system of law and the judiciary began to work in our favor and, one after another, legal barriers started to fall.

SNCC's distinctively idealistic belief that fortitude, determined action, and fearlessness would result in momentous social change stemmed to a great degree from the Protestant upbringings of most of its workers. Even if one were in rebellion against a church that provided insufficient witness or failed to challenge the status quo, still at work was the fundamental influence of the Christian tradition. Translated into political action, John Wesley's belief that through grace and redemption each person can be saved reinforced our belief that the good in every human being could be appealed to, fundamental change could correct the immorality of racial segregation, and new political structures could be created. This was not new. What may have been novel was the sense of timing influenced by the sweep of anticolonialism—we wanted it now and not in the hereafter; we were not willing to wait for "the kingdom to come." Even if each SNCC field secretary did not use the term *redemption* in everyday conversation (but in the earliest days of the group I venture to say everyone did), the concept abounded in the biblical ethos of the southland, black and white, and was part of the climate in which the movement was working.

Strictly speaking, the civil rights struggle was not a religious phenomenon. Yet individual religious leaders of all creeds were among the first to come to its assistance and assert that the movement was raising a critical moral choice before the nation. Although organized Catholicism and Judaism did not take stands in the same unified and official denominational sense that most of the large Protestant denominations did—partly for structural reasons and partly because there was less influence from what was in Protestantism called the social gospel—many brave priests and rabbis joined their Protestant colleagues in putting themselves personally on the line, and individual Catholic churches and synagogues gave some support.

I have been asked why Judaism was not more of a force in the struggle and I will offer some observations, for it is true that, despite its traditional emphasis on social justice, Judaism remained in the background. Perhaps in part because its congregations were fighting their own battles against discrimination, its support of the civil rights movement was manifested by individual action. Jews were themselves a minority group. Fellow Jews in the South were not as discriminated against as were blacks. Most American Jews, or their parents or grandparents, were relatively recent arrivals in the United States, often having come between the time of the Civil War and World War I. Their background in Europe had been that of a repressed minority. Demonstrating in a Russian or Czech ghetto for their rights would have been unthinkable. Few connections compelled those of Jewish extraction or from northern synagogues to go South to take part in a movement so entrenched in the moral suasion and spiritual force of a black Christian culture closely linked to resistance. The national Protestant denominations, on the other hand, had black constituencies in the South and, along with the Quakers, their missionaries had worked to establish a high proportion of the southern black colleges and universities; some of them were still helping to fund these institutions of higher learning. Awareness of the problems suffered by black congregations in the region was thus more functional.

The number of Jews or individuals of Jewish extraction on SNCC staff was perhaps 5 percent, counting Chuck McDew's conversion. This meant a fluctuating figure of up to one quarter of the white SNCC workers, a percentage showing a concern for justice much higher than their presence in the overall population. No one in SNCC thought of Jews as a separate group, however; they were simply considered white. Dr. King and SCLC made a point of enlisting rabbis and priests as well as ministers in direct-action campaigns. In Mississippi, we had clerical involvement, particularly through the National Council of Churches which was a vital source of support, but this pattern was in general less applicable for SNCC because religious leaders were not our constituency and our long-term organizing was less likely to lend itself to symbolic presence. On the other hand, in SNCC we had more Jews on our staff than did SCLC, although not, I should think, as many as CORE, which was urban- and northern-based.

SNCC was more secular than SCLC, but even within our group theological terminology was commonplace and the influence of specifically Protestant thinking was pervasive, again reflecting the cultural milieu of the South, black and white. I

remember some workers talking frankly of the undertaking as a
"Christian movement." We openly thought of ourselves as working toward "reconciliation" and used the phrase "the beloved
community" as a golden image representing an America that would
one day reject racism. For many, it was the fundamental assumption of the "redemptibility" of America that gave rise to our confidence that the appeal of nonviolence would be successful. Anyone
who put himself or herself on the line, subjected to humiliation,
brutality, arrests, beatings, or even torture, *had* to believe that
America as a nation could experience shame and remorse and would
repeal its history of oppression.

When I was studying at Union Theological Seminary in New
York, immediately before moving to Atlanta, in a seminar led by
my philosophy and religion professor Miriam Willey who was on
the faculty at Union that summer, I was introduced to the works
of Dietrich Bonhoeffer. He was a German theologian who had
studied at Union and who publicly denounced Hitler and abandoned the safety of the United States to return to Germany and
work for the "confessing church." He wrote to his adviser, the
ethicist Reinhold Niebuhr, in 1939, "I will have no right to participate in the reconstruction of Christian life after the war if I do
not share the trials of this time with my people." Believing that
being a Christian meant taking sides, Bonhoeffer became actively
involved in the resistance against Hitler and participated in a bomb
plot to kill him. He was arrested on April 5, 1943. In February
1945, he was taken to Buchenwald. While in prison, he wrote
profoundly moving letters explaining his stand that were to have
a great impact on me. He wrote, "We must confront fate . . . as
resolutely as we submit to it at the right time." In the early morning of April 9, 1945, he was hanged by the Nazis. Strangely,
Americans overlook the fact that disproportionately large numbers
of Protestant church leaders and theologians suffered the same
fate as did Jews, political dissidents, homosexuals, Gypsies, and
communists in Nazi Germany. I cannot remember having had a
single doubt about joining the civil rights movement, but if I did
it was resolved after studying Bonhoeffer.

There was one other way in which the Judeo-Christian tradition had an underlying influence on this very American movement. Professor Benjamin Spencer, a man of gentle humor and
my favorite teacher, one day challenged the students in his liter-

ary-criticism seminar. He posed to the group of seven students, all in our senior year, the question, "Isn't it true that before you can write, you must decide first whether or not you believe in original sin?" I did not understand, not normally thinking in terms of original sin. What did he mean? Then I realized that he was asking, Don't you have to decide first whether you believe in the inherent evil or the inherent goodness of human beings before you take any position because this fundamentally influences all other assumptions, values, and beliefs? He didn't care which position one took but he thought one must consciously decide whether one believed human beings were intrinsically evil.

For most of the staff of SNCC, Dr. Spencer's question would have been an easy one. An astonishing number were, like me, the children of ministers. Some were themselves ministers. I think this shared background gave us something in common, white or black; at an early age I, imperceptibly, absorbed the belief that there is good in every human being and that people can change. Although we were a diverse group, the great majority of us working for SNCC shared this prevalent liberal Protestant view, which supported the conclusion that the institutions of society can change.

Ours was not a revolution nor was it pressing for exotic ideals; it was a movement to assure basic rights and to allow blacks to participate in their own governance. The reason it was threatening was race; the fact that it was blacks who were seeking fundamental rights is what activated the machinery of obstruction, the violence, and the charges that it was communist. Our movement was affirming in a naked and tangible way the promise of the Constitution. Not only was this not revolutionary, it was, in a pure sense, conservative.

Indeed, that it was not revolutionary was troubling to some. Jane Stembridge wrote me from Greenwood, Mississippi, in November 1963, saying, "One thing bothers me—the movement is reformistic. It is not revolutionary."

Yet, given the burden of institutionalized racism and its penetration into nearly all aspects of American life, simply to implement the founding principles of the republic would have a revolutionary effect. So entrenched was the hypocrisy of racism that when the movement called for affirmation of basic democratic rights and making the truths and platitudes of the Constitution a reality for black people, it terrified many white Americans.

* * *

To the extent that there was an ideological nucleus or nerve center for SNCC in the early years, when a vision of an integrated society achieved through nonviolence still permeated our thinking, it was found in a group of student leaders from Nashville. Embodying SNCC's commitment to direct nonviolent confrontation with segregation was a cadre of highly motivated and informed students. Primarily from Fisk University, they included Diane Nash, John Lewis, Marion Barry, and Bernard Lafayette. This group met in workshops every other Tuesday night during 1958 and 1959, led by divinity student James M. Lawson, Jr., the black doctoral candidate at mostly white Vanderbilt University who was expelled because of his advocacy of nonviolence.

The students studied Mohandas Gandhi's two major doctrines: nonviolent resistance and civil disobedience. They traced the origin of nonviolence to the doctrine of *ahimsa,* the Hindu concept of nonviolent passive resistance. They learned that Gandhi had read Henry David Thoreau's essay "On Civil Disobedience," while he was in jail in South Africa in 1906 for refusing to carry a special fingerprinted identity card; they found that his thinking was deeply affected by this essay, which protested the United States government's condoning of slavery and its waging of an unjust war on Mexico. They also learned of the influence of Christianity on Gandhi that started his meditating on nonviolence—specifically the impact of the passage in the New Testament (Matthew 5:38–42) in which Christ admonishes his disciples to turn the other cheek to their aggressors. They read that Gandhi had considered becoming Christian until he was turned away from the door of a Dutch Reformed church in South Africa because he was "colored." The group's analysis also covered the example of Christ and the lessons of the Montgomery bus boycott of 1955 and 1956, and included writings from the boycott by Martin Luther King, Jr.

Although they did not know about each other's deliberations until later, the preparations of the Nashville student leaders antedated those of the four students in Greensboro by two years. When the North Carolina sit-ins started, the Nashville students had already held some "test sit-ins" at Nashville department stores, although they had not used that term, and they immediately followed the example of the Greensboro activists with sit-ins in Nashville.

"Each member of our movement must work diligently to understand the depths of nonviolence," the first issue of *The Student Voice*, SNCC's regular newspaper, admonished in June 1960. It carried a statement of purpose that was written by Jim Lawson:

> We affirm the philosophical or religious ideal of nonviolence as the foundation of our purpose, the presupposition of our faith, and the manner of our action. Nonviolence as it grows from the Judeo-Christian traditions seeks a social order of justice permeated by love. . . .
>
> Through nonviolence, courage displaces fear; love transforms hate. Acceptance dissipates prejudice; hope ends despair. Peace dominates war; faith reconciles doubt. Mutual regard cancels animosity. Justice for all overthrows injustice. The redemptive community supersedes systems or gross social immorality.
>
> Love is the central motif of nonviolence. Love is the force by which God binds man to himself and man to man. Such love goes to the extreme; it remains loving and forgiving even in the midst of hostility. It matches the capacity of evil to inflict suffering with an even more enduring capacity to absorb evil, all the while persisting in love.
>
> By appealing to conscience and standing on the moral nature of human existence, nonviolence nurtures the atmosphere in which reconciliation and justice become actual possibilities.

Although in its emphasis on love and reconciliation the student movement showed its basic reliance on Christianity, the derivation of the techniques of nonviolent resistance and civil disobedience from Gandhi also reflected the influence of anticolonialism.

Nonviolence required careful tactical preparation. "Roll up in a ball! Protect your vital organs!" How can I forget those training sessions led by Cordell Reagon and Matthew Jones and other meetings steered by James Bevel of SCLC. "Curl up! Protect your head and your neck with your hands," Cordell barked at us, trying to prepare us for a hostile encounter. We were taught to roll into the fetal position if attacked, so as to protect our abdomens, or to kneel, arching over to protect our skulls and faces, but not to hit back, not to run, and to accept whatever happened. This meant a prepared state of mind as well as physical training.

Cordell and Matthew seemed to have no doubts. They stated bluntly that whoever was watching would be moved by the sight of a polite group nonviolently protesting a moral wrong but not attempting to defend themselves against violent attack, and that this could lead to a change of heart. It often did.

In 1960, rules were developed by John Lewis and other Nashville students for those who were sitting-in, based on a similar approach that had been used in Montgomery: "Do show yourself friendly at the counter at all times. Do sit straight and always face the counter. Don't strike back, or curse back if attacked. Don't laugh out. Don't hold conversations." The better instincts of adversaries and the basic humanity of onlookers were to be touched by this polite demonstration of morality in a way no words could express.

The Nashville group was disciplined but this did not mean that the sit-ins lacked humor. Perhaps they partially expressed the innocence of a more expansionist period when Americans were less aware of the finite nature of resources and before the cynicism of the era of the war in Vietnam suffused our national consciousness. Perhaps they reflected the optimism of the black community whose very survival has always required hope. Jokes were frequent. A waitress approached a group of young people who were sitting-in. "I'm sorry, but we don't serve Negroes here," she told them. "That's all right," came the reply. "We don't eat them either."

The students who sat-in and formed SNCC's base did so not out of ideology but from a moral insistence that there was a higher law, the "natural law," Howard Zinn had emphasized, under which racial segregation of public facilities was wrong and should be challenged. In violating existing law by civil disobedience, we would be rising to a higher morality. "Demonstrations" were not solely protests against something—they actually demonstrated or showed the immorality of existing law.

Eventually a major debate would develop within SNCC over the question of whether nonviolence should be merely a tactic, although most of the Nashville group continued to regard nonviolence as a total philosophy, "a way of life." This debate was never resolved in SNCC, and, as the organization suffered a series of disappointments beginning in 1964, by the following year, adherence to nonviolence largely was tactical.

It would be a grave error for anyone to examine the life of the Reverend Dr. Martin Luther King, Jr., and his organization, the Southern Christian Leadership Conference, and not see SNCC in the background. It would be as serious a mistake to view SNCC without seeing it shadowed against SCLC. Yet, when many people think of the civil rights movement, they have in mind only Dr. King and SCLC. The church-based leadership conference was led by ministers who were traditionally the least dependent on white power brokers of all leaders in the politically disenfranchised black communities.

SNCC was more controversial—in its tactics, its rhetoric, its concept of leadership, and its disdain for convention. It was also fiercely democratic, extremely idealistic, inventive, and visionary. Writing in *SNCC: The New Abolitionists,* Howard Zinn termed it "the most serious social force in the nation."

Unlike Dr. King's organization and most institutions and organizations of the 1960s, SNCC was racially and sexually integrated. There were a handful of whites involved with the NAACP and SCLC, and a few others served on the staff of CORE. Of all these organizations, SNCC had the most significant representation of women. Ella Baker's parting from SCLC was, without question, because Dr. King was uncomfortable with such a strong woman. Indeed, although never more than 20 percent white, SNCC had more whites and women than all the other organizations combined.

As SNCC progressed from direct action to voter registration and into political organizing, SCLC remained steady in its attempt to build an activist organization through the southern black churches, later mobilizing coalitions that reached into labor unions and elements of the Democratic party. Although we were acutely aware of subtle differences, in many areas of belief the underlying philosophical assumptions of SCLC and SNCC were actually the same, with variations occurring in strategy and tactics. Casey Hayden once remarked at a staff meeting, "SNCC doesn't really have a philosophy different from SCLC's—we're just younger and madder!"

There was, however, one vital distinction of enduring significance that existed between SNCC, on the one hand, and SCLC and the rest of the civil rights movement, on the other, and it persisted throughout the organization's existence—SNCC's nontraditional view of leadership, which was rooted in the tradition of the southern black grass-roots resistance discussed earlier. This viewpoint also reflected the composition of the organization. SNCC was made up of young people, many of them *very* young people, who were, with few exceptions, not from elite backgrounds.

In late 1963, writing in *SNCC: The New Abolitionists*, Professor Zinn checked the backgrounds of forty-one SNCC workers, approximately one third of the total staff then at work in the Deep South. Thirty-five of them were black and twenty-five came from the Deep South. All the southern blacks left homes where their mothers worked as domestic servants and their fathers were farmers, truck drivers, factory workers, bricklayers, or carpenters. Twenty-nine of the Mississippi staff (about three fourths of the SNCC staff based in that state) were between fifteen and twenty-two years of age while twelve were between twenty-two and twenty-nine. One person each was aged in his or her thirties, forties, or fifties.

What the SNCC staff shared most was a willingness to risk their security; many had not undertaken any formal training, or even selected the fields for their life work; many had not finished college, a matter of indifference in a cadre where action based on belief was all that counted.

SNCC was grounded in the purest vision of democracy that I have ever encountered. A spirit of egalitarianism permeated the organization and, even if every individual did not always speak out, everyone's opinion counted. No one was unimportant. As much as possible, policy decisions were made by consensus.

What caught me up emotionally and intellectually in my first encounter with Jim Forman, Julian Bond, John Lewis, and Bernard Lafayette was SNCC's bold perception of human worth and the feasibility of democracy. No matter how humble someone's circumstances or how far ground down by poverty and racism, in the eyes of SNCC that person was a potential leader. Mahatma Gandhi expressed this principle thus: "There go my people. I must follow them for I am their leader." Leadership to us was a matter of development, something that could not be bestowed, and a process that in and of itself brought forth innate strength. Our role as organizers was to release and accentuate the leadership potential that existed in communities and individuals. Our job was to help others develop their potential and assert themselves, thereby nurturing new leadership.

From its reformist moral vision, seeking nonviolently to break

down the system of segregation, SNCC was determined to produce new leadership for a new order. This would, however, require that black people control the specific political and social
institutions that served them, not merely that they were let in at
the front door; it would also mean the development of indigenous
leadership. Here, SNCC stood in sharp contrast to the more traditional approaches emphasizing a single leader of stature, such as
SCLC's ulitization of Martin Luther King, and earlier the leadership of A. Philip Randolph of the Brotherhood of Sleeping Car
Porters and Roy Wilkins of the NAACP (who was, incidentally, a
Methodist lay preacher).

The other civil rights organizations and, of course, Dr. King
would have protested that they, too, were committed to leadership development. But by virtue of their composition—in SCLC's
case, mostly ministerial, or, as I call it, priestly and patriarchal—
they were not so free as SNCC to define leadership as something
also inherent in women and the uneducated. Fannie Lou Hamer
would never have been projected nationally as a leader by SCLC,
which could not even handle the educated Ella Baker.

Indeed, SNCC's perspective on leadership was in large part
attributable to the philosophy of Miss Baker and her conviction
that "you must let the oppressed themselves define their own
freedom," and was given added definition through her influence
on Bob Moses and his impact on others.

Nonetheless, when Dr. King's assassination removed this giant
of a figure from the scene, it left a vacuum that was never filled.
Aside from an awesome human loss, it also meant that a variety
of groups and individuals lost their ability to pose themselves in
contrast to him, for Dr. King had provided a stable point around
which other polarities could express themselves.

Between them, SNCC and SCLC represented almost the full
spectrum of black life, and both were an undeniable part of the
successes of the civil rights movement. It would be specious to
consider one without the other. SCLC was more establishmentar-
ian and SNCC more indignant, and both were—relative to those
who had been struggling before them—comparatively new organizations that came into being after the Montgomery bus boycott.
Together, they formed an unplanned (and usually quite uncoor-
dinated) pincers movement, the total strength of which can now
be seen to have been critical for the gains that were made.

* * *

The underlying belief that the existing laws of segregation were morally wrong and should be disobeyed under the tenets of civil disobedience led to one other logical conclusion: No one else's theory or another's "ism" was ready-made for our situation. There was no reason for the American movement to look for another ideology. To move beyond parliamentary processes and outrace litigation, to assert the power of popular will and organization, meant that the last thing we wanted was the warmed-over thinking of the German who had written *Das Kapital* in a dusty corner of London's British Museum over a century before. Our own thinking would do.

Opportunists of varying political viewpoints found it convenient to try to discredit this indigenous protest by raising the specter of communism. Looking back through my files and papers, I see that we were forced (more than I remember) to spend time and energy refuting efforts to link our actions to alien infiltration and the "Red menace."

It was a handy method of attack for our opposition, some in the news media, sources in the federal government, and others to label us Marxist in order to undermine us, but in fact there was no role for communism in SNCC. Two good reasons Marxism was not a feasible theoretical framework for us are that, first, we were not educated in it, and, second, we would not have survived had we adopted it.

The northern student protest and action groups, including the Students for a Democratic Society (SDS) and the Northern Student Movement (NSM), were more familiar with the doctrines of socialist revolution and Marxism. Some in SDS and NSM were suspicious of SNCC because it was based on organizing and mobilization rather than on theoretical analysis. The activists of the northern student movement of the 1960s were sophisticated, well educated, and sometimes doctrinaire.

The youth of the civil rights movement, however, despite our audacity, tended to come from church backgrounds. The Reverend Henry Hobbs told my father that Stokely Carmichael had, as a youth, been a member of his church, the Westchester Methodist Church in the Bronx. SNCC workers respected the Church. Furthermore, with few exceptions, the black southerners who made up the majority of SNCC in the early years—before northern black influence came to dominate SNCC's leadership in 1967—were not well educated; they were often the victims of underdeveloped, segregated rural school systems. Their teachers and instructors, having themselves been products of the same severely limited education, would have had little if any exposure to Marxist theory, yet they all came out of the Church. This pattern reached back into the last century, when, according to Frederick A. Norwood in *The Story of American Methodism*, Sojourner Truth, Frederick Douglass, and Harriet Tubman "were either members of or associated with the [AME] Zion Methodists."

We didn't need a foreign ideology. SNCC workers were, before the disillusionments and reversals that began in 1964, proud that ours was an American movement, that we were fighting for constitutional rights. While standing in the Judeo-Christian tradition and resting our case on natural law, we owed no debt to any political theory other than Jeffersonian democracy. In the same way that jazz is an Afro-American gift to the world's music, ours was an American contribution to making democracy real. Some in SNCC were arrogant, but it was the arrogance of youthfulness, part of our energy and momentum. "I would take ideas from the youngest of them," Ella Baker told Joanne Grant.

Despite what our detractors said, we knew barely anything about Marxism. I remember occasional visitors from the Young Socialist League of Ypsilanti, Michigan, and similar organizations calling on us in Atlanta. They received nothing more than the politeness that an occasional foreign press correspondent received. Had you judged us by the smearing and "Red-baiting" done by some reporters and newspapers, this cool reception might have surprised you. We felt little affinity with such callers and many SNCC workers thought these visitors were weird. Ignorance combined with a certain streak of anti-intellectualism also influenced our indifference to Marxist theory in the southern movement.

Several visitors from the North who had studied intensively the Russian Revolution spent some time talking with Juilian Bond and me in our small Atlanta office. They were determined to interpret the civil rights unrest in their terms. I was fascinated because I knew very little about Marxism or Leninism. In fact, my formal education in the cold war period scantily mentioned these political philosophies and, when it did, it was as though they could be touched only with sterile gloves. One could study comparative religion in the 1960s, but only with difficulty could one study comparative political theory.

One wealthy Californian, whose family fortune was derived from mining extractive minerals in southern Africa, began sending subscriptions for socialist literature to the Mississippi field offices during the summer of 1964. I presume this bizarre contribution was supposed to expiate his guilt. SNCC, in its pragmatism, was by then developing libraries in new community centers in twenty towns throughout the state, soliciting donations of essential literature and reference books from our supporters. Basic magazine subscriptions would have been useful. Those of us who knew about the arrival of the strange subscriptions were mystified by such insensitivity. Any sheriff's deputy or law officer wandering through a movement office and finding this material could use it to create tension, harass local civil rights workers, fuel fires in the press, and, by brandishing socialist literature, raise the specter of communism.

It would have been a deadly strategy had we adopted Marxism as the basis of our thinking. In the early years of SNCC, the furthest thing from our minds was to use obscure language describing goals that most Americans feared. Rather, we desperately wanted to communicate and to cause an outpouring of sympathy. For us the issue was not only to prevent police brutality but to obtain police protection for black communities and to get black officers into police forces. The issue for us was not free speech as in the later free speech movement at Berkeley, California, led by one of our 1964 volunteers, Mario Savio, but admission of blacks to good colleges and universities. The issue was not that electoral politics did not work because the "system" was corrupt, but that more black people needed to participate in electoral politics. The issue was not the destruction of capitalism but the creation of opportunities to allow blacks to reap some of its profits. Except where "consent by the governed" would democratically have resulted in the removal of racist white officials, the issue was not overthrowing the ruling class or the government but forcing those in power and in the government to provide protection when black people tried to exercise constitutional rights. Mostly, we wanted "in" for blacks on the benefits enjoyed by the rest of the society.

Although our rhetoric sometimes became a little ruddy with references to blood in the streets, we didn't favor armed struggle nor did we want any more bloodshed than had already occurred. At times, we poetically used the term "revolutionary" in describing ourselves and our goals, but we did so with romantic imprecision and probably because no one in our ranks had seriously studied revolutionary societies where change had required armed struggle. Having now traveled in several countries that achieved their metamorphosis by means of such revolution, I blush to remember how loosely we used that term.

Furthermore, Marxism was not pertinent. It claimed to respond to the brutality of the economics of industrial oppression, but it did not speak to agrarian poverty or to the underdeveloped conditions of the American South. It was not clear on race. Africa was never featured in Karl Marx's analysis of class society.

We were also vaguely aware that the United States had been in opposition to every major revolution after it achieved its own independence in 1776; this is still our unstated policy, even if the conflict means that a resultant democracy would replace a dictatorship or an oligarchy. Had we ever seriously advocated revolution in the framework of Marxism, we would have been squashed like bugs.

The only Marxist thinker I encountered who had serious influence on civil rights workers was W.E.B. Du Bois, and I am not certain that he should be labeled as such. At the age of seventy-five, at the height of McCarthyism, he formally joined the Communist party and announced it to the world as a gesture of defiance against the senator. A pioneering black sociologist, born in Massachusetts in 1868, he was intelligent enough to have been graduated from Harvard University in 1898 during the period when Jim Crow was being firmly entrenched. He repudiated what he considered the appeasement of Booker T. Washington who was urging the pursuit of manual skills and avoidance of conflict over segregation as shifting "the Negro problem to the Negro's shoulders . . . when in fact the burden belongs to the nation." He believed that blacks should not ask for that to which they were entitled but should affirm and seize every right that others enjoyed. He founded the NAACP and edited its organ, *Crisis*, a center of intellectual thought in the black community for almost fifty years.

In 1919, far ahead of his time, Du Bois convened the first of several Pan-African conferences during a period when only Ethiopia and Liberia, of the entire African continent, were not under colonial rule. He anticipated SNCC's later advocacy of "Black Power" by arguing for "Negro self-sufficiency," and was an early articulator of the unique character of black culture and identity as it had evolved through the struggle and suffering of generations of Afro-Americans. He saw that the combination of historical experience and cultural characteristics brought from Africa had combined to produce in North America a new people. In 1903 in *The Souls of Black Folk* he wrote, "To attain his place in the world, he must be himself, and not another." Again anticipating SNCC, he affirmed the value of black initiative in creating autonomous institutions so the community could assert its priorities and values, and work for its own aspirations striving together as " 'people of color,' not as 'Negroes.' "

What I recall most from the SNCC discussions of Du Bois was his aching and heavyhearted articulation of a distinct identity of blacks.

> We the darker ones come even now not altogether empty-handed: there are today no truer exponents of the pure human spirit of the Declaration of Independence than the American Negroes; there is no true American music but the wild sweet melodies of the Negro slave; the American fairy tales and folklore are Indian and African; and, all in all, we black men seem the sole oasis of simple faith and reverence in a dusty desert of dollars and smartness.

Du Bois marked a point in the history of black thinking from which there was no turning back, and he is still considered the preeminent personality of the twentieth century to many who were active in the civil rights movement. What made him of interest to SNCC was partly the human tragedy of this internationally renowned scholar who lived his ninety-five years without being accepted as one of the great American thinkers of this century because he was black and had what some would consider a Marxist orientation, and partly his intellectually aggressive philosophy that sharpened and defined the black identity. He died the day before the march on Washington in 1963, self-exiled in Africa.

As in the case of Marxism, another philosophy was also alien in the early years of SNCC—that of the Black Muslims. The Black

Muslims represented a northern, urban-based approach with none of SNCC's early egalitarianism or idealism. Until midway through the decade, we reacted to the occasional black separatist in the same way that we reacted to the strange irrelevancy of visitors enamored of the Russian Revolution. Some SNCC workers were intrigued to read or hear of Malcolm X and the Black Muslims. But most SNCC workers were disdainful. We knew better than anyone else that the Black Muslims were not to be found in the dangerous Black Belt counties where we worked. Later the Black Muslims came south in small numbers, evangelizing on the by-ways and circuits opened by the civil rights movement. By 1966, however, this would change and the rhetoric of Malcolm X would appeal strongly to some of the SNCC staff, especially blacks from the North, many of whom had come into the movement comparatively late.

The women of SNCC would have been disgusted with the secondary role that the Black Muslims with their patriarchal hegemony imposed upon women, restricting them to the family.

On July 1, 1964, I issued to the news media a statement by John Lewis that shows how most SNCC workers felt at the time:

> I understand a New York newspaper has linked me today through inference with a new movement which espouses black nationalism and armed self-defense. The group, I understand, is called The Organization of Afro-American Unity and is headed by Malcolm X. I am completely surprised that a responsible newspaper would not contact me to confirm my membership in such a group, knowing the historical position of the Student Nonviolent Coordinating Committee and my often-stated personal position with regard to nonviolence.
>
> I have no connection with this group. I would like to reaffirm my philosophical adherence to nonviolence both as a means of protest and as a way of life. SNCC believes today, as it has since its formation in 1960, in achieving an interracial democracy through peaceful protest.

On the other hand, any balanced account must also note that the Black Muslims made it easier for the strivings of the civil rights movement to be accepted, and Martin Luther King, Jr., in particular benefited by being seen as the preferable alternative to

Malcolm X. If we have to choose between two evils, the nation seemed to say, Martin Luther King is the lesser of the two and the goals of the nonviolent movement are easier to swallow than are those of the Black Muslims.

Neither communists nor the Black Muslims seemed willing to put themselves on the line in the Deep South. Indeed, being called a communist seemed faintly amusing. The more sophisticated among us knew that the Communist party had been rendered ineffective well before we came onto the scene. One simple question, Are you willing to put your body on the line? decided whether someone, assuming he or she had persistence, would be accepted in SNCC. Other considerations bowed before this measure. This was in large part due to Ella Baker who urged that SNCC resist those who cried Red scare; it would introduce fear, she believed, if we started worrying about "associations." We were, furthermore, working under such austere circumstances and taking such grave risks that what would have otherwise been a rhetorical standard was actually a significant index. Warding off frequent efforts to Red-bait SNCC by holding to our position that anyone willing to make the ultimate sacrifice was welcome, we knew that attacks on us as communist-infiltrated were based on malice or sought to create a diversion to siphon off our energy.

Jimmy Garrett, the lean and brilliant black SNCC staff member who ran our Los Angeles office, spoke at one staff meeting about how weak and ineffectual was the Communist party in California. "We're more revolutionary than the communists!" he declared. Jimmy may have been the first person I had ever known who had actually had political contact with the present-day party. While the Southern Christian Leadership Conference had a "firm policy" against hiring communists, SNCC had a firm nonexclusion policy. SCLC's policy grated on me. It was a source of pride to me that SNCC was more adamant than other civil rights groups in defying those who tried to smear us. SNCC would not allow anyone to be discredited because the FBI or a newspaper called someone a communist. The issue for us was, literally, whether one was willing to die for one's beliefs.

It was much later before I figured out why we were able to take this stand and refuse to ask about personal political beliefs. During the McCarthy era academicians, writers, and speakers with a left-wing perspective on American politics had been purged and driven from positions of influence in civil-liberties organizations, universities, publications, and the entertainment industry. The progressive elements in all sectors of our society were intimidated, harassed, jailed, and brutalized by job loss and denial of expression. Many individuals were hurt because of guilt by association. The resulting vacuum allowed us to work in a state of bliss. By the time SNCC came into being in 1960, there was in fact no political Left in the United States of any consequence—just as there is not now—especially in comparison to the European democracies. Our purism and lack of concern in resisting Red-baiting was in large part possible because the Left had already been silenced. Few of us in SNCC remembered, because of our youth and because most of us were the first of our families to challenge the status quo, how liberal organizations had systematically cleansed themselves of socialists and reputed communists. This is why we could be more nonchalant in our resistance to such labeling, and why we lacked fear about false charges and blithely dismissed the witch-hunts. The high price that others had already paid during the 1950s in the loss of their freedom of speech made possible our insouciance.

Laughing out loud, Jim Forman walked into my office one day in Atlanta carrying a photograph I had sent to John Doar, deputy director of the Civil Rights Division of the U.S. Department of Justice. It was a picture of a sympathy demonstration held on our behalf in California. Chuckling, Jim pointed to one of the participants in the picket line who, he told me, was from a family that had many communist members during the 1930s. "Did you have to pick the one picture with *him* in it?" Jim asked, sagging with mirth into a chair.

Perhaps one of the reasons that relatively little attention has been paid to the civil rights movement in scholarly research and in historical studies is that we were so American. In fact, our democratic system has such extraordinary flexibility, and the creation of wealth is so much more important than any transient sociological phenomenon, that the United States can eventually absorb almost any change in attitude, behavior, or life-style that a protest might inspire. Ironically, had ours been a movement based on Marxism, it might now occupy a more significant place in scholarship, research, and history. Indeed, I believe we could have been stronger and have avoided some of our internal foundering if we had had more historians and theoreticians in our ranks with training in different streams of thought and experience; this was one of our shortcomings.

The American Revolution was misnamed. It was a "devolution" rather than a revolution because the same established classes —in the South the privileged slave-owning landed gentry— remained in control. The American Revolution is listed in my Merriam-Webster's unabridged dictionary under the table of wars, not in the full-page listing of modern revolutions. Furthermore, to vote in eighteenth-century America, you had to be, in the South, a white male and landowner.

As the Western democracies have evolved since the eighteenth century, it is unfortunate that there have been so few new words coined for describing social change within the context of flexible democratic systems such as ours. As Andrew Young put it to me, "Either you speak like Karl Marx or you talk as if you're in the General Motors boardroom. We need to develop some other vocabularies."

What finally brought about the capitulation of the nation to many of the demands of the civil rights movement was precisely that it was not a revolution but a reassertion of fundamental rights and democracy. Because of the racism woven into the warp and the weft of the nation, when the United States was called upon to apply the Fourth of July rhetoric to black people, many reacted as if this were a revolutionary demand since it would result in the crumbling of a way of life. Indeed, it meant dismantling the historic deal that had been cut during the time of President Rutherford B. Hayes that the nation would look the other way when it came to the treatment of black people in the South. Thus, the net effect of implementing democracy in Black Belt counties was that, at the micro level, there would be a renunciation of the racist oligarchies controlling many courthouses. In such counties, the impact of voting rights would mean a shift of power across race and class lines and would therefore be none other than revolutionary. The movement was, therefore, revolutionary insofar as making the pieties of Jeffersonian democracy real to people of color meant overturning the institutions that perpetuated racial division.

One enduring significance of the civil rights movement, as it was represented by both SNCC and SCLC, is that it was a southern undertaking. Its genesis was in the South, its theoretical framework was rooted in the southern black church experience, it was for most of its life composed primarily of southerners, and it therefore reflected in a most profound sense the desire for governance by "consent of the governed."

It is strange to me, looking back, how isolated we were, even from those who should have been our friends. We were committed to democracy and human rights and were prepared to die for it, but, in addition to violent opposition, we faced many predicaments from unexpected quarters. Yet, I felt a strangely sweet feeling of pride in our loneliness; it made me feel good, perversely.

The American Civil Liberties Union (ACLU), in existence since 1920 and considering itself the watchdog of civil liberties and guardian of free speech, did not open an office for the southern region of the United States until 1964 when it finally picked the experienced civil-liberties lawyer Charles Morgan, Jr., who had defended SNCC workers and others in the movement. The fact is, however, that by the summer of the year that the ACLU decided to set up shop in Atlanta, we already had 150 lawyers in the state of Mississippi alone from several law groups, and in many ways we were past the point of our most acute need for the ACLU's intervention.

Amnesty International, an international human-rights organization founded in 1961, which later won a Nobel Peace Prize, ignored the pleas that Jim Forman and I made from Atlanta in late 1963 to its London headquarters. We asked Amnesty to take up the cause of the American prisoners of conscience incarcerated as a result of the civil rights movement in jails all over the South. I don't remember what reason they gave us, but they declined to help.

The federal government was a major force for the status quo that had allowed the local tyranny and terror of American-style colonialism to persist unchecked. We had a president, John Fitzgerald Kennedy, and an attorney general, Robert Francis Kennedy, who interpreted their executive powers so cautiously that they failed to observe the requirements of the constitutional federal-state balance and the demands of the Fourteenth and Fifteenth amendments, as they affected the day-to-day protection of blacks against infringement of their rights.

Many Americans consider that President Kennedy set an important moral tone to the struggle with a major speech on June 11, 1963. On that day, five hundred commando troops of the 31st National Guard ("Dixie") Division were placed in federal service by President Kennedy and began moving into Tuscaloosa. Three black students—Vivian Malone, James Hood, and David Mc-Glatnery—had presented themselves for enrollment at the University of Alabama. In Tuscaloosa, Malone and Hood were blocked by Governor George C. Wallace who "stood in the schoolhouse door." (McGlatnery entered the university branch in Huntsville peaceably the next day.) Deputy Attorney General Nicholas deB. Katzenbach brought with him a presidential proclamation commanding Governor Wallace to "cease and desist" from unlawful obstruction of a federal court order handed down by U.S. district judge Seybourn H. Lynne in Birmingham on June 5, causing the governor to step aside when requested by the commander of the federalized national guard. Yet, to us, there were dozens of other situations that called for federal balancing of state denial of constitutional rights.

That night, I watched President Kennedy as he told the nation in a twelve-minute television address that when Americans "are sent to Vietnam or West Berlin we do not ask for whites only." He called civil rights primarily a "moral issue" and asked, "Are we to say to the world—and more importantly to each other—that this is the land of the free, except for the Negroes; that we have no second-class citizens, except Negroes; that we have no class or caste system, no ghettos, no master race, except with respect to Negroes?" He announced that he would soon submit to the Congress additional civil rights legislation.

Although I was impressed by his presence, I considered the President's speech to be rhetoric, responding to an embarrassing provocation by Governor George Wallace in Tuscaloosa. I observed that Kennedy had not taken the initiative but had responded. I remembered that while still the senator from Massachusetts, on October 26, 1960, John F. Kennedy had telephoned Coretta Scott King while her husband was in Georgia's Reidsville prison, and Robert F. Kennedy had telephoned De Kalb County's Judge Oscar Mitchell asking him to reverse his decision to deny bail. Yet I considered this speech—like those gestures—to be sound public relations. For a couple of hundred staff members of SNCC and SCLC on the front lines in the Black Belt, this speech seemed too little and too late. So many sacrifices had already been made. Yet, for perhaps one hundred million people across the country, and millions more around the world, an American president had taken a moral rather than a legal stand on civil rights and, in so doing, he made the cause respectable.

Look clinically at the chronology of President Kennedy's actions and you will see why I considered him reactive rather than "proactive." In September 1962, Mississippi governor Ross Barnett turned away black student James Meredith from the doors of the University of Mississippi at Oxford. President Kennedy followed President Eisenhower's lead (Eisenhower had sent federalized national guard troops into Little Rock five years earlier); on October 1, he had the students escorted onto campus by 250 U.S. marshals. Subsequently, about 2,500 regular Army military police were sent to Oxford but not until after rioting resulting from Meredith's enrollment.

In January 1963, Governor George Wallace was inaugurated, vowing "segregation now and forever." In April, news coverage of Birmingham police chief Eugene "Bull" Connor unleashing police dogs on Dr. King and SCLC, and power-spraying demonstrators with fire hoses, caught world attention. On May 20, the U.S. Supreme Court ruled the segregation of Birmingham to be unconstitutional. After testing some of his themes in a speech to the Council of Mayors in Honolulu on June 9, and following Cabinet debate, Kennedy made his famous June 11 civil rights speech. That night, Medgar Evers was killed by a sniper's bullet in Jackson. Eight days later, Kennedy's bill calling for an end to segregation of interstate public accommodations, the Civil Rights Act of 1963, reached Capitol Hill.

"Vigor" was a word employed to describe the Kennedys, but President Kennedy was not vigorous enough to depart from the tradition of Senate confirmation of segregationist judges in judiciary appointments. President Kennedy appointed to the federal bench a number of judges who compiled notorious records of indifference to the constitutional rights of black people—Harold Cox, Clarence W. Allgood, J. Robert Elliott, and E. Gordon West. If he had left those seats vacant, as the moderate Southern Regional Council suggested at the time, it would have at least been a statement.

Our beliefs about the feasibility of change were unrelated to President Kennedy, and his record of accomplishments has been overrated in this area. What sustained our faith was the deeply ingrained biblical mandate influencing most of the movement's participants, the model of Gandhi, and the example of other anticolonial movements. Yet, our feelings of *hope* for change were greatly affected by the mood swing of the Kennedy era following the lusterless Eisenhower years. President Kennedy was a young man and the youth of the southern civil rights movement felt themselves important. Belief in American invincibility related to the space race was replacing the stodginess of the 1950s, and the economy was buoyant although, some would later assert, in large part because of the war in Vietnam.

President Kennedy presented the civil rights movement with a major paradox. He perplexed me when his words thundered across the early 1960s, "Ask not what your country can do for you; ask what you can do for your country." Wasn't that precisely what we in this indigenous movement were doing?

Yet, I saw with my own eyes that the Kennedy administration's legal actions were ineffectual. The President refused to use a federal presence to deter official lawlessness far more often than he acceded. He declined to send federal marshals to protect voting places far more frequently than he agreed to utilize them. He refrained from using the injunctive powers of the Justice Department. He was unable to reorient the FBI so that it would enforce the law rather than its own interpretation of the law, and the bureau remained the private principality of its potentate, J. Edgar Hoover. Neither the President nor his brother, the attorney general, fully used the authority and powers deeded to them by their offices except in small measure.

David J. Garrow's historical survey of Dr. King and the SCLC, *Bearing the Cross*, quotes President Kennedy as saying that Dr. King's greatest asset was his relative moderation and nonviolence: "If King loses, worse leaders are going to take his place"; the President also told a group that they should be grateful that Dr. King and not SNCC was involved. "SNCC has got an investment in violence," the President averred. "They're sons of bitches."

Historian Harvard Sitkoff has written of President Kennedy in his book *The Struggle for Black Equality, 1954–1980:*

> He prided himself on being pragmatic, tough-minded. Idealists and romantics annoyed him. Quixotic crusades interfered with his careful plans and cautious timetables. Only in

the battle against Communism did he think the United
States should "pay any price, bear any burden, meet any
hardship, support any friend, oppose any foe." Never in the
struggle for black rights would he ask the American people
for a commitment or sacrifice approaching that. . . . He believed in using the absolute minimum force in this sensitive
matter. "I don't think we would ever come to the point of
sending troops," Kennedy confided to an aide just a month
before the Freedom Rides began.

The position of the Kennedy administration at the time of
the 1961 Freedom Rides was described by Sitkoff:

> They could no longer tolerate either the deliberate failure of
> local authority to preserve civil peace or the open defiance
> of federal law. Yet they still sought to walk the tightrope
> between, as the Kennedys viewed them, the unreasonable
> militance on both sides. . . . Racial prejudice and the ine-
> qualities it fostered bothered them. They hoped to better
> the life of Afro-Americans—but slowly, and at the proper
> time. They thought demands for freedom *now* to be just as
> irresponsible as calls for segregation forever.

I remember feeling that, until his speech of June 11, 1963,
President Kennedy seemed personally detached from the struggle.

Yet President Kennedy's position on civil rights was more
ethical than that of anyone who preceded him—in word if not in
deed. He was flawed in his grasp of how to use the powers of his
office to change a heinous system, but he was better than the
overall governmental structure allowed him to be—his party was,
after all, the party of the racist oligarchies of southern courthouses. Although he underestimated the strength of the opposition, in his administration's backing of the Field and Taconic
foundations' support of black voter registration, he was the first
national political leader to recognize that the demography of his
party, perhaps as much as 40 percent Dixiecrat, could benefit from
black political participation.

He was the first president to recognize the lasting effects of
the end of colonial rule and that the face of the planet's leadership was immutably changing. Even if we in SNCC could not feel
it tangibly and nothing changed in our work, he made it clear to

the rest of the world that the policies of the United States government no longer favored segregation.

I have written of the shared perspective held by SNCC workers and of the ethos of the organization. Yet there is an important aspect of the group with which I worked and lived that has only over time become clear to me. This element was so fundamental and played so central a part in the eventual disintegration of our group that it must appear extraordinarily naïve of me not to have been aware of it at the time. The failure to see, respond, and address this reality, however, was not simply naïveté on my part, but was interwoven with the attitudes and hopes of the young people of SNCC. Furthermore, if it was a key weakness that ultimately helped to destroy the group, it was also, ironically, our greatest strength. This fundamental aspect that I began to see only much later is the diversity of race, class, background, and experience of the staff members.

What does that mean? We saw ourselves, black and white together, as a "band of brothers and sisters" and "a circle of trust." The spirit that united us—not even the most worldly and cynical of my colleagues would today qualify or disagree—was such that we would have died for one another. What this fierce, all-embracing vital force of loyalty disguised was the real and ultimately unassimilable differences in class, race, gender, and experiential backgrounds in our circle.

Black and white together. Really? Who were the whites? There were some from influential homes of famous writers and lawyers, and from private schools. Some were the children of white ethnic workers in mills and factories. Many of us came from middle-class Christian homes. Others of us came from conservative or reactionary white southern segregationist families. There was one now legendary SNCC hero whose father had been an Alabama Klansman. Some represented the New England Puritan abolitionist tradition of the Unitarians and Quakers. Some were urban Jews. Some came from the "little red schoolhouse" tradition of the American Left.

And the blacks? Anyone who looked at the black staff as a homogeneous group could not have been more wrong. A few were the children of northern black professionals, college-educated, confident, and upwardly mobile even within a segregated society.

Some had been born in the Caribbean and others were but one generation removed from its cane fields, mostly from the North. A few were the children of that painfully small class of southern professionals that made them a true elite. A vast majority were southern college students, frequently the first of their families to reach university but who put that aspiration aside to do battle. The rest were our shock troops. They were our kamikazes, our heroes and heroines, southern kids, scrappy, many of them academic dropouts working in the cotton fields of the Black Belt, all of them rebellious, the "local folk," plucky, in their teens and early twenties, many of whom had had members of their families lynched, who responded to the call of the movement—and made it work.

In retrospect, it is clear that while the passion and sacrifice of SNCC united us and made us all equal, the more basic differences in our perspectives, outlooks, and vision of possibilities, while initially masked, would ultimately have to be confronted. That so profound a reality escaped us for so long should not be judged a flaw; it was, rather, ultimately a testament to the strength and power of the civil rights movement during its finest hours.

Journalists were fond of categorizing SNCC as "radical." Radical compared to what? An October 1960 edition of *The Student Voice*, in the year of SNCC's founding, carried an editorial:

> Nonviolence has real healing potential. It says that the only "place to stand" is in relation. To what? To the self and the other. Nonviolence says that each person has personhood, that each of us is capable of entering into relation. Consequently, nonviolence refuses to manipulate. It refuses to regard persons as things, as "its." If we lose sight of this basic concept of nonviolence, we will lose the ultimate potential of the student movement. For, without this commitment to the validity of the other person, the movement will become an institution and persons will become things. . . . To retain personhood will be the hardest battle of all in a world where a mass movement is necessary to save the South and America. But the South and America will not be worth saving unless there are persons, real selves, left to live there. This retaining and creating of personhood is the great and final goal of the student movement.

Jane Stembridge, probably the author of those words as
SNCC's first executive secretary, put an additional twist on this
germinal concept of SNCC's when she quoted a black Mississippi
woman to me in one of her letters from Greenwood: "An old lady
the other night told me this line that would solve the whole problem. She said we must act like this: 'Do unto others as you would
be did.' " SNCC's first chairman, Chuck McDew, was often heard
to pose the Talmudic query: "If I am not for others, then who is
for me? If not now, when?"

SNCC was in fact radical during the period about which I
write in its spirit of self-sacrifice, its vision of human worth, and
its heterogeneity. Its radicalism expressed itself in its ferocious
insistence that ideals should be made reality, the obstinacy of its
existential position that belief and action were one, and its puri-
tanical determination that ideas came from action and that rhetoric should never precede behavior.

CHAPTER 8

NONVIOLENCE

I was standing by my window
On a cold and cloudy day
When I saw that hearse come rolling
For to take my mother away.

Chorus after each verse:
Will the circle be unbroken
Bye and bye, Lord, bye and bye
There's a better home awaiting
In the sky, Lord, in the sky.

Lord, I told that undertaker
Undertaker please drive slow
For this body that you're hauling
Lord, I hate to see her go.

I followed close behind her
Tried to hold up and be brave
But I could not hide my sorrow
When they laid her in the grave.

I went home, my home was lonely
Now my mother she has gone
All my brothers, sisters crying
What a home so sad and alone.

Will the circle be unbroken
Bye and bye, Lord, bye and bye
There's a better home awaiting
In the sky, Lord, in the sky.

—Traditional southern hymn, black and
white, used for reassurance whenever there
was internal strain within the movement

One warm night in the early autumn of 1963, following a southwide staff meeting in Atlanta, Casey and I
brought four black male fellow workers back to our apartment for
a glass of wine and further discussion. We continued to talk strategy for the program in Mississippi.

Suddenly, there was scuffling in the hallway. We stopped talking. A bang at the front door was followed by muffled sounds. The door burst open. Three black men whom I had never seen before were standing, bent-kneed, in the front door. One of them held a sawed-off shotgun and another had a broad butcher knife. They slinked into the apartment. Seeing the three armed men sidling in, shifting their weight from leg to leg, three of our fellow workers fled out the back door; the fourth had fallen asleep at the back of the apartment and did not wake up until the episode was over.

The screen door flapped, banging after them, leaving Casey and me standing there facing the strangers holding their sawed-off shotgun and long knife, as they rocked nervously from side to side. Grimly hiding how scared we were, and looking them steadily in the eye, we asked them to go. "You have to leave. You have to leave," I kept repeating in the most calm voice I could muster, never letting myself break eye contact with our assailants. After what seemed like a long time but was probably only moments, they looked at each other and left.

I guess I will never know the full story. I did not expect special treatment but neither did I anticipate that our friends would run out the back door. I was initially surprised by their reaction, for these were men who were not afraid of physical danger and they were not cowards. One, a former Freedom Rider, had been incarcerated more than twenty times and had been bloodied in numerous police beatings. Another was the director of a project in a dangerous part of the region; it had required both physical and emotional courage for him to handle the brutalization of the black community that occurred in response to the movement there. The third had been tested in vicious encounters on the Eastern Shore of Maryland where police dogs had been used to rebuff peaceful demonstrators.

This peculiar episode is, I think, revealing, but only if you look deeply. It is not heroic, yet, for the reader who is interested in understanding what it was like to work in the civil rights movement, it discloses something about the nature of nonviolence that romantic accounts may distort and it lays open a dimension of the environment in the South.

First, although nonviolence specifically means *not* running away, it requires systematic forethought, planning, preparation, sometimes meditation; and it has to have meaning. This was street violence and our fellow workers were not prepared for nonviolent resistance in this unexpected situation. Nonviolence also demands a deliberate and conscious decision with cohesion in the group. It is not reactive. Our three friends acted without advance planning in a situation where a nonviolent response would have lacked meaning. The willingness to subject oneself to abuse by hostile white onlookers in a demonstration had to have a specific political point, but here it would have been meaningless fighting if they had stayed, with no payoff at the end.

Why the unplanned response to leave us standing there? This incident occurred while there was still widespread prevalence of "lynch law" in the Deep South, when a black man who committed a crime against a white woman knew he was in real danger of being hunted down and killed without trial. In those days, a black man would hardly dare to hurt a white woman because of the malign reaction. But black-on-black crime was punished mildly if at all. Our three fellow workers knew they were in mortal danger of being cut with the knife or shot by the accosters for they were unarmed and protected by no taboo. The second reason for their flight is that our fellow workers probably concluded that the three black strangers would not harm Casey and me given the forbiddance by the culture, whereas they were vulnerable and there would likely be no justice.

Completely based on instinct, Casey and I tried to disarm the three intruders by appearing to be unafraid and by our wits. I never figured out the original motive for the forced entry into our apartment although I suppose it was robbery. The next day we were back into our staff meetings and no one ever mentioned the episode. I did not bring it up, in part because I sometimes find confrontation difficult, although I continued to feel confused and miffed until I had reasoned it out. I believe it was they who felt *they* were the ones who were at risk.

"Lynch law" still set the tone for an incident like this. Despite the inadequate nature of reporting on lynchings, the U.S. Department of Commerce logged 4,733 lynchings nationwide from 1882 to 1962, three quarters of them black victims, mostly in the South. Prior to 1904, a number of whites were lynched, many of them petty criminals or horse thieves, but from then on, lynching became tantamount to a crime only against blacks, although there were exceptions. My father remembers being told of a teenage white boy who was lynched in Patrick County, Virginia, in the early part of this century. My step-great-grandfather, a Confederate veteran, had taken him from an orphanage, in an arrangement similar to indentured servitude, onto his farm where there was also a white tenant family. The boy stole something from the tenant family and was discovered by the teenage daughter, whom he killed with a hoe when she said, "I'm gonna tell Mr. Cranford on you." A lynch party was formed and he was hanged. Lynching was an illegal form of group killing under the pretext of serving race, pride, or the group's idea of justice. Legal evidence that the person was killed, however, was required for the lynching to be included in official statistics and thus many lynchings, especially those involving black families already living under fear, went unrecorded.

I learned through the experience with the three men with the sawed-off shotgun and butcher knife an important lesson—you cannot plan exactly how you will act in the face of danger or disaster. Your reaction may well up from inside you unpredictably and uncontrollably, and much faster than you can think. The most important teaching for me from this experience was that in every situation I should trust my instincts. I discovered that I would not freak out. I saw that my defenses were self-protective. I learned that I could trust myself in peril. Ever since then, I have noticed that when I feel threatened or in danger, often a strange sense of calm comes over me. It is not control; it is an internal process going on as if I am mobilizing all my resources and lining up my wits. In the long run, this incident helped my self-confidence and it enabled me to handle many dire situations.

As the summer of 1964 approached, the apprehensions of everyone rose with the coming heat. One steaming June day in Atlanta, when circles of perspiration formed dark-blue rings on the underarms of work shirts, and women with long hair tied it up high leaving wisps trailing wet on the backs of their necks, we emptied out the Raymond Street office and straggled to the basement of Frazier's Lounge. There were approximately two dozen of the core SNCC staff meeting together that day, many of them from headquarters, but some of the state directors and field secretaries were there too. We laughed and joked quietly among ourselves as we walked down Hunter Street, with passersby staring at this strange, racially integrated group. We strolled past the stand where I frequently bought a "half-smoke" frankfurter for my lunch and went on by Pascal's, a restaurant and nightclub that served the best fried chicken I've ever eaten.

We sauntered past the corner drugstore where two incidents now stand out in my memory. A few months earlier I had seen a man gunned down by one of Atlanta's few black policemen not far from the pharmacy. Atlanta was more progressive than the rest of the South, then and now, and had a small number of black policemen, but this didn't lessen my shock at seeing a black law officer shoot point-blank at a fleeing black man who, I presume, had been stealing. The other memory was of November 22, 1963. It was in that drugstore that I heard over the radio that President John Fitzgerald Kennedy had been shot in Dallas.

The staff assembled around tables with pitchers of iced tea to discuss the Mississippi Summer Project, the largest single organizing feat yet undertaken by the civil rights movement, which would involve one thousand volunteers. It was June 10, 1964. All of the key issues we were grappling with came out in that meeting, with five major concerns having priority: the national reaction of the established civil rights leadership to SNCC's dominance in Mississippi; the relationship between SNCC and the new umbrella entity called the Council of Federated Organizations (COFO); the role of the Greenwood headquarters for Mississippi, which would soon be usurped by the Jackson office of the summer project; tensions between blacks and whites as a result of hundreds of white volunteers coming into Mississippi; and the relationship of SNCC programs in other states to the larger Mississippi project.

This was also the time when our philosophy of nonviolence was being put to the test, and when fears and anxieties about the imminence of death began to be expressed openly.

As the staff meeting opened, I sat looking at Jim Forman. He was reporting on the "unity council," a loose ad hoc grouping of all the large civil rights organizations, that had met two days earlier. Jim was a good representative, with a calculating mind and well-channeled anger. His traumatic experience of being beaten in Monroe, North Carolina, had left a deep impression on him. His scalp wound healed but his memory was scarred by the experience; unvented anger seethed beneath his affectionate surface. Jim was completely down-to-earth, although he had a somewhat cranky way of making interjections with an edge of complaint about them. Jim did something that won him my admiration—he swept the Raymond Street office floors. This simple action showed that he was willing to share in all aspects of taking responsibility for the organization; it also demonstrated that everyone on staff should be willing to do whatever had to be done.

As the meeting started, I thought once again about SNCC's nonhierarchical organization and how our attempts to operate with consensus often produced chaos. Highly democratic forms of organization are often infuriating because decision making is slow. They allow for indulgence of personal whims and require high motivation of the individuals involved as well as honesty in interaction, or else commitments aren't met, agreements are broken, and responsibility is shirked. There was determination among the SNCC staff and we worked very hard, but Jim's periodic sweeping the floor was a signal that we all had to share the dirty work and that one kind of activity was not better than another. He was not advocating no division of labor, however; on the contrary, he was a sharp observer of people's strengths and knew how to encourage individuals to use best their abilities. Ever since, I have tried to follow Jim's example; perhaps this is one reason why I don't like to stand on ceremony.

Jim opened the session by describing the reaction of the major civil rights leaders to our Mississippi Summer Project. The plan was to have twenty Freedom Schools with volunteers teaching civics, the Bill of Rights, the system of law in the United States, and the responsibilities and rights of citizenship. Voter registration would be used to organize dozens of local drives in different neighborhoods and on plantations. The third feature of the summer project would be community centers, which in some areas would be renovated abandoned buildings and in other sites would have to be built from scratch. Overall decision making would be coordinated by Bob Moses, Mendy Samstein, and Jesse Morris of SNCC, and Dave Dennis of CORE. Organizations of lawyers and ministers were expected to join us. An alternative political party, the Mississippi Freedom Democratic party, was being developed and would formally "challenge" the all-white regular Democrats at the Democratic National Convention in August.

Jim described how Roy Wilkins of the NAACP had spoken

in the "unity council," a group composed of most of the national black leadership figures, against the Mississippi Summer Project. Wilkins had said that he had "grave misgivings" and that the only result would be that "one thousand white volunteers would be exposed to 'civilization' in Mississippi." He said that the summer project had "potential for embarrassing President Johnson and may further the political goals of Goldwater." This didn't surprise me. Roy Wilkins was the doyen of the established black leadership and I remembered reading in *The Washington Post* something that Wilkins had said the year before: "All the rest start a little and then rush somewhere else. They are here today, gone tomorrow. There is only one organization that can handle a long sustained fight—the NAACP." Although there was sibling rivalry with SCLC, it was with the NAACP that SNCC felt most at odds.

Seventy young people were upstaging everyone else in the civil rights movement by this project in Mississippi, a place everyone talked about "going into" as if it were a combat zone. The project flamed new jealousies among SCLC, CORE, the Urban League, and the NAACP, although less so with the "Inc. Fund" which had earlier separated from the NAACP. The competitiveness was due to fund-raising overlaps, the struggle to build and maintain constituencies, philosophical differences, and varying histories. When it came to SNCC, there was a love-hate relationship. The established groups liked the way we were stirring things up, awakening communities, mobilizing a new constituency among upwardly mobile college-age youth and others, penetrating rural counties where they had no base, and producing more inflammatory statements than any other organization. We made them look the picture of moderation. But they didn't like our obstreperousness or our irreverence and, worse, they considered us uncontrollable. Furthermore, despite the civil rights movement being by and large about assimilation of blacks into American society, SNCC went one step further and talked about structural political change and new leadership. This might concern an older organization, for who knew how much influence they would lose if there was much progress on that front.

I was surprised when Jim Forman went on to report that the Reverend Dr. Martin Luther King, Jr., had been very supportive of us at the "unity council" meeting. Sensing the opposition of the other groups, Dr. King had asked, "Couldn't there be a reconciliation?" I was amazed to hear Jim's report, expecting that Dr. King's reaction would be the same as that of the other leadership figures trying to stop us. I thought he would fear that SCLC would be preempted by SNCC. At the very least, I thought, Dr. King would have tried for some control of our planning and program. Instead, he had generously stated, "The Mississippi Summer Project is the most creative thing happening today in civil rights."

Our interaction with Dr. King was through two of SCLC's younger staff members. One was the Reverend Andrew Jackson Young, from New Orleans, an emotionally open and sympathetic United Church of Christ minister with a rounded cadence to his speech who showed a talent for negotiations; Andy was then in his early thirties. The other was the Reverend James Bevel, a capricious young minister from Nashville who had an energetic gait and intense eyes and, whether indoors or out, wore a skullcap with his overalls. Whenever we struck outright conflict or needed open lines of communications between the two groups, we called on Andy and Jim as mediators or intermediaries.

SCLC's headquarters were on the other side of town, on the east side of Atlanta on Auburn Avenue, a black business thoroughfare known as Sweet Auburn Avenue for its string of self-made black-owned businesses, so we weren't bumping into each other. I remember how, when SNCC was planning a demonstration in Atlanta, early in the winter of 1964, a group of us that included Jim Forman, Andy, and Jim Bevel stood at night on a street near Atlanta University talking about the plans. We wanted SCLC's support for the demonstration because we shared the same city and we considered Andy and Jim to be close enough to us that we could count on their word.

SNCC workers for the most part, except for Jim Forman and John Lewis when taking part at large events, had no interaction with Dr. King until the Selma, Alabama, march in 1965, and later through a Mississippi march in May 1966. Other than hearing him speak, I did not know him. Yet, despite our rivalries, SNCC had come up with something bigger and bolder than anyone else and Dr. King, alone among the major national figures, was the one to recognize its potential positive impact.

Jim said the "unity council" had asked him to come back to SNCC with the recommendation that "an advisory group with

substantive powers in Mississippi" be formed. This was a flimsily
disguised move to create a mechanism to manipulate SNCC in
Mississippi, and the suggestion died of its own weight. We wanted
resources for the Mississippi project, not a long-distance power
play. Jim continued to astonish me when he reported that Dr.
King had suggested SCLC might give money to assist the summer project. Part of me responded cynically. There would be strings
on that money, wouldn't there? I asked myself. But Jim didn't
feel suspicious and he was shrewd.

The next topic was the statewide umbrella organization Bob
Moses had revived from its origin at the time of the Freedom
Riders to bring together the national civil rights organizations in
Mississippi. Ideally, the Council of Federated Organizations
(COFO) would have been a coalition, but coalitions are difficult
because it is impossible to make decisions rapidly when each
member organization's internal formulation process is different.
Bob's concept of COFO was simpler—it would function as a
framework for cooperation, and create a climate in which differences among the various civil rights groups could be minimized
and some collaboration achieved.

Now I watched Bob as he listened while Jim quoted Roy
Wilkins's declaration at the "unity council" meeting that "the national NAACP is not involved in COFO." Wilkins had grumbled,
"We're a part of COFO at all only because there is an individual
who happens to be our state person there," alluding to Aaron "Doc"
Henry, the black pharmacist in Clarksdale to whom Bob had drawn
close to unify the diverse organizations, and the man who had
been our candidate the previous autumn for governor in the mock
election. I could see Bob brooding over the official stand of the
NAACP.

Suddenly in the meeting, something began to change. From
discussing the hesitation of the other major organizations to join
us wholeheartedly and their resentment of SNCC, some members
of the staff shifted and seemed to question Bob's loyalty to the
organization. How could Bob set up a confederation like COFO
through which these other groups would work in Mississippi—
even raise funds for their own operations and use the publicity
that would be attracted—if Bob really cared about SNCC?

"So if these other organizations are not a part of the Mississippi Summer Project, why are they raising money around it?"

Ivanhoe Donaldson demanded angrily. He complained that the rest of the national organizations were simply "gotten off the hook for any responsibility of what happens" by these disclaimers. "Medgar Evers certainly speaks as a representative of the N double A when he tries to raise funds based on the project." Ivanhoe had no way of knowing that Medgar would be killed by a sniper's bullet fired from ambush the day following this meeting.

Bob had opened the door to these groups, some of those present wondered, but would they now take advantage of SNCC without assuming any moral obligation? Whose interests did Bob really have in mind? some were asking themselves.

Never defensive, Bob rose quietly, his gaze steady and his shoulders thrown back in stability and strength, and quietly said, "My commitment is basically as a SNCC person. The energy that makes COFO positive comes from SNCC; and SNCC is committed to the development of this kind of a group because we need coordination." Bob went on patiently, reassuringly, to explain once again the need for an umbrella organization if the summer was to succeed even though SNCC would do most of the organizing.

This was not what Prathia Hall, strong, proud, and always a moving speaker, wanted to talk about. "There are undercurrents not far below the surface that should instead be discussed at this meeting, such as violence and nonviolence, black and white tensions, and Jim Forman's role." Prathia knew that internecine struggles with other groups were superficial compared to what really troubled the staff.

I was sure that the prospect of one thousand white volunteers being incorporated into the movement was what was bothering people and that was why they had turned on Bob.

The meeting became more rambunctious but also more open after Prathia's intervention. Charlie Cobb, a thoughtful and popular twenty-one-year-old graduate of Howard University and the son of a United Church of Christ minister in Springfield, Massachusetts, was preparing to speak. Even-tempered, a good writer, and possessing a flair for program development, Charlie was doing much of the preparatory work for the Freedom Schools to be opened that summer. I admired and respected Charlie. He stood up and said:

> People are breaking into the Greenwood office for food and
> clothes but that's not the real reason. White citizens are or-

ganizing against us. There's a group organizing in Cleveland near us in the Delta. A truck filled with guns and ammunition and headed for Mississippi was stopped in Clinton, Illinois. Threats of violence have been made to five of our Negro staff around Greenwood. Two of them had guns given to them. One gun was placed in the office and two guns were placed in the Freedom House. Dick Frey, the only white member of our staff, is the only nonnative Mississippian against guns. The sheriff's riding around the county warning local black families that they should not house the civil rights workers.

Charlie, who was considerate and had an attractive quality of ingenuousness about him, had zeroed in on what we needed to discuss and urgently had to clarify at that meeting: SNCC's policy on nonviolence. All of the other subjects were either impossible to resolve in one meeting or they could be dealt with once we reached consensus on a policy relating to the new circumstances in Mississippi. I realized that our staff there had been living under pressure that the rest of us did not fully understand and it had to surface before we could come together in agreement on a policy. I also felt the Mississippi staff was asking for emotional support from the headquarters and SNCC people in other projects; we needed more than intellectual resolution on this issue.

Willie Peacock was burning to say something. One of several local youths from the Delta who had gone to work with Bob, he personified the natural leadership that Ella Baker, Bob Moses, and many in SNCC believed was latent in every community, ready to be thrust up by careful behind-the-scenes organizing. Hardy, dark, good-looking, slender, and one of the original organizers in Mississippi, Willie had shown courage so often that he had become a hero to us from within our own ranks. He now spoke of some of the dilemmas he faced on a day-to-day basis as he tried to live out his commitment to nonviolence:

I asked a local man to fire on anyone who broke into our Freedom House, so that neither I nor any other SNCC staff person would be compromised by using arms. But he would not agree. So, instead, I placed guns there so that we could at least guard the Freedom House at night. We have done this since January. The Freedom House is accessible to three alleys and there are no dogs there. Violence is not being preached about, but the local people all say that the white man thinks it's war and he is preparing to defend his home. I think an organization should be set up to halt whites. I was shot at on March sixteenth, 1963, in front of the office on McLaurin Street. People were there observing it and I presented evidence to the FBI including a picture of the car from which I was shot at drawn by a taxi driver. They haven't found them yet! Whites in Greenwood are more convinced than ever that they can kill a Negro and get away with it.

Willie also mentioned that our communications system was effective:

If a collect call had not been placed to the justice of the peace in Columbus, Mississippi, where some of our people were being held, at the right moment, by a SNCC worker claiming to be an attorney, they would have shipped them off to the county penal farm. It's only because SNCC bluffed the justice into thinking someone knew where they were that they got released.

Don Harris pointed out that people were getting shot at in other parts of the South besides Mississippi, namely, the twenty-two counties in southwest Georgia where he was now directing our project. For the sixth time in eighteen months, someone had been shot down in one of those counties that comprised Georgia's Second Congressional District. "At a mass meeting two nights after the last shooting," Don continued, "we talked about nonviolence but the people walked out angry and frustrated." Afterward the staff got together among themselves, he said, and "questioned what right they had to stop the local people from whatever they wanted to do."

Any organizing brought out violent tendencies in Deep South white communities that were stimulated to even greater excesses as the black community began to resist. In that sense, someone could argue theoretically that we were antagonizing the violent impulses of white communities and provoking a violent response. Yet such conflict was a prerequisite for permanent change in white communities with rabid elements. It was axiomatic in the movement that confrontation always preceded reconciliation. The fatuous contention of white politicians that there would be no trouble were it not for "outside agitators," had no credence in the black community; it was a cliché in black pulpits that to get rid of the dirt you had to have an agitator in your washing machine.

"Aren't we," one field secretary asked, about to "lead people into the fire, then ask them to sing a song and return to church?"

Frank Smith was angered by this remark and abruptly rose. He was an astute realist, perceptive and tenacious. The meeting became quiet. "You should decide," Frank said brusquely, his arms akimbo, "that if you go to Mississippi, you're going to get your ass whipped, go to jail, and get shot. You'll be functionally useless if you can't decide this. If you get hung up in your own personal safety, we're not going to get anything done."

It was natural in the rural South that the black community should consider arming itself for self-defense. Courtland Cox, tall, burly, broad-shouldered, urbane, a leader of the Nonviolent Action Group (NAG) of Howard University, agreed with Frank. "The question of arming ourselves is larger than Mississippi," he stated. "To the extent we think about self-defense, we are immobilized." It was significant that Courtland took this position at that moment. The group from Howard University formed a subgroup within SNCC. The Howard students, such as Bill Mahoney who ran our Washington office, were self-assured and theoretically oriented; they carried themselves easily and were highly articulate. It was from this group that, first, Stokely Carmichael and, later, H. Rap Brown moved into the role of spokesperson for SNCC. Now, in this staff meeting, if "the Howard group" had taken a position favoring armed self-defense, it might have changed the Mississippi Summer Project and thereby the civil rights movement as a whole. The Howard group was composed of such self-possessed, intelligent, and sophisticated individuals that it was disproportionately influential.

The discussion raged. SNCC staff meetings were never composed. Anxieties were raised about other ramifications of a policy of nonviolence. Charlie Cobb asked if SNCC would defend its own staff if they were arrested in a house where local people defended themselves even though they didn't shoot. Ruby Doris Smith asked if SNCC workers actually wanted local people defending them with arms and whether this was an appropriate posture for us as organizers.

Sam Block, like Willie Peacock, was a highly respected twenty-four-year-old black youth from Cleveland, Mississippi, muscular and lean, who had joined Bob Moses after the Freedom Rides to become a SNCC field secretary. Jim Forman used to brag that Sam and Willie Peacock would sleep in hollow logs upon arriving in a community until they found a local family to give them housing. When he had first gone to Greenwood, he spent two nights sleeping in a junkyard on the backseat of a crushed car. Sam told us that white vigilantes had come to Greenwood from one of the northern states a few weeks earlier. "They had one hundred sub-machine guns, two units of twenty-five bombs each, and fifty or sixty pistols—enough ammunition for a small army," Sam declared. In the Delta, Greenwood was the focal point of vigilante, terrorist, and Ku Klux Klan activity as well as the location of our state office. Sam was on edge. He played a wild card, saying, "I would back nonviolence if the whites coming for the summer would go into the white community and preach nonviolence."

Several other staff members voiced similar statements that the white volunteers should work to dissuade the white community from violence. This was an unrealistic suggestion given the racial polarization of the state at that time, and Sam knew it, but as a rhetorical rejoinder it sounded more reasonable that it was.

Prathia Hall spoke again. An independent thinker, she did not typify any school of thought, yet she represented well the theologically based pragmatists that composed so much of early SNCC. "No one can be rational about facing death," she mused. "What is happening now is that for the first time we as a staff are coming to grips with the fact that this may be *it*," Prathia said solemnly. "I don't have a martyr complex; I'm fighting because I want to live. Living in this system has not been life for me," she glowered. "But," she continued, "I can't take someone else's life knowingly. We must decide what is life and what is defense of it."

Prathia paused, her head held erect. She had everyone's concentrated attention:

> Willie said he was concerned for the people around the office who might die. But at the same time you shoot a person breaking in to plant a bomb, you might shoot someone who broke in because of hunger. I thought we were going to Mississippi because people have been getting killed there

for years and no one cared. I thought we were going there to say to the world that if any of us dies, it was not a redneck who shot us but the whole society that had us killed.

Waves of emotion undulated across rapt faces. "Lastly," Prathia said as a practical afterthought before she sat down, "I want you all to think about the fact that there's a direct relationship between the fact that we don't have money and we're doing something real."

I wondered about this point. To what extent was our precarious financial position related to our being more daring and more militant than the other civil rights organizations? Perhaps it was our very independence from moneyed sources that allowed us to aim for targets of boldness. Our funds came from mailings to individuals, events featuring The Freedom Singers, speeches by members of the staff, fund-raisers organized by celebrities like Harry Belafonte, Ossie Davis and Ruby Dee, and from the Friends of SNCC support groups across the country. Other entertainers also lent their talents. Joan Baez gave concerts to raise money and sang for the staff in Atlanta and Jackson, and I remember walking along a dirt road in the Delta on a torrid summer day with Judy Collins when she came to sing for us in Mississippi. In addition to the consistent help of key Protestant denominations and church groups, we also received funds from two predominantly black labor-union locals in Detroit. I once discussed the uncertainty of our funding with Howard Zinn. "Nothing of value," he told me, "ever goes under for lack of money. If you are doing something worthwhile, you will not cease to exist because of lack of funds. Organizations go under for other reasons and fund raising dries up if they're not addressing real need."

Prathia was making us confront the probability that there would be deaths as a result of the Mississippi Summer Project. All of us were suddenly alone with ourselves. It was not the first time each of us had examined the possibility of dying for our commitment, because everyone had to come to grips with that possibility before joining the staff. But this was the first time, in preparation for the Mississippi Summer Project, that we had sat together and probed our responsibility for one another, acknowledging how much we cared about each other, the likelihood that one or more of us would die that summer, and the loss of other lives because of our plan.

* * *

Ruby Doris Smith, plucky, unabashed, filled with energy, and one of the major figures in SNCC, reminded us that we had always known what the consequences of our actions might be. "There's no one in this room who thought of this project as not involving bloodshed," she said. Ruby Doris was among the earliest activists in the sit-ins and was one of the most spirited leaders of the student movement. She was headstrong and tough. It is worth pausing to consider how Ruby came to play a central role in SNCC.

As a sophomore at Spelman College in 1960, Ruby Doris had participated in the Atlanta sit-ins and helped to organize the Atlanta student movement. In that same year, she had attended the founding conference of SNCC in Raleigh, North Carolina. One year later, in February 1961, ten students had been arrested in Rock Hill, South Carolina. SNCC's executive committee made a pivotal decision that four individuals would go to Rock Hill to sit-in, be arrested, and refuse bail as the first ten students had done, in order to bring attention to the arrests. They elected three veterans—Diane Nash from Nashville; Charles Sherrod from Petersburg, Virginia; and Charles Jones, from Charlotte, North Carolina—as well as Ruby Doris, who was, compared to the others, taking on her first big assignment. After the four demonstrated there, joining students from Friendship College, Ruby Doris and the others served a thirty-two-day jail sentence in Rock Hill.

This was, I believe, the first time that anyone in the sit-in movement had served out the full sentence, and many SNCC staff and Ella Baker subsequently marked Rock Hill as the true beginning of the organization because of the way it blended SNCC people with a local movement. "It was not until four outsiders joined with the Rock Hill students to fight a common enemy—segregation—that we realized that until all are free, no one is free," said one SNCC worker. The action by Ruby Doris and the others of remaining in jail for thirty-two days also reinforced SNCC's "Jail—No Bail" policy adopted after Jim Lawson's October 1960 speech, a feature of militancy differentiating SNCC from the other organizations.

Ruby Doris played another historic role. On May 1, 1961, two buses, one Greyhound and the other Trailways, left Washington, D.C., for New Orleans, Louisiana. The buses were carrying seven blacks and six whites on the first Freedom Ride, an ordeal of conscience organized by CORE. To reach New Orleans, they had to travel across states where segregation was frankly buttressed by terrorists and their frequent collaborators, the police. Harassed and beaten along the way, and therefore requiring long stopovers, the Freedom Riders did not reach Alabama until May 14. Outside of Anniston, one bus was burned to its iron frame and eight white men climbed aboard the other as it arrived, violently beating the integrated group of riders. James Peck of New York, a white Freedom Rider, was beaten unconscious and required over one hundred stitches. Walker Bergman, a white schoolteacher from Detroit, was to spend much of his life in a wheelchair following the beating he received. The police, who knew of the arrival of the buses in Anniston, never appeared. Assembling in Birmingham, the group boldly prepared to go on to Montgomery; and when they could not find a driver, some went to New Orleans by plane to participate in a mass rally. Birmingham police commissioner Eugene "Bull" Connor explained the missing lawmen: "They were home with their mothers" (referring to its being Mother's Day).

CORE wanted to discontinue the Freedom Rides because they had become too dangerous, and these were the same sentiments expressed by the Kennedy administration. CORE's Jim Farmer had ridden one of the first buses that finally reached Jackson, and the organization had sent its own lawyer to join attorney Wiley A. Branton in defending the Freedom Riders; notwithstanding, CORE's willingness to drop the rides was the beginning of the eventual fading of CORE into the background of the movement.

Ruby Doris's significant action was that she telephoned all the SNCC affiliates at campuses across the South to mobilize support. As a result, SNCC took over the Freedom Rides. They continued their passage through bloodthirsty crowds in Montgomery and on into Jackson. Other students joined the protesters and kept coming throughout the summer of 1961—by train and by bus, black and white, men and women—until more than three hundred of them were held in Mississippi's notorious Parchman penitentiary for forty-nine days. Ruby Doris was one of the original Freedom Riders to arrive in Jackson, where she was again jailed and served a two-month sentence, first in the Hinds County jail and then in Parchman penitentiary. There she, like all the others, had plenty of time to think, and Parchman, the fifth largest prison in the United States, hardened her intentions. On eight other occasions she was to be arrested and serve an additional seventeen days in southern jails.

At the time of our June 10, 1964, staff meeting, Ruby Doris was, as always, feisty. "Let's face it. When the four children were killed in the church bombing in Birmingham last year, there were no thousands of volunteers to take their place," Ruby said, adding, "It's our hands and our minds that created a project that's going to stimulate violence." Violent reprisal would indeed worsen before the situation would improve.

There was no turning back now. We were committed to a course. Bob Moses and the Mississippi staff had been contemplating for months the concept of the Mississippi Summer Project based in large part on the November 1963 mock election. It was at just such a solemn moment as this that I expected Bob to speak to the most basic questions.

"I think it's best to discuss the controllable things," he stated, trying to focus on what was directly in our hands at that meeting, moving away from general apprehension.

"I don't know if anyone in Mississippi preached to local Negroes that they shouldn't defend themselves," Bob continued. "Probably the closest is when I asked Mr. E. W. Steptoe not to carry guns when we go together at night. So, instead, he just hides his gun, and then I find out later." Mr. Steptoe was the pivotal figure in Amite County on whose farm one of the first voter-registration schools was set up. He paused. "Self-defense is so deeply ingrained in rural southern America that we as a small group can't affect it," he went on. "It's not contradictory for a farmer to say he's nonviolent and also to pledge to shoot a marauder's head off. The difference," he said, speaking very slowly and carefully, "is that we on staff have committed ourselves not to carry guns."

Just how pervasive was arming for self-defense in rural Mississippi communities is shown indirectly by a memorandum I wrote in August 1964, where I described Hartman Turnbow from Holmes County. Mr. Turnbow was one of the most interesting individuals that I had met. He was a large, stocky dark man who spoke each syllable slowly but volubly and who lived in a part of the state where black families had been able to obtain title to land after the Civil War. I wrote:

> Mr. Hartman Turnbow represents the landed gentry of the movement. Holmes County is 70 percent Negro, and 70 percent of the land in this county is owned by Negroes. Coming south from Tchula, his house is across railroad tracks just before you turn left to the Mileston community center . . . *get directions or an escort as he may shoot.*

In the South, closer to the American-frontier mentality than the rest of the East, learning to use arms was part of growing up. When I was twelve years old, my father took me into the Virginia forest and taught me how to shoot his shotgun and his Smith and Wesson .32-caliber revolver. My targets were tin cans and tree stumps. As each of my three brothers reached this age, they too were taught how to use these guns to defend themselves or kill a poisonous snake. On my own, while I was alone and aged fourteen, I shot a copperhead snake in Virginia.

As usual, Ella Baker had said little at this meeting, but now she spoke. "We have a responsibility to live up to an agreement," she said. "The agreement is not that the white volunteers are coming as emissaries to the white community. One of the reasons we're going into Mississippi is that the rest of the United States has never felt much responsibility for what happens in the Deep South. The country feels no responsibility and doesn't see that as an indictment." Her posture erect and her voice orotund, she said, "Young people will make the Justice Department move." Miss Baker never overstated anything; she understated. Her comments tended to be observational and nondirective. "If we can simply let the concept that the rest of the nation bears responsibility for what happens in Mississippi sink in, then we will have accomplished something," she said.

Bob turned the subject back to the other gnawing worry. "In discussing whites," Bob said, "we have always tried to locate positive elements in the white community to speak out—not to infiltrate segregationist White Citizens Councils to try to change them. The people who're being invited to work with us this summer were not asked to do that nor were they recruited for that purpose. Will Campbell has been traveling in the white community for one month. The American Friends Service Committee and the National Council of Churches have been doing work. The Society of Friends has sent someone down to visit in the white community to mediate. There's a tiny trickle beginning to flow that could expand as a result of the Mississippi Summer Project with teachers working with teachers and ministers working with ministers—counterparts to counterparts."

The thousand volunteers were needed, Bob said, as the spearhead of an offensive to confront and break open legalized oppression and terrorism of the state. Only then could more moderate strategies be brought into play. "Otherwise, if we're not willing to take this approach," Bob continued, "we should just think about keeping the pressure on the federal government.

"John Doar and Burke Marshall of the Justice Department went out to Mr. Steptoe's farm in McComb in early June. We're now trying to follow up to get the FBI to track down violence that is controllable and keep the leads on the predictables," Bob said. Speaking against the option of putting pressure on the federal government, which he said never produced anything significant, Bob suggested that it was hard enough to get this minimum response from a federal bureau let alone expect any serious initiatives to be taken. No one responded and the meeting turned to another topic.

Dick Frey wanted to talk about greater autonomy for the Mississippi staff from the Atlanta headquarters. Tension between headquarters and field offices was inevitable. "The present status of the movement in Greenwood is that the staff is demoralized," Dick asserted. "There's less rapport now between our staff and the local people in the town. This is one reason for decentralization of personnel," he maintained.

Willie Peacock disagreed, saying that money was the reason for morale problems. "Greenwood is immobilized," he said, "because there's no money." He explained that he, as an individual, was now too recognizable to hitchhike and he needed a car to meet with Hartman Turnbow and other local figures. But, Willie said, the movement's credit had been destroyed because of an unpaid four-hundred-dollar food bill and a five-hundred-dollar car bill. These were huge sums to us in those days. "Mississippi staff from all over the state pass through Greenwood," Willie charged, "because it's a central location in the Delta and they expect to be fed and gas up their cars."

These were the nagging day-to-day problems of our movement, with field offices feeling shortchanged of resources, and new strains were being added by preparations for the summer project. Ruby Doris, viewing the situation from her standpoint as the administrator of the Raymond Street headquarters in Atlanta, responded, "The problems of Greenwood are universal SNCC problems. There has been a lack of communication. The problems of Greenwood are the problems of SNCC."

The organization had grown from fifteen staff members in 1961 to seventy at this June 1964 meeting. On April 27, our Communications office had documented that large wooden crosses had been burned on the lawns of homes and churches in sixty-four out of a total of eighty-two counties in Mississippi alone, most probably the work of the Ku Klux Klan. (The origin of the practice of burning crosses as the mark of the KKK is obscure. It may have been adopted as "the old Scottish rite of the Fiery Cross" described in the 1905 novel *The Clansman,* by Thomas Dixon, Jr.: "In olden times when the Chieftain of our people summoned the clan on an errand of life and death, the Fiery Cross, extinguished in sacrificial blood, was sent by swift courier from village to village." This novel formed the basis of the script for the noted motion picture *The Birth of a Nation.*)

Jim Forman wanted to return to the topic of SNCC's isolation from the other civil rights groups and gave examples of how the leaders of those groups were not ready to do what Ella Baker had suggested—to take responsibility for addressing the situation in Mississippi—or even to recognize SNCC. Some of them acted as if we didn't exist. Jim reported that several other civil rights leaders had attended a one-and-a-half-hour discussion on civil rights the previous Sunday with Senator Jacob Javits in which, astonishingly, no one had raised the question of Mississippi. He gave as one positive example, however, what happened when Attorney General Robert F. Kennedy had recently telephoned Harry Belafonte and novelist James Baldwin to tell them he was coming to New York City to talk with them. They had both responded, "No. You've got to deal with SNCC."

Jim talked about how the federal government was still reluctant to use its legitimate authority. "Burke Marshall cynically told me," Jim said, "when I called him about one of the field secretaries being beaten in Columbus, Mississippi, 'Well, I guess we have to do something about it since you have the police officers' badge numbers.' "

Always eager to make connections between what we were doing and liberation movements elsewhere in the world, Jim became playful and said with a grin, "You know, SNCC is not the end-all and be-all. There are many areas where people can work. We need people in the Congo and in South Africa." His voice trailed off, giggling.

Jim Forman's worries reflected his national role and were not primary to others on the staff. Courtland Cox pulled the group back to our central concern: Should we follow a policy of nonviolence or have permission to arm ourselves for self-defense where necessary? "The expression of frustration can't be solved by talk of violence," Courtland said. "The Negro community is fundamentally American and the majority are not going to go along with violence. We're an organization trying to mobilize to bring pressure for change." Harping on a frequent theme of his that we needed long-term programs as opposed to mere protest, he stated, "Both violence and nonviolence are irrelevant without a program."

Courtland was reflecting a perspective shared by many of "the Howard group." Having had his baptismal into direct action on the rigidly segregated Eastern Shore of Maryland with SNCC's dynamic affiliate leader there, Gloria Richardson, he and other young intellectuals would later advocate a strategy whose goal was political power. The development of their concepts paralleled the turn toward political goals—in many cases, spearheading it—that the organization as a whole would make during the next two years. Courtland's comment showed that he already thought of nonviolence as tactical. When he asked for a "program," he was hinting that SNCC should reach for a more significant mark than heretofore. This would later be defined as political command of its own institutions.

"No one here has lived the life of Gandhi," Sam Block blurted out. "Amzie Moore has reported that vigilantes will kill Fannie Lou Hamer, Bob Moses, Aaron Henry, Dave Dennis, and himself." His voice rising, he cried, "Bob's too valuable to be killed in Mississippi, because there's nothing in Mississippi worth dying for! I'm not going to carry a gun but if someone else is going to protect himself, then let him protect me as well!"

I thought the meeting might shatter like a piece of glass.

This was the problem with making decisions by consensus. Until you achieved consensus, there was no way to settle a disagreement except to gravitate toward others who felt as you did; we lived with a high level of unresolved dissent in SNCC until we reached consensus.

Beginning to flail about, we seemed to be overcome by our own powerlessness to control the results of the summer project. Charlie Cobb tried to pinpoint the issue specifically, to achieve resolution, but, instead, he added a dimension of greater complexity: Should SNCC allow for defense of others who were vulnerable?

"Where does SNCC stand when Mr. Steptoe is killed while defending his home, with his two daughters there and his rifle laying on the floor?" Charlie asked. "Where does SNCC stand when I pick up the gun—as I will—and, then, when the police arrest me?"

There was a long silence broken by Ella Baker: "I can't conceive of the SNCC I thought I was associated with not defending Charlie Cobb." Speaking with her steady clear voice, she asked, "What is the basis on which it is now necessary to raise this question? In my book, Charlie would not be operating outside of SNCC if he did what he said." I wasn't sure I had heard her correctly. Did she mean that armed defense was acceptable? I believe she was actually saying that the organization avowed nonviolence but the society at large hadn't, and SNCC couldn't require the ultimate sacrifice or insist on martyrdom or suicide in certain situations.

"I won't carry a gun," Charlie said in response to several comments, "but what's different here is the presence of Mr. Steptoe's daughters. If I were there alone, I'd head out the back door. The question for me here is purely one of protection of the daughters," he said.

Matthew Jones, one of The Freedom Singers, was dismayed and jumped up, sputtering, "If I picked up the gun, that would be the day I'd be leaving SNCC." Matthew, still possessing the fervency of the Nashville vision of nonviolence as an all-embracing philosophy of life, fairly yelled, "I'm in SNCC because I believe in nonviolence."

Will the circle be unbroken, I wondered.

Lawrence Guyot, who would later become the first chairman

of the Mississippi Freedom Democratic party, spoke from the perspective of local Mississippians. Guyot, as we called him, had been graduated from Tougaloo College in 1963, and was the eldest of five brothers. He reminded the group that twenty-three local people who were active in the movement had languished in Parchman penitentiary for two months the previous summer, with no national campaign to bring attention to their plight. Guyot thought there was no course other than nonviolence. He was an impassioned speaker. "If I decide to take up arms, I'll leave Mississippi. The only reason I ask others to work in voter registration without arms," he continued, sputtering impatiently and jabbing his fingers, "is that there's some protection in it."

By "protection," Guyot was referring to the civil rights legislation that already authorized federal intervention but was rarely used. The Civil Rights acts of 1957 and 1960 were intended to reverse discrimination against blacks in voting, but the control of the Congress by the powerful Dixiecrats guaranteed that the law would not be seriously enforced and was therefore in sheriffs' hands. Guyot believed we had the moral upper hand as long as we stuck to voter registration and disdained self-defense. "Don't you see?" he bellowed, his large arms waving. "They'll shoot us quicker if we're armed!"

Having discussed these questions intensively for several hours, at last I had the feeling that we might be coming together. Guyot's was a decisive summary point—if we armed ourselves it would destroy the potency of our petition for national pressure on the state and provoke even greater violence.

Courtland Cox must have also sensed we were on the edge of accord. "It seems to me that there's consensus that there will be no guns permitted in any Freedom House or office in any SNCC project and that no one on staff is to carry guns or weapons." Glancing around the sticky room, I saw heads nodding with a sense of resolve. No one contested Courtland's statement. The question stayed open for another moment.

Someone suggested that we needed a further modification: "It will also be our policy that volunteers recruited for the Mississippi Summer Project who carry weapons will be asked to leave." Again, there was silence, assent, and no one spoke against it.

We had finally achieved that elusive group state of mind—consensus. It was not something that could be forced, and the feeling of congruence, once achieved, was difficult to define. When we achieved it, however, everyone knew it.

A question was raised: "Wait a minute, don't we need an administrative procedure to carry this through?"

Backs stiffened with exasperation. Why open another set of choices and interminable discussion? Couldn't we leave well enough alone?

"That's irrelevant," snapped Courtland coldly, reflecting everyone's impatience with the question. "What we need is a policy!"

Now we had one.

Despite SNCC's impetuosity, temerity, adventurousness, and its madcap quality, it was a thoughtful and pragmatic group of bold young Americans with a sense of mission. There were profound pressures to capitulate to armed self-defense in the early years because SNCC staff were so intrinsically rooted in rural southern communities with their traditional frontier perspective that cherished possession of guns. But these pressures were warded off again and again by staff meetings similar to this one. We would continue the struggle as the Student *Nonviolent* Coordinating Committee.

More than two years later, however, when the rhetoric of violence had captured some of the newer, more vocal northern SNCC staff, H. Rap Brown would protest, "Violence is as American as cherry pie."

CHAPTER 9

POLITICS

If you miss me from the back of the bus
and you can't find me nowhere,
Come on up to the driver's seat
I'll be driving up there.

If you don't see me in the cotton field
and you can't find me nowhere,
Come on down to the courthouse,
I'll be voting right there.

If you miss me from the old plantation
and you can't find me nowhere
Come on down to the precinct meeting
I'll be speaking-up there.

If you miss me from knockin' on doors
and you can't find me nowhere
Come on down to the circuit clerk's room
I'll be the registrar there.

If you miss me from the movement
and you can't find me nowhere,
Come on over to the graveyard,
and I'll be buried there.

—Adaptation of a spiritual

In the spring of 1964, Mayor Allen Thompson of Jackson, Mississippi, ordered and deployed a "tank," a blue armored car with machine guns that could carry twelve policemen. Jane Stembridge wrote me from the Delta:

On the other side of the wall people are getting ready too—their baby-blue riot helmets, their baby-blue tanks, their shotguns and motorcycles are for real and their horrible hate and fear. So we're over here on our side of town and they're over there on theirs and nobody can cross the line. We are two sides and we never can speak together or even cry.

In early May, the state legislature passed several bills in response to our planning for the Mississippi Summer Project. House
Bill 870 prohibited entry into the state for purposes of violating
its laws and made it a felony "to advocate change by force, violence, or willful violation of state laws." Senate Bill 2027 forbade
assemblage for purposes of "criminal syndicalism," which it defined as any doctrine or precept for "effecting any political or social change." Another piece of legislation, Senate Bill 1969, required
anyone operating a school to be licensed by the county superintendent of education. By May of that year, the governor of Mississippi had signed into law five separate bills that limited First
Amendment rights and were directed at curtailing voter-registration activity and curbing the scope of the summer project. They
prohibited picketing, banned distribution of boycott literature, allowed cities to extend their police forces to other municipalities,
permitted cities to restrict the movement of groups and to set
curfews, and provided increased penalties for violation of city ordinances.

Arms were flowing toward the state and into the hands of
white vigilantes. The increased almost-military preparedness of
the police of Jackson and other cities showed up in our daily WATS
Line Reports. This activity, however, only intensified our determination.

Jane Stembridge wrote me:

> There is just enough of a wind blowing over a just-cut field
> to make us know that there is nothing ultimate about Mis-
> sissippi as a state and nothing ultimate about the Mississippi
> legislature, although it seems so at times, realizing that they
> will never be able to issue an injunction against April nor
> legislate a leaf.

To some participants and observers, the summer of 1964 was
the climax of the civil rights movement. Yet it was the political
organizing of March, April, May, and June of 1964 in Mississippi
that marked a crossing of the Rubicon. Political organizing became the top priority in the state and, shortly afterward, mere
voter registration—with its implied passive acceptance of whoever
happened to be running as candidate—was expanded. Up to that
point we had gingerly stepped onto the path of political action

with only one foot; now, with political organizing, we planted both feet firmly on the road to electoral politics. We found ourselves facing the choice of making an effort to realign the Democratic party to include blacks or organizing separately for political power.

My parents had avoided talking partisan politics with my three brothers and me because they did not want us discussing it with my father's parishioners. This is one reason I had so little political sophistication when I joined the movement. They had not wanted people in the congregation to discuss how the pastor voted for fear it would divide the congregation or interfere with my father's ability to serve the needs of the community. As a consequence, I had to make up my mind for myself. It seemed to me that the party that might open up to black participation was the Democratic party, and that despite its domination by blatantly racist politicians in the South, if blacks could vote and participate in the party, its character could change. Perhaps it's just as well that I had no preconceived ideas about partisan politics, because I had a lot to learn.

Casey had originally moved to Mississippi to work on a literacy project with three black Mississippi staff, John O'Neal, Doris Derby, and Helen O'Neill. Once there, however, she began to concern herself with plans for a "Challenge" to the Democratic party. With some of her ties to Students for a Democratic Society still intact, she was listening from a distance to the discussion then taking place within SDS on whether it was better to try to make existing political institutions realign themselves, or preferable to work outside the framework of what already was in existence by organizing separate political entities. This distant discussion influenced her thinking and discussions with Bob Moses. This is clear from a letter she wrote me in November 1963, at the time of the Freedom Ballot mock election of Doc Henry:

> It is wild here, really well organized, lots of good work
> going on. The Henry campaign really should be seen as cru-
> cial, I think, since it is forming the whole organizing nexus
> for the state and will have real repercussions on the kind of
> political organization that will develop here—in or out of the
> Democratic party is debated here now with vigor.

The decision to move toward a formal Challenge fell within the concept of seeking realignment. Casey began working full time on the Challenge including several laborious steps leading up to it.

The first aspect of this strategy was a series of "Freedom Day" celebrations designed to awaken interest in voter registration. These took place in several towns including Greenwood, Hattiesburg, and Canton in March, April, and May of 1964. With 6 or 7 percent of Mississippi's nonwhite population registered to vote, or, at most, about thirty thousand out of over four hundred thousand black adults of voting age, the Freedom Day events were meant to reduce the likelihood of danger by bringing voting activities into the open and also to desensitize the intimidation in the minds of black people by making registration seem less formidable.

In the second step of the new political strategy, for the first time since Reconstruction four blacks announced their candidacy for the U.S. Congress—in protest write-in candidacies. Kick-off rallies in three congressional districts promoted Fannie Lou Hamer, James Houston, and the Reverend John Cameron as write-in candidates for Congress, and Victoria Gray was the statewide entrant for the Senate. Trucks with public-address systems rigged on their backs crawled sluggishly like giant snails through black sections of towns, inviting people to attend evening mass meetings.

The Boston Friends of SNCC sent ten thousand pounds of food to Ruleville by truck in March. Mrs. Hamer helped to distribute it, and, as a result of the contacts made during its distribution, sixty-five more individuals were registered to vote. (Ivanhoe Donaldson, driving alone twelve separate times from Michigan to the Delta, had in 1963 brought a dozen truckloads of food and clothing. Such supplies always made it easier to earn the confidence of the local people because it showed we were sincere about alleviating their suffering.)

On March 25, one of the first Freedom Days was held in Greenwood, because our office there had the biggest concentration of staff and leadership. The night before, at midnight, in response to the attention being attracted by the Freedom Day leafleting and the public-address systems circulating through the black community, a cross was burned four doors from our headquarters. Reflecting the rising mood in the black community, staff members Dick Frey and Iris Greenberg who were working late, sallied out, surrounded the flaming cross, and sang freedom songs around it. On Freedom Day, between two hundred and three

hundred individuals picketed the courthouse, including seventeen ministers from northern parishes who were part of a team
sent by the National Council of Churches. Approximately two
hundred people attempted to register to vote before 11:30 A.M.,
but only sixty were actually allowed to take the test. By midafter-
noon, all those on line had to leave the courthouse because a
chemical placed on the radiators turned to gas when heated, causing everyone's eyes to smart and some to become dizzy. Danny
Lyon telephoned to say he believed it was mustard gas that
was used.

The following day, approximately sixty individuals sought to
register to vote but only twenty-nine of them were permitted to
take the test. Again, a chemical gas was released inside the courthouse to discourage people from making the effort. What of the
news media? Only NBC-TV saw fit to send one correspondent.

Both nonofficial and official retaliation greeted the Freedom
Day. A twenty-two-year-old local black man named George R.
Davis, employed by C & J Transportation, was fired the day after
Freedom Day because the White Citizens Council had shown slides
taken at the courthouse and his photograph had gone up on the
screen five times. George, who also moonlighted with David Shaw
Tire and Oil Company, was advised by his second employer that
he would never be able to get another job in Greenwood.

The report telephoned to me in Atlanta noted that fourteen
individuals had been arrested (they would remain in jail for two
weeks). All of them had been involved in voter registration, most
of them driving others to the courthouse in their private automobiles. Six were held in the city jail where someone banged on the
metal doors all night preventing them from sleeping; the other
eight were removed to the county facility. On April 2, the charges
of disorderly conduct were changed to obstructing public streets,
carrying a maximum sentence of six months or a $500 fine.

Because of the success of Greenwood's Freedom Day it was
repeated on April 9. This time, I learned by telephone, forty-six
picketers were arrested; all but seventeen of them were released
by late afternoon and by evening the rest were let out of jail. At
the same time, fifty-five were arrested for voter-registration activities in Hattiesburg, including one local and two northern ministers. Momentum was building in Mississippi communities as a
result of the Freedom Day tactic. Even Liberty, in Amite County

where Herbert Lee had been killed, reported a Freedom Day on April 15.

A rash of cross burnings occurred in Hinds and Rankin counties, in the center of the state. An anonymous telephone caller to *The Jackson Clarion-Ledger* claimed that the cross burnings were part of a drive "to fight integration and communism." April 11 saw ten separate five-foot-high crosses burned in Simpson County alone, in the southern part of the state; the crosses were burned on the lawns of black families who had recently become active in the movement and in front of black schools and churches.

In response to the burgeoning interest being shown by potential black voters, there were increases in the number of injunctions, beatings, sideswipings of cars, bombings, dynamitings of cafés and meeting places, as well as many arrests of individuals who were held at both city and county jails all over the state. The charges applied by the police included improper mufflers, improper lights, unlawful picketing, refusing to obey a law officer, contributing to the delinquency of minors, running a stop sign, "arrest as a suspicious person," and breach of the peace—a medley of trumped-up charges. In Meridian, Lenore Thurman was charged with "interfering with a man's business" for encouraging a boycott of a store and her bail was set at $500.

Attorney Ben Smith, a Tulane-educated white lawyer from New Orleans who had come to Mississippi under the auspices of the National Lawyers Guild, dashed from one courthouse to another filing writs of habeas corpus. Attorney John Conyers, a black lawyer later that year elected to the U.S. Congress from Detroit, arrived to offer his assistance. A trickle of outside lawyers began coming into the state but, since there was a two-year residency period for admission to the bar, their help had to be behind the scenes. (Wiley A. Branton, head of the Voter Education Project and originally from the Arkansas Delta, seemed to be an exception to this rule; he had moved in and out of Mississippi courts from Atlanta for years and was never required to be a member of the Mississippi bar.) Marian Wright was acting out a fiction that she was the clerk to three local civil rights lawyers while waiting out her residency requirements. Volunteer lawyers coming into the state worked in support of resident attorneys R. Jess Brown, Carsie Hall, and Jack Young, and others by gathering affidavits, preparing depositions, and writing briefs.

Several of the newly active local black ministers in Greenwood called a meeting on April 21 with representatives of SNCC, SCLC, and the NAACP and formed a social-action committee in which they agreed to open more churches for mass meetings and pledged to preach "freedom sermons" on Sundays. They agreed to enlist ministers who had not been willing to take a stand and offered to sponsor indefinitely at least one mass meeting a week. They also asked SNCC field secretary Sam Block to invite eight pastors from northern parishes to help with door-to-door canvassing and agreed to house the clergy.

Although concentrating staff and resources in preparation for the Mississippi Summer Project, SNCC was still supporting its other programs. Spurred by the congressional campaigns in Mississippi, write-in candidates were fielded in other states. In Selma, Alabama, Amelia P. Boynton went through the paces of filing to run for senator in the Democratic primary and eventually got more than four thousand write-in votes in contrast to forty-eight thousand votes cast for the regular candidate. In southwest Georgia, black attorney C. B. King entered the race as a candidate for Congress. He was an amazing man, self-contained, poised, and unflappable, a person of redoubtable strength. I had watched him being addressed by judges with abusive manners in southwest Georgia courtrooms as "boy," but he did not flinch or blink at their crude efforts to humiliate and intimidate him.

I would not say that there was a split over differences in approach, but the two schools of thought coexisting within SNCC since 1961 were nowhere more visible than by the contrast between the activities of SNCC staff in Nashville working on direct action in the late spring of 1964 with those of our staff across the state border in Mississippi organizing voter registration. These two adjacent efforts showed different methods and divergent although compatible goals.

"Nashville just might be the place to start the long hot summer a little early," John Lewis said with excitement as he telephoned me from Nashville and reported the headline from one of the city's newspapers to me. Over three hundred students from Fisk University, Tennessee A & I, Vanderbilt University, Scarritt College, and Peabody College for Teachers marched downtown to the metropolitan courthouse on April 28, calling for desegregation of restaurant chains such as Morrison's and Krystal's. They had been intercepted by police, who beat them with sticks and clubs. Ten were arrested and twenty-three were hospitalized. This protest was typical of the direct action of SNCC's early years, integrationist and assimilative, based on the concept of nonviolence as a redemptive force. By mobilizing large numbers on the streets and with moral persuasion, one created a confrontation, and, the theory held, if enough people were rallied often enough, then the greatness of American society would be touched, it would awaken to the evil, and would reverse itself. SNCC's fundamental credo of May 1960 still held in Nashville in 1964, as Jim Lawson had expressed it: "By appealing to conscience and standing on the moral nature of human existence, nonviolence nurtures the atmosphere in which reconciliation and justice become actual possibilities."

The demonstrations were, John Lewis rushed to tell me, "aggressive nonviolent action—perhaps the most potent the South has seen yet." Describing the day's activities as "very serious," he said that the power of nonviolence was so strong that "the cops are out of their minds." He asked the Atlanta headquarters to send workshop leaders to Nashville, and in response Ruby Doris Smith and Cordell Reagon were dispatched.

Demonstrations continued with close to three hundred individuals picketing at Morrison's on May 1, when John was hit in the mouth and knocked down. *The Nashville Banner* headlined the story, RACIAL SCUFFLE HURTS LEWIS, yet a tiresome editorial in the same newspaper cited a report from Louisiana alleging there were communists in the movement. Meanwhile, the dean of Fisk University's chapel joined the demonstration, and Nashville's leading rabbi prepared to add members of his synagogue to the lines the next day. By May 5, more than two hundred clergymen had marched on city hall, many of them white and most of them local. So strongly ensconced was the Nashville concept of nonviolence that a new tactic was devised that day. More than two hundred white students conducted a "sip-in": After they were admitted to Morrison's cafeteria, they ordered coffee, and then remained in their seats—for hours. When they finally departed, they handed the cashier slips of paper with individually prepared messages saying, for example, "As a white citizen of Nashville, I urge you to desegregate this restaurant."

In Mississippi, however, the objectives were those of creating the conditions for a political awakening, with the longer-term
goal of political realignment. Direct action had never been the
centerpiece of the Mississippi movement for the simple reason
that Bob Moses had different goals based on his earliest discussions with Amzie Moore, the man who made it clear that desegregation was not what Mississippi needed. A beefy, heavyset man
of courage and modesty, Amzie had, despite decades of intimidation and reprisal, continued to fight as head of the NAACP
chapter in Cleveland, Mississippi. I saw Amzie through Bob's eyes,
and to Bob he was heroic. Voter registration was the issue, he told
Bob, and he asked Bob to bring student volunteers to help canvass. Amzie ruled out direct action for two reasons, I assume.
First, the state's outlaw elements were out of control and attempts to desegregate public facilities would have resulted in more
ruthless and severe repression than in the mid-South states. Second, public facilities were all but irrelevant to the economic and
political conditions of blacks in that state, who did not have sufficient money to eat at lunch counters to say nothing of restaurants.

On the eve of the Freedom Day in Hattiesburg on June 21,
1964, Ella Baker addressed a mass meeting:

> Even if segregation is gone, we will still need to be free; we
> will still have to see that everyone has a job. Even if we can
> all vote, if some people are still hungry, we will not be free.
> . . . Singing alone is not enough; we need schools and
> learning. . . . Remember, we are not fighting for the free-
> dom of the Negro alone, we are fighting for the freedom of
> the human spirit, a larger freedom that encompasses all
> mankind.

Bob hoped to confront and diffuse the fear of the violence
against blacks in Mississippi, to nurture a new indigenous leadership, and to reverse the emigration of blacks from the state. He
also wanted to open up the political process and to prepare black
citizens for public office to challenge the inequities of the archaic
economic system and the pathetic educational arrangement that
existed for blacks. This view led to tactics of community organizing, voter registration, mock elections, write-in ballots, and other

forms of educational and political action that were used in Mississippi. We still used shorthand to describe this divergence of goals and tactics and called it "direct action versus voter registration." Even though Ella Baker, at the staff meeting at Highlander Folk School in Tennessee in August 1961, had resolved the conflict by pointing out that SNCC could do both, there remained some self-consciousness about the division.

Many of the political gains of blacks and other groups such as women in the United States over the last two decades can be traced directly to these activities in Mississippi in June 1964.

A watershed event was the entry of the four local black leaders in the June 2 Democratic primary as write-in candidates in three congressional districts and the statewide race. Fannie Lou Hamer was put up against Congressman Jamie Whitten in the northwest quadrant of Mississippi's Second Congressional District and became, because of her personal power and the inspiring quality of her humility, our standard-bearer. Sandy Leigh of our staff was her campaign manager. In the southwest, where James Houston from Vicksburg was a candidate, Jesse Harris of SNCC was his campaign director. Hattiesburg was the campaign headquarters and home for the Reverend John Cameron, the write-in candidate for Congress in that district, and also for Victoria Jackson Gray, our nonofficial candidate for the Senate. Mrs. Hamer and the other candidates worked tirelessly, traveling throughout their districts or, in the case of Mrs. Gray, throughout the state, making appearances and speeches. In five days in April, for example, Mrs. Hamer spoke at mass meetings in Greenville, Holly Springs, Holmes County, Greenwood, and Itta Bena.

The June 2 write-in ballot voting had no binding effect, but it raised awareness in the black community and allowed us to reiterate the case for stronger voting-rights legislation. Victoria Gray had been one of the first blacks allowed to register to vote in Forrest County in October 1962. At the time of the 1960 census, of 7,495 voting-age blacks in the county only 24 had been permitted to register. This attractive, articulate, and fully accredited Hattiesburg teacher had been failed five times before she was finally accepted. Of the 850 blacks in Hattiesburg who, along with Victoria Gray, had sought to register in the spring of 1964, only 145 were actually enrolled.

Fannie Lou Hamer's candidacy provoked the strongest reaction from white officialdom, perhaps because of the audacity of a black woman who had been a plantation timekeeper and sharecropper contesting the seat of a member of Congress.

Near midnight on March 2, 1964, one of our staff, a young white history instructor with riveting blue eyes and steady determination named Mendy Samstein, was arrested in Ruleville. Mendy had been graduated from Brandeis University and was a doctoral candidate in history at the University of Chicago. I first met him in Atlanta in 1963 at Bobbi Yancy's apartment, when he was teaching history at Morehouse College, and it was immediately clear to me that there was a tug-of-war going on within him about whether to remain in academia or to go to work full time for the movement. It wasn't long before Mendy resolved the conflict, his idealism winning; he became one of SNCC's most conscientious and reliable field secretaries. This night Mendy was arrested along with a black SNCC worker from Greenwood, George Greene, whose home had been fired into by a shotgun exactly one year earlier, while three children slept in the bedroom as its walls were blasted. The Ruleville police slammed their pistols several times into George's stomach, apparently because he was black, and finally, after harassing Mendy and George on the side of the road, took them to the police station. One of the officers asked Mendy for whom they worked. When Mendy responded that they worked for the Council of Federated Organizations, the policeman, a surly patrolman named Officer Mileston, sneered, "You must be connected with that Fannie." Then he snorted, "We don't have any nigger politics in Ruleville." Mendy and George were put into separate cells and not allowed to telephone a lawyer. The next day the mayor informed them that they were charged with violating the curfew. When Mendy explained to the mayor that the Supreme Court had ruled that curfews for adults were unconstitutional, the mayor replied, "That law hasn't reached here yet."

On June 16 and 17, 1964, after weeks of preparation spearheaded by Casey, plans for blacks to attend the regular Democratic party precinct meetings were put into effect across the state. In groups of two, three, eight, twelve, or even fifteen, black citizens attempted to attend the standard party functions occurring on those two days that would select delegates to attend the county meetings of the party. Those sessions chose delegates to the state convention where, in turn, delegates were slated for the national convention. In many instances, only one black citizen could be found who was willing to overcome trepidation, conditioning, and fear sufficiently to attempt to attend the meetings.

Casey got on the WATS line to me in Atlanta to report on the results from across the state. Describing the precinct-meeting encounters, she recounted a variety of maneuvers used by the white Democrats to prevent blacks from participating, including canceling sessions or changing the meetings at the last moment to secret places other than the advertised location. Despite the obstacles, the attempt was a victory because the local people had overcome their intimidation and acted, at the same time aiding the process of documentation that would support the challenge to the seating of the all-white regular delegation at the Democratic National Convention in Atlantic City, New Jersey, later in the summer. Casey was excited and happy, laughing in her hearty and throaty way.

In Ruleville, eight blacks, including Mrs. Hamer, went to the customary place at the announced time, found the door locked, conducted their own meeting, and elected their own delegates to attend a counterconvention being organized for later that summer. In Thornton, a local white banker stood up and said, "I will not stay where there are Negroes"; and when the blacks were asked to leave, they did, intimidated. In Batesville, where twelve blacks showed up, the three white participants stalled for twenty minutes until they could bring in twelve more whites to give themselves a majority. In Clarksdale, fifteen blacks, including Doc Henry, were allowed to participate but were defeated on all counts by forty-nine to fifteen. One or two blacks attended the other three precinct meetings in Greenville, and, in each instance, they were allowed to participate but were defeated in their nominations of delegates. In Greenwood, the police denied to our group that a precinct meeting was taking place; however, noticing that there seemed to be some sort of a gathering in the regular meeting place in city hall, the twelve blacks (only four of whom had previously been allowed to register to vote) held their own session in front of the building and elected their own delegates to the Mississippi Freedom Democratic party convention. In Library Precinct in Hattiesburg, seven blacks and three whites came out; six of the blacks were not allowed to participate because they had not paid the poll tax and were questioned about whether they were registered to vote, while the three whites were asked no questions at all. In several of the precinct meetings Casey described, blacks appeared at the regular place, were told the meeting was not occurring there, went to look at another logical site, then returned to the original location, and were informed that the meeting had already ended.

There were some surprises. Anticipating another walkout like that of the Dixiecrats in 1948 from the Democratic National Convention, or a regional bolting from the party's platform and nominations at the forthcoming convention in Atlantic City, black participants in some precinct meetings presented a loyalty resolution binding the state's delegation to support the party's national platform and nominees. Casey said that in Precinct 3 of Greenville, a comparatively more progressive river town in the Delta, a Mr. Williams, who was black, presented the loyalty resolution and, astonishingly, it passed.

In Precinct 24 in Jackson, because 299 registered voters had voted in the last election, the precinct was one vote short of qualifying for two delegates, instead of one, to the regular county convention. Since ten blacks and only four white women attended the precinct meeting, Casey said, a black man, listed in my records only as Mr. Herrington, and a white woman, listed as Mrs. Black, were elected, the group then deciding to allot half a vote to each of them. The ten blacks, surprised at their success, did not bring up the loyalty resolution. They later said, shyly, that it was because they felt it would be "impolite."

In precincts where they conducted their own alternative election of delegates, black citizens took an important step in the unfamiliar world of electoral politics. Something more subtle was occurring in the June 16 and 17 precinct meetings; even though most of the state's blacks were still disenfranchised, the ante had been upped from mere registering to vote to running for delegate. If blacks failed individually they succeeded collectively, because of the learning and experience gained. Our staff also drew confidence from this coordinated initiative and were now more certain of the overarching political purpose of the summer project. Bob, Casey, Guyot, Jesse Morris, Frank Smith, Mendy Samstein, Jesse Harris, Charlie Cobb, and other staff became political operatives overnight and learned the Democratic party rules in detail; they assembled a mass of data to be presented to the Credentials Committee in Atlantic City at the Challenge at the upcoming Democratic National Convention. To mount the Challenge, careful documentation of legitimate black attempts to participate in the regular Democratic party was crucial.

The attempts to attend the regular party precinct meetings were followed by separate precinct meetings and district caucuses to organize a new entity, the Mississippi Freedom Democratic party (MFDP). Midway through July, the emphasis shifted from actual voter registration to "Freedom Registration" to enlist registrants in the infant alternative party.

In the book *Letters from Mississippi*, published in 1965, the editor, Elizabeth Sutherland, compiled letters written by the volunteers in the Mississippi Summer Project. One letter from Carthage described an early meeting of the budding party:

> I went to Meridian Sunday for the District Caucus—4th
> District . . . there is an aware, sophisticated group creating
> the party, so the extreme lack of sophistication on the part
> of the delegates was, for now, unimportant. It would be
> very easy for a small group of people to control the party,
> but there is no such group and the leaders really want this
> to be a learning event for the people. . . . It was a vision of
> things to come.

When the regular all-white party's state convention met on July 28, it resolved: "We believe the southern white man is the truest friend the Negro ever had; we believe in separation of the races in all phases of life."

Unbeknown to the regular party, efforts were under way across the state to establish a new party. There was no effort to make it a black party, but door-to-door solicitations of whites to join were invariably rebuffed. One volunteer's letter home from Vicksburg, included here from Elizabeth's book, read:

> Fear reigned at first—but soon people were excited about
> the prospects of the party and neighbors were talking to
> neighbors about this "New Thing." Block parties and mass
> meetings were being held many times a week in various
> parts of town. Spirit grew. Hundreds of people risked their
> lives and jobs to come. Representatives were elected after

the election of a permanent chairman and secretary. Resolutions were introduced, minutes were kept . . . The precinct meeting was one of the most exciting events of my
life.

The "New Thing" held its state convention in Jackson on
August 6, 1964, at the black Masonic Temple up the street from
the Lynch Street COFO headquarters. This historic event was
attended by more than three hundred delegates who were elected
in the precinct meetings and observers, and was the high point of
the summer for me. It was the heyday. It was another tremor in
the middle of the iceberg of Bob's letter from the Magnolia jail. I
was moved by the sight of over three hundred delegates, few of
whom had ever been able to cast a vote in their entire lives, holding their floor passes and presenting their credentials, in their
Sunday-go-to-meeting clothes, the women in their best dresses,
the men in starched shirts, their faces earnest and serious. Joust-
ing placards representing their counties, they lobbied for resolutions, and reluctantly seated themselves as Guyot gaveled the
convention to order. Ella Baker gave the keynote address and told
the delegates to prepare themselves for a new type of fight—
political battle. The convention elected the sixty-eight delegates
and alternates who would represent the Freedom party in Atlantic
City in the Challenge.

Another volunteer's letter published by Elizabeth Sutherland read:

> Right after Miss Baker's speech, there was a march of all
> the delegates around the convention hall—singing freedom
> songs, waving American flags, banners, and county signs.
> This was probably the most soul-felt march ever to occur in
> a political convention, I felt, as we marched with a mixture
> of sadness and joy—of humility and pride—of fear and cour-
> age, singing "Go Tell It on the Mountain," "Ain't Gonna
> Let Nobody Turn Me 'Round," and "This Little Light of
> Mine."

I felt completely alive, sparkling with good humor, buoyant
with confidence, filled with hope, exhilarated, and lighthearted.
It was a moment of high jubilation and vindication. Having been
growing steadily more political in my thinking, now I could savor

the sweet results. The convention passed a loyalty resolution pledging its support to the national party, unlike the state regular Democratic party, which had not, and this convinced me that the national party would receive the Freedom Delegation with open arms. I, and I think everyone else in SNCC, believed the two-party political system could be realigned and that the state Democratic party would be required to open up to blacks if a lawful Challenge was presented.

Elizabeth Sutherland's volume includes a letter written on August 9, 1964, from Moss Point:

> This is the stuff democracy is made of. All of us here are pretty emotional about the names of the counties of Mississippi. Amite and Sunflower and Tallahatchie have always meant where this one was shot, where this one was beaten, where civil rights workers feared for their lives the minute they arrived. But on Thursday, Amite and Tallahatchie and Sunflower and Neshoba didn't mean another man's gone. They meant people are voting from there, it meant people who work fourteen hours a day from sun-up to sun-down picking cotton and living in homes with no plumbing and no paint, were casting ballots to send a delegation to Atlantic City. As the keynote speaker said, it was not a political convention, it was a demonstration that the people of Mississippi want to be let into America.

The success of the new alternative party, in that atmosphere of fear, was a tribute to consolidated effort, including Bob's perspicacity, Casey's diligence, and the hard work of Guyot as the first chairman of the new party, and the Mississippi staff. But, even more, it was an expression of the resourcefulness and heart of some of the bravest people in the country—local black Mississippians who defied history and their own experience of violence to put their lives on the line.

Sitting in that convention, I thought of Chuck McDew's frequent paraphrasing of the popular slogan justifying World War I—to make the world safe for democracy. His words summed up my state of mind at that moment: "We must fight in America," Chuck would say, "not to make the world safe for democracy but to make democracy safe for the world."

*   *   *

The Mississippi Freedom Democratic party delegates who would present the Challenge boarded buses in Jackson and reached the Democratic National Convention in Atlantic City on Friday, August 21. The atmosphere was exhilarating for the delegation and the staff members who accompanied them. There was, first of all, the scale, the feverish activity, and the aura of excitement on the boardwalk that dazzled and bewildered them. In addition, there were platoons of national and international news media, electronic and print, and all the rituals associated with this most quintessentially American political phenomenon, the national convention of a major party. For our delegation, it was intoxicating. Politically speaking, it was a dull convention—almost a ceremonial coronation rally for Lyndon Baines Johnson who was draped in the mantle of the slain President Kennedy—and there was no opposition. The only questions of interest were who would be chosen as his vice-presidential nominee, and the Challenge represented by the black Mississippians.

The events of the summer had been important. Only a short time earlier, three of our fellow workers, James Chaney, Andrew Goodman, and Michael Schwerner, had been lynched. That tragedy plus the presence of nearly one thousand volunteers from mainstream America had attracted world press attention; the struggle in Mississippi had been in the national consciousness all summer. When our gallant delegation of rural Mississippians got off the buses, many of them were greeted by members of the national and international press corps as old friends, or at least as familiar faces. It is unlikely that anyone arriving from anywhere in the country with a state delegation for the convention did not have some awareness of the Mississippi issue; it had been on the airwaves all summer.

As if that were not enough, the summer project volunteers had been writing to their families, friends, churches, and members of Congress about conditions in Mississippi. Many volunteers made fast trips home to lobby for support for the Freedom party by local Democratic leaders and then routed themselves back to Mississippi by way of Atlantic City. Outside the convention hall, these volunteers, along with their friends and supporters, maintained a constant vigil shadowed by huge portraits of our three dead colleagues mounted on tall poles. The burned-out car in which they had last been seen was on exhibit. The vigil on the boardwalk grew from eighteen people to three thousand. The volunteers engaged every delegate going into the arena, distributing material describing the Challenge and their experiences in Mississippi. More important, they testified to any who would listen, and their earnestness, passion, and sincerity visibly moved many a delegate, some of them to tears.

Thus, the vast majority in the convention knew, at least abstractly, of the issues surrounding the Challenge. What they may not have had was the personal experience of the force, the power, the spirit, the dignity, and the presence of the black people of Mississippi. They had not encountered the simple eloquence and mighty determination of a Fannie Lou Hamer, Annie Devine, E. W. Steptoe, or Hartman Turnbow. Once they did, and if the convention was called upon to choose between the regular all-white delegation and the Freedom party, it was inconceivable that we would not have been seated. At the worst, we thought, they might seat both delegations and divide the votes allocated to Mississippi equally between them. This would doubtless have caused the regulars to reject such a compromise, because their commitment to white supremacy would not have permitted them to share authority with "our nigras." Governor Ross Barnett and Senator James Eastland accorded equal status with Mrs. Hamer and Mr. Steptoe? They would, we thought, certainly have felt it necessary to stalk out even if they secretly preferred to stay. Alabama, Georgia, South Carolina, and Louisiana might have felt honor-bound to follow them. That these states ended up, predictably, voting for Goldwater was something the Democratic leadership did not seem to consider. But, as events were to show, the Johnson leadership did not really need the Dixiecrats' votes, and it would have cost nothing politically for both delegations to have been seated.

Led by Fannie Lou Hamer, the Freedom party delegation began approaching members of the Credentials Committee, asking them directly to unseat the racially exclusive state party's delegation. Several state delegations passed resolutions in their daily caucuses supporting the MFDP. Overall, however, the Freedom party delegates were disappointed by the response from their contacts with Credentials Committee members and thought they would have a better chance if the national audience could hear their appeal and watch as each state delegation voted on the Challenge. They decided to try instead to get onto the floor of the convention and did so with borrowed passes from sympathizers.

One of the volunteers working to help the delegation get onto the convention floor wrote a letter that is included in *Letters from Mississippi:*

> At 7 P.M. we met . . . and arranged a system of runners to bring badges from regular delegates inside the hall to FDP delegates outside. I was appointed to receive badges inside and carry them outside to a person who passed them on to delegates waiting in small groups on street corners near the hall. I made about four or five trips in and out—it was really exciting. I felt like Mata Hari and the French Resistance rolled into one. I had very little trouble getting back into the hall because I wore a press badge which was honored.

Absolutely convinced that the delegation was right and that their case rested on solid documentation of their efforts to participate in the June precinct meetings and legitimate open elections for their own delegation as opposed to the illegitimate elections of the regular state party's representatives, it never occurred to us that our delegation would be turned down. As Miss Baker had said, the black Mississippians simply wanted to be let into America, let into the state party. The delegation was exuberant and confident that they had properly held openly advertised precinct and county elections, that at every step of the cumbersome process they had carried out the procedures with faultless attention to detail, and that they, not the regulars, had legitimately elected their sixty-eight delegates and alternates.

On the next day, Saturday, August 22, Fannie Lou Hamer made a passionate speech before the Credentials Committee, which was chaired by the attorney general from Minnesota, Walter F. Mondale. She told how blacks in Mississippi were excluded from the most basic rights of democracy, and included the story of her beating in Winona one year before. The validity of the MFDP's presentation was starting to put great pressure on President Johnson who, as a sitting president occupying his office after a tragic assassination, had mastery and control of the convention. He was said to be afraid of a walkout by all the southern delegations if the Freedom Delegation was seated and he gave Vice-President Hubert H. Humphrey the task of deflecting the Challenge. He asked him to offer the fledgling party a compromise: two at-large seats, to be selected by him, and a guarantee from the regular party that it would, beginning in 1968, never again bring an all-white delegation to a national convention; in return, the regular delegation would be seated after taking a loyalty resolution.

Tuesday dawned after a fretful night. The Credentials Committee was to meet at 2:00 P.M. At ten o'clock in the morning, the Freedom party caucused. Bob Moses slowly and deliberatively asked the delegation if they would be willing to take the two seats offered in President's compromise. Led by Fannie Lou Hamer, the delegation voted overwhelmingly to reject the lamented compromise and the two seats, although Doc Henry favored it. In doing this, Mrs. Hamer was taking on President Johnson and Vice-President Humphrey, but neither the men nor their offices impressed her—the struggle to her was not symbolic; it had life-and-death consequences. She knew that members of the delegation might be killed returning home. Furthermore, the promises for 1968 referred only to blacks who were already registered and laid no groundwork for future patronage.

Pressure to accept the proffered compromise from the entire leadership of the Democratic party was overwhelming, and it was of this force that SNCC workers retained their most lasting memories. Years later, former SNCC staff members are still rankled by the recollection of an assortment of figures ranging from Vice-President Humphrey, to Roy Wilkins, to Martin Luther King, to Bayard Rustin, to James Farmer, to attorney Joseph L. Rauh, Jr., of Washington, D.C., claiming that the compromise was a "great victory" and trying to induce Mrs. Hamer and the delegation to take the token seats. They lobbied the delegation hard in favor of the compromise. Mrs. Hamer later reported the details of how one mighty figure after another tried to coax her. According to her, Roy Wilkins, executive secretary of the NAACP, said to her, "Mrs. Hamer, you people have put your point across. You don't know anything. You're ignorant of politics. You don't know anything about politics. I've been in the business for over twenty years. You people have your point across, now why don't you head on home?" Yet Mrs. Hamer held her position, standing up to the giants who were unleashed on the Freedom Delegation.

Was the sharecroppers' contesting of the seats so threatening to Lyndon Baines Johnson, Hubert H. Humphrey, and Walter F.

Mondale that it shouldn't be allowed to go through as the case warranted? Or, was there something more at work?

Joseph Rauh was the powerful counsel to the United Auto Workers in Washington, D.C. During the preceding spring, when virtually every other civil rights and liberal figure said that our Challenge wasn't feasible and couldn't be mounted, Joe Rauh had told Bob he thought it could. In reality, the only reason we got to Atlantic City was because Rauh helped to take us there. It was he who assured us that the backwoods Mississippians and threadbare staff would be received seriously. Yet his exact role in the final outcome has remained a mystery and a source of resentment to many SNCC workers. By summer, concerned as were others that Humphrey might not be chosen as Johnson's running mate, Rauh moved into the role of lawyer for the MFDP. Perhaps it was a shrewd move to preempt the Challenge from promoting discord and hurting Humphrey's chances. For, in the final moment, instead of acting as advocate for the Freedom Democrats, Rauh ended up acting as middleman trying to sell the compromise offer to the delegation. In one meeting with Humphrey, Rauh told Mrs. Hamer that if the delegation didn't back off, Humphrey would not be nominated for vice-president. Mrs. Hamer glared at the Vice-President, "Mr. Humphrey, do you mean to tell me that your position is more important than Mississippi's four hundred thousand black lives?"

The Reverend Edwin King, who, as a white leader in the alternative party, would probably have been handpicked to fill one of the two seats, later said that Vice-President Humphrey told him about Fannie Lou Hamer: "The President has said he will not let that illiterate woman on the floor of the Democratic convention."

To the SNCC staff who were following Ella Baker's stance and trying to be nondirective, the tendered offer in response to their labors and anguish represented anything but a compromise. Yet they said little. Casey later remarked to me, "The local people knew they had done it right and they didn't buckle. The SNCC staff didn't have to influence the delegation. They didn't yield to the pressure to accept the compromise because they knew they had legitimately elected their delegation and were correct. The pressure from the other civil rights leaders was inappropriate. The Challenge had absolutely nothing to do with the NAACP or

SCLC. I don't even know why Roy Wilkins or SCLC and Dr. King lobbied us."

Seventeen members of the Credentials Committee were committed to bringing a minority report to the floor on the Mississippi Challenge, more than the number of votes required. If such a document was to be presented, it would surely mean a floor fight. It was at this juncture that long knives came out to prevent a minority paper from reaching the full convention. Each member of the Credentials Committee suddenly found him- or herself being buttonholed in hotel lobbies, elevators, crowded corridors, and lavatories, and being pressured to vote against the minority report. The leverage of the White House was surgically applied as government contracts were threatened to be withheld, judgeships were rumored to be pulled back, and other forms of intimidation were brought to bear. Congresswoman Edith Green of Oregon held out for the minority report despite insistence that she change her vote. It had been her idea that the convention seat all members of either delegation who would take an oath of loyalty to the national party and presidential ticket, a move that the white Mississippians would probably have disdained, and the subject of the minority report. Curiously, it was at this critical point that Joe Rauh erroneously reported to the committee that the Freedom party had voted to accept the compromise. Many of my fellow workers believed he did this as a calculated, opportunistic move to snuff out the Challenge. I tend to think he had been misinformed or misled about the delegation's intentions, because I don't believe Rauh would have lied only to be found out twenty minutes later. But by then, the committee had voted down the minority report which demolished the Challenge.

Many accounts, including Theodore White's *The Making of the President—1964*, imply that the Freedom party delegation accepted the compromise and the two seats. This is not true. For people who had been forcibly denied participation in the selection of the all-white delegation to accept two seats and then watch as that supremacist delegation occupied Mississippi's seats and cast the state's votes was offensive and invidious. What was particularly galling to us was that the reason given for offering the compromise was fear of losing the South because the MFDP delegates knew that the Republican presidential nominee, Senator Barry Goldwater, was going to carry the region.

True, the Challenge brought the specifics of disenfranchisement before the nation in a way that had not been possible before, and started rules reform within the party. Yet the offer of
two seats, given the enormity of the Freedom party's efforts against
daunting odds, and the raw power of its protest, will be remembered with bitterness, to their dying day, by the dozens of SNCC
staff and COFO volunteers who had helped to mount the Challenge.

After the convention was over, SNCC worker Mike Thelwell
was given three hundred dollars and asked to open a Washington
office for the MFDP. Mike was a willowy, handsome, fair-skinned
Jamaican writer from Kingston. He had a lilting accent and a strong
sense of irony, and was, I believe, the only person on the SNCC
staff who was not a U.S. citizen, having come to Washington on
a student visa to study literature at Howard University. The first
piece of mail to tumble through the slot of the new Washington
office was an eleven-thousand-dollar invoice for reproduction copies
of the MFDP legal briefs used by Joseph Rauh at Atlantic City.
Mike telephoned him and said that they hadn't ordered any printing and that "the poor folk in Mississippi, like the printer who
had sent the bill" had assumed this was to be a contribution of
the wealthy United Auto Workers. "Well," Rauh retorted, "you're
independent," leaving the budding party to raise the money for
the bill, which, said Mike proudly, they finally did.

What happened in Atlantic City was the beginning of a division within the civil rights movement that posed SNCC, CORE,
and the MFDP on one side, and the NAACP and Urban League
on the other, with SCLC hovering in between. The SNCC staff
became disillusioned, not only with other civil rights groups, but
also about the capacity of existing political institutions for reform.
Thus began SNCC's move toward independent and separate institutions. Inside the organization, the belief grew that local and
state governments in the Black Belt couldn't change on their own
initiative but had to be democratically taken over by the black
majority. Language changes first, and our rhetoric began to alter;
it would not be long before we started talking about "taking over
the courthouse." And, as we became more politicized, adopting
the goal of developing separate and independent political parties,
cooperatives, and credit unions, we started to speak of the radical
restructuring of society.

With the myopia of intense youthful idealism, we would willingly have sacrificed the election of Lyndon Baines Johnson, something I now see as too rigid an insistence on purity. It did not give us much pause that the Republican party's nominee, Barry Goldwater, who campaigned unabashedly for the racist vote in the South, would have been a more serious setback for blacks and other Americans. But, of course, as the election showed, there was no way that the Goldwater candidacy could have won in a national election in 1964.

Jane Stembridge wrote a poem about Mrs. Hamer and the compromise:

> the
> revolutionary
> element remained
>
> intact.
>
> they
> simply
> stood, she said
>
> no sir
>
> (for emphasis)
>
> we didn't come
> for no two
> seats
>
> since
>
> all of us
> is tired.

Fannie Lou Hamer, the granddaughter of slaves, came to the fore nationally as a central figure in the civil rights movement in Atlantic City and perhaps best represented the natural leadership that Ella Baker and Bob Moses saw as the linchpin of the civil rights struggle. Growing up with her nineteen sisters and brothers in circumstances only one small step removed from slavery, Fannie Lou Hamer had received scarcely any formal education. Yet, she often said, her sharecropping mother had taught her to "stand up no matter what the odds." She was a woman of wisdom, grit, and discernment. Jane Stembridge observed:

> Mrs. Hamer is more educated than I am. That is, she knows more.
>
> Not the clear line between justice and injustice. I know that, too. Not what to say in Atlantic City. I know that, too. Not what a citizen is entitled to receive, as citizen. Not what a human being deserves. I know these.
>
> Not how to speak with congressmen, nor how to make a speech. I know that. . . .
>
> Not how to endure pain. I can endure pain—my pain, pain of the ends of things, relationships, failures; even physical pain.
>
> She knows more. What? She knows *she is good*.
>
> If she didn't, she couldn't sing the way that she sings. She couldn't stand, head back, and sing. She couldn't speak the way that she speaks—she *announces*.
>
> It is not the story she tells—dramatic, true, terrible, real. It isn't the facts, but the way that she stands to announce.

Mrs. Hamer often aroused the SNCC staff by rising and announcing, "I'm sick and tired of being sick and tired." No one wearied of hearing her utter this phrase, it was so matter-of-fact. Despite her circumstances and the sadness in her mournful eyes, she had a deep well of self-assurance; she believed that no one was better than she. But there was also the other side of Fannie Lou Hamer, her humility; she was not better than anyone else.

Whenever she was strongly moved, she would stand spontaneously, radiant, her face glistening, defiant in her compact, rounded physical frame, and lead us in her favorite spiritual: "This little light of mine, I'm gonna let it shine." She started singing alone, mellifluously; then our voices would one by one mingle with hers as we let her lead us. The "light" of the spiritual served as a metaphor for one's life, and "this little light of mine" was a pledge of her life's purpose. Fannie Lou Hamer sang it as an expression of her personal commitment, but it was also a call to reaffirmation for others. Largely because of how Fannie Lou Hamer sang this spiritual—stirring and simple, yet profound—it became a mainstay of the movement's freedom songs.

The MFDP delegation departed from Atlantic City asserting that they would nonetheless remain loyal Democrats and returned to Mississippi to campaign for the Johnson-Humphrey ticket. With a twist of rare calculated irony, they knew that their support would lose white votes, yet they would prove their fealty. MFDP posters supporting Johnson were sprayed with bullet holes around the state. The rationale for rejecting the Challenge in Atlantic City was that the party might lose the South. Yet there was no doubt that the Democrats would lose the white South in 1964 against a conservative Goldwater—it was the only region where he did well.

That autumn, the MFDP decided to mount another "Challenge"—this time to the Congress. In the Second Congressional District, Fannie Lou Hamer was slated as the "Freedom Candidate." In the Third Congressional District, Annie Devine from Canton was to run, and, in the Fifth Congressional District, Victoria Jackson Gray was the protest candidate. In these three districts, black candidates once again challenged the all-white party in protest.

There is a humorous footnote to this account that bears noting. In January 1965, after Lyndon Baines Johnson had been elected in a landslide, the Freedom party office in Washington was organizing the Congressional Challenge. One morning, the office coordinator, Mike Thelwell, happened on a feature story in *The Washington Post* detailing the elaborate arrangements being made for the inauguration. The White House staff member in charge of the operation was identified. Out of a sense of mischief, Mike wrote him a tongue-in-cheek letter, describing the distress of the Freedom party. The only group that had campaigned for the national ticket in Mississippi had been the MFDP, the letter decried, and yet no one from the alternative party had been invited to the inauguration. At best, Mike had hoped to cause some bureaucratic discomfiture. Having forgotten all about the letter, he was surprised when the phone rang one morning and he heard

Hartman Turnbow languidly drawl, "Mike, you know that white fella run the post office in Tchula? This mornin' he come to my house to wake me up. He had this *big* envelope." Elsewhere in Mississippi as well, large engraved invitations to the inauguration with the presidential seal were similarly being delivered to Fannie Lou Hamer, Victoria Gray, Annie Devine, E. W. Steptoe, Doc Henry, Ed King, Susie Ruffin, and others. With only seven dollars in the party treasury, a decision was made to telephone Lucy Montgomery in Chicago, one of SNCC's most loyal financial supporters and a white southerner, to ask her help in raising the money necessary to allow the Freedom Democrats to attend.

Mr. Turnbow wanted to go to whichever of the five inaugural balls Governor Paul B. Johnson of Mississippi and his wife would attend, "So's I can ask Mrs. Johnson to dance wid me," he said, with a wink in his eye. The invitees, most of them sharecroppers or farmers, went to Washington where MFDP lawyer Jan Goodman took the women to Woodward and Lothrop department store to buy ball gowns at the expense of the party. Jan later said, "When we got to the store, a sales clerk looked at the group of poor, country black women and sniffed, 'And what may I do for you?' 'You may,' said Mrs. Devine with great dignity, 'take us to your better dresses department, please.' " When they tried on the dresses, Jan reported, "I saw poverty; their worn-out slips and petticoats were pinned up with safety pins and everything was tied together." Later, when Mrs. Devine was asked by a young woman journalist, "That's a nice dress, Mrs. Devine, but where on earth can you wear it in Mississippi?" she answered, "Why, to the executive committee meetings of the Freedom Democratic party and I can't think of nothing more important than that."

Pursuing the concept of a Congressional Challenge, MFDP organizers sought and found a member of Congress who was willing to rise at the swearing-in of the new Congress to challenge the credentials and seating of the Mississippi delegation. He was William Fitts Ryan, a reform Democrat elected from Manhattan's Upper West Side Twentieth Congressional District in 1960. The first member of Congress to condemn American involvement in Vietnam and vote against the war, Ryan agreed to make the challenge. Since only the House can vote on its own membership, the actual challenge had to come from within that body. None of us thought Fannie Lou Hamer, Annie Devine, and Victoria Gray would be seated. By making the fight, however, we hoped to keep the three seats vacant and send a signal to all southern districts. Organizers from SNCC and the MFDP fanned out to rally other members of Congress to Ryan's side, but this was a difficult task since Congress was not yet in session. As a consequence of President Johnson's victory and his long coattails, the Eighty-ninth Congress had the largest incoming Democratic class in years, some from districts that had never before elected a Democrat. It included John Conyers and Patsy Mink, and they and other newly elected members agreed to join with Ryan when the SNCC and MFDP workers surrounded them in a hotel suite adjacent to their freshman orientation session.

Because Congress was not in session, we were unable to secure other votes and were at a loss as to how to garner more support. Knowing that most of the members going to the initial session would walk through the long underground passage connecting the Capitol with the House office buildings, however, the MFDP decided to line the artery with individuals like Hartman Turnbow, E. W. Steptoe, Robert Miles, and other black Mississippians. The tunnel was queued with poor rural Mississippians, approximately ten feet apart. With their work-worn overalls, faded dresses, and their posture bowed from physical work, they held themselves solemnly. They stood with such dignity and such presence, saying nothing but looking each member of Congress straight in the eye as he or she passed. Mike Thelwell recalled, "I watched as the equilibrium of the elected representatives was visibly affected by the presence of the Mississippians."

With a sense of drama, Mrs. Hamer, Mrs. Devine, and Mrs. Gray went through the motions and were brought to the door of the chamber to claim their seats. As we expected, they were turned away. When the House convened, Ryan rose and objected to the seating of the Mississippi representatives. Astonishingly, some 60 members of Congress rose with him, half of them, we believed, as a result of the walk through that tunnel. When the actual vote was taken, 149 members voted not to seat the regular Mississippi delegation on the first vote.

The next day, the governor of Mississippi sent a letter to state patrolmen and sheriffs across the state saying that incidents of violence against civil rights workers must cease and nothing should occur to give Congress reason to take punitive action. Mississippi newspapers ran editorials saying that the House of Representatives had turned against them and that the name of the state had been traduced by radicals.

They were not the only ones offended. Mike recounted:

> The NAACP was outraged. The whole liberal establishment had turned against us at Atlantic City and now they maintained that the Congressional Challenge was not serious. Joe Rauh was stunned when I told him of the one hundred forty-nine votes. It was a serious blow to the prestige of the NAACP and the labor groups in the Leadership Conference of Civil Rights that we students and sharecroppers—supported by the Protestant church denominations and the National Council of Churches—could get those one hundred forty-nine congressional votes.
>
> The NAACP and other civil rights groups used to say that it was their expertise, contacts, and influence in Washington that would swing congressional votes. This time we did it without them.

We subpoenaed the Mississippi members of Congress, the head of the state Democratic party, and the former governor of the state as well as their lawyers to hearings on the Congressional Challenge. The Lawyers' Committee for Civil Rights enlisted dozens of volunteer lawyers as counsel for the MFDP to establish the obvious—that blacks were not permitted to vote. In dusty little tucked-away weatherboarded black churches, black people cross-examined the Mississippi powers. Now, however, they were no longer addressed as "girl" or "boy" but as "ma'am" and "sir."

The Congressional Challenge did not pass, but I believe it made possible the passage of the Voting Rights Act later that year. The Democrats in the Congress at heart preferred not to vote to unseat the Mississippi representatives and alienate the South, especially those southerners chairing committees whose average tenure, if I recall correctly, then ran something like twenty-two years. SNCC and MFDP organizers maintained pressure on the House throughout the year. Prior to meetings, they went into the hearing rooms of committees of which the Mississippi representatives were members and wrote boldly across the second pages of the paper pads waiting at the members' seats, "Unseat the Mississippi Congressmen." When the members tore off the top page, the slogan leaped out at them. The organizers mobilized high school students to insert leaflets with the same message under the windshield wipers of congressional cars. "Some of the members talked about a highly financed communist plot—they said they couldn't move in Washington without being confronted with leaflets," our Washington staff said. In the whole year and a half Congressional Challenge, though, SNCC didn't raise and spend more than ninety thousand dollars for everything connected with it, and eleven thousand dollars of that went for Joe Rauh's briefs.

At meetings of the coalition of civil rights and labor-union groups composing the Leadership Conference on Civil Rights, Mike Thelwell sometimes represented either SNCC or the MFDP:

> The other groups were narrow and vindictive, and actively worked against us and the Congressional Challenge. We didn't have any influence, they said. It was a hostile arena; they tried to ostracize us from the political community. What saved us was the support of the churches—they took an evenhanded approach.
>
> The NAACP Washington representative, Clarence Mitchell, who chaired the coalition in the absence of Roy Wilkins, came to the meeting one day and reported that President Johnson was thinking about introducing voting-rights legislation in Congress. He went over the bill's provisions. It was atrocious. It said that only in towns and communities where less than 10 percent of the black population is registered the President *may* send federal voting registrars.
>
> Dr. King said he would support it but I later telephoned him and said, "This bill says that ninety percent disenfranchisement is good; it's only when it's ninety-one percent that they *might* send registrars. It means that in communities where people have risked their lives struggling to vote and gotten eleven percent of the black community registered, they won't come under the law—they're being punished for the courage and bravery they showed. Even then, the registrars will only be sent at the President's discretion."
>
> When Dr. King realized what the legislation meant, he reversed his position and signed with Jim Forman, Lawrence Guyot of the MFDP, and James Farmer of CORE, a statement that if the climate in Congress wasn't right, we would take to the streets again and create the climate. Dr.

King's name gave legitimacy when we rejected the proposal.
Evans and Novak attacked us for irresponsibility, adventur-
ism, and "trying to destroy the Leadership Conference on
Civil Rights." I think either the NAACP or the AFL-CIO
was leaking to them. Four days after that memo was circulated, without any real planning, Selma broke out.

Another legislative package was prepared in Washington. This
time, in consultation with our new friends in Congress, members
of the SNCC staff were able to participate in preparing the language and suggested that the law's provisions should be automatic, with registrars able to go anywhere in the South to register
whoever wished to vote.

The MFDP Washington office organized a constituent letter-
writing campaign entailing national mailings and a conference attended by the Friends of SNCC, church representatives, and civil
rights and peace groups. One after another, the members of Congress who had said they would support the Congressional Challenge began responding to the orchestrated queries of their
constituents. They wrote back in response to the incoming letters
that while they supported human rights, they planned instead to
vote in support of the new Voting Rights Act thus making the
need to unseat the Mississippians moot. The Voting Rights Act
passed in the Congress as emphatically as it did—77 to 19 in the
Senate and 333 to 85 in the House—because we had kept up our
pressure for more than one year, with volleys of affidavits, constituent visits, leaflets in the parking lots, and messages on writing pads. From inside SNCC and the MFDP, it seemed clear to
us that the legislation itself had come about in large part, although
certainly not solely, as a consequence of the Congressional Challenge.

The Atlantic City Challenge not only brought Fannie Lou
Hamer and others like her into national view; it is now possible
to see that this Challenge began a process of rules reform within
the Democratic party that moved in four-year segments, from 1964
to 1968 to 1972, accompanied by a steady rise of black voters.
These reforms later made it possible for an outsider to the party
structure, Governor Jimmy Carter, to obtain the presidential nomination in 1976, as the party had become more open to popular
participation.

Following Jimmy Carter's 1976 election, a Voter Education Project poster appeared saying, THE HANDS THAT PICKED THE COTTON PICKED A PRESIDENT. Certainly, the dramatic turnout of black voters in that election was a major factor in the Democratic victory. This process was helped by the imprimatur of the first black member of Congress from Georgia since Reconstruction, Andrew Young. After Andy saw that then Governor Carter could win against the segregationist Alabama Governor George Wallace, in the Florida primary (and was therefore able to beat racist appeal in the South), Andy began to travel on Carter's behalf. President Carter has said that he could not have won the nomination without enthusiastic support from the black community in key primary states. This support was essential in the major cities that played an even more vital role in determining the delegates sent to the national convention after the end of the winner-takes-all primaries, because urban votes could now swing a state. In the general election, black response was critical to the Carter win. This turnout was a direct result of the political changes that had begun in Mississippi in 1964 and had steadily developed in the South throughout the following years, gathering black political strength until it could actually determine the outcome of a presidential election. No white southerner could have achieved the American presidency in the twentieth century without the support of southern blacks.

It would be twenty-two years before Fannie Lou Hamer's 1964 protest candidacy in the Second Congressional District would bear fruit; it was not until November 1986 that Mike Espy, a black lawyer, was elected to the 100th Congress from the 53-percent black Delta district. To the extent that there is a starting point, a moment, that marked the beginning of the still-growing impact of black voting on American politics, it was June 16 and 17, 1964, the all but unnoticed dates of the precinct meetings in Mississippi.

John Lewis *(left)*, summer 1962, Cairo, Illinois © *Danny Lyon/Magnum*

Organizing in "Terrible" Terrell County, Georgia, 1962. Charles Sherrod *(standing right)*, Randy Battle *(sitting right)* © *Danny Lyon/Magnum*

Above: The twenty girls, aged nine to thirteen, arrested in Americus, Georgia, August 9, 1963, and transferred to the Leesburg stockade. They were held for a month with no beds, mattresses, or commodes.
© *Danny Lyon/Magnum*

Dorie *(left)* and Joyce Ladner at the March on Washington, August 28, 1963 © *Danny Lyon/Magnum*

The sit-in where I was
arrested at the Toddle
House coffee shop in
Atlanta, Georgia,
December 21, 1963

Judy Richardson *(center)*,
Chuck Neblitt *(right, facing
camera)*, George Greene
(standing, right)
© *Danny Lyon/Magnum*

"Big Rock," the Atlanta
city jail, where we were
locked up just before
Christmas 1963, and where
Nancy Stearns and I were
separated from the others
© *Danny Lyon/Magnum*

Bob Moses training the volunteers at Oxford, Ohio, prior to their departure for Mississippi, June 1964 © *1964 Steve Shapiro—Black Star*

Volunteers learning freedom songs, Oxford, Ohio, June 1964. Liz Fusco *(center)* coordinated the freedom schools. © *1964 Steve Shapiro—Black Star*

Arriving in Mississippi, volunteers joined with local residents to sing "We Shall Overcome," June 1964 © *1964 Steve Shapiro—Black Star*

Mississippi Freedom Democratic party meeting at the Indianola, Mississippi, freedom school, July 1964, to prepare the Challenge to the National Democratic Convention in Atlantic City, New Jersey. (SNCC's insignia is painted above the freedom-school door.) © *Bob Fletcher: a SNCC Photo*

Above: After Leake County officials tried to stop the freedom school in Harmony, Mississippi, in July 1964, the local residents, staff, and volunteers built a new community center. © *Bob Fletcher: a SNCC Photo*

Inset: Mendy Samstein Mississippi Delta, 1964 © *Danny Lyon/Magnum*

CHAPTER 10

MISSISSIPPI

They say that freedom is a constant struggle,
They say that freedom is a constant struggle,
They say that freedom is a constant struggle,
O Lord, we've struggled so long,
We must be free, we must be free.

They say that freedom is a constant crying,
They say that freedom is a constant crying,
They say that freedom is a constant crying,
O Lord, we've cried so long,
We must be free, we must be free.

They say that freedom is a constant sorrow,
They say that freedom is a constant sorrow,
They say that freedom is a constant sorrow,
O Lord, we've sorrowed so long,
We must be free, we must be free.

They say that freedom is a constant moaning,
They say that freedom is a constant moaning,
They say that freedom is a constant moaning,
O Lord, we've moaned so long,
We must be free, we must be free.

They say that freedom is a constant dying,
They say that freedom is a constant dying,
They say that freedom is a constant dying,
O Lord, we've died so long,
We must be free, we must be free.

—Song of The Freedom Singers first used at a
1964 Oxford, Ohio, training session after it was
learned that three civil rights workers were missing

The Mississippi Freedom Summer of 1964 was on a
larger scale than anything thus far attempted by the
civil rights movement. At the Mall in Washington, D.C., the previous summer, one quarter of a million individuals had gathered

for the march on Washington, but this was a single protest and its primary result was to focus national attention on the issue of race through a media event.

The Mississippi Summer Project was to begin in June and last until one thousand or so volunteers returned to their university campuses, law practices, or jobs the following September. Some, it was expected, would stay. The project had several dimensions—educational programs, political organizing, and community self-help. Despite months of preparation, many of our plans were just that—plans.

Inspired by SNCC's earlier voter-registration schools in Amite, Pike, and Walthall counties, and "Nonviolent High School" in Pike County, the concept was born for Freedom Schools to be developed in twenty-five areas of Mississippi. The schools were to be under the overall direction of Professor Staughton Lynd, who was leaving Spelman College in Atlanta for Yale University to teach social studies in the fall. Jack Minnis, a deft analyst who had taught social sciences at Louisiana State University before joining the Voter Education Project and then became director of research for SNCC, convened a conference of educators in New York City on March 20 and 21. They put together the curriculum. Until the arrival of the volunteer teachers, though, the Freedom Schools existed only in the minds of Bob Moses, Charlie Cobb, Mendy Samstein, and other Mississippi staff who were planning them.

The local people need the vote, Amzie Moore had told Bob Moses; would he please bring student volunteers into Mississippi to help? Amzie's clarity on this issue—combined with the news coverage and the protection and leverage brought by the Stanford and Yale students to the mock election of November 1963—led directly to the concept of the Mississippi Freedom Summer. Bob also believed it would take a sustained strategy to enlarge the number of those concerned and engender the sense of national responsibility that Ella Baker talked about. Bob's idea was similar in nature to the still-novel Peace Corps, which was three years old. Just as the 1960 sit-ins were a catalyst for the Peace Corps concept, the 1964 Mississippi volunteers were to be the inspiration for the federally supported VISTA program—Volunteers in Service to America—that began one year after the Mississippi Summer Project.

Yet, as we in the Atlanta headquarters and the Mississippi staff in the field awaited, hour by hour, the arrival of the volunteers, we were held together only by our belief in Bob and each other.

With a thousand volunteers, we could turn the eyes of the country onto the state of Mississippi and its legal reign of terror. Some accused us of using the 99 percent white volunteers as cannon fodder. Yet we were not asking the volunteers to do anything that the staff wasn't already doing or to take risks that we weren't already taking. One of our brochures exclaimed, "A Domestic Freedom Corps will be working in Mississippi this summer. Its only weapons will be youth and courage. We need your help now." With that strength of numbers—and paradoxically by capitalizing on the double standard and racism of the news media that found whites more newsworthy than blacks—we hoped to attract human and material resources and bring the case of black people living in a vestigial system of slavery to the attention of the nation and the world.

Almost all of us felt ambivalence, in my case a feeling of dread, at the thought of the arrival of one thousand innocents. How could we be certain of their motivation, we first asked ourselves—before backing away from the question, because they were, after all, "willing to put their bodies on the line." Some white staff members felt threatened; it meant that their specialness would be gone. Some black members of the staff were frightened; they might lose control. The delicate balance between the white minority and black majority on the staff might be undermined. Others feared the unknown consequences of working with the uninitiated. We wondered to ourselves, How do we know they are coming for the right reasons? Some of the staff openly resented the volunteers and thought they would not be pure enough. Others feared that lives would be lost.

Jane Stembridge voiced her apprehensions in an April 21, 1964, letter to me from Greenville, Mississippi:

Those who think it is glorious to put on Levi's and identify
with the people, whatever the hell they think that means,
are full of shit. The people don't want to be identified with
dirt, poverty and absolute boredom. We work on Lynch
Street about which there is nothing good. It is dirty and hot

and full of vacant lots and greasy-spoon joints with loud
noise and boring people. . . . There is nothing great and
glorious about dead people and nothing particularly important about dirty Levi's and SNCC buttons. It is unbelieva-
bly absurd to think that 2,000 bright and eager youth are
coming down here to help—and what in the name of God
can they help with? . . .

   Mary, please forgive me for this. I am too afraid. Please
do not despair of me soon.

Jane was not the only one confused or troubled by the plans
for the summer. Everyone was anxious. In my deepest feelings, I
worried that it was one thing for a small committed core of seventy staff members to accept the possibility of being killed; it was
quite another to lead someone else to slaughter. For me, Mississippi, as a state of mind, remained the foul-smelling crater with a
putrefying stench, gangrenous vortex, and uncertain eruptions. I
did not know where it would end or who would be lost in it.

   I was also afraid that Bob would would be singled out and
killed.

> These kids aren't any good . . .
> a lot of them are even idealists.

—Governor Paul B. Johnson of Mississippi, July 2, 1964

Michael Schwerner was already distinguishing himself as a
conscientious staff worker for COFO by early May of 1964. Twenty-
four years old, he had a heavy build, brown hair, warm eyes, a
goatee, and was from Brooklyn, New York. He was a professional
social worker who was on the CORE staff. He was known within
our circles to be responsible and to have good judgment. On May
4, he was arrested along with Leroy McCall and Lenore Thurman
in connection with a boycott organized to induce Bill's Dollar Store
in Meridian, Mississippi, where large numbers of blacks shopped,
to integrate its staff. Mickey was arrested while sitting in his car
in front of the store and charged with two counts of blocking the
crosswalk and was told there would be a five-dollar fine when the
trial was convened a few days later.

   On June 13, Mickey telephoned me in Atlanta from Meridian
with his account for the evening WATS Line Report. While pick-

eting Woolworth, Kress, and J. J. Newberry stores in Meridian, thirty-five individuals had been arrested. The first group had arrived at 9:30 A.M. and were arrested as they stepped out of their automobiles. "They weren't even allowed to take their picket signs out of the cars," Mickey said. The second group was arrested at 12:35 P.M. The boycott of the three stores had been "fairly successful," Mickey reported. Attorney Larry Warren was in Meridian working on these arrests, most of which were of teenagers. Ten of those arrested were adults and one twelve-year-old girl had been released. "Attorney Warren has advised me not to go down to the jail to check on them because he believes that I will be arrested on charges of contributing to the delinquency of minors," Mickey told me.

Little more than one week after Mickey gave me this account, he disappeared. He and James Chaney, a twenty-one-year-old local black youth who had recently been added to CORE's staff, and Andrew Goodman, a twenty-year-old white volunteer, a student from Queens College in New York City, whose father was a civil engineer and whose mother was a psychologist, were missing. Andy was described in our files as solidly built, having dark, sandy hair and a "strong face." He was from Manhattan.

On the morning of Sunday, June 21, Andy Goodman had just arrived in the first contingent of volunteers. From the Atlanta headquarters, I prepared a sketchy report on the progress of two buses that had left the orientation program in Ohio the night before to take volunteers to Mississippi. My account was based on telephone calls I made that morning to the places in Mississippi where new volunteers were expected. I wrote in hastily truncated sentences for our internal records:

Sunday June 21, 1964—before noon
The two buses which left Oxford, Ohio, yesterday at about 4 P.M. have discharged all passengers safely. . . . No trouble in *Cleveland*, debarked at Amzie Moore's house, volunteers all in church. Debarked at Mrs. Hamer's house *Ruleville*—Charles McLaurin says everything all right. The first car that arrived with volunteers, however, was taken down to station and police took all names. CBS camera crew stopped by police, will shoot mass meeting at Williams Chapel Church tomorrow and workshops, canvassing. Plan to canvass Ruleville next couple of days, then move into

Drew and then *Indianola. Clarksdale:* bus let volunteers out in front of Doc Henry's. Police car drove in front of bus into town and pulled over when kids debarked. Police questioned one person for the group, told them to get their stuff off the street. Volunteers went into church, two cars of police parked in front. No trouble apparently. All ten for *Batesville* got there OK. They were dropped off in front of state police station. All in church. *Greenville.* All OK. . . . Charlie Cobb and Claude Weaver in charge. *Greenwood,* everyone in. No trouble. *Holly Springs:* everyone in all right. Volunteers in church.

Claude Weaver was a black student from Harvard University who drew fetching cartoons that were circulated with amazing speed throughout the SNCC network. He had joined the Mississippi staff after the Freedom Ballot in November 1963. The subject of the series was a shuffling black janitor with averted eyes who turned into "Supersnick" on demand, bursting into his blue jeans and cambric work shirt to fight for justice and save all the good SNCC workers. Each new "Supersnick" cartoon sped from hand to hand across the southland. Eagerly anticipated, Claude's cartoons brought mirth and self-deprecating humor to every office.

A special orientation program of one week for each of two cohorts of new volunteers was taking place at Western College for Women in Oxford, Ohio. The sessions were financed and supported by the National Council of Churches, with training meetings conducted by Bob Moses, Jim Forman, and Mendy Samstein.

It is worth including here a few excerpts from the reports of volunteers to family and friends in Elizabeth Sutherland's book *Letters from Mississippi,* because they were written while the volunteers were still in training in Oxford:

Monday, Jim Forman . . . stood up during one of the general sessions and calmly told the staff (who already knew) and the volunteers that they could all expect to be arrested, jailed and beaten this summer, and, in many cases, shot at. There is a quiet Negro fellow on the staff who has an ugly scar on his neck and another on his shoulder where he stopped .45 slugs. . . . Another fellow told this morning how his father and later his brother had been shot to death.

I'd venture to say that every member of the Mississippi staff
has been beaten at least once and he who has not been shot
at is rare. It is impossible for you to imagine what we are
going into, as it is for me now, but I'm beginning to see.

An assortment of speakers were enlisted in addition to SNCC
and CORE staff that included the Reverend Vincent Harding, a
much-admired black clergyman with the Central Mennonite
Committee; the Reverend Edwin King, the white Methodist
chaplain of black Tougaloo College; and Bayard Rustin. The white
Alabama lawyer Charles Morgan who was forced out of Birmingham for his condemnation of the 1963 bombing deaths of four
black children spoke, and was quoted in another volunteer's
letter:

He warned us gravely about the dangers of Mississippi. Said
he thought that atrocities don't soften but harden the local
people. . . . He laid the slow movement of the civil rights
cause in the South not to the strength of southern opposition but to the weakness of the North on the issue. . . . He
ended by solemnly stating that he admired our courage.
. . . We have all lived under the increasing weight of fear
and the struggle to come to terms with the possibility of
death consumes much of our emotional energy.

The volunteers were briefed on security precautions: Beware
of cars without tags; never go out alone; never be the last to leave
a mass meeting; keep your ears tuned for car accelerators outside;
watch for cops without badges; if you awaken suddenly thinking
there is danger, wake everyone up. They were told about types
of retaliation employed against local people who became involved
in the movement. In meetings with the project directors of the
counties to which they were assigned, the volunteers learned the
specific details of conditions where they would be living. They
were taught techniques for survival such as playing dumb with
law officers. Workshops and role playing were used to prepare
them for hostile reactions and police brutality.

They were offered the theory of nonviolent resistance:

Wednesday, the Reverend James Lawson presented and
skillfully defended Christian revolutionary nonviolence as a

way of life. Most of the staff and volunteers were agnostic nonviolent technicians. The discussion was hot but very real. It became clear that not all nonviolent techniques could be practiced by certain personality types. Only perhaps ten percent can talk successfully with someone who is going to beat you. For the rest, withdrawal seems the best reaction.

They were also given practical training:

We staged one situation, a screaming mob lining the steps to the courthouse while a small band of registrants tried to get through. The inevitable happened . . . the chanting mob (instructed to be as brutal as possible, and to pull no punches) turned into a clawing, pounding mob, and we volunteer registrants were down in our crouched-up ball. Casualties? A couple of scratches, a sprained ankle, and one cameraman who got swept up was a little bit shaken. . . . We've got to be ready for anything, and we must prepare for it ourselves. Once we get South we are nonviolent. . . . Some of the staff members walk around carrying sections of hose. This strangely terrible training in brutality may well save lives.

Some volunteers had lied to their parents about their plans or went to Oxford secretly and then had to explain:

I am sure that you are convinced that I have fallen in with agitators and a dangerous brand of screwballs. Well for some time I feared the same thing for myself. I have found the facts to be otherwise. . . . I am, of course, living hand to mouth now. I expect that you are so disgusted with this whole business that you will try to starve me out. You may succeed. I receive no pay from SNCC.

The distinctive quality of SNCC took some volunteers by surprise:

These SNCC people . . . really stand out against the background of a lazy dead-end society.

Another volunteer wrote:

Most of the regular SNCC workers don't show much emotion in the open. To us it was something new, something
unbelievable, that we were putting our lives on the line.
. . . I got the impression that their feelings did not differ
much from those of a soldier who sees death around him.

One SNCC staff member in particular impressed one of the
volunteers who wrote home about him:

Jimmy Travis, who has been in the movement for years and
has been shot up with a machine gun, suddenly opened up
and started to give one of the most moving statements I
have ever heard. . . . "It's hell in Mississippi," he repeated
again and again. "We've got to change the system, to
change the system!" he cried repeatedly. He talked for
about a half hour, saying the same things over and over
again, but each time it struck each of the listeners or at least
me like a poison dart filling each of us with the realization
of what we were getting into and the dedication needed to
do it. . . . After his words, everyone broke out in applause
and Travis left the room in disgust. Another SNCC worker
stood up and said that no one should have clapped—that
Jimmy was not giving a speech.

Another wrote about SNCC to a friend:

The organization here is a real student movement. And it
looks like it will be around a long time. I would not be surprised if it really does, with time, influence the course of
American history through the leaders it produces and develops—for that is one of its main objectives. . . . The savvy
of the organization is a marvel. It is shrewd, calculating, and
geared for years of struggle. Its members . . . have the
strange ability to discuss, plan, scheme, openly and honestly
disagree, and then come to a definite decision which all follow. . . . They have acted when few others would. They
are speaking about a festering sore in this nation.

Still another observed:

These people—the Mississippians and the SNCC staff
members—are the ones who are really free. . . . Maybe

you have to see the people's faces, hear them talk and sing
and struggle, to understand the movement. You should—
you must—understand this movement for it is the most important thing involving people in America today.

The volunteers met all the key COFO figures including one
of the directors of the Freedom Schools, a talented and vibrant
young woman volunteer named Liz Fusco. The volunteers themselves were an extraordinary and diverse sample of serious young
people who had been moved by the struggle in the South to endanger themselves. One year earlier, in 1963, Eleanor Holmes
Norton, who later became one of the country's leading civil-liberties
lawyers, had left her clerkship with federal judge Leon A. Hig-
genbotham of Philadelphia for the summer to assist the SNCC
staff. The Mississippi volunteers of 1964 presented an incredible
array of talents. They included Barney Frank, elected to Congress
in 1980 from the Fourth Congressional District of Massachusetts;
Bob Beyers, the director of public relations for Stanford University; Fred Ickes, the son of President Roosevelt's secretary of the
interior; Irene Strelitz, editor of *The Stanford Daily;* Paul and
Geoffrey Cowan, sons of the former head of CBS; earnest and
gifted young writers like Kathy Amatniak and Nan Grogan; Bob
Berger, who later became editor of the *Los Angeles Times* Pulitzer
Prize-winning editorial page; Len Edwards, son of Congressman
Don Edwards; Professor Florence Howe of Goucher College; and
Stephen Bingham, nephew of Congressman Jonathan Bingham.

"A certain amount of bluffing has to be expected," Mendy
warned the assembled trainees. "If you're arrested, remember that
there's a bluff factor. Not always, but often, you'll find local law
enforcement tries to intimidate people by talking very roughly.
Try not to overreact. It'll help you to maintain your sanity if you
just remember that they do occasionally bluff you into an emotional reaction."

The volunteers were taught how to use the SNCC Communications system, how to telephone Atlanta or Jackson collect, and
what essential information should be included in their accounts
for our use with the national news corps. They were advised not
to reveal the names of the local families they were staying with,
if apprehended, but to say simply that they lived at the COFO
office, so that they would not put their hosts in danger.

During those two, week-long sessions at Oxford, the news media awakened to what was happening—exactly as we had planned. A main group of 650 students from thirty-seven states recruited from the nation's best colleges and universities were now available for the news media to write about or interview. Because most of them were white, they provided a screen of protection by bringing with them national attention and, behind this nonviolent human armor, spread across eighty-two counties, local blacks could become more assertive and begin to work toward self-determination.

Julian Bond and I spent most of our time working with the print and broadcast reporters during the orientation sessions. Patiently, we presented the facts on how the black community in Mississippi faced not only terror and violence, but also problems that much of the rest of the country had solved twenty years earlier: hunger; illiteracy; high infant mortality; lack of health services and family planning; lack of rural electrification; virtually no access to federally supported programs such as Social Security, extension services, and soil-conservation assistance from the U.S. Department of Agriculture or other federal agencies. Of all the reporters and correspondents I met at the orientation in Ohio, Jack Perkins of NBC impressed me the most with his intelligence, inquiring mind, and ability to grasp the subtleties involved in our situation.

At one news conference, a reporter asked Julian if it wasn't true that SNCC was the counterpart to the Ku Klux Klan. Julian, masterful and calm, explained the absurdity of the question to the naïve journalist without offending him.

In the second week, while Julian remained in Oxford, I returned to Atlanta to coordinate the activities of the Communications office. In the early evening of Sunday, June 21, I received a distressing telephone call from Louise Hermey, one of the first group of volunteers who was assigned to work on communications in the Meridian office. She told me that Mickey Schwerner, James Chaney, and Andrew Goodman had left Meridian at 9:00 A.M. to drive to Philadelphia in Neshoba County in the central part of Mississippi, to investigate the recent burning of Mount Zion African Methodist Episcopal Church and the beating of three local black individuals there. Philadelphia itself was a city settled soon after the Treaty of Dancing Rabbit Creek, which gave away the

Choctaw land, on the location of an ancient Indian town, Aloon Looanshaw, meaning "Bullfrog Place." Mickey, Jim, and Andy were expected back by 4:00 P.M. but nothing had been heard from them. I became alarmed immediately upon receiving the telephone call. We didn't know the exact extent of the lawlessness but we knew there were elements in Mississippi more villainous than anywhere else in the country.

Perhaps it was the absence of interference with the morning's arrival of the volunteers that aroused my feeling that there was something terribly amiss when Louise telephoned. Robert Weil in Jackson had already told me that the state WATS line had been cut off for several hours in the afternoon, and I had been having difficulty getting through by telephone from Atlanta to the Jackson headquarters on the two regular lines. I felt a prickly sensation and had an awful feeling of foreboding. There was a gap of six hours between the time that the Meridian office notified Jackson of the disappearances and the time that Atlanta was advised, although it was still the communications hub because it was where the regional wire-service bureaus were located. (By July, the nexus of communications activity would move to Jackson where the national news corps would by then be based.) In response to learning of this gap, I decided that we had to be more aggressive and that the initiative would now have to come from Julian and me, rather than assuming we would be informed of the unusual.

After Louise's telephone call that Sunday, I began systematically telephoning every jail and detention center in the counties surrounding Philadelphia—Lauderdale, Kemper, Leake, Winston, Neshoba, and Newton counties. I used our standard SNCC technique. Following my usual custom, I made the inquiries using the pseudonym of Margaret Fuller, one of the New England Transcendentalists and an associate of Ralph Waldo Emerson's whose essays and letters I had studied. It was a name that had meaning for me. I had also frequently used the name Margaret Fuller to write letters to the editors of various newspapers to lodge complaints about slanted coverage. So, on June 21, 1964, posing as Margaret Fuller of *The Atlanta Constitution*, I meticulously telephoned every police headquarters and each sheriff's office, and the mayors of smaller towns in the six-county area, to ask if they were holding the three men. These telephone calls took several hours. Under customary law, officers were supposed to acknowledge whomever they had in custody and to indicate the charges under which they were held. By acting as if I were a reporter for the legitimate press, I was hoping to create a measure of protection for Mickey, Jim, and Andy. This was a ruse that had worked in the past to prevent harm, but now I had no idea if it would be effective.

One of my earliest telephone calls was to the Neshoba County, Mississippi, jail where I spoke with Deputy Sheriff Cecil Ray Price. Price was a gum-chewing, flabby, dark-eyed, and slovenly liar who denied to me what was later proved in court—that they were then in his custody.

I also notified the FBI as did the Meridian and Jackson offices. An attorney in the Civil Rights Division of the Justice Department who was in Mississippi on other business and was staying at a Holiday Inn in Meridian, Frank E. Schwelb (later a District of Columbia Superior Court judge), was contacted by the Meridian office. He said quite bluntly that he wasn't sure that there was any federal violation and therefore wouldn't investigate the matter. When the FBI was telephoned in Jackson, they said they would not do anything until morning, after they checked with the Justice Department in Washington. More than two days were to pass from the time I first contacted the FBI until there was any sign of activity from their agents in Philadelphia, Meridian, or Jackson.

Even though by this time it was 1:00 A.M., I telephoned John Doar, deputy director of the Civil Rights Division of the Department of Justice, at his home, to tell him about what had happened and my telephone calls that had turned up nothing. I said that I feared the worst. He suggested that I telephone the state highway patrol. I got back on the phone to Jackson and asked someone there to make those calls.

I decided that I must telephone the parents of Andy Goodman. The fact that I called only Andy's parents at this point was a tribute to his special status as a volunteer. Since Mickey Schwerner and Jim Chaney were CORE staff, they had, to my mind, made a commitment on a different order of magnitude and must have reckoned with the possibilities of foul play in a more ultimate way. Andy, however, had been in the state for only a few hours and was, I felt, vulnerable. It was 1:40 A.M. Atlanta time, on Monday morning June 22, one hour ahead of Mississippi time, when I began the grim job of calling the Goodmans in New York. I told them about the telephone calls I had been making and something about my fears. They seemed to appreciate the call and were obviously apprehensive. They asked me to call back immediately, no matter what the time, if there was any further word. Then I telephoned Mickey's wife, Rita Schwerner, in Oxford, Ohio; she was a professional teacher and a volunteer herself in the second contingent of volunteers undergoing orientation.

The last thing I did that night was telephone Claude Sitton of *The New York Times*, who was already standing by in the Jackson COFO office on Lynch Street.

"It isn't necessarily a news story yet, Claude," I said, "but I am very troubled that my telephone calls to all the jails, county farms, mayors' offices, and so on in the five-county area have turned up no information. It doesn't seem possible that they would disappear and no law officer would be able to tell me anything. Someone's lying, I'm certain."

Always the professional, Claude responded, "I appreciate knowing the ground you've covered, Mary."

"Well, at least I wanted you to know what we've been doing," I said.

"I may file a story anyway. I'll think about it," Claude said.

At 2:30 A.M., when I left the headquarters to get some sleep, Ron Carver took over, compiling from telephone sources the license-tag numbers of cars circling the Meridian office. Throughout the night, he stayed in contact with the offices in Meridian and Jackson, and with Rita in Oxford, Ohio. At 3:45 A.M., he telephoned the Goodmans again in New York, who were by then at work trying to reach Attorney General Robert Kennedy, New York's senators Kenneth Keating and Jacob Javits, and Congressman William Fitts Ryan. Andy's mother suggested contacting all hospitals in the area and this was done.

Lawyer Schwelb was telephoned again at 5:00 A.M. This time he said he was in touch with the Justice Department in Washington. The state highway patrol was contacted again. They reacted with irritation, saying, "Our job is to patrol highways and we don't know anything about the three men." One of our Jackson telephone lines remained out of commission throughout the night because of a crude form of harassment—tape-recorded White Citizens Councils racist messages were played into the phone, presumably with the assistance of the telephone operators. Rita suggested from Oxford that a Reverend Mr. Porter, a local minister in Meridian that her husband had told her about, be brought over to the Meridian office for moral support, and he came immediately. The Reverend Mr. Porter was also sent to talk to Jim Chaney's mother in Meridian.

At approximately 6:00 A.M., Rita telephoned Mickey's parents in Pelham, New York. The Jackson staff called the highway patrol for the third time. The officers said they had talked to our Meridian office but added, "We haven't called Philadelphia because we don't want to wake anyone up." Claude Sitton had filed his story although he doubted it would be run in *The New York Times,* and said that he thought it would be carried by radio, television, and other newspapers. CBS put the story on its world-news roundup, and UPI and CBS both started telephoning Jackson periodically to be kept up to date. Ron Carver had called back to John Doar during the night requesting the FBI to get in touch with the state highway patrol.

I was back at the office by 8:00 A.M. on Monday, June 22, in time to learn that the Neshoba County jailer's wife, Mrs. Herring, had told the Jackson office that the three workers were picked up late on Sunday, ostensibly for speeding, and were fined twenty dollars. They were brought to the county jail in Neshoba County and, she said, released after paying the fine. Her husband had flatly denied to me that he knew anything of their whereabouts the previous evening. A call to John Doar with this information resulted in this response: "I have invested the FBI with the power to look into this." But FBI agent H. F. Helgesen in Jackson denied that there had been any word from John Doar, said he had no authority to ask the state highway patrol to act, and sputtered that he took his orders from the bureau in New Orleans. Bill Light in the Jackson office telephoned Sheriff Lawrence A. Rainey, a 225-pound, jowly, crude, and tobacco-chewing man, in Philadelphia, and was told that his deputy, Cecil Ray Price, saw the three young men looking through the wreckage of the burned church, and that they were picked up for speeding when they got back in the car.

Andy's father, Robert W. Goodman, was on an early morning plane that Monday to Washington and spoke with Nicholas deB. Katzenbach, deputy attorney general, as well as John Doar at the

Justice Department. By noon, UPI carried a report that officials in Philadelphia, Mississippi, claimed to have released the three men at 10:00 P.M. the night before. However, Ed King at Tougaloo College, the white chaplain and early supporter of the Mississippi Freedom Democratic party, told me that friends of his in Philadelphia had telephoned to say they heard that the three workers had been beaten in jail and that Sheriff Rainey of Neshoba County was a member of the Ku Klux Klan there. Before noon, all the jails in Neshoba, Newton, and Lauderdale counties, the city of Philadelphia, and the city of Meridian had been telephoned again and all said that they had held no one overnight who fitted our descriptions.

At 8:30 A.M., new information from the wife of the jailer of Neshoba County suggested that the three had been released at 6:00 P.M. on Sunday. This word was given to Agent Helgesen, who said, with the foot-dragging characteristic of the bureau, that he could do nothing until contacted by the New Orleans FBI office. At 9:00 A.M., Robert Weil in Jackson telephoned the state highway patrol again. Though they had been telephoned four times during the night, they claimed to have no knowledge of the case. At 11:00 A.M., Ed King's information about the possible beating was given to Agent Helgesen to see if this would rouse him. He responded that "this casts a new light on the FBI's role" and that the FBI "would take necessary action." An hour later, as he grew impatient, Helgesen was telephoned again; he said he had called New Orleans but had received no orders to investigate.

At noon on Monday, UPI reported that officials in Philadelphia had released the three workers Sunday night at 10:00 P.M. That same morning, we got in touch with an FBI agent named Mayner in New Orleans, who said he had received no orders from Washington. James Farmer, executive director of CORE, and Marvin Rich, CORE's public relations director, spoke with Agent Cartha D. "Deke" DeLoach, second-in-command of the FBI in Washington, as well as with President Johnson's appointments secretary Lee White and with Burke Marshall, director of the Civil Rights Division of the Justice Department. The Meridian office tried unsuccessfully to get local Air Force bases to carry out an air search. Marvin Rich worked to get the Defense Department to institute an air search but, as if in consternation and chagrin, the skies darkened and the weather had become turbulent and stormy.

Between 1:45 P.M. and 2:45 P.M. on Monday, I attempted to contact John Doar and Burke Marshall, but to no avail. I was angry that I couldn't reach them. So I left extensive messages with their offices about the inactivity of local officials as well as the FBI. I said that we were calling a news conference in the COFO office at 1017 Lynch Street in Jackson at 3:00 P.M. I mentioned that a chronology of attempts to reach the Justice Department and the FBI would be distributed to the press and that a mailing was going out to the parents of all the volunteers asking them to put pressure on the federal government. "We do not comprehend how three individuals could be lost for almost twenty-four hours and over fifty telephone calls made to find them," I stated, "and yet we have received no information on their whereabouts from the FBI, the state highway patrol, law officers, or the Justice Department."

At 3:05 P.M., Bob Moses, still in Oxford, Ohio, training the second group of volunteers, received a call from Meridian and was told that a highway patrolman had advised the COFO office there that Sheriff Rainey had released the three men the previous night and that he had an unofficial report that they were headed south on Highway 19 toward Meridian. There was supposed to be a general alert out for them from the FBI and state highway patrol, Bob was told.

Following the news conference in Jackson, Claude Sitton of *The New York Times* and Karl Fleming of *Newsweek* went to Philadelphia, county seat of Neshoba County, and were allowed to look through the jail. There was no sign of our co-workers.

Toward 5:00 P.M., on Monday, Bill Light telephoned from the Jackson office to the highway patrol. He reported that they were very hostile to him. The patrolman with whom he spoke said the state troopers would not go into a case unless called in by the sheriff or unless there was evidence of foul play, and they normally wouldn't undertake a search in less than seventy-two hours. They said they were about to issue a missing-person alert— but they minimized its importance, saying that it was due to pressure from the press. The FBI agent in Meridian still insisted that he had no orders to initiate an investigation and therefore would not do so.

At 5:20 P.M., John Doar finally called me back and said he had been informed that the three men had been in jail from 4:00

P.M. until 10:00 P.M. Sunday and had been released at that time. He also told me that the state highway patrol had advised him that they had an all-points alert out for the missing men, and that the sheriffs of Neshoba and adjoining counties were looking for them. But he did not specifically address the question of whether or not the FBI was investigating.

At 8:00 P.M., there was an exchange by telephone between Agent Helgesen and the Jackson office in which he was asked five times whether the FBI was investigating. Five times he answered that "all inquiries are to be directed to the Justice Department in Washington."

Practically everyone working in the civil rights movement knew from firsthand experience of the duplicity of the FBI. In many instances, FBI agents could be seen watching a demonstration while fraternizing with sheriffs and local law officers. I decided once to test the closeness of communications between local police and the FBI as well as whether our telephones were tapped. I called a friend and deliberately gave incorrect information that we were planning a demonstration for a particular time and place. Then I went surreptitiously to that location and found both the uniformed local police and FBI agents, the latter of whom were recognizable in their look-alike nondescript plain clothes, waiting for us. Because the FBI employed primarily local men as their agents, and because of indifference or complicity in the senior levels of the bureau, FBI investigators often worked in collusion with local law-enforcement personnel. It has now become commonly accepted that some of these agents were themselves members of the Ku Klux Klan, and used both legal and extralegal means to control or intimidate the black community. The venality of many of the agents in the FBI led to cooperation between the bureau's agents and white vigilantes. As a result of documentation by us and other groups of the nonresponse of the FBI following the disappearance of the three young men, a much wider group, starting with the Friends of SNCC in northern cities and families of the summer volunteers, were now becoming aware of the unscrupulousness of the FBI.

I spoke with Rita Schwerner at 8:00 P.M. Monday night. She had talked with James Farmer, the national director of CORE, who told her he would contact New York's Senator Kenneth Keating and attempt to speak with President Johnson. Rita had made plans to travel from Oxford, Ohio, first to Meridian and then to Neshoba County and hoped to be accompanied by a delegation including Michael Harrington; Harold Stassen; Alan Cranston, later senator from California; Congressman William Fitts Ryan; and Mark DeWolfe Howe of the Harvard University School of Law. These individuals in fact never did accompany her, although Congressman Ryan was involved in other ways. The fact that Rita had access to such people showed the superior resources and contacts that many of the summer volunteers brought with them.

Finally, at 10:00 P.M., on Monday, June 22, thirty-seven hours after they were last seen alive by a member of our staff, UPI carried a story that Edwin Guthman of the Justice Department had announced the FBI was being ordered into the case to determine whether the three civil rights workers were being held against their will and whether the case involved a violation of civil rights. This was the first sign we had that a tangible change of orders was occurring within the FBI.

On Tuesday, June 23, Andy's parents and Mickey's father met with Attorney General Robert Kennedy for one hour, accompanied by Congressman William Fitts Ryan, Congressman Ogden Reid, Stan Neuman, and attorney Martin Popper. The attorney general told them that the FBI was acting on the assumption that the disappearance was a kidnapping—that is, kidnapping was the basis of the FBI's assuming jurisdiction. The parents' delegation told the attorney general that they wanted the federal government not only to find the three men but to protect the rest of the civil rights workers in the state. They said that investigation and protection were both needed. Showing personal sympathy but also a lack of full awareness of the intransigence of his federal bureaucracy, Kennedy apparently told the parents that there would be federal protection and that he would personally report to the President on new developments.

Jim Monsonis, a conscientious SNCC staff member in Washington, D.C., telephoned from our office in the capital and said that the parents' meeting with the attorney general, which also included Nicholas deB. Katzenbach and Burke Marshall, had gone well. "Everyone came away convinced that the feds were doing all that they can," Jim told me. The group was informed that President Johnson had several times contacted J. Edgar Hoover, director of the FBI. Jim stated, however, that the meeting had produced no commitment for federal involvement or action in the future.

Jim also said that, in a separate hour-long meeting with Burke Marshall, a recent bombing in McComb was discussed and the deputy attorney general had asked that the whole project in the southwest part of the state be called off. Jim told me that between forty and fifty congressional offices had been visited that day by parents of volunteers to make certain that individual members of Congress were aware of the summer project. In each case, the visiting parents advised the elected congressmen of exactly who, among their constituents, was serving as a volunteer. At last, federal authorities were beginning to recognize the umplumbed lawlessness and terrorism that ran rampant in the state and were becoming alarmed at the possibility that the volunteers might be killed.

The group then went to the White House and met with presidential assistants Lee White and Myer Feldman, who told them that the President had asked Secretary of Defense Robert McNamara to advise J. Edgar Hoover that Army personnel was available to the FBI and that Navy helicopters were already in use.

At 10:10 A.M. that morning, our Meridian office informed us that FBI agents John Proctor and Harry Saisan were in the office, asking questions and obtaining photographs. Despite what the attorney general had told the parents, the appearance of these two agents was the first evidence that we had of federal action.

I sent a telegram over John Lewis's signature to Walter Reuther of the United Auto Workers, with whom we had a fragile alliance, that reflected our feelings at the time:

> WE URGE YOU, ON BEHALF OF TWO HUNDRED STUDENTS
> ALREADY IN MISSISSIPPI, WHO MAY AT ANY MOMENT BE
> BEATEN, BOMBED, FOUND MISSING, OR KILLED, AND ON
> BEHALF OF SOME FIVE HUNDRED MORE YET TO ARRIVE,
> TO SEEK AN AUDIENCE WITH THE PRESIDENT, THE JUS-
> TICE DEPARTMENT, AND OTHER FEDERAL AGENCIES TO
> ASK FOR STATIONING OF SPECIAL TEAMS OF FBI AGENTS,
> THE PLACEMENT OF FEDERAL MARSHALS IN CRITICAL
> AREAS, AND WHATEVER OTHER MEANS ARE NECESSARY TO
> ENSURE THAT ALL AMERICANS HAVE EQUAL VALUE UNDER
> THE LAW. DELAY BY FEDERAL AUTHORITIES IN SETTING A
> VISIBLE PATTERN OF FIRM COMMITMENT TO UPHOLD BA-

SIC PROTECTION OF VOTE WORKERS WILL HAVE AN IRRE-
MEDIABLE EFFECT ON WHAT HAPPENS LATER THIS
SUMMER.

That same evening, UPI ran a story that the FBI had found
Mickey's charred and burned station wagon, by now cold, in a
swampy part of Bogue Chitto Creek fifteen miles north of Philadelphia. Bob Moses was told—probably by Burke Marshall, my
records say—that the door had been pried open. There was no
trace of our co-workers. The road near the spot where the blue
1963 station wagon, with license tags H25503 from Hinds County,
was found, off Route 21, was a remote road, in a farming region,
that apparently went nowhere but linked Routes 15 and 45. The
Goodmans, Nathan Schwerner, and congressmen Ryan and Reid
learned this news during a twenty-minute meeting with President
Johnson, who assured them that the federal government was doing
everything it could.

Meanwhile, Francis Mitchell, a tolerant and seasoned black
SNCC staff member from Los Angeles, called me from Jackson
to say, "All of the press people in Philadelphia have been threatened and told to get out of town." Francis said there were reports
that Claude Sitton and Karl Fleming had received direct threats.

At 8:00 P.M., President Johnson telephoned Robert Goodman at his home in Manhattan and told him that bodies had not
been found but that tracks were seen leading away from the car
used by the three young men. He said he had ordered more FBI
and Defense Department personnel to "comb the countryside."
Mr. Goodman's attorney, Martin Popper, told the Jackson office
that he had been informed that 60 percent of the agents for the
FBI now being assigned to the case were special personnel moved
in from elsewhere in the country and not local agents.

At seven o'clock, Wednesday morning, as I was dressing to
go to the Communications office, I heard a radio report that Allen
Welsh Dulles, former chief of the Central Intelligence Agency
and brother of John Foster Dulles, President Eisenhower's secretary of state, was being sent to Mississippi as President Johnson's
personal investigator. Yet, even as Dulles must have been preparing to fly to Jackson during the small hours of Wednesday morning, the home of the Reverend R.L.T. Smith of Moss Point was
shot into, and a Molotov cocktail exploded in the basement of the

Sweet Rest Church of Christ Holiness in Rankin County, both of whose congregations were active in the movement. At 8:30 A.M., the President's emissary arrived in Jackson; and, about the same time, John Lewis and James Farmer came to Philadelphia in Neshoba County along with the comedian Dick Gregory and thirty others.

John reported that there were now 235 state patrolmen and approximately 50 FBI agents in Philadelphia as well as some personnel specially deputized. He said that people were standing around the streets, especially near the courthouse, armed with rifles and guns. Shortly after, by 9:30 A.M., Rita Schwerner arrived in Philadelphia from Oxford, Ohio, accompanied by Art Thomas of the National Council of Churches and Bob Zellner of SNCC. President Johnson had telephoned Mr. Goodman himself but only Lee White from the White House had bothered to call the mother of James Chaney, the one black among the three young men. While a presidential telephone call was considered appropriate for the parents of the white men, the parent of the black youth seemed worthy of only a call from one of his assistants.

During that day, the work of the Friends of SNCC offices as they swung into action across the country began to show. Elizabeth Sutherland, the savvy writer and editor who was active with the Friends of SNCC in New York City, called me to say that there was a picket line around the federal building in Manhattan from 11:00 A.M. to 6:00 P.M., with seven hundred people there at noon. A vigil was to be held that night.

A round-the-clock picket line was thrown up around the federal building in Boston by the Friends of SNCC with between one hundred and two hundred individuals picketing. Over seven thousand leaflets, with a statement by our adviser, Professor Howard Zinn, had been distributed in the area and huge crowds were reported to be watching. A mailing with a call for a demonstration at an upcoming speech by President Johnson was being sent to three hundred people in Detroit.

Bobbi Yancy telephoned from Chicago where fifteen or twenty individuals were about to go into the U.S. Attorney's office led by staff member Marion Barry to issue statements. Marion didn't always enjoy the nuts and bolts of organizing but he was a highly effective public representative for SNCC. Outside the federal building, a picket line of fifty had formed and there were television crews, radio commentators, and journalists. Bernard Lafayette was in the building, as well as Curtis Hayes and Chuck McDew. They were pressing a demand for "federal protection for the rest of the project participants." By 7:25 P.M., officials in the building had locked the group inside, tarpaulined the windows so that press photographers could not take pictures of them, and turned off the electricity so that television crews couldn't shoot film footage.

Marion was handcuffed and "dumped" into a police squad car, Bobbi bitterly reported, while six others were carried out bodily and laid on the sidewalk. She didn't know whether it was the Chicago police or federal marshals who had taken custody of Marion. He later ended up in Chicago's first district police station but under federal custody. Marion telephoned from the jail to say that he was being unfairly charged with assault of a federal marshal and resisting arrest. He said he had been tricked into going into a corner to talk with the marshals by himself and then he was roughed up and arrested.

This episode exemplified our quandary. There ought to have been federal marshals in all eighty-two of Mississippi's counties. There was nothing in the federal statutes to prevent the FBI or federal marshals, if they were on the scene where a violation of existing civil rights legislation had occurred, from arresting the violator on the spot. Instead of protecting civil rights workers fighting for voter rights, federal marshals were assaulting Marion Barry in response to the plea for federal marshals in Mississippi.

Our supporters across the country were frustrated. A storm of outrage was beginning to build at federal inaction, even though a corner had been turned in Mississippi. When Bob Moses heard reports that there were several different forms of protest being contemplated in Washington, D.C., he quietly let it be known that he thought civil disobedience in Washington should be avoided. The Reverend Robert Spike of the National Council of Churches had just arrived in Oxford, Ohio, from Washington and had told Bob that among the civil rights support groups in the nation's capital there was a growing feeling that the Mississippi Summer Project had been designed specifically to embarrass the federal government. If this belief became more widespread, Bob reported, they would begin backing off. Bob sensed that we were starting to see a more appropriate federal response in Mississippi.

He suggested that rather than civil disobedience, the organizing of a steady stream of individuals to meet with Burke Marshall, Attorney General Robert Kennedy, and President Johnson would be the most successful approach, because there was already a sufficient statutory basis for the federal government to act. What seemed to be missing was the intention of the federal government to act. Dinky Romilly, I, and others started to put out the word to northern callers and the Friends of SNCC that civil disobedience would not be as useful as maintaining the pressure of visits to government leaders.

Besides, there was no denying the facts. One of the primary purposes of the summer project was being accomplished. An imperfect but important shield of protection for local Mississippi black people, behind which they could begin to assert themselves, was being ratcheted into place. Life would never be as threatening for them again, although it was uncertain how they could achieve anything approaching self-determination.

Rita Schwerner was proving to be plucky and indefatigable. I admired her tenacity and courage. On Thursday, June 25, she chose the Reverend Edwin King and Bob Zellner to go with her in an attempt to meet with Mississippi's Governor Paul B. Johnson because she felt that an all-white group stood a better chance of reaching him. They tried first at the capitol in Jackson. An obese man saw them coming and zoomed ahead of the three into the governor's reception room, slammed the door, and leaned on it to keep it shut. A few seconds later, he opened it. Rita had barely introduced herself when the man yelled back, "He's not in." The group then spoke with the governor's special assistant, State Senator Frank Barber, who was, Rita told me, "extremely rude." They left after he said the governor could not be reached and wouldn't be back, and they went to a downstairs office to try again. There, the receptionist started telling Rita what a beautiful state Mississippi was. Next they went to the governor's mansion. They arrived just as Governor Johnson was escorting Governor George Wallace of Alabama and Mayor Allen Thompson of Jackson up the steps. Rita, Ed, and Bob walked quickly up the steps and reached the top in time for Bob to overhear a news reporter inquire about the three missing men. Governor Johnson pugnaciously replied with what was supposed to be humor, "Governor Wallace and I are the only two people who know where they are, and we're not telling." At that point, Bob Zellner stepped forward to introduce himself. The governor stretched out his hand to shake hands but suddenly realized who Rita was. Dropping his arm, he turned, walked away, and slammed the door to the mansion; the delegation of three heard the door lock. Rita spoke to a state trooper standing nearby and asked him to deliver a message to the governor that she had attempted to see him, but the patrolman refused.

The group left the governor's mansion and headed for the federal building to see Allen Dulles. They spoke with him, according to Rita, for about two minutes. The President's personal investigator assured Rita that the federal authorities were doing all that they could. Bob reported the wisecrack he had just overheard Governor Johnson make to the reporter, but Dulles insisted twice that it must have been a misunderstanding. Rita, growing perturbed and frustrated, replied tersely, "You may be sure that before we bring you any information, we check, since we know you'll try to discredit it." She also said she was quite sure that anything she told him would not leave the room—in other words, she doubted that the federal government was taking serious action. Her remarks reflected how little credibility federal representatives had at the time. She was, of course, too emotionally involved to see that there had been a slight change in the federal response—even if it was not all we hoped for.

Rita telephoned both the AP and the UPI to report these two encounters. But she told me dejectedly that she felt the news media had, in general, not used her numerous statements and the tapes she had made because she refused to be maudlin, sentimental, or tearful, and had instead tried to discuss the issues involved. Rita had a good point there. The strengths of the American press remain its technological capability and its immediacy. Its weaknesses, however, are notable. In contrast to the British or European news media, for which news analysis and interpretation of issues are considered a high priority, analysis takes second place to facts in American news sources—and the facts are often presented in sensationalized form, with stories skimmed for their entertainment value or emphasizing the instant emotional reactions of participants. It is easy to understand why Rita felt the news media disdained what she had to say.

The following day, Friday, June 26, marked the sixth day

that the three men had been missing. There was a discernible change in the federal response to the situation, although one might well ask, at what cost? Allen Dulles issued a statement to UPI saying that he had made the following recommendations to the President: First, more FBI agents should be ordered to Mississippi; second, there should be more contact between the President and Governor Johnson to facilitate local, state, and appropriate federal action to endeavor to control and prosecute terrorist activities, particularly the acts of clandestine groups in the state like the Ku Klux Klan; and, third, state and local officials should bear the main burden. His first two recommendations were fine but I dismissed his third comment as a rhetorical gesture. Had state and local officials not been deeply sympathetic with terrorists in Mississippi, there would have been no disappearances and no need of a summer project.

In late afternoon, for the first time in the history of the FBI so far as I know, agents arrested three men in Itta Bena for interfering with distribution of voter-registration materials. John Lyon Daul, twenty-one years of age and a volunteer from Hamilton College, and Roy Bernard Torkington, twenty-four years old and a volunteer from the University of California at Berkeley, were handing out leaflets in Itta Bena announcing a voter-registration rally. The FBI arrested Merritt Ely Randall, forty-five; James E. Hodges, thirty; and Lawrence N. McGraw, thirty-seven, as they were interfering in the leafleting. John Doar told me in the early hours of Saturday, when I telephoned him on another matter, that the arrests were made because the U.S. Commissioner in Oxford, Mississippi, issued a complaint. When their bail was set, it was $1,000 for McGraw and $2,000 each for the other two men. This was a minor but perceptible change.

I had actually been telephoning John Doar about a series of arrests in Columbus, Mississippi. Our policy about informing him had altered and now he came first. The Communications office, as a first step, was calling the deputy director of the Civil Rights Division of the Department of Justice immediately and automatically about any arrests of civil rights workers and was, secondly, telephoning the FBI in New Orleans, Jackson, or Memphis according to which geographic section of the state was involved. The news media now came third. We maintained our procedures for intermittent calls to jails. Deciding to alter our routine, in part because we had more leverage with the FBI as a result of national clamor, we also concluded that we had now interested the news media to the extent that reporters and television-network crews were based in Mississippi and able to pick up their own leads on stories.

Just before noon on Friday, June 26, four local volunteer workers had been arrested in Columbus, in the Black Prairie region of the state, for passing out leaflets without a permit. They were taken to the city jail where the police questioned them and tried to get them to implicate other members of the black community. At 2:25 that afternoon, five additional local people were arrested along with one summer volunteer, with their bail each set at $400. An hour and a half later, three more were arrested. Some of those taken into custody were released; eight remained in jail. Bomb threats started coming by phone to the Columbus COFO office. This was not particularly noteworthy; Don White, the local COFO director, called it an "everyday occurrence." But the situation was ironic, I told John Doar, because the pamphlet that was handed out was on the newly passed Civil Rights Act and emphasized voting. Furthermore, Don had tried to obtain a permit from both the mayor and the chief of police the previous November during the mock-election campaign and again this afternoon an attempt had been made. Both times the permit was refused.

I maintained a very formal relationship with Mr. Doar and said to him somewhat indignantly by telephone, "We are requesting the Justice Department to file suit to enjoin against the use of, and to declare unconstitutional, any statute requiring a permit to distribute leaflets. The FBI should be requested to investigate and arrest those who are denying people their constitutional rights by enforcing statutes violating the First Amendment." He and I then went on to discuss the Itta Bena arrests by the FBI which had been made on exactly that basis. I acknowledged that the report from Itta Bena was welcome news. John Doar seemed to care. I had the feeling that he was one man in the Justice Department who worked to his limits.

Even though someone with my vantage point could see that a turn had been taken, it did not yet look that way to others in the state. Stokely Carmichael and Charlie Cobb were arrested at Durant in Holmes County the night before, when they stopped to repair their car. The reason was that the police had found COFO leaflets in their automobile.

In Clinton, a town in which only one black was registered, at 1:30 A.M., the Holy Ghost Church was set on fire. This was the fifth burning of a black church to occur in the state in eleven days, including churches in Philadelphia, Rankin County, Moss Point, and Ruleville where Williams Chapel across the road from Fannie Lou Hamer's house was burned. Each of these churches was the scene of voter-registration meetings. In Greenwood, Hunter Morey, a serious and meticulous white SNCC worker, reported that an 11:45 P.M. telephone threat was worded, "Don't go to sleep, you black bastards, or you'll never wake up." Similar messages were reiterated at 1:47 A.M. and 2:00 A.M. Emmie Schrader reported that attorney Paul Scheregny of New York, accompanied by law students Mike Smith of Los Angeles and Sherwin Kaplan of Chicago, had left Jackson to drive to Belzoni to investigate a report that police were clubbing local blacks. On June 27, Ed Hollander, a white volunteer, was beaten by white prisoners in the Hinds County jail under exactly the same circumstances as Pete Stoner, a white SNCC field secretary, who had been beaten on April 21. Both Ed and Pete had been transferred to the Hinds County jail under federal custody before they were assaulted. To all outward appearances, it looked as if their being transferred under these auspices had been to facilitate their beatings. John Lewis's question that had been removed from his speech at the march on Washington, echoed in my mind: "I want to know: which side is the federal government on?"

Northern support activity continued to accelerate. A picket line at the FBI office in Urbana, Illinois, brought good publicity, as did a vigil for the three men—now missing for six days—and a mass rally. In Carbondale, there was a demonstration on the Southern Illinois University campus and at the post office (the only federal facility in town), which SNCC supporters pledged to continue every day. In New York City, there had been a round-the-clock vigil for three days and three nights, Julie Prettyman reported; and a meeting was planned at the Community Church in Greenwich Village to decide on the placement of major advertisements in *The New York Times* to present the situation in Mississippi with recommendations for action.

From different parts of the country, groups and individuals

were suggesting that perhaps they should send carloads of people to Mississippi. The NAACP in New York City was suddenly talking about one thousand individuals going to the state, the New York Friends of SNCC reported. Rushing to stanch the flow of new people, Bob Moses went on record with the news media giving our official position—"People coming into Mississippi will not help the program as it has been developed and will not help black people in Mississippi; the way in which those who want to help can best help is to remain in the North and act as a force for political pressure." Both Bob and Jim Forman prepared to go on television requesting that individuals not pour into the state. On Saturday, June 27, I issued a news release with a statement from Bob:

> OXFORD, Ohio—An urgent appeal for transient volunteers not to attempt to join the Mississippi Summer Project was made here today by Robert Moses, Program Director of the Council of Federated Organizations (COFO).
>
> Informed that northern offices of the Student Nonviolent Coordinating Committee (SNCC) were being flooded by phone calls from persons determined to head south in the wake of violence in Mississippi, Moses declared that, "a wave of untrained, and unoriented, volunteers into the project areas would serve only to disrupt what is now a well-controlled plan of operation throughout the state.
>
> "In addition," he said, "no matter how well-intentioned these new volunteers may be, it is impossible for us to house them, supervise their activities, or protect them from violence on the part of the white community.
>
> "Although our trained volunteers are open to hazard," he added, "at least their orientation has provided them with the ABC's of those kinds of protection available through our own security system. Their movements are constantly supervised in an effort to minimize the risks, and our staff people are already hard pressed to provide those safeguards which are available to us. Absolutely no one else can be accepted," he said.
>
> Moses's statement came as Navy personnel, the FBI, and state and Neshoba County police continued their search for Michael Schwerner, James Chaney, and Andrew Goodman, missing since Sunday following their release from jail in Philadelphia, Mississippi.

Each one of us had a different way of coping with the steadily increasing sense that the three men had been killed. As helicopters whirled, fifty-five miles of the Pearl River were dredged, and the Bogue Chitto Swamp was combed, we each began to conclude that they must have been murdered. Some of the staff foundered; others clustered with each other. As the days passed we—each of us—newly confronted ourselves. My tendency is always to try to cope with disaster by throwing myself into my commitments, exerting more discipline, expending even more energy than usual, and thereby trying to wring something good from the predicament. I think this pattern was established then as I wrestled with how I could be most effective when three of my coworkers had probably been killed. Something else bothered me profoundly, but I was stretched so thin that I was unable to do anything about it—in the course of dredging the Pearl River, several black bodies turned up, one of them decapitated, as I recall. These corpses did not even receive cursory treatment from the law enforcement establishment and the press.

Jane Stembridge's way of handling the situation was to write a missive on June 30 that she sent to me. I could find no one to publish it, but saved it along with my other papers. It shows how estranged, as a white Georgian, she felt from much of the southland. Yet, it was Jane's cry, her howl, that we had to make the entire country answer for what had happened. It couldn't all be blamed on the South; as Ella Baker had earlier challenged us in the June staff meeting, "If we can simply let the concept that the rest of the nation bears responsibility for what happens in Mississippi sink in, then we will have accomplished something." Here is what Jane sent me:

Open Letter to America

America, if Jim Chaney had gone to Neshoba alone and disappeared somewhere out there, it would not have made very much difference. Because, America, Jim Chaney is black. Black men have disappeared for three hundred years across the length and width of this nation. You did not care. If you had cared, you would have done something about it. . . .

You may have known a very long time that the South is filled with sickness and death. You have not helped to heal

it. You have not protected the Negro. You have not helped
the poor white. You have done nothing about it. The South
is responsible for death. Yes, for death and sickness and
murder and hate. But who is responsible for the South?
America, do not blame the white South alone.

You have noticed Mississippi now, because two white
men are missing along with Jim Chaney. Andy Goodman
and Mickey Schwerner had to come down here before you
heard of Jim Chaney, or Meridian, or Neshoba County. Negroes died out there before and died down in Natchez; they
died at night in the Delta. Andy Goodman and Jim Chaney
and Mickey Schwerner are missing. America, we have paid
a high price for your attention.

We are in Mississippi this morning because we believed
what we learned in the schools of this country—freedom
and justice for all—but we did not *see* freedom and justice.
We are here *because* we believe in this nation. . . . We are
your children, living what *you* taught us as Truth.

Forty-four days after their disappearance, on August 4 and
following a nationwide search, after payment of twenty five thousand dollars to an informer, the FBI found the three bodies of our
lynched co-workers buried fifteen feet apart and twenty feet under the dam of a newly constructed cattle pond on a farm, in a
densely wooded area, south of Philadelphia between Highways 21
and 488. A bulldozer had been used to heap tons of red clay soil
over their bodies.

The dam was free of grass and vegetation. The pond had
been drained of water by a pipe during the construction of the
dam, and was intended for fishing and watering of cattle. The
farm was owned, Claude Sitton confirmed, by Olen L. Burrage, a
trucking company operator in nearby Philadelphia. The official
autopsy said there was no evidence of beatings. But it was later
revealed after an examination by Dr. David M. Spain that Jim
Chaney had been savagely beaten before being shot three times,
twice in the head and once in the chest. Mickey and Andy died
from shots through or near the heart.

On January 16, 1965, the chief law officers of Neshoba County
and sixteen other men were arrested. Bail for Sheriff Lawrence
Andrew Rainey and Deputy Sheriff Cecil Ray Price and fourteen
others from the local area was set at $5,750 each.

The day before their arrests, a federal grand jury in Jackson composed of twenty-three individuals, one of them black, returned indictments against Sheriff Rainey, Deputy Sheriff Price, and the sixteen other defendants. They were charged with conspiracy to deprive our three co-workers of their civil rights.

Seven defendants were convicted on October 20, 1967, in the case prosecuted by John Doar. Since murder is a state crime, they were brought to trial under federal civil rights statutes. The defendants included Deputy Sheriff Cecil Ray Price and Sam Holloway Bowers, Jr., of Laurel, who was identified as the Imperial Wizard of the White Knights of the Ku Klux Klan of the Sovereign Realm of Mississippi. Also convicted were Horace Doyle Barnette, on whose confession the government's case heavily rested; plus Jimmy Arledge, Billy Wayne Posey, Jimmie Snowden, and Alton Wayne Roberts. The maximum penalty was ten years in prison and a $5,000 fine. Eight of the men were acquitted and mistrials were declared for three of the defendants.

Jack Nelson's account in the October 27, 1967, *Los Angeles Times* quoted testimony from one of three former Klansmen who had turned FBI informants. According to Jack, the Reverend Delmar Dennis said that Bowers—the Imperial Wizard and mastermind of the lynching—had declared his satisfaction that this "was the first time that Christians had planned and carried out the execution of Jews." This comment referred to Mickey and Andy.

In New York, Andy's mother issued a statement that the important thing about the conviction "is not the number of men punished but that the social forces of society in the South are changing. . . . The decision gives a real meaning to the reasons that Andy went south with Michael Schwerner."

CHAPTER 11

SUMMER

Hear that freedom train a-comin', comin', comin',
Hear that freedom train a-comin', comin', comin',
Hear that freedom train a-comin', comin', comin',
Get on board, get on board.

It'll be carrying nothing but freedom, freedom, freedom, . . .
Get on board, get on board.

They'll be coming by the thousand, thousand, thousand, . . .
Get on board, get on board.

It'll be carrying freedom fighters, fighters, fighters, . . .
Get on board, get on board.

It'll be carrying registered voters, voters, voters, . . .
Get on board, get on board.

It'll be rolling through Mississippi, Mississippi, . . .
Get on board, get on board.

Hear that freedom train a-comin', comin', comin', . . .
Get on board, get on board.

—Originally "Old Ship of Zion," a traditional black sacred song
reshaped by Lee Hayes into "Union Train" and adapted
for use in Mississippi by Sam Block and Willie Peacock

Jim Chaney, Andy Goodman, and Mickey Schwerner
had disappeared on June 21, 1964; their bodies were
missing for a month and a half. During that gloomy period with
its overhanging portent of tragedy, the summer project, nevertheless, had to continue. According to my records, not one volunteer
left Mississippi because of fear of the same fate. One was physically removed from a Gulf Coast town by his father since he was
a minor; the boy had enlisted even though he was only seventeen
years old. Most SNCC staff had been psychologically preparing
themselves for the possibility of their own deaths for so long that
they were not surprised at what happened.

My parents were worried but they did not let their fears intrude on me. My mother wrote, "We are proud of what you are doing. We hope that you are safe and that you will be unharmed!" My father's letter said:

> Ever since you left . . . you have been far away and yet so near. You are my only daughter. The ties of love are the steadying controls. My anxieties about you from time to time . . . find a reward in the beautiful closing portion of your last letter. . . . I am so proud of you and the stand you take and the work you do and the things you say. And I like to feel that I had some little part in planting the germ of some of these ideas in your restless mind and compassionate spirit.

My youngest brother, Edward, wrote in his ten-year-old hand of his fears for me and said he got "sad stomack ake." His letters cried out wrenchingly, "Please write me the day that you get this letter. Write me every day. It will help me feel better."

During those weeks, I felt despondent but I never wallow in such feelings long. I worked hard to turn that emotion around to give me energy to redouble my efforts. I thought it was poignant that those who were missing were relatively new activists and sometimes I wished it had been I who was killed. I transformed my feelings of isolation, believing I was doing something special. Turning around the clammy feeling that we had no one else but the local people sharing our vulnerabilities and our cleavage from the nation, I converted this exposure into a conviction that I was part of a unique company, a circle that was unbroken, an elite group.

That same year, my brother William had gone to Thailand with the Peace Corps. My mother wrote me, "Bill plans to go into the Peace Corps. When we raised objections—he is still twenty-one—he said, 'But Mary went into SNCC.' " Whatever the merits of the Peace Corps, it seemed unconscionable to me that our government would send hundreds of volunteers overseas while responding to our efforts at home with such disinterest, and, to make matters worse, I knew that my brother was safer than I was.

My father sent me an August 16, 1964, clipping from *The New York Times* containing a letter from the renowned lawyer Grenville Clark:

Much has been said in deserved praise of our Peace Corps volunteers in foreign countries. But, save in a few instances, their fine service cannot compare in the risks involved and hardships borne with the arduous and self-sacrificing duty undertaken by the Mississippi volunteers. . . . Three of their number were brutally murdered at the outset, and the virtually unanimous resolve of the others to persist in the face of this tragedy is the most striking evidence of their unselfish purpose.

My brother and the other Peace Corps volunteers had the federal government behind them morally; but the Mississippi volunteers had only the SNCC staff and the shell called the Council of Federated Organizations (COFO). But whom did we on SNCC staff have behind us but ourselves?

Whatever each of us felt, however, we had to get on with the work of the summer project. In July 1964, Jim Forman asked me to leave Atlanta and move to Mississippi to coordinate the efforts of the Communications office, managing the information we gave to the national news corps for the summer project and COFO. That month I turned twenty-four years of age. My pay was $10 a week, or $9.64 after deductions.

I moved into the tidy white weatherboarded house outside Jackson, where Casey was living. It had a shingled roof and a small porch whose ceiling was painted robin's-egg blue. It sat up on cinder blocks across from the rococo entrance gates of Tougaloo Southern Christian College later called simply Tougaloo College. *Tougaloo* was a word in the language of the Choctaw Okino-Ftuk Lo Indians that meant "where the waters divide" and applied to the fork of two streams on the campus. The school was established for freed slaves in 1867 by the American Missionary Association, now affiliated with the United Church of Christ. In that year the missionaries bought five hundred acres of Boddy's Plantation, a cotton estate owned by a John Boddy. The old antebellum mansion for the Boddy family, built by slaves, was turned into the administration building. Many of the other buildings were erected by students trained in the industrial arts department, with red bricks made in the school's own brickyard.

Living at the entrance of the college meant that Casey and I were surrounded by a black enclave. This offered us protection;

the black community enveloped us much as the kudzu vine smothered the Mississippi roadside. We were able to live in this house because Bob Moses had obtained a grant for the literacy project on which Casey was working. Based on the intervention of a former philosophy professor of his, the Diebold Group in New York offered a corporate contribution; I had accompanied Bob to one of his meetings at the Diebold headquarters to make a presentation. I don't recall any other corporation giving us a grant in those years. Bob found a decaying house with splintered floorboards that was rotting from leaks and broken windows and used money from the grant to have it fixed up as a Freedom House, where Casey could live and others could stay, because, out of fear of reprisal, so few in the black community would rent to SNCC workers.

The house was located at 177 County Line Road, bordering Madison and Hinds counties, just off U.S. Route 51. Hardly a night went by without itinerant field secretaries like Reggie Robinson, traveling volunteers like Abe Osheroff, or visiting northern support staff like Elizabeth Sutherland sleeping on our floors. Casey and I were not far off the floor ourselves. We laid mattresses on the pine floorboards but at least we each had a room of our own. Having my own room was an incredible luxury in the movement, and I later realized that it helped me to tolerate stress. Even now, I seem to require physical space that is unshared and utterly mine. I fixed up my room at the front of the house with dried wild flowers arranged in empty Chianti bottles and an Indian cotton spread sent by my mother. Casey and I bought tables, chairs, and chests of drawers secondhand for a dollar or two in junk shops in Jackson and then painted them flat black.

The community surrounding Tougaloo College called us Freedom Riders. Local black communities had been stunned by the daring of the Freedom Rides of 1961 into the mob-packed segregated bus stations of Anniston, Birmingham, Montgomery, and finally into Jackson. For years afterward, the local people in southern hamlets called any and all civil rights workers by the stock name Freedom Riders. Throughout the Alabama and Mississippi Black Belt, the Rides had been such a shocking challenge to the old order that even though Casey and I never rode a bus and always drove to the Jackson office in a donated car, we were "Freedom Riders" to the people of Tougaloo. Years later, the president of the college told me that our house is now called the Civil Rights House. Our neighbors at Tougaloo, themselves hard-working but very poor, would sometimes bring us a platter of fried chicken, greens, black-eyed peas, yams, and okra. At other times, if we had a little pocket money or a visitor offered to take us out, we would walk a few hundred feet down County Line Road to Washington's Place where the jukebox had Motown records or Mississippi blues. Its needle stuck on "Sugar pie, honey bun, you know I love you." If we were willing to wait a long time, listening to moaning blues, we could have a delicious greasy hamburger.

There were several periods during which I lived on nothing more than popcorn accompanied by Fanta orange soda, sarsaparilla, or Dr Pepper. Jane Stembridge stayed with us for a while and taught me that, if we had absolutely no food in the house, the caffeine and sugar in a bottle of Coca-Cola the first thing in the morning would give me the jolt that my system needed to start another day. I had no delusions of invincibility but I was ruthless in the way I overlooked fundamental nutrition, other concerns seeming much more important.

I decided a garden was the answer to our food needs, since with careful planning it was possible to have three harvests a year in Mississippi. I convinced Curtis Smith, the owner of our house, to plow the gently sloping half acre behind the house, and I planted okra, beans, corn, tomatoes, greens, lettuce, cucumbers, watermelon, and muskmelon. The heat rose so early and so unyieldingly, however, that I had to get up at five o'clock with the cooing of the doves to be able to chop, weed, and water the garden.

Neither Casey nor I could cook very well but we slowly developed a bill of fare that fitted our limited circumstances. Casey knew how to curry cheap cuts of meat. From Maria Varela we learned how to make chili con carne as Rennie Davis of SDS had taught her. Abe Osheroff came from Los Angeles and told us tales of fighting Franco in Spain while he taught us how to use fresh basil that grew easily in Mississippi. Francis Mitchell showed us how to prepare catfish. Mike Thelwell added a Jamaican dish. Dona Richards showed us New York deli-style tuna fish with chopped onions and olive oil. Emmie Schrader and Theresa del Pozzo showed us other meals.

Occasionally shipments of food arrived from the North. The Jackson office was scrupulous about giving out such boxes to the local people under the direction of Jesse Morris, the clever black administrator of the Jackson office. Like Cassius, Jesse had a lean and hungry look and wore a permanently disgruntled expression. His seeming discontent hid from view his shrewd capability as an astute manager. He occasionally passed on to Casey and me a box that was unsuitable for distribution. Some of Jesse's boxes included improbable and phantasmagoric items such as anchovies, marrons glacés, smoked oysters, and tinned pâté sent by well-intentioned people who were obviously out of touch with life in Mississippi. Either I could feel guilty about eating these absurd fantasies or I could enjoy them. I chose the latter, deciding that while an oath of pure poverty might make me feel self-righteous, it would not necessarily improve my effectiveness. Whenever, for one brief instant, I got to live well, I did it with gusto.

At night, over a bottle of cloying cheap Italian wine, with the cicadas and katydids chirping in the background and the tallow-hued moonlight shining through the chinaberry tree in our front yard, Casey and I continued our discussions. Intellectually, I was still growing. A white Radcliffe graduate who worked with us, Emmie Schrader, had traveled extensively in Africa and talked to us about the *troisième monde*, the "third world." The terminology had begun to be used in 1947 during the cold war by nations that did not want to be aligned with the Soviet bloc and the East or with the industrialized West. It had first reached me through Jean-Paul Sartre and the French existentialists we were reading who used the phrase. On January 20, 1965, Emmie gave me a long detailed exposition, forecasting, "The *troisième monde* will include American Negroes, Africans, South Americans, Middle Easterners, and maybe eventually Asians." That was when the term *Third World* became a functional concept for me. It was in these discussions among Emmie, Casey, and me in the Freedom House at Tougaloo that my vision of our struggle in the American South was framed: I began to see this struggle as an integral part of the change sweeping the globe since World War II, wresting freedom and political authority from colonial powers.

Our political, emotional, and spiritual lives were inseparably bound to the movement. It was all-consuming and I was consumed. There was no line where the movement began and our personal lives left off. In a sense, I didn't have a life of my own. The movement was too encompassing. It was about personhood,

no matter what your race. It was about human promise and democracy. It was about empowering new indigenous leadership. It
was about transforming potentiality into actuality. These goals were
so close; yet they were so far. They grabbed me up, sucked me
in, and took over.

You couldn't go to work for SNCC as if you were signing up
for a regular job, even less as if you were embarking on a career.
This was not a job or a career; SNCC demanded total commitment. We weren't even paid a salary, but a subsistence stipend.
Nearly all of us were unmarried. Many SNCC field secretaries
didn't even have a home base but were moved from one project
to another. In contrast, the SCLC staff, almost all of whom were
men, tended to be married, they were paid salaries, and they owned
cars. Working for SNCC meant signing up your life.

Relationships were intense and bonds deep. When we gathered for staff meetings, or reunited after an absence, we always
greeted one another with emphatic rocking embraces, wrapping
our arms around each other in bear hugs. This was a typical SNCC
greeting. As if enacting the spiritual, "It May Be the Last Time
We See Each Other," these were great gripping expressions,
characteristic statements of how much we cared for each other.
We wrapped ourselves in each other's arms, pressing together,
exhilarated to be together again. At the start of every SNCC staff
meeting, we had to allow time to greet each other in unself-
conscious embraces. There were never any wan handshakes or
limp greetings at SNCC meetings.

Within this community we had created, we satisfied our emotional needs from the group more than from the solace of separate
personal relationships.

Maria Varela, whom we then called Mary, a highly disciplined SNCC worker with a strong Roman Catholic background
who organized a pilot literacy project in Selma and was of Mexi-
can extraction, wrote in a letter to me: "With my working hard
now, I find that even the pull of private life is at times too much
of a pressure—what I mean is the pull of sharing my private life—
being alone is sometimes a great relief."

Yet another element in daily life was described by Casey years
later: "There was a lot of going home with someone or bringing
someone home with you." This was not predatory or grasping,
however; it was a reflection of the itinerancy and innocent com-

munalism of our lives. After driving at night across a state or even from one end of the southland to the other, we would stumble out of a church mass meeting or a SNCC strategy session, hot and exhausted, and at that point turn around and try to figure out where to stay. "If you were lucky enough to have a bed, you might feel bad if you didn't share it," Casey recalled.

Concluding that not to be sexually involved with any of the major male players in SNCC was an easy way for me to avoid conflict, this was the decision I made. Besides, I think my personal style was not inviting. Twenty years later, a pivotal figure in the movement would say to me, "It was not that I did not think of making love to you. I thought about it many times. But you were always so serious and earnest that I never tried."

Unrelenting, the movement drove out everything else in its wake. You couldn't reserve private time or put the demands of the movement aside. It not only intruded on my sleep, it invaded my dreams. I was awakened from sleep one night by a frightening dream in which I had to organize a trip to the morgue. Standing around in the darkened ice-cold chamber with me were ten or twelve civil rights workers who were friends of mine. Stokely Carmichael and Julian Bond were there as well as Jean Wheeler and Casey. They were standing somberly. I recognized the voice of my youngest brother, Edward, upstairs, where he was weeping. I could tell that he was crying for me. There were corpses strewn about the morgue, some stretched out on slabs and tables. One was cut in half. Elsewhere in the shadows there were boxes containing human organs and one row of heads stared down at me from a shelf. Then, with great difficulty and overwhelming sadness, I started to unload my own body from a box on the floor. I struggled to lift the heaviness of my own body up into my arms and onto a shelf. As I was trying to lift it, struggling against gravity, suddenly I awoke, distraught.

For as long as I was involved, the telephone rang at all hours of the day and night. I felt like the switchbox on the Illinois Central Railroad whose tracks ran from New Orleans to Chicago a tenth of a mile east from our house, receiving signals and sending them. As a result of the unrelieved demands of the movement I developed a need—which has continued to the present time—for some private moments alone with myself every day.

Even when dealing with the minutiae of daily life, I was often afraid, although I learned to accept my fears. We were surrounded by situations like that to the north in the Delta town of Clarksdale where the police that summer wore no badge numbers and the town's motorcycle cops had electric cattle prods strapped to their waists. There were some uninhabited stretches of road between Jackson and Tougaloo, and so I carefully worked out ten different road routes from the Lynch Street office to the Freedom House at Tougaloo. Each day I took a different route. I thought this might frustrate anyone who might be keeping me under surveillance, in order to try to force me off the highway, or shoot into the car as happened when Viola Liuzzo was killed in Selma, Alabama, the following year.

On July 2, 1964, the Civil Rights Act, pending since President Kennedy had introduced it the previous year, was passed by the Congress. The entire congressional delegations of Alabama, Arkansas, Georgia, Louisiana, Mississippi, North Carolina, South Carolina, and Virginia voted, without any deviation, against the omnibus bill. We had summer volunteers from thirty-seven states representing a good portion of the congressional districts of the country working in Mississippi that summer. Close to midnight on that day, Dinky Romilly filed a small item in the WATS Line Report to the effect that Jim Forman, our executive secretary, had left Jackson that morning to attend a meeting of the Council of United Civil Rights Leadership in New York City. As the group was about to begin its meeting, it received an invitation to fly to Washington to attend the signing of the bill. Jim witnessed President Johnson's signing along with A. Philip Randolph, the Reverend Dr. Martin Luther King, Jr., Whitney Young, Roy Wilkins, Dorothy Height, Attorney General Robert Kennedy, Burke Marshall, Nicholas deB. Katzenbach, and presidential aides Lee White and Louis Martin.

The WATS Line Reports remain as indisputable evidence that the legislation didn't offer much immediate comfort. That day and the next, accounts of harassment were filed from Selma, Alabama; Atlanta, Albany, and Americus, Georgia; and Greenwood, Canton, Laurel, and Holly Springs, Mississippi. They concerned beatings, arrests, bomb scares, shootings, and clubbings directed against local blacks and civil rights workers. Governor Paul B. Johnson of Mississippi responded, more frank than bitter, saying, "This comes at a very bad time. Of course, as far as we're concerned, any time is a bad time." Fannie Lou Hamer's reaction to the new legislation was to get on a plane to speak at a mass rally in Chicago.

Although few said so publicly, there could be little question that the disappearance of Jim Chaney, Andy Goodman, and Mickey Schwerner, and the resulting world attention and national outcry, had stimulated a recalcitrant Congress to pass this legislation.

Immediately after the signing of the Civil Rights Act, however, there was no discernible difference for us. In Enfield, North Carolina, our field secretary, J. V. Henry, reported a number of hooded Klansmen driving up and down the highway.

In Gulfport, Mississippi, a seventeen-year-old black COFO volunteer, George Johnson, and a twenty-one-year-old white volunteer, Gibbs Von Kinderman, a senior at Harvard University, were canvassing for voter registration when they were stopped by a dirty, unshaven, greasy-clothed white man in a red pickup truck who harassed them, knocking them about and using profanity. In response, we made the first request to the FBI that the assailant be arrested under Title I of the new Civil Rights Act.

From Selma, Alabama, SNCC field secretary John Love reported that Eric Farnum, a nineteen-year-old white student from Raleigh, North Carolina, had been arrested after talking with Maria Varela. When Julian Bond telephoned the jail, he was told that Eric had been charged with disturbing the peace and was being held under $500 bail.

Don Harris, director of the twenty-two-county Southwest Georgia Project, reported that he was apprehensive about the outdoor rally for attorney C. B. King to be held near Albany and plans to test whether a swimming pool would remain segregated in Tifton.

In Meridian, Mississippi, Ben Chaney, the eleven-year-old brother of Jim Chaney, had his arm broken when a car ran through a red light, causing a collision. In the automobile with Ben were two white summer volunteers, twenty-four-year-old Walton Hackman from Eastern Mennonite College in Harrisonburg, Virginia, and Ronnie de Sousa, a twenty-four-year-old graduate student at Princeton University who was from Switzerland, as well as another local black youth, Larry Martin. When the driver of the car at fault and the driver of a third car involved in the collision saw the integrated car and learned the four were working on voter registration, they had Walton Hackman arrested.

In Greenwood, however, there was good news: The Freedom School began operation on July 3, construction had started on the community center, and block-by-block voter-registration canvassing was proceeding well.

Four members of Congress arrived in Jackson for the Fourth of July weekend. Congressmen Augustus Hawkins of Los Angeles, William Fitts Ryan of New York, Phillip Burton of San Francisco, and Don Edwards of San Jose, California. Congressman Edwards's son Len, a twenty-one-year-old law student at the University of Chicago, was a COFO volunteer in Ruleville. It was decided that Francis Mitchell would accompany the four members of Congress to Greenwood.

The delegation, flushed with the victory of the passage of the Civil Rights Act, visited the voter registrar of Leflore County. According to Francis, they stood by as silent observers while Sam Block and Mary Lane, two local black SNCC field secretaries, faced Circuit Clerk Martha Lamb and sought to register to vote. Francis said the clerk was accompanied by four lawyers, one of whom was known to be a member of the executive committee of the White Citizens Council. Nine times in three years twenty-four-year-old Mary had attempted to register. The congressmen watched, amazed, as she failed on her tenth try.

A volunteer writing home was quoted about this incident in Elizabeth Sutherland's *Letters from Mississippi:*

> When we asked her to try again, she broke down in tears, saying she just couldn't take any more degradation. However, Bill Ryan, one of the Congressmen, decided to see her back tests. (We were never allowed to see them ourselves.) He felt strongly that her answers were better than some of the whites who had passed. So Ryan convinced her to try again. (We learned later that she *did* pass, with Congressman Ryan breathing down Martha Lamb's neck. She was the only Negro to be registered in Leflore County all summer.)

On the night of July 3, a mass rally was held in Ruleville at which John Lewis and the four representatives spoke. It was attended by over one hundred twenty-five individuals who squeezed into Williams Chapel, across the road from Mrs. Hamer's home, where only a week and a half earlier a Molotov cocktail had been thrown. The four members of Congress walked up the still-charred steps onto the chancel of the church and joined in the singing of freedom songs.

> Ain't gonna let nobody turn me 'round,
>   turn me 'round, turn me 'round,
> Ain't gonna let nobody turn me round,
> I'm gonna keep on a'walkin', Lord,
>   keep on a'talkin' Lord,
> Marching up to freedom land. . . .
>
> Well, have you been to jail,
>   Certainly, Lord,
> Well, have you been to jail,
>   Certainly, Lord,
> Well, have you been to jail,
>   Certainly, Lord,
> Certainly, certainly, certainly, Lord. . . .
>
> Come and go with me to that land,
>   come and go with me to that land,
> Come and go with me to that land,
>   come and go with me to that land,
> Come and go with me to that land, oh,
>   come and go with me to that land,
> Come and go with me to that land
>   where I'm bound. . . .

Irene Johnson, president of the Ruleville Citizens Club, the local black civil rights organization, chaired the event, emotionally welcoming "the people we thought would never be here." Congressman Ryan told the volunteers in the audience that they were "on a mission of conscience." To the local people present he expounded, "There is no reason why Mississippi should not join the rest of the nation in living up to the ideals of this country." Congressman Burton acknowledged two volunteers in the audience who were from his district in California. Congressman Edwards, a member of the House Judiciary Committee, who had helped to draft the new legislation, was introduced by his son, and then said that he had come to visit his son and "to lend whatever support I can." Congressman Hawkins asserted, "I go back to Washington with the feeling that what we are doing there is insignificant in comparison to what you are doing."

John Lewis gave a characteristic SNCC speech and told the crowd, "The Civil Rights Act is not the end—it is just the beginning. Just as the Interstate Commerce Commission regulations became meaningful only with the bodies of the Freedom Riders, it will still take our bodies and our efforts to make the Civil Rights Act meaningful."

The highlight of the meeting came when six individuals were introduced from the nearby Delta town of Drew. Like Ruleville, and only six miles away, Drew was a town of shops and merchants that serviced the surrounding plantations. During the week preceding the mass meeting, COFO staff and volunteers from Sunflower County had concentrated their voter-registration activities on Drew, which had until then seen no civil rights activity. Our project director for Sunflower and Bolivar counties, twenty-three-year-old Charles McLaurin, was one of the first local black SNCC field secretaries to join Bob Moses in Mississippi. Round-faced with soft features, he was thoughtful, serious, and intense. He had a heavily muscled frame and close-cropped hair. At the time, I wrote that he was the "staff person I think most important to talk to of all in the Delta." McLaurin told the rally that the very presence of six persons from the town of Drew "symbolizes a real breakthrough." He explained, "We have been working in Drew to overcome the fear and intimidation there." Picking up the theme of the little light that Fannie Lou Hamer sang about letting shine, he continued, "These people will be a light to Drew just as a few people were the light in Ruleville a couple of years ago. The reason so many are coming to Ruleville to see what is happening is that that little light did not go out."

On July 4, Nan Grogan, an enterprising white volunteer from Mary Washington College in Fredericksburg, Virginia, and I composed the unusually lengthy WATS Line Report together. It filled four legal-size and two letter-size pages, all single-spaced, and concerned the following: four arrests and several brutal beatings by the sheriff and his posse in Selma, Alabama; severe beatings of four SNCC workers at a stadium in Atlanta; two black youths hospitalized as a result of a beating and brick-throwing in Laurel,

Mississippi; ten arrests in New York City for distributing leaflets about the situation in Mississippi; a mob's beating of a SNCC field secretary in Americus, Georgia; and the beating of a local black who went to a drive-in restaurant in Tifton, Georgia.

Amidst the dense telephoned accounts of atrocities was a glimmering and joyful report from Bill Light that 575 individuals had signed up for the Freedom School in Hattiesburg, Mississippi. The students who had registered to attend the program spanned eighty years in their ages. The first to sign up was an eighty-two-year-old local black man who had taught himself to read and write and now wanted to prepare himself to register to vote. At least thirty-three summer volunteers were teachers along with several recruited local teachers. COFO staff and volunteers offered to teach at night because of the unexpectedly high registration, although they were already busy handling voter registration for the new Mississippi Freedom Democratic party, gathering the data for the Atlantic City "Challenge," and keeping track of incidents for Communications.

Students who were aged eight to twelve years had no choice in their courses and followed one curriculum: language arts (reading, writing, and spelling), black history, and mathematics. Those aged thirteen and over could choose three courses from among the following: language arts embracing basic skills, public speaking, and creative writing; American history including Mississippi history and black history; social studies covering geography and the U.S. and Mississippi constitutions; a science survey course; and general mathematics. One third of the registrants were over thirty-five years of age. Two-hour night sessions were planned, some with provision for instruction in advanced science and mathematics. Typing was available, too, to be taught on twenty-five donated typewriters.

Meanwhile, Mendy Samstein telephoned to report on the activities of the local black citizens of Carthage near the center of the state. They had spent four days scrubbing an abandoned school building in the nearby town of Harmony that had been closed by the county, to prepare for the summer's Freedom School, and had also built a library.

It is worth considering the tale of the forsaken school in Harmony. Prior to the advent of public education in Mississippi, the black citizens of the town had provided the land and property for a school so the community could have a bit of schooling. In the 1930s, the Rosenwald Foundation, established by the former chairman of Sears, Roebuck and Company, gave money to support the school. The foundation was then leading the creation of schools and clinics in many rural areas in accordance with Julius Rosenwald's concepts of marketing and morality, which he did not think were in conflict, ideas that were perhaps unique for their time. Rosenwald thought that education and improving the standard of living for blacks and poor whites in the South would mean that they would have more money to purchase Sears products. As they purchased more goods from Sears, he reasoned, the development of their communities would improve, and this in turn would lead to even more purchases. Programs were instituted that gave heifers and piglets to poor families based on an agreement that they would return the best of the livestock offspring to Sears for distribution to other families. By 1935, the foundation had built half of all the public schools for blacks below the Mason-Dixon Line. Unfortunately, this commonsense approach of improving communities in order to increase sales has not caught on with other corporations, and even U.S. foreign assistance to developing countries is not viewed as market development. When the Harmony school was incorporated as a public school, black citizens served on the board of trustees. After the state in 1953 brought the school under the authority of a county school board, however, the black trustees were ousted, and, in 1956, the county closed the school altogether.

After eight ghostly years of sitting unused, the Harmony Freedom School opened on July 2 in the rejuvenated school building with fifty students and twenty more expected. Trying to junk the Freedom School, the county school superintendent suddenly proposed a summer-school session solely for blacks that would have been the first such session in the memory of local residents. Under Mississippi law, holding a summer session meant the county would not have to offer an autumn session for black students in the public schools. The sheriff of Leake County and the school superintendent posted NO TRESPASSING signs on the Freedom School building but the classes simply moved to private homes and one of the churches. Aghast at the county's belligerent response to its self-help efforts, the black community remembered well that the original land and property for the school had been donated by some of its members for the general welfare of the town. Harassment began. According to Mendy's account, between five and six pounds of large roofing nails were poured on roads in the black community. A large cross was burned on the main thoroughfare in the black section of town. Police went from house to house at night shining flashlights into homes of black citizens. Nonetheless, when Mendy telephoned, he said, "Morale in the black community is very high even though warnings have been issued that any youth who does not attend the county's gimmicked-up summer session will be set back one grade in school."

One by one, the twenty-five projected Freedom Schools opened. Classes were taught by summer volunteers under trees, in chapels, in church basements and Sunday-school annexes, in parish halls, in lodges, on shady lawns, in private homes, in abandoned buildings, and in structures that had been inventively converted into Freedom Schools. By July 9, 1964, there were fifteen hundred students of all ages in Freedom Schools across the state, mostly in morning and evening sessions because of the afternoon heat. Six more schools were to open; this would bring the enrollment that summer to over two thousand.

I remember Batesville's striking bright red-brick courthouse walls that fronted on a wharf on the Tallahatchie River, looking like a movie set. The county seat of Panola County, Batesville, was the scene of an important voter-registration success in early July when the United States Court of Appeals for the Fifth Circuit overturned a decision by the District Court of Northern Mississippi, "opening" registration books to blacks, effectively saying that the same standards that were applied to whites had to be applied to blacks. Over 85 percent of Panola County's eligible white voters were already registered to vote. The appeals court ruled that voter-registration applicants must be twenty-one years of age or older, might apply for registration without paying a poll tax, might register without the registrar or the deputy being present, and that as many applicants as physical space allowed might take the test. Of 7,250 eligible blacks in Panola County, only 1 was registered before the court's ruling. Within one week of the court's erasing the double standards, 237 blacks were added to the rolls.

The federal appeals court noted that a Negro Voters League in Panola County, formed in 1955, had attempted to register black voters but had been able to enroll only one. Throughout the first half of the century, black citizens had organized, had sought to vote, had contributed land for education, and had tried to alter the patterns of discrimination. In small communities like Batesville, the Supreme Court's *Brown* v. *Board of Education of Topeka* ruling of 1954 ordering integration of schools, the Little Rock crisis, the Montgomery bus boycott, the Greensboro sit-ins, the Freedom Rides, as well as quiet and undocumented organizing efforts undertaken by individuals, plus the buoyancy of the Kennedy period, all came together. People were willing to act. The Civil Rights acts of 1957 and 1960 had been intended to end discrimination against blacks in voting but they had little effect because the President and the Justice Department pursued only rare and cautious lawsuits. Where the attorney general had specific statutory authority to intervene in voting, he had failed to act vigorously to enforce the law. Not until the disappearance and deaths of our three co-workers was there a catalyst for passage of the Civil Rights Act of 1964, which became the basis of the Panola County ruling and a host of other subsequent litigation victories.

In short order, U.S. District Court judge Sidney Mize took under advisement a request from the Department of Justice for a preliminary injunction to halt discrimination in Lauderdale County. District judge Claude Clayton agreed to hear voter-discrimination cases against the Carroll County and Humphreys County circuit clerks, who in Mississippi served as voter registrars. In addition, as the news release I wrote on July 6 reported, a three-judge federal panel was appointed to hear a suit challenging the state's election laws, asking for an injunction to prevent registrars from administering voter-application tests to blacks that were not given to whites. That same suit asked the judges to set aside state Democratic precinct and county meetings and to delay the state Democratic convention until blacks were assured a greater role in the state party's activities.

That same day, a young woman was shot at in Moss Point, Mississippi, as she left a voter-registration meeting at the Knights of Pythias Hall. Twelve shots were fired, also at Moss Point, from a circling carload of whites, and another young woman, Jessie B. Stalworth, nineteen years of age, was shot in the side and was hospitalized. Journalists telephoned from Mobile to the New Orleans bureau of the Associated Press to say that the same carload of whites had shot at a passing car of reporters who were driving in for the meeting. The sheriff's office confirmed it: "There's bin some shootin' at the coloreds' meeting."

Later that day I spoke with Matt Herron, the sympathetic photographer with the Black Star Agency, who was in Selma, Alabama, and asked him to pass a message to the chief SNCC photographer, Danny Lyon—if he could locate him. "Tell Danny that we'd like him to take four days cruising the Mississippi Delta photographing anything that strikes his fancy," I told Matt. "Julian says our one requirement is that he stay in close touch with one of our offices there." We needed photographs for new materials.

Crucial litigation was beginning. Our WATS Line Reports, however, were little changed—there was violence against civil rights workers in Pine Bluff, Arkansas; an arrest in Itta Bena, Mississippi; and a shooting in Americus, Georgia. In Selma, Alabama, electric cattle prods were used by state troopers against would-be voters, and the shock-giving prods were even pressed up under the dresses of young women.

One thing that had changed were the resources that were now available to us. Lawyers could be found in Mississippi, which had never been possible before. From the early 1950s until this point, the much-loved black lawyer from Pine Bluff, Arkansas, Wiley Branton, was often the only attorney handling civil rights matters in the Delta of Mississippi, in Arkansas, and northern Louisiana. He early won the trust of SNCC workers because he was the first of four lawyers to take up the defense of the Freedom Riders when they arrived in Jackson in 1961. Later, as director of the Voter Education Project funded by private philanthropic foundations in Atlanta, Wiley was often the sole lawyer called in to provide legal remedies across a southland that had few such professionals. Once castigated as an "outside agitator" for addressing a mass meeting in Greenwood, he boldly announced to the audience, stunning the sheriff and his posse who ringed the church sanctuary, that he was descended from a Greenwood family. "My great-grandfather was the Indian chief and plantation owner Greenwood Leflore, after whom both the town of Greenwood and Leflore County were named," Wiley stated, "and I'm just down here to see can't mama's folks and papa's folks go down

to the courthouse to register together," which made the audience roar.

Wiley Branton had his own one-man communications system,
sometimes using the telephone to bluff civil rights workers out of
jail. By long-distance from Atlanta, he was the one who had arranged to bail out Fannie Lou Hamer, Annelle Ponder, and the
others from the Winona, Mississippi, jail after Mrs. Hamer was
beaten so severely that she could not walk.

My favorite Wiley Branton intervention was when he telephoned the sheriff of "Terrible" Terrell County, in southwest
Georgia, who was holding two SNCC workers in Dawson. Wiley
had been told that if the sheriff called you "Cap'n," it meant that
he not only thought you were white, he believed you to be a good
old boy. Wiley got on the phone to the sheriff as if he were an
old friend.

"Sheriff, you're talkin' to ol' Wiley Branton up heah in
Atlanta. Lawyer, ya know. Been down there a few times,"
Wiley said.

"What kin I do for you, Cap'n?" responded the sheriff.

"You've got two boys down there. One's a white boy and
one's a colored boy," Wiley declared.

"That's right, Cap'n. They're involved in that civil rights
mess," the sheriff replied.

"Well, Sheriff, I don't care 'bout the white boy—it's the colored boy I'm interested in. That colored boy's mother works for
me and I ain't gettin' a damned bit of work out of her 'cause she's
so worried 'bout her boy. I'd like to git him out. I'd be much
obliged for anything you can do."

"Cap'n, tell you what I'll do," the sheriff responded. "I want
a thousand-dollar bond on that white boy 'cause he oughta know'd
bettah, but I'll let you have the nigger for five hundred."

Knowing the answer, Wiley asked, "You don't have any
professional bondsmen down there, do you?"

"You don't need that, Cap'n," the sheriff said. "Your word
is good enough for me."

Wiley completes this story by saying, "That was the only
time in my life I was ever willing to concede that a black man
was worth only half the value of a white man. And I want you to
know that I took that brother for half price and never protested!"

Now, however, things on the legal front were different. A

Lawyers' Constitutional Defense Committee (LCDC) was formed, consisting of Jack Pratt of the National Council of Churches; Howard Moore, who was affiliated with SNCC; Carl Rackland of CORE; Mel Wolf of the American Civil Liberties Union; Leo Pheiffer of the American Jewish Congress; Father Robert Drinan of the School of Law of Boston College; Robert Carter of the NAACP; and Clarence Jones of SCLC. They worked out of the offices of the Inc. Fund in Memphis and Jackson. Other legal resources were available through the Lawyers' Committee for Civil Rights, a separately formed group that enlisted lawyers nationally.

The situation was similar with health care. I recall one black physician in Jackson, Dr. Robert Smith, who handled an enormous patient load, sometimes seeing sixty to seventy patients in one day, a staggering responsibility. I turned to him for care on a minor health matter and was amazed at his energy and the length of his day. I would have consulted only a black physician, fearing indifference or worse at the hands of any white clinician who learned that I worked for the movement. As late as the early and mid-1970s throughout many parts of the South, black patients were treated with contempt, usually not asked to disrobe for examination, and were customarily given indifferent care.

By mid-July 1964, however, a Medical Committee for Human Rights was established and came on the Mississippi scene with physicians and nurses. They offered health services to local black people who could not obtain care, as well as to staff and volunteers. Mickey Leland, a pharmacist by training who was subsequently elected to the U.S. Congress from Houston, Texas, and later became chair of the Congressional Black Caucus, led the Medical Committee for Human Rights chapter in his state.

In McComb, on July 7, the night after Congressman Don Edwards stayed overnight at the local COFO headquarters at 702 Wall Street, the office was bombed and a number of people were injured. Field secretary Curtis Hayes, a slender, twenty-one-year-old black native of McComb who had spent seventy-four days in the Pike County jail, and who was one of the original team of local youths that Bob Moses had assembled, was the worst hurt. He was knocked unconscious and received glass cuts all over his face, arms, and body.

On July 8, at Columbus, Mississippi, three summer volunteers—Joel Bernard, Steven Fraser, and Warren Galloway—were arrested. In Ashland, Mississippi, SNCC field secretary Cleveland Sellers, an irreverent twenty-year-old student from Howard University who strutted about in swashbuckling boots with d'Artagnanlike flaps, and later wrote a book about his experiences, was driving two white volunteers. He was arrested for reckless driving. In the Delta—at Ruleville, Indianola, and Drew—COFO staff and volunteers were tossed out of circuit clerks' offices, jeered at by police, verbally harassed by election officials, and threatened by police. The summer went on, the violence banal and demented.

Journalist John Herbers reported in *The New York Times* our exact count, issued from the COFO headquarters at 1017 Lynch Street, for the summer's violence. I was pleased that he used our figures, as it showed the credibility we had achieved. In addition to the deaths of the three young men, he cited: "At least 80 persons were beaten, 35 churches burned, more than 1,000 persons arrested, and 30 homes and other buildings bombed. There were also 35 shooting incidents in which three Negroes were wounded, according to a Council tally that has not been disputed."

The heat was as unrelenting as the harassment. It couldn't be blamed on the weather, however, or even on poverty, although that may have made it worse. Less than half of the reported black births in Mississippi in 1963 took place in a hospital with a physician in attendance. As late as 1970, Issaquena County had an infant mortality rate of 70 (this index of the number of babies that die for every 1,000 born offers the best single measure for an area's level of development), putting it at the same level as many developing countries in Africa, Asia, the Middle East, and Latin America. But few countries—despite comparable levels of poverty and underdevelopment—showed the malignancy and venality of Mississippi's strictly racial repression. This ingrained contempt for blacks by whites in the United States could therefore be interpreted only as a legacy of slavery.

"Whatever terror there is in Mississippi is the terror and tragedy of an entire state," Dr. Robert Coles said, deliberately choosing his words. The Harvard University psychiatrist, speaking at the SNCC staff meeting at Tougaloo College on August 7, 1964, impressed us with his quiet and respectful method of analyzing the effects of segregation and desegregation on southerners, both black and white. Dr. Coles, who was frequently seen at SNCC staff meetings, was trying that day to make the staff of seventy-odd members see that everyone in Mississippi suffered because of the oppression of blacks. Enough of the early SNCC ethos of the sit-in period was still present among the staff, that, for one brief suspended moment, with Bob Coles's analysis, the group allowed itself to feel sympathy for the Mississippi white community with its wanton upper hand. Bob said he was convinced that there was "a moment of hesitation before those who perpetrate brutality strike out." If it were possible "to create an indication of concern from the whole community, then the people of the street may hold back from violence," he asserted.

The state was polarized. There was no middle ground. Brakes on violence against blacks scarcely existed. Despite the sincerity of Bob Coles's assertion, I didn't know where in Mississippi to look for "an indication of concern from the whole community." Countless acts of compassion and respect may have been shown by individual white Mississippians toward black Mississippians over the years, but only the smallest of small constituencies in the white community had emerged in favor of progress.

The past hung like a heavy burden over the southland, yet throughout the region there were white homes that sought to overcome its ponderous weight. My father, Luther Waddington King, was taken by his father and uncle during the early 1930s and shown the exact oak tree in Patrick County, Virginia, where the white boy from the orphanage had been lynched for killing a girl with a hoe. This was to be a lesson for my father, then a young man, against lynching. "I was the only mourner at his funeral," my great-uncle Benjamin Cranford, who had been a boy at the time of the hanging, told my father. "He'd been kind to me; he gave me a penknife." Like many white families, they were against "justice" being handed out by lynch parties.

Yet the fact remains that pockets of enlightenment and idiosyncratic acts of mercy do not constitute a culture. Such acts had had no discernible effect on Mississippi's truculent treatment of its black citizens. In retrospect, I think Bob Coles's words were meant not so much to analyze the situation as to try to help us feel less impotent against the violence.

A July 1, 1964, letter written to the U.S. Civil Rights Commission by its Mississippi Advisory Committee included recommendations for the immediate dispatching of federal marshals into arcas of violence and witholding federal funds where there was acknowledged discrimination. It also suggested that information about the state's denial of civil rights should be disseminated to Mississippi's professional groups such as physicians, teachers, and lawyers. The letter opined that many Mississippians did not realize how much of a "closed society" they lived in and were unaware of its deprivation of rights. The committee's assumption that brochures or leaflets might affect the thinking of professional groups was a simpleminded one, given a situation that was so polarized. The state's underlying massive conspiracy of silence that existed among the white community was shown, however, by the fact that the advisory committee's issuance was not even made public at the time.

That summer of 1964, I was privileged to know a few white Mississippians who were openly against the repression of blacks or publicly opposed to the state's vigilantism and terrorism. These were individuals who took personal risks and often paid a heavy price for acting on the basis of conscience. My father and Bob Coles shared a valid view that it was not only southern blacks who were the losers in the segregated South—everyone had lost his or her freedom. Unless one understands the odds faced by such individuals, it is impossible to comprehend the dimensions of the struggle in the early 1960s.

I remember several times visiting Winifred Green's apartment in Jackson with Jane Stembridge. It was, so far as I can remember, the only home in the white part of town where any SNCC workers regularly visited. Winifred, along with Patricia "Patt" Derian and some thirty other white citizens, formed Mississippians for Public Education in the autumn of 1962, after James Meredith desegregated Ole Miss. The committee worked to keep the public schools and parks open and to monitor housing-code violations. Patt, later Assistant Secretary of State for Human Rights in the Carter administration, recalled to me how they had managed to put up three billboards in different parts of the state with a picture of a girl and boy of indeterminate race walking together with the slogan, THEIR TOMORROW DEPENDS ON YOU TODAY. This gesture resulted in scathing attacks to the effect that the committee had "covered" the state with billboards.

Winifred later ran the American Friends Service Committee

(AFSC) Family Aid Fund in Mississippi, part of a southwide program set up to assist families whose participation in desegregation
of schools had resulted in loss of jobs or eviction. Connie Curry
had run this regional program out of Atlanta with the support of
the Ford Foundation, originally to help keep black children in
schools. Connie described the fund to me:

> Right after the Civil Rights Act was passed in 1964, as local
> blacks were trying to put their children into white schools
> and register to vote, the harassment and intimidation of
> those families was gross. In Issaquena County, thirty-five
> kids went into formerly white schools. The next morning,
> all thirty-five sets of parents lost their jobs or were removed
> from Social Security or welfare or veterans' pensions. We
> gave small grants to the thirty-five families to help them
> keep their kids in school because if they withdrew their
> children, it was all over.
>
> The Carters in Drew had their house shot into and
> burned, the owner of the plantation plowed their cotton un-
> der, and their credit was cut off. But they put the five black
> children into Sunflower County schools. For four years,
> these were the only black children in the Sunflower County
> schools. For years after, not another family would do it. We
> found them a house in Drew because no one, white or
> black, would sell to them out of fear, and we gave them
> small grants until Mrs. Carter got a job. . . . It was one of
> the best things the Ford Foundation ever did.

Later, as SNCC organizers began setting up cooperatives and
credit unions, the AFSC program helped these and other offshoot
groups. The Lowndes County Christian Movement and a cooperative in Simpson County each received two-hundred-dollar grants
that paid electricity bills and kept these struggling economic-de-
velopment efforts alive until they were viable. Connie, Winifred,
and others later located markets, including Western Electric and
Sears, Roebuck, for the products from new companies and cooperatives manufacturing wood pallets. "A tiny bit of money, from
AFSC or, later, from the antipoverty program, gave black families
the means to organize," Connie told me, "and for the first time,
they had some power. That's what Senator Eastland and the others were opposed to."

The Greenville newspaper owned by Hodding Carter III and his family, *The Delta Democrat-Times*, was subjected to long-term boycotts from 1955 through 1970 because of its moderate editorials on race. The term "moderate" was often used as an epithet by segregationists who attacked first his father and then Hodding, official spokesman for Secretary of State Cyrus Vance in the Carter administration, for their attempts at a reasonable editorial position.

At the same August 7, 1964, staff meeting at Tougaloo College where Dr. Coles had spoken, Bob Moses stood before us and introduced a white couple, Malva and Red Heffner. "I want everyone to meet the Heffners from McComb," Bob said, peering at us thoughtfully. We had already heard their story by word of mouth. "Three weeks ago, the Heffners invited two COFO workers—two *white* COFO workers—into their home for dinner. Since then, the entire state has turned against them and there's some fear they might not be able to remain in McComb."

Mention of Pike and Amite counties adjacent to Louisiana touched a chord in every staff member present. These counties held a special place in SNCC history and raised a host of associations, chief among them Bob's deep study caused by the death of Herbert Lee, gunned down by the state representative at the cotton gin in Amite County in 1961. I remembered the beatings of Bob, Travis Britt, and John Hardy. Hearing about McComb made me shiver on a torrid August day.

Red Heffner was an insurance salesman and a highly successful one. My eyes, however, were on Malva. She was a slender, attractive brunette, perfectly groomed, and wearing a white-lace sheath dress. She must have been the most neatly coifed person ever to attend any SNCC staff meeting. Malva's father had been in law practice with Governor Paul B. Johnson. Bob asked them to introduce themselves. Without hesitation or self-consciousness, Malva plunged into her story. "Well, one of my daughters, Jan Nave, has been Miss Mississippi this past year and her term is ending this month." She proceeded to tell us, "On July 17, Red and I went up to a wedding in Greenville in the Delta and stopped at a restaurant called Doe's Place."

Doubtless the reason I remember this part of the meeting so clearly is that this restaurant was well-known. Since I was always in search of a good meal, I remembered hearing journalists and northern visitors talk about the wonderful food there. No one on the SNCC staff, however, even if white, would have gone to Doe's Place for the simple reason that it was segregated—I would not have even considered crossing its threshold. I remember being astonished to learn that whites on the periphery of the movement didn't feel similarly compromised and that some of them patronized the establishment.

"I bought three or four dozen tamales," Malva continued, "which I then froze." It was incongruous to see them standing before our robust and uncomplying group talking about tamales. Yet there was such innocence in the way Malva talked about the menu that everyone listened attentively. "Later, Red and I served the tamales to two COFO volunteers whom we invited to our home, the Reverend Don McCord and Dennis Sweeney.

"They were the first civil rights activists Red and I ever met," Malva explained of their encounter three weeks earlier. "And to think that it only took three weeks for the state to turn against us for entertaining two white COFO workers." Years later, Malva told me that the Tougaloo staff meeting was the first time she had ever been in a racially integrated group and that she had felt "overcome." The three people she especially remembered from that day were Ella Baker, Bob Moses, and Jim Forman. At the time of our staff meeting, however, although there had been no news reports, the story of the Heffners of McComb had seeped out and Red would soon lose his job. In short order, the combined forces of the Ku Klux Klan and the city leadership in McComb would run the Heffners out of town for serving those tamales.

There were other individuals who showed similar mettle. The Reverend Edwin King and his wife, Jeanette, at Tougaloo College, made their campus home an oasis for me and everyone else in the movement. Ministers, journalists, foreign visitors, and civil rights workers wandered through their huge residence at all hours of the day and night. Jeanette brewed what I thought of as a magic pot of coffee—it never ran out.

The first time I met Virginia Foster Durr she was loping up the steps into the SNCC headquarters on Raymond Street in Atlanta behind her longtime friend, the British-American author Jessica Mitford, the mother of Constancia "Dinky" Romilly. Dinky was my friend as well as co-worker and we lived together as room-mates in Atlanta near Raymond Street after Casey moved to Mississippi. She was a loquacious young white woman who had recently been graduated from Sarah Lawrence College. She had droll blue eyes and the receding chin of the Hapsburgs, to whom she was said to be related. Possessing a distinctive and irrepressible sense of humor, playful and teasing, Dinky had an insouciance all her own. I loved her spontaneity and irreverence, and her seemingly endless supply of good humor. She wore dresses without waist-lines that dropped from the bodice straight down in fabric like homespun, often in orange. Her mother was one of the prominent Mitford sisters of England and her father was Esmond Romilly, the nephew of Winston Churchill. Jessica had run off with Esmond Romilly to join the Republican forces fighting Franco in the Spanish Civil War, and Prime Minister Neville Chamberlain sent a battleship to bring the couple back to Britain at Dinky's grand-mother's request. Esmond, a Royal Air Force pilot, was subse-quently killed when his plane was shot down over Germany.

On that day when I first met Virginia Durr bounding up the SNCC steps, she was coming for Dinky so that she and Jessica Mitford could take her out to dinner. Virginia came into the office striding animatedly, her face beaming triumphantly. She was wearing a powder-blue, wide-brimmed portrait hat covered with blue flowers, each the size of a clenched fist. Never before had anyone entered the pandemonium of our rough-and-tumble of-fices dressed in this fashion. Virginia declared, her eyes shining with mischievous defiance, that she was "thrilled to be in the heart of the movement." Outwardly, she appeared to be the ar-chetype of traditional southern civility, but she was instead an iconoclastic advocate of civil liberties and racial equality.

Whenever Dinky and I stayed with Virginia and her hus-band, Clifford, in their roomy home in Montgomery with its Bar-bados-style slatted blinds, to break the long drive from Atlanta to Jackson, she gave both shelter and advice. I suppose Virginia of-fered the same kind of guileless, unreserved counsel to dozens of others who stayed in their home in the 1940s, 1950s, 1960s, and on into the 1980s. One night she served us a gallon of boiled shrimp in a cut lead-crystal punch bowl, verifying my opinion that everything Virginia did was inventive. I felt affection for her. If the Durrs also had other guests, as they often did, Dinky and I would sleep on the living-room floor. Years later, at the Washington, D.C., home of Charles and Camille Morgan, Virginia greeted me effusively, embracing me, and gleefully announced to the dinner party that I used to sleep on her floor! Although nothing unusual for a SNCC worker, to Virginia this was a source of merriment.

Virginia was the sister-in-law of Supreme Court justice Hugo Black and had been an early champion against the poll tax in the South. It was Virginia who had arranged for Rosa Parks to attend Highlander Folk School, after which her decisive action launched the Montgomery bus boycott. Clifford Durr was a lawyer who had gone to Washington from Montgomery, Alabama, to work for the Reconstruction Finance Corporation and later was appointed by President Franklin D. Roosevelt to the Federal Communications Commission. The couple were outspoken and forthright on matters of race to a degree that was extraordinary for southern whites in that period. I and others cherished the hope that, first, President Kennedy and, then, President Johnson would appoint Clifford to a federal judgeship or the Supreme Court but neither ever did.

Although the Durrs were often ostracized, had crosses burned on their lawn, and were subjected to continual retaliation, they and their outspoken frankness represented a sobering influence in the white community in Alabama that was missing in Mississippi. What was more surprising was that the Durrs had achieved enough credibility to be able to reproach us and other SNCC staff right to our faces. When we stayed in her home, Virginia never shied from chastising Dinky and me, lecturing us on where we had gone wrong, and lapsing into homilies to show us our errors.

She startled me, causing me to sit bolt upright in the chair when she started castigating Dinky and me one night. "Really, it's terrible, the way I hear SNCC staff talk about Dr. King and the Southern Christian Leadership Conference. You're just wasting your time and energy," Virginia said. "Can't you all see that this is a diversion and a drain and absolutely pointless?"

"You have to admit that our criticism is well founded, Virginia," I said. "After SNCC workers have done the spadework and taken the greatest risks, Dr. King and SCLC roar into town, make a power grab, and will be given all the headlines on the evening news. It's happened before and it'll happen again, but I don't think it can happen in Mississippi because the program's too diffuse and too political for SCLC. There's no single point of confrontation."

"It doesn't matter, Mary. Don't you see?" Virginia upbraided me. "It's what you produce that matters. It may be that SNCC's boldness is more important at the start. But don't ever forget that people are inspired by Dr. King. He's a great speaker. He makes people forget their fear, and he puts the cause across nationally the way no one else can."

"Yes, Virginia," I countered, "but SCLC doesn't dig in for the long-term organizing that brings true change or develop lasting local leadership. It feeds its own leaders and creams local movements. It uses them for their news value. It relies on traditional leadership—the same clergymen who've been accommodating segregation all along."

"You're wrong. The problems are so immense," Virginia remonstrated, "and the solutions are so far down the road, that you all are very silly to spend even one instant worrying about SCLC and Dr. King."

"Virginia, you don't deny what I said," I insisted. If I hadn't cared what she thought, I would have politely demurred. I respected her and so I argued.

"Maybe so," Virginia continued. "But it's dead wrong for SNCC staff to go around criticizing. The movement is big enough for all of you. It's going to take all of you and more to do the job. It pains me to hear the SNCC people talking about Dr. King and SCLC the way you all do."

Fairly typical of how SNCC staff felt about SCLC was this comment in a letter sent to me by Maria Varela on April 20, 1964. In it she wrote about the dashed expectations she anticipated in Gadsden, Alabama, if the black community invited Dr. King and SCLC in to work with them:

> Gadsden is a small replica of . . . SCLC posture: raped
> hopes, ravaged faith in those "outside organizations" which
> promise, promise, promise. Not irrevocable is the posture.
> They'll [the local people] work with others remembering
> that they trusted and relied well—though not wisely.

While SCLC was organizing a network of ministers, SNCC workers believed they should come into a community to stay until local leadership was ready to take the full brunt of responsibility. "You can't fly into town one weekend, make a speech about civil rights, and expect local people to carry the ball from there," one Mississippi SNCC staff member had said, early in 1962, summarizing our difference in viewpoint. "If people are afraid to register to vote, you've got to go with them. If they think their house is going to be burned down, you've got to sleep with them on their living-room couch. And if someone wants to beat them, then you've got to take their beatings."

Within our own ranks, the SNCC staff referred to Dr. King as ML. Privately, when we were out of hearing, SNCC workers often called him "de' Lawd." Partly a play on his name, it was as if we were antimonarchists displaying irreverence about a king. Reflecting the differences in life-style between the two organizations, we joked among ourselves, saying, "When ML goes to jail, it is with fried chicken and silk pajamas." Giving modern-day meaning to the biblical verse, "A prophet is not without honor except in his own country," the SNCC staff from Atlanta did not regard Dr. King as unique; indeed, his father, "Daddy" King, was the more respected pastor of the two in the city.

My observation to Virginia was accurate: Dr. King usually arrived after a local movement had been organized. But I might have gone on to say that this was often because of how he was invited into a community. He was, for example, asked into Albany, Georgia, specifically to bring publicity, a task that he accomplished to the satisfaction of the local movement leaders who had this very purpose in mind for him.

At the heart of SNCC repartee, which we did not make public, was actually a plea for acknowledgment. We wanted admission of SNCC's verve, creativity, daring, political progressiveness, and, in comparison to SCLC, its willingness to work without frills and with minimum support and recognition. It was one thing to call Dr. King the spiritual leader—which he was for every black family in the South that knew someone with a television set—and another thing when the news media treated him as the vanguard. It annoyed us that the press was simplistic; we considered ourselves the shock troops. Indifference by the national news corps affected our fund raising and fueled everyday jealousy and resentment. As irrelevant as such feelings may now appear, they are part of the story of the civil rights movement and should not be construed as petulant carping at the fringes of the civil rights movement but as a persistent and unresolved tension.

From 1956 on, most of the major direct-action campaigns of the 1960s—except the Freedom Rides—involved Dr. King as a symbolic figure at some stage. The exception was Mississippi prior to 1966. The reason for this was that programs built around voter registration would not necessarily benefit from an emblematic presence, and this, coupled with the sheer scale of the Mississippi Summer Project, meant that a certain parity with SCLC had been achieved. Dr. King was the most gifted orator but it was harder to treat a complex process through the comments of a symbolic personage or the phrasing of a speech. Our feelings of sibling rivalry softened during the Mississippi Summer Project.

At last, SNCC was automatically included in any national strategy meetings of civil rights leaders, and comments by some old-line leadership in the NAACP minimizing SNCC's importance were no longer heard. Coverage became more balanced. It was less likely that Dr. King would appear alone on the evening news. When the situation in Mississippi was covered, it included the people of Mississippi, justice in Mississippi, and the volunteers of Mississippi. Many news accounts began to give SNCC appropriate recognition. Once the national news corps based itself in Mississippi, its correspondents filed dispatches from Jackson and our role was more clear. Mississippi news stories demanded investigation. The almost feudal economic situation for blacks was blatant and reporters on the scene were more inclined to look into who was behind what. No reporter could file an in-depth story from Mississippi without concession to SNCC's role. It was acknowledgment we craved, not glory.

Yet the news media preferred a single spokesperson. Dr. King genuinely filled this role better than anyone else. I believe he had modesty, was a reluctant leader, and was not seeking publicity for himself. Indeed, he was probably more aware of being only a part of a larger whole than was anyone else, but this awareness was never conveyed by the media, *if* they understood it.

The first occasion when Dr. King lent his presence to an initiative in Mississippi, and the first time SNCC workers actually worked side by side with him, was a May 1966 march in Mississippi after James Meredith had been shot down. Concerning this event, Cleveland Sellers wrote in his book *The River of No Return:*

> Although SNCC people were dominating the march, Dr.
> King was enjoying himself immensely. Each day he was out
> there marching with the rest of us. His nights were spent in
> the huge circuslike sleeping tent. For one of the first times
> in his career as a civil rights leader, he was shoulder to
> shoulder with the troops. . . . One of our most important
> accomplishments was the deep friendship that developed
> between Dr. King and those SNCC workers who partici-
> pated in the march. I have nothing but fond memories of
> the long, hot hours we spent trudging along the highway,
> discussing strategy, tactics and our dreams. I will never for-
> get his magnificent speeches at the nightly rallies. Nor the
> humble smile that spread across his face when throngs of
> admirers rushed forward to touch him.

SNCC, with its ethic of developing leadership in individuals
and communities, and its emphasis on consensual and collective
leadership, presented almost insuperable problems for the simple
framework of the media. The news media also had structural
problems in covering a process as opposed to an event.

When Dr. King wasn't involved and they couldn't find a leader
or a spokesperson, the news media created one. This pattern
amounted to the fabrication of leaders by repetitively citing one
individual as a source. It bothered Ella Baker because of her philosophical commitment to leadership development as a major purpose of the movement, and it disturbed Bob Moses more than
anyone else because of what happened when the national news
corps concentrated on Mississippi. Although Bob was our state
director, he did not want to be "an important leader." He was
willing to be accountable and take responsibility, but philosophically he did not want to be fashioned by the press into "the leader."
He was in Mississippi to assist local black Mississippians to assert
their own leadership. To Bob, the only difference between the
leader and the led was a matter of becoming.

At a staff meeting at Old Gammon Seminary in Atlanta in
December 1964, Bob found the compulsion of the news media to
make him a leader so discomforting that he announced, in a fashion unforgettable and touching to everyone who heard it, that he
was changing his last name to his mother's name, Parris, in symbolic repudiation of this tendency of the press. He resigned at the
end of 1964 as COFO director because he felt the Mississippi

staff and local residents were becoming too dependent on him and that he was, therefore, blocking their development.

Virginia Durr pinpointed a shortcoming of mine and others' in being too preoccupied with the actions of Dr. King and SCLC. With the benefit of time and maturation, it is now possible for me to say that even though there was genuine disagreement on our concepts of leadership, and even if we felt alienated from Dr. King and the leadership conference, we should not, however, have compromised our own dignity by allowing ourselves to feel antipathy when we were minimized or upstaged.

Having admitted this, I must, however, go on to say that contemporary historiography with its longer and more patient view, its freedom from deadlines, and its standards of scholarship, has not always offered a fair perspective. The entire civil rights movement with all of its complexity, its local variation, its lack of predictability, and its serendipity, is inaccurately being swept up by some writers as merely the actions of King's followers. Although we and SCLC fundamentally trod the same path, there were legitimate differences, and, furthermore, SNCC raised a host of major philosophical questions that remain unresolved. These differences and issues are part of the story in any honest portrayal. "If contemporary histories are thus false," Thomas Jefferson wrote in 1787, "what will future compilations be?"

The personal example of Dr. King, brought home to thousands of poor black individuals through the coverage of television, enabled untold numbers to rise above their fears. A single television set might be watched by four or five families with maybe twenty-two adults and children gathered around on a porch after supper. Dr. King's resonant voice provided essential nourishment arousing people to take action, inspiring them in their isolation. It did not organize them but it energized them. SNCC field secretaries could be more effective precisely because Dr. King provided sanction to a black community that was conservative in the way of rural folk of all continents, who are skeptical about change. The use of television in this specific instance marked a threshold in its effects on attitudinal change in the United States.

Considering the pressure to cover the news while events were taking place, I can understand the failure of the news media to report a quicksilver process involving hundreds of local communities. I have even conjured up some patience in accepting the slanted angle of the current media when commenting or televising segments about those years. I understand the perplexity of covering the ingenuity, the risk taking, behind-the-scenes organizing, and a certain amount of chaos in SNCC. But I have less patience with some of the chronicling being done by writers, historians, and documentary filmmakers.

Virginia Durr was right. It was, in the end, what we produced that mattered. Yet, by that standard alone, some of the histories now being written are biased by slighting SNCC, its base, and some of its figures including Ella Baker.

Perhaps, too, the subsequent history of SNCC has negatively overshadowed its earlier ethos and accomplishments.

Together, SNCC and SCLC reflected the prism of black protest in America. The one organization could not have succeeded without the other. The leadership conference was strategically sound in developing a network of activist leadership in the esteemed institutions of the black church. Our group was strategically correct in digging in to do the tough organizing that would in time lead to political power. Both approaches had to be utilized in order for the civil rights movement to achieve the goals that it realized.

SNCC made SCLC look so reasonable!

Although a larger gulf existed between SNCC and the NAACP, it was inevitable that Dr. King and the leadership of SCLC would at some point be challenged by a more radical group and that a chasm would open between young militants and older leadership.

Looking back, SNCC deserves its rightful place, partly out of fidelity to facts and accuracy in the recording of history. Far more important, however, SNCC should have proper treatment historically because of its generative vision of leadership inherent in the humblest hamlet as the basis of new political power. This distinguishing perspective is in danger of being forgotten in historical summaries of the period. Yet this concept of authentic and truly democratic leadership, expressed so cogently by SNCC, goes to the heart of what the civil rights movement was about and is part of its enduring significance.

No final resolution of the question of leadership from the top versus leadership from below is conceivable. Many Americans, white and black, yearned for a great spiritual leader on whom they could model their lives and were touched by Dr. King. The spirit of his leadership propelled members of both races who would otherwise never have been moved. Decades after the march on Washington, Dr. King's speech articulates values that still guide individuals. He found the basic wisdom that reached millions who were indifferent or not involved and uplifted his listeners by awakening their noble qualities. The basic contradiction between the two types of leadership represented by SNCC and SCLC is an irresolvable duality and, in the end, we needed both.

William Ferris was one of the very few white Mississippians I came to know in 1964. I had studied with him at the seminar at Union Theological Seminary in New York just before moving to Atlanta. After graduating from Davidson College near Charlotte, North Carolina, he later became a folklorist and taught at Yale University before returning to Mississippi to direct the Center for the Study of Southern Culture at the University of Mississippi. It was Bill's respect for the richness and variety of the blues and other indigenous music and art forms of Mississippi that led him to develop the center at Ole Miss to help preserve these musical expressions.

In July 1964, Bill telephoned me at the Lynch Street headquarters of COFO and invited me to have lunch and spend the day with his family at their farm, Broadacres, on the bluffs of the Big Black River. It is almost impossible to recall now that the state was then so polarized that inviting a SNCC worker to your home—any SNCC worker—took courage if you were white in Mississippi.

Bill's mother was gracious but painfully nervous and in a state of controlled agitation about this pariah that her son had inflicted on her. Somehow, she managed to serve the turkey tetrazzini without spilling it. I remember the dish clearly because it was a welcome break from the forty-cent gumbo at Eddie's Chicken Shack near the Jackson office that was my frequent lunch. Bill's younger brother and sisters were handsome teenagers and too refined to say much; they watched me, remaining cautiously observant. I sensed that Bill's father was curious over what we were about, but he was reserved because Bill's mother was so tense.

After we had struggled politely through the meal, she blurted out, "Don't you know that you're destroying our state, destroying our way of life?" Her comment cleared the air but my response didn't change her mind. I replied, using some of the points I had made in my campus speeches in the Y human-relations project. Perhaps two years earlier I might have been able to converse effectively with her and help her see the situation differently. But I was by then in another camp, literally, and so far out of touch with her thinking that I did not know how to be persuasive. I could no longer see through the eyes of moderates because I had come to feel that not only were gradualists irrelevant, but, worse, they blocked and stymied the conflict and outpouring of dissension that were necessary prerequisites to significant change. I had come to believe that the polarization of the state preceded its alteration. Her sense of vulnerability, however, touched me. Finally I was almost speechless, not knowing what to say, yet I couldn't help wishing that I could reach out and hug her and tell her that Mississippi might represent the worst degradation of American democracy but it was only the worst, and not the only one.

Bill and I were glad to leave the main house and be off on our own. I needed this respite from the movement. I was in a state of deprivation and was beginning to feel like a rubber band that had been stretched to the point where it has no more give. This one day was my first release from the responsibility of the Communications operation since I had been in jail the preceding Christmas. We went horseback riding through the large, exquisitely cultivated farm, swam in the storybook swimming hole ringed by gnarled trees, and walked through dense woodland trails. Bill wanted to know the details of what we were doing.

It was a day I can never forget because I had been admitted to a white Mississippi family's private torments over racial change. I could see Bill's face contorted and his eyes filled with pain over the terrible conflicts he faced, for I believe he would have liked to join us. The previous summer he had worked with migrant workers in California and Oregon, harvesting watermelon and pea crops. He kissed me long and movingly when I left, not wanting to let go of the day in the same way I have not wanted to relinquish its memory.

Bill wrote me later that fall, on October 15, 1964, from Northwestern University, about the bombing of the building that housed the Vicksburg COFO headquarters:

We were really upset about the bombing in Vicksburg. It made me sick to my stomach and very helpless to think the brutal stamp of violence has been placed on Vicksburg along with so many other Mississippi towns. Daddy drove by the home after the bombing and saw several of the workers whom he had met earlier this summer who waved. He waved back and was going to stop and ask them about the incident, but Mother refused to let him.

Mother sent me a pamphlet of hate issued by the KKK which was thrown all over our place and into the yards of several Negro families who live on our farm. They were also littered throughout Vicksburg and on the lawns of several Jewish families there. I've never read such an open call to violence leveled against Jews, Catholics, and others who question the white supremacy which they are determined to maintain. The ironic part of their arguments is that they are all based on the Bible.

Still another incident involved the Ferris family. After the Mississippi summer had turned to autumn, Bob Moses was musing one day, reflectively, with a group of staff in Jackson. It had amazed him how little interest had been expressed in the summer project or COFO by white Mississippians.

"I expected a lot of curiosity about the summer project because of all the publicity about it," Bob remarked. "But do you know that only one white Mississippian this entire time has asked to meet with me to find out what we were doing and discuss our efforts?" he continued. "A man asked to see me one day at the Vicksburg office and politely said, 'I have come because I am interested in knowing what you are trying to accomplish and how you are going about it. I want to know for myself what this project is all about and what your goals are,'" Bob recounted. "We sat down and talked for a while. He was very polite and thanked me and said he appreciated my explanation and left. Strange, isn't it, that he was the only white Mississippian to approach me like that."

"What was his name?" I asked Bob.

"His name was Bill Ferris," Bob answered.

He was Bill's father.

In the temper of those times, these two acts of the Ferris family—entertaining me at their farm and meeting with Bob

Moses—were exceptional. The fact that they took bravery proved Bob Coles's point that the entire state was locked into terror.

I noticed recently in the newsletter that Bill sends me from the Center for the Study of Southern Culture at Ole Miss that three out of the four literary artists honored that semester were black women.

CHAPTER 12

MANIFESTO

This little light of mine, I'm gonna let it shine.
This little light of mine, I'm gonna let it shine.
This little light of mine, I'm gonna let it shine,
Let it shine, let it shine, let it shine.

The light that shines is the light of love,
Lights the darkness from above,
It shines on me and it shines on you,
And shows what the power of love can do.
I'm gonna shine my light both far and near,
I'm gonna shine my light both bright and clear,
Where there's a dark corner in this land,
I'm gonna let my little light shine.

—Traditional spiritual

As the autumn of 1964 approached, SNCC had behind it in Mississippi the mobilization of nearly one thousand nationally enlisted volunteers including lawyers, thirty-one Freedom Schools across the state, the letdown of the Challenge to the regular state Democrats at the Atlantic City national convention by the Mississippi Freedom Democratic party, and the worldwide attention that accompanied the deaths of Jim Chaney, Andy Goodman, and Mickey Schwerner. The civil rights movement in Mississippi was operating under the umbrella of COFO, the bulk of whom were SNCC staff. The other civil rights organizations were more cooperative and had stopped trying to assume remote control.

Now we were at loose ends. Because of the rejection of the Challenge, some of us were bitterly disenchanted with the prospect of changing the American political system that excluded blacks from governance. We were uncertain of the next act in the drama. On the other hand, our support base had broadened to include some new allies, and we now had impressive backing—the Protestant church denominations such as the Methodists, Presbyteri-

ans, United Church of Christ, and Episcopalians, two or three
labor unions, the Medical Committee on Human Rights, several
nationally supported committees of lawyers, teachers' associations, and campus support organizations. We had a working relationship with John Doar of the Justice Department; a number of
entertainment figures considered themselves part of our network;
and the Friends of SNCC groups were becoming more vital in
their role of fund raising and with the news media.

   We did not yet comprehend that we had dealt a crippling
blow to the violence in Mississippi. Tension still permeated our
world. We operated in awareness of Mississippi's underbelly of
terrorism, but we didn't know how much worse it might become.
"We never knew when the bloodbath would come," Mike Thelwell recalled. "We kept waiting for the pogrom to begin. Malcolm
predicted a war and, on the basis of history, there was a lot to
suggest that there might be a war." In the city of Birmingham
alone, there were fifty-six unsolved bombings. Fear hovered over
us still and we bantered, "If you aren't paranoid, you're crazy."

   A researcher visiting the Jackson COFO office showed me his
documentation revealing that in neighboring Louisiana, during the
two weeks preceding the 1868 presidential election, eighteen
hundred people were assaulted and manhandled, many of them
tortured to death, most of them black. The Ku Klux Klan, he
told me, had been the single most powerful political organization
in the United States from 1921 to 1925. Its operations in 1964
were still strong.

   For the first time, the fervent sense of community that had
bound us together was straining. Splits were beginning to appear.
There was confusion about administration of the staff. We now
had a far-flung operation in place across Mississippi with local offices, WATS lines, Freedom Schools, transportation networks, local political organizations, an alternative state political party, and
assorted local and county self-help groups that were springing into
being. Our automobiles were operated and repaired by the Sojourner Motor Fleet, named for Sojourner Truth. Our signal corps
had sixty-two citizens-band radio transceivers. Territorial anxieties that preceded the summer flared up again, this time with new
concerns. To whom did this mechanism belong? Were these
resources now the property of Mississippians—the new local political party might be the logical inheritor. Did they belong to COFO—

it was an ersatz coalition. Weren't they SNCC's—the organization had, after all, contributed the major personnel and material resources?

For some of the staff who had traveled north to raise money, there was the additional weight of newfound self-consciousness. Several now felt themselves celebrities from having been feted at the soirees of stylish northern fund raisers.

The staff was overworked. One night I awoke to answer the telephone at Tougaloo at 3:00 A.M., and on the way back to bed I fainted in the hallway. The cold pine floorboards pressing against my cheek finally brought me back to consciousness.

Despite the jostling over domain, possessiveness over project turf, and lack of clarity concerning direction, there was also something that had been there all along but now showed itself in stronger form—a feeling of exclusivity about being part of SNCC. Running through the organization, like a low-voltage current, was a sense that being part of the SNCC staff set you apart from everyone else. I certainly felt it. I don't think there was anyone who didn't believe that he or she was part of a singular American phenomenon. SNCC's isolation during the years leading up to the summer project and the bittersweet feelings of pride probably reinforced this sensation. It was a conviction that no one could match us; and indeed within the overall civil rights movement, no one could equal our passionate belief in democracy, our concept of indigenous leadership, our unwillingness to bow to authority—or our irreverence. This was more than a feeling of novelty or of being original. I was convinced that there was something so exceptional about being a part of the SNCC staff that anyone who was not a staff member could not possibly understand or grasp it. Although I can now see our many deficiencies, I also have to admit that, despite the passage of more than twenty years, I still feel I was part of something so extraordinary that it almost defies description. I did not picture myself a fugitive, nor did I any longer have the sensation of being under siege as I had in Danville. I felt that we were inimitable. I was sure that we were closer to the truth than anyone else.

Unfortunately, at the point where, strategically, we most needed to find ways of involving significantly larger numbers of people and becoming inclusive, we were becoming exclusive. For example, volunteers had less standing than staff. As I look back,

I can see that at the moment we had the eyes of the nation on us we were starting to become insular. I was not the only one who noticed this. Jane Stembridge wrote:

> The maintaining of SNCC for its own sake, the creation of an institution, the maintaining of an institution, the party line, the values, the isolation of each other, of non-SNCC people, the judgments, the conformity, the rigid refusal to burst
>
>   is because enough people in SNCC are afraid to be free!
>
> Absolutely threatened by the possibility of becoming free . . . people in SNCC *prefer revolution to freedom.* . . .

Jane was also dismayed by the growing bureaucracy in SNCC. As essential as she knew Communications to be, she saw WATS lines, the motor fleet, the signal corps, walkie-talkies, news releases, cameras, print shops, automobiles with shortwave radios and whip antennae, and all our other gear as intruding into the fundamental purposes of the movement. She thought (there were echoes of Ella Baker in this) we should be working toward something larger than desegregation—we should be working toward *freedom*, an all-encompassing state of mind in which human relationships would be liberated from the artificial constraints of hierarchies and prejudice including this sense of exclusivity and its bite. Jane began to fear that we were paying more attention to procedures, operations, gadgetry—what she called "apparatus"—than to our basic goals and objectives embedded in the early SNCC radical concept of nonviolence and its regard for persons. So she wrote:

> where
> in all
> the awful
> apparatus
> we acquired
> to hasten
> freedom
> is
> the flute
>
> the
> fine

thin
flute
the flute
thin
thing
the
thin
thin
thing
which
thinner
than
the
rain
rings
freedom
in

Jane had written the manual used by several hundred teachers in the thirty-one Freedom Schools set up in Mississippi in the summer of 1964. This was an important contribution, and one that Bob Moses regarded as important—she had written me, elated, when he approved the text. Yet Jane confided to me that she was not sure whether her poetry and writing were useful for the movement and that perhaps they were not programmatic enough.

Jane was not alone in wondering about her effectiveness. Almost everyone was concerned about his or her role after that summer. I too was worried and bewildered. We were floundering, adrift, and unclear about where we were going. I felt doubt and perplexity.

Years later, I turned up a shard of rhyme among my papers. Hacked out with a manual typewriter on a torn piece of paper, it was written by a shy young volunteer from Arkansas named Dov Green. What he wrote was not factually accurate—Bob Moses never turned to drink, and Mississippi's fledgling Freedom Democratic party (MFDP) was too green to have a defined political direction—but this fragment of doggerel brings to life some of the instability and doubt of this period following the successes of the summer:

Moses is drinking
And Forman's in bed.

Now the whole world is thinking
That SNCC has gone red.
Well, we've lost our picket lines,
FDP has gone right,
We're all showing signs
Of losing this fight.
N double A's a-gambling
That our next breath will be our last.
Now the whole world is crumbling
And I'm sitting on mah ass.

Tensions manifested themselves in many ways, including debates among the staff about the structure of SNCC. At the conclusion of the Mississippi Summer Project of 1964, a large retreat of all SNCC staff members who were then on payroll (still about ten dollars a week) was called for Waveland, Mississippi, near Bay St. Louis. The purpose of the meeting was to discuss the future of the organization, its goals, and the structure that would allow it to do what it decided to do. The word went out that we could each bring position papers on whatever issue we wished to present for consideration by the entire staff. As a staff committee started preparing for the Waveland meeting, position papers on scores of subjects were produced across the South. Although the overriding concern was the functional definition of SNCC following the summer of 1964, consistent with its democratic principles whoever wanted to write a paper on any topic could send it in to the Atlanta headquarters to be mimeographed for distribution.

Many of us had ideas growing out of the experiences of the summer. There were bitter frustrations as well as an awareness of soaring possibilities as the changing spirit of our movement settled in on us like cloud cover. One paper distributed in advance of the retreat said, "It would be ironic and tragic if SNCC were able to survive outside pressures—beatings, killings, terrorism—and choke and strangle on its own size and affluence."

This was still a formative stage in the development of my political consciousness, and my politics was as yet grounded in a radically democratic, idealistic, and nonideological perspective growing out of my campus activism and the period of the sit-ins in which one simply acted out one's beliefs. I was convinced I was making a lifelong commitment based on the ideals of popular democracy and self-determination. But slowly, and perhaps inevitably, self-determination was coming to mean not only politics but also literally self. For both Casey and me, this translated into our growing conviction that we had an obligation to find ways to communicate our deepening sense of political definition, which included the political identification of ourselves as women.

I wrote one "working paper" for the November 1964 Waveland meeting based on my role in Communications in which I commented about SNCC's fear of bureaucracy and the conflicting need for a better communications system. (See Appendix 1.) I recommended that there should be six distinct sections operating under our Communications program: the news department; publications; flyers, political primers, and literacy materials; promotion; signal corps; and an audiovisual section; with print shops and photography falling under two of these categories.

"My position," I wrote, "is that there are some jobs that have to be done well, and doing them well does not necessarily mean changing movement values." I continued:

> Fear of bureaucracy is valid. We all shun organizations and civil rights groups which seem intent on building the organization and fund raising. We even pride ourselves that other groups do the talking while we do the hard dirty work. Yet SNCC has grown larger and larger and has created its own needs. . . . We can use skills and organization in some areas without letting *them* use us.

I then decided to write another paper on women for the November session. In the spirit of the preparations for Waveland, I desperately wanted to share some of my thinking on our organizational direction and within that context lift the question of how my growing perception of myself as a woman might affect the structure and program of SNCC. When it came time to sit down at the typewriter, I was shaken with doubt. The issue was enormous. I was afraid. The reaction, I was convinced, would be one of ridicule. There was also a technical problem of how to write about some of my concerns involving women because—within the framework of the civil rights movement and the fields of human rights and civil liberties at the time—women's rights had no meaning and indeed did not exist.

For a period of over one month, I quietly gathered examples of how the movement's style and practice conflicted with its rhetoric when applied to women. I watched bulletin boards, listened carefully in staff meetings, noticed what came across my desk, took notes and talked with women friends on staff like Ruth Howard, Maria Varela, Dona Richards, Muriel Tillinghast, and Emmie Schrader. Finally, I made a list of examples using civil rights metaphors. I had no trouble finding examples. They were everywhere. Then I drafted a position paper. I consulted with Casey. She said she would join with me in it and made some suggestions.

We decided not to venture into the profound implications of the worldwide second-class status of women which Simone de Beauvoir had sharpened for us, but to limit the paper to behavior in the movement. I thought there was no use raising the bizarre twist of history that man, born of woman, had, with primeval arrogance, relegated her in virtually all cultures to secondary status. We would instead try to draw simple, clear-cut analogies between white treatment of blacks and the movement's treatment of women, because we thought the points would be better understood. Fearing a mirthful reaction, I prepared it secretly, to be presented anonymously. (See Appendix 2.)

I wrote the paper using the male gender for pronouns, and I remember thinking that someday this would have to stop. All my life I had been troubled by the use of the male gender in referring to human beings of both sexes. Sitting in church as I did for so many hours of my childhood listening to the King James Version of the Bible and later the Revised Standard Version with their unbroken use of male references for the supreme being and the human race, I used to wonder if that didn't leave me out. Perhaps I was not subject to all the dos and don'ts of biblical admonitions and proscriptions! Now, writing this position paper I did not want to say "he," "his," and "him" referring to women and men or use "man" for human beings of both sexes. Beginning in the fifth grade, I used to sit in church and school and think about these language patterns. Indeed, as a teenager I had figured out—although I would not have phrased it this way—that as long as English provided a different word for each gender, one of those words could not be universal except by obliteration and disparagement of the other. (Beauvoir wrote almost an entire book, *The Second Sex*, on woman as "the other.") But I had not yet figured out any alternative usage, and I was afraid it would be distracting from the main points I was trying to make. There was also a limit to how much I could encompass. The paper was sketchy and I did not feel secure raising these questions. My heart was palpitating and I was shaking as I typed it. My fear of a joking response was making me unsteady in my resolve.

I wrote:

> The average white person finds it difficult to understand why the Negro resents being called "boy," or being thought of as "musical" or "athletic," because the average white person doesn't realize that *he assumes he is superior.* And naturally he doesn't understand the problem of paternalism. So too the average SNCC worker finds it difficult to discuss the woman problem because of the assumption of male superiority. Assumptions of male superiority are as widespread and deep-rooted and every [bit as] . . . crippling to the woman as the assumptions of white supremacy are to the Negro.

While the paper drew analogies between the movement's rhetoric and the exploitation of blacks, it grew out of and reflected a deeper concern for where our movement was headed. Would SNCC's visionary spirit and idealism be able to encompass Casey's and my concerns? Already there were hints of a narrowing of vision that would preclude such expression.

By floating this anonymous position paper, Casey and I believed we would be reasserting the basic values of the early sit-ins and SNCC's original concept of leadership. We were asking if SNCC's view of leadership as something inchoate and inherent in every community, and furthermore in every person, didn't also mean that the rights of women should be among the concerns of the movement. The early SNCC values of personhood had nourished Casey's and my changing sense of ourselves. As old-timers, relatively speaking, Casey and I also thought we should take some responsibility to influence the debate on SNCC's identity and future. Sooner or later we would have to reveal our new awareness as political beings who were concerned with the status of women, if we were to be honest with ourselves and with each other.

In preparation for SNCC's open forum at Waveland, the first of several meetings that would be held there, debates were occurring among the dispersed staff on different questions concerning its organizational structure and its program for the coming years.

Other themes figured in the many position papers being written—
the war in Vietnam, responses to the war of liberation in Algeria
and other African national liberation movements, approaches to
leadership development, and concepts of political organizing.

Long-term planning in SNCC was always difficult because of
our youth. Although our goals were high and we were dauntless,
for approximately three quarters of the SNCC staff a five-year
plan would have represented 20 or 25 percent of a lifetime!

A staff committee sent around a list of open-ended questions
to stimulate preparation of the position papers: "What is SNCC?"
"What do we organize?" "Where do we organize?" "How do we
organize?" "Why do we organize?" In response, at least thirty-
seven papers, which I still have among my files, were circulated
prior to the meeting. In answer to the question, "What do we
organize?" one staff member from the rural South wrote:

> We organize groups of people who feel the same needs. We
> organize them so they can gain enough power to get their
> needs met by people in this country who can meet their
> needs. These groups should be as independent as possible,
> should be led by people from within the group (rather than
> by the organizers or "civil rights leaders") and should de-
> velop programs themselves with our help.

In answer to the question, "Why do we organize?" the same
person wrote:

> We hope for this world, all of us. Even though we and our
> programs are sometimes dull, or ugly, or impatient, the
> hope is beautiful. Maybe we would be more patient with
> each other—and our organization would therefore become
> more democratic—if we remember that while we are all very
> different, we are joined together by a hope that is very
> beautiful.

Two main schools of thought were evolving on the underlying structural issues as we moved toward the November 1964
Waveland meeting. They were represented on the one hand by
Jim Forman and on the other by Bob Moses. Each of them worked
in different environments and was under certain daily pressures,
which he reflected in his views of how to address the issues.

Jim, who was based in Atlanta, represented SNCC at national meetings and with national leaders. He was expected to
speak for us, as the most politically militant among the civil rights
organizations. He raised money and oversaw the handling of it,
was responsible for relations with the churches and the black labor
unions, and sought to sustain the morale of a far-flung group of
highly individualistic field secretaries and project directors. There
were many personal needs of the staff he also had to consider. All
of this he did with a warm sense of humor.

Bob Moses was based in Mississippi, spending his time in
the hamlets of the Delta and rural counties of the state. The people he saw daily were survivors of a stygian system that had been
discarded by most of the Western world over a century ago, a
system that mocked their dignity as human beings. He believed
that the greatest need was to meet and facilitate change among
those living in this state of semislavery, and he had to cope with
the pressures of operating programs amidst the poverty of plantation economies. He was deeply influenced by Ella Baker and her
supportive behind-the-scenes approach. He thought that enabling
uneducated provincial people to rise to their full potential and
speak on their own behalf was a requirement for lasting change.

Jim Forman wanted a more coherent structure and a base to
support him in working with the world beyond the staff circle. I
recall Jim's saying in the autumn of 1964 that we had 161 full-
time staff members. They were spread across the South, and we
had support offices in a score of northern cities. Jim wanted the
money to come into the center of the structure in Atlanta where
there could be accountability and the programs could be reviewed
by a central decision-making body. To solve these problems, he
believed, a more hierarchical structure with clear-cut lines of delegation was critically needed.

Those of us around Bob favored a loosely confederated structure akin to that of SNCC's early days, a coordinating unit linked
to autonomous affiliates. We thought the money should be allocated to state-based programs and local communities, with the
accountability for the use of the funds in local hands. "Do we
build a SNCC machine," Bob asked at this time, "or do we organize people?" Those of us who wanted a decentralized arrangement also wanted a clear acknowledgment that only a radical
commitment to democracy among ourselves, as the catalysts, fa-

cilitators, and organizers, would help us retain the sense of community that would allow us to maintain our vision and also sustain us for what lay ahead.

These tensions over SNCC's structure and its future course came together for Casey and me in a blast of energy, as between us we prepared to speak out, anonymously. In preparing to raise the question of women, we believed we were also broadening the debate in favor of a decentralized and manifestly democratic SNCC. In breaking open difficult and unasked questions on the role of women, we thought a decentralized SNCC would be better able to respond.

At about this time, I remember, I was beginning to feel other conflicts. The movement was exposing me to the worth and dignity of humble Black Belt people in a dramatic way, suggesting that existing institutions needed not only to open up but also to change in order to accommodate them. I could see that no sheriff's posse and no gun could smother the desire for dignity and self-determination. On the other hand, I was sometimes walking on tiptoe to do what had to be done, skirting the edges—to use a metaphor obviously describing a traditional female stance—and occasionally acting through others because I was white in a mostly black movement.

"The sit-ins were very existential," Casey used to remind me about the movement of 1960 and 1961. "It was about desegregation but, more important, the sit-ins were about enacting your beliefs. The purpose of life was in living as you think. There were no other ultimates except doing that and communicating in that way," Casey would say. "The sit-ins had a quality of charisma and basic humanism."

So, when she and I prepared to step into the Waveland debate on how to structure SNCC and whether there would be room for a variety of political and social concerns including those of women, we were really asking whether there would be room for us to act out our beliefs.

Our November 1964 staff retreat was held at a church center, the Gulfside Methodist Assembly grounds in Waveland, near Bay St. Louis, on the Mississippi Sound, beyond which lay the deeper waters of the Gulf of Mexico. This was a somewhat more tolerant section of Mississippi, perhaps because the French Canadians—

Acadians expelled from Nova Scotia—settling the bay in the eighteenth century had intermarried with the Indians and Spaniards, forming a group called the Creoles on the Gulf Coast. Only at Waveland was it possible for a racially integrated group to stay together and not trigger violence in Mississippi. It was located on the sea-wall drive of the southernmost county of the state, Hancock County. The summer home of many New Orleans whites during the hot months of June to September, by November the town had closed up for the winter. We were housed in simple frame bungalows and dormitories on the water's edge. A pier extended into the bay.

Jim Forman's opening remarks were revealing:

> No one is questioning the fact that everybody within SNCC is a decision maker. . . . There is no superstructure which sits in Atlanta or Jackson and constantly says this project must do this and must do that. . . . No one has ever questioned the right of the staff to make decisions in the field, except for certain decisions dealing with fund raising. In this respect we have been different from other organizations that have attempted to control decisions made by staff people in the field from a central point. On the other hand, that freedom to make decisions has created many problems and many strains within the organization. . . .
>
> I call for internal cohesion. . . . We are on a river of no return. . . . It also becomes imperative that we ask ourselves why do we exist? . . . We must continue, not necessarily to work for the redemptive society, but to work toward a new spirit of brotherhood, a spirit that transcends both black and white, a spirit that supersedes, a spirit that goes above and a spirit that sees all of us simply as men and women, struggling for a sense of dignity. . . . We must decide if the circle will be unbroken.

The position papers distributed at the meeting varied from polemical tracts to vague musings to solid programmatic proposals on the variety of structures available to SNCC, some highly democratic and decentralized, others more strictly defined in conventional terms. The papers did not comprise the agenda for the meeting but were circulated on the side, to inform the discussion. There was little reasoned dialogue, however. This meeting turned out to be explosive. Racial tensions surfaced openly in a blunt and assaultive way, with cutting acidity. Some of it was too much for me. For the first in my life, I walked out of a meeting because of the brutally aggressive hostility being expressed. Many staff members were bitter, accusatory, and confrontational. The process of achieving consensus—our standard method for conducting business—was impossible. Passionately concerned for SNCC's future, I felt uncertain and confused. The whole retreat seemed catastrophic. I was depressed.

When the document on women was distributed informally at the meeting, the reaction to the anonymous position paper was one of crushing criticism. I had been right about the ridicule. People quickly figured out who had written it. Some mocked and taunted us. There were, however, some exceptions. I will never forget standing at night alongside a parked car on the assembly grounds with the moon shining through the ring of scrub-pine trees and learning that Bob Moses and Charlie Cobb liked our paper and respected it. Their approval was important to me. Mendy Samstein said he admired it. Maria Varela and Dona Richards were warm and appreciative. Emmie Schrader and Theresa del Pozzo already knew about it and supported it. Julian Bond smiled wryly about it, noncommittal, with his sidelong glance. A few others here and there talked about it with interest. Some minimized it, but for the most part it was disdained. As Bertha Gober's freedom song went, I felt as if I'd "been 'buked" and I'd "been scorned."

Once change has occurred, it becomes part of you and it is difficult to remember the state of mind that preceded that alteration. Yet I can never forget how lonely I felt in putting that paper out and how afraid I was of derision. We were raising a foreign issue. Very few women were interested in it. It may now seem contradictory that risk-taking, independent, farsighted women organizers were not yet able to articulate these concerns; yet it is my obligation not only to detail the facts but to place them in context. Casey and I were trying to communicate that someone felt treated unjustly and that this concern was compatible with our cause. SNCC had the potential to see itself both as the oppressed and the oppressor, an insight that not every organization had the capacity for, and the women of SNCC were uniquely poised to respond but in many cases couldn't.

SNCC staff were known for always working very hard, and

we partied equally hard. This was part of the release mechanism
for coping with tension and adversity. Even if our meetings were
intense and there were hostile interchanges, afterward there was
always music, with beer and dancing late into the night, and our
basic affection for each other would flow across the wounds of the
day's diatribes. Waveland was no different.

One night, in the charged atmosphere of the retreat, a group
of us gravitated toward the pier with a gallon of wine. Under
a bright, cloudless sky, we talked and laughed among ourselves
as we walked to the bay seeking humor to salve the hurts of
the day.

Stokely Carmichael, handsome, gregarious, and sinewy, had
an elongated frame and an easy smile that flashed across his face
warming up the environment around him. Stokely's mind was sharp
and incisive. A graduate of the famous Bronx High School of Science and Howard University, he originally came from Trinidad.
Stokely had the ability to joke like a professional stand-up comedian, a facile wit accompanied by an amazing capacity for sustained humor that reflected his high intelligence. He had been
called Stokely Starmichael the summer before in Mississippi because of his natural celebrity. Cracking jokes one after another,
he usually made fun of himself and the people of Trinidad more
than of anyone else. It was the same this night. Casey, Mendy
Samstein, Carole Merritt, a beautiful black woman who had formerly worked with the United Negro College Fund and sometimes went out with Stokely, and several others of us were
beginning to mellow after the traumatic meetings. We were soothed
by the gentle Gulf winds that were still warm in November, the
lapping waves, and the wine. The moon was bright enough to
read by.

Stokely started one of his monologues. He led slowly and
then began to warm up. One humorous slap followed another. We
became more and more relaxed. We stretched out on the pier,
lying with our heads on each others' abdomens. We were absorbed by the flow of his humor and our laughter. He reveled in
our attention as we were illuminated by the moon. Stokely got
more and more carried away. He stood up, slender and muscular,
jabbing to make his points, his thoughts racing. He began to ges-
ticulate dramatically, slapping his thighs and spinning around,
thrusting his arm, silhouetted against the moon like a Javanese

shadow puppet. His dashing smile baring his perfect teeth, he made fun of himself and then he dressed down Trinidadians. He started joking about black Mississippians. He made fun of everything that crossed his agile mind. Finally, he turned to the meetings under way and the position papers. He came to the no-longer-anonymous paper on women. Looking straight at me, he grinned broadly and shouted, "What is the position of women in SNCC?" Answering himself, he responded, "The position of women in SNCC is prone!" Stokely threw back his head and roared outrageously with laughter. We all collapsed with hilarity. His ribald comment was uproarious and wild. It drew us all closer together, because, even in that moment, he was poking fun at his own attitudes.

Casey and I felt, and continue to feel, that Stokely was one of the most responsive men at the time that our anonymous paper appeared in 1964.

Later-published accounts, such as Robin Morgan's book *Sisterhood Is Powerful*, asserted that Ruby Doris Smith Robinson had written our position paper. Other versions reported that Ruby Doris stood up to read the paper at Waveland and Stokely shouted her down with his comment.

At the end of 1973, I received a telephone call from Gloria Steinem, who had been told by Julian Bond that she should talk with me. *Ms.* magazine was considering publishing an article on Ruby Doris, Gloria told me, "because we understand she wrote a pivotal paper presented at a civil rights meeting that raised some vital issues on women for the first time. We want to track down the paper." Overlapping each other, Gloria's longtime associate Joanne Edgar wrote me, on January 31, 1974, about Ruby Doris: "Certainly she is a lost heroine for all of us. And we would like to honor her." To Gloria's credit, she took the trouble to seek verification. I explained the actual situation both to her and to Joanne and showed them our original position paper when I next went to New York City. *Ms.* magazine never enshrined the error.

How on earth Casey's and my document was ever ascribed to Ruby Doris by Robin Morgan is a complete mystery to me. She herself would never have taken credit for it. Far from it. Ruby, along with a great many of the women in SNCC and certainly the majority of the black women in SNCC, repudiated it when it first appeared.

Ruby Doris had little sympathy for the questions Casey and I raised during the debates on SNCC's structure. As an administrator, she felt strongly, along with Jim Forman, that SNCC needed centralization for tighter management, and she considered the issue of women to be a diversion.

Nevertheless, when a group of us women in the Atlanta headquarters conducted a sit-in of our own around Jim Forman's tiny congested office, in January 1964, Ruby Doris joined us and held her placard high, her spirits fueling our tongue-in-cheek and jocular demonstration. Judy Richardson, vivacious with her pert topknot of hair; Betty Garman, the capable liaison to northern support groups; and I had rounded up women working in the headquarters to sit-in both outside and inside of Jim's cubicle. It was more of a show of force than a demand for redress of specific wrongs, and perhaps our demonstration was also a plea for recognition.

Jim later wrote in his book *The Making of Black Revolutionaries* that he had been told by Kathie Sarachild, the feminist editor, that "the awareness of a sit-in in the SNCC office in 1963 or 1964 by some women tended to light a prairie fire in the women's movement." His response was to say:

> That sit-in grew out of a discussion between some women in the SNCC national office in Atlanta, Georgia, and myself about the conditions of women in general and in the SNCC. Many of those who worked in the office stated they felt they could not discuss with some men how they felt about certain matters or grievances they held about various situations.
>
> I suggested at that time that women should begin to become more militant in their demands and that they could start the process by emulating the lunch counter sit-in movement. . . . I proposed that they role play, using me as a target. I also suggested they should make a sign or signs and develop a plan of action along with the sit-in in my office.

It is not true, however, that Jim invited this demonstration. It was certainly not his idea. Perhaps what he meant was that he did not feel antagonized by it. That was true; he was very good-spirited about it and entered into the humor of the situation. We had many laughs.

Slowly the questions that Casey and I had raised were beginning to find receptivity and the issues were gradually being discussed openly. Most of the time, however, Ruby Doris regarded
the new consciousness with regard to women, which was emerging in SNCC after Waveland, as disruptive and divisive. An impatient manager, eager to bring order out of SNCC's ad hoc
procedures and hectic pace, she wanted to get back to the demanding reality of building a tightly run SNCC. I respected Ruby
Doris and I believe she respected me. She often bristled with
antagonism toward white women, perhaps because they represented a standard different from the ideal cherished by black
women. But Ruby and I had a territorial standoff. We left each
other alone except when business matters required contact, until
late 1965. That was when Ruby Doris and the personnel committee took steps to cut me off the payroll because I was beginning
to include opposition to the war in Vietnam and concern for the
impact of economic poverty into my thinking. These were issues
she regarded as diversionary.

Ruby Doris died of cancer in October 1967. She suffered from
cumulative health problems and traumas that started in the Rock
Hill jail and were exacerbated by her subsequent incarceration
and lack of proper treatment. In its obituary in the October 1967
SNCC newsletter, the staff wrote:

> Ruby's passing is especially tragic for all those involved in
> the struggle for human rights and the liberation of black
> people. During her seven years in the movement, she was
> the heartbeat of SNCC, as well as one of its most dedicated
> administrators. Her memory will be a shining light to all
> who continue the battle to which she dedicated her life.

Unfortunately, we will never know whether Ruby Doris, who
was elected executive secretary in June 1966 when Stokely Carmichael was elected chairman, might not ultimately have been
proud that a grass-roots movement to assure equality for women
in the United States would be sparked among activist women and
organizers from within the civil rights movement. So many others
who were antagonistic or indifferent at the time have since then
come to see in a new light the questions Casey and I were raising
and have expressed their deep satisfaction that SNCC played a

generative role in the modern women's movement. I venture to
say that Ruby Doris, too, would have been pleased.

Fully one year after the first Waveland retreat, Casey and I
together wrote another document, this time signing our names.
Like the first paper, this manifesto was intimately tied to the
deepening ferment within SNCC on fundamental issues of leadership, organizing, political vision, institution building, and self-
determination.

My having worked with Ella Baker was one of the most important factors in my wanting to share the ideas expressed in the
two documents, and she has had a lasting impact on my life. In
Miss Baker, I saw a uniquely liberated human being at work with
consistent creativity. She was a great listener and synthesizer. Her
concepts of strategy, leadership, and organizing laid the groundwork for my later thinking; they are part of the person I was to
become and they enrich me every day.

Occasionally Bobbi Yancy and I would go shopping and load
up Ella Baker's freezer in her apartment at 239 West Lake, in
northwest Atlanta, with little steaks so she wouldn't have to go to
the market to shop. On one of many evenings Bobbi and I spent
talking with her there, she told me that she had been married at
one time. "I have always been very happy that I didn't change
my name," she said to me. "I didn't think that I *belonged* to any
man," she stated, eyes crinkling and her lips downturned in her
characteristic smile.

Perhaps some of Miss Baker's concern for the burden of
working in isolation came from her own feelings as she traveled
throughout Mississippi and the rest of the Deep South in the 1920s,
1930s, and 1940s—alone—speaking in churches, clubs, and lodges,
or wherever she was allowed to appear, for the purpose of encouraging individual memberships in the NAACP or other organizations. She must have learned painfully how much more could
be accomplished if one was confident one was working in con-
junction with others.

Ella Baker was a thoroughly principled person. One of her
convictions sounds deceptively simple but it is difficult in imple-
mentation—she believed that individuals should make their own
decisions. This was not the predominant view in the paternalistic
atmosphere of the black community, which had learned its les-

sons well from the paternalism of whites toward blacks. As an example, black women's colleges like Benedict and Spelman, at the time I visited them on the human-relations project, required their students to wear white gloves, to have letters of permission from home to leave campus after 5:00 P.M. or for a few hours on Saturday, and forbade chewing gum. Miss Baker believed that most people were submissively ready to follow authority; therefore, she convinced SNCC that a fundamental purpose of the civil rights movement was to teach people to make their own decisions, to take responsibility for themselves, and to be ready to accept the consequences.

A minor but profoundly revealing episode concerning Ella Baker occurred when Fannie Lou Hamer described to the entire SNCC staff, assembled in the Old Gammon Seminary in Atlanta in February 1965, how the Mississippi Freedom Democratic party rejected the compromise at Atlantic City. Mrs. Hamer gave her account without realizing how much it said about Miss Baker. "I asked Miss Baker if we should accept the compromise," Fannie Lou Hamer told the staff, "and she said that we should make our own decision."

Perhaps the most important principle for Miss Baker was that "you must let the oppressed themselves define their own freedom." This tenet, combined with her belief that individuals should make their own decisions, was a dominant factor setting SNCC apart from the NAACP and other groups with more traditional views of centralized and personalized leadership. Miss Baker supported SNCC's evolution toward the policy of creating organizations that local people could control themselves.

Through Ella Baker's influence on me, these principles also gave rise to the two documents on women. Wasn't that in fact what we were seeking to do, to define our own freedom?

Our second document was written when Casey and I were spending a few days at my family's cottage in a remote tract of woods in Spotsylvania County, Virginia. There, in the quiet isolation of a forest, and with woodsmoke from the cottage fire scenting our walks, on November 18, 1965, Casey wrote the first draft and then together we polished our challenge to women who were involved across the spectrum of progressive organizing. This call would go out to women in Students for a Democratic Society, the

National Student Association, the Northern Student Movement, and the Student Peace Union as well as SNCC. Working from notes from conversations we had had with Dona Richards, we composed our message and mailed it to forty women activists across the country. We wrote:

> We've talked a lot to each other and to some of you, about our own and other women's problems in trying to live in our personal lives and in our work as independent and creative people. . . . In particular, women we've talked to who work in the movement seem to be caught up in a common-law caste system that operates, sometimes subtly, forcing them to work around or outside hierarchical structures of power which may exclude them. Women seem to be placed in the same positions of assumed subordination in personal relationships too. It is a caste system which, at its worst, uses and exploits women. . . .
>
> A very few men seem to feel, when they hear conversations involving these problems, that they have a right to be present and participate in them since they are so deeply involved. At the same time, very few men can respond nondefensively since the whole idea is either beyond their comprehension or threatens to expose them. The usual response is laughter. That inability to see the issue as serious, as the straitjacketing of both sexes, and as societally determined, often shapes our own response so that we learn to think in their terms about ourselves and to feel silly rather than to trust our inner feelings. . . .
>
> The reason we want to try to open up dialogue is mostly subjective. Working in the movement often intensifies personal problems, especially if we start trying to apply things we're learning to our personal lives. Perhaps we can start to talk with each other more openly than in the past and create a community of support for each other so we can deal with ourselves and others with integrity. . . .
>
> All the problems between men and women functioning in society as equal human beings are among the most basic that people face. We've talked in the movement about trying to build a society which would see basic human problems (which are now seen as private troubles) as public problems and would try to shape institutions to meet human needs rather than shaping people to meet the needs of those with power. . . .

Given the brooding silence of that time concerning these issues, we were still concerned about the reception of this second
manifesto; and although we were no longer afraid of ridicule, we
purposely downplayed it by calling it "A Kind of Memo." (See
Appendix 3.) We also threw a sop to those who would be critical
of us for being divisive, by saying that most of us would probably
want to work full time on problems of war, poverty, and race.

Since the term *liberation* was not then widely used pertaining
to women, the word *sexism* had not been coined, *feminism* was
rarely heard, and other now familiar argot of the women's movement did not exist, we searched for the best term to use to describe the condition of women. We liked the concept of a *caste
system* because it suggested an arbitrarily imposed method of val-
uation in which rigid taboos forbade certain behavior and lines
were drawn that could not be crossed, based on involuntary status
acquired at birth. One year after the earlier attempt at breaking
open this issue, the racial analogy seemed to have limitations
(women, for example, are not a minority but a slight majority) and
caste system seemed the most accurate characterization.

Even in our fantasies, we had no hope that a movement would
develop. "Objectively the chances seem nil that we could start a
movement based on anything as distant to general American thought
as a sex-caste system," we wrote. Instead, we wanted to provoke
the reaction of a selected group of women including some of the
black women in SNCC to whom we felt drawn. We wanted the
support of other women who were politically involved with civil
rights and antiwar issues, women who were risk takers and who
shared a commitment to fostering social change. We hoped that a
network would evolve. What developed was far beyond our expectations.

As we were writing our missive, Casey said, "I am concerned
about how to be independent and creative. I can see how racial
taboos in the black community block that potential for blacks.
The movement's soul is that of a caste grouping in a larger indifferent culture. I used to wonder what happened to suffering people who have a shared view of the underside of society and what
specific knowledge and benefits come from it. The people we've
been working with are incredibly rich spiritual human beings. Their
spirit is what's kept me going."

Casey and I could not yet see the wheel of change beginning

to turn for women. Reflecting a feeling of hopelessness, we confided that we weren't absolutely certain that the end results, if there was massive change, would be any better than things as they were then. We could see there was a cultural grouping in which women had a perspective on birth and death, endurance, love, and basic human values that was often different from that of the dominant culture—and that should be exalted. We were just as concerned for employed mothers who were locked into low-paying, dead-end, meaningless jobs providing little means for caring for their offspring, as we were for women who needed the gratification of stimulating work for their sense of fulfillment and personhood. The point was, simply stated, that women should be able to define freedom in their own way.

As Casey said, with her vibrant, throaty laugh, "You've got to have a choice before you can choose."

Misconceptions have developed along the way, perhaps because so few books have been written by direct participants in the civil rights movement. One damaging notion implanted in the literature, even by such pathfinding authors as history professor Sara M. Evans of the University of Minnesota and author of *Personal Politics*, was that in the years after 1965 the movement became increasingly alienating for women. This was true for me, but *not* for the reasons given. As this story goes, women in the movement were relegated to typing, running mimeograph machines, preparing and serving coffee, washing dishes, and being available for sex. This is not correct and is not an explanation of Casey's and my protests. Our status in the movement was never the issue. Furthermore, this distortion overlooks the truly significant roles women played, the responsiveness of SNCC to women leaders before such an issue had been articulated, and the fact that, by and large, the movement was peopled by women; worst of all, it belies the seriousness and earnestness with which women in SNCC were involved and denies the important debate within SNCC that gave rise to our two documents.

This distorted characterization represents an imposition of a later feminist construction on a period of ferment. While the civil rights movement and the people in it mirrored the conventions and stereotypes of the larger society, that movement was at the same time giving rise to a challenge from within it that would contribute to producing a successor movement.

Within the context of the turbulence of SNCC at the time, Casey and I were not inquiring about our roles but about whether there would be room in the civil rights movement for differing political and social concerns, as various groups and, in our case, women defined them.

Specifically, we were asking whether we would be able to act out our beliefs and make decisions based on our convictions, beliefs grounded in our definition of freedom and self-determination as women, stemming from what we had learned in the movement. The questions Casey and I raised ran parallel to the larger debate about SNCC's future course. The organizational structure for SNCC that we supported, one of democratization and decentralization, would have allowed this. Autonomous local movements as opposed to a centralized hierarchy would have supported diversity and variation; this was the view that Bob Moses personified, and it was broadly compatible with a concept about which there *was* consensus: the increasing conviction that SNCC organizers should dig in and help local people develop institutions they controlled.

Our second document was in part a call for a return to the fundamental values of the sit-ins and the early vision of SNCC, according to which any community should be free to define its own political agenda, spark its own local movement, and raise up its own leaders. Ten years later, when I told Sara Evans that I had felt "relatively powerless" as a member of the SNCC staff, I was referring to a general feeling that I was losing ground within the movement with regard to the principles and beliefs of the early SNCC years that I valued.

Correct about much of what we said in our declaration to the forty women activists, Casey and I were also wrong on some points. We were about as wrong as we could be, for example, when we said, "The caste system is not institutionalized by law." In 1965 the body of case and statutary law that legalized a variety of forms of discrimination against women had not yet been uncovered and was certainly not being taught as such in law schools. Casey asserted at one point, "It's not as bad for women as it is for blacks legally." But it was. It was actually much worse.

We were also wrong in another way: Our document underestimated the causal economic forces at work. The entry of Amer-

ican women into the labor force in significant numbers was not
caused by the women's movement; it had actually begun during
World War II. The entry of women into the labor force created
the preconditions and economic climate that would produce in
America a mass movement of women. We could not in 1964 anticipate that numerous industries, such as life and health insurance, baby foods, and toy industries, would subsequently fight
hard against constitutionally guaranteed equal rights for women,
sometimes financing opposition groups working against an equal
rights amendment, or that there would be reactionary counter-
movements attempting to reverse those gains that had been made.
By the same token, we did not realize that our asking, Who defines whom? was a revolutionary question.

Even our straightforward arguments concerning the economic
inequity between the sexes were threatening. Within the American economy, where for decades women had received less than
62 percent of the pay of men for the same work, to ask for equal
pay was also a revolutionary demand because of its potential de-
stabilizing impact on an entire system of interconnected parts. The
solution to this lingering inequity will elude us for many years.

The greatest mistake we made was believing that the caste
system was volitional—that is, we thought men and women together could agree it should not be that way in private relationships. That was utterly naïve. The caste system for women,
bolstered by law and tradition, and erected on rigid economic
structures of differentiated pay and opportunity, has a profound
effect on personal intention. Although many men want relationships that do not hold women to second-class status, it is undeniable that legal and economic strictures have a compelling effect
on personal relationships, to say nothing of self-image based on
custom and conditioning.

Our manifesto that was sent to the forty activists came from
the heart of the civil rights movement and may, in its own way,
have helped to redress an imbalance that had dated back to the
period of abolition. The constitutional exclusion of women from
suffrage and other rights, despite the visible and significant leadership of women of both races in the effort to end slavery, has
been a travesty to women who are aware of the history. After the
Civil War, former male slaves were given the vote, in statute if
not in practice, while both white women and black women were

legally excluded. This inequity, in which black men got the vote several decades before white women—so many of whom had been active in the abolition movement—had continued to fester.

Healing a rift that was developing between black and white women was an important objective for Casey and me. Particularly in Mississippi, a number of competent young black women had become directors of field projects by 1964 and Casey and I were close to most of them. Muriel Tillinghast was the project director in Greenville; Ruth Howard directed voter registration in Greenwood; and Janet Jemmott coordinated voter registration in Natchez. While Cynthia Washington was in charge of the community center in Cleveland, Gwen Robinson was the project director in Laurel. Jean Wheeler Smith was a field secretary and campus traveler in Virginia and Tennessee. Prathia Hall was spearheading the program in Selma, Alabama. Gloria Richardson was the charismatic head of the SNCC affiliate in Cambridge, Maryland. Dorie Ladner became a key field secretary in 1962 and had been dispatched to many projects in Mississippi; her sister, Joyce, although still a student at Tougaloo College, was active in the Mississippi movement. Bernice Johnson Reagon had been pivotal in the Albany, Georgia, movement, and was one of The Freedom Singers. Fay Bellamy, Lorne Kress, and others were part of a long list of talented women staff members.

Silas Norman, a graduate of Paine College in Augusta, Georgia, had circulated a position paper at Waveland in November 1964 that spoke of an "ethnic relationship" between black staff and local communities, and stated, "I do not feel that this relationship can be entered into by whites." Over the next few months, some started speaking of wanting whites out of the movement. Tensions aroused by such arguments began to affect personal relationships—even with those who were not enthusiastic about this argument or did not agree—and some of Casey's and my friendships with key black women began to tear. She and I were at least partly responding to this estrangement in our second document.

The black women of SNCC were slow to respond to our missives. While some had reacted with indifference or antagonism to the 1964 anonymous Waveland position paper, others were interested but appeared reluctant to speak out. One exception was Jean Wheeler Smith, one of the first black women in the United States at that time to leave her hair natural and unstraightened as a political statement. I was strongly drawn to Jean and admired her as much as anyone with whom I worked and, during the intervening years, I have continued to hold her in high esteem. She was honest, open, and unpresuming. She had no complexes and seemed completely in touch with her own strengths and weaknesses. When Jean was a student at Howard University, she had come into conflict with Patricia Roberts Harris, then dean of women, who asked her not to wear her hair natural (but later became her friend and mentor). She had a gentle manner and a shy halting in her speech that was appealing in its ingenuousness, yet Jean was a visionary and a genuinely freethinking person. She would stand in staff meetings and say the unpopular thing or make comments that others were afraid to say. Utterly lacking in trendiness and wary of fashionable phrases, Jean remained aloof from factionalism. She sympathized with the deeper questions Casey and I were raising.

Another black woman who was in accord with us was Dona Richards, a plucky graduate in philosophy from the University of Chicago. Always wearing snugly fitting blue jeans, Dona's small frame was topped by broad shoulders. I thought Dona guileless with her high, rounded forehead and engaging smile. I remember her walking about with a textbook on metaphysics by Alfred North Whitehead under her arm for several months one autumn. For reasons that I could never fully discern, Dona was considered controversial. I think that she was simply ahead of her time—a woman of the 1990s living in the 1960s. Some of her adversaries were rankled because they couldn't appreciate why she had retained her birth name after marrying Bob Moses. She was almost ostracized by others because of her desire for independence within the marriage, although jealousy of her proximity to Bob may also have been a factor in this antagonism. Smart, feisty, free-speaking, and energetic, Dona was openly in agreement with our position paper at Waveland and had in many discussions helped to stimulate Casey's and my thinking.

Perhaps one reason that we heard nothing from our black women friends other than Jean and Dona was that, within the black community, women since the days of slavery had often been the primary responsible person in many families and were not constrained by the harsh gender-stereotyping of middle-class white women. Although formal leadership roles might go to men, and the most prestigious professions such as those held by the clergy and morticians were for males only, there was no question about the authority or clout of women in the family and community. If any generalization can be made, it is that black women had too little support for the responsibility they carried.

Lillian Smith of Rabun County had described in *Forbidden Fruit* the taboo in the South against black men having sexual contact with white women, and, for more than two centuries, lynching had often been justified by saying that the miscreant black man had looked at a white woman. Such a cultural history naturally added an emotional charge to the forbidden liaison of a black man and a white woman in the civil rights movement, and perhaps a greater lure. Because of that taboo, some black men found white women more interesting.

Sexually aggressive styles of behavior are more acceptable in some strata of the black community than in the white. Most of the handful of white women who were members of the SNCC staff understood this. But for the several hundred white women who came as volunteers during the summer of 1964—in their newness and also because they did not have to work their way laboriously into the movement to gain trust, having been recruited—they sometimes found themselves the focus of blandishments. Wittingly or unwittingly, a number of them found themselves attracted by the sexually explicit manner of certain black men in the local community and also on the SNCC staff. Many wore décolleté necklines and dangling earrings, not realizing that these would be provocative in southern rural communities, and seemed sometimes to strike an incautious pose. In contrast, women on the SNCC staff were plain; we wore little or no makeup, cut one another's hair, and had no possessions or clothing worth mentioning. Lack of awareness coupled with sudden exposure to the sexual frankness of some of the black men meant that a few of them fluttered like butterflies from one tryst to another. Sexual dalliances were one way for a volunteer to prove she was not racist and I'm certain any number of black men manipulated this anxiety.

This complex dynamic created stress between the veteran black women and white women on the SNCC staff, because the black women could see the allure of the white women volunteers to black male staff. Such desire was unacceptable intellectually, but, psychologically, for some men, it was compelling. I have often wondered whether resistance to this pattern might not have contributed to the surge toward black nationalism that showed itself in SNCC after the November 1964 Waveland meeting. Black men, suddenly exposed to large numbers of white women volunteers—with many of the local men talking to a white woman for the first time in their lives as an equal—suddenly had the real or hypothetical opportunity to break an old taboo. Black women who were field secretaries and project directors, working side by side with black male colleagues all day, found that after hours some of the latter sought the company of the white women volunteers.

This behavior was denounced and bitterly attacked during tormented sessions in a second meeting at Waveland in May of 1965. It was termed "backsliding," because the rhetoric of black pride seemed inconsistent with the reality for some black men. Insofar as I know, this was the only time that sex and politics affected each other during the civil rights movement.

This tension inevitably spilled over and affected Casey's and my relationships with treasured black women friends; nevertheless, we included some of them among the forty activists to whom we sent our second document at the end of 1965.

In my case, there was no undercurrent of sex affecting my experiences in the civil rights movement. Not one of the black men and only one of the white men that I have written about in this book—all the men who were central to SNCC—ever made an explicit sexual advance to me during the years I was involved in the civil rights movement.

Yet, our lives defied conventional morality. For the most part in our twenties and unmarried, peripatetically moving from one crisis to another, from one meeting to another, from one county to another, our toothbrushes in our pockets because of the possibility of being locked up, survival required that we be flexible, sleep anywhere, and make do.

Of course there was flirtation and repartee. This created play in the middle of unrest and provided the gaiety of comic relief. The ebullient field secretary from Baltimore with a cherubic face, Reggie Robinson, constantly flirted with me, but this was part of his exuberance and he still flirts with me. When Reggie stops flirting with me, I will be upset. James Jones, a strikingly handsome and quietly tenacious black field secretary from the Arkansas project, arrived at a staff meeting in Atlanta and shyly came to tell me that he and William Hansen, our white Arkansas state director, had a competition going. The purpose of the contest was to see which of them was the more attractive to me! Yet those with whom I worked the longest, and in some cases the closest, never asked to become sexually intimate, and these were men for whom I felt, and still feel, love—Julian Bond, Jim Forman, Bob Moses, Stokely Carmichael, Bob Zellner, Ivanhoe Donaldson, and many more.

Immediate reaction followed the November 1965 mailing of the second document to the forty activists. Jan Goodman, of the International Ladies Garment Workers Union, told Casey, "I was very turned on by the memo and want to do some kind of exposé on male leadership of the ILGWU." Elizabeth Sutherland, a former editor of *The Nation,* was excited and offered to rewrite the memorandum "making it more popular, less heavy" for publication in magazines. Harriet Stallman wrote us, on December 26, 1965, a four-page, single-spaced letter-response on family and childhood, transmission of values, the mass media, and legal problems, and concluded by proposing institutes for training women and men.

Years later, when I was a presidential appointee in the Carter administration, the writer Barbara Raskin visited my office and told me she would never forget the day, fifteen years earlier, that her copy of our communication had arrived in the mail. She said:

> It was stunning in its effect on me. I read it and reread it, and shared it with all my friends. Eventually we started a group in Washington and met on a regular basis to discuss the issues you and Casey raised. From reading and rereading it, the letter became creased and dirtied. Finally, I could hardly read it anymore but by then I knew it by heart.

On December 10, 1980, toward the end of the Carter years, a telephone call came to my speechwriter, Judith Axler Turner. It was from Janis Kelly, a writer and journalist. Judith dashed off a memorandum to me with an account of the call:

> Janis Kelly said you and Casey have been heroes of hers since the 1960s. She was an organizer and activist at Cornell

and your essay was an incredible catalyst for her and so
many others. She said the Merv Griffin types always track
the women's movement to Betty Friedan or the National
Organization for Women, founded in 1966, or to Simone de
Beauvoir, but Janis Kelly says that the radical segment of
the women's movement tracks directly back to your memo.

From our black women friends to whom we had sent the
missive, however, we heard nothing. Not one responded.

In December 1965, one month after we had dropped our
manifesto in the mail, the women attending the Students for a
Democratic Society convention in Champaign and Urbana, Illinois, who had received it and had been studying it, stood up and
walked out. They called a separate meeting of themselves and
termed it a "Women's Caucus"—the first time that phrase had
been used. Sara Evans—the first historian to call attention to the
role played by our documents—noted that the only man attending
the SDS convention to rise in defense of their walkout was Jimmy
Garrett, the articulate black SNCC organizer who ran our Los Angeles office.

Sara Evans's conclusions about the catalyst provided by our
manifesto were correct. Yet, since she did not have the benefit of
direct experience, she identified a wider group of women as being
involved in the process of writing than was actually the case. She
also emphasizes our status in the movement as the genesis of our
protest, although this was not a source of contention at the time;
rather it was the driving discussions about the structure and purpose of SNCC.

But Sara was not nearly so incorrect as was Jim Forman in his
book, and he was in the middle of everything. He wrote about
what he described as "the paper on women in the SNCC that was
written by three female SNCC staff members and presented at
the Waveland, Mississippi 1965 meeting." He continued:

> Instead of permitting the body to discuss the paper the
> three women withdrew it. I urged them not to do this insist-
> ing that body would most likely be criticized for not discuss-
> ing the paper. Unfortunately history proved me correct. It is
> very regrettable that the three women withdrew it instead of
> letting those in attendance discuss it.

Jim is wrong about what happened, when it happened, and who was involved, and history has certainly not proved him correct. How could Jim have asked us two, not three, *anonymous* writers of the first paper in the November 1964, not the May 1965, Waveland meeting to do anything?

Liberation magazine, published by the War Resisters League, carried our second manifesto in its April 1966 issue. It caused a hue and cry among those in pacifist circles who did not want to admit that anyone involved in the civil rights movement might have feet of clay. The publication of our document in this periodical, however, increased by a quantum leap the number of people circulating it. With widening distribution and study, it was often employed as a kickoff for consciousness-raising groups in what would become a grass-roots women's movement across the country.

Jimmy Garrett was not our only sympathizer. In a small notebook containing random personal observations, I wrote a note to myself on December 28, 1964: "Bob Moses is the only man I know who has made the connections between women and the larger world of political struggle and can be counted on. Bob is liberated in all the important ways."

Some reactions were understandable. Francis Mitchell told me, and I respected the sincerity of his comment, "Mary, I didn't understand. I always thought—before reading what you and Casey wrote—that white women had absolutely everything, that there wasn't anything more that they could possibly wish for."

One day in 1965, I walked into the Freedom House in Tupelo, Mississippi, and someone recognized me who had heard about the two position papers on women. I no longer remember his name, but he pulled from his pocket a piece of paper with a quotation by Frederick Douglass he had typed out and gave it to me: "When I ran away from slavery, it was for myself; when I advocated emancipation, it was for my people; but when I stood up for the rights of women, self was out of question, and I found a little nobility in the act."

Many men who had been active in the civil rights movement were subsequently to take pride in its legacy to the women's movement. One story will illustrate how, little more than a decade later, this point of view was locked firmly into place. In 1978, Stoney Cooks, who had worked with Andrew Young in SCLC, telephoned me in Washington from the U.S. Mission to the United Nations in New York City, where he was still associated with Andy, then ambassador to the UN. Fannie Lou Hamer had just died.

"Andy has asked President Carter for a presidential jet to attend Mrs. Hamer's funeral in Ruleville and President Carter said yes," Stoney told me. "He would like you, your husband, Patt Derian, Hodding Carter, Vernon Jordan, and Charles Diggs to accompany him to the funeral."

At the appointed time, my husband, Peter Bourne, and I waited at the West Wing entrance of the White House as the group gathered to leave for Andrews Air Force Base. As the small, neatly appointed jet with its emblazoned seal of the United States took off with its seven passengers, I saw Andy, who was sitting opposite me, thumbing through a Bible. He was preparing Mrs. Hamer's eulogy. As we had started our flight to the Delta, memories were refracting through my mind like the hues of the sunlight prism glinting at the airplane's windows. I was reeling dizzily, Mississippi memories racing. This was the first time I had returned there after leaving SNCC.

Something about the sight of Andy studying the Bible brought back the memory of Bob Moses's message that had been sneaked out of the Amite County jail in Magnolia in November 1961, in which he had written, "This is a tremor from the middle of the iceberg—from a stone that the builders rejected." I thought of Bob and the August 1961 death of Herbert Lee and what it meant to him. His haunting reference to Psalm 118:22 also seemed to describe Fannie Lou Hamer: "The stone which the builders rejected has become the chief cornerstone."

Flying across the southland in the presidential jet fifteen years after I had sat with Mrs. Hamer on her front porch in Ruleville, my heart overflowing, I opened the Bible to Psalm 118 and showed it to Andy.

"Doesn't this make you think of Mrs. Hamer?" I asked him.

"Umm. That's good," Andy responded, nodding. But I could see that he had something else in mind.

"Women were the spine of our movement," he told the rapt congregation in the small, reconstructed white weatherboarded Delta church that had been burned to a blackened brown in 1964.

It was women going door to door, speaking with their neighbors, meeting in voter-registration classes together, organiz-

ing through their churches, that gave the vital momentum
and energy to the movement, that made it a mass movement. Mrs. Hamer was special but she was also representative. Hundreds of women spoke up and took leadership in
the movement, and from the civil rights movement learned
the lessons that inspired the women's movement. It was
from our movement that a catalyst came and now, it is now
a global upsurge from the village level to parliaments, asserting the rights of women.

Andy concluded his eulogy to Mrs. Hamer by declaring:

W.E.B. Du Bois, the great black thinker, once said, "The
problem of the twentieth century is the problem of the color
line—the relation of the darker to the lighter races." But I
say, the problem of the twenty-first century will be the
problem of relations between men and women. From right
here in the sharecroppers' cabins of the Delta, with Fannie
Lou Hamer, we have seen the start of the promise of the
twenty-first century unfold.

I listened attentively. Subsequently, and only from working
with him years later, was I to realize that he is one of the few
men I know who is willing to talk openly about his prejudices
toward women and his ambivalence about full equality. Andy is
able to be honest without being hostile. He explains his candor
by recalling how much it used to aggravate him when whites denied their prejudice about blacks. He says the first step toward
reconciliation is honest admission of differences. "Women ought
to know just how reluctant men are to share power with them in
anything more than a symbolic way," he has said to me. I have
come to prefer the approach of Andy's honesty to polite tolera-
tion, so often nothing more than controlled hostility.

What conclusions do I draw? In the last century, the abolition
movement had a similar catalytic effect on a number of women.
The period after 1890 in the United States was marked by severe
racial repression and is the time when most of the laws of segregation were implemented. This regression in the progress made
by blacks since the Civil War served to heighten the consciousness of a group of women who began agitating for the vote. Wom-

en's suffrage was finally established in 1920. So too, for me, my proximity to the suffering of blacks in the South and the creative ferment within the civil rights movement prompted a deep personal awareness of the condition of women.

The documents Casey and I wrote reflected a dynamic interrelationship between the nourishment we were receiving from the movement—the political consciousness, boosts to our self-confidence, and encouragement of our native willingness to take risks—and the internal SNCC debates and confusion that caused us to speak out.

Having deeply internalized Ella Baker's lesson that the oppressed themselves must define their own freedom, I felt I could not allow the civil rights movement to overlook fundamental questions that remain unanswered by our and other movement protests, conflicts, and revolutions: Who defines what it is to be a woman? Why must women form a second class? Who decides whether men or women are superior or inferior? Who determines the validity of another's existence?

It has been a revelation to me, in my continuing intellectual growth since the civil rights movement, to observe how little has been written describing this period. Yet, it is important to clarify the role that the civil rights movement played in the genesis of women's organizing as a launching pad for the changing awareness of contemporary women.

After the death of the Reverend Dr. Martin Luther King, Jr., which enervated the civil rights movement, the unbidden and still unseen women's movement became the logical inheritor of its struggle. Genuine civil rights issues are at the core of the women's movement. They include the stereotyping of women, the question of equal pay, lack of constitutional guarantees, problems of self-perception, the feminization of poverty, and a variation on the theme of disenfranchisement—the fact that few women are elected representatives.

It is an error by subsequent historiography not only to fail to recognize the role played by SNCC in the American civil rights movement but also to omit the role of that movement in building an American concern for the rights of women. This is all the more true because these two causes are historically linked. It takes nothing away but adds to the depth of the women's movement to acknowledge that part of its inspiration was in the civil rights cause.

This connection even brings with it a sense of righteousness, for it implies that justice rather than selfishness was the tinder for the organizing done by many women in the late 1960s. Furthermore, it was a woman—Ella Baker—who was catalytic to the start of SNCC and who became its single most important philosophical and strategic influence, and she is one of this century's key voices in American political struggle. Her vision of the leadership potential in each person, the ability of each of us to take responsibility for him- or herself rather than submit to authority, and the necessity for the oppressed to define their own freedom will be as pertinent tomorrow as these insights were to us then.

In addition, the leadership issues raised by SNCC should be of current and future interest to women. The direction of the women's movement should be more squarely aimed at including uneducated, rural, and unaffiliated women in the heartland of the country, and, indeed, were this done, perhaps it would become a more deeply rooted mass phenomenon. The key to an Equal Rights Amendment to the U.S. Constitution lies in the state legislatures. Rural American women must understand why equal-rights protection would help them rather than threaten them and believe so strongly in its correctness that they condition their votes on this issue in electing their representatives to the state capitol. The opinions of women in cities will not be sufficient to win a constitutional amendment because it is the states that must ratify constitutional amendments.

The women's movement in the United States could at present also listen harder to the issues that were raised in SNCC, because otherwise it could become an elitist endeavor. If we are not careful, the women's movement could come to be seen as concerned only with what I call "equal pay for all the lawyers in the corporate boardroom." More attention must be paid to women in mills, factories, on family farms, and at home. Just as Ella Baker and SNCC perceived the role of the civil rights movement as liberating the leadership inherent in "the least of these," so the women's movement must concern itself with the release of leadership inherent in women of every walk of life. If SNCC could thrust up Fannie Lou Hamer, the twentieth child in a family of uneducated sharecroppers and the granddaughter of a slave, as its standard-bearer, why can't the women's movement deliver a union leader from a canning plant, a farmer, or a textile worker among its spokeswomen?

"If you let it," Bob Moses said, "the news media will tell you who your leaders are instead of your telling the news media who your leaders are." A kind of symbiotic relationship can grow up between the leadership of the women's movement, on the one hand, and the communications industry, on the other. Ella Baker and Bob Moses knew that the news media destroy true community leadership by demanding and creating spokespersons. Phyllis Schlafly would not necessarily be considered a "leader," for example, were it not for the need of the media to present an opposite point of view.

Finding a principle equivalent to the Nashville concept of the "redemptibility" of those who are in opposition to equal rights for women (the counterparts of segregationists), who number among themselves both men and women, might help to minimize the antagonism and fear that accompany social change.

The women's movement could also learn from SNCC to address more cogently the question of power and how to achieve power. This process might explore that mentality whereby some women seek to cut down other women. Instead of supporting and nourishing emerging female leadership, as SNCC workers tried to do, usually from behind the scenes, there is sometimes a tendency on the part of women to bring down another woman who begins to rise. In fact, another woman's having power does not diminish the first woman; if you think about it politically, it enhances and strengthens her.

Women also have to continue to work to end racism even when there is no coherent organizational avenue for doing so. Collective unconsciousness or lack of awareness is almost as destructive as the overt presence of racism. The best gauge of the success of our democracy and the true measure of justice in the United States is still the status of America's black community. Covert forms of racism need the attention of women, and no women's movement in the United States can be viable without a strong alliance to overthrow racial injustice and a clear presence of black women. It is still easier for white women than for blacks to achieve positions based on merit in the academic and business worlds, in government, and in other fields.

I believe it will eventually be shown that, over the long run, sexual prejudice is more deeply ingrained than racism. Women's reproductive capacity defines women as a class and is therefore the cause of their oppression and repression. For the future survival of the species, however, this capacity should result in status, not degradation. The implication of Andrew Young's remarks at Fannie Lou Hamer's funeral is that it may take longer to root out the presumption that women are inferior than it will to change the idea that people of dark skin are of less value than those of light complexion, even though most of the world is dark-skinned.

Casey and I were pleased that the documents in which we presented our concepts helped lead to the kind of grass-roots, often leaderless, organizing that the women's movement has done for itself. For this social protest belongs to all women and men who are concerned about becoming fully human. Its work has just begun. It will, over the next century, change the patterns of national and international leadership throughout the world, as women worldwide achieve the eradication of female illiteracy, greater access to education, control of reproduction, control of venereal disease, improved health care, equity in income, and participation in the political and economic life and institutions of their cultures.

This worldwide movement may ultimately be as significant in the twenty-first century as the end of colonialism has been in the twentieth century, as far as leadership is concerned. Still using its basically leaderless approach, the American women's movement must direct itself to the plants, farms, factories, schools, churches, synagogues, mills, clubs, and homes of women who are struggling quietly to improve their lives and those of their families.

Indeed, the women's movement has the potential to do what eluded us in the most progressive branch of the civil rights movement, despite our rhetoric, organizing, political mobilization, challenges, position papers, and manipulation of the news media: To take the leadership out of the hands of leaders and put it into the hands of everyone.

CHAPTER 13

FREEDOM

O freedom, o freedom, o freedom over me,
And before I'll be a slave, I'll be buried in my grave
And go home to my Lord and be free.

No more weeping, no more weeping, no more weeping over me,
And before I'll be a slave, I'll be buried in my grave
And go home to my Lord and be free.

No more shootings, no more shootings, no more shootings over me,
And before I'll be a slave, I'll be buried in my grave
And go home to my Lord and be free.

—Traditional spiritual adapted by the civil rights movement

Jimmy Lee Jackson, a pulpwood cutter, was part of a group that attempted a night march in Marion, Alabama, on February 18, 1965, when state public-safety director Al Lingo's state troopers attacked them. As the twenty-five-year-old black man sought to help his grandfather and his mother, who had been clubbed, a state trooper shot him in the stomach with a revolver. Jimmy Lee's death eight days later aroused the community, and, early in the month of March, Jim Bevel of SCLC announced that on March 7 there would be a march from Selma to Montgomery, the capital of Alabama. This gigantic event eventually turned out to mark the end of innocence for SNCC in more ways than one.

A few words will summarize how work started in Selma. The city had been chosen by SNCC for a voter-registration project in 1963 when Bernard Lafayette and his wife Colia moved there, soon to be joined by field secretaries Worth Long and John Love. Maria Varela was based there for one year, living underground at a white Roman Catholic church. Since 1963, our voter-registration activities showed trivial results—despite the tenacity of our field staff, good local leadership, and litigation by the Justice Department—because of entrenched opposition. In July 1964, a state judge issued an injunction forbidding meetings. This was enforced by Sheriff Jim Clark with his huge deputized posse. In 1965, Silas Norman, a graduate of Paine College in Augusta, Georgia, became SNCC project director.

On February 1, 1965, Dr. King and two hundred fifty demonstrators were arrested as part of what SCLC announced as a major voter-rights campaign. SNCC staff were deeply ambivalent about his and SCLC's efforts in Selma. Dr. King provided important leverage against the sheriff and his posse, many of whom were known to be members of the Ku Klux Klan. He enthralled community people as no one else could. Yet we knew he would be moving in and out of town, even more so now that he was a Nobel laureate and had more demands on his time. Furthermore, his ministerial style of mobilizing for highly visible public protests of great intensity and short duration, although part of a direct-action tradition shared with SNCC, was not directly compatible with SNCC's concept of constant presence and slowly developing indigenous leadership. Touched by his arrest, one thousand people, a large number of children among them, demonstrated and were arrested. President Johnson announced that he intended to assure that the right to vote was "secured for all of our citizens." Before long, three thousand people were in jail in Dallas County and Dr. King had brought about a confrontation with Alabama that attracted national attention.

We debated in one contentious staff meeting after another whether SNCC should support a huge march with other than the staff and resources already in Selma. Our Alabama staff were against it but decided that because of their personal bonds with local Alabamans, they could not be absent. In Mississippi, with staff roles lacking clarity in the aftermath of the 1964 summer project and without the compass of Bob Moses pointing our direction since he had resigned from being state director out of concern that there was too much dependency on him, the question of whether to go to Selma was particularly problematic. I and many other SNCC workers were opposed to the organization's putting resources and personnel into a stagy protest in Selma. I thought that a march, although providing brief gratification and the exhilaration of a mass mobilization, was unrelated to our long-term objectives and would produce few serious political results in the hamlets of Alabama. I decided the march was regressive and, along with others in Mississippi, refused to participate.

When the executive committee met in Atlanta, it decided that the organization would remain neutral about the march but said that the staff were free to participate as individuals. It was later disclosed that Jim Forman had, on his own initiative, moved five thousand dollars of SNCC funds into Selma to support the march.

The SNCC staff who decided to join the march found to their astonishment that Dr. King was not present when nearly six hundred marchers started out on Sunday, March 7. He had gone back to his Atlanta church to preach. This left the throng to be led by Hosea Williams of SCLC and John Lewis and Robert Mants of SNCC. As the crowd surged toward the Edmund Pettus Bridge that arched over the Alabama River on the outskirts of Selma, Sheriff Jim Clark and Major John Cloud greeted them on horseback with deputies and state troopers three-deep across the four-lane highway, wearing gas masks and helmets, and carrying billy sticks. Through a bullhorn came the order to disperse within two minutes. When the marchers remained in place, police waded into the demonstration, smashing the front lines with billy clubs. John Lewis's skull was fractured. The state troopers regrouped and attacked the marchers again, firing canisters of tear gas. Amelia Boynton fell, unconscious from blows and tear gas. Sheriff Clark's mounted posse rode out from behind some buildings with a Dixie Rebel yell, whipping the demonstrators with rubber tubing wrapped in barbed wire and with bullwhips.

Beaten, bleeding, gasping, and choking, the marchers were led back to Brown Chapel.

Literally within minutes after the word of John's being bludgeoned reached us in Mississippi from the church, carloads of SNCC staff were bound for U.S. Highway 80 out of Jackson, on their way to Selma. A group in Atlanta chartered a plane rather than take the time to drive. The old SNCC spirit of direct action was touched, and there was an instantaneous resurgence of SNCC's crisis orientation. I would have gone had I sensed there would be a role for me. Wrestling with what in my mental shorthand I called "feel good versus effective," I finally decided not to jump into one of those cars.

Although Dr. King stayed home from what came to be known as Bloody Sunday, SCLC ran a full-page fund-raising advertisement in *The New York Times* the next day with a photograph of

John Lewis being hit on the head. As *our* chairman lay hospitalized with a brain concussion, having led the march when Dr. King
did not appear, *they* raised money for their coffers with a picture
of John going down. SNCC would soon be caught in a downward
spiral of disenchantment with SCLC more serious than any to
date. Once our staff in Selma had decided to march, they wanted
to proceed with it. If they stumbled or showed signs of uncertainty, they thought, it would confuse the local community that
had put its trust in them. In Selma, SNCC staked out a position
in opposition to Judge Frank M. Johnson's request in the U.S.
district court for postponement of the march as a prerequisite for
hearing SCLC's request for an injunction against state officials.
On Tuesday, March 9, Dr. King greeted the marchers and led
them in prayer, but he then asked the crowd to return to the
church and fight it out in the courts. The march was discontinued
despite the objection of SNCC staff who were by then enraged
because the community had already been aroused. The SNCC
staff got angry at this "turn around." Although John Lewis remained pledged to continue in support of SCLC's efforts, Jim
Forman and most of the other SNCC workers pulled back.

Three white ministers who had joined the march were attacked by four white men that night after eating at a black café.
They were clubbed, and one of them, the Reverend James Reeb,
a white Unitarian clergyman from Boston, died two days later.
Labor unions, religious groups—Protestant, Catholic, Greek Or-
thodox, Jewish—and national associations sent telegrams to the
White House in protest. Supporters by the thousands came from
across the country for Reeb's memorial service. President Johnson
and his wife both telephoned the widow and the President sent
Air Force One to transport her back to Boston. In response to the
Selma crisis, President Johnson gave a major address on Monday,
March 15, calling for new and stricter voting-rights legislation. He
referred only to the death of Reeb and ended the speech by saying, "And we *shall* overcome!"

I was watching television in Jackson. Perhaps it will seem
strange now, but, rather than feeling gratified by his invocation of
the title of the movement anthem, I was depressed. I was annoyed. The President may have been sincere, but it sickened me
that it had taken so much suffering to bring passion to the simple
issue of voting rights.

Jim Forman had gone on to Montgomery to organize black students at Tuskegee Institute and other colleges and was joined by Bill "Winky" Hall, Bill Ware, and Willie Ricks. On March 15, there was a violent confrontation with police, and the following night six hundred demonstrators were attacked by mounted police with billy sticks and electric cattle prods. Officials from the Johnson administration and staid moderate leaders of the black community tried to dissuade Jim and the students from further confrontations. A rally was called on March 16 at Beulah Baptist Church by SCLC officials, who were vying for command. In wrath at the police, in fury at the moderate leadership, seething at SNCC's loss of control in Selma to SCLC and therefore angry at Dr. King—Jim roared at the audience that was filled with ministers, nuns, and reporters, "If we can't sit at the table of democracy, then we'll kick the fucking legs off!"

When the famous march finally occurred, it had a celebratory mood, and many thought it was like a carnival in contrast to the turbulence of the preceding month. Judge Johnson had handed down the order allowing the march and ordering state officials not to interfere. Starting out on Sunday, March 21, three thousand individuals—many of them celebrities and religious leaders who had flown in from all over the country—walked to the state capital, heading for a rally on March 25 to be addressed by Dr. King. Some of them camped along the way; most drove back to Selma at night by car and bus, with volunteers providing transportation. At the end, their ranks would reach approximately twenty-five thousand as they triumphantly marched through Montgomery. The nation watched as Governor Wallace refused to step out of the capitol to receive their petition.

That night, after the throng abated, Viola Gregg Liuzzo, a white volunteer from Detroit who had driven a load of protesters back to Selma, was shot and killed in Lowndes County by Klansmen during a high-speed chase as she returned alone on the road to Montgomery.

The Selma march was clearly a national victory for King and SCLC. It produced a level of national accord on the need to address voting rights and a breach in the official resistance in Alabama (much as had the three deaths in Mississippi). The march produced sufficient nationwide pressure on the federal government and on a Congress that had already been subjected to year-long lobbying that passage of President Johnson's voting-rights bill was assured.

Perhaps I was shortsighted and lacked perspective in not appreciating the value of these accomplishments—even against my own standard of political effectiveness—for if you examined the score from a national perspective, it was a win.

Yet, paradoxically, if you looked at the Selma march from the point of view of the SNCC staff, it was a failure. We saw a besieged black community that was left in chaos, with its expectations raised, and its frustrations sharpened, but with no improved or additional instruments for permanent change. Our fundamental objection was that an intense, well-publicized turning out of a community for the purpose of national news exposure produced only short-term gains. This did not in any way obviate the difficult job of following through later. The community would be momentarily aroused, but then would be left confused and deflated; there would still be people in jail, cases would move slowly on appeal for years afterward, and morale would be reduced to a shambles. SNCC favored the patient, low-key creation of community organizations that could carry on a long-term struggle "for the duration." Internally, also, within SNCC, the march represented a setback by further enhancing the disorder in our process of making policy. Moreover, it would be a final knell for direct-action protest in the struggle.

A raw fact underlay the feelings of SNCC staff: The response to Jimmy Lee Jackson's death—about which the protest started—was muted, while the death of a white minister drew thousands and a presidential address. Even in so small a gesture as President Johnson's sending flowers to James Reeb's widow but none to Jimmy Lee's mother, the cold Tartuffery of the White House showed. We had seen it before—a similar thing had happened the year before when only a presidential assistant telephoned Jim Chaney's mother. But then SNCC workers had believed they would be able to expose such hypocrisy and gain tangible achievements. Now there seemed to be bizarre and discouraging redundancy. Little seemed to have changed.

Some, however, were exhilarated by the return to militancy and the confrontation of the march; and the Nashville school of thought had a temporary resurgence. Less than three weeks after the march, Marion Barry excitedly told SNCC's executive committee in Holly Springs, Mississippi, "I think our problem is that we no longer mobilize around direct action." Other SNCC workers began to admit that they were getting tired of being beaten with so little to show for it. Many thought the march's disruption of the organization of projects aimed at long-term political goals was not worthwhile. John Lewis's forbearance was visibly tried. He was good-humored, but I could see that even he wondered if the results justified the effort. Then, too, there was the question of how decisions had been made and about Jim Forman's unilateral allocation of five thousand dollars to the disputed march. We were also faced with the irony that so many who had spoken out against the march had subsequently joined it. Ivanhoe Donaldson had been one of the most vocal against SNCC's participation and ended up serving as a marshal in the demonstration.

The disenchantment within SNCC that had begun after the doors were slammed in the face of the Mississippi Freedom Democratic party delegation in Atlantic City the summer before deepened after Selma. Jim's comment about kicking off the legs of the table of democracy brought astonishment and protest from his listeners at the time. Yet it accurately expressed the frustration and consternation of the SNCC staff. Almost unnoticed at the time, the circumstances of the Selma march would also end up furthering the hierarchical thinking within SNCC of those who favored bureaucratic structures and central control. It was from this camp, too, that the expulsion of whites from SNCC would begin.

By the spring of 1965, although SNCC's Communications office had grown more sophisticated, taken on wider functions, and saved lives, there was less need for the function it had formerly performed. A wrap-up article on Mississippi by John Herbers on November 16, 1964, in *The New York Times*, reported "significant breaks in the state's organized resistance." He said that COFO had projects in thirty communities involving 250 workers of whom 160 were staff from SNCC. Herbers reported, "The council [COFO] is now trying to get Negroes elected to agricultural stabilization and conservation committees in several counties where Negroes outnumber whites. These committees administer federal crop programs and have been controlled by local whites." Commenting on the Waveland staff meeting then taking place, Herbers quoted me as the spokesperson, saying that emphasis in the future would be put on "organizing local Negroes around the needs that they feel, so that it's not our giving direction to the local people so much as their giving us direction." (When I came across the yellowed article by Herbers among my papers two decades later, I had totally forgotten something else he noted. He said that in Mississippi the national defeat of Barry Goldwater in November 1964 had "left many whites in a state of shock and confusion. They had been told that the cause for segregation had been gaining throughout the nation and that it would be only a matter of time before the Civil Rights Act would be repealed.")

Scrawled in tiny notes on both sides of an envelope addressed to me, postmarked December 22, 1964, from Tchula, Mississippi, were my notes on remarks by Amzie Moore. (I guess this was the only paper I could find.) His perspective on what had been accomplished was important because it was he who had framed the parameters of SNCC's organizing in Mississippi. His comments provide a unique summary of the situation in Mississippi by a man of stature whose words may otherwise go undocumented. His remarks also show a practicality that two years later would be dissipated by stresses on the movement:

> Before Bob Moses, we had what the army calls morale boosters—meetings and rallies—for years. In the 1950s, we were talking about "separate but equal" and restrooms. But with the 1954 Supreme Court decision, our outlook changed and we thought in terms of a complete revolution of the social structure in education, politics, and everything else. There was a series of killings in 1955—on May 5, Jack Smith in Brookhaven; on May 7, the Reverend George Lee; Gus Coats was shot in Belzoni because he attempted to vote. In 1955, the White Citizens Council took over the Mississippi power structure with a program to bring about an exodus of ten million black adults from the South over ten years. Bob Moses came in with SNCC and started to set up education programs for voter registration and literacy. He brought one thousand copies of the Constitution. He set up schools. Bob came to see me in Cleveland, recruiting for a conference in Atlanta in 1960. A church had been burned. I sent him to see C. C. Bryant in McComb. . . .
> You can't go in with guns and bombs and win the hearts and souls of the people. You can't do it with refrigerators either. . . . You can't buy your way in around the world.

> We've got numbers, that's all we've got, numbers.
> We've got poor, poverty-stricken illiterate sharecroppers but
> we've got numbers. The Freedom Democratic party is our
> only salvation even though we know we'll eventually be
> controlled by some power structure. The Mississippi Sum-
> mer Project was the best thing that's happened here since
> the 1940s. The FDP can save the soul of America.
> We'll need ten thousand volunteers here for four years
> for real political leverage. . . . It will take maybe fifteen or
> twenty years to build a balance of power between Demo-
> crats and Republicans in the Black Belt. . . . There's not
> much economic security for Delta Negroes. . . . We know
> that the federal government is not going to do more than
> you make it do.

Casey and I believed we could make a real contribution by developing materials for training of local organizers. The Challenge that Casey helped to organize in 1964 was over, and Communications no longer required the same involvement by me. We thought we could build on the creative work done by Maria Varela in her literacy project. The concept was simple—people could learn to read and write from materials that offered information useful for economic survival, and one could better learn to read from a pamphlet or filmstrip about organizing a county political party or an okra cooperative, or how to sign up for Social Security, than from meaningless pap. In this way, literacy efforts could be an organizing tool. Maria welcomed our involvement. Casey and I developed a series of proposals and supplements that we sent to Atlanta, detailing plans and timetables. We determined to learn photography and set up a darkroom at Tougaloo. We raised the money ourselves, so it would not come from SNCC's central funds or the Mississippi state budget, to produce printed materials and filmstrips after testing with local individuals. Black Star photographer Matt Herron agreed to teach us photography and, working with us eight or ten hours a day at his studio in New Orleans, gave us an intensive course. The local people helped us with the construction of the darkroom at Tougaloo, and within record time we were in production.

By identifying a need and moving to fill it, we were operating within a prime decision-making tradition in SNCC. The group's momentum had always depended on SNCC staff's being self-starters. Our credo was that those who do the work should have the greatest say in its execution. Within democratic SNCC, one person did not give directions and another carry them out; while there was a division of labor, there had always been mutuality and shared decision making. SNCC was built on what you might call an existential theory of organization—you are what you believe.

From the other "camp" now, there came an alien and different drumbeat. Bob Moses, Casey, I, and others were disparaged as "floaters" and "freedom highs," the implication being that we were high on personal freedom. Cleveland Sellers described us, admitting that it revealed his bias, in his book *The River of No Return:*

> The most flamboyant faction was composed of a group of "stars," who at various times were referred to as "philoso-phers, existentialists, anarchists, floaters and freedom-high niggers." Most of them were well educated. And they were almost evenly divided between whites and blacks. . . .
> They loved to bring meetings to a screeching halt with open-ended, theoretical questions. In the midst of a crucial strategy session on the problems of community leaders in rural areas, one of them might get the floor and begin to hold forth on the true meaning of the word *leader.*

Those who used the disparaging phrase "floater" favored the hierarchical concept of a pyramidal and authoritarian structure. They, including Cleve Sellers, called themselves "hard-liners."

The question before us since the first Waveland meeting was difficult: Should SNCC operate through locally autonomous decentralized movements linked by a network of organizers providing catalytic support and encouraging local leadership? Or should it institutionalize itself into a "disciplined," centrally administered structure?

Despite the intricacies and difficulties posed by this question—a major issue for movements in the late twentieth century—the debate was clouded by a new element. Until late 1965 it was possible to disagree in SNCC and yet not feel reviled, because the underlying bonds were strong. Personal hostility was now being expressed. This did not feel like SNCC to me. It was foreign—dissonant.

As Casey and I were fund raising in New York City in February 1965 for the materials-development project, a special-delivery letter arrived from one of our friends in Jackson. It described the other group, the "hard-liners":

> There is some very ugly business going on within the staff and I think you should know about it. . . . The rumor follows this form: "Look at the people at Waveland who supported loose structure; look what they've been doing since Waveland; don't you think it's strange that the very people who don't want structure are off doing whatever they like without anyone in a position to ask them for an account of their actions?"
>
> A second form stresses the Waveland "conspiracy" and sounds something like this: "All the people at Waveland who don't want structure are white, intellectuals, and not doing any specific job, they claim to speak for the people who don't talk-up; but do they? They claim to believe in democratic structures but don't the ideas they present really amount to anarchy and just pave the way for dictatorship or amassing power?" (Bob Moses is included in this version but explained away because he's in a power struggle with Jim Forman.)
>
> The third version, which I first heard last night, came via Cleve Sellers: "There was a conspiracy at Waveland between Casey, Mary, Francis Mitchell, Mendy Samstein, Dona Richards and possibly Emmy Schrader and some others which he wouldn't name. They filibustered during the first part of the staff meeting so that structure wouldn't come up till the end by which time most people would have left, and then they would pull a coup to gain power for personal reasons. This conspiracy began in Atlanta after the staff meeting there." There are apparently several people who overheard your plottings and they include Bill ("Winky") Hall, Bill Hansen, Stanley Wise, and Roy Shields.
>
> All of this seems very insane. However, people are talking this up quite a bit in the most malicious way. I hope you guys can react coolly to such stuff. . . . I find it hard to tell you this because it's so sick, but I'm trying to convey the spirit in which this is being done. How can we create a better society while people are so full of hate?

These hints of SNCC's coming dissolution began immediately after SNCC's period of greatest accomplishment, and, as life has since taught me again and again, the moment of triumph can also bring vulnerability. How SNCC, five years after the start of the sit-ins at the opening of the decade of the 1960s, would handle the internal and external stresses of 1965 would determine whether it would be around when two more years had passed and, if so, what kind of a group it would be.

Racked by the contentious political and philosophical issue of decentralized democratic organization as opposed to centralization and strong bureaucracy, SNCC was increasingly confronted by other issues. An example can be seen from just before the Selma march, in early March 1965, in a meeting at a Hattiesburg church, where we were wrestling with the question of whether or not to join the march. The staff was cantankerous. One diatribe led to another. A personal attack was made on Marian Wright, one of the first representatives elected to SNCC in 1960 when it was still but a coordinating committee and one of the first black women to receive a law degree from Yale University.

Casey and I were sitting next to each other listening as Marian was accused of disloyalty by some of the staff, who said she was afraid to endanger herself. Marian handled the situation crisply. She stood up, her usual clear determination marked by anger, and spoke through tightly clenched teeth grinding the words out with exasperation: "I'm fed up with being attacked because my way of working for the movement is through litigation. My tools are those of a lawyer. I can't get arrested because it would keep me from being admitted to the Mississippi bar. There are only four black lawyers practicing in Mississippi now as it is."

The meeting was rife with bitterness, marked with some of the first stirrings within SNCC of the rhetoric of black nationalism. The debate turned to the issue of white participation and discussion of incipient white control. My temples began to throb and my scalp to tighten. My head ached as I became aware that Casey was preparing to speak. She stood up, with her curious combination of fragility and strength, pulling herself together. The church sanctuary fell silent. She was struggling with what she wanted to say. My throat thickened in empathy with her. Putting both hands on the pew in front of her, she spoke each word slowly and tremulously: "I think that many blacks *hate* whites." She paused. "And I think that many whites *fear* blacks." Casey was not intimidated, as shown by her two simple but penetrating statements. In naming the closely interlinked emotions of hate and fear so accurately, she weakened for a moment their distorting effects.

Along with this increase in personal attacks that began to rend the fabric of the organization, serious programmatic questions were in need of resolution in 1965. One such issue was whether political organizing should encourage and create parallel structures like the Mississippi Freedom Democratic party, or whether SNCC should organize to take over and change political entities from inside. My notes for one small staff meeting in Mississippi at this time contain a series of "Questions to Myself" about the future of the Mississippi Freedom Democratic party:

> How will the MFDP be staffed, by SNCC or from its own resources? Should it enlarge and develop a national arm? How do we work where there is already a black political machine? Does the MFDP want to broaden its reach into "party out-of-power" areas? What programs further the goal of involving people in decision making so they learn they have power? How do we feel about being linked to the national Democratic party? What do we do where a black machine is part of the Democratic party?

The meeting also mirrored the staff's disillusionment after Atlantic City and its uncertainty about direction. A paralyzing question had arisen after the Challenge: Should COFO or SNCC organizers continue to register local people to vote, where they had little real *choice*, or should we direct that energy into the parallel structure of the MFDP, where they had little real *power*? As Margaret Burnham, a young black lawyer, phrased it: "Is it honest to tell people they can change things if they have a black party when they may not be able to?" In a typical SNCC rejoinder, Courtland Cox stated, "The people should decide what they want."

The executive committee meeting held for three days in April 1965 at Holly Springs, Mississippi, told a story of growing distrust, suspicion, uncertainty on program, and internecine strife. I have included a few lines on the meeting here because it sheds light on the internal stresses and tensions in the aftermath of the Mississippi Summer Project and Selma march. During this meeting, the personnel subcommittee of the executive committee considered the case of each member of the staff. Foremost in their minds was whether or not each person was "floating," and in retrospect it can be seen that the groundwork for later purges was being laid.

Stokely Carmichael's voice on the use of this pejorative term was decisive and reasonable. He defended an organizer's right to develop a workable program where the original purpose could not be fulfilled. "I personally know a lot of people who are 'floating' now, but have worked very hard in the past in Mississippi," Stokely said. "This is because there are no programs. . . . Why do we call people 'floaters' who want to work and have no jobs assigned to them?"

Jim Forman supported him, saying, "We have many staff who are oriented to breaking ground and mobilizing people. . . . Breaking ground used to be a program; now it is no longer needed in Georgia or Mississippi. We don't have the same problem as yet in Alabama because it is virgin territory."

Field secretary Ralph Featherstone, the thoughtful black elementary-school teacher who had taught in the Mississippi Freedom Schools and had later become their coordinator, asked, "How do you decide who's producing or who's not producing?"

"The staff in Mississippi is tired," Muriel Tillinghast said. "They just don't have the energy to start over knocking on doors." Muriel was a prudent, plain-speaking Howard student with commonsense gentility. Strangely, she was the only one to acknowledge the singeing stresses of the previous year and to admit that many people needed a change of pace; the one who had the most need of rest was Bob Moses. But this meeting revealed the group's inability to handle its collective exhaustion.

After Bob Moses had resigned from the position of COFO director, he and Dona Richards had gone to Birmingham. Not only was Bob concerned that his leadership was blocking others, but he and Dona needed distance from Mississippi and time to recover from the terror and traumas of the experience.

"How did Bob and Dona get to Birmingham?" John Lewis asked, strangely cold.

"Bob says he wants to see what it is like to organize in a city," Ruby Doris responded.

Marion Barry sparred, "If it was anybody else, we'd be raising hell."

Abruptly, it was suggested that the executive committee mandate the personnel subcommittee to "look into the situation of the floaters." Bill "Winky" Hall, a relative newcomer, said, "This should include all floaters," who ought to be contacted and asked "what they are doing and where they are working; they must be told that they have to do a specific job." He made a motion that "they must work within the discipline of the state project." His motion was seconded by Doug Smith. "People don't have the right arbitrarily to decide to work in an area," Bill said.

Stokely recoiled at this, saying that Bob and Dona were among those who had committed themselves to go to Alabama to work on independent political-party organizing, and, offended, he objected to the attitude expressed in the motion and the discussion. Jim mildly protested as well, saying the motion with regard to "floaters" was premature. Bill agreed to withdraw the motion if it was "understood that we will come up with a list of problem people for the personnel committee."

When it came to Casey, Marion Barry said offhandedly, "She should get in a project or resign," and John Lewis said, surprisingly detached and I guess lost in his own fatigue, "Some people want to do what they want and go where they want. They want to experiment with personal freedom."

Bob, Casey, I, and others were now considered "problem people" seeking "personal freedom." From a trusting and supportive community that backed the initiative and creativity of its self-selecting organizers, SNCC had reached the point where a latecomer could declare that Bob didn't have the "right" to be in Birmingham, and only Stokely and Jim would protest. I did not understand it yet, but this meeting was the first clear sign that, because of forces from within and without, our circle could not remain unbroken.

With only a sleeping bag, a little cash, and the name of a contact, Stokely Carmichael was dropped off in Lowndes County the day after Viola Liuzzo was shot and killed, at the place of her death. After the Selma march, SNCC decided to launch a new strategy for organizing county political parties in Alabama. Out of this would grow the Lowndes County Freedom Organization, soon to be known as the Black Panther party. Stokely Carmichael was in large part responsible for this decision. In contrast to the Selma debacle, I thought this had some real potential.

By 1965, it had been decided within SNCC to narrow its focus specifically on the Black Belt counties that girthed the South. Whether to organize separately or to try to move into established political institutions was still under debate.

Many SNCC staff had come to feel that the state-supported system of repression of black people was so venal and impervious to reform that it should not be opened up, mended, desegregated, or repaired, but that alternative institutions in different phases of a community's life should be developed. The idea of locally controlled entities to achieve distinguishable power began to replace notions of assimilation. This approach grew directly out of our experiences in Mississippi and Selma, but it also coincided with two of Ella Baker's convictions: her belief in self-determination and the right of people to make their own decisions without relying on those with authority, and her credo that the oppressed should define their own freedom. Echoes could be heard in the advocacy of nation building and defining oneself for oneself being made by Malcolm X, and there was, as always, the shadow of Du Bois in the background.

One key difference would exist between the Alabama undertaking and our Mississippi political organizing. In Mississippi, the Freedom Democratic party was a parallel structure that existed alongside the regular party and, while not part of the system, was designed to make the regular party realign itself. In Alabama, however, SNCC research director Jack Minnis had discovered that state law allowed for the formation of county political parties and, sixty days before an election, a county party could certify a nominee and place that person directly on the ballot of the regular elections. (Through SNCC's materials, Jack single-handedly popularized the term *power structure* that resounded throughout the decade of the 1960s and beyond, a phrase originally conceptualized by political scientist Floyd Hunter.)

Lowndes County was singled out as the logical place to build the new political party because its population was slightly over 80 percent black. It had a reputation for being extremely rough, and therefore it could be psychologically useful to start there in laying a foundation for parties elsewhere in the state. The symbol of the new party was chosen after deliberation. The emblem of the all-white regular Democratic party in the state was a white rooster. What might eat a white cock? The panther. The new party's in-

signia would be a springing black feline silhouette, and the party's
name, the Black Panthers. (Not two years would pass before two
young black Californians, Huey Newton and Bobby Seales, would
come to meet with Stokely to ask him if they, too, could form a
Black Panther party in California.)

The major problems for the new party, according to the Alabama staff, were: illiteracy, the newness of politics in the black
community, and the lack of self-confidence of blacks. The new
party's objectives? Control of the courthouse, combating terror for
the future, and building an instrument of power for the people.
It was not to be all black initially, something that would have
been a detraction with some local blacks; however, no white people from Lowndes County wanted to join it. At one staff meeting
in the autumn of 1965, Jack Minnis observed that by having control of the power in the courthouse, it would be possible to challenge tax assessments and hold fair instead of rigged elections,
because, he said, "we still think democracy is possible."

"We've got to center our attention on one problem—Negroes
feel they're not worth shit," Courtland Cox stated at a staff session. "We have to help them overcome their fear. We have to
leave something behind and the political arena is the easiest for
organizing. This is not a radical idea. . . . Parallel structures are,
in the long run, tragic. We need a way to get real power. Our
strategy should be to go for the courthouses."

Marion Barry agreed, saying, "People feel powerless but
they're not antigovernment. We need to begin a sense of power,
starting with black officers, developing a sense of growth and dignity. It's hopeless and futile to discuss blowing up courthouses;
we're not revolutionary or radical. Let's talk about what we can
concretely do. What if we take over? What's our alternative economic program to go along with our political program? Cooperatives?" He continued, "We lost the Atlantic City Challenge because
we had no power, not because the political process didn't work."

Frustrations in purpose, program, future, and structure were
expressed in that meeting. You could hear the difficulties reson-
ating when Muriel Tillinghast said:

> What's important are people, not SNCC. . . . People learn
> freedom on different levels. . . . There are Unita Black-
> wells everywhere. . . . The frustration is that as a group,

we are not revolutionary. We continue to stumble through
processes. . . . We have to work with poor people including
whites and Mexicans. We need a sense of proportion, a
sense of internationalism, and perhaps we should consider
harvest strikes. I keep losing this group with too many programs building too rapidly.

Jim Forman responded, "I want to discuss harvest strikes and
what organizational forms we can use so that when I leave, the
people can continue in power. I see 'the courthouse' as an organizing technique to build Black Belt political parties and also to
deal with other problems such as welfare and cooperatives. It's
not just power in 1966 that we need, but responsible broad organization. It may take seven years to build a self-help welfare fund."

In addition, the same meeting showed the breadth of concerns battering the organization: activities in Arkansas, administrative controls in Atlanta, and personnel policies. Ivanhoe
Donaldson introduced an urban-organizing concept for consideration in which, he said, three hundred thousand dollars a year would
pay one hundred local organizers three thousand dollars a year, or
enough jobs for a whole neighborhood of organizers in Chicago.
SNCC was never to realize that notion.

Feelings of desperation surfaced that had not been there in
the past. Assertions were made that people in the room were carrying guns. There was discussion of staff stipends being cut off
and hostile letters being sent out from headquarters. "Fear," said
one participant; "I feel fear because people feel powerless. We
can't deal with SNCC as a corporate empire. SNCC is becoming
just like an oppressor in some of our minds. We then cover it up
with being hostile."

I had been going to SNCC staff meetings for almost four
years, half the time struggling to stay abreast of what was happening. In 1965, I told Casey cynically that they were beginning to
remind me of the Marquis de Sade's account of an eighteenth-
century French insane asylum. John Perdew, a white staff stalwart
in southwest Georgia for several years, declared, "I've given up
hope that the problems we're talking about can be solved. We
keep losing. We have no money. I strike out at the nearest target.
When I hear a rumor about someone I don't like, I eat it up. We
are succumbing to our frustrations."

Lawrence Guyot, who walked a narrower line between SNCC and the MFDP than anyone else, and who always spoke elliptically and in paradoxes, said, "SNCC has cut the Freedom Democratic party off and SNCC people are attacking the FDP." Others thought that Guyot was attacking SNCC. Legitimate administrative concerns underlay this. If the party was an independent party, then shouldn't it do its own fund raising, have its own cars, and pay its own staff? On the other hand, it was still new and tied to SNCC. There was a need to work out an arrangement for solving this dilemma, but the meeting spun around on its axis. Guyot roared, provocative as always, "SNCC should be destroyed. This is what happens when people bring about change that they then can't keep up with."

Like so many SNCC people, I never again after the end of 1964 found my fit as satisfying as it was when I was working in Communications with Julian Bond in Atlanta and later when I was in charge of Communications at Jackson. It was a period of gloomy ambiguity; everyone felt confusion. I reached the point that when I saw someone adamantly taking a stance of certainty, I thought it signified doubt.

Jane Stembridge and I collaborated on a filmstrip about the impact of the war in Vietnam on Mississippi blacks and the fact that those who made the decisions about the war were not doing the fighting. I had observed at dusty crossroads and at Mississippi train platforms the aluminum coffins bearing bodies arriving from southeast Asia. I noticed that, at least where I was, they were overwhelmingly met by black families. We also made a filmstrip called "The Peoples Wants Freedom," in the vernacular of sharecroppers, about economic and political issues. I helped Frank Smith organize a special workshop for Mississippi black leaders in Washington, D.C., and arranged for them to meet officials of the Congress, the Department of Agriculture, and other federal agencies.

Increasingly concerned about poverty and the war in Vietnam, both of which, although not strictly racial in content, were racial in impact, I began planning a series of workshops to help volunteers who had been involved in the movement to remain active on civil rights and related issues when they returned home. The circular said the workshops were "to discuss ways of using new skills, experiences, and lessons learned from community organizing in other parts of the country and in other phases of the movement." They were to include discussion of how Mississippi "relates to broader issues of human freedom such as free elections in the South and Vietnam, poverty, and organized terrorism."

The first workshop was to be held at Mount Beulah Center at Edwards, twenty-five miles west of Jackson, Mississippi, from July 30 through August 1, 1965, for those leaving for the West Coast. Others were to follow for volunteers departing for other parts of the country. Volunteers were to be enlisted in Mississippi by Dennis Sweeney, Bill Light, and me, along with Dick Jewett of CORE; in Arkansas by Ed Hamlett; and in Louisiana by Mike Lester and Rudy Lombard of CORE. These workshops were to dovetail with similar efforts under way in Washington, D.C., involving Bob Moses and Dona Richards, who had now moved there, Staughton Lynd, Eric Weinberger, Walter Tillow, Courtland Cox, and Francis Mitchell, planned collaboratively with Students for a Democratic Society and several of its offshoots plus a number of peace groups.

Underlying these new activities in the nation's capital and the southern states was a fresh concern that the civil rights movement should broaden itself to encompass other causes. SNCC had rarely addressed collateral issues and, indeed, this was one of its strengths; unlike other movements and many leftists of the Depression era, SNCC was resistant to embracing the questions of totalitarianism, imperialism, and peace. By and large, it stuck to racial equality. But Ella Baker in April 1960 had called upon the sit-in movement to focus on "more than a hamburger and a Coke," and, increasingly, SNCC's experiences over the years were demanding that it recognize the tentacles that reached from racial injustice into other areas.

A letter that I sent a friend on August 19, 1965, shows how SNCC's internal debate about its structure was spilling over into other concerns:

> It seems difficult for organizers to get discussion going
> around deeper human issues that so often determine the di-
> rection, structure, and amount of community participation in
> the little community groups that we start. Specifically, we
> have been trying to open discussion on human questions

that are rarely discussed but affect people most . . . such as
authority, authority figures, bravery, fear, feeling unquali-
fied, women and men. . . . Another personal factor . . . is
my increasing anguish over Vietnam. I have felt that I had
to direct more of my attention to what could be done on
Vietnam.

I was not alone in saying that we should include poverty and
the war in Vietnam on our agenda, but this position was controversial and not popular. Bob Moses took a leave of absence from
SNCC to step out of the way of criticism from those who challenged opposition to the war as diversionary. In planning workshops to keep the volunteers active not only on civil rights but on
other issues, I was moving outside the framework now gaining
sway within SNCC.

I took my position against the war a year before SNCC would
declare in a news release that the civil rights movement was a
"valid alternative to the draft." SNCC had been reluctant to declare itself against the conflagration in southeast Asia because hard-
liners within the organization said that would represent a diffusion
of efforts. Not until January 5, 1966—two days after the killing of
Sammy Younge, a twenty-one-year-old voter-registration worker
who was attempting to use a white rest room in Tuskegee, Alabama—would SNCC speak. Then it charged in a news release:

> The United States government [has] been deceptive in its
> claims of concern for the freedom of the Vietnamese people,
> just as the government had been deceptive in claiming con-
> cern for the freedom of colored people in such countries as
> the Dominican Republic, the Congo, South Africa, Rhode-
> sia, and in the United States itself.

Following Sammy's death, which followed the deaths of the
summer of 1964 and that of Jimmy Lee Jackson in 1965, the
implications of a war against a Third World country in a battle for
self-determination were now too compelling for SNCC to remain
silent. That statement, in turn, was issued more than a year before Martin Luther King, although long troubled by the war, would,
in April 1967, formally take a public stand in opposition to the
conflict in southeast Asia.

For me in 1965, however, discouragement and a murky sense

of dislocation were deepening as I realized how many of the SNCC staff were against the organization's speaking out in opposition to the war. I was beginning to feel estranged from the group that was so close to me that I felt it was part of me, like my lungs. Instead of creatively building on past successes to move forward, SNCC seemed now to be consumed with staving off disabling internal dissension.

In notes to myself I wrote:

> I look around in the mass meeting and see more and more clearly there is no place for me, no real place for others like me. I struggle much of the time between retreating and its opposite, to rush ahead. . . . I am almost numb. There is so much emotional entanglement, so little sense and so little stamina that it's either be numb and cope, or do not cope. . . . Who can predict what will come of taking what personal happiness there is in the movement? It happens so rarely.

By the end of that year, although I maintained many personal relationships, I was lost to SNCC and, after I left, for a period of three whole years I was almost lost to myself.

Race, always important in America, was crucially so in SNCC, and, in the next few pages, I will give an account, as I saw it at the time, of the impact of race inside SNCC, within our ranks.

By 1965, an argument was being made that white staff members should leave SNCC and organize in the white communities of the South. This idea had surfaced earlier but had been rejected because large numbers of white volunteers brought with them accompanying news media and, therefore, protection and survival.

One brief story will show the roots of the issue of white participation as I remember its first surfacing and how it had been dealt with at an earlier period. It begins with a meeting that had occurred two years earlier, in November 1963. For three days the SNCC staff in Greenville, Mississippi, had discussed the massive summer project that was planned for the following summer. Consideration of restricting the role of whites had been precipitated by reports that the Stanford and Yale students taking part in the protest Freedom Ballot that November had rushed into the limelight seeking publicity. In the meeting, Bob Moses stated his po-

sition: It was important to involve whites, who could "break down
the depersonalization of people"; if you had whites working
alongside you, then it was "a question of rational people against
irrational people." Someone made the argument that there must
be *something* in America where Negroes themselves could lead, to
wit, SNCC. Bob responded quietly, "I always thought that the
one thing we can do for the country that no one else can do is to
be above the race issue."

After the martyrdom of our three co-workers in 1964, with
brute violence checked, there was no longer need for the protection afforded by white volunteers and the attendant news corps.
But what about other concerns? What about Sherrod, still in
southwest Georgia, believing tactics always should reflect goals
and that blacks needed to be reminded that not all white people
in America were cruel.

Allusions were made that white staff or volunteers had "taken
over" various programs in the Mississippi Summer Project. This
was, in fact, an unfounded assertion, although it might have felt
this way to the local staff who suddenly saw themselves displaced
by the attention paid to whites.

What was probably happening was a rite of passage. Not one
black could be truly free without reckoning with what the shackles of racism had done to one's soul and with the resulting way
one felt and thought about oneself. No one in America, white or
black, escaped being deformed in some way by racism. Perhaps
the only way to come to grips with the profound psychologica
effects of second-class citizenship was for blacks to redefine their
self-image. That is what blacks in SNCC started doing.

The thrust for racial consciousness represented the frustration of the northern black staff more than it articulated a need of
black southerners. Blacks growing up in the South where it was
assumed that the pains and troubles of "colored people" didn't
hurt as much because they were of a lower order of life were
primordially aware of their blackness. There was no ambiguity
about their place, no uncertainty about their lack of status, no
doubt that they were not considered fully human, no question
that they were believed to be genetically inferior.

Northern blacks who entered the organization in greater
numbers after the summer of 1964, however, had grown up in a
situation marked by dusky ambiguity. In the North, there were

illusory hints of freedom and equal rights. Blacks could make eye contact with whites, shake hands with whomever they met, and ride where they pleased in public transportation. They could vote. It was in the circumscribed areas of jobs and housing that the all-too-real obstacles lay. There were indeed severe strictures—residential segregation that affected education, tokenism in admission to universities and in jobs, covert racism, and earning power tied directly to race—but there was a certain amount of subtlety in confirming race as the causal factor of lowered opportunity. Integration and a prejudice-free environment were goals that seemed distantly within reach.

The northern blacks who came to work for SNCC after 1964 had few shared bonds with whites in the organization, some of whom—like Bob Zellner and Bill Hansen—had sustained as many physical and psychological wounds from the struggle as anyone. They had not been steeped in the Nashville tradition of nonviolence, with its vision of an integrated society to be accomplished through radical redemptive nonviolence. When they came south to work for SNCC, they learned with wrenching finality exactly how barbarous and animalistic a system the United States of America had been tolerating in the Deep South.

The new emphasis on "blackness" may have also been accentuated by the accumulation of power and resources in the Atlanta headquarters and the state offices of SNCC after 1964. It was in these offices that fund raising, liaison with northern support groups, conversations with national figures, and other communications were handled. These offices, with their control of resources, had more white staff than the project and field offices. Casey, Betty Garman, Hunter Morey, Dottie Zellner, Dinky Romilly, Nancy Stearns, Mark Suckle, Jerry DeMuth, I, and other whites in offices had elected to work in positions that were necessary and used our skills; yet, paradoxically, this resulted in a concentration of white influence where the money went in and out.

I believe that, ironically, things would have worked out differently in SNCC if, after the first Waveland retreat, the school of thought that favored a decentralized SNCC had prevailed. Autonomous and freestanding local movements and projects could have controlled their own priorities, their own funds, and they could have resolved personnel questions, including racial ones, and determined policies themselves.

The contention that whites should organize in white communities had little to do with practical necessities. Politically, it was invalid because in the white community in the South there was no base for resistance, no incipient rebellion, no inchoate uprising, no potential for insurgency. To organize for change, there must be a perceived need in a community. Brave and iconoclastic exceptions didn't make the rule. Most white southerners didn't want change, especially in more impoverished areas where poor whites, themselves victimized by segregation's by-products of poor education, inadequate health care, and political manipulation, didn't even know that their standard of living had suffered as a result of racial segregation and that they had been prey to racial demagoguery.

Casey was one of the first white SNCC staff to take seriously the assertion that whites should work with whites. She went to Cleveland, Ohio, in May 1965, on loan to Students for a Democratic Society—an idea planned with Jim Forman—to work on transferring the organizing skills developed by SNCC to the SDS staff in northern industrialized states. She worked with Paul Potter, Sharon Jeffries, Ken McEldowney, and Charlotte and Ollie Fine. Discouraged with the results, however, she moved to Chicago and joined with Rennie Davis, Harriet Stallman, Leni Wildflower, Todd Gitlin, and Nancy Hollander of SDS. There, she managed to organize a welfare-recipients union composed mostly of southern white women who had emigrated to Chicago. By autumn, dismayed by the prospects, Casey returned south, convinced that the women's issue had first to be raised within our own organizing community in SNCC. Having followed the admonition to organize whites, it was ironic that Casey should be one of the first to be criticized as a "floater."

In 1966, a newly formed Atlanta Project, directed by Bill Ware, outrightly abandoned SNCC's strong ethic that ideas emerge from action, and began to promote a doctrine of racial separatism. Bill was a black Mississippian who had been educated in Minnesota and served for one year in the Peace Corps in Ghana in 1962. He had been exposed to the black scholar St. Clair Drake during Peace Corps training and adopted a Pan-Africanist philosophy calling for unification of blacks worldwide. Historian Clayborne Carson has noted that approximately half of the staff of the Atlanta Project were from the North and observed that "Atlanta separatists unhesitatingly rejected many of SNCC's prevailing values." Perhaps in one way they did manifest a root SNCC premise—they thought that unabashed commitment to their ideals would bring about significant change.

The Atlanta Project, based in a ghetto called Vine City, a few blocks beyond Alex's Barbecue, rejected several applications from white staff who wanted to be assigned to work in it because of the project's implications for urban organizing, a new area for SNCC. Mendy Samstein was one of those turned down. The group came into outright conflict with the headquarters staff over a three-thousand-dollar contribution that was meant to build black support for Julian Bond's campaign but which they had witheld from SNCC accounting. Asked formally to explain, they bluffed, and, using a procedural hedge, presented instead a position paper to a March 1966 staff meeting. It was a pastiche by different writers, including Bill Ware, Donald Stone, and Roland Snellings, in which they argued that "the form of white participation, as practiced in the past, is now obsolete." White people, the paper asserted, were inherently incapable of comprehending the black experience. For SNCC to become the type of organization they desired, it would have to rid itself of white staff members and become "black-staffed, black-controlled and black-financed." Although there were fewer than two dozen whites left in the organization by the spring of 1966, the elimination of those remaining was viewed as a crucial step toward racial identity. The paper called for a general move toward black separatism, saying, "If we are to proceed toward true liberation, we must cut ourselves off from white people. We must form our own institutions, credit unions, co-ops, political parties, write our own histories."

These concepts and the document itself were to be picked up and flashed back and forth across the United States throughout the late 1960s in the speeches of black militants, and many of the paper's ideas were adopted even by those within SNCC who did not agree with the purging of white staff. By forcing the issue, however, and by using it to block the discussion of all other problems, the Atlanta separatists deeply undermined the trust and communality that bonded SNCC together and produced a torque that would irrevocably change its course.

In May 1966, at Kingston Springs near Nashville, in a repudiation of the Nashville ethos, John Lewis was defeated as chairman of SNCC and was replaced by Stokely Carmichael, who was then twenty-four years old. Jim Forman had already indicated he wanted to resign, and twenty-three-year-old Ruby Doris Smith Robinson was chosen as executive secretary. Cleveland Sellers, the newest and youngest of the new leadership trio—only twenty-one years of age—having joined SNCC in 1964, was reinstated as program director. They represented a heightened militancy.

Despite the many misconceptions that would form about him, Stokely opposed the Atlanta separatists and later told Clay Carson that he viewed them as opportunists trying to be "blacker than thou" to gain control of SNCC. Like other veteran black staff, Stokely rejected the expulsion of white staff, but he already believed in developing institutions to meet the needs of the black community. This was evident from his successes in Alabama with the Lowndes County Freedom Organization or the Black Panther party, and he was drawn to many of the ideas put forth by the Atlanta Project staff. Ironically, because Stokely was smart, articulate, capable of dramatic eloquence, and a natural performer, it was he who would go on to popularize nationally many of the concepts of the Atlanta group.

At the same meeting in Tennessee, the first resolution was passed to the effect that white SNCC organizers should work in southern white communities. In his book *The Making of Black Revolutionaries*, Jim Forman writes disingenuously as if there were no struggle for power or control of SNCC under way:

> Following the Mississippi Summer Project of 1964, some of
> the leadership of SNCC became even more insistent that
> the conditions were ripe to begin organizing in white south-
> ern communities. The resistance, however, was so great that
> some of us felt we should pass a rule that SNCC white orga-
> nizers should work in white communities. . . . At our
> Kingston Springs, Tennessee, meeting in 1966 the SNCC
> did pass such a resolution. As the maker of that resolution,
> it was not my intent that white or black organizers should
> work in complete isolation or without any consultation with
> each other.

What was really happening? Jim was a competent analyst but his normal political acuity is not evident here. He asserts that the advice to white staff to work full-time in southern white areas was "usually rejected on the grounds that it was easier for white peo-

ple to work in black communities than white communities." It
was self-evident that it was more dangerous to work in white communities, yet Jim knew that the question of ease or difficulty of
organizing was not the issue for the whites who elected to join
SNCC staff. There was an element of truth to what he said, but,
shrewd tactician that he was, Jim was also aware that there was
little potential for defiance, resistance, or mobilization in southern
white communities. Jim was opposed to the new group of black
nationalists. Yet he had to address the concerns of the opposition,
and so he said that whites found it easier to organize in black
communities, with his accommodation to their position based on
an extraneous reason. He was bowing to extreme internal political
pressures.

If one operated from a class analysis and saw the issue as the
poor versus the rich, one might believe in an initiative to organize
in the white community. The dream of poor whites and blacks
joining together in the fight against oppression had rarely been
mentioned in SNCC. We had traditionally operated on a single-
issue basis. The Southern Conference Education Fund (SCEF),
through which Bob Zellner and Sam Shirah entered SNCC, and
the Southern Student Organizing Committee (SSOC), which enlisted the talents of Sue Thrasher, had always held to such a hope,
but this concept was never SNCC's. Even with regard to the war
in Vietnam, when SNCC finally took a position, it was based on
the racial implications of a superpower's suppressing an indigenous internal struggle among nonwhite people in the Third World.
The argument that whites should organize in white communities
served the political-power objectives of the Atlanta group whose
paper historian Clayborne Carson called "the initial volley in a
struggle among blacks over the control of SNCC and the future
direction of black struggles."

It would be an error to doubt that blacks were always in
control in SNCC, and not one white whom I knew thought it
should be any different or sought leadership. Never at any time
was SNCC more than 20 percent white. Yet it was not numbers
that were under discussion here. It was, rather, the perception of
some blacks who were convinced they had to free themselves of
any dependence on whites, perhaps feeling in the process less
angry about their fundamental condition. The Atlanta Project paper even hints that they felt that by following this course they

would prove they could run things. The analogy is wildly inexact, but Mohandas Gandhi once remarked that it would be better to let the Indians run things and make a mess of India than to continue under British rule. "For many SNCC workers," Clay Carson observed, "racial separatism met psychological needs that were not as easily satisfied through patient efforts to mobilize black communities to achieve concrete goals."

After the passage of the resolution that whites should work in white communities, and in the tumult of related internal struggles, personal bonds in SNCC were to be severed with wanton disregard and emotional brutality. Bob Moses announced that he was breaking all relationships with whites. Along with black separatism came the discarding by SNCC of more than its few remaining white brothers and sisters. It lost the redemptive vision of human worth, the image of a future free from barriers of race, the passion for democracy, any quest for reconciliation, and its rare radical creativity.

Believing that nothing is more precious than personal relationships, I was appalled as abstractions were put ahead of relationships hewn under obdurate conditions.

Was black separatism to be the cause of SNCC's deterioration, or, rather, was the group's degeneration mirrored by the emergence of this problem? The question of white participation was a protean issue. It exemplified one critical weakness in SNCC's decision making after 1965—its inability to determine whether policy should be made on the basis of political principles and achievable objectives, on the one hand, or on the ground of emotional need, on the other. The issue of white participation was unstable, continually changing because it brought out other conflicts and differences. It was not subject to logic or reason. Once resolved, this question would, fugitivelike, move to another place to hide, later to reemerge, stimulated by some other disunity. Sometimes masquerading, clownishly obscuring more urgent contemplations, this problem could obliterate—in its power to preoccupy and obsess—the purposes that had brought SNCC into being.

The black separatists construed the minimal continuing white participation in SNCC as indicating an inability to break with its past; at the same time, they made the claim that early SNCC had been too anarchistic and that only harsh discipline coupled with the ideology of black unity could correct this. By late 1965, the

question of white involvement had lodged as an irreconcilable source
of internal conflict for SNCC.

Intellectually, I could comprehend the aesthetic affirmation
of the value of black identity and culture that was at the heart of
racial separatism. Yet I also knew that part of its energy came
from the difficulties the organization was having in resolving in-
ordinately complex issues such as centralized organization as opposed to a decentralized structure. As a result, the debate became
an ordinary power struggle, so that people stopped listening to
what others were saying.

Black separatism represented a short-term strategy. It showed
a tragic inability to sustain a coherent political philosophy. It was
a triumph of personal need over political purpose. On the scale of
priorities, organizing for significant political gains was placed, by
1966, below ruminating on black consciousness. The softness of
militant rhetorical expostulation replaced the hard tasks of organizing.

In the beginning of January 1966, Charlie Cobb sent me a
letter that showed how SNCC's original ideal, of providing catalytic backup through a network of organizers mobilizing around
local needs and building new political institutions, had withered
while the Atlanta Project's rhetorical advocacy of black unification
based on separatist themes was winning. Although Charlie had
initially been supportive of decentralization, the concept had taken
hold that only by tightening internal controls could SNCC solve
its problems. The letter reflects the influence of the Atlanta group:

> About SNCC: Well, I guess the major thing is we are tight-
> ening up (or becoming more coherent) both structurally and
> programmatically. . . . A major problem is that rhetoric
> leaps so far ahead of program (and communities).
>
> I think that we've pretty much concluded (and I know
> that I have) that we cannot save the country, and even that
> it's contradictory to talk about salvaging the country or aim-
> ing that way, and at the same time say that our responsibil-
> ity is to the black community. We no longer assume
> America ignorant of what it is, or what it is based upon, but
> that it is very conscious of, and dependent on its white
> power—which of course is our worldwide oppression.
> Therefore, America must be treated as an enemy—an en-
> emy to humanity in fact, and cut loose from. SNCC experi-

ences, from Amite County, Mississippi, in 1961, to the
Vietnam war in 1967, teach a hard lesson. . . .
  People are holding on anyway, but the country is so
powerful (and out to get us).

A friend who attended the February 1966 funeral of Malcolm
X in New York City said that one third of SNCC was there.
Whether or not that count was apocryphal, Malcolm's interest in
nation building was compelling to many SNCC staff who were
trying to do something similar in the Black Belt. Malcolm had
broken his ties with the American Black Muslims headed by Elijah Mohammed, and having made a pilgrimage to Mecca he had
converted to traditional Islam. He had abandoned the Black Mus-
lim position on the "blue-eyed white devil." The more Malcolm
staked out a position of independence, and began to sever his ties
with the New York mosque of the Nation of Islam, the more
appealing became his political beliefs—not his religious convictions—to SNCC staff. For those who had not been in early SNCC
and missed its original concept of achieving an integrated society
and who had never heard Charles Sherrod expound on how the
means should at all times reflect the ends, some of the thinking
of Malcolm X urging the raising of racial consciousness rather than
its eradication must have been irresistible.
  Malcolm's sense of internationalism also excited SNCC, as
well as the attention that he called to links with the developing
countries of the Third World. In this, he was echoing Du Bois's
Pan-Africanism. From the beginning, SNCC had sought to foster
networks. Starting with the sit-ins and Ella Baker's strong encouragement, SNCC tried to link groups, local movements, and organizers who were working in isolation. SNCC had come into being
as a "coordinating" committee; its many stormy staff conferences
reflected this concept. Once SNCC staff became used to thinking
about linkages between their individual work and that of others,
it required only a small change in orientation to think of networks
internationally as well as domestically. Malcolm's personal charisma and the international connections that he made fascinated
SNCC workers against the preexisting backdrop of interest in anticolonial movements and the influence of Frantz Fanon's perspective on Algeria.
  A few months later, on June 5, 1966, James Meredith was

wounded by three shotgun blasts and hospitalized in Memphis after he undertook a walk across Mississippi to show that blacks could exercise their rights. Stokely and Cleve Sellers drove in from Arkansas, along with Stanley Wise, even though they thought Meredith's idea was impractical. Stanley was a swarthy and stocky North Carolinian built like a fireplug who had attended Howard University and been active on the Eastern Shore of Maryland in 1964 through Howard's Nonviolent Action Group.

Two days later a group assembled at Centenary Methodist Church in Memphis whose pastor was the Reverend Dr. James M. Lawson, Jr., the author of SNCC's original statement of purpose. In addition to the three SNCC workers, there were in attendance CORE's new national director Floyd McKissick, Dr. King, Roy Wilkins, and Whitney Young, Jr. Although grave ambivalence marked SNCC's reaction to another march because the march on Washington and the Selma march were both remembered as fiascos, Stokely argued that, if they were to continue the march, it should deemphasize the involvement of white dignitaries and celebrities, push the theme of freestanding black political entities, and should allow the Louisiana-based Deacons for Defense who carried arms to join. Roy Wilkins and Whitney Young, Jr., opposed Stokely's concept, but Dr. King held the deciding vote, which he declined to use against Stokely. The march went forward with Stokely, Dr. King, and Floyd McKissick in a feeble alliance, differences barely concealed from public view.

When the march reached Greenwood, Stokely was arrested and held in jail for six hours. That night, as the last speaker at the mass meeting, he moved out in rhetorical combat with Dr. King's more moderate approach, declaring that he had been arrested that day for the twenty-seventh time. Then he shouted, "What we are gonna start saying now is Black Power." Willie Ricks, a gnomic and unpredictable SNCC field secretary of great energy and drive, powerful instincts, and charisma, who had come into the movement as a high school student in Chattanooga, had given Stokely this tool to use in his speech. It was a shortening of "black power for black people," a phrase that SNCC staff had used in organizing in Alabama. Rousing the crowd still further, Willie jumped up on the podium, yelling, "What do you want?" With each repetition, the audience roared back, "Black Power!" louder each time.

The term scared whites across the nation, but the fact that it conjured up a frightening specter only added to its allure within SNCC. CORE, with its northern base close to the growing strength of urban black militancy, was the only civil rights group formally to support SNCC in its appeal for Black Power. In 1967, however, in Dr. King's last published work, *Where Do We Go from Here: Chaos or Community?*, he wrote movingly regarding the necessity for black pride. Years later, Andrew Young would tell me, "Martin understood Black Power but he disagreed with it"—a position not dissimilar from mine.

The use of the Black Power slogan also brought such notoriety that it rendered SNCC's behind-the-scenes organizing impossible. SNCC had had national attention before, but now its creative tension and controversial tactics were no longer aimed at community change. Many staff people instead became preoccupied with the question, What is the proper black consciousness? Sheer militancy moved in to fill the vacuum left by the absence of ideas for building significant programs. This obsession further smothered resolution in areas of program confusion.

Black Power was not new and it had been proposed before. This poetic phrase had been used by writers and politicians for almost twenty years before Stokely made it a national refrain for blacks (and choke word for many whites). It evocatively combined two familiar themes that had long been present in the black community, a positive emphasis on pride in being black and the hope for real and significant political power. Primed by Willie Ricks, Stokely caught the saying at the right instant and with his brilliant rhetorical style, he popularized it overnight, soon making the term *Negro* obsolete. Stokely said that black people would define Black Power for themselves. Yet it was soon clear that it meant something different to every ear. It also was becoming evident that SNCC, in this ever more complex milieu, did not have the capability to build programs that could accomplish major concrete political goals.

From 1961 until 1966, all but a fraction of SNCC workers were assigned to projects in Alabama, Arkansas, southwest Georgia, and Mississippi. By October 1966, as Clayborne Carson documented in his history *In Struggle: SNCC and the Black Awakening of the 1960s*, two thirds of the SNCC staff were near SNCC's Atlanta headquarters or in cities outside the South.

Few of the officers and project directors of 1964 remained by the autumn of 1966. John Lewis resigned in June of that year, reminding a press conference of his more than forty arrests, and saying that he could not give up his "personal commitment to nonviolence." Julian Bond resigned later that summer to put his full energies into his campaign for the Georgia State Assembly. Field operations were badly deteriorating as SNCC's most experienced field secretaries departed, one by one. Charles Sherrod, SNCC's first field secretary, resigned when his submitted plan, which included the bringing of white students to work in southwest Georgia, was turned down. He set up another organization and remained there. Bill Hansen left Arkansas. Even in Alabama, where the Black Power strategy originated, only one SNCC staff member, Hubert "Rap" Brown, the younger brother of a field secretary from the Howard group named Ed Brown, remained by the autumn of 1966.

Clay Carson observed of this period:

> Instead of immersing themselves in protest activity and deriving their insights from an ongoing mass struggle, SNCC workers in 1966 stressed the need to inculcate among urban blacks a new racial consciousness as a foundation for future struggles. Those who joined SNCC's staff during 1966 generally were urban blacks attracted more by SNCC's militant image than by its rural southern projects . . . few wanted to engage in the difficult work of gaining the trust and support of southern black people who were older than themselves and less aware of the new currents of black nationalist thought.

In December 1967, after days of debate at a New York staff meeting, SNCC decided to expel the handful of remaining white staff by a vote of nineteen in favor, eighteen opposed, with twenty-four abstentions. Cleve Sellers wrote in *The River of No Return*:

> We were surrounded by contradictions. While establishment leaders denounced our spiraling influence, we were doing everything possible to keep the organization from collapsing. . . . Our support of Black Power and criticism of the Vietnam War virtually eliminated all our funding sources. By December, 1967, SNCC had fewer than ten offices in full

operation. And one of our most difficult tasks was keeping the seventy-five to eighty people still on staff fed, housed, and clothed.

The Atlanta separatists had been expelled by Stokely in February 1967, although the emotional weight of their arguments had by then infused the organization. In the spring of 1967, little-known H. Rap Brown was elected to replace Stokely as chairman and Stanley Wise was chosen to take the place of Ruby Doris as executive secretary. Ralph Featherstone became program secretary instead of Cleve Sellers.

In May 1967, the organization rejected support for Bob and Dottie Zellner's proposal to organize in the white community in New Orleans as members of SNCC staff. It is hard to know when the period of final deterioration began, but that action marked the end of the time when I stayed in touch with SNCC. The organization subsequently sank into doctrinaire feuding and the beginning of SNCC's demise.

Rap Brown, who believed in armed self-defense and had been arrested for carrying a concealed weapon in Alabama in 1966, issued a call to arms in response to heavy provocation by police in Prattville, Alabama, a few weeks after his election. "At another time in its history," Cleve Sellers wrote, "SNCC would have flooded Prattville with organizers prepared to break the will of the white community. Unfortunately, we were no longer in a position to launch such a campaign. We didn't have the staff, the money or the support from outside sources." Apparently unable to think of anything else, what was left of SNCC authorized Rap to release a statement that was full of sound and fury but signifying nothing, for there was no program behind the utterance: "We will no longer sit back and let black people be killed by murderers who hide behind sheets or the badge of the law. . . . We are calling for full retaliation from the black community across America."

Stokely Carmichael was expelled from SNCC in July 1968 by a new group, none of whom I had heard of or worked with; and by December of that year Cleve Sellers and Willie Ricks were fired.

Among my papers I found a quotation from Miguel de Unamuno that I had written out in longhand: "The real, the really real, is irrational."

In the long run, separatism doesn't work and is unnecessary in a flexible democracy except as a transient political statement; and even then it is charged with self-indulgence, for anger cannot be the basis of policy. Although an evocative and thrilling symbol for an idea, the use of the word *power* does not produce it. Separatism has little to do with the achievement of power, although it may be fleetingly useful as a pole in staking out an extreme.

In the final analysis, the American system was realistic. Blacks were a minority that was not going away, could not be repressed by force, and was capable of creating explosive dissension, and the nation started to accede to this reality.

Yet there is more that must be said. I must try to answer the question of what ended SNCC—and so fast. When I return to this vexing question, instead of describing how I felt and saw it at the time, as I have thus far done, I will account for it with the maturity and reflection that the years have brought me. But, first, I shall complete my personal narrative.

I was briefly married to Dennis Sweeney, a volunteer in Mississippi whose name would not be recognized by most people. Fifteen years later, he shot and killed Allard Lowenstein, his former mentor and the man who recruited him for Mississippi. It had not occurred to me that my short marriage was relevant to this story until I was advised by some whose judgment I respect that failure to comment on this episode—the marriage, not the homicide—would be seen as evasion. This is unfortunate, because it occurs to me that others might conclude that my reasons for including it here are inspired by sensationalist impulses. I am, classically, damned if I do and damned if I don't.

The tragedy of Dennis Sweeney has sources and implications that legitimately reflect the tension, agony, and psychic dislocation experienced by many young people in the movement and so may be appropriately discussed in these pages. This account is not the story of Dennis Sweeney or of that tragedy. The relevance of my marriage is that it illuminates my situation emotionally and politically at a moment crucial to my life and in the movement's history. The forces that drove and tormented Dennis to the stage of psychological disintegration may well have been generated by his experiences in the struggle, because there are others of my colleagues who have suffered similar symptoms and pathology.

They say that freedom is a constant sorrow.

Dennis was an engaging and handsome Stanford University student. We first met at the second Waveland staff meeting in May 1965. He was clearly interested in me, yet I had been keeping my head in the sand, ostrichlike, concerning personal relationships with men. Initially, I did not reciprocate. I had first heard of Dennis by telephone through Communications when the COFO office in McComb was bombed in July 1964 and I had given his name, age, and address to the news media as one of those hurt in the blast. Subsequently, at the staff meeting in Tougaloo, I learned about the tamales served to him by Malva and Red Heffner that resulted in their being run out of McComb. After the summer project, in the autumn of 1964, Dennis changed his status from that of a volunteer and became a SNCC field secretary in Mississippi. He seemed to be highly respected among the Stanford students; his major field of study had been political theory, which brought him into contact with some of the university's most famous professors who, apparently liking him, had given him standing among the other students. He was also known to be a protégé of Allard Lowenstein's and had first come to Mississippi with Al in November 1963 for the protest Freedom Ballot. That was the extent of the information I had about him.

I noticed him working with Bob Moses and saw the unusual rapport he seemed to have with Bob. I was intrigued by the questions Dennis asked. He had a distinctive way of revealing his position on an issue by asking analytical questions. His sandy hair was inclined to curl and his blue eyes had a far-gazing quality to them. The blue jeans and T-shirts that he wore over his medium build were always fresh, and his shoes were constructed for walking. He was shyly aggressive. Every once in a while, his clean-cut demeanor was interrupted by a flash of insight. This, and his quality of charisma, interested me. On the other hand, he also had an intense introspective air, and was occasionally brooding, withdrawn, and diffident.

Dennis talked often about the connection between what we were trying to do in the American South and the U.S. position in the war in Vietnam. He spoke of his disdain for the misuse of authority by those in positions of power—an abstraction that included university administrators, Mississippi sheriffs, or the Johnson administration's defense establishment—and it was the abuse of authority that bothered him more than anything else. He placed a premium on honesty and talked about how he was trying to achieve a higher standard of integrity—in interactions with others, in his political analysis, and in his willingness to admit flaws in himself.

Dennis invited me to assist a film crew, friends of his, in the southwestern part of Mississippi. They were making a *cinéma vérité* documentary about black leadership to be called *Black Natchez*. I thought the theme was consistent with our purpose, and, since I was uncertain whether the Atlanta headquarters was going to support the workshops for departing volunteers, I agreed, thereby putting the workshop proposal on hold. No one—including Bob, Jim, or Julian—had suggested clearer alternatives to me and this project at least had a beginning, middle, and end. It was not my first choice for my work, but there was so little clarity in the placement of staff at that moment that it seemed attractive. At least there would be some tangible result. In Natchez, the film crew of two, Dennis, and I stayed in a house reached through a single road that led across a deep-cut marshy bayou into the labyrinth of unpaved streets that composed the black community of this old flatboat city on the Mississippi River. This access road reminded me of Danville because, once on the other side of the bayou, police cars would not follow us.

Two local youths, "Otis" and "Jackson," took it upon themselves to protect us from night riders. One slept on the roof with a shotgun, the other under the front porch with a rifle. I did not want this kind of protection, and it created great tension for me. I thought it begged for violence. What really troubled me, was that the youths bought "dumdum" bullets for the rifle, which would burst upon contact, tearing flesh, and leaving a more serious wound than a clean bullet hole. The additional angle of retaliation bothered me even more, compounding all my other problems.

In Natchez, my relationship with Dennis grew into one of personal involvement. I began to see more facets of his personality and, never having been in love before, thought that the attraction I felt for him must be love. He was tender and kind, and concentrated his attention on me. We shared much in common politically and his values and mine were similar. He had qualities that I admired and treated me as if I were an extraordinary prize. There was no hint of abnormality. Although I was sometimes troubled by his brooding, I thought that these interludes were caused by his efforts to explore his deficiencies and weaknesses. I liked his willingness to examine himself and felt that it brought forth from me a stronger effort to improve myself.

A heavy-handed letter arrived in Natchez by mail on July 25, 1965, from Muriel Tillinghast in Atlanta, sent to Dennis and me and asking for an explanation of our activities. Four days later Cleve Sellers, who was now program director, sent me a letter from the personnel committee saying that my paychecks were being held in Atlanta pending an evaluation. When I telephoned the office to inquire, I was told that Ruby Doris Smith Robinson had given the instructions. This was a real threat to me. I had no savings and felt I could not call on my parents, whose chosen professions gave them limited means.

Dennis asked me to marry him and talked about it often but I demurred. "This is not the right time to think about that," I said.

I sensed that the group I had joined was imperiled, but I could not fully admit consciously that I might no longer belong there. My decision to go to Natchez was not made with enthusiasm but I barely recognized that this reflected my anxiety about the deterioration of the situation within SNCC. Looking back now, I can see that I was starting to grieve for a movement that had meant everything to me.

Distressed over the demoralization I felt, I tried to figure things out and differentiate my role in SNCC, and I sat down and wrote out what "work" meant for me:

—It needs to be done
—I can do it
—There is room (it is not competitive)
—I can grow from it, be creative, and deepen my sense of self

These words evoke sadness in me even now because they throw back at me the feelings of confusion, inadequacy, and stifling of growth that I was experiencing at the time.

I had joined the movement because it was an affirmation of my own beliefs, and I had discovered in *its* search for political self-determination the tool kit for my own self-definition. Now, SNCC was no longer a naked affirmation of democracy. Although lip service was increasingly given to the questions about women that Casey and I had raised in Waveland, insofar as the larger dimensions and structural issues of our memoranda were concerned, I felt that we had lost.

What had sustained SNCC through the summer of 1964 was our belief in each other. Instead, now, little over one year later, others no longer seemed to believe in me or in one another. I wasn't sure what anybody believed or what we stood for. My ability to work, as I had described it, on the things I thought important, was impaired. I saw nothing but imponderables. I had always felt that we were isolated from the rest of the country, with the exception of the churches, remembering when we couldn't count on the traditional labor, civil rights, or liberal groups. Now even the support of the Protestant denominations was beginning to fade. As I thought about the options, my sense of estrangement deepened. I now had only Casey and a handful of other close friends, and I started to feel alienated within SNCC. Bob and Dona were working in Washington on an Assembly of Unrepresented People, and Francis Mitchell and Mike Thelwell, along with other friends, were there with the Mississippi Freedom Democratic party. Yet, while I considered joining them, those efforts did not seem right for me.

The holding of my paychecks in Atlanta, small as they were, moreover, was shattering to me and forced a crisis.

Dorie Ladner, a frisky black SNCC field secretary from Mississippi with a dashing smile and wild hair arrived one day, agitated, to tell me that she had heard rumors that Ivanhoe Donaldson, Cleveland Sellers, and Ralph Featherstone were visiting projects and dismissing staff. It sounded like a self-appointed troika. Dorie was someone I had always been fond of and trusted and I couldn't dismiss her alert. "They're firing people left and right if they don't like what they're doing," she blurted. Her account was confirmed as telephone calls came from other field offices.

On September 2, 1965, a demonstration was turned back when Governor Paul B. Johnson, Jr., sent six hundred fifty national guard troops into Natchez armed with rifles and bayonets. On top of this, the language of black consciousness ricocheting through SNCC seemed less an urge to pride in being black and more a call to be antiwhite. Since the May 1965 Waveland staff meeting, the decibel levels of this revolt were rising.

In the midst of this internal disintegration, unclear objectives, estrangement, troops, Dorie's alarm, the traveling troika, and the clangor of black-separatist rhetoric, Dennis held out marriage. "We'll go to California, to Stanford, where, I'm certain, something will work out wonderfully for you," he said, caring and confident.

His pressure was healthy in one sense; it produced a tentative admission in me that I should leave. But that moment of uncertainty was no time to make a decision about marriage.

My father, normally supportive and nondirective about my specific decisions, had been since April 1964 writing occasionally to encourage me to think about leaving SNCC. "I think I have understood all along, better than you have imagined, what you were trying to tell me about the meaning to you of your work with SNCC," he had written in November 1964. He talked about my "term of service" being up. In retrospect, he was quite right, but my immersion in SNCC and my identification with it was to the exclusion of all self-interest. Because of my state of mind, he inadvertently produced conflict in our relationship that had the effect of deepening my sense of alienation. In addition, he had always said he hoped I would marry by my twenty-fifth year and, try though I might to fight it, I could feel this admonition influencing me.

I was lost, feeling that the SNCC I had cared for so deeply was defaced and scarred, and yet at the same time I felt disaffected and like a wanderer in my own country. I was now, indeed, a "pilgrim soul" but with pathos that Yeats had not envisioned. Dennis offered an escape from this miasma that seemed bleakly without options. He and I brought together Casey, Bob Moses, Dona Richards, Miriam Willey of Ohio Wesleyan, his friend Fred Goff who later became my friend, and a few kinfolk at my family's place in Virginia and my father married us.

Not knowing where I was going, I developed a fantasy that was nine tenths hope that Dennis and I could re-create the conditions of movement and community that I had had in SNCC. Little did I know that nothing would ever again fill the place of SNCC in my life.

A few months later, I received a letter from Casey in which she said, "Lots of talk about violence. Everyone is gone. Enclosed is a list of who's on staff. Also enclosed is some other stuff since you have files and I don't, Meticulous Mary."

Dennis and I lived in East Palo Alto, close to and sometimes house-sharing with David Harris, president of the student body of Stanford University, and another of the volunteers recruited to Mississippi by Al Lowenstein, and also with Ira Arlook, subsequently to head the Ohio Public Interest Corporation of Citizen Action. Dennis and David Harris, in coordination with Mendy Samstein, began organizing the resistance to the draft for the war in Vietnam. David would later marry Joan Baez and go to prison for three years for his opposition to conscription for Vietnam. Although these friends were generous and sympathetic to me, I was bereft of happiness and barely able to cope with my deprivation of the movement. Dennis could not allay my grief because, going through his own separate process, he was now plunged into an interval of what he called self-doubt.

I think that those I met in California knew how unhappy I was; one friend of Dennis's told me that I had the saddest eyes he had ever seen. A friend from Students for a Democratic Society, Leni Wildflower, a warm and inquiring brunette from Hollywood, lived in Berkeley and opened her apartment to me as did another friend, Lynn Phipps, a gifted photographer. I started spending more and more time in Berkeley, where these two friends provided understanding and solace that Dennis, because of his own difficulties, was not able to give. As I was able, little by little, to talk with them about the transition in SNCC, I started building a bridge that would eventually lead me back to a society from which I felt dislocated.

One day, I simply did not return from Leni's apartment in Berkeley to our place in Palo Alto. My marriage had been based on a political decision more than a personal tie. I had married Dennis more out of hope for a bond, an affiliation, that might substitute for the loss of SNCC than out of deep commitment to him. He couldn't help me solve the problems I had living outside of SNCC and defining my purpose anew, and I couldn't help him resolve his separate feelings of isolation upon returning to Stanford. Although we each tried to be sensitive to the other, we were both besieged by our own turmoil. Little more than a year after marrying, I divorced him. (Whenever someone tells me they have divorced, I never say that I am sorry, for I have learned it may be a positive step.)

I never saw Dennis again. During the intervening years I did not even hear anything about him or his whereabouts until October 4, 1977, at a United Nations luncheon given by Ambassador Andrew Young for President Jimmy Carter and the African heads

of state at the General Assembly. I sat down—flushed with pleasure from Andy's introductions of me to Lieutenant General (later
President) Olusegun Obasanjo of Nigeria, President Samora Machel
of Mozambique, and other heads of state, for such events still
excited me then—and found that I had been seated next to Allard
Lowenstein. By then a former congressman from New York, Al
was there as part of the U.S. delegation to the UN. He brought
me to earth with a thud. He said that he had recently been to
Philadelphia and had seen Dennis, who had filed his teeth down,
apparently believing that the CIA had wired his brain and was
controlling him through his teeth.

I was shocked and dismayed but later learned that this was a
mental aberration that has been experienced in similar terms by
at least four individuals I knew in SNCC.

In a terrible encounter in New York City, on March 14, 1980,
Al was shot and killed by Dennis, who had apparently spent most
of the previous ten years tormented by the hallucinations of schizophrenia and by voices that he couldn't control. He had easily
been able to buy a weapon in Connecticut, which had no effective handgun control law.

There was in the Dennis of earlier years no hint of this eventual psychotic state. Several psychiatrists acquainted with the situation consider him a classic paranoid schizophrenic suffering from
a condition that normally develops over a long period of time. It
is true that there were major unresolved tensions in his relationship with Al, dating back to the period before I knew either of
them; yet nothing in Dennis's behavior when I was with him even
remotely hinted at this severe and progressive psychopathological
condition. It is hard to tell what might have triggered it. Perhaps
he would have become schizophrenic no matter what he had done.
Not having communicated with Dennis for fifteen years by the
time of the killing, I found it hard to comprehend how someone
who was once so discerning and probing could have sunk into
such a psychological abyss. In addition to the sorrow and grief that
I feel about this tragedy, I must also add that my anger at having
been obliquely connected, even if only through the dissolved formality of my past relationship with Dennis, makes it difficult for
me to think about him objectively.

Perhaps the shocks and interludes of living in fear that we all
experienced in Mississippi precipitated the progression of his condition. Many who knew him have no explanation for his disinte-

gration other than the playing out of stresses he endured, including a concussion suffered in the July 1964 McComb bombing. The death of Al Lowenstein and the ruination of Dennis Sweeney may have been caused by the traumas of the civil rights movement, battering what may have already been a fragile balance, as were sufferings of others and the deaths of the individuals to whom this book is dedicated—part of the high price the nation has paid for equivocation in the ending of racism.

What brought about SNCC's agony? What killed it? Why did it die so quickly? What transformed a bold, self-confident, highly creative, and fearless organization into a floundering, backbiting, and paranoid group? Why didn't the circle stay unbroken? What caused a man like Bob Moses, once so justifiably hero-worshipped, to make the extreme statement he made about severing all relationships with whites?

If one recalls the genesis of this struggle—workshops every other Tuesday night in Nashville studying Gandhi, the Bible, and Thoreau; the surprise of the sit-ins; the invocations of nonviolence and belief in the beloved community of a raceless society; the "band of brothers and sisters" and "circle of trust"—then one has to engage fully with the question of what changed SNCC and finished off this extraordinary group so fast? Finding the answers to this difficult query will involve looking at economics, geography, race, class, history, and the adamantine intransigence of American political institutions. It also requires the full weight of any insight I might have derived from subsequent experience. In these final pages, I no longer tell the story as I saw it then but will bring to bear all that the years since have taught me.

SNCC's funding sheds light on the group's internal problems and, since it is the simplest element in answering the perplexing question of what brought about SNCC's demise, I will look at it first. A few financial figures will show the phenomenal growth from what had in the beginning, a few years earlier, been a group of less than twenty full-time staff operating on a budget of less than twenty thousand dollars a year.

Up until 1964, SNCC was almost entirely southern-based. By the autumn of 1965, however, 35 of its 129 staff members were located in New York, California, Michigan, Pennsylvania, Massachusetts, and Washington, D.C.—outside the region. The staff in the South was based as follows:

Atlanta	33
Southwest Georgia	6
Alabama	12
Arkansas	16
Mississippi	26
North Carolina	1

The weekly payroll for the brothers and sisters had risen to $5,096 by the fall of 1965.

Most of SNCC's annual budget was raised by the Friends of SNCC. Here's how our income looked in the first ten months of 1965:

Friends of SNCC groups	$408,243
Personal contributions	77,432
Organizations (church denominations, black trade-union locals)	56,273
Sales of books	10,509
Other	13,744
	$566,201

Adding money carried over from 1964, the funding for 1965 reached $616,784 through the end of October.

Here is how we spent our money during the first ten months of 1965:

Payroll	$257,977
Field-office expenses	81,397
Sojourner Motor Fleet	31,404
Conferences	33,933
Freedom Democratic party	6,360
Travel (individual)	3,440
Speaking, fund-raising travel	7,953
Organizing buses	4,741
Building construction	34,576
Costs of sale items	10,792
Loans	20,448
Office supplies and upkeep	61,880
Printing costs	22,195
Photography	4,917
	$582,013

The prominence that SNCC occupied for several years in the consciousness of the country meant that financial resources from whites of conscience were available; still, SNCC was receiving funding that none of us would have earlier dreamed possible. Most of it was from the North and from white contributors or largely white institutions. SNCC was thus exceedingly vulnerable to any lessening of white goodwill. While it was precisely because of SNCC's connections with wealthy friends and the imprimatur of powerful individuals and groups that our budget and paid staff grew astronomically, once whites were expelled from SNCC the budget plummeted, so that I can see now that there had been an artificial quality to our growth. SNCC's financial support was not based in the black community; the poor blacks of Mississippi could never have sustained us.

Not only did the expansion of staff and projects carry attendant financial burdens; it meant the end of a highly personal and free way of operating, in which we had been like an extended family. Many staff members were unable to adjust to the requirements of what had become a large and complex entity. The situation called for increased accountability. Yet, when not handled adroitly, particularly with old hands who had been part of SNCC when it was an oasis of personal trust in a hostile southland, the new measures seemed authoritarian.

In the early days, going to work for the movement required serious self-selection and ominous confrontation with oneself because of the risks and isolation. There was no prestige and nothing fashionable about SNCC when I joined it. It was small, steeped in its own world-view, proud in its isolation, and as yet struggling to bring press attention to the oppression of blacks. Recall from the beginning chapters of this book that, in addition to ourselves, we possessed only donated cars and typewriters, a mimeograph machine, and the telephone! We couldn't even meet the modest payroll every week. Yet, paychecks or no, SNCC was independent, self-supporting and self-generating, with a deep synchronization between belief and action, rooted in the bonds among its members, and anchored in its own reality.

In addition to rapid growth in 1964, reverberations from the society at large must be considered. The character of the organization changed once it had grown large, bringing volunteers in by recruitment. The organization became fashionable and chic in literary, art, entertainment, professional, and political circles. I never savored such treatment in East Coast and West Coast parlors myself, but I remember Marion Barry, The Freedom Singers, and other staff members going off to what Bobbi Yancy and I called the cocktail circuit.

At that time, too, a number of gifted and flamboyant advocates and lawyers traveled the country on our behalf, recruiting and expostulating, some of them like barkers for a show. A few of them acted as if *they* were Bob Moses and as if the Mississippi Summer Project were *theirs*. Never knowing of Amzie Moore, Annie Devine, or E. W. Steptoe, unconscious of the local black staff like Jesse Harris, Bob Mants, or Hollis Watkins, they made the involvement of the white volunteers sound like a southern experience for the children of the privileged—the equivalent of a junior year abroad, perhaps in Paris, an excellent moving experience of exposure and discovery. That it may have been. But this verbiage did not reflect the reality of the civil rights movement with its roots in a century and a half of black resistance, faith, and endurance, and the volunteers should not have been sung as its heroes and heroines. The perspective and point of view of the movement's true stalwarts receded, the poor black Mississippians almost like objects against which the perceptions of enlightened northerners could be sharpened.

In the Mississippi Summer Project, there were few working-class volunteers. Those who participated were from some of the most elite and prestigious colleges and universities of America. They were students who had the decency and the sensitivity—as well as a certain freedom from want—to elect to use their summer confronting the beast of racism.

A more important aspect of the impact of class was that black southerners in the movement noticed that when northern whites came in large numbers—with their educated speech, access to the influential, and with the news media following them—the definition and role of the local folk changed. This was a hidden, unanticipated, and sad outcome from the summer project. The white volunteers unintentionally took authority, and sometimes roles, from local blacks. Hypothetically speaking, even if all of the volunteers had been black and from prestigious colleges, it is probable that similar although less stinging displacement would have occurred because of their sophistication and differences in skills.

Many of the 1964 summer volunteers decided that they wanted to stay, even though they did not necessarily meet SNCC's organizational needs. They thought they had earned their spurs in the movement and were entitled to remain, and SNCC, open and free, and erringly for its own interests, accepted them, so that our staff almost doubled, to 160, in Mississippi alone right after the summer. Having grown so much so quickly, we possessed no mechanism to evaluate personnel against program. Many local black SNCC field secretaries, believing that they had become peripheral, felt they either had to adopt the new perspectives reflected in the larger SNCC staff or they would become marginal. Yet, this was *their* struggle.

I can now also see that the 1964 summer project, despite its many significant accomplishments, was, ironically, like SCLC's siege of Selma at the time of the march from that city. Although we had at the time strenuously criticized what had happened in Selma, something similar occurred in Mississippi as huge numbers of outsiders and dignitaries descended, although on a protracted basis. The project not only brought close to seven hundred volunteers, lawyers by the gross, and the national news corps; it also commanded the presence of political figures, religious leaders, and entertainers, who came to the state on weekends. Like Selma, the project brought concrete breakthroughs and justified attention; in addition, again like Selma, it left chaos, frustration, confusion, and deflation.

I wrote earlier of a factor wholly unrecognized by us at the time—the cultural diversity of SNCC's staff, which included individuals who were first-generation college-educated southern blacks, rural local blacks, northern middle-class blacks, upper-class southern elite blacks, middle-class Christian whites, privileged whites, New England Quakers, Jews, white ethnics, members of the Left, and southern conservative whites. Within the staff, the divisions inherent in such variation in background and perspective were overcome—an enactment of our belief in one another, in raw and naked testimony to the power of the movement. Our heterogeneity—a strength while we were small and a factor that made ours an imperfect but sincere attempt at a society free of race, class, and gender discrimination—was strained to the breaking point when we expanded quickly. It resulted in irreconcilable schisms.

We must also look at the evidence from SNCC's own short political history as an organization. By 1964, we had reached the point where everything we tried, no matter how creative, ran aground on the obduracy of America's political institutions. The national Democratic party rejected the "Challenge" at Atlantic City, a repudiation ironically supported by most of the other civil rights organizations. Three of our fellow workers were murdered in Mississippi; subsequently we learned that it was law officers who killed them. The reaction of the White House to Jim Chaney's death was different from its response to the murder of Andy Goodman and Mickey Schwerner. The stresses and terror of the summer in Mississippi left SNCC exhausted. At Selma, once more, the White House had one reaction to Jimmy Lee Jackson's killing and another to the death of the Reverend James Reeb.

The difference in the responses accorded to the black and white deaths in Neshoba County and at Selma was an essential element in the deterioration of SNCC. Not only the White House but reporters and television crews—and therefore the nation—emphasized, in ways that SNCC's own egalitarian ethos was powerless to contradict, a simple but stunningly clear message: White people were still of more consequence than blacks, and white lives were still more important than black lives. Emotionally and mentally depleted, we received this as the national signal. It was here that the drift toward SNCC's end began.

America had broken the hearts of the young idealists of SNCC. Where now did the movement, as we knew it, turn? SNCC's ideas had always come from action, its rhetoric evolving from experience, never in advance of its ability to behave. When, however, SNCC had to interpret this series of disappointments and defeats, it became vulnerable to the forces and tendencies lurking in the history of black Americans.

In addition, Mississippi, in which most of SNCC's staff and resources were concentrated, suddenly in 1965 had a government antipoverty program called Headstart with lots of federal money—a program that attracted attention and employed many, a program that in some ways rendered redundant the role that SNCC and COFO had played.

Questions of program were vital to the movement's future, as well as the issue of growth. Even had all other things been equal, SNCC would still have gone through an intense crisis in

1965 and 1966. My preference in the question of structure had been for SNCC to operate as a democratic partnership. Yet this would have required immense and prolonged self-discipline. I reacted to proposals for a strong central organization as a *putsch* for the advocates of bureaucratization of SNCC. This conflict was not impossible to mediate and talk through; however, for reasons of personal exhaustion and depletion, instead of discussion it degenerated into a polarized debate, dividing us into camps, making us suspicious and paranoid. SNCC had indeed outgrown its earlier forms; it needed organization and it needed clear programs. But because of the too-rapid expansion, the overlay of race and class issues, the desperate quality and diatribe in the debate, and the twisting of perspectives, we could not achieve that much-needed clarity, and the trust that was essential to SNCC's functioning was destroyed.

I can now see that it would have been a miracle if the question of racial separation had not emerged to obscure already difficult issues, given our emotional exhaustion after 1964 and the unresolved ironclad reality of race and racism in America. Understanding the loss of status of local black southerners that resulted from the involvement of large numbers of sophisticated young people from the North; recognizing that in the ghettoes of the North a radical black nationalism was arising that talked of an irredeemable white society; and seeing that SNCC's own political experience had disillusioned it about reform and the morality of America's white power blocs, what resulted was inevitable.

SNCC had become incredibly effective at raising the money to pay its staff stipends. Yet, because of this funding base, it had also become a creature of the chic constituency that financed it. The Sojourner Motor Fleet existed because someone in SNCC knew someone at General Motors who could sell us automobiles at a cut rate. SNCC also had cachet. Fannie Lou Hamer left the actress Shirley MacLaine at her stove stirring a pot of beans while she went to a Freedom Democratic party meeting one day. We could mount the "Congressional Challenge" with most of the civil rights and liberal community against us. We would be received by members of Congress virtually whenever we wanted.

Nevertheless, the experience of being trapped by an alliance with a Joe Rauh—dependent but some felt betrayed—echoed with

brassy tintinnabulation as the field staff looked at the white contacts and allies who had brought about SNCC's enormous growth.
The local black staff had another perspective on the movement.
The more unwieldy SNCC grew as a consequence of involvement
of the white and powerful, the more the MacArthur Cottons, Dorie Ladners, and Willie Peacocks felt excluded—yet it was they
who had made SNCC what it was, distinctively, in American history. SNCC's very strengths had become its weaknesses.

Whether the aspirations of SNCC's Thoreauvian idealism could
be meshed with the sheer organization needed by a large group
was the question at the heart of SNCC's structural dilemmas beginning in late 1964. This intrinsic issue got lost, knotted in the
vines of race. Reports from the 1967 meeting where whites were
ultimately expelled held that Stokely waffled for hours, that Jim
Forman filibustered into the small hours of the morning, and that
the few old-timers who were present lobbied frantically when the
time for that close vote drew near. "It never would have gone
down," some say to this day, "if more of us had been there,"
pointing to the lateness of the hour, two o'clock in the morning,
after the remainder of the staff had left the meeting or gone to
bed, exhausted after days of tempestuous debate, when the vote
was taken. Had there been more participants in the meeting then,
perhaps they would not have voted out a Mendy Samstein or a
Dottie Zellner.

As I have reported, the vote was nineteen in favor of the
expulsion of the remaining whites, eighteen opposed, with twenty-
four abstentions. What caused more abstentions than the vote on
either side? The figures fascinate. Not having been at the meeting, I do not know how the handful of whites voted. Why were
so many blacks, whom I assume to have been the bulk of the
abstentions, unable to make a decision—in a group where I had
never known anyone to be afraid? Did they believe that expulsion
was unworthy of the loyalty and sacrifice of their white colleagues
and therefore of SNCC? On the other hand, given the patterns of
re-emerging separatism in modern black history, did they feel unable to resist the inevitable? It is said that Bill Mahoney brought
breakfast in bed to Elizabeth Sutherland Martinez the morning
after that tally. Why this expression of contrition?

Looking back, I can now see that there was an inevitable
historical logic that drove SNCC in this direction. As I have stated,

segregation in the South persisted into the second half of the twentieth century only because of a rapprochement with the rest of the nation, an implicit concord that let the South do as it pleased, an agreement enforced by the incredible power of southern members of Congress who often stayed in office until they died, while chairing the most important Senate and House committees and using their clout within the Democratic party to protect the system with legal and political sway. SNCC—whose experiences demonstrated that this national deal might well continue, still offering political impunity to the region—had no way of knowing that South Africa's draconian measures would not be used. Thus, the originally integrationist organization would, sooner or later, have been caught up in the other tendency in black history: to separate.

We come now to an intriguing possibility in our query about SNCC's demise: the use of agents provocateurs. The Philadelphia-based Revolutionary Action Movement was a northern black group, professing violence and condemning passive resistance, imbued with nationalism, and defining itself as Marxist and revolutionary. RAM enlisted ghetto youth who were on the wrong side of the law. Disenchanted with the lack of freedom of thought, absence of action, and religiosity of the Nation of Islam, RAM's members were nonetheless enthralled by the personality of Malcolm X. They were disciples and students of Mao Zedong, studied Marxist revolution as interpreted by European and Vietnamese theorists, and read Marcus Garvey and Du Bois. They were also admirers of Frantz Fanon, concerning whom they said, "Not Marxist but he had theory." RAM's program included civil war and envisaged armed rebellion starting in Boston and spreading down throughout the East Coast.

One of the key members of the group in the mid-1960s, Professor Playthell Benjamin, presently a historian of Afro-American studies, told me years later:

> We sent four Philadelphians into SNCC in late 1965 and 1966. Two of them were intellectuals who came out of Temple University and two were gunmen who were disaffected members of the Philadelphia mosque. Their mission was to give SNCC a "correct" revolutionary posture and get rid of what RAM perceived to be white domination.

Roland Snellings, also from RAM in Philadelphia and later known as Mohammed Toure, had already moved into place within SNCC in the Atlanta Project. He had helped to draft the ideology section of its pivotal separatist position paper described earlier.

Two of the RAM members proceeded—under explicit instructions from the group's leadership including Professor Benjamin—to organize a conference in New Orleans at black Xavier University. They specifically sought out SNCC staff for attendance. The meeting was intensely ideological and black nationalist in the views presented, according to Dr. Benjamin, one of the speakers, and its purpose was to cause a questioning of the direction of the movement. Other speakers included Professors John Henry Clark and Keith Beard. "Black consciousness was discussed and the role of whites and nonviolence was questioned. These issues were particularly focused on in a long session on Frantz Fanon and the purifying influence of violence for the oppressed," recalled Benjamin, formerly professor in the W.E.B. Du Bois Department of Afro-American Studies at the University of Massachusetts, in an interview. "Xavier, being close to Mississippi and Alabama, allowed many SNCC staff to attend. I remember meeting Bob Moses, Ralph Featherstone, John O'Neal, and the Free Southern Theater," he recollects. "The Xavier conference marked the turning point in SNCC's thinking as I saw it."

A purposeful infiltration of SNCC? This was the sort of thing that a group like RAM might do, having a wildly distorted sense of the origins and history of SNCC and not understanding what made it unique in the arena of political struggle in America. According to Benjamin:

We had dismissed outright the possibility of infiltrating SCLC. The Christian willingness to suffer was odious to us and I personally thought it was a challenge to my manhood.

We were confused about SNCC's nonviolence. We didn't understand that many in SNCC saw nonviolence as tactical, nor did we understand that there was a philosophical conflict within SNCC on this issue. To us, the idea of nonviolence in the movement invited terror, and we had to respond, operating under Frederick Douglass's dictum, "He who is whipped easiest is whipped oftenest."

We saw SNCC as secular and decided it was the youngest, most intellectual, most independent group in the movement. SNCC's style, its dedication, its presence in the most dangerous parts of the South, the fact that SNCC workers lived with the people, and lived on nothing—SNCC seemed to us to personify Mao's teaching that a revolutionary must swim among the people like a fish in the sea.

The only thing missing in SNCC, we believed, was correct revolutionary ideology.

RAM had much of that and cells from east to west in cities like Philadelphia, New York, Pittsburgh, Chicago, Cleveland, Detroit, and Los Angeles, but it had no popular base; I doubt whether it could have put fifty people in the street. Professor Benjamin today concedes that if the black community had followed RAM's advice at the time, it would have resulted in unmitigated disaster, a catastrophe for black people. Benjamin recalls:

We had arguments with Stokely when he came to Harlem right after the Black Power slogan and before the Black Panthers organized in the West. None of us knew Stokely or anything about him until he started saying Black Power. We were northern; he was from a southern movement. The RAM members he was meeting with were Maoists but Stokely was talking about electoral politics.

We thought that the southern movement would eventually come to our point of view because this was the "classic" path of revolutions. We met with Stokely hoping that he had arrived at our position, but he hadn't. We thought we were onto the "science" of revolution; we were arrogant.

To us, Stokely was a bourgeois pork-chop nationalist, halfway there, outer trimmings, but not at the nitty gritty. We decided to set up a Black Panther party in Harlem but give it a different twist. This was front politics. The party in California had no resemblance to the original one in Lowndes County [Alabama] either.

"In infiltrating, RAM astutely chose a time when SNCC was vulnerable and when the currents of nationalism were changing," Mike Thelwell later noted to me, adding, "That timing might have been RAM's only astute act."

According to Mike: "Someone who had experienced the valor

of a Bob Zellner, the perception of a Casey Hayden, and the tenacity of a Bill Hansen could never have accepted RAM's mission to get rid of whites." Ideologues and gunmen who trafficked in nationalist abstractions of white and black, however, might. As another one of many ironies affecting SNCC's end, it was precisely the openness and freedom of the organization that would have allowed such penetration.

One question left unanswered is whether U.S. government infiltration had anything to do with RAM's foray into SNCC. Clayborne Carson writes in *In Struggle* that the FBI's J. Edgar Hoover "did not single out SNCC for inclusion in the FBI's Counterintelligence Program (COINTELPRO) until 1967, but concerted FBI surveillance of SNCC's activities had begun several years before," although "none of the FBI reports from 1964 to 1967 presented evidence that any member of SNCC's staff was or had been a member of the Communist Party." The Stanford University historian quotes an August 25, 1967, order from Hoover to FBI field offices "to expose, disrupt, misdirect, discredit, or otherwise neutralize the activities of black nationalist, hate-type organizations and groupings, their leadership, spokesmen, membership and supporters" of groups including CORE, RAM, SCLC, and SNCC. "No opportunity should be missed," the memorandum read, "to exploit through counterintelligence techniques the organizational and personal conflicts of the leaderships of the groups and where possible an effort should be made to capitalize upon existing conflict. . . . You are urged to take an enthusiastic and imaginative approach." Stokely Carmichael, in particular, was targeted, according to Carson, because he had what the bureau considered to be the "necessary charisma" to be a new black messiah, and, on one occasion, Carson writes, FBI agents were encouraged to discredit him by spreading a rumor that he was a CIA agent. Thus SNCC's difficult internal problems were exacerbated by documented external pressures, although of an unknown scope.

One could clearly see the divided perspective in the black community: Are we Americans or are we Africans? Do we integrate or do we separate? That dichotomy in the stream of the history of black people in America was at first seeping and later flooding under the back door of SNCC. By then, most of those who might have tempered that strain were gone, either worn out or squeezed out. The tensions in black history and the ambivalent relationship of blacks with white America resonated in SNCC's course and became explicit.

This leaves the question of Bob Moses. A few years after this period, in 1970, I talked with Ivanhoe Donaldson and told him how I had felt about SNCC's rejection of me. "Oh, but we weren't talking about you," he protested. His comment was not disingenuous. He meant it. Of that I am certain. I think I now understand exactly what he was saying. What the young black people in SNCC were doing, despite the resistance of some, was declaring: In the same way that the society has rejected us, we now reject it and withdraw ourselves and our resources for our own salvation.

The few white members who remained in SNCC at the end understood this declaration, and I think this explains why there was no cry of anguish. Not one white person from SNCC protested or spoke with the press, which was, incidentally, clamoring aggressively for material on this denouement.

While not justifying the racial rejection of the brotherly and sisterly sharing of sacrifice and comradeship, and not praising sectarianism and intolerance, I can only observe that, in a profound way, a new generation of younger black people in SNCC, as well as whites, and the old hands, were all victims in a curious, ironic, and absurd danse macabre caused by America's racism.

I am struck by the fact that Bob Moses did not stay in a SNCC that had expelled whites but left the United States and went to Africa, where he lived for several years in a small Tanzanian village and taught in a humble school in total obscurity. I know that he was anguished by the deaths of people that he led in SNCC. I know that he was deeply hurt by the indifference and callousness of the social order toward blacks. I know that he had internalized pain and the responsibility for the grief of others. He was probably emotionally, spiritually, and physically depleted. Indeed, some of our group have not recovered to this day. Now, in reflection, I see that his refusal to have anything to do with whites was not directed at his personal associates but was a rejection of his acculturation and the overwhelming and downpressing constructs of white culture. At that moment, the world—the white world—was too much with him.

When I think back, quietly, with my own wounds healed and with the benefit of twenty years' perspective, I see and I feel, like a nightmare that repeats itself, recurring images of the local black field secretaries. We must consider how the changes in SNCC and the movement in the years 1965 and 1966 felt to someone like Jesse Harris, a young man who typifies the black Mississippi and Alabama staff. In order to make my point, I must pause for a few lines to tell one last story.

Jesse Harris was a tall, slender youth from Jackson, with the nose of an Apache warrior, and deep-set, intense eyes. He was somber, serious, and very brave. Jesse joined the movement when the Freedom Rides reached Jackson in 1961. He had heard that the riders were coming, went to greet them, and ended up accompanying them to a lunch counter. At the sit-in, he was swept up in the group as if he were one of them and was locked up in Parchman penitentiary. There, he refused to say, "Yes, sir," or "No, sir," to the guard.

"Damn it, nigger, don't you know how to say 'sir' to a white man?"

Violating mores by looking him straight in the eye, Jesse replied, "I only say 'sir' to my father."

Enraged, the guards circled around him, and pushed him down across a log, his buttocks rising up exposed into the air. They began to whip him viciously across his rump with a long, thick leather strap.

When they had finished, Jesse slowly, tenderly, and painfully eased himself up until he was standing, teetering from the pain.

"Guess that'll teach you to say 'Yes, sir,' " the guard jeered.

Jesse gazed at him silently, looking at him, dazed. Then, saying nothing and revealing nothing in his face, wearily and awkwardly, Jesse lay back down on the log.

I have written of my disorientation in 1965 and 1966, when the world of SNCC that I knew came to an end. How did the local staff like Jesse Harris feel? These extraordinary young black people, frequently with only a high school education, many of them having had members of their families killed, having grown up in a society that informed them in every way that they were less than human, had suddenly found in the movement comradeship and genuine equality with young people from other regions and different classes and backgrounds—some of them white and some of them black. For a glorious period of four, five, or, at most, six years, they were welded together into a union—risking, daring, and struggling together.

For the Jesse Harrises of the movement, the $9.64 weekly SNCC paycheck was the first regular income in their lives, but, more important, they achieved a sense of themselves and their own worth. Emboldened, they came to have confidence in their steeliness, knew the joy of tangible achievement, and realized they could count on themselves and each other under duress. They were part of a circle whose members believed that through their own courage, their own valor, and their own flinty resourcefulness, they could change their lives, the reality of others, and affirm a new meaning and definition of their existence. They became heroes and heroines to each other.

Suddenly, as SNCC grew and changed, infused with gargantuan white involvement, things all about them altered, including their sense of themselves. Jesse and the others found their movement threatened. They saw it vanishing as though SNCC itself were an ephemeral gift of white society. As SNCC's murky structural debates made the already difficult problem of developing coherent programs seem like a power struggle, as racial clots blocked its bloodstream, and as the disappointments it experienced set the staff back emotionally, they found themselves on the sidelines, in a vacuum. Jesse and the others bore the physical and psychological scars of the conflict but had no place to flee. In their passionate concern for the continuation of their movement, many of them sided with the group that called for strong central organization; there seemed more security in it. The skein of SNCC's successes was unraveling; yet for them the fight was just beginning. They were still living in a Mississippi that, although changed, held no real opportunity for most of them.

The local black field staff of SNCC were prepared to live and die for each other and for the struggle. But, as they watched, powerless before the unwieldiness of SNCC, the organization that had brought them value and self-worth was inexorably slipping away from them. Disappearing. "We ain't freed nobody, yet!" I remember one of them shouting.

I have since heard that some of the bravest and most courageous of the local black field staff have ended up dislocated, severely disoriented, alcoholics, on drugs, or in prison. That brings me to another conclusion about the dissolution of SNCC. The pain and alienation of the valiant Jesse Harrises who personified this unique organization and were the guts of the civil rights movement must have been many degrees more grave than mine.

"The real question," Charles Sherrod wrote in his position paper for the Waveland meeting in November 1964, "is whether SNCC is born to die or to live in the new society or to be the new society."

Yet, in the view of many SNCC workers, the organization was not meant to last. When I first went to work with Julian Bond, he would say that SNCC was designed to put itself out of business in five years. Implicit in SNCC's thinking was the notion that if we did our work well, there would be no need for such an organization. Some said that once we had empowered local leadership, it would turn around and run us out of town, and the better we had done our job, the faster this would happen. Reflecting the high speed at which SNCC operated—"We're an organization of organizers and we've got to move on"—you could glimpse a certain evanescence in SNCC's early philosophy: Not only was the organization never supposed to become a bureaucracy, it came into being in response to a particular historical circumstance and should not endure.

"SNCC went dead on schedule," said one SNCC friend from southwest Georgia. "I only hoped, as I saw those shrill people coming in later, none of whom I knew, that it would hurry up and die so that *they* couldn't go around saying that *they* were SNCC."

Nonetheless, I have subsequently worried that my own anguish about the loss of SNCC might have altered my ability to see and evaluate the later progress of American blacks working in their own idioms. I comfort myself by thinking that it is only if I am not concerned about this that I should worry. There is no gainsaying that some aspects of the experience of black nationalism were destructive, but others were useful.

Black nationalism should never have come as a surprise. It was the expression of a long historic thread in the dynamic relationship between the black community and white America. It reflected the dichotomies represented by Frederick Douglass and Dr. Martin Delaney, W.E.B. Du Bois and Marcus Garvey, and that of Martin Luther King, Jr., and Malcolm X. In the face of intractable racism, there always has been a significant black response that preached: We must separate. In the early days of SNCC, we did not recognize it, most likely because we did not know about it; it surfaced to confound us because it appealed so strongly to many stalwart workers after 1965.

Some say SNCC's black nationalism was the phoenix arising

from its ashes. Indeed, for many individuals who participated in the civil rights movement, black nationalism was a rite of passage—something to be partaken of and moved through. Many of them are now involved in diverse coalitions, enhanced by that perspective.

Two quotations have continued to haunt me as I have sought resolution for this enigmatic question. One is from Jean-Paul Sartre in his introduction to *The Wretched of the Earth:* "We only become what we are by the radical and deep-seated refusal of that which others have made of us." The other is from a young Alaskan, an American Indian woman named Margaret Nick. She was quoted after this period by Senator Edward M. Kennedy in *Look* magazine on June 2, 1970: "Some people say that a man without education might as well be dead. I say, a man without identity—if a man doesn't know who he is—he might as well be dead."

On the day that Dietrich Bonhoeffer learned of the failure of the plot to assassinate Hitler in which he participated, knowing that retaliation would be inescapable, he made an accounting of his life in a poetic essay called "Stations on the Road to Freedom." Still believing that to be Christian meant taking sides, it was about the freedom that is expressed in the willingness to assume responsibility. Most significant to me is his belief that freedom without responsible action is not freedom. He was convinced that discipline was decisive:

> If you would find freedom, learn above all to discipline your
> senses and your soul. . . . None can learn the secret of
> freedom, save by discipline.
>   Not in the flight of fancy, but only in the deed is there
> freedom. Away with timidity and reluctance! Out into the
> storm of event, sustained only by the commandment of God
> and your faith, and freedom will receive your spirit with ex-
> ultation.

Preparing for his imminent death at the hands of the Nazis, he penned:

> O freedom, long have we sought thee in discipline and in
> action and in suffering. Dying, we behold thee now, and
> see thee in the face of God.

What became of my fellow workers? Many settled in Georgia. John Lewis was elected to the 100th Congress from Georgia's Fifth District in November 1986 after having served for several years on the Atlanta City Council. He worked for me as the head of domestic operations for ACTION, in the independent federal agency containing the Peace Corps and four domestic national volunteer service corps programs to which President Carter appointed me as deputy director during his administration.

Julian Bond served in the Georgia state legislature for twenty years. I have already told how his was the youngest name ever placed in nomination for the vice-presidency at a national party's convention. He has had a distinguished career as a nationally known commentator on television and radio, and he became a much sought-after public speaker, writer, and celebrity. Charles Sherrod remained in southwest Georgia in community-development work and was elected to the Albany, Georgia, city commission, on which he still serves. Casey Hayden (Sandra Cason), the mother of two children, went to work for the city of Atlanta under Connie Curry, both of them serving in the administration of the city's mayor, Andrew Young.

Others went to Boston, New York City, or other points northwest and south. Bob Moses and Dona Richards were divorced. Bob taught in Tanzania, married SNCC field secretary Janet Jemmott, and they have five children. He returned to complete his doctoral studies at Harvard University and was honored with a five-year "genius" grant from the John D. and Catherine T. MacArthur Foundation of Chicago to allow him to continue his research.

Bob and Dottie Miller Zellner, although divorced, both live in New York. Dottie went to work for the Center for Constitutional Rights. Donald Harris went to work first for the mayor of Newark and later for the Philip Morris Corporation. Nancy Stearns has spent her adult life in the practice of civil-liberties and public-interest law, lately in the New York State Attorney General's Office handling environmental cases.

Professor Michael Thelwell established the W.E.B. Du Bois Department of Afro-American Studies of the University of Massachusetts, which now houses the papers of W.E.B. Du Bois, and has published several articles and books, both fiction and nonfiction. Professor Howard Zinn, having been forced to leave Spelman College because he was too much of an activist, taught government at Boston University for over twenty years and became a playwright of social-issue drama.

Ella Baker died on December 13, 1986, in New York City. It was her eighty-third birthday. At the funeral, Bernice Johnson Reagon led the congregation, which included many former SNCC workers, in the old song that Miss Baker always asked Bernice to sing: "Guide my feet while I run this race. . . . For I don't want to run this race in vain." A few months later, in March 1987, E. D. Nixon died, aged eighty-seven.

SNCC people turn up in all facets of community work. I was surprised one day in Philadelphia to run into Gwen Robinson and Ed Nakawatase, both of them working for the American Friends Service Committee in Philadelphia.

A full complement moved to Washington, D.C. Marion Barry was elected mayor of Washington and took office in 1979; Ivanhoe Donaldson managed his campaign. Courtland Cox became Mayor Barry's deputy mayor for economic development. Jim Forman married and then was divorced from Dinky Romilly. He completed graduate studies, wrote several books, and became a neighborhood commissioner in Washington, D.C. Dinky lives with their children in Atlanta, has remarried, and is a nursing supervisor. Charlie Cobb became a journalist with special expertise in covering developing countries and is on the staff of the National Geographic Society magazine. Lawrence Guyot became a lawyer, also residing in Washington. Marian Wright married Peter Edelman, an aide to Robert F. Kennedy whom she met in 1967 when he advanced a trip for Kennedy and the House Education and Labor Committee before whom she testified. Marian later founded and has for many years directed the Children's Defense Fund based in Washington.

Dr. Bernice Johnson Reagon became director of the Program in Black American Culture of the Smithsonian Institution. She was also the founder of The Harambee Singers and Sweet Honey in the Rock, both professional singing groups that evolved out of the experience of The Freedom Singers. Bernice still considers herself to be a Freedom Singer, in a direct link with what she did in the movement. Frank Smith was elected a member of Washington's school board, went on to win a seat on the city council, and served as a local elected official for many years. Dr. Jean

Wheeler Smith, having been graduated from Georgetown Medical School, became a privately practicing psychiatrist in the capital. Dr. Joyce Ladner became professor of sociology at Howard University and chairs TransAfrica Forum, which is concerned with ending apartheid in South Africa.

Jane Stembridge remained, as she always was, a gypsy poet. Her last letter to me carried an Iowa address.

The Reverend Dr. James M. Lawson, Jr., became minister of the Holman United Methodist Church in Los Angeles. Francis Mitchell has worked with venture capital in appropriate technologies also in Los Angeles.

Most of my fellow workers survived the tempests of SNCC and were tempered as a result of their experiences, becoming stronger. There were, however, cruel tragedies. Dennis Sweeney is *not* the only SNCC worker who went crazy. At least two others of whom I am aware suffered from paranoid schizophrenia, some became psychotic, and others have had to cope with pernicious emotional afflictions including alcoholism and drug abuse. On March 9, 1970, Ralph Featherstone was killed near Bel Air, Maryland, when a bomb exploded in the car he was driving. Some say it was planted by police, but many believe that he was planning to use it at the courthouse where Rap Brown's trial was to have occurred. Sam Shirah was shot to death in 1978; Bob Zellner told me that a man whom Sam was trying to help had turned on him in a demented state. Two men who played prominent roles in SNCC and are figures in this book have served time in federal prison for financial improprieties. They have suffered enough for their crimes. Since I fervently hope they will be able to reconstruct their lives to use their talents, I see no reason to identify them or to catalog the reasons why they had to pay this debt to society.

Stokely Carmichael has lived for many years in Conakry, Guinea, under the name of Kwame Toure, is head of the All-Africa Peoples party, and speaks frequently in the United States to promote Pan-Africanism. Cleveland Sellers, after writing his book, became an administrator of a government unemployment program in Greensboro, North Carolina.

Mine is but one account of experiences in the American civil rights movement of the 1960s. Everyone who participated has a different story. No one could experience everything in this galactic awakening of hundreds upon hundreds of towns and hamlets involving millions of people. No one saw every facet. No one can elicit from it all of its lessons. No one was there from the beginning of SNCC to its end. No one can debate what I lived. Others can only tell you that they agree or disagree. Then, insist that they give you their stories. Ask them to write down their accounts.

SNCC was heroic and it was humdrum. It was romantic and it was sweaty. It was uplifting and it was brutalizing. It was powerful disproportionately to its numbers. It was inspiring and valiant. It was filled with all the contradictions, frailties, paradoxes, and vexations that accompanied confrontation with its own power and, conversely, its own powerlessness. It was magnanimous in its response to meanness, terror, and killing. It could be joyful, nurturing, tender, and loving. The bonds forged among us gave incredible strength and built resilience that defied ordinary limits. Sometimes SNCC was playful and exhilarating. Yet, in its tragic inability to hold to its vision in the face of disappointments and defeats, and to determine a constructive course through the shoals of ideological hardening, it was enervating. When I left, I felt it suffocating me and depriving me of hope.

It took me many years, first, to accept and, then, to come to peace with the conflicts and pain that I experienced in the tormented year of 1965. For a long time after leaving SNCC, I dreamed at night as if I were still there—about continuations of staff meetings, struggles within SNCC, and of violence against me or against others. I dreamed in reenactment, reliving my impotence and our inability to resolve internal conflicts.

I dreamed in November 1966 that Charlie Cobb, Bob Weil, Mike Sayer, Betty Garman, and I were listening to a tape recording of local people talking among themselves of their fears of violence and terror and of their wish to arm themselves in self-defense. In the dream our staff group debated arming ourselves and we tried to spur a staff meeting to reach a decision but Jim Forman refused. The dream closed with a series of frantic telephone calls by which we overrode him and pulled the session together but, by then, everyone was drunk.

Even a full year after I had gone, in January 1967, I dreamed that I was with Stokely Carmichael on a bright hazy day. We were surrounded by people jostling, none of them supporters. Suddenly he was shot, and as I threw myself down beside him, the hole in his chest from the bullet slowly widened until it was the size of a dinner plate. Distraught, I put my face next to his, convinced there would be no breath coming out. As happens only in dreams, he started talking to me calmly, and asked me to help him escape from there.

Much of the trauma of 1965 had to do with absorbing the expressions of suspicion, bitterness, and hostility concerning white participation that I encountered, sometimes from people I loved, and the aching discussion of this issue. Yet, along the way, I learned something about the depths of the effects of racism.

The organization had been destroyed by the polarization that resulted from the dispute involving personal freedom and discipline; by factors of race, class, money, power, and apparently infiltration; and, finally, in the face of its disappointments following confrontations with the obdurate political institutions of America, by deaths and exhaustion, by the logic in black political thought toward separation.

Yet, failure is not a term that ever should be used for this small organization whose name was synonymous with the word "radical" in the 1960s. SNCC straddled deep philosophical ravines. The value of our experience is not in showing how to do it better next time; it lies, rather, in the validity and universality of our quandaries. These have reasserted themselves in the experience of movements in Poland, South Africa, the Philippines, the Middle East, Africa, Asia, and Latin America.

Starting with relationships between the dark-skinned majority and the white-skinned minority on the planet, SNCC grappled with some of the major issues of the twentieth century: the use of nonviolence as opposed to violence in resistance, whether leadership should proceed from a single charismatic figure or from the people, the choice between centralization or decentralization of power, democratic means in contrast to more authoritarian approaches, the power and psychology of relationships between women and men, the question of reform or revolution, and the degree to which institutions of governance should lead in social change. No group addressing all these paradigmatic issues could last. It was inevitable that we would destroy ourselves in the process of trying. Years later, Black Power is the only memory that many have of SNCC, but this does not mean that this concept was our most important and lasting contribution to political struggle.

Although SNCC could not resolve these profound and vexing questions, what made it remarkable in the American context was that a small band of very young men and women raised them. Its relevance is that these perplexities are still unresolved—and they still rend and break causes, organizations, and movements.

SNCC directly influenced an entire generation of protest. It helped to catalyze not only the women's movement but also the movement against the war in Vietnam. The free speech movement and the "Yippies" were both led by young men such as Mario Savio and Abbie Hoffman, who had been volunteers in the Mississippi Summer Project of 1964. In one sense, SNCC led the New Left, not in the intellectualism of Students for a Democratic Society and its offshoots, but in the way it broke from the Old Left—radical in its lack of confidence in the establishment and liberal goodwill, but resting its faith on the struggle itself and on local people, sometimes anarchistic in its distrust of centralization and suspicious of centralized power. Echoes of these tenets are found in later New Age movements.

In some ways, I have never recovered from the loss of SNCC. I grieved for three years. It was even longer before I could talk without choking about what my experiences meant.

I began the hard work of taking the lessons of the movement and constructing my life around them. I did this, aware of the probability that, because it had been a unique convergence of forces and people, there would never be another SNCC in my life. I determined to live out the values of the early years of SNCC, but I knew that I would have to do this without its support. I did not lose my idealism, but I tried to learn the secrets of effectiveness and sought to integrate the hard knots of realism from my experiences into my optimism. I broadened my goals and enlarged my scope. I became increasingly international in my thinking and work. With steadiness, I became more effective. I took a serious interest in other movements that were similar to ours and became informed about them.

Working with a team of ingenious young professionals tucked away on an all but unnoticed floor of the federal government in Washington, I spent four years during the Johnson and Nixon administrations in a novel and fast-paced initiative. I was part of a maverick group in the U.S. Office of Economic Opportunity that included Dr. Arthur Frank, Lucia S. Hatch, Dr. Stephen C. Joseph, Dorothy H. Mann, Donald Pugliese, and Dr. Franklin L. Stroud. Racing under rare Congressional legislation that mandated the setting up of demonstration neighborhood health services, this shrewd staff group created facilities where they had never existed for America's rural and urban poor. An inventive bureaucrat named Daniel I. Zwick who, like my mother, believed that the word *can't* does not exist in the English language, taught me how to accomplish goals within the labyrinthine workings of the federal bureaucracy and much of what I know about public administration. Our director in OEO, Dr. Thomas E. Bryant, an exceptional lawyer and physician from Demopolis, Alabama, personified the progressive leadership that the civil rights movement had unleashed in white southerners. It was from him that I learned that *how* you achieve your goals is as important as what you are trying to achieve.

In 1972 I left the federal government and set up my own business, and in 1974 I joined with five outstanding women in Washington to establish the National Association of Women Business Owners, a still-flourishing organization. I was its president in 1976.

Before leaving the federal government, however, in 1969 I met Dr. Peter Geoffrey Bourne while visiting one of the programs I helped set up—a neighborhood health center that served thirty thousand people in southside Atlanta. He was a professor in Emory University's psychiatry department and was about to leave that position to go to work for his friend, Georgia's new governor, Jimmy Carter. As Peter and I came to know each other, he would occasionally talk to me of his belief that Governor Carter should seek the American presidency. My initial reaction, remembering the counties the governor had once represented as a state legislator, was reflexively negative. I couldn't forget the cruel, sometimes bestial, attempts to suppress the movement in southwest Georgia, or the seven hundred people in jail there in Albany. I couldn't forget the use of cow prods or the twenty young girls in the Leesburg stockade cell forced to stand in their own excreta. I couldn't forget Americus and the bail set at $120,000 for my fellow workers Don Harris, John Perdew, and Ralph Allen. Yet, as I came to know the governor and his remarkable wife, Rosalynn, I became convinced that Peter was right. In August 1972, Peter showed me a twelve-page memorandum he had drafted, suggesting to the governor that he run for the presidency and outlining a strategy for the campaign. He asked me, hesitating, his eyes inquiring as to whether I thought his concept too farfetched and unrealistic: Should he give it to the governor, even at the risk of having the idea rejected out of hand? I said yes.

I joined with Peter and a small group of individuals who set about to win the White House. In 1974, days before Governor Carter publicly announced his decision to run for the highest office in the land—because we knew that from then on there would be no time in the hectic pace of our lives for it—Peter and I were married by my father. In the campaign, my business office, until we outgrew it, served as the initial Washington headquarters, and I helped manage the mid-Atlantic primary elections and ran one of the campaign's policy task forces. I also set up a policy and strategy arm of the campaign for women, having convinced Governor Carter that women were becoming more consequential politically and did not necessarily vote as men did. Once elected, the new president called me to breakfast at Blair House and asked me what responsibility I would accept in the administration. I told him I wanted to run the Peace Corps, VISTA, and three other programs of the ACTION agency, and he appointed me deputy director of the independent subcabinet federal agency that housed those national programs. My appointment was confirmed by the unanimous vote of the Senate, and I was sworn into office in the Rose Garden. Peter was one of the President's assistants in the White House and later became assistant secretary general at the UN.

After the end of the Carter administration, I helped to organize the first "summit" meeting of leaders of mass movements from Asia, Africa, and Latin America. For the last several years, I have worked through a variety of organizations in international development to open up new markets for American technology and expand trade relations with Africa and the Middle East.

Charlie Cobb wrote that he had given up thinking that SNCC could save the country. Yet, in some ways, even with its painful inability to resolve internal conflict and its bent for self-destruction, SNCC salvaged the image of the United States in the eyes of the world. Over a period of ten years, my work with international development has taken me to more than seventy-five countries. I have learned that the American civil rights movement and its successes represent that part of the American experience with which a great proportion of the world's population identifies. I have experienced vividly how my having participated in the movement opens doors and hearts, communicating something unique with few words. Even with the most grave and erratic foreign-policy errors made by the government, our civil rights movement remains a persuasive and redeeming feature and a live declaration of human rights for countries in whose eyes the democracy and foreign policy of the United States are a conundrum.

SNCC as an organization and many of the individuals within it were ahead of their time in another way. SNCC was able to promote and respond to the leadership of women in a manner that antedated an articulated and coherent struggle for women's rights. Even if not fully ready for the questions we raised, SNCC provided the crucial nourishment that allowed Casey and me to pose our concerns.

The civil rights movement, with all of its strengths, weaknesses, and paradoxes—and particularly SNCC—has proved to be the most significant part of my life. Most of the major lessons that I have learned in life are based on foundations that I constructed during that period. Many of the principles I have since used to guide me in other fields and endeavors started with my deductions from my experiences in that struggle.

Along the way I came to believe that there must be defiance in the days of one's youth. One must stake out a forceful position early, for it is unlikely that one can modify a flaccid and weak-kneed position with later experience to find the balance between ideals and effectiveness.

The lessons I learned in the movement about social change in the United States began a process that has continued for me over the years. Among those original lessons were the following: There are many avenues for political and economic progress and there is no single doctrine or right way. In a democracy, a very few people, working together, can accomplish significant change. In a society dominated by communications, effective political strategies depend on good communications. If people have organized conscientiously within a democratic framework, they can resist immense pressure. The self-indulgence of internecine struggle that will not effect external reality must be avoided. If a group does not choose its leaders, the press will choose them for it. Anger should not be allowed to frame policy or get in the way of accomplishing goals. Individuals and groups should preserve their energies for fights that will lead to changes in power and policy.

The lifting of the onerous weight of white supremacy and segregation came with refreshing relief to the southland. Many would say that Bob Moses's prediction has already come true and that relations between the races are better in the South than in other regions of the country.

Those who sardonically claim "not much has changed for American blacks" must not know how bad it was. Such a comment reveals—making me want to avert my eyes, as if from some shame I should not see—that the speaker was not on the front lines in the southern civil rights movement and never experienced the brutality that was directed against blacks and their supporters at that time. Twenty years later, the word *integrated* has lost significance in the American lexicon. To say that "the car was integrated" or "an integrated group drove by" was once a frightening statement; its meaning has now become obscure. Similarly, the term *northern* no longer has the meaning it did twenty years earlier in the South, and the word *southerner* has all but lost its stigma in the North.

The black and white children of the South today are the first racially diverse southerners to grow up with completely legal contact with each other. Yet, America for the most part remains a segregated society. Commitment to the possibilities and promise of the American democracy must be vigilant. Problems as they arise must be kept under surveillance. The accomplishments of the southern civil rights movement were not a fulfillment of the final goal; they were what Bonhoeffer would call stations on the road to freedom.

When Du Bois said that the problem of the twentieth century was the problem of the color line and the relations between the darker and lighter races, he accurately perceived that we would still be wrestling with race at the end of the century. The struggle for justice is not won. We may need to build new movements to complete this task if it cannot be accomplished within the framework of litigation and electoral politics.

It is, sadly, possible for young people in the United States today to grow up never knowing what life is like for people such as Hannah, the hardworking woman in the Delta. Yet, discussion of a national youth service corps to enlist the energy of the young in solving problems is rarely mentioned in public-policy debate. Without exposure to others, how can Americans comprehend the fact that three quarters of the world's population of five billion live in impoverishment as bad as or worse than the poverty of black people in the Mississippi Delta twenty years ago—conditions under which exploitation and oppression flourish—or that most of the world is dark-skinned? If Americans don't concretely and viscerally understand these basic facts, will not our foreign policy, inevitably, be flawed?

Women and their male supporters must develop kaleidoscopic strategies capable of long duration, because here is a fundamental question that transcends differences between rich and poor and all ideologies, governments, and political systems: What does it mean to be a woman, to be a man, to be human? It may take movements within movements, in forms unrecognizable to us today, and be well into the twenty-first century before the ancient injustices toward women are eradicated. Perhaps we will need to nail another set of ninety-five theses on the door of the world—and to have a new Reformation pertaining to women.

So, should you and I happen to sit together on a long plane flight someday, perhaps to Khartoum or Baghdad or Dhaka, and if we talk about anything and everything as travelers do, you will know before we have gone far that my preparation for later growth and for understanding other struggles in Africa, South Africa, and North Africa, Latin America, Asia, and the Middle East came from the civil rights movement. You will hear how, whether in politics, foreign policy, development, or trade, my basic understanding of human behavior and political systems, and their dilemmas, vexations, and vulnerabilities, was molded by my experiences in the civil rights struggle. You will see that my fundamental principles are those with which we wrestled on Raymond Street and Lynch Street and carved out at Tougaloo, in Danville, and in the Delta. You will realize that my finest teachers were individuals like Ella Baker, Bob Moses, Casey Hayden, Julian Bond, John Lewis, and Jim Forman. You will sense my conviction that freedom is expressed in the willingness to take responsibility, and that without responsible action it is not freedom. You will know that I believe we must build more movements, and write new verses for old freedom songs, to continue to press for social justice and the fulfillment of the promise of democracy; and these movements, too, like ours, will be stations on the road to freedom.

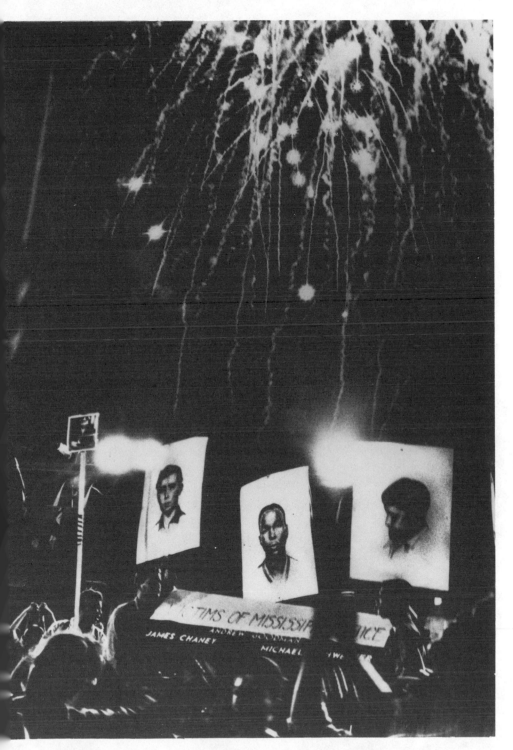

Placards showing our missing fellow workers, *(left to right)* Andy Goodman, Jim Chaney, and Mickey Schwerner, at a boardwalk demonstration, Atlantic City, New Jersey, August 1964 © *Bob Fletcher: a SNCC Photo*

Fannie Lou Hamer
Atlantic City, New Jersey,
August 1964
© Bob Fletcher: a SNCC Photo

Fannie Lou Hamer *(center)*, Doc
Henry *(above right)*, and Miss
Baker *(lower right)* at an
impromptu boardwalk event,
Atlantic City, New Jersey,
August 1964
© Bob Fletcher: a SNCC Photo

Staff and volunteers in the Communications section of the Lynch Street COFO headquarters, Jackson, Mississippi, watching a televised speech by Dr. Martin Luther King, summer 1964

(Left to right, approximately) Casey Hayden, Joanne Grant, Emmie Schrader, Irene Strelitz; *(center right)* Courtland Cox, Jimmy Bolton, Dona Richards, and Walter Tillow

© *Bob Fletcher: a SNCC Photo*

Lawrence Guyot
Chairman, Mississippi
Freedom Democratic party
© *1965 Bob Fletcher: a SNCC Photo*

COFO volunteers singing freedom songs in the community center at
Meridian, Mississippi, July 1964 © *1964 Steve Shapiro—Black Star*

"Woke up this morning with my mind stayed on freedom!"
Left to right: Dona Richards, Euvester Simpson, and Gwen Gilliam, Hattiesburg, Mississippi, 1964 © *Danny Lyon /Magnum*

Mary King *(far left)* taking some of the notes upon which this book is based at the first Waveland, Mississippi, staff retreat, November 1964 © *Bob Fletcher: a SNCC Photo*

Ruby Doris Smith
Robinson
Waveland, Mississippi,
November 1964
© *Bob Fletcher: a SNCC Photo*

Stokely Carmichael
Lowndes County,
Alabama, 1965
© *1987 Flip Schulke*

Mary King in the late 1960s

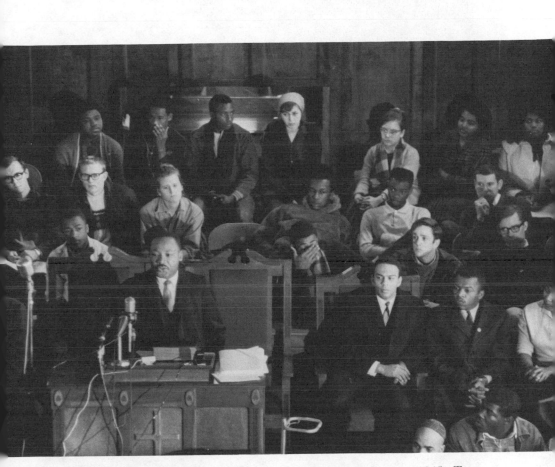

Dr. King addressing a Selma, Alabama, mass meeting, January 1965. *To his left:* Andrew Young, John Lewis, and Dorothy Cotton. Ringed around him on the church chancel are SNCC staff and volunteers working in Selma, including Prathia Hall *(second from upper right).* © *Bob Fletcher: a SNCC Photo*

Julian Bond, finally allowed to take his seat in the Georgia State Assembly, Atlanta, Georgia, January 9, 1967 © *1987 Flip Schulke*

AFTERWORD

With honesty and sensitivity, Mary King corrects widely held misconceptions of the black freedom struggle of the 1960s. Recalling the easily forgotten details that distinguish history as lived from the diligent editing of the past that is history as usually written, she portrays a nurturing movement community composed of self-questioning, constantly changing individuals rather than media-inspired stereotypes: "demonstrators," "Martin Luther King's followers," or "black-power militants." Instead of focusing on the dramatic mass marches in Albany, Birmingham, Washington, and Selma that prompted the passage of national civil rights legislation, her memoir emphasizes the unpublicized small gatherings where ordinary individuals came to understand the sources of their shared oppression and acquired confidence in their ability to overcome.

Mary's story reflects her unique background and experiences while also offering important insights regarding the evolution of a historic social movement. Much has been written about black protest and militancy in the 1960s, but most previous accounts have betrayed a misunderstanding of the distinctive values that emerged in the course of the black struggle. SNCC, in particular, has suffered from distortion and ignorance. If mentioned at all in histories of the 1960s, the nature of its contribution to the struggle is rarely defined and its mystique within what was once called The Movement is inadequately explained.

To be sure, many accounts have noted that SNCC was more

radical than the other major civil rights organizations. SNCC workers gained a reputation as the shock troops of the southern struggle, because they were willing to attack southern racism in its Deep South strongholds—predominantly rural counties, such as Terrell in Georgia, Lowndes in Alabama, and the Delta counties in Mississippi. Their militancy was honed by the beatings, jailings, and killings inflicted upon them and the local residents with whom they worked. SNCC's radicalism is only partially explained, however, by references to the violence its workers suffered.

While becoming increasingly aware of the brutal nature of southern racism, SNCC workers also became disillusioned with the federal government because of its failure to provide protection for those involved in civil rights activities. As Mary makes clear, they were more willing than those in other civil rights groups to criticize the Kennedy and Johnson administrations. Ready to risk their lives on behalf of southern blacks, SNCC workers had little sympathy for liberal politicians who were unwilling to take political risks in order to promote the values they espoused. Nevertheless, although John Lewis's censored speech at the 1963 Washington march and Stokely Carmichael's black-power speeches of 1966 were the most visible manifestations of SNCC's radicalism, such militant statements were not the most distinctive aspects of SNCC's radicalism.

SNCC workers' uncompromising insistence that all people—regardless of class, race, sex, or education—should participate fully in American political life and in SNCC's internal discussions comprised the essence of their radicalism. Black radicalism has been often equated with the militant public oratory of a few firebrands, but SNCC's radicalism was best displayed through the unpublicized activities of its field staff, who firmly believed in leadership from the bottom up, rather than through the speeches of its officers. Indeed, Carmichael's image as a racist, perhaps sexist, demagogue of the late 1960s contrasts sharply with Mary's portrayal of his work during the early 1960s as one of SNCC's corps of dedicated community organizers.

Unlike most organizations, SNCC cannot be understood from a top-down leadership perspective. One of its defining qualities was a distrust of institutionalized leadership and an openness to influences from the grass roots. Most Americans saw the black struggle simply as a civil rights movement in which objectives were determined by national civil rights leaders and implemented by sympathetic politicians at the national level. SNCC's contribution, if recognized at all, was viewed as a small element in a larger reform process in which a few leaders, most notably Martin Luther King, mobilized mass activism on behalf of long-standing civil rights goals. To the extent that SNCC's objectives were perceived as extending beyond the liberal civil rights agenda, the group was criticized as a counterproductive, ostensibly subversive, force to be controlled and even destroyed.

SNCC's contribution cannot be measured, however, merely through its impact on national civil rights policies. To call SNCC a civil rights organization is to restrict severely the broad vision of a new society that once blossomed within the group. Mary's memoir reminds us that the southern struggle not only prompted the passage of civil rights legislation; it also transformed the lives of many participants in ways more profound than was ever possible through legislation.

The increasingly militant public statements of SNCC's spokespersons departed from rather than reflected the radical values manifested in SNCC's organizing activities. Some of the ideologues identified with SNCC during its final years ironically and unwittingly gave support to the FBI's assumption that the black movement could be destroyed by eliminating its potential "mesiahs."

Understanding SNCC requires that we look beyond the rhetoric of its much publicized leaders and even beyond its contribution to the achievement of civil rights reforms. Other organizations possessed far more financial resources and had more access to institutionalized power, but SNCC's historical importance was based on its success in releasing the untapped energies of ordinary people who discovered their ability to do extraordinary things. Although SNCC has been described as becoming more radical through its moving from an integrationist perspective to a separatist one, its organizing activities during the first half of the 1960s were themselves truly radical departures from conventional approaches to social reform, and they stimulated unprecedented feelings of racial consciousness. Southern black people were never so united and militant as they became during that period of sustained activism.

Although white activists in SNCC clearly played a supportive rather than dominant role in the group, black separatist sentiments ultimately led white activists to leave. Mary's narrative does not focus on the complexities of the black-power era, but it does suggest that, in some important respects, even as SNCC workers adopted black-nationalist ideas, the group became less directly involved in the daily experience of racial oppression and collective struggle that had fostered the emergence of a militant racial consciousness among southern blacks. The rise of separatist ideologies, often drawn from sources outside the South, coincided with the decline of southern grass-roots mass activism thus involving all classes of blacks. In contrast to SNCC workers who had once acquired political insights from the southern black people with whom they lived and worked, doctrinaire SNCC radicals after the period about which Mary writes competed with self-appointed leaders from other groups who were seeking to bring about the ideological conversion of increasingly discouraged black people.

Although SNCC was often portrayed as a group of protesters and dissenters, its main goal during its years of greatest effectiveness was to mobilize black communities for long-term struggles. While resisting the tendency to become bureaucratized and hierarchical, SNCC fostered the emergence of strong, locally based, black-controlled institutions such as the Mississippi Freedom Democratic party and the Lowndes County Freedom Organization (better known as the Black Panther party). SNCC organizers saw themselves as catalysts rather than leaders of the black struggle. They endeavored to undermine the widely held assumption that better-educated, affluent individuals should exert dominance within a movement including ill-educated poor people. Believing that they had failed if local residents became dependent upon their presence, they sought to enhance the skills of residents, asserting that their job was to work themselves out of a job. For SNCC's most successful organizers, mass demonstrations were among the outgrowths of community organizing rather than ends in themselves.

Despite their generalized distrust of institutional leaders, the best SNCC organizers were leaders of an unusual kind. They exercised their leadership carefully and selectively, recognizing that their wisdom was based on an understanding of their social context and a careful reading of their experiences. The Montgomery bus boycott and the lunch-counter sit-ins demonstrated to them that movements can be initiated by individual unplanned acts of courage. They learned from their own experiences that leaders are more likely to emerge from social movements than to launch them. They also learned that all communities contained people with unexploited capacities for leadership and that organizations can stifle as well as facilitate these capacities.

The black struggle changed American society, and, more importantly, it transformed the way participants thought about themselves and their social roles. SNCC organizers provided many black people with their first opportunity to imagine and assume social roles that were not defined by racial subordination. Within the movement, black people were able to relate to whites as equals, sometimes even as superiors. Rather than continuing to feign acquiescence in white racial domination, they could begin to perceive themselves and white people in new ways. In areas of the deep South far from the American mainstream, young activists created prototypes of a society in which all people would have the opportunity to participate in decisions that affected their lives.

Mary's memoir demonstrates that the ideals of SNCC workers were implicit in their daily activities rather than empty slogans. SNCC was an imperfect model of an alternative society, but, during its best years, it embodied the dream of an egalitarian society in which freedom was not limited by racism or any other form of elitism. Although the "beloved community" that early-1960s activists saw as their goal was an unachievable ideal, it was taken seriously within the southern movement. SNCC workers did not simply bring the values of modern America to the backwater areas of the South; they were transformed and educated by the southern blacks with whom they worked. Their experiences provide us with a valuable legacy: an awareness of what democracy and freedom might mean in a future and restructured America.

Mary's depiction of SNCC's distinctive character helps us recognize that the southern black struggle achieved far more than the Civil Rights acts of 1964 and 1965. In addition to seeking changes in the surrounding society, SNCC workers sought to transform the movement community into a model of a better world. They demonstrated that ordinary people could identify and overcome the varied and sometimes subtle sources of their oppression. SNCC worker Bob Moses once compared the liberation of personal energies that took place inside SNCC to the energy released by the splitting of the atom. The analogy aptly explains how such a small organization could have such an enormous impact on the surrounding society. SNCC has now passed into history, but its legacy remains worthy for those of us who are still able to believe that it is possible to build a better world.

—CLAYBORNE CARSON
Associate Professor of History, Stanford University,
Stanford, California, and
Director, Martin Luther King, Jr., Papers Project,
Martin Luther King, Jr., Center
for Nonviolent Social Change,
Atlanta, Georgia
December 2, 1986

APPENDIX 1

WORKING PAPER, NOVEMBER 1964

"Communications Section" means many things to different people in SNCC. To some it is a network of citizens band radios in Mississippi, to others *The Student Voice*, and to others it is the immediate dispatch of news to the national press, and the limited protection that results from publicity. Still others think propaganda is "70 percent of the fight." Communications is all these things and more, and by next summer it will be different from what it is today.

Some of the plans for an enlarged Communications operation should be discussed by the staff since there are some basic questions posed. My position is that there are some jobs that have to be done well, and doing them well does not necessarily mean changing movement values.

Suggestion: There should be six distinct sections operating under "Communications."

1. NEWS DEPARTMENT. The job of gathering and dispatching news (that is, gathering information for public use, releasing news of incidents to the press, the mailing of releases and fact sheets, and pre-publicity) is the most important day-to-day activity of Communications at present. Very few people now do news work although it is very important. The Communications offices of Atlanta and Jackson have established a good reputation for reliable news reporting. It is not easy to achieve a level of documenting daily events so that stories are straight on the beam and maintain it. It is 24 hours' work. It requires scrupulous checking out of every incident. We should not have to do it ourselves because America and the American press should be interested enough in accurate reports of what is happening to maintain an adequate and

honest press corps throughout the South. That is not the case as we all
know. By next summer the news department should be separated from
the other functions of Communications. And because the basic job is
documenting, writing up in news "copy" and releasing, people who are
committed to news as news can be used to help if they have the skills,
and if they work closely with someone who has a strong movement orientation who can point out the issues involved.

A great deal of time spent by the people handling news is spent on
the phone. Others, like the Northern Coordinator, spend much time on
the phone getting the same news to support groups which help to get
news placed in local press. At present the Communications office neither
in Atlanta nor Jackson can handle more than one crisis at a time ade-
quately because of the time required to dispatch one item. We should
investigate a teletype system that would *simultaneously* dispatch news to
maybe twenty points around the country (both Friends groups and news-
rooms) so that in five minutes the wires would be cleared and ready for
the next dispatch. To some people the complex system of WATS line
calls and the citizens band radios (SNCC SIGNAL CORPS) is already
technological. Because it is often inefficient, people do not always think
of it that way, but it requires trained people to use such a network,
which has become the very nerve center of the operation in Mississippi.
Teletypes are one step further toward fast communication with distant
parts. Speed is often the difference between life and death in SNCC.

2. The second section could be called PUBLICATIONS. At present the people who prepare publications are often those who handle
news. This happens less and less because those administrating different
programs (in Mississippi, for example) often do their own reports. The
haphazard result is that we have publications of sorts on some things and
not on others. What gets published is not necessarily because of a pre-
determined need, but often because of the aggressiveness of a special
interest group, or because one person has better access to the people
who run the presses. We could have one person chiefly responsible for
developing literature as the need arises; who sees that things get published according to a carefully thought out timetable; who determines
what should get a fancy layout with pictures and what should get mimeographed; who develops a good mechanism so that materials reach those
for whom they are destined. A distinction is implied from publications
we might call "propaganda," that is, interpretative pieces which tell our
story to those outside the movement, which pinpoint the issues that our
action is directed toward.

3. MOVEMENT MATERIALS. The flyers, political primers, and
literacy materials, etc., should go in a different section since, again, materials for internal use ought to be shaped in accord with needs rather

than by other factors. Movement materials and publications should be shaped by people whose main job is to feel out those needs and develop materials to fit them.

4. PROMOTION. The same people who basically do news do promotional work now, although if we were to analyze carefully the job of Northern Coordinator we would see that most of that job is promotion and public relations. Under the umbrella Communications, there could be a section called "promotion." The job of the one or two people in that section would be to make personal appearances on TV shows, be available for interviews, set up interviews, and develop news media contacts. As it is now, there is one person in Atlanta and one in Jackson who informally serve in this capacity, but they also do news, publications and other work interspersed with briefings of newsmen. If there is a southwide project next summer, there will be a real need for a key person to travel and develop news contacts and do the hard job of talking issues with the press—which now gets done only incidentally.

5. SIGNAL CORPS. There are at present sixty-two citizens band radio transceivers in the state of Mississippi. They must first be installed and then maintained by specially trained people, and they are. Some of these people came out of the movement or from the Jackson community. They too are technocrats now. Others were already trained when they came. Presumably, expansion into the Black Belt will mean more of the same.

6. AUDIO-VISUAL. We have a photography department with photographers and a dark room. Running a dark room is a skill, and taking useful pictures is a skill. There have been field secretaries taken out of the field to learn still and movie photography. More should be similarly trained. Other dark rooms should be set up. It is no accident that SNCC workers have learned that if our story is to be told, we will have to write it and photograph it and disseminate it ourselves.

In Mississippi, Freedom Schools are aided by circulating educational films. There is much more that can be done. We can develop film strips on different aspects of political organizing for local workers who are already stretched thin over several counties. A tape-recording library with tapes that can be lent to Friends groups is already being developed. We could make a real effort to develop audio materials, not only for spot-radio news as is already done but for tapes explaining programs, literacy, and interviews with people like Mrs. Hamer, Mr. Agnew James, Mr. Steptoe, and others. The photography department is now closely connected to news functions. The marketing of photos and placement of photos in newspapers through quantity mailings which are cheap, is already done though not so much as should be by next summer. Much more can be done to use pictures within the movement. Again, placement of persons in positions where their job is to work with their ear to the ground to fill movement needs is required. That may mean recruiting or training people to handle either the content or the technical end. But one traveling FDP worker with specially developed film strips may be able to do the job of five people.

The PRINT SHOPS fall under the direction of several of these areas and are not distinct in themselves. The chief job of the print shops in Atlanta and Jackson should be the technical work involved in getting things printed. It's a dirty word, but in order to run an offset or multilith press, you have to be a technician. When the print shops determine the ideological content of materials, as well as production, they can do neither job well.

* * SNCC COMMUNICATIONS * *

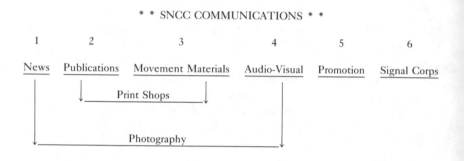

Some of the people needed to fill the positions described above are already in SNCC. Training or relocation may be involved, but they are here. For some of the others, recruitment of people who already have the skills may be needed. This does not mean we have to enlarge our staff with professionals who care nothing about the movement, do not understand SNCC thinking, or require large salaries. However, it may mean we should experiment with special recruitment.

We should be ready to admit that in the course of daily field work, in the course of giving up school or professional career, and developing ways of working that have never been tried before in areas that have never been tried before, we are ourselves highly skilled, and we may have to develop more efficiency in some areas in order to do our total job well.

Fear of bureaucracy is valid. We all shun organizations and civil rights groups which seem intent on building the organization and which spend their time image-building and fund raising. We even pride ourselves that the other groups do the talking while we do the hard dirty work.

Yet SNCC has grown larger and larger and has created its own needs—needs for its own internal communications system, and needs within its specially developed programs. Organized and unorganized Friends of SNCC groups (international now) depend on us for up-to-date information. (It was almost embarrassing this past summer to pick up newspapers from across the country and read line for line the news reports that were written in the Jackson Communications office.)

There are some things that need reorganizing, retraining, and recruitment before next summer if Communications is to do the job it must. We can use skills and organization in some areas without letting *it* use us.

—MARY KING

A P P E N D I X 2

SNCC POSITION PAPER, NOVEMBER 1964

(Name witheld by Request)

1. Staff was involved in crucial constitutional revisions at the Atlanta staff meeting in October. A large committee was appointed to present revisions to the staff. The committee was all men.

2. Two organizers were working together to form a farmers league. Without asking any questions, the male organizer immediately assigned the clerical work to the female organizer although both had had equal experience in organizing campaigns.

3. Although there are women in the Mississippi project who have been working as long as some of the men, the leadership group in COFO is all men.

4. A woman in a field office wondered why she was held responsible for day-to-day decisions, only to find out later that she had been appointed project director but not told.

5. A fall 1964 personnel and resources report on Mississippi projects lists the number of people in each project. The section on Laurel, however, lists not the number of persons but "three girls."

6. One of SNCC's main administrative officers apologizes for appointment of a woman as interim project director in a key Mississippi project area.

7. A veteran of two years' work for SNCC in two states spends her day typing and doing clerical work for other people in her project.

8. Any woman in SNCC, no matter what her position or experience, has been asked to take minutes in a meeting when she and other women are outnumbered by men.

9. The names of several new attorneys entering a state project this past summer were posted in a central movement office. The first initial and last name of each lawyer was listed. Next to one name was written: (girl).

10. Capable, responsible, and experienced women who are in leadership positions can expect to have to defer to a man on their project for final decision making.

11. A session at the recent October staff meeting in Atlanta was the first large meeting in the past couple of years where a woman was asked to chair.

Undoubtedly this list will seem strange to some, petty to others, laughable to most. The list could continue as far as there are women in the movement. Except that most women don't talk about these kinds of incidents, because the whole subject is not discussable—strange to some, petty to others, laughable to most.

The average white person finds it difficult to understand why the Negro resents being called "boy," or being thought of as "musical" and "athletic," because the average white person doesn't realize that *he assumes he is superior*. And naturally he doesn't understand the problem of paternalism. So too the average SNCC worker finds it difficult to discuss the woman problem because of the assumption of male superiority. Assumptions of male superiority are as widespread and deep-rooted and every much as crippling to the woman as the assumptions of white supremacy are to the Negro. Consider why it is in SNCC that women who are competent, qualified, and experienced are automatically assigned to the "female" kinds of jobs such as: typing, desk work, telephone work, filing, library work, cooking, and the assistant kind of administrative work but rarely the "executive" kind.

The woman in SNCC is often in the same position as that token Negro hired in a corporation. The management thinks that it has done its bit. Yet, every day the Negro bears an atmosphere, attitudes, and actions which are tinged with condescension and paternalism, the most telling of which are seen when he is not promoted as the equally or less skilled whites are.

This paper is anonymous. Think about the kinds of things the author, if made known, would have to suffer because of raising this kind of discussion. Nothing so final as being fired or outright exclusion, but the kinds of things which are killing to the insides—insinuations, ridicule, overexaggerated compensations.

This paper is presented anyway because it needs to be made known that many women in the movement are not "happy and contented" with their status. It needs to be made known that much talent and experience are being wasted by this movement, when women are not given jobs commensurate with their abilities. It needs to be known that just as Negroes were the crucial factor in the economy of the cotton South, so too in SNCC, women are the crucial factor that keeps the movement running on a day-to-day basis. Yet they are not given equal say-so when it comes to day-to-day decision making.

What can be done? Probably nothing right away. Most men in this movement are probably too threatened by the possibility of serious discussion on this subject. Perhaps this is because they have recently broken away from a matriarchal framework under which they may have grown up. Then, too, many women are as unaware and insensitive to this subject as men, just as there are many Negroes who don't understand they are not free or who want to be part of white America. They don't understand that they have to give up their souls and stay in their place to be accepted. So, too, many women, in order to be accepted by men, on men's terms, give themselves up to that caricature of what a woman is—unthinking, pliable, an ornament to please the man.

Maybe the only thing that can come out of this paper is discussion—amidst the laughter—but still discussion. (Those who laugh the hardest are often those who need the crutch of male supremacy the most.) And maybe some women will begin to recognize day-to-day discriminations. And maybe sometime in the future the whole of the women in this movement will become so alert as to force the rest of the movement to stop the discrimination and start the slow process of changing values and ideas so that all of us gradually come to understand that this is no more a man's world than it is a white world.

APPENDIX 3

A KIND OF MEMO FROM CASEY HAYDEN AND MARY KING TO A NUMBER OF OTHER WOMEN IN THE PEACE AND FREEDOM MOVEMENTS. *

November 18, 1965

We've talked a lot, to each other and to some of you, about our own and other women's problems in trying to live in our personal lives and in our work as independent and creative people. In these conversations we've found what seem to be recurrent ideas or themes. Maybe we can look at these things many of us perceive, often as a result of insights learned from the movement:

• Sex and caste: There seem to be many parallels that can be drawn between treatment of Negroes and treatment of women in our society as a whole. But in particular, women we've talked to who work in the movement seem to be caught up in a common-law caste system that operates, sometimes subtly, forcing them to work around or outside hierarchical structures of power which may exclude them. Women seem to be placed in the same position of assumed subordination in personal situations too. It is a caste system which, at its worst, uses and exploits women.

This is complicated by several facts, among them: 1) The caste system is not institutionalized by law (women have the right to vote, to sue for divorce, etc.); 2) Women can't withdraw from the situation (a la nationalism) or overthrow it; 3) There are biological differences (even

*As reprinted in *Liberation*, April 1966

though those biological differences are usually discussed or accepted without taking present and future technology into account so we probably can't be sure what these differences mean). Many people who are very hip to the implications of the racial caste system, even people in the movement, don't seem to be able to see the sexual-caste system and if the question is raised they respond with: "That's the way it's supposed to be. There are biological differences." Or with other statements which recall a white segregationist confronted with integration.

• Women and problems of work: The caste-system perspective dictates the roles assigned to women in the movement, and certainly even more to women outside the movement. Within the movement, questions arise in situations ranging from relationships of women organizers to men in the community, to who cleans the freedom house, to who holds leadership positions, to who does secretarial work, and to who acts as spokesman for groups. Other problems arise between women with varying degrees of awareness of themselves as being as capable as men but held back from full participation, or between women who see themselves as needing more control of their work than other women demand. And there are problems with relationships between white women and black women.

• Women and personal relations with men: Having learned from the movement to think radically about the personal worth and abilities of people whose role in society had gone unchallenged before, a lot of women in the movement have begun trying to apply those lessons to their own relations with men. Each of us probably has her own story of the various results, and of the internal struggle occasioned by trying to break out of very deeply learned fears, needs, and self-perceptions, and of what happens when we try to replace them with concepts of people and freedom learned from the movement and organizing.

• Institutions: Nearly everyone has real questions about those institutions which shape perspectives on men and women: marriage, childrearing patterns, women's (and men's) magazines, etc. People are beginning to think about and even to experiment with new forms in these areas.

• Men's reactions to the questions raised here: A very few men seem to feel, when they hear conversations involving these problems, that they have a right to be present and participate in them, since they are so deeply involved. At the same time, very few men can respond nondefensively, since the whole idea is either beyond their comprehension or threatens and exposes them. The usual response is laughter. That inability to see the whole issue as serious, as the straitjacketing of both sexes, and as societally determined often shapes our own response so that we learn to think in their terms about ourselves and to feel silly rather than trust our inner feelings. The problems we're listing here, and what others have said about them, are therefore largely drawn from conversations among women only—and that difficulty in establishing dialogue with men is a recurring theme among people we've talked to.

● Lack of community for discussion: Nobody is writing, or organizing or talking publicly about women in any way that reflects the problems that various women in the movement come across and which we've tried to touch above. Consider this quote from an article in the centennial issue of *The Nation:*

> However equally we consider men and women, the work
> plans for husbands and wives cannot be given equal weight.
> A woman should not aim for "a second-level career" be-
> cause she is a *woman;* from girlhood on she should recognize
> that, if she is also going to be a wife and mother, she will
> not be able to give as much to her work as she would if sin-
> gle. That is, she should not feel that she cannot aspire to
> directing the laboratory simply because she is a woman, but
> rather because she is also a wife and mother; as such, her
> work as a lab technician (or the equivalent in another field)
> should bring both satisfaction and the knowledge that,
> through it, she is fulfilling an additional role, making an ad-
> ditional contribution.

And that's about as deep as the analysis goes publicly, which is not nearly so deep as we've heard many of you go in chance conversations.

The reason we want to try to open up dialogue is mostly subjective. Working in the movement often intensifies personal problems, especially if we start trying to apply things we're learning there to our personal lives. Perhaps we can start to talk with each other more openly than in the past and create a community of support for each other so we can deal with ourselves and others with integrity and can therefore keep working.

Objectively, the chances seem nil that we could start a movement based on anything as distant to general American thought as a sex-caste system. Therefore, most of us will probably want to work full time on problems such as war, poverty, race. The very fact that the country can't face, much less deal with, the questions we're raising means that the movement is one place to look for some relief. Real efforts at dialogue within the movement and with whatever liberal groups, community women, or students might listen are justified. That is, all the problems between men and women and all the problems of women functioning in society as equal human beings are among the most basic that people face. We've talked in the movement about trying to build a society which would see basic human problems (which are now seen as private troubles), as public problems and would try to shape institutions to meet human needs rather than shaping people to meet the needs of those with power. To raise questions like those above illustrates very directly that society hasn't dealt with some of its deepest problems and opens discussion of why that is so. (In one sense, it is a radicalizing question that can take people beyond legalistic solutions into areas of personal and institutional change.) The second objective reason we'd like to see discussion begin is that we've learned a great deal in the movement and perhaps this is one area where a determined attempt to apply ideas we've learned there can produce some new alternatives.

INDEX